# KNOWLEDGE-BASED SYSTEMS FOR MANAGEMENT DECISIONS

## Other Books by Robert J. Mockler

*Knowledge-Based Systems for Strategic Planning*

*Business Planning and Policy Formulation*

*Using Microcomputers* (with D. G. Dologite)

*Developing Information Systems for Management*

*Management Decision Making and Action in Behavioral Situations*

*The Business Management Process: A Situational Approach*

*Guidelines for More Effective Planning and Management of Franchise Systems* (with Harrison Easop)

*The Management Control Process*

*Business and Society*

*New Profit Opportunities in Business Publishing* (editor and contributing author)

*Putting Computers to Work More Effectively in Business Publishing* (editor and contributing author)

*Readings in Business Planning and Policy Formulation* (editor and contributing author)

*Readings in Management Control* (editor and contributing author)

*Published by Prentice Hall.

# KNOWLEDGE-BASED SYSTEMS FOR MANAGEMENT DECISIONS

ROBERT J. MOCKLER

PRENTICE HALL, *Englewood Cliffs, New Jersey 07632*

Library of Congress Cataloging-in-Publication Data

Mockler, Robert J.
    Knowledge-based systems for management decisions / by Robert J.
Mockler.
        p.   cm.
    Bibliography: p.
    Includes index.
    ISBN 0-13-516907-0
    1. Management--Data processing.   2. Decision making--Data
processing.   I. Title.
HD30.2.M63 1988
658.4'03'0285416--dc19                              88-4020
                                                       CIP

Editorial/production supervision
 and interior design: Editing, Design & Production, Inc.
Cover design: Diane Saxe
Manufacturing buyer: Margaret Rizzi

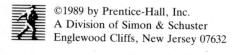 ©1989 by Prentice-Hall, Inc.
A Division of Simon & Schuster
Englewood Cliffs, New Jersey 07632

Unless otherwise specified all figures are copyrighted by the author
(©1987 by R. J. Mockler) and are reprinted with his permission.

Printed in the United States of America
10  9  8  7  6  5  4  3  2  1

0-13-516907-0

Prentice-Hall International (UK) Limited, *London*
Prentice-Hall of Australia Pty. Limited, *Sydney*
Prentice-Hall Canada Inc., *Toronto*
Prentice-Hall Hispanoamericana, S.A., *Mexico*
Prentice-Hall of India Private Limited, *New Delhi*
Prentice-Hall of Japan, Inc., *Tokyo*
Simon & Schuster Asia Pte. Ltd., *Singapore*
Editora Prentice-Hall do Brasil, Ltda., *Rio de Janeiro*

*TO*

*Kim, Nicky, Chris, Matt, Brad,*
*Kathleen, MaryBeth, Chrissy, JoJo,*
*Barbara, Michael, Joanna, Emily, Andrew—*

*a new generation of computer users*

# Contents

# Preface

This book is about knowledge-based systems, a branch of artificial intelligence (AI). It gives an introduction to knowledge-based systems, and how to develop these systems in a wide range of business situations.

The book is intended for anyone—business manager or student of business management—interested in the subject. It will help readers learn how to develop knowledge-based systems for management decision making. It will also help them improve their general management decision-making skills, as well as specific job-related skills, in such areas as marketing, finance, operations, and accounting. No background in computers is needed for developing the systems described in this book.

The book should also be of interest to corporate managers looking for well-defined, simple ways to

- Encourage the development of knowledge-based systems throughout their organizations
- Get those systems used to improve operations
- Generally improve middle management decision-making skills

Those thinking about becoming knowledge engineers will also find the book useful. It covers one area of knowledge-based systems development in particular that is given little attention elsewhere—analyzing and reconstructing decision situations. The book is not, however, for computer scientists. It is an introductory book for managers, and so is not highly technical.

The book can be used for

- Courses in knowledge-based systems development

- Advanced courses in any business discipline—from accounting and finance to marketing, operations management, and business policy
- General management decision-making courses
- Training seminars for managers who want to learn knowledge-based systems development
- Individual managers interested in studying the area on their own

The book is based on courses given at the author's university and on seminars and consulting work done for industry.

If artificial intelligence is to have wide application in business, it is necessary to take the development initiative out of the hands of the computer technicians, and put it into the hands of business managers.

Experience has shown that it is easier in the long run to teach a manager how to develop a knowledge-based system, than it is to expect a computer technician to acquire the skills and experience of business experts. Whether this works in practice in your own company, of course, will depend on the competence and training of the individuals involved, and on the organizational atmosphere.

In mid-1985, for example, DuPont undertook a major knowlege-based systems development project. The project's organization was based on the premise that middle and lower level manager's best know how decisions are made in their jobs. Training and helping these managers acquire knowledge-based systems development skills appeared, then, to be the fastest and most effective way to put AI technology to work to make money for DuPont.

Within two years DuPont reported that hundreds of useful AI applications had been developed (or were under development) using this bottom up, hands-on approach. Experience then shows this to be the quickest way to get practical and useful knowledge-based applications that work to help run a company better. It would seem, therefore, that lower and middle level management have a great role to play in the AI boom.

Successful knowledge-based systems development efforts, such as DuPont's, have taught us a lesson. The rapid growth of AI applications in industry will come only from

- First, putting knowledge-based systems development tools and expertise in the hands of middle and lower level management
- Then, training and helping these managers to seek out and develop opportunities for knowledge-based systems development in their own jobs

This book is part of the effort to put the power of AI into the hands of these nontechnical managers.

Using this approach is especially important today because it is at the lower and middle management levels that shortages arising from the "baby bust" will be occurring over the next twenty years. These shortages are already showing up in the retail and service areas today. A wide range of knowledge-based systems will be needed to help fill this management gap.

The unusual aspect of knowledge-based systems, which distinguishes the area from other computer areas, is that 80 percent of the work involves understanding and modeling a manager's decision processes used in doing a specific management job. This helps explain why these managers are the most effective medium for building knowledge-based systems. These managers also benefit in another way from participating in developing these systems because it helps them learn how to do their jobs better.

Several aspects of the relationship between knowledge-based systems and decision making and problem solving in various business areas are discussed in this book:

1. The nature of knowledge-based systems, and how to develop them to support management planning and decision making in various business areas
2. The use of knowledge-based systems and their development to improve management decision-making skills in such business areas as marketing, accounting, finance, operations, and business policy development

The examples of knowledge-based systems given in this book fall into two categories.

1. *Small prototype systems*. A number of small prototype systems are described in detail in Part 2. This was done
   □ To introduce the reader to knowledge-based systems development technology and concepts
   □ To introduce the reader to applying this technology to developing knowledge-based systems in specific business areas
   □ To provide a basis for the study of the concept, structure, and design of larger systems
   Within the context of these objectives, such small prototype systems are appropriate and useful. An experienced manager in any of the specific business areas involved may, however, find some of these systems somewhat trivial.
2. *Larger knowledge-based systems*. These are designed to give the reader a feeling for how larger systems work. These are not trivial systems. They are described only in general terms for several reasons:
   □ A detailed study of them would be beyond the introductory scope of this book
   □ Documenting the larger systems in detail would take as many pages as there are in this book
   □ They are proprietary systems that cost hundreds of thousands of dollars to develop

The book is divided into three parts. The first part introduces readers to knowledge-based systems, and how to develop them. The second part describes a variety of knowledge-based prototype systems that were developed by managers guided and assisted, by the author, for their own use on the job.

The third part, the Appendixes, gives examples of several systems developed by others and described in periodicals. In addition, the Appendixes provide some technical information on expert systems shells and several studies of knowledge engineering.

Comments and enquiries are welcome. For information about some advanced systems in these and related management decision-making areas or about any other aspect of this book, the reader should contact me through the publisher.

I wish to thank Steve Thompson of Micro Data Base Systems for his assistance in helping me learn GURU and develop some of the sample systems discussed in this book. Extensive development help was provided by Kenneth Chou, who was involved in the project from its inception. I also extend my thanks to the many managers, students, and fellow workers who provided help, including May-Mei Wong, Sweelim Chia, and Nancy Ward, and to my graduate assistants, including Yuan-I Lin and John Merseburg.

Substantial contributions and considerable assistance in developing the knowledge-based systems described in Part 2 was also provided by T. Connelly and E. Hagerty (Chapter 8); P. Sinaly, A. Barbera, and A. Wojcik (Chapter 9); B. Daly (Chapter 10); C. Zavala and G. Rosenfeld (Chapter 11); S. Memis (Chapter 12); L. First and P. Borocco (Chapter 13); E. Portnoy (Chapter 14); L. Lutzak and D. Chatman (Chapter 15); C. Ochs and J. Nelson (Chapter 16); J. Morison (Chapter 17); W. Holsten and D. Popper (Chapter 18); E. Conlon (Chapter 19); K. Zick and H. Gindin (Chapter 20); J. Merseburg (Chapter 22).

I wish to thank the following companies for furnishing software and other materials for research: Analytica Corp.; Ashton-Tate; Alacritous Inc.; Borland International; Decision Support Software Inc.; Digitalk Inc.; Experiences in Software Inc.; EXSYS Inc.; General Optimization Inc.; Human Intellect Systems; IntelligenceWare; Level Five Research; Lightyear Inc.; Meridian Education Corporation; Micro Data Base Systems Inc.; Microsoft Corporation; Neuron Data; Paperback Software International; Personal Computer Engineers; Programs In Motion; Reality Technologies Inc.; SPSS International; Texas Instruments Inc.

Last, I wish especially to thank D. G. Dologite who participated in a substantial way in all phases of the systems development work (and its underlying basic research) described in this book.

# 1

# Introduction

The introductory discussion in this chapter is divided into four parts:

- What knowledge-based (artificial intelligence) systems are, how they are developed, and the role played by computers in their development
- The role of prototyping in the development process
- The manager's role in developing knowledge-based systems
- The potential applications of these systems to a wide range of business decision-making areas

## KNOWLEDGE-BASED SYSTEMS

### What They Are

As shown in Fig. 1-1, knowledge-based systems are a branch of artificial intelligence (Bonnet 1985; Charniack and McDermont 1985; Harmon and King 1985; Keller 1987; Hart 1986; Rauch-Hindin 1985; Rauch-Hindin 1986(a); Rauch-Hindin 1986(b); and Waterman 1986). Such systems can function at the assistant, colleague, or expert level.

Knowledge-based systems are designed to replicate the functions performed by a human expert. For example, the systems developed at DuPont perform such tasks as selecting the right kind of rubber product for customers, diagnosing equipment failures, and scheduling machines on the factory floor. At other companies similar systems exist that give expert advice in auditing, sales management, media selection,

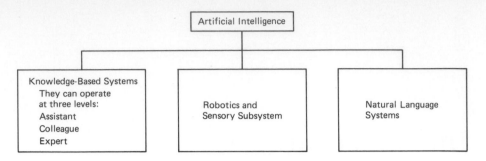

**FIGURE 1-1 Branches of artificial intelligence.**

configuring computer systems, repairing telephone line breakdowns, and many other areas of management planning and decision making.

Typically knowledge-based systems enable a user with a problem to consult the computer system as they would an expert advisor to diagnose what might be causing a problem or to figure out how to solve a problem or make a decision. This is done through a consultation with the knowledge-based system at the computer, in much the same way a manager might a human expert.

Like a human expert such a computer system can extract additional information from a user by asking questions related to the problem during a consultation. It can also answer questions asked by a user about why certain information is needed. It can make recommendations regarding the problem or decision at the end of the consultation, and when asked by a user it can explain the reasoning steps gone through to reach its conclusions.

## How Knowledge-based Systems Are Developed

Knowledge-based systems are developed by

- *Analyzing, or decomposing, the decision situation under study*
- *Reformulating or reconceptualizing the decision situation*
- *Putting the system onto the computer*

The *analytical phase* requires breaking the decision situation down into its smallest components. For example, even in a simple decision like whether or not to cut the grass, considerable scenario development may be required in order to recreate the actual situation encountered on a given Saturday morning.

For someone not trained or naturally skilled to do so, it is often difficult to specify every step involved in making a decision, each piece of information needed, and all the many alternative decision paths the mind pursues in the decision process. It has been said that a good journalist or story writer is best trained for this phase of a knowledge-based system's development.

As the decision situation is analyzed, diagrams are often constructed to get a picture of just how the decision is made. This is the *reformulation phase*. Figure 1-2 gives an example of such a diagram made for a decision on cutting the grass.

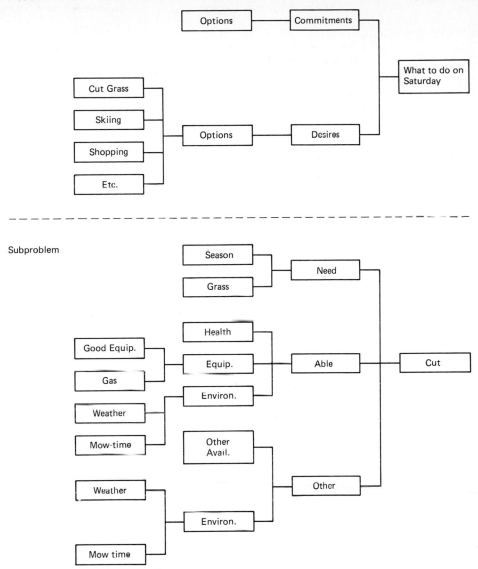

**FIGURE 1-2 Structured situation diagram or model for grass-cutting decision.**

This diagram is referred to as the definition of the knowledge needed to make the decision, or the *structured situation diagram or model.* These diagrams are sometimes referred to as knowledge domain models.

The diagram in Fig. 1-2 is not a *decision diagram.* It does not specify and follow all the reasoning paths that the decision maker follows in making the final decision, nor does it specify the criteria for each decision phase.

```
            Column 1                      Column 2
        Plain English Version         Condensed M.1 Version

rule-1:
   if the grass doesn't need to be cut    if need = no
   then the grass will not be cut         then cut = no.

rule-2:
   if the grass needs to be cut and       if need = yes and
   if I am able to cut it                    me-able = yes
   then I will cut the grass              then cut = me.

rule-3:
   if the grass needs to be cut and       if need = yes and
   if I am not able to cut it and            me-able = no and
   if another person can cut it              other-can = yes
   then another person will cut it        then cut = other.

rule-4:
   if I am not able to cut it and         if me-able = no and
   if another person can't cut it            other-can = no
   then the grass will not be cut         then cut = no.
```

**FIGURE 1-3  Knowledge-base segment—rules for grass-cutting decision.**

For example, in actually making this decision a number of decision rules (called heuristics) are used. These can be stated in "if-then" form, as is shown at the left of Fig. 1-3, where a few plain English examples are given.

Questions are also developed to ask a user of the system during a consultation for input information about the situation under study. Plain English examples of these are shown at the top of Fig. 1-4.

Another reformulation technique used is to develop decision charts, as shown in Fig. 1-5. This particular chart was developed for the final rule set in the small grass-cutting prototype system.

Based on this study of the decision processes involved, it is now possible to expand the knowledge domain model in Fig. 1-2 to give a sense of how the decision is made. Figure 1-6 shows such an expanded diagram. It includes the

- Specific alternative solutions that are to be considered
- Possible alternative values at each phase
- Knowledge needed to make the decisions
- Rules used to process the knowledge
- Information sought from the system user

Such diagrams are called *dependency diagrams*. Creating these diagrams, and the decision charts and statements of rules and questions, are generally referred to as the *documentation* phase of knowledge-based systems development.

The above is, in very simplified form, the process involved in creating a knowledge-based system—excluding the final stage. The final stage, *putting it onto the*

```
'Is the equipment available for mowing the grass in good
 condition?'

'Do you have enough gas to run the mower for the entire cutting
 job?'

'Is the weather good or bad?'

'Is the time available for mowing the middle of the day, or
 is it the early or late part of the day?'
```

---

```
Condensed GURU Version


VAR:    GOODEQP
 FIND:  input goodeqp with "Good Equipment: y or n? "

VAR:    GAS
 FIND:  input gas with "Enough gas: y or n? "

VAR:    WEATHER
 FIND:  input weather with "Weather: good or bad? "

VAR:    MOWTIME
 FIND:  input mowtime with "Time of Day: early, middle, or late?"
```

**FIGURE 1-4  Knowledge-base segment—questions for grass-cutting decision.**

*computer*, involves changing the plain English statements, where required, into a computer readable format.

    An example of a condensed computer compatible form for rules is shown at the right of Fig. 1-3. This particular example is taken from a small illustrative system developed on M.1, a microcomputer development program, which is also called an expert system programming shell. *Expert system shells* are software applications that have preprogrammed routines that can relieve the user of most of the programming

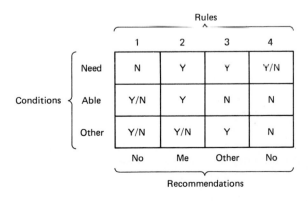

**FIGURE 1-5  Decision chart for final rule set—grass-cutting decision.**

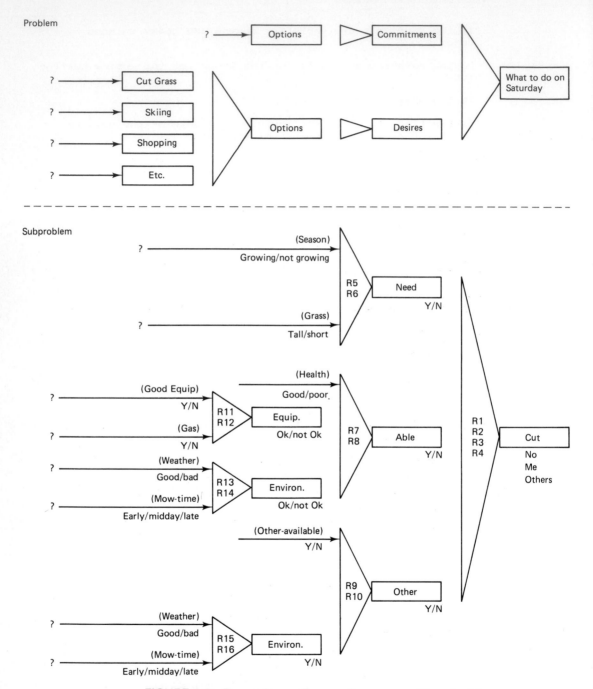

**FIGURE 1-6  Dependency diagram for grass-cutting decision.**

chores associated with developing a knowledge-based system. (See Gevarter 1987 for a complete review of the major currently available expert system shells.) The exact final form of the rules will depend on the programming language or programming shell used.

Examples of user questions rewritten for a computer are shown at the bottom of Fig. 1-4. These were written for GURU, another microcomputer expert system programming shell from Micro Data Base Systems (Holsapple and Winston 1986).

As is suggested by the above example, the computer is often of secondary importance during the initial phases of knowledge-based systems development. This is especially true in situations where an expert system shell, such as GURU or M.1, is used for creating test systems, often called *prototype systems*.

The key ingredients in developing the structure and design of knowledge-based systems are (1) to understand and articulate how the decision works in very precise, detailed terms and (2) to translate that decision into a format the computer can work with.

The description presented here of the knowledge-based systems development process is discussed in much more detail in Part 1 of this book. The discussion there provides the basis and structure for the discussion of specific knowledge-based systems in Part 2.

## THE ROLE AND IMPORTANCE OF PROTOTYPING

Since knowledge-based systems are relatively new and costly to develop, it is usually prudent to develop them in stages, starting with a small prototype of the actual system. This enables testing the basic structure and concept of the system before committing substantial resources to its development. It also enables developers to become familiar with knowledge-based systems technology before undertaking larger, more costly systems (Kauber 1985).

Prototypes can take many forms. At times prototypes are done of the overall system. For example, in the personal investment planning system described in Chapter 8, the total system was first outlined and then a prototype developed of the general approach. A diagram of this prototype is shown in Fig. 1-7. This approach was used to enable testing the general structure of the system and the interrelationships of its components.

At other times prototypes will be done of different segments or modules of a system, as in the development of a marketing strategy for international affiliates system in Chapter 18. An overview of the overall situation for which the system was being developed is shown in Fig. 1-8. The segment of that system being prototyped initially is shown in Fig. 1-9. Such prototyping enables building a system incrementally, adding modules or segments to it as they are developed.

These prototypes also enable initial development of ideas about questions, rules, and decision charts, as is shown in Figs. 1-10, 1-11, and 1-12, which are extensions of Fig. 1-8, the marketing planning system.

Since this is an introductory book, almost all the systems described in detail

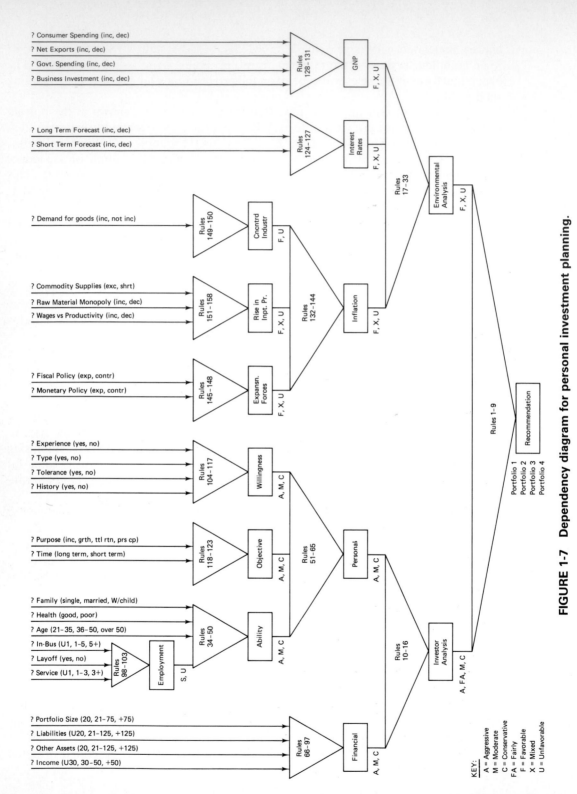

**FIGURE 1-7** Dependency diagram for personal investment planning.

8

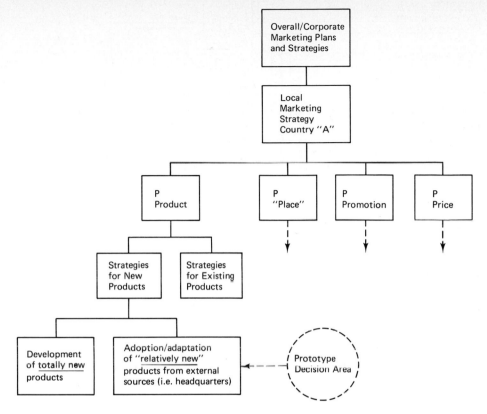

**FIGURE 1-8** **Diagram of situation under study—international local affiliates marketing strategy**

here are prototype systems. Some larger systems are described, but only in more general terms.

Prototype systems are by definition trivial, since they are testing and development tools. Their function in the development process is not trivial, however. They are a necessary ingredient of a prudent, cost efficient, well-planned and executed development project.

In developing prototypes, an effort is made to select only the most critical factors in the decision and to show only their most basic relationships in order to test the underlying structure and concept of the system. For this reason most prototype systems do not, and cannot be expected to, capture all the rich complexities involved in the actual situation. That is the function of later, more advanced versions of the system.

Although often a crude first effort, prototype systems serve useful purposes:

□ They provide a preliminary analysis of the decision situation. Since they isolate the essence of the structure and concept of the system, they give a

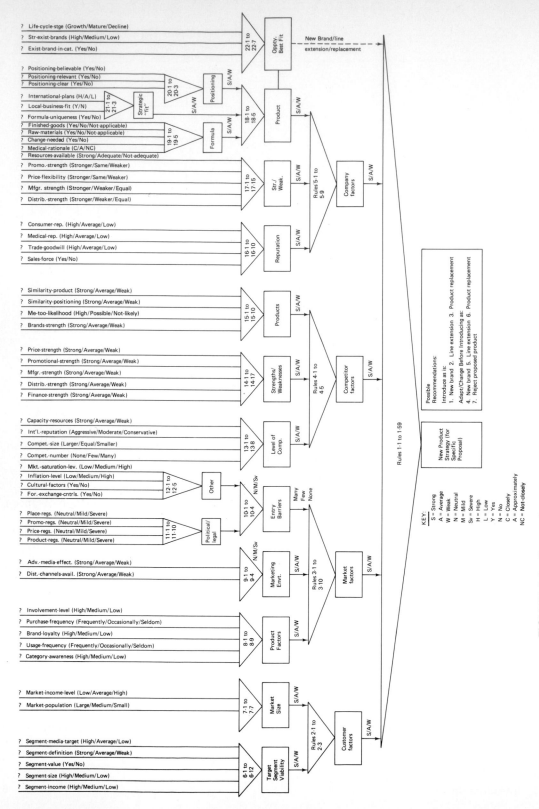

**FIGURE 1-9  Dependency diagram for new product strategy selection for local country product proposal—initial prototype.**

```
question(foreign-exchange-controls) =
[nl,nl,nl,nl,nl,nl,nl,nl,nl,'
Are there any controls on foreign exchange that would present
major problems to successfully obtaining the required raw
materials or finished goods for the proposed product?'
,nl,nl,nl,nl,nl,nl,nl,nl].
legalvals(foreign-exchange-controls) = [no, yes].

question(cultural-factors) = [nl,nl,nl,nl,nl,nl,nl,nl,nl,'
Are there any specific cultural factors that would present
serious problems to the successful introduction of the proposed
product?'
,nl,nl,nl,nl,nl,nl,nl,nl].
legalvals(cultural-factors) = [no, yes].

question(inflation-level) = [nl,nl,nl,nl,nl,nl,nl,nl,nl,'
What is the current or anticipated relative level of inflation in
the coming 2 years?
[low (not a problem), mild (minor but manageable problem) high (
major problem)] '
,nl,nl,nl,nl,nl,nl,nl,nl].
legalvals(inflation-level) = [low, mild, high].

question(market-saturation-level) = [nl,nl,nl,nl,nl,nl,nl,nl,nl,'
To what degree is the market for the proposed product saturated?
[low (room for major growth), mild (room for growth and market
share competition), high (vary saturated, high entry cost)] '
,nl,nl,nl,nl,nl,nl,nl,nl].
legalvals(market-saturation-level) = [low, mild, high].
```

**FIGURE 1-10    Sample questions from segment of knowlege base—initial prototype.**


developer and users a chance to evaluate the overall approach before getting too deeply into the system development.

□ They enable doing a preliminary analysis quickly. Not only does this help sustain interest at a high level, it also whets the developer's appetite for expanding and enhancing a system.

□ They encourage building a system in a modular, incremental way, that is at the same time well coordinated. In larger projects, this enables using a development team, and still maintaining the integrity of the unified, overall system.

In addition to its practical value in actual business situations, prototype development is also an important learning and teaching tool:

□ It reduces the situation to a manageable size, so that it can be included in a seminar or course on a specific business subject.

□ It introduces a manager or potential manager to knowledge-based systems and to expert system shells in a very compact, efficient, and realistic way.

```
rule-19-3:
    if change-needed = no and
        formula-uniqueness = yes and
        formula-medical-rationale = closely or
        formula-medical-rationale = approximately and
        not (formula-raw-materials = yes and
            formula-finished-goods = yes)
    then formula = strong.
rule-19-4:
    if change-needed = yes and
        formula-uniqueness = yes and
        formula-medical-rationale = closely or
        formula-medical-rationale = approximately and
        not (formula-raw-materials = yes and
            formula-finished-goods = yes)
    then formula = average.
rule-19-5:
    if formula-raw-materials = yes or
        formula-finished-goods = yes
    then formula = weak.

    /* Rule set twenty: Determining Positioning Factors */
rule-20-1:
    if positioning-believable = no or
        positioning-relevant = no
    then positioning = weak.
rule-20-2:
    if positioning-clear = no and
        positioning-relevant = yes and
        positioning-believable = yes
    then positioning = average.
rule-20-3:
    if positioning-clear = yes and
        positioning-relevant = yes and
        positioning-believable = yes
    then positioning = strong.
```

**FIGURE 1-11  Sample rules from segment of knowledge base—initial prototype.**

Competitor Factors Rule Set

| RULE NO. | TRGT. SEG. | MKT. SIZE | OUTCOME STRONG/AVG./WEAK |
|----------|------------|-----------|---------------------------|
| 1 | S | S | S |
| 2 | S | A | A |
| 3 | S | W | W |
| 4 | A | S | S |
| 5 | A | A | A |
| 6 | A | W | W |
| 7 | W | S | W |
| 8 | W | A | W |
| 9 | W | W | W |

**FIGURE 1-12  Sample decision chart—initial prototype.**

## A MANAGER'S ROLE IN DEVELOPING
## KNOWLEDGE-BASED SYSTEMS

The approach used in this book, and in conducting seminars and courses based on this book, replicates the way many successful knowledge-based systems development projects are actually conducted at companies. For example, DuPont promotes the widespread development of knowledge-based systems by operating managers. The theory is that the operating managers know both the problems and the solutions in their areas better than any systems developer ever could. DuPont essentially took the specific systems development initiative out of the hands of the computer technicians and put it into the hands of business managers.

Using this approach, operating managers do the bulk of the actual situation analysis, reconstruction, and documentation with the assistance and guidance of a knowledge engineer from the systems development department. A systems development department does a substantial part of the computerizing of the system, where an operating manager does not have the time or experience to do it. This approach works, where the objective is to develop a large number of relatively circumscribed systems. A somewhat different method is used for very large systems development (Evanson 1988; Hoffman 1987; Leonard-Barton 1987; and Prerau 1987).

The approach used here has the added benefit of giving an operating manager a proprietary interest in a system, and so ensures its use in actually achieving the intended benefits.

Many consulting assignments are also conducted using this approach, with the consultants serving as knowledge engineer and systems development department. Classes and seminars based on this book are often run exactly as such a consulting assignment would be conducted.

The approach is most effective where readers or participants work fulltime, as is the case with seminar participants, individual managers reading this book on their own, and MBA students working full time and taking their degree evenings and weekends.


## A WIDE VARIETY OF POTENTIAL APPLICATIONS
## TO BUSINESS DECISION MAKING

Knowledge-based systems have been developed for a wide range of management decision areas, including financial investment planning; auditing and other accounting areas; most operations management decisions; marketing and sales management; general decision making; and even interviewing, negotiations, and business law.

Using the approach described in this book, for example, operating managers have developed knowledge-based systems for their jobs, covering such decisions, tasks, or problems as

- □ Configuring computer systems (operations)
- □ Capital investment planning (finance)

- Personal investment planning (finance)
- Customer service representative training (marketing)
- Sales management quota setting (marketing)
- Commercial loan application screening (finance and banking)
- Tax planning (accounting and taxation)
- New venture decision making (marketing and management)
- Career planning (management)
- Auditing (accounting)
- Strategic planning (management and business policy)

The primary objective of these managers was to develop systems useful in assisting them do their jobs more effectively and efficiently. The benefits of these systems, however, go beyond the expert guidance these systems provide managers in making decisions and the cost savings and operating efficiencies the systems themselves provide.

The development process also affords managers an opportunity to sharpen their management and decision-making skills and increase their competence in their job area. For example, in the finance area asking for an explanation and disciplined outline of how an expert loan officer goes about reviewing and deciding on a commercial loan application is a valuable learning experience, even for someone who has worked a long time in the field. The same benefits accrue to managers in all areas.

These very real benefits to on-the-job managers, such as making them better managers and giving them sophisticated computer tools to do their job better, may help explain why companies like DuPont have been so successful in relying on lower and middle level managers to develop knowledge-based systems.

The potential for applying knowledge-based system technology both to providing decision support to working managers and as teaching and learning aids to managers and potential managers in almost every business area seems wide ranging at this time.

One major roadblock to the more rapid and widespread development of knowledge-based systems for management decision making is the proprietary nature of the knowledge-based (and other AI) systems now under development in industry. Considerable work has been done, for example, in strategic corporate planning, marketing, and accounting systems by major corporations. This work is not today widely available, because it is looked upon as a competitive advantage for the company developing the system.

Another roadblock is technical. More sophisticated and more user friendly expert system shells are still under development. In addition, personal computer (PC) technology has yet to break the 640k working memory barrier in PC machines that are widely available today. These decision-making systems require substantially more storage space in working memory. And, the faster microprocessors (such as Intel's 80386) are only now beginning to be introduced in low cost PCs. Such speed is needed in decision-making systems because of the more complex thinking processes involved. Software development to enable full use of the newer hardware developments will probably be the major roadblock during 1988 and 1989 once the new microcomputer hardware is in place.

These technical roadblocks will be overcome in the near future, however, opening the door for more rapid growth in knowledge-based systems development in all management decision-making areas.

## EXERCISE QUESTIONS

1. Define knowledge-based systems.

2. Identify and describe the key ingredients in developing the structure and design of knowledge-based systems.

3. Describe the steps involved in developing a knowledge-based system.

4. What is a dependency diagram? Describe its function in the knowledge-based system development process.

5. What is the role of a nontechnical manager in knowledge-based system development?

6. Describe the function of prototyping in knowledge-based systems development. What are some of the drawbacks?

7. List some of the kinds of knowledge-based systems that have been developed.

8. In addition to leading to the creation of a knowledge-based system, describe some of the other benefits of participating in the knowledge-based systems development process.

9. Describe some of the technical problems that inhibit the growth of knowledge-based systems development.

10. What are expert system shells? What function do they serve?

## REFERENCES

Bonnet, A., *Artificial Intelligence*, Jack Howlett, trans. Englewood Cliffs, NJ: Prentice-Hall, 1985.

Charniack, E., and D. McDermont, *Artificial Intelligence*. Reading, MA: Addison-Wesley, 1985.

Evanson, Steven E., "How to Talk to an Expert," *AI Expert*, February 1988, pp. 36–42.

Gevarter, William B., "The Nature and Evaluation of Commercial Expert System Building Tools," *Computer*, May 1987, pp. 25–41.

Harmon, P., and D. King, *Expert Systems*, New York: Wiley, 1985.

Hart, Anna, *Knowledge Acquisition for Expert Systems*, New York: McGraw-Hill, 1986.

Hoffman, Robert R., "The Problem of Extracting the Knowledge of Experts from the Perspective of Experimental Psychology," *AI Magazine*, Summer 1987, pp. 53–67.

Holsapple, C. W., and A. B. Winston, *Expert Systems Using GURU*, Homewood, IL. Irwin, 1986.

Kauber, Peter G., "Prototyping: Not a Method but a Philosophy," *Journal of Systems Management*, September 1985, pp. 28–33.

Keller, Robert, *Expert System Technology: Development and Applications*, New York: Yourdon Press, 1987.

Leonard-Barton, Dorothy, "The Case for Integrative Innovation: An Expert System at Digital," *Sloan Management Review*, Fall 1987, pp. 7–19.

Prerau, David, "Knowledge Acquisition in the Development of a Large Expert System, "*AI Magazine*, Summer 1987, pp. 43–51.

Rauch-Hindin, W. B., *Artificial Intelligence in Business, Science and Industry* (*Volume II– Applications*), Englewood Cliffs, NJ: Prentice-Hall, 1985.

Rauch-Hindin, W. B., *Artificial Intelligence in Business, Science and Industry* (*Volume I– Fundamentals*), Englewood Cliffs, NJ: Prentice-Hall, 1986.

Rauch-Hinden, W. B., "Software Integrates AI, Standard Systems," *Mini-Micro Systems*, October 1986, pp. 69ff.

Waterman, D. A., *A Guide to Expert Systems*, Reading, MA: Addison-Wesley, 1986.

# 2

# Knowledge-Based Systems: What They Are and How They Work

Four aspects of knowledge-based systems of interest to this study are discussed in this chapter:

- ◻ What knowledge-based systems are.
- ◻ The way knowledge is represented in a knowledge-based system.
- ◻ The ways these systems "think" or "reason" or "infer." The mechanism through which a knowledge-based system reasons is called an "inference engine."
- ◻ What knowledge-based systems programming languages and shells are.

## WHAT EXPERT KNOWLEDGE-BASED SYSTEMS ARE

As shown earlier in Fig. 1-1, knowledge-based systems are one branch of artificial intelligence. Such systems can function at the assistant, colleague, or expert level.

*Artificial intelligence* (AI) is the capability of a device, such as a computer, to perform functions or tasks that would reasonably be regarded as intelligent if they were observed in humans.

An *expert system* is a computer system that attempts to replicate what human experts normally do. Human experts make decisions and recommendations, such as what company strategy to follow or who to give bank loans to, and do tasks, such as adjust temperature controls in a manufacturing plant. They also assist (or help) and train others to do tasks and to make decisions. So do expert systems.

The term *expert* is used here only in a relative sense. It refers to persons who do their jobs well or professionally. The actual job can range from order entry clerk to troubleshooting repair person, to product planner, to strategy developer. The absolute importance of the decision, problem, or task is not what makes it expert.

*Knowledge bases* are collections of expertise or expert knowledge. They can include anything from basic information about a field of knowledge to guidelines for reasoning about that information, in order to make decisions and do tasks.

Some computer systems that are called expert systems are not knowledge-based systems. As an example, some traditional financial planning systems, which are used to analyze and evaluate alternative strategies, have been called expert systems. Several other types of decision support systems, such as some decision-tree software applications that are used for alternative strategy evaluation, have also been called expert systems. These types of computer systems are not discussed in this book. Only knowledge-based systems are covered here.

It should also be noted that the knowledge-based systems discussed in the later sample system chapters in this book are not large, multimillion dollar systems. Rather, they are the smaller systems that can be developed by managers and that can help them in their day-to-day work.

The concept of artificial intelligence has been around for a long time. Meaningful development work on knowledge-based systems only began, however, in the 1960s. During the 1970s many knowledge-based systems were developed.

Early knowledge-based systems were developed mainly at major universities such as Stanford, Carnegie-Mellon, and the Massachusetts Institute of Technology (MIT). These systems involved such areas as agriculture, chemistry, computer systems, electronics, engineering, geology, information management, law, manufacturing, mathematics, medicine, meteorology, military science, physics, process control, and space technology. By far the most popular areas were medicine and chemistry.

More recently increased attention is being paid to developing knowledge-based systems for a wide range of business applications.

Typically knowledge-based systems enable a user with a problem (for example, how to find the cause of machine failure and a way to repair it) to use a computer system as they would an expert advisor to guide them through diagnosing what might be causing the problem and how to solve it. This is called a consultation.

Like a human expert, the system can extract additional information or data from the user with questions related to the problem. During a consultation the system can also answer questions about why certain information is needed and the reasoning steps gone through to reach a conclusion, and it can make recommendations for solving the problem at the end of a consultation.

Knowledge-based systems are often integrated with traditional computer systems. For example, financial planning systems often have traditional quantified financial analysis applications, such as those mentioned in Chapters 8, 9, and 10, that are combined knowledge-based systems that evaluate the more subjective decision criteria, such as planning assumptions.

Knowledge-based systems are sometimes classified by the area to which they can be applied, such as medicine and chemistry. They are also classified by the generic problem areas they are applied in, such as those given in Fig. 2-1. These generic categories range from well-defined areas, such as diagnosis, monitoring, and

| Category | Problem Addressed | Types of Systems |
|----------|-------------------|------------------|
| Diagnosis | Infers system malfunctions from observations | Medical, electronic, financial analysis, auditing, machine repair |
| Monitoring | Compares observations in order to plan vulnerabilities | Management control, nuclear, power plant regulation |
| Debugging | Prescribes remedies for malfunctions | Computer software |
| Repair | Executes a plan to administer a prescribed remedy | Automobile, computer, telephone |
| Instruction | Diagnoses, debugs, and corrects student behavior | Tutorial, remedial |
| Control | Interprets, predicts, repairs and monitors system behaviors | Air traffic control, battle management, manufacturing process control |
| Prediction | Infers likely consequences of given situations | Weather forecasting, crop estimation, financial forecasting |
| Interpretation | Infers situation descriptions from sensor data | Speech understanding, image analysis, surveillance, mapping |
| Design | Configures objects within situation constraints | Circuit layout, budgeting, automatic program generation |
| Planning | Develop guidelines for action | Strategic planning, process scheduling, military planning |

**FIGURE 2-1  Generic categories of expert system applications.**

debugging, to less well-defined areas, such as planning, design, and interpretation. Such a generic classification system helps potential users to determine if their own problem might be a potential application for knowledge-based systems technology. Knowledge-based systems for management decision making generally fall into the less well-defined categories listed in Fig. 2-1, such as planning, designing, and interpreting.

Well-known early systems had such names and applications as:

| NAME (AND UNIVERSITY OR INSTITUTE) | APPLICATION |
|------------------------------------|-------------|
| DENDRAL (Stanford) | Chemical analysis |
| HASP/SIAP (Stanford) | Military ship identification |
| HEARSAY-II (Carnegie-Mellon) | Speech understanding |
| INTERNIST/CADUSEUS (University of Pittsburgh) | Medical diagnosis |
| MACSYMA (MIT) | Algebraic simplification and integration |
| MYCIN (Stanford) | Medical diagnosis |
| PROSPECTOR (Stanford Research Institute) | Evaluation of mineral deposit potential |
| PUFF (Stanford) | Medical diagnosis |

Thanks largely to popular works of fiction, such as the movie *Star Wars*, the most widely recognized knowledge-based systems are those involving robotics and government weapons systems.   Robotic applications of AI techniques are fairly common today in manufacturing and the military.

Although most of the early systems were developed for research, many of them being thesis research projects, considerable progress has been made in the 1980s in developing commercial business applications. For example,

- ACE (AT&T) provides troubleshooting reports and analyses for telephone cable maintenance
- COMPASS (GTE Corporation) also troubleshoots telephone circuit break-downs
- DELTA (GE) helps diagnose and repair diesel electric locomotives
- DRILLING ADVISOR (Teknowledge) advises drilling rig supervisors on ways to avoid problems related to drilling and sticking
- GENESIS (IntelliCorp) assists genetic engineers in analyzing DNA molecules
- (R1)XCON (Digital Equipment Corp. and Carnegie-Mellon) configures computer systems to meet individual customer specifications.

In addition to those cited above, knowledge engineering companies such as CGI (Carnegie Group), Inference Corporation, Computer Thought Corporation (C*T), Production System Technologies, Smart Systems Technologies (SST), Syntelligence, and Software A & E, are active in the knowledge-based systems development field. Developing systems for business is a significant part of their work.

Major development activity is also evident within business firms. In 1987, there were many thousands of knowledge-based systems in existence or under development. The exact number is not known because most of the systems being developed by corporations provide a major competitive advantage in the market place. These companies, therefore, are unwilling to discuss them in any detail.

For example, Ed Mahler of DuPont noted at a June 1986 Texas Instruments AI Symposium that his company already had 50 knowledge-based systems under development, even though the project was only a year old. In October 1986, he was quoted as saying 150 such systems were already in use at DuPont. By 1990, he expects DuPont to have developed over 2,000 such systems. These systems cover the spectrum from manufacturing to marketing to decision-support applications. IBM announced in late 1986 that it is developing 70 knowledge-based systems for internal use and expects to become a major supplier of them.

A great deal of work is also being done in the accounting and auditing area. Many major accounting firms have an active AI development program. At the 1986 Texas Instruments AI Symposium, for example, Bruce Johnson of Arthur Anderson described their involvement with knowledge-based systems as "extensive." He stated:

> We first of all have our internal applications for each of our major operating divisions: our audit, tax and systems practices. And we have tools—and are continuing to develop more tools—that support each of those practices, to make our services more productive, or to provide us with a competitive advantage. We also work with our clients, through our consulting division, to develop systems for their internal use, to usually help with their competitive advantages—occasionally to help them reduce costs.

The Internal Revenue Service (IRS) is actively developing knowledge-based systems. They have gone so far as to send a large number of employees, at full pay, to spend two years studying AI theory and applications at the graduate level.

Many major banks and insurance companies have an in-house knowledge-based systems program. So have other financial services companies, such as American Express and Lazard Freres. Major industrial companies are also working on financial systems. For example, General Motors is reportedly working on a wide range of financial knowledge-based systems, including ones that integrate strategic planning applications with financial applications.

Several general purpose financial planning systems are commercially available. Applied Expert Systems (APEX) has developed PlanPower, which helps create financial plans for wealthy people. Palladin Software's Financial Advisor advises business executives on capital investment projects. Syntelligence has developed expert systems that help insurance underwriters analyze and rate commercial risks and assist lending officers with the evaluation of commercial loans. Sterling Wentworth Corporation's Businessplan advises self-employed professional and business owners about all aspects of financial planning.

Manufacturing applications are fairly advanced. Westinghouse Corporation, for example, took five years to develop a major AI system to detect potential steam turbine generator failures. During that period the basis was created for developing a wide range of other knowledge-based systems in the manufacturing area.

Although there has been and continues to be substantial progress in developing knowledge-based systems in the manufacturing area, much remains to be done. There is still a shortage of sophisticated software application packages available commercially in the manufacturing area. Palladin's Operations Advisor was one of the few commercially available in 1987 that assists strategic and operational decision making in the manufacturing area.

The marketing area is rich in potential, but it still lags behind manufacturing and financial services in both proprietary and commercially available knowledge-based systems. Knowledge-based systems have been developed to support a company sales operation. These systems help transfer the expertise of superior salesmen to others in the field. Other knowledge-based systems have been developed to assist sales management decision making; guide consumer buying decisions; manage retail operations; and increase the effectiveness of service, warehousing, and distribution.

Very little work appears to have been done to date in the strategic planning areas. This is probably because the area is less well-defined and because the payoffs there are not as visible, measurable, or immediate as in manufacturing, operations, marketing, and finance.

It appears that companies will be turning out a continuing flow of knowledge-based systems. For example, DuPont expects to be developing more than one new system a week during 1988. The need, *especially at the lower middle management level*, is there. The shortages at the lower and middle management levels caused by the baby bust following the baby boom will accelerate this need. Knowledge-based systems technology is in place, and its availability will expand substantially at the PC level over the next eighteen months. People are being trained in increasing numbers to catch up with that need within corporations.

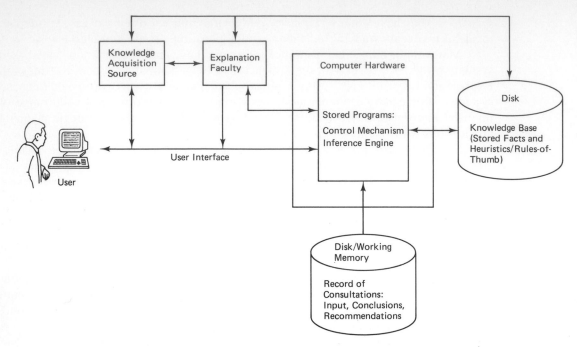

**FIGURE 2-2   Essential components of a knowledge-based system.**

Overall the evidence indicates that corporations are on the threshold of a major expansion of knowledge-based systems development.   Most likely this will eventually be followed by a growth in commercially available applications.

This book is an effort to encourage and extend this development activity into more management decision-making application areas.

The distinguishing characteristics of knowledge-based computer systems are that they

- Contain symbolic programming and reasoning capabilities
- Contain a knowledge base about a specific decision domain or situation that is in large measure distinct from the inferencing mechanism
- Contain an inference engine, or inferential reasoning capability, that is in large measure distinct from the knowledge base
- Can handle uncertain, unknown, and conflicting data
- Allow a programmer or user to modify segments of programs relatively easily
- Have a facility to explain their advice or reasoning process
- Use if-then rules (heuristics) extensively, but not necessarily exclusively

Figure 2-2 shows the components of a knowledge-based system: knowledge base, inference engine and control mechanism, user interface, and computer hardware. The following sections discuss these components.   The discussion provides a basis for the sample systems development work described in detail in later chapters.

## KNOWLEDGE REPRESENTATION

The following discussion covers the ways knowledge is represented in knowledge-based systems. It also describes some applications of these representation techniques to strategic corporate planning.

### If-Then Rules (Heuristics)

The most common way that knowledge is represented in knowledge-based systems is by if-then rules. An example of if-then rules is given in Fig. 2-3. Such rules contain premises or conditions in the "if" clauses and conclusions in the "then" clauses. The example in Fig. 2-3 shows an if-then rule used in a strategic company planning knowledge-based system.

If-then rules in knowledge-based systems differ from similar ones in conventional computer systems. They are more flexible since they can be modified much more easily to meet changing needs. Digital Equipment Company, for example, first used conventional programming if-then statements for a computerized system that was designed to configure computer equipment into complete units (or systems) appropriate for specific customer needs. Digital found conventional programming rules could not meet the requirements of their production process, since their product line required frequent changes and modifications to meet individual customer needs. They

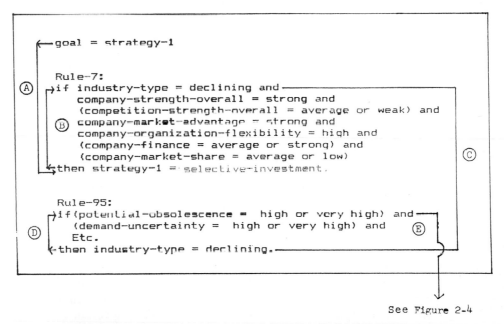

See Figure 2-4

**FIGURE 2-3  Sample of "if-then" rules from a knowledge base and of the inference engine search process—strategic planning prototype system.**

```
question(potential-obsolescence) = 'How would you characterize
                                    the potential for technological
                                    obsolescence in this industry
                                    segment [very low, low,
                                    average, high, very high]?'

question(demand-uncertainty) = 'How would you assess the
                                uncertainty of future demand in
                                this industry segment [very low,
                                low, average, high, very high]?'
```

The first question above, which is stored in the system's knowledge base, causes the system to print the following on a user's computer screen:

```
    How would you characterize the potential for technological
obsolescence in this industry segment [very low, low, average,
high, very high]?

    >> (A user types an answer in here.)
```

**FIGURE 2-4    Sample of knowledge-base questions and a user query—
strategic planning prototype system.**

switched to a knowledge-based system (called XCON) with if-then rule capability, since it was more adaptable to change and easier to maintain and update.

Rule-based systems, as well as other kinds of knowledge-based systems, also have the capability during consultations to ask users questions about information needed to deal with specific decision problems.   Figure 2-4 gives an example of such questions.

### Frames (Also Called Structured Objects)

Frames are a kind of template for holding related clusters of data, facts, rules, hypotheses, or any other knowledge in a single conceptual unit.   They therefore require conceptual reorganization of situation data around key controlling concepts.   For this and other reasons frame systems appear to have many potential applications to strategic corporate planning.   An example of a frame is given in Fig. 2-5.

Frame-based, also called object-oriented, systems enable dealing with more complex decision situations than can be dealt with in systems that contain just rules and questions.   Since people generally think in clusters, especially in decision situations

```
┌─────────────────────────────────────────────────────────────────┐
│                          PRODUCT                                   │
│                                                                    │
│  Characteristics - Type: Specialty cookies                         │
│                    Name: Brand X                                   │
│                    Specifications: Low volume, high margins,       │
│                                    appealing to specific           │
│                                    market segments                 │
│                                                                    │
│  Factors affecting success: Familiarity with local market and     │
│                             specific market segment tastes;        │
│                             flexible manufacturing operations;     │
│                             ability to obtain outlets, and good    │
│                             store position and shelf space;        │
│                             market intelligence gathering          │
│                             networks; new product development      │
│                             capability                             │
│                                                                    │
│  Opportunities: Growing customer market, with rapidly expanding   │
│                 disposable income, whose demographics favor spe-   │
│                 cialty and convenience products                    │
│                                                                    │
│  Interconnecting-              Rule-6-1, Rule-7-2, etc.             │
│    Procedures-Pointers                                             │
│                                                                    │
│  Rules:                        Rule-5-1, Rule-5-2, etc.            │
│                                                                    │
│  Questions:                    Question (...), etc.                │
│                                                                    │
└─────────────────────────────────────────────────────────────────┘

┌─────────────────────────────────────────────────────────────────┐
│                          CUSTOMER                                  │
│                                                                    │
│  Category, Name, Type:                                             │
│                                                                    │
│  Attributes - Demographic Profile:                                │
│               Number/Size:                                        │
│               Motivation:                                         │
│               Location:                                           │
│               Buying Patterns:                                    │
│                                                                    │
│  Interconnecting-              Rule-8-1, etc.                       │
│    Procedures-Pointers                                            │
│                                                                    │
│  Rules:                        Rule-9-1, Rule-9-2, etc.            │
│                                                                    │
│  Questions:                    Question (...), etc.                │
│                                                                    │
└─────────────────────────────────────────────────────────────────┘
```

**FIGURE 2-5   Knowledge representation using frames.**

such as strategic planning, frames can sometimes come closer to mimicking the ways human beings reason and remember.

Frames make use of slots to hold information about an item or object.  This information usually covers its attributes and values as well as procedures and pointers

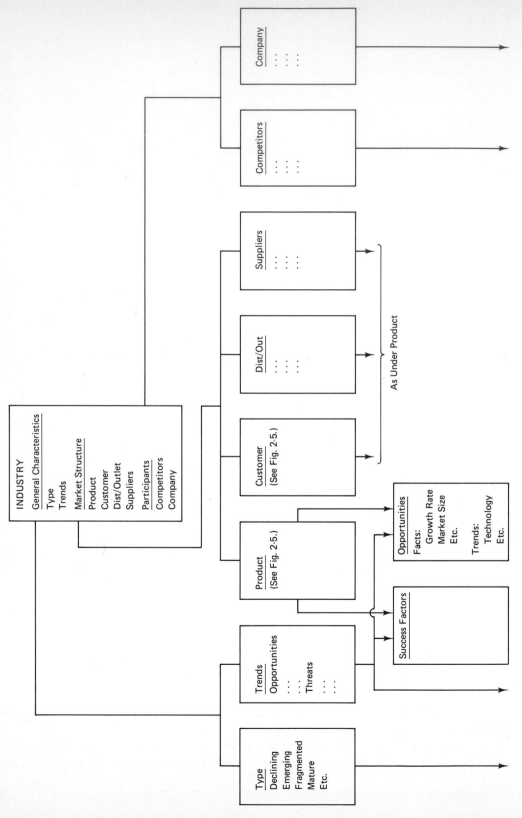

**FIGURE 2-6** Frame hierarchy chart.

for getting facts from other frames in the knowledge base. Frames may also contain rules and questions involving information in the frame. In addition to the items shown in Fig. 2-5, they can contain display and graphic material. They may even contain a default value, which is a value assumed when no other value is available.

Frames can be linked to other frames, to form a frame hierarchy. Pointers and procedures can, for example, direct the system to search other frames for related data. They can even be manipulated by the inference engine to draw new information from other frames. An example of frame hierarchies is given in Fig. 2-6.

Since frame-based systems are more complex than simple rule-based systems, they are not yet as widely used in PC applications.

## Semantic Networks

Semantic networks are used in many knowledge-based systems. They are similar to frame hierarchies. They differ primarily in the way the knowledge is represented. Semantic networks use groups of nodes and arcs instead of groups of text and pointers, which are used in frame hierarchies. An example of a semantic network is given in Fig. 2-7.

## Hierarchies and Inheritance

Objects can inherit information or attributes from other objects in a frame hierarchy or semantic network. For example, in the semantic network shown in Fig. 2-7, since Company X is in the consumer food products industry everything generally true about that industry is also true about Company X. Inheritance relationships can be designated by inheritance indicators or pointers in a frame.

Inheritance relationships are important in these systems for several reasons. When industry attributes change, for example, inheritance capabilities make it unnecessary for a system developer to rewrite any new industry-wide attributes for every individual company in the industry, including Company X. In addition, inheritance capabilities give new nodes, frames, or objects in a system the ability to know information about many attributes, capabilities, and constraints as soon as these nodes, frames, or objects are created. For example, when new companies are added to an industry model, they automatically inherit general industry characteristics without a system developer having to write them for each new company.

At the same time, new information can be added to the data describing any company in the industry without disturbing the rest of the system's knowledge base. For example, the fact that Company X introduces new product lines can be added without disturbing the other frames of knowledge.

## Other Representations Used

Knowledge-based systems also use other forms of knowledge representation. Two of the most commonly used are described here.

One is called *logic representation*. The most familiar form of logic representation

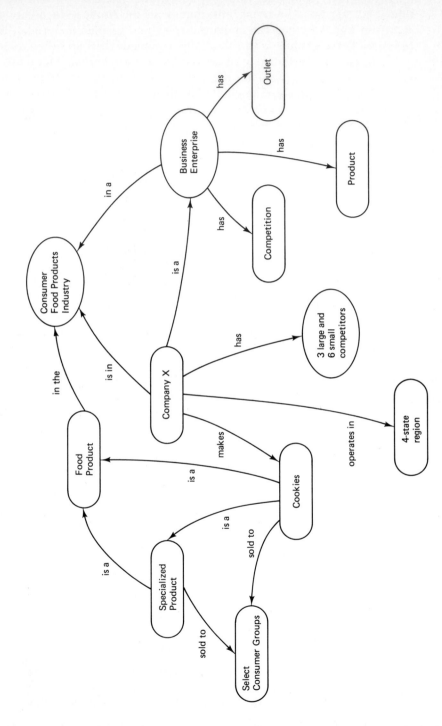

**FIGURE 2-7  Knowledge representation using a semantic network.**

is predicate logic statements, such as "is-regional (company)." The statement literally means a company is regional. The answer can only be yes or no.

Another related representation format is called *object-attribute-value triplets* (O-A-V). These are knowledge-base entries that give information about an object. For example, in Fig. 2-5 the O-A-V would be:

Object     = Product, specialty cookies
Attribute = Factors affecting success
Values     = Familiarity with local markets and specific market segment
             tastes, flexible manufacturing operations, and the like

As seen in Figs. 2-5 and 2-7, these representation forms can be used in conjunction with other forms of knowledge representation.

### Certainty and Uncertainty

Knowledge-based systems can represent degrees of certainty and uncertainty. Certainty factors, for example, identify the confidence that one has in a statement or piece of evidence. There are many different ways to represent certainty factors. For example, MYCIN, a medical diagnosis knowledge-based system, uses numbers ranging from $-1$ (definitely false) to $+1$ (definitely true). Others use numbers 1 to 10, 0 to 1, or some other range. Certainty factors are not probabilities. They are informal measures of confidence or certainty. They represent the degree to which one believes that the knowledge represented is, in fact, true.

### Ease of Modification

Because the inference engine is separate from the knowledge base, it is possible to modify the knowledge base without disturbing the inference mechanism or control program. It is in this sense that it is easier to modify knowledge-based systems than conventional computer programs.

Rules, frames, frame hierarchies, semantic networks, inheritance, logic statements O-A-V triplets, and certainty factors are all tools that are mixed and matched in different combinations (or in some cases used all by themselves) in creating a knowledge base. The exact combination used will depend on the situation under study, and on the hardware and software used.

## THE INFERENCE ENGINE: INFERENTIAL REASONING

The inference engine is a computer program that guides the manipulation of knowledge contained in a knowledge base. The inferential reasoning mechanism is distinct from the knowledge base. There are many ways that the inference engine in a knowledge-based system *reasons inferentially* and *controls* the reasoning processes and manipulation of the data represented in the knowledge base.

In deciding where to start a search for an answer, an inference engine can be either goal driven (called *backward chaining*) or data driven (called *forward chaining*). This search is often called a *reasoning process* in a knowledge-based system.

## Backward Chaining

Backward chaining involves starting with one or more possible goals. In a rule-based system, for example, the inference engine tests each goal to see whether or not the if clauses in the rule containing each possible goal are all true. It tests each rule in turn until an answer is found (that is, it finds a rule in which all the if clauses are true) or until all possible rules are examined and no answer can be found.

Following the arrows in Fig. 2-3 shows how this process works. The program begins its search for a solution with the *goal* it is seeking, a strategy (strategy-1). It seeks the first then clause in a rule in the knowledge base that contains the key word "strategy-1," as is indicated by the arrow line (A) on the left of Fig. 2-3. The inference engine then backward chains to the first if clause (or premise) within that rule and finds the key word "industry-type," as shown by the line (B) in the figure. The process continues in this way through the entire knowledge base until an answer is found. The answer is assumed found when (1) an answer is found for all of the if clauses in a rule containing "strategy-1" in its then clause, or (2) all the rules have been examined and the system determines an answer is not possible. The process shown in the figure is discussed in more detail in the discussion of the STRATEGIC PLANNER I system in Chapter 21.

## Forward Chaining

Forward chaining involves working from the other direction. It starts with the data, examines the if clauses, and searches for a solution by working from the data toward a goal. Using this reasoning process, the system builds its case working from the data toward a solution from the data. When an answer is found to all of the if clauses in a rule containing a goal word in its then clause (for example, "strategy-1"), the system gives the user its recommended solution. It will report that no solution is possible, if after an exhaustive search no answer is found.

Forward chaining searches can expand very rapidly, since a virtually unlimited number of rules may be examined. For this reason controls are needed to set limits on the search process. In today's systems, therefore, forward chaining usually is combined with backward chaining, which sets limits on the number of goals examined, in order to reduce the time and computer capacity required for processing.

Forward chaining is a familiar reasoning strategy in strategic company planning. In many situations planners work from the situation data to a conclusion. Very often a planner combines forward and backward reasoning processes, moving from the data to several hypotheses, and then back from the hypotheses to the data to retest initial thoughts.

Since forward chaining searches usually require much more processing capacity than is required for backward chaining, economic factors have set major limits on the application of forward chaining in the strategic corporate planning area.

## Other Search and Reasoning Techniques

In addition to different search directions, there are several other search techniques that can be used by an inference engine. Procedures can be written to do so-called *depth* and *breadth* searches through the knowledge base. In depth searches, the search mechanism first explores a line of reasoning up or down through the knowledge base; the backward chaining example discussed earlier is one kind of depth search. A breadth search, on the other hand, would first move across the knowledge base before moving up or down a rule or frame hierarchy structure.

## Reasoning with Uncertainty

Inference engines can present solutions that are uncertain by combining certainty factors when searching a knowledge base. For example, they can make recommendations such as: A selective product investment strategy has a 75 percent certainty factor of working. In this way they can provide guidance in estimating risk.

## Control Mechanisms

Knowlege-based systems also have operators and control programs, like other computer systems. For example, rule-based systems have an executor (operating program) that determines which rules are appropriate (matches), chooses one to execute (select), and executes (or fires) the chosen rule. Object or frame-based systems have executors that can determine inheritance, traverse networks, and query and modify data given in frames. In addition, procedures can be written into frames to print, edit, handle messages, trigger default values, check restrictions, and manipulate values. A variety of controls can also be included to handle the variables contained in many knowledge-based systems.

Some knowledge-based systems developers consider such control mechanisms to be part of the inference engine. Others treat them as a separate component of the program.

## Explanation Facility

An inference engine may also provide an explanation facility. This enables it to explain to a user *why* a question was asked or *how* a conclusion was reached. In this way, during a consultation, a user can study the search processes the system followed to make a recommendation. It helps a user to understand the logic used and the assumptions upon which a decision was based. For example, it can show users the rules used to reach a conclusion or an explanation of why certain questions were asked. This feature is a powerful one, which is extremely useful in dealing with strategic company planning decisions where certain assumptions have such a significant impact on decisions. With the explanation facility, a user can identify the root assumptions and reexamine their validity.

### Natural Language Capabilities

Many knowledge-based systems can communicate with a user in English, so they are said to have natural language capabilities. They are not, however, natural language systems. Natural language systems are another subset of AI research. Natural language systems are computer systems that explore speech understanding and replication. One of the better known ones is INTELLECT (Artificial Intelligence Corporation), a natural language system that is used to interface with commercial data bases, such as FOCUS.

## KNOWLEDGE-BASED SYSTEM PROGRAMMING LANGUAGES AND SHELLS

Knowledge-based systems were originally developed using programming languages such as LISP and PROLOG. This kind of development requires knowledge of, and experience with, these programming languages. For this reason they are beyond the scope of this book.

Many other development tools and expert system shells are available. They range from development versions of programming language (such as OPS5 and INTERLISP), which contain prepackaged routines, to mainframe shells (such as ART, ESE and KEE) to more limited microcomputer shells (such as M.1). A number of these are described in Chapters 5, 6, and 7. Because of its nontechnical orientation, this book is concerned almost exclusively with expert system shells, especially those used on microcomputers.

During the early 1980s, a variety of preprogrammed expert system shells were developed. They contained such components as inference engine programs, programmed control mechanisms, programmed external software interface routines, and capabilities for storing knowledge bases. A user of a shell is expected to create only the knowledge base. This allows people to create knowledge-based systems without knowing programming languages. These so-called expert system "development shells" or "development environments" triggered the current surge of work in knowledge-based systems.

Some shells developed require the use of a mainframe computer, for example, ART (Inference Corporation). Some shells have been designed for use on LISP and other special purpose (dedicated) machines. Many shells have been developed for PCs.

Expert system shells are discussed in some detail in Harmon and King (1985) and by Rauch-Hinden (1986b) and Gevarter (1987).

Of most interest to this study are the shells available for PCs. They are the ones that will stimulate widespread development of knowledge-base systems for business applications, including those for strategic company planning.

Advanced microcomputer shells have been and are being developed. Teknowledge, for example, has such a microcomputer expert system shell (called M.1, version 2). It uses backward chaining, but also has some limited forward chaining capabilities. It can handle up to 2,000 rules in its knowledge base. Texas Instruments' most advanced microcomputer shell is called PERSONAL CONSULTANT PLUS. It also has backward and forward chaining capabilities and expanded rule capacity.

Micro Data Base Systems' GURU is one of the more advanced and versatile expert system shells available for PCs. Among its more interesting features are spreadsheet and relational data base systems integration capability, math and certainty factor capabilities, and on-line knowledge base editing facilities (Holsapple and Whinston, 1986).

Microcomputer expert system shells are especially good for developing small systems that test the feasibility of proposed larger systems. Such smaller, developmental test systems are called *prototype* systems.

Knowledge-based systems developers almost always create a prototype of proposed larger systems. These prototypes are used to test the soundness of a system's design before undertaking expensive development efforts.

The growth of PC technology, combined with the emergence of expert system shells, has set the stage for rapid growth in knowledge-based systems development in the late 1980s.

Expert system shells, such as GURU and M.1, are putting into the hands of users, both computer systems developers and managers who are fairly knowledgeable about computers, powerful development tools. This should draw into the development process many more managers and businesses, who in turn will be able to perceive many more possible applications of knowledge-base systems technology to actual management jobs than could computer technicians. The development pattern anticipated here is similar to the one that occurred after the major spreadsheet and data base management programs were introduced.

A manager obviously needs some computer background to put these shells to work. They are sophisticated tools and require some computer expertise. In addition, shells have a long way to go to be truly "user friendly." What these shells do is just make the widespread development of knowledge-based systems more feasible for a new generation of managers. These managers, on the whole, have had more training in computers than any previous generation of managers.

All knowledge-based systems development described in the sample system chapters involves the use of PC expert system shells. Some of the major PC expert system shells are discussed later in the book. Several languages, such as PROLOG, are briefly described, but only to provide background.

Before discussing systems design and documentation, knowledge engineering tasks, such as structured situation analysis and situation model development, are examined.

# REVIEW QUESTIONS

1. Define artificial intelligence and its major components.

2. The term *expert system* has caused considerable confusion. Discuss the ways in which the term *expert* is used in relation to knowledge-based systems and artificial intelligence. Why is it best to consider it a relative, not absolute, concept here?

3. What is a knowledge base? What is a knowledge-based system?

4. Describe the different ways to classify knowledge-based systems. Give examples of each.

5. Discuss the major applications of knowledge-based systems technology today.

6. Describe the distinguishing characteristics of knowledge-based systems.

7. What are the major ways to represent knowledge in a knowledge base? Describe if-then rules.

8. Define "inferencing" and "inference" engine as related to knowledge-based systems. Define different kinds of inferencing found in knowledge-based systems.

9. What are expert system shells? How do they work? What is their impact on knowledge-based systems development?

10. Describe the ways in which expert system shells make it possible for nontechnical managers to develop knowledge-based systems.

11. In what ways is it easier to modify knowledge-based systems than conventional computer systems?

12. What are prototype systems and why are they important in knowledge-based systems development?

# REFERENCES

Gevarter, William B., "The Nature and Evaluation of Commercial Expert System Building Tools," *Computer*, May 1987, pp. 25–41.

Harmon, P., and D. King, *Expert Systems*, New York: Wiley, 1985.

Holsapple, C.W., and A.B. Winston, *Expert Systems Using GURU*, Homewood, IL: Irwin, 1986.

Rauch-Hinden, W.B., "Software Integrates AI, Standard Systems," *Mini-Micro Systems*, October 1986, pp. 69ff.

# 3

# Structured Situation Analysis

This chapter concerns structured situation analysis. The situation involved can be a business problem, a task, or a decision. It is often referred to as the "expert's knowledge domain" or the "area of expertise."

The structured situation analysis phase involves studying and organizing the decision situation for which a knowledge based system is being developed. This phase of the systems development process is variously referred to as knowledge, problem, or situation engineering. Its objective is to develop a framework or basis for the next development phase, the systems documentation-engineering phase, which is described in the following chapters.

The aspects of the development process covered in this chapter are

- Selecting a decision, problem, or task to work on
- Acquiring the knowledge or expertise
- Probing how the situation works and how decisions are made
- Narrowing the focus
- Defining or structuring the decision, problem, or task for which a knowledge-based system or prototype system is being developed

The study of the strategic corporate planning area in Part 1 of this book is an extended example of this exploratory phase of expert knowledge-based systems development—getting to know the area of expertise.

## SELECTING A DECISION, PROBLEM, OR TASK
## TO WORK ON

Business needs should be the major factor in selecting a knowledge-based systems development project.

Sometimes selecting a business decision, problem, or task for knowledge-based systems development can be easy, for example, if you are hired to do a specific systems development project, such as a system to guide customer service representatives in handling billing complaints. There, the situation is preselected for you.

At other times an AI consultant (or company personnel experienced in related AI areas) may be asked to review all company operations to see where AI tools might be of help. This can initially involve a study ranging across many company operating areas. Eventually an area to be worked on is selected from those examined.

The selection process involves examining such factors as

- □ Is human expertise about to be lost?
- □ Is human expertise scarce?
- □ Is human expertise expensive in relation to the job needs?
- □ Is the expertise needed in a variety of locations?
- □ Is the expertise needed in a hostile environment?
- □ Do the job requirements (such as speed and precision) exceed the capacity of normally available experts?

Such overall business needs studies are being continually done today at major banks, insurance and other financial services companies, accounting firms, and manufacturing companies.

The situation could also involve an individual operating manager with some computer training who selects a problem from among the many faced daily. For example, it might be a problem concerning poor performance in the telephone screening of car insurance applicants. In this case there was a shortage of trained people available at a reasonable salary level. High turnover and poor performance had resulted.

The problem or decision to be studied was how to guide each phone operator through the applicant screening process and have the system make recommendations as to whether or not to approve the application.

The solution to reconciling performance requirements and budget constraints was for the manager to spend several weekends developing a knowledge-based system. The manager who developed and introduced such a system in this situation was able to increase performance consistency substantially. In addition, the system reduced training time and cut training costs by a third.

More and more frequently younger managers are taking the initiative in this way to solve their immediate problems and gain recognition and promotions.

After considering the business need, the next consideration is to determine whether or not a knowledge-based system is feasible and appropriate in the situation. In order to consider doing a knowledge-based system, the answer should be yes to most of the following:

- □ Do recognized experts exist?
- □ Can experts do the task better than amateurs and can their skills be taught to others?
- □ Do experts agree on solutions?
- □ Does the task require reason and informed judgments, as opposed to just common sense?
- □ Can experts articulate their methods?
- □ Is the task well understood?
- □ Is the task of manageable size?
- □ Are typical example cases or situations readily available?
- □ Does the task require symbolic manipulation?

A major consideration encountered frequently involves the decision as to whether or not to use a conventional computer application instead of a knowledge-based application for the problem, decision, or task under study. If the answer is yes to the following question, then you would probably not use a knowledge-based system application.

Does the task have such a quantitative or procedural content or structure that it would best be done using a more conventional computer tool, such as a spreadsheet or data base management application?

Another consideration is whether or not a knowledge-based system is justified in the situation. This involves determining if the benefits or payoffs from introducing the system justify the costs of developing the system.

Where a situation involves a decision or task encountered only a few times a year, then it is probably best handled by a human expert.

Selecting a problem, decision, or task area for expert knowledge-based systems development, then, involves studying (1) the business need (does it seem needed?), (2) the feasibility of it (can you do it most effectively using a knowledge-based system?), and (3) the benefits versus the costs (is it worth it?).

As seen in the discussions of the sample systems later in this book, sometimes (though not always) the selection process is a narrowing process, during which a general situation area is studied and then a specific area selected for initial prototype system development. In the following discussion this narrowing process is treated on two levels: (1) the general situation under study and (2) the specific situation for which the actual system or a prototype system is being developed.

The complexity of the actual situation under study and the objective of your systems development project will dictate how many levels are dealt with in your situation. Structured situation analysis techniques are applied at all levels.

## ACQUIRING THE KNOWLEDGE OR EXPERTISE

Expertise can be acquired in a variety of ways. Experts may develop the system themselves in narrowly defined situations. In these instances they are their own source of knowledge about the field. This was the case in the insurance applicant screening situation mentioned above.

On the other hand, a systems developer (or knowledge engineer) may analyze the expert field and organize it for computer input. Acquiring expertise in such situations normally first involves some reading and studying about the expert's field. At times a large part of the expertise can be acquired from written sources. This is often the case in fault diagnosis situations where much of the expertise is contained in technical and repair manuals.

Where the knowledge engineer must acquire a large part of the expertise directly from an expert, a variety of problems can be encountered. Experts usually have regular jobs to do and time is limited for them to work on other projects. On average, up to 25 percent of an expert's time is required, over an extended period of time, to develop an expert knowledge-based system. In such situations some organizational commitments are required from higher management in order to relieve the expert of some regular work. Without such commitments it is best not to start the project.

Committing an expert this extensively to a project can be an especially good idea if the expert will be involved in putting the system to work and using it. It gives the expert a proprietary interest in the system, which helps assure that it will actually be used effectively.

In addition to organizational roadblocks to the knowledge acquisition and to the subsequent use of these systems, there are many psychological and emotional roadblocks.

- It is hard to articulate concisely and precisely how we make decisions. The more competent experts are, the less able they often seem to be to describe the knowledge and reasoning processes they use. To overcome this it is best to focus at first only on the most typical situations. The initial prototype system can be built around the typical situations.

- It can appear to be a bothersome job that seems pointless. If you know your job, why bother to write down how to do it? Special incentives are needed to overcome this problem and the other negatives cited below.

- There appear to be no payoffs or benefits to the expert, only potential loss of status, ego satisfactions, and possibly the job when knowledge-based systems are developed. If everyone knows how you do your job, the magic is gone. And, if the computer can do your job, you may no longer be needed. Some of these fears are well-founded, since mediocre people will possibly be replaced. But for the true professionals these systems only take over the more routine, typical jobs leaving the more interesting work for the human professional. In addition, many of these systems are designed to assist the expert to do a more professional job. In spite of these potential benefits, sufficient rewards and satisfactions, both real and psychological, must be provided to the expert helping develop the system and getting it used, or the perceived negatives will prevent effective system development.

Because of the many potential organizational and other problems, good interviewing skills, tact, and at times a little creativeness are prerequisites of successful knowledge acquisition. In one situation, for example, the experts found it so difficult to work with the knowledge engineers that the experts had to be observed at work through a see-through mirror.

The following are some useful guidelines to keep in mind during the expert knowledge acquisition phase:

| | |
|---|---|
| □ Expert observation | Watch the expert solving real problems at work. |
| □ Problem analysis | Explore the kinds of data, knowledge, and procedures needed to solve problems in the expert's area. |
| □ Problem description | Have the expert describe a typical problem for each category of solution in the expert's area. |
| □ Problem refinement | Present the expert with a series of realistic problems to solve, probing for the rationale behind the reasoning steps. |
| □ System development and refinement | Once a description of how the expert works has been developed, have the expert give you a series of problems to solve using the rules acquired from the interviews. |
| □ System testing | Have the expert examine and critique a prototype system's rules and control structure as well as the results of a prototype system consultation. |
| □ System validation | Present the cases solved by both the expert and the prototype system to other outside experts. |

The same guidelines, in modified form, would be followed by individuals developing systems on their own.

## PROBING HOW THE SITUATION WORKS AND HOW DECISIONS ARE MADE

The objectives in examining a situation are (1) to identify what kind of knowledge is needed (the problem space), (2) to determine how one goes about manipulating the knowledge to come to a decision or recommendation (the reasoning process), and (3) to specify the kinds of decisions and recommendations possible (the solution space). These objectives are achieved through studying how a human expert actually works and developing typical scenarios of how the expert goes about doing the job. This is often referred to as the *decomposition* or *analysis* phase.

The following describes how a knowledge engineer in an oil spill situation went about expert knowledge acquisition (Hayes-Roth, Waterman, and Lenat 1983, 133–135).

The knowledge engineer first had several preliminary meetings with the expert to narrow the scope of the problem. During the meetings that followed, the knowledge engineer attempted to understand what concepts, relationships, and definitions were important and relevant to the problem by asking the expert to explain and justify the reasoning used to deal with specific types of spill problems. For example, the following is a segment of one of the early interviews:

> KNOWLEDGE ENGINEER: Suppose you were told that a spill had been detected in White Oaks Creek one mile before it enters White Oak Lake. What would you do to contain the spill?

> EXPERT: That depends on a number of factors. I would need to find the source in order to prevent the possibility of further contamination, probably by checking the drains and manholes for signs of the spill material. And it helps to know what the spilled material is.

> KNOWLEDGE ENGINEER: How can you tell what it is?

> EXPERT: Sometimes you can tell what the substance is by its smell. Sometimes you can tell by its color, but that's not always reliable since dyes are used a lot nowadays. Oil, however, floats on the surface and forms a silvery film, while acids dissolve completely in the water. Once you discover the type of material spilled, you can eliminate any buildings that don't store the material at all or don't store enough of it to account for the spill.

During these meetings, the knowledge engineer defined specific terms that the expert used (such as odor and color) as well as identifying other knowledge-structuring mechanisms that the expert used. For example, there were classes of compounds with distinguishing generic properties. Such classifications helped organize the hundreds of actual compounds that were stored on-site.

The oil spill expert also grouped or classified locations of spills (which sites are prone to a spill, which are potentially more hazardous). These conceptual classifications seemed to form the basis for certain types of inferences the expert made when solving problems. This identification of terms used in a technical way and the descriptions of how situation components are organized and structured constitutes the *structure of the expert knowledge* or *knowledge segments* in the situation.

A second kind of knowledge the knowledge engineer listens for is the *basic reasoning strategies* an expert uses when searching for a solution to a problem, making a decision, or performing a task. What facts does the expert try to establish first? What kinds of questions does the expert ask first? Does the expert make initial guesses about anything based on tentative information? How does the expert then determine which questions to use to refine the guess? In what order does the expert pursue each of the important tasks, and does this order vary according to the case or kind of case?

In addition, the knowledge engineer also identifies the expert's justifications for the associations, terms, and reasoning strategies the expert uses. These justifications are important to record not only for the knowledge engineer's own clarification, but also for maintaining adequate systems documentation and allowing accurate systems explanations. These kinds of knowledge ease the task of designing, constructing, and later modifying the expert system.

As seen from the above quoted conversation, the knowledge engineer develops these so-called *typical reasoning scenarios* of how the expert works through tracing actual typical decision situations from start to finish. Generally speaking, *it is best to focus on the most typical situations during these early phases of the study*, and *to avoid the exceptional cases*, until reasonably good diagrams or models of the situation have been structured. Trying to incorporate all the nuances of the job into these early models very often impedes progress. The initial prototype systems will generally be designed to handle only the most typical situations.

As part of this process the knowledge engineer also defines the possible *recommendations or actions* that might be made or taken by the expert in the types of situations under study.

Not all knowledge engineers (or systems developers) have an expert available who can articulate all aspects of a problem as clearly as did the oil spill expert. In addition, some areas are not as well defined or are too broad in scope or too subjective to be easily defined. Organizing the problem situation can be a major undertaking in these instances.

Based on these studies of typical situations, the structure of the situation begins to emerge. These early ideas of the situation structure can be fairly rough, as is seen in Figs. 3-1 and 3-2. The diagrams shown in the figures are not to be taken as examples of good models. They are examples of rough and imperfect diagrams and are given here to illustrate how the more fully developed models (such as the versions shown in Figs. 3-3 and 3-4) evolve later from very rough beginnings.

The process of structuring the situation in a way useful for knowledge-based systems development is a continuing, evolving one, involving

- *Reviewing typical decisions made in each area*, and developing typical scenarios of the expert at work. This is the situation analysis or the decomposition phase.
- *Drawing initial diagrams of the typical decisions*. This is the beginning of the reconceptualization or reformulation phase.
- *Reviewing additional test case examples and revising the diagrammed structures*, as often as needed or as time permits, the recycling phase.

This approach is a common one in knowledge-based systems development projects, and is at work at all levels of the situation analysis.

Figures 3-3, 3-4, 3-5, and 3-6 give examples of several more fully developed general situation diagrams. The situations these diagrams represent range from very large and complex situations, such as the strategic company planning and the new venture planning ones shown in Figs. 3-3 and 3-4, to a fairly circumscribed one for personal investment planning shown in Fig. 3-5, to the very basic grass-cutting situation diagrammed in Fig. 3-6, which is used throughout this book for instructional purposes.

In some instances these models were developed over several years, based on work done on many smaller prototype systems within the area. This was the case

(*Text continues on p. 48*)

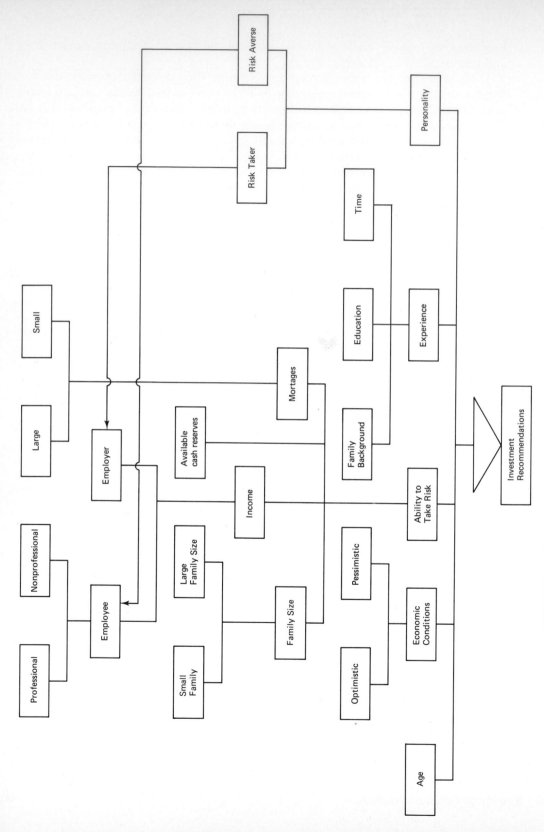

**FIGURE 3-1** Preliminary rough decision situation diagram for personal investment planning.

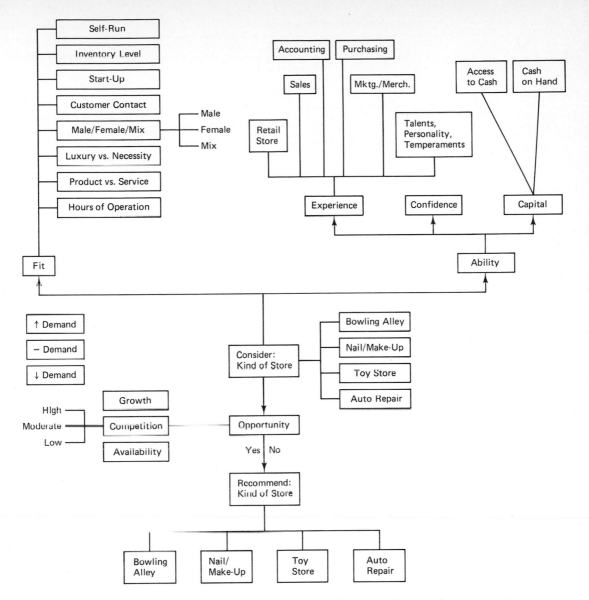

**FIGURE 3-2  Preliminary rough decision situation diagram for new venture planning decision.**

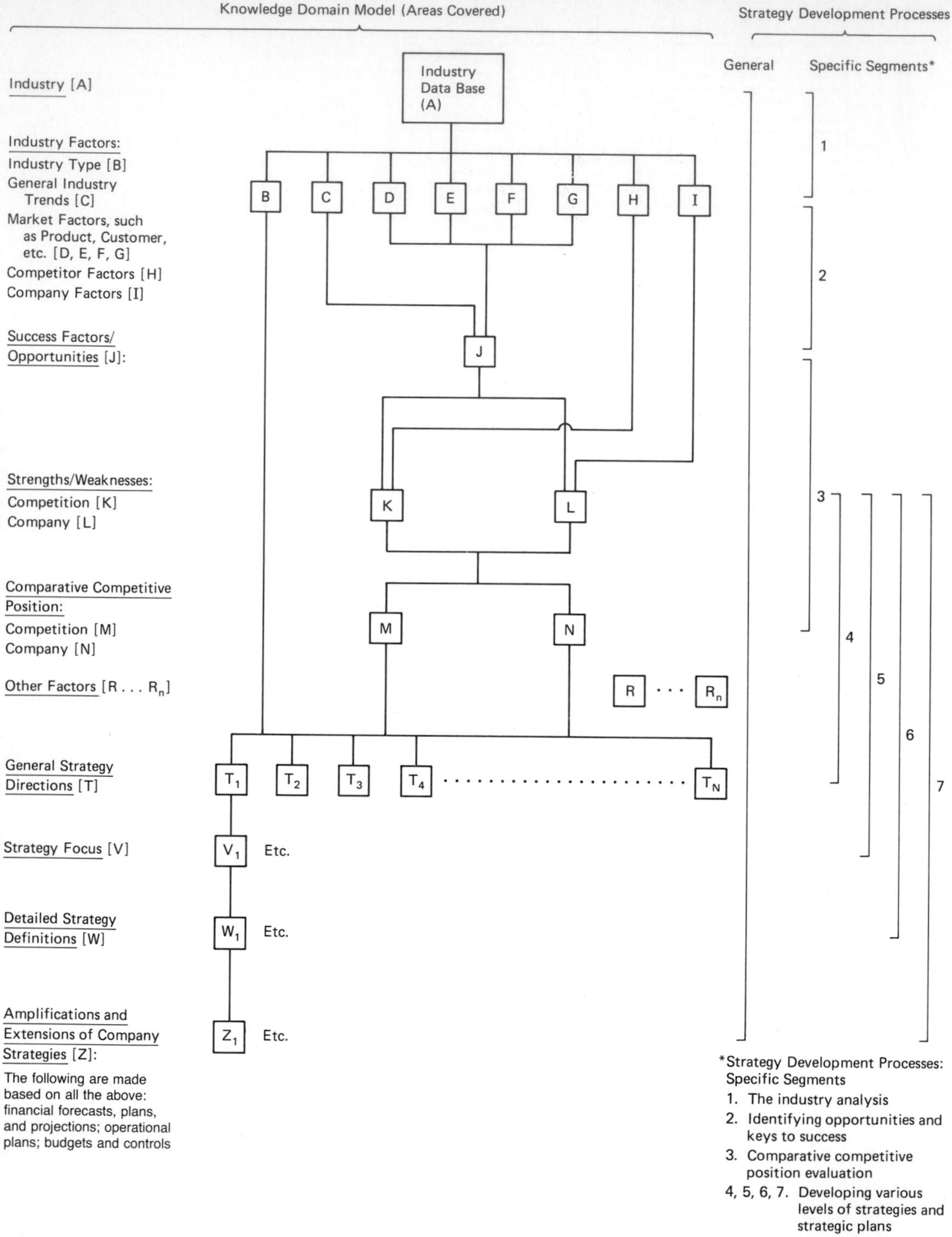
Knowledge Domain Model (Areas Covered)
Strategy Development Processes
General
Specific Segments*
Industry [A]
Industry Data Base (A)
Industry Factors:
Industry Type [B]
General Industry Trends [C]
Market Factors, such as Product, Customer, etc. [D, E, F, G]
Competitor Factors [H]
Company Factors [I]
B
C
D
E
F
G
H
I
Success Factors/ Opportunities [J]:
J
Strengths/Weaknesses:
Competition [K]
Company [L]
K
L
Comparative Competitive Position:
Competition [M]
Company [N]
M
N
Other Factors [R . . . R_n]
R · · · R_n
General Strategy Directions [T]
T_1
T_2
T_3
T_4
T_N
Strategy Focus [V]
V_1
Etc.
Detailed Strategy Definitions [W]
W_1
Etc.
Amplifications and Extensions of Company Strategies [Z]:
Z_1
Etc.
The following are made based on all the above: financial forecasts, plans, and projections; operational plans; budgets and controls
1
2
3
4
5
6
7
*Strategy Development Processes: Specific Segments
1. The industry analysis
2. Identifying opportunities and keys to success
3. Comparative competitive position evaluation
4, 5, 6, 7. Developing various levels of strategies and strategic plans

**FIGURE 3-3 Decision situation diagram for enterprise-wide strategy development—knowledge areas covered and strategy development processes.**

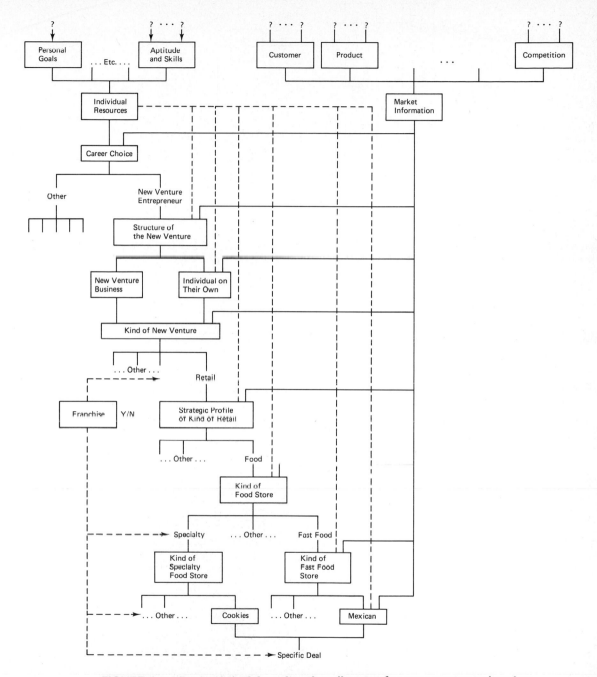

**FIGURE 3-4   Revised decision situation diagram for new venture planning decision.**

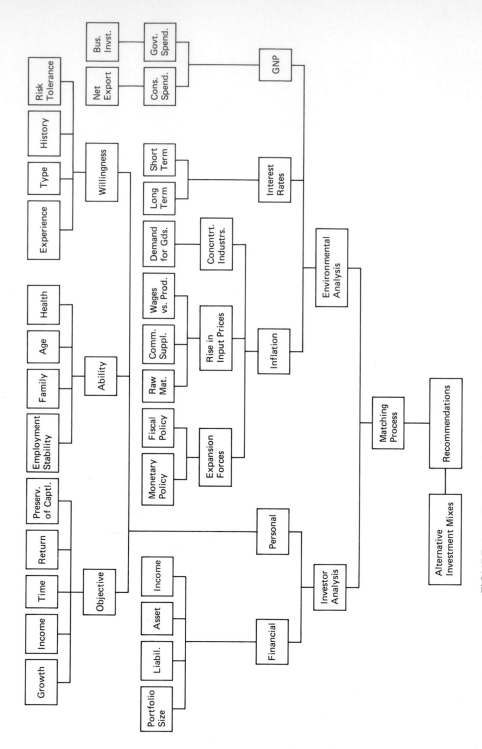

**FIGURE 3-5  Revised decision situation diagram for personal investment planning.**

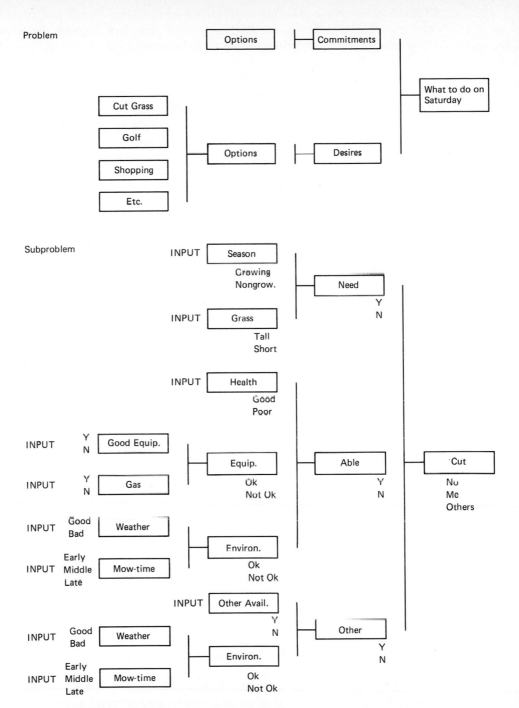

**FIGURE 3-6   Decision situation diagram for grass-cutting decision.**

with the new venture-planning model in Fig. 3-4. Once developed, these models in turn served as a structure for further specific prototype systems development. In other cases, such as with the grass-cutting decision in Fig. 3-6, models are developed in a few hours.

Developing such overview models can also help to coordinate and give direction to complex development projects, where that is an important consideration. Where that is not a major consideration, for example when developing isolated operational support systems such as the one described earlier for telephone loan application screening, such large overview models are not needed or used.

In all situations some degree of narrowing, refinement, and amplification is needed during the early development phases. It is always needed to define areas for initial prototype development.

## NARROWING THE FOCUS

Narrowing the focus of a decision, problem, or task is something you do continually, from the beginning of a project. In the oil spill situation, for example, the knowledge engineer first did a few weeks of independent study about the field, before interviewing the expert. He then met with the expert to learn more about the expert's job and agree on ways to restrict the scope of the proposed system in order to make the problem more manageable. These early preliminary sessions led to a very precise definition of what the system would accomplish—identifying, locating, and containing the spill.

During the process of narrowing the focus in the strategic-planning study, specific segments of the planning process were identified within the context of the overall planning process. These are shown on the right side in Fig. 3-3. This segmentation enabled concentration in more narrowly focused areas and so the more rapid development of specific prototype systems.

A similar refining process occurred in the grass-cutting example. As is shown in Fig. 3-6, the general decision was "what to do on Saturday." This was narrowed to one segment, grass cutting, for prototype development.

In the new venture-planning situation in Fig. 3-4, prototype systems were initially developed at many levels of the decision situation, including the entrepreneurial career planning and franchise selection systems described in the later chapters of this book.

The narrowing process in the personal investment planning situation shown in Fig. 3-5 was somewhat different, since there it was decided initially to develop a very general prototype system of the basic decision. Later separate systems were developed for each major investment instrument area, such as bonds and stocks. For the initial study the narrowing involved limiting the situation to four specific portfolio mixes to enable studying the dynamics of the concept and structure of the overall system.

Business managers and experts want to see results quickly, so you want to have something to show them that is specific, works, and is useful as soon as possible. A narrowed focus leads to faster development of a working prototype system.

## DEFINING OR STRUCTURING THE DECISION, PROBLEM, OR TASK FOR WHICH A KNOWLEDGE-BASED SYSTEM OR PROTOTYPE SYSTEM IS BEING DEVELOPED

Like the study of the more general situation areas described above, this phase of the structured situation analysis involves

- Not only a very careful analysis (or *decomposition*) of how a situation typically works
- But also organizing (*reconceptualizing* or *reformulating*) a situation in a fairly comprehensive, systematic, structured way

The process is a continuing one, which in complex situations can involve repeating the cycle many times.

Continuing the refinement process, more detailed models are developed for specific areas being studied for possible prototype system development. For example, Figs. 3-7 through 3-10 show diagrams for a franchise selection decision situation. This system is a segment of the overall new venture-planning decision situation shown in Fig. 3-4. Figure 3-11 shows an example of a prototype system in the planning area for general strategy direction development; it is a segment of the overall planning model shown in Fig. 3-3.

### Identify All Possible Recommendations That Can Be Made in the Situation

Identifying the specific recommendations the system might make has proved to be a very helpful device for guiding beginners through the situation analysis.

For example, in a grass-cutting situation the possible recommendations might initially be limited to: don't cut the grass, I will cut the grass, or someone else will cut the grass. In the strategic-planning situation involving identifying general strategy directions, several possible strategic focuses might be: get out of the business, hold position, niche concentration, and the like. The ones identified in a personal investment planning situation, which is also described below, were four portfolio mixes:

- Stocks (100 percent)
- Stocks (60 percent), T-bonds (30 percent), money market funds (10 percent)
- Stocks (30 percent), T-bonds (50 percent), money market funds (20 percent)
- T-bonds (10 percent), money market funds (90 percent)

Besides helping systems developers focus quickly on a specific frame of reference, thinking about actual recommendations encourages testing one's thoughts against actual examples—the expert scenarios. At each stage in the guidelines that follow, thinking in terms of actual typical situations keeps the study's focus on *how the situation actually works*.

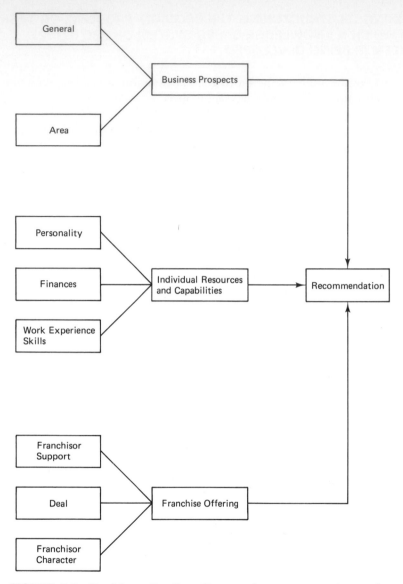

**FIGURE 3-7  Decision situation diagram for a new venture using franchising.**

## Specify Conditions That Are Examined in Coming to Conclusions and Alternative Values of These Conditions That Dictate the Solution

For example, in the grass-cutting situation in Fig. 3-6, the conditions affecting the choice among the possible solutions are need, my availability, and the availability of others. The controlling values for these conditions are all yes or no.

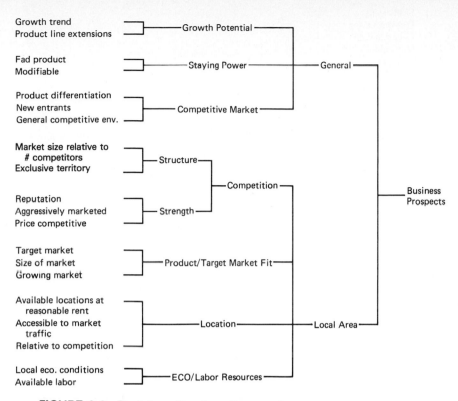

**FIGURE 3-8   Decision situation diagram for a new venture using franchising—business prospects area segment.**

In a strategic-planning situation, the conditions affecting a decision include industry type, comparative company and competition strengths in key-to-success areas, special company and market factors and the like, as seen in Fig. 3-11. The values for these conditions would, for example, be for industry type: fragmented, declining, emerging, and mature.

At this point, the developer is beginning to define with more precision the heuristics, or reasoning process, the expert uses.

### Trace the Reasoning Back to Its Roots and Isolate Specific Segments of the Problem

It is necessary to trace how the expert reasons from the situation facts to solutions. As an illustration, in the grass-cutting situation shown in Fig. 3-6, the process would involve probing the conditions of health, weather, and equipment to determine a person's ability to do it.

In the development of the personal investment planning system, the developer focused at one point on how to determine the individual investor's capacity for risk taking. It was determined that risk capacity depended on both the investor's *will-*

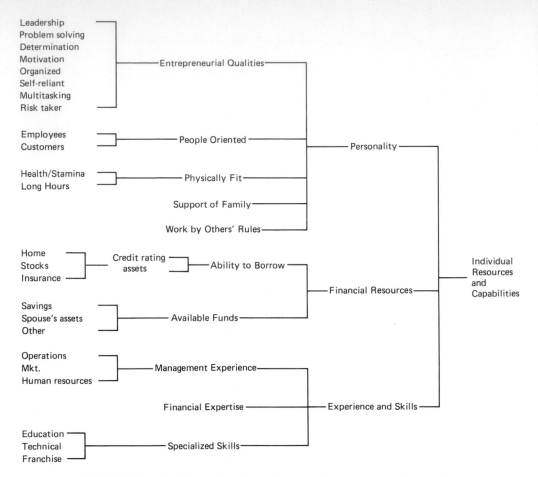

**FIGURE 3-9 Decision situation diagram for a new venture using franchising—individual resources and capabilities segment.**

*ingness* and *ability* to take risks. In turn, ability would depend on a number of other conditions.

The line of reasoning identified, which is roughly sketched out in Fig. 3-1 and in a more structured way in Fig. 3-5, therefore, went from

- Recommended investment (such as portfolio mix of stocks and bonds) to
- Factors affecting the choice (such as individual investor and environmental factors) to
- Factors affecting the individual investor situation (such as personal characteristics and financial resources available) to
- Defining personal characteristic (such as willingness and ability to take risks) to
- Identifying those factors affecting ability to take risks (such as employment stability, age, health, and family situation)

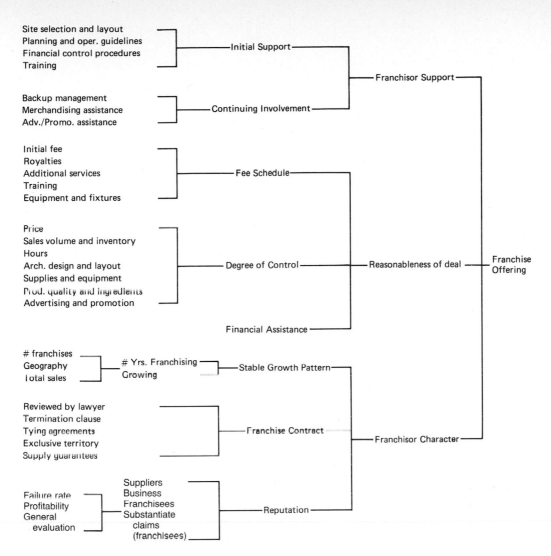

**FIGURE 3-10  Decision situation diagram for a new venture using franchising—franchise offering area segment.**

As is seen from this brief example, the process of examining decision situations in depth involves analyzing the reasoning process and knowledge segments in extraordinary detail.

### Develop Detailed Diagrams of the Structure of the Situation to Be Prototyped

As the study progresses, a systems developer develops more and more structured and detailed diagrams of the situation.   Figures 3-8 through 3-10, for example, give more detailed segments of the franchise selection decision outlined in Fig. 3-7.

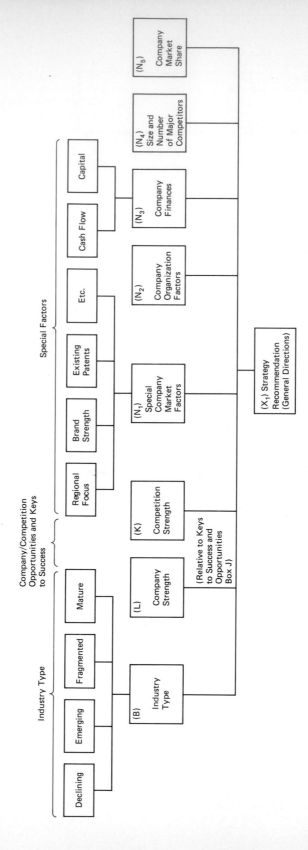

**FIGURE 3-11  Strategic planning decision situation diagram—general strategy directions segment.**

A variety of examples of ways in which such structured situation models are developed are given in the sample system chapters. Structured system models, such as those shown in Figs. 3-7 to 3-10, are the key link between the expert situation and the computer system representing it. They are intended to reconceptualize and reformulate the situation in a way that facilitates systems development. On the one hand they must accurately represent the way an expert actually works. On the other hand they must be structured in a way that can be handled by an expert knowledge-based system shell.

One way to help yourself find fresh insights and keep your focus on reality during this difficult phase of the development process is to *write down a scenario of a typical expert situation observed*. For example, this might involve a four- or-five-paragraph description of how an expert consultant reasoned about a franchise offering for a client in coming to a recommendation. Examples of these scenarios appear in all the sample system chapters, including the one for the franchise selection.

Then a diagram is drawn of that specific decision. The diagram would be what is called a knowledge domain diagram or model, such as the ones shown in Figs. 3-7 through 3-10. This is the beginning of the *modeling* phase.

The scenarios would be rewritten based on what the diagram (or structured model) looks like and any revisions in the scenario that may have occurred to you while constructing the diagrams. In turn, the diagrams are revised based on the rethinking of the scenario. Revisions always occur, because something always seems to be omitted or not said right the first times through and because you usually think of better ways to structure and represent the way the expert thinks as you study the situation in more depth.

The cycle is repeated as often as necessary or as time permits. This is not only because it is hard to represent reality within the confines of diagrams and written scenarios. It is also because there can be several pretty good ways to draw a diagram. So you may want to experiment with alternative diagrams.

The purpose of this back-and-forth exercise is to keep the diagram (or technical tool) close to the reality of the situation (the scenario of how an expert works). This back-and-forth process continues during the systems development stages described in the following chapters, so that the scenario continues to function as a reference point in reality for the systems developer.

> This test case scenario writing has proved in practice to be the single most useful method for keeping knowledge-based systems (which are based on the structured diagrams) true replications or emulations of actual experts at work.

Subsequent model development phases involve writing scenarios of other, different typical situations and going through the model adjustment process again to make the model have applicability to a wider variety of tasks, problems, or decisions. For example, the general auditing model shown in Fig. 3-12 was developed by studying a series of specific auditing situations and gradually expanding the diagrams of initial typical situations analyzed. Once developed, this in turn served as a framework for stimulating further specific systems development work in the auditing area.

The diagrams (or models) of decision, problem, or task situations exactly du-

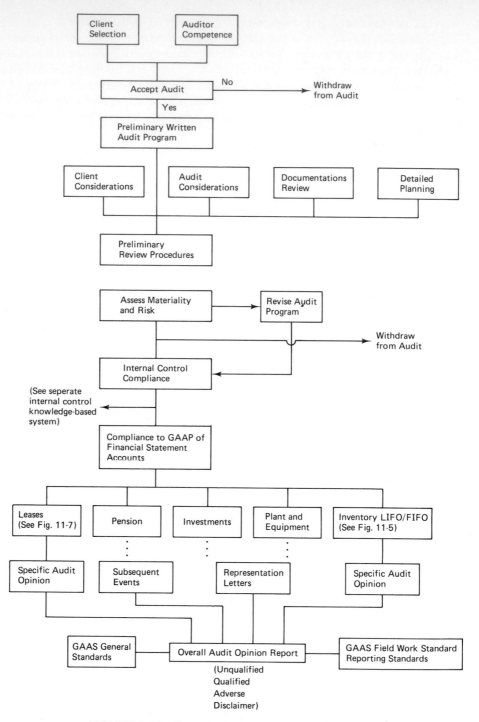

**FIGURE 3-12  Overall diagram of the audit process.**

plicate human reasoning processes only in very simple situations. Most of them only replicate, imitate, or approximate aspects of human thinking. They do not duplicate human thinking or capture the exact way the expert's mind moves back and forth continually among the different frames of knowledge—even after many revisions. Management decisions simply are not that easy to represent graphically.

The reformulation of the situation, therefore, is always an imperfect compromise that tries to strike a balance. For example, in many management decision situations the reformulation or reconceptualization is not necessarily a *prescription* for the best way to solve a problem or make a decision. Nor is it merely a *description* of how one person, a presumed expert, does it.

Rather, in management decision situations *the objective is often to replicate or emulate a composite description of how one pretty good expert might do it reasonably well*. In major systems this replication would be based on the judgments of a variety of experts in the field as to the best compromise among

- The different ways different experts actually do it
- The theoretical best way to do it
- The limitations inherent in graphic representation techniques
- The limitations inherent in the expert system shells used to computerize the system

### Define the Information That Is Needed to Put the Decision or Reasoning Process to Work to Solve an Actual Problem

For example, in the grass-cutting situation, to make an actual decision, information has to be obtained on the weather, the height of the grass, who was available to cut the grass, the level of gas in the mower, and the like. In the strategic-planning situation, specific information about the industry conditions and competitor and company resources has to be obtained. This is done in each specific situation by answering questions about each competitor's market share and financial and marketing resources, the company's strengths and weaknesses in the same areas, the direction of industry sales, and the like in the specific situation under study.

Similar definitions of specific input information required for making actual decisions are made in every study.

### Recycle, Refine, Retest

From the beginning, the knowledge-based systems development process has been described as an evolutionary one. The developer keeps going back and refining what is done, no matter what the stage of the development process. As this refinement process continues, a developer gradually builds a more and more precisely structured definition of how the situation works. At some point this becomes the basis for the beginning of the documentation stage described in the following chapter.

This phase ends, therefore, with fairly good diagrams or models of the situations, decisions, or tasks.

STUDYING THE OVERALL SITUATION: UNDERSTANDING
THE EXPERT'S DOMAIN

Selecting a Decision Area to Work On

Probing How the Situation Works and How Decisions Are Made

Narrowing the Focus of the Study

Getting More Specific and Defining Interrelationships (This section is needed only in larger
development projects)

STUDYING THE SITUATION TO BE PROTOTYPED

The precise decision situation under study is defined.

The knowledge segments or influencing factors are defined.

The decision process is defined, usually through specifying the recommendations an expert
normally makes and then describing how the knowledge segments are manipulated in making
each recommendation. An example of how a typical decision is made must be included here.

At each of these phases, *when probing, when getting more specific*, and *when studying the situation
to be prototyped*, always:

- Review a specific test case in typical situations
- Draw a generalized model (or diagram) of it
- Review additional test or typical cases and revise the diagrams

While the approach described above is generally used in each system development chapter, some
minor variations in the approach occur where individual situation circumstances warrant them.

FIGURE 3-13   Outline used in sample system chapter discussions.

# CONCLUSION

The discussion in this chapter provides a framework for the systems development
discussions in all of the sample system chapters later in this book.  The outline used
in those discussions, as given in Fig. 3-13, is the basic outline of the structured situation
analysis process described in this chapter.

The work done during the structured situation analysis provides the structure
for the development of the actual prototype knowledge-based system.

During that systems development work, which is described in the next chapter,
reference is continually made to the typical scenario and situation models described
in this chapter.  This is done to make certain that the system finally developed is
based on and so replicates the reality of an actual expert at work.  In addition, as
that system development proceeds, situation structures (models and scenarios) described in this chapter may also be revised as the system requirements are reconciled
with the system-engineering requirements.

# REVIEW QUESTIONS

1. What factors should be examined when selecting a knowledge-based systems development
project?

2. Describe the conditions under which a business situation might be appropriate and feasible for a knowledge-based systems application.

3. Explain why the analysis described in this chapter is called "structured" analysis. What is involved in it? In what ways does this structured analysis impact on the actual computer system development?

4. What are structured situation models or diagrams? Describe their function within the knowledge-based systems development process.

5. Describe the interrelationships between scenario writing and model development when doing structured situation analysis.

6. Discuss why this type of analysis is sometimes referred to as "knowledge engineering."

7. Discuss the process by which general overall situation models are developed from the study of typical actual expert work situation observation.

8. Discuss some of the organizational, psychological, and emotional roadblocks to knowledge acquisition and how they might be overcome. Under what conditions would it be prudent to refuse to undertake a knowledge-based systems development assignment?

9. Discuss some of the potential problems with worker displacement arising from introduction of knowledge-based systems.

10. What are prototype systems, and how are they developed?

11. Describe the difference between knowledge engineering and systems engineering.

## REFERENCE

Hayes-Roth, F., D.A. Waterman, and D.B. Lenat, *Building Expert Systems*, Reading, MA: Addison-Wesley, 1983.

# 4

# Designing and Documenting
# a System

This chapter concerns designing and documenting a knowledge-based system and covers the following:

- System proposals
- Description of the system
- Dependency diagrams
- Decision charts
- Designing and constructing the knowledge base
- A situational approach to knowledge-based system development
- Selecting methods of putting the prototype system on computer

These steps are part of the engineering of a computerized knowledge-based system. They are done within the framework of the situation structures discussed in the preceding chapter.

The discussion in this chapter focuses on the documentation required in developing the smaller prototype systems for management decision making covered in this book. As with other parts of this book an experienced computer technician may find this discussion very limited. That limitation is intentional, since only enough of the subject is covered here to enable a working manager to get a useful prototype system up and running in a reasonable period of time.

In addition, this discussion is limited to prototype systems designed for use on expert system shells. Nontechnicians would not be expected to know any programming languages or development tools.

Specific examples of everything discussed here are given in each sample prototype system chapter later in this book.

## SYSTEM PROPOSALS

Even if you are just doing a system for yourself, it is a good idea to define in a few sentences exactly what you are trying to accomplish and the resources required to do it.

Where you have to convince a client to undertake a system development project, or your employer or company management to support it, such a systems proposal is mandatory.

The following are some of the areas such a proposal might cover:

- □ Nature and purpose of the system
- □ Why it is needed
- □ Who will use it
- □ Benefits to be derived from the system and problems if it is not developed
- □ What it will cost to develop
- □ How long it will take us to develop it
- □ Who will develop it and to what extent will others be involved
- □ Knowledge sources to be used
- □ What additional resources must we acquire to do it
- □ What controls will there be for monitoring progress of the project
- □ Potential problems

This list might be expanded or condensed, and the proposal itself vary in length and detail, depending on the actual situation under study. For example, the proposal for a small prototype system designed to test the feasibility of doing further work may be only a few paragraphs. Extensive four- to five-year projects costing several millions of dollars might require several volumes and many layers of feasibility studies.

## DESCRIPTION OF THE SYSTEM

The following topics are covered in system descriptions:

- □ System overview and objective
- □ Nature of the user interface
- □ Recommendations to be made by the system
- □ Description of the knowledge structure and reasoning processes

The decision description briefly describes the structure or outline of the system. Like the system proposal it will vary in length and detail, depending on the decision, problem, or task situation under study.

As an example, a very simple description was written for the system developed to aid in the grass-cutting decision.

- A knowledge-based system was designed to help a user decide on whether and how to cut the grass. The system is intended solely to illustrate knowledge-based systems concepts and techniques and is for instructional purposes only.
- The system would ask the user a number of questions about such things as the weather, season, and condition of the equipment.
- The recommendations would be not to cut, user cuts, or someone else cuts.
- The recommendations are based on three critical factors: the user's ability, another's ability, and the need to cut. In turn, these factors are based on other factors, such as health, availability, and weather conditions. If-then rules and backward chaining inferencing are used to determine the values and make recommendations.

Examples of prototype systems descriptions are given in all the sample system chapters later in this book.

## DEPENDENCY DIAGRAMS OF THE SYSTEM

Dependency diagrams graphically model a knowledge-based system. They show the knowledge segments and their interrelationships. They also indicate some of the basic reasoning processes by which the knowledge is manipulated. Dependency diagrams are a very powerful tool for understanding a knowledge-based system and guiding its development, since they give a complete and accurate picture of the entire system or system component they represent.

These diagrams are based on the structured situation models or diagrams described in the preceding chapter and are often developed and reviscd along with them. The versions described below are the final dependency diagrams that document the actual prototype systems.

Systems documentation often includes a separate diagram of the *knowledge segments* of a knowledge-based system. These diagrams are based on, and in smaller systems can be very similar to, the detailed situation diagrams illustrated in the preceding chapter.

These diagrams are tree-type diagrams, which are in many ways similar to conventional programming hierarchy charts. They give a summary view of the knowledge segments involved in a system. For example, Fig. 4-1 shows two levels of knowledge for the grass-cutting system described earlier—one overall and one for a specific segment or component for which a prototype system is developed.

Because the example is a small one, the relationship between structured situation diagrams (for example, Fig. 3-6) and prototype systems models (Fig. 4-1) is very easy to see. They are almost the same. This is an ideal that is normally achieved only in smaller prototype systems projects.

*The more focused and detailed the structured situation analysis is, the more likely these diagrams are to be similar and the easier the actual system development will be.*

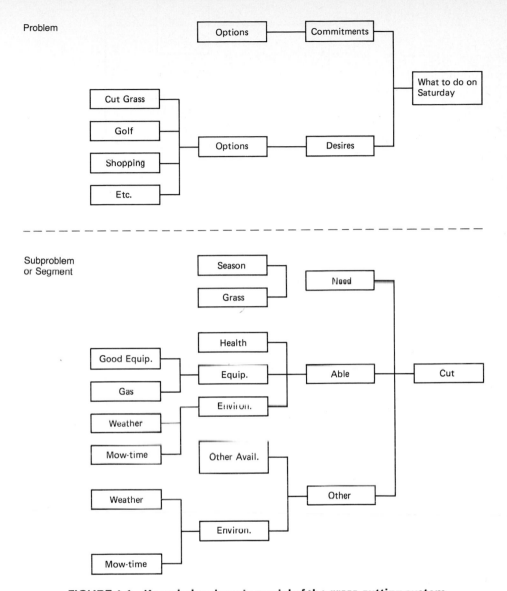

**FIGURE 4-1   Knowledge domain model of the grass-cutting system.**

This point is illustrated again in Fig. 4-2, where the knowledge domain model of the small prototype strategic-planning system is given.   It is identical to the situation model given in the preceding chapter (see Fig. 3-11).

The structured situation models for the franchise selection decision and personal investment planning decision given in the preceding chapter could also be considered knowledge domain models for systems documentation purposes.

Although in larger systems separate models of the *reasoning process* are developed, in smaller systems these process models can be combined with the knowledge

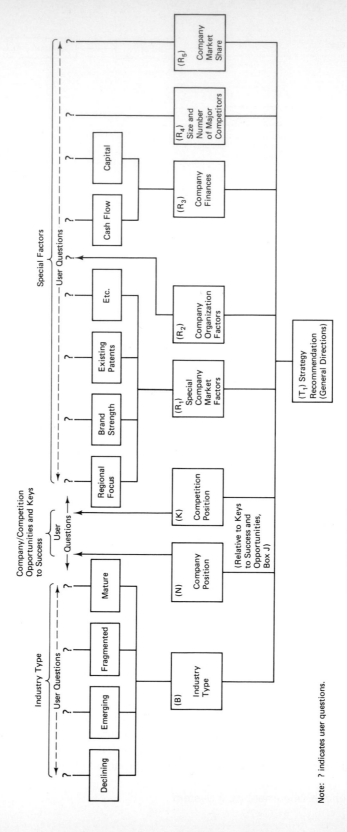

**FIGURE 4-2  Strategic-planning decision situation diagram for general strategy directions segment—initial prototype.**

Note:  ? indicates user questions.

domain model diagram. These *combined* diagrams are often referred to as *system dependency diagrams*.

An example of such a system dependency diagram is given in Fig. 4-3. In the figure, the grass-cutting model shown in Fig. 4-1 has been modified to show

- The situation-specific information that is sought from a system user during a consultation. This was done by adding input arrows preceded by question marks and by inserting the topic of each question in the parentheses above the input arrows.
- The values or conclusions are arrived at for each stage in the decision process. This was done by adding all the values used in the system at the point where they are determined (for example, tall/short, ok/not ok, no/me/others.
- The points in the process where heuristic reasoning occurs. This was done by adding triangular rule-set boxes that indicate where if-then rules are used.

In addition to showing the *knowledge segments*, this dependency diagram shows exactly where each knowledge segment is manipulated in coming to a decision. It also indicates the *reasoning paths* followed through a knowledge hierarchy to arrive at a final decision or recommendation. For these reasons it can also be considered a decision process model.

Such a diagram is an indispensable tool for anyone trying to understand a system or to coordinate and control its development. The diagram contains a complete picture of the prototype system and of the other documentation needed for the system. It is a master coordinating and control document for the entire system.

The following summarizes the basic components of these full system dependency diagrams:

- The triangles have numbers that refer to the rules in the knowledge base that manipulate the knowledge segments adjacent to the triangles. There will be a decision chart for every triangle.
- The boxes and arrows adjacent to a triangle show the name of the knowledge segments to which they are related and which they manipulate.
- The question marks indicate questions asked by the system in order to get information input from users into the system.
- The subject of the questions is given in the parentheses.
- Acceptable values for each phase in the process are given under the input arrows and boxes.
- The recommendations to be made by the system during a consultation are named under the final box in the diagram, the decision to be made.

This document, or one like it, serves as a complete reference outline for understanding, controlling, and coordinating a knowledge-based system and its development effort. Such diagrams are mandatory for any well-planned and executed system development effort.

Diagrams, such as the one shown in Fig. 4-3, are clearly not the only kind of decision process models. Many systems are simply too large to enable creating such a detailed picture of them in a single document. Figure 4-4, for example, shows the

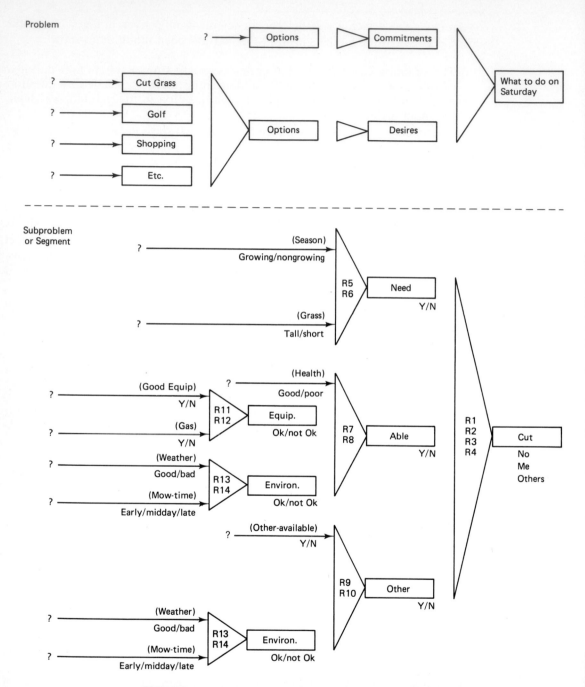

**FIGURE 4-3   Dependency diagram for grass-cutting system.**

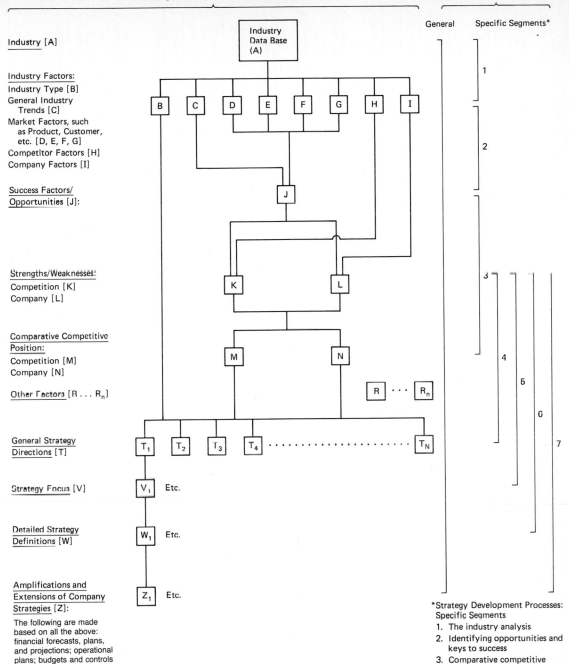

Knowledge Domain Model (Areas Covered)

Strategy Development Processes

General    Specific Segments*

Industry [A]

Industry Factors:
Industry Type [B]
General Industry Trends [C]
Market Factors, such as Product, Customer, etc. [D, E, F, G]
Competitor Factors [H]
Company Factors [I]

Success Factors/ Opportunities [J]:

Strengths/Weaknesses:
Competition [K]
Company [L]

Comparative Competitive Position:
Competition [M]
Company [N]

Other Factors [R ... R_n]

General Strategy Directions [T]

Strategy Focus [V]

Detailed Strategy Definitions [W]

Amplifications and Extensions of Company Strategies [Z]:

The following are made based on all the above: financial forecasts, plans, and projections; operational plans; budgets and controls

*Strategy Development Processes: Specific Segments
1. The industry analysis
2. Identifying opportunities and keys to success
3. Comparative competitive position evaluation
4, 5, 6, 7. Developing various levels of strategies and strategic plans

**FIGURE 4-4  Dependency diagram for overall strategic company planning strategy.**

4:   Designing and Documenting a System

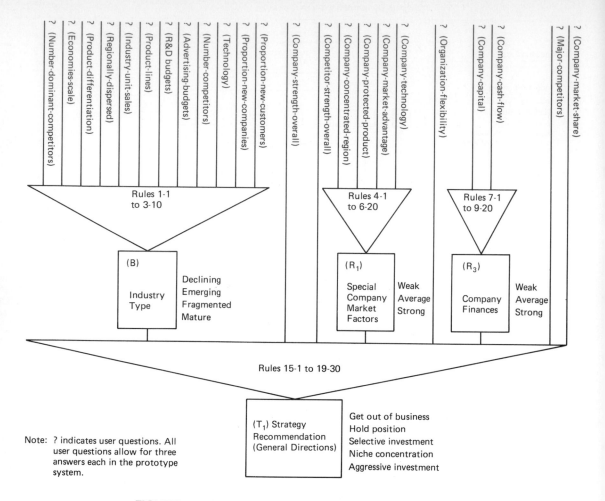

**FIGURE 4-5** Dependency diagram for strategic company planning system—general strategy directions segment (initial prototype).

Note: ? indicates user questions. All user questions allow for three answers each in the prototype system.

processes involved in an overall strategic-planning knowledge-based system only in summary on the right hand side of the diagram. The knowledge segments are shown on the left hand side. The decision processes are shown in this way in Fig. 4-4 because the size and complexity of the overall system did not permit showing the processes in more detail in a single document.

More detailed diagrams, such as the one shown in Fig. 4-5, were then developed for different segments of the system.

Figures 4-6 through 4-9 show the dependency diagrams from the franchise selection prototype system. In this case there is an overview diagram of the system, followed by detailed diagrams of specific segments.

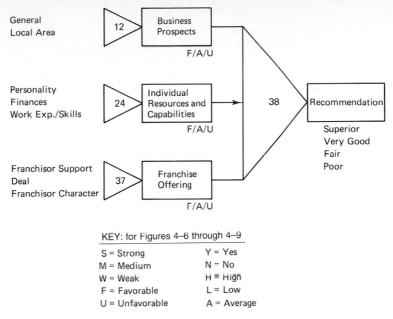

General
Local Area

Personality
Finances
Work Exp./Skills

Franchisor Support
Deal
Franchisor Character

12 ▷ Business Prospects
F/A/U

24 ▷ Individual Resources and Capabilities
F/A/U

37 ▷ Franchise Offering
F/A/U

38 ▷ Recommendation

Superior
Very Good
Fair
Poor

KEY: for Figures 4–6 through 4–9

S = Strong    Y = Yes
M = Medium    N = No
W = Weak    H = High
F = Favorable    L = Low
U = Unfavorable    A = Average

**FIGURE 4-6   Dependency diagram overview for new venture using franchising decision situation—initial prototype.**

The diagrams in Figs. 4-6 to 4-9 are *system dependency diagram* versions of the *knowledge segment* diagrams shown in Figs. 3-7 to 3-10 in the preceding chapter.

## DECISION CHARTS

Decision charts are another graphic way to represent the knowledge segments and reasoning contained in the rule-based prototype systems discussed in this book.

*A decision chart is prepared for every rule-set triangle in the dependency diagram.*

A decision chart in the grass-cutting example is given in Fig. 4-10. It represents the final rule set of the system (rules 1 to 4 in Fig. 4-3). The note at the right of Fig. 4-10 indicates that the original version of this final rule set had nine rules instead of four rules. The earlier version of the chart would therefore have had nine columns.

An example of a decision chart from a small segment of the strategic-planning system is shown in Fig. 4-11.

Another example of a decision chart, or table, is given in Fig. 4-12. It involves a prototype knowledge-based system for franchise selection, which is described in full in a sample system chapter later in this book.

The timing of when the decision charts are developed, as well as their design,

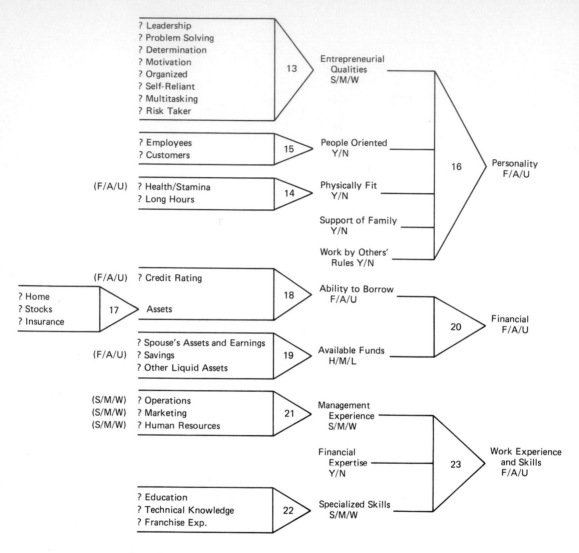

Note: All answers to questions are
yes or no except where indicated.

**FIGURE 4-7 Dependency diagram for individual resources and capabilities segment—initial prototype.**

depends on both the situation and the preferences of the system developer. For example, the decision charts may be prepared *after* the major rules are written. In this way the charts are used to check out the variations on each rule and to make sure nothing is missed. Alternately, decision charts can be prepared before the rules are written.

Usually, however, the development process is not so structured. Rather, the

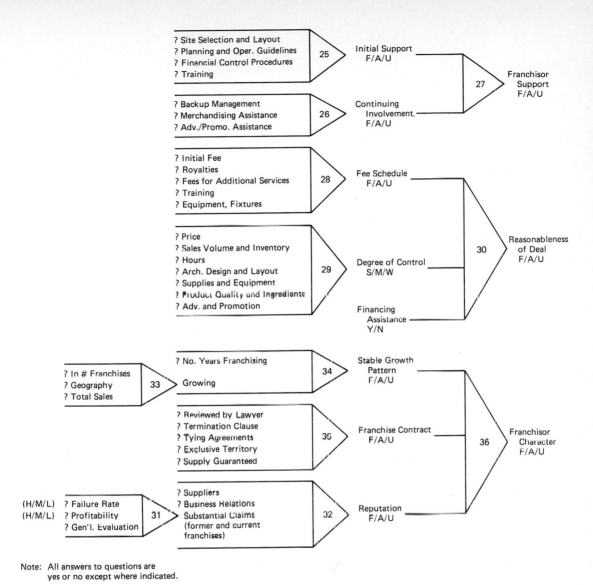

Note: All answers to questions are
yes or no except where indicated.

**FIGURE 4-8   Dependency diagram for franchise offering segment—
initial prototype.**

decision charts, dependency diagrams, and knowledge bases are compared, restudied, and revised in a variety of different ways continually during the course of the development process.   The process even includes going back to the *typical situation expert scenarios* and *structured situation diagrams*, and revising them during the process. The development process is basically a fluid, evolutionary one.

However used, decision charts are important documentation for use in later

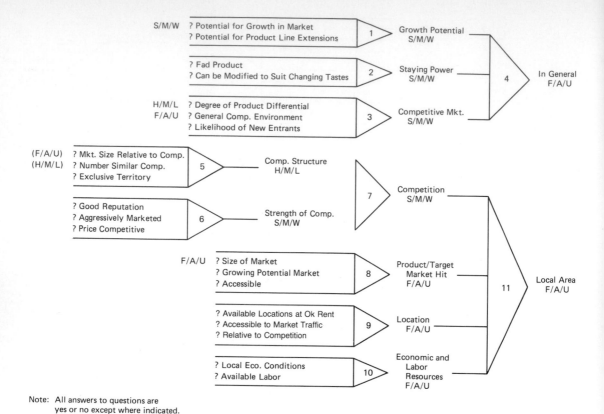

Note: All answers to questions are yes or no except where indicated.

**FIGURE 4-9** Dependency diagram for business prospects area segment—initial prototype.

stages of system development when layers of complexities have been introduced. They are a good way to verify that modifications of the system are consistent and accurate. Decision charts are absolutely necessary to determine the completeness of rule sets.

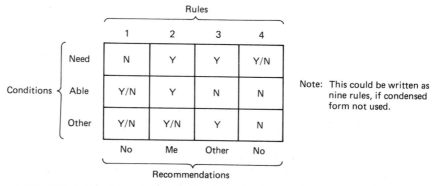

Note: This could be written as nine rules, if condensed form not used.

**FIGURE 4-10** Sample decision chart for final rule set of grass-cutting decision.

PART 1: KNOWLEDGE-BASED SYSTEMS

| PREMISES | RULES | | | | |
|---|---|---|---|---|---|
| | 1 | 2 | 3 | 4 | 5 |
| number-dominant-competitors | high | med | | | |
| economies-scale | and high | and med | | | |
| product-differentiation | or high | or med | | | |
| regionally-dispersed | or high | or high | | | |
| industry-unit-sales | | | decreasing | stable | increasing |
| product-lines | | | decreasing | stable | increasing |
| r&d-budgets | | | decreasing | stable | increasing |
| advertising-budgets | | | decreasing | stable | increasing |
| number-competitors | | | decreasing | stable | increasing |
| technology | | | mature | mature | emerging |
| proportion-new companies | | | low | average | high |
| proportion-new customers | | | low | average | high |
| INDUSTRY TYPES | | | | | |
| Fragmented | x | x | | | |
| Declining | | | x | | |
| Mature | | | | x | |
| Emerging | | | | | x |

**FIGURE 4-11  Sample decision chart for strategic company planning system—industry type segment (initial prototype).**

| IF { | | 108–110 FFF FFF FAU | 111–113 AAA FFF FAU | 114–116 UUU FFF FAU | 117–119 FFF AAA FAU | 120–122 AAA AAA FAU | 123–125 UUU AAA FAU | 126–128 FFF UUU FAU | 129–131 AAA UUU FAU | 132–134 UUU UUU FAU |
|---|---|---|---|---|---|---|---|---|---|---|
| | BUSINESS RES-CAP OFFERING | | | | | | | | | |
| THEN { | SUPERIOR | x | | | | x | | | | |
| | VERY GOOD | x | x | | | | | | | |
| | FAIR | | | x x | | x x | x x | | | |
| | POOR | x | | x x x | | | x | x x x | x x x | x x x |

KEY:

F—Favorable
A—Average
U—Very good
S—Strong
V—Very weak
FA—Fair
P—Poor

FIGURE 4-12 Sample decision chart for new venture using franchising decision situation—initial prototype.

## DESIGNING AND CONSTRUCTING THE KNOWLEDGE BASE

Designing and constructing a knowledge base involves selecting a representation form to be used, writing out the knowledge for the knowledge base, and putting that knowledge into a form acceptable to the expert system shell or computer language chosen.

### Selecting a Representation Form

The kind of decision, problem, or task situation can dictate whether a rule-based system or frame-based (object-oriented) representation form is used. These two types of knowledge representation were discussed in Chapter 2. Either one or the other, or some combination of two, may be selected. A rule-based structure is used in the following illustration, since it suits the reasoning (or heuristics) involved in the example situations, is easier for the nontechnician to follow, and is the representation form used in most expert system shells.

For illustrative purposes here, the examples of knowledge bases given below are designed for use on M.1, Teknowledge's expert system shell. M.1 uses conventional English, and so is easy for the nontechnician to read and work with. M.1 also uses simple syntax. Rules and questions can be written on any conventional word processor. For these reasons, M.1 is a convenient expert system shell for developing smaller systems, especially prototype systems.

A computer technician might argue that such a development environment introduces processing inefficiencies. From a systems development viewpoint such inefficiencies are very often the price paid for making a system easier for a nontechnician to understand, develop, and use. This is almost always the trade-off required, if the objective is to bridge the gap between the technique and the nontechnician in a way that makes less work for the nontechnician during the development stage.

The trade-off is not always that simple, however, since the longer processing time required by an easy-to-use shell may alienate a system user later on. The systems development process therefore requires considerable judgment to reach a balanced final system solution.

## Writing the Knowledge Base

Figure 4-13 shows the knowledge base (rules and questions) written for the grass-cutting situation. In developing this knowledge base, the first phase was to specify the objective (decide on how and if to cut the grass), what values of recommendations the system will make (I cut, someone else cuts, or cutting is not done), and what the structure of the final rule set (rules 1 through 4) will look like. These were the elements shown at the right side of Fig. 4-3. Additional rules were then developed all the way back through the decision or reasoning paths until the questions were specified.

A knowledge base is developed with continuing reference to the decision charts and dependency diagrams, how the expert thinks, the typical sample situation scenarios, and the structured situation diagrams. The knowledge base as much as possible will be written to conform with the documentation.

This is not always possible, however. The charts, diagrams, and scenarios are therefore often used to test the modifications and compromises that may be required to meet the needs of the expert system shell limitations. For example, experts do not always think in terms of backward chaining inferencing or if-then rules. Although it may not be the way all experts think in all situations, however, in many situations if-then rules can represent the way a competent expert is able to reason to a conclusion. If that is the case, then such an if-then rule-based system can validly replicate expert thinking in the situation.

One effective way to tell if your knowledge base does replicate actual experts at work is to translate it into the typical expert situation scenarios written earlier and observe whether the revised scenario sounds right. Another more direct way is to review your knowledge base structure documentation with an expert.

The scenario review process is needed mainly for the smaller systems, where managers are developing systems on their own. It is, however, also sometimes useful to reduce the amount of time a knowledge engineer has to spend with the expert.

The process of developing the rules shown in Fig. 4-13 began with the structured situation analysis described in Chapter 3. The rough sketches developed there were gradually revised as the situation was studied further, until they were in the form of useful dependency diagrams. As part of this development process, many drafts of the decision charts and rules were written simultaneously along the way. Review sessions were held with the experts involved, and, where appropriate, typical decision scenarios were rewritten and retested.

It is important to remember that the situation diagrams and typical situation scenarios may be reviewed and refined during this phase.

/* Rule set one: the Final Decision */

rule-1:
if the grass doesn't need to be cut
then the grass will not be cut

```
if need = no
then cut = do-not.
```

rule-2:
if the grass needs to be cut and
if I am able to cut it
then I will cut the grass

```
if need = yes and
    me-able = yes
then cut = you.
```

rule-3:
if the grass needs to be cut and
if I am not able to cut it and
if another person can cut it
then another person will cut it

```
if need = yes and
    me-able = no and
    other-can= yes
then cut = other-can.
```

rule-4:
if I am not able to cut it and
if another person can't cut it
then the grass will not be cut

```
if me-able = no and
    other-can = no
then cut = do-not.
```

/* Rule set two: Determining the Need */

rule-5:
if the grass is long and
if it is the growing season
then the grass needs to be cut

```
if grass = long and
    season = growing
then need = yes.
```

rule-6:
if the grass is short or
if it isn't the growing season
then the grass doesn't need to be cut

```
if grass = short or
    season = non-growing
then need = no.
```

/* Rule set three: Determining User's Ability */

rule-7:
if my health is good and
if the equipment is working and
if the environment is favorable
then I am able to cut it

```
if health = good and
    equip = ok and
    environ = ok
me-able = yes.
```

rule-8:
if my health is bad or
if the equipment isn't working or
if the environment is unfavorable
then I won't be able to cut it

```
if health = bad or
    equip = not-ok or
    environ = not-ok
then me-able = no.
```

*(continued)*

**FIGURE 4-13  Knowledge base for grass-cutting decision.**

```
                    Column 1                      Column 2
              Plain English Version          Condensed Version


          /*  Rule set four: Determining Other's Ability */

  rule-9:
      if another is available to cut it and    if oth-avail = yes and
      if the environment is favorable             environ = ok
      then another can cut it                  then other-can = yes.

  rule-10:
      if another is unavailable to cut it or   if oth-avail = no or
      if the environment is unfavorable           environ = not-ok
      then another can't cut it                then other-can = no.


          /* Rule set five: Determining Condition of Equipment */

  rule-11:
      if the equipment is in good shape and    if good-eqp = yes and
      if gas is available                         gas = yes
      then equipment is working                then equip = ok

  rule-12:
      if equipment is not in good shape or     if good-eqp = no or
      if not enough gas is available              gas = no
      then equipment is working                then equip = not-ok.


          /* Rule set six: Determining Environmental Conditions */

  rule-13:
      if the weather is good and               if weather = good and
      if midday mowing time is available          mowtime = midday
      then the environment is favorable        then environ = ok.

  rule-14:
      if the weather is bad or                 if weather = bad or
      if midday mowing time is unavailable        mowtime = early or
      then the environment is unfavorable                   late
                                               then environ = not-ok.
```

**FIGURE 4-13**  *(continued)*


## Putting the Knowledge Base into Computer Acceptable Form

Using a very abbreviated version of this development cycle, fourteen rules were created for the grass-cutting system.   They are shown in Fig. 4-13, first in plain English (column 1) and then in condensed form for M.1 usage (column 2).   The transition from column 1 to column 2 represents the transition from English to a computer acceptable language, as required for M.1.   The headings in between the rules are for documentation purposes, so anyone reviewing the system can follow its structure.

The questions that are asked a user, in order to obtain needed information, were also identified and written out. First they were written in English (the English sentences within the reversed single quotation '. . .' marks below). Then they were put into the M.1 format as shown here.

```
question(season) = 'Is the present season the growing or
                    non-growing season?'
question(good-eqp) = 'Is the equipment available for mowing
                      the grass in good condition?'
question(gas) = 'Do you have enough gas to run the mower
                for the entire cutting job?'
question(weather) = 'Is the weather good or bad?'
question(mowtime) = 'Is the time available for mowing the
                     middle of the day, or is it the early
                     or late part of the day?'
question(oth-avail) = 'Is someone else who has working
                       equipment available to cut the
                       grass?'
question(health) = 'Is the condition of your health good or
                    bad?'
question(grass) =  'Is the grass long or short?'
```

Developing user-effective questions can be more complex than this example indicates. For example, in the franchise selection system the questions were used to guide the user to study the local market more carefully. To do this, the version of one question

How appropriate or suitable is the area for the proposed franchise?

was rewritten as follows:

After identifying the target market for the franchise product and analyzing the demographics of the population in the area selected for the proposed store, how you would rate the appropriateness of the franchise for the area under consideration?

In addition to guiding the user's information search more than did the first question, the rewording avoids ordering the user to "go do something (analyze the market, turn on the computer, or some other order)," something that speaks down to the user. Rather, the wording "after analyzing" carries the implication the user is bright and competent. It seems to be more user friendly.

In larger knowledge bases the questions are often placed directly after the rule sets to which they are related in the knowledge base. This makes modification, reading, and control of the knowledge base easier and more efficient.

## Compromises Are Necessary

As in almost every system development project, in order to create these rules and questions, some compromises were needed. They were needed to reconcile the way an expert thinks with the way a computer works. For example, a person making a grass-cutting decision may not always check the environment twice, as the diagram in Fig. 4-3 indicates:

- □ Once when considering their ability to cut the grass
- □ Again when considering the ability of someone else to cut the grass

Some people may do it this way; some may do it differently.

You will find that in developing prototype systems, it is more efficient to have as few (three to five) conditions as possible leading into the final decision (here: need, able, other available). In the grass-cutting situation the efficiency of the system, making the final rule set less cumbersome, dictated showing the environment checking twice farther up the decision tree.

Developing effective compromises when building a knowledge base is very hard to learn and to do, especially in management decision situations. Nontechnical managers just starting out in knowledge-based systems development are often frustrated by the fact that there is rarely *one best way* to diagram a decision. They feel that since several ways may be equally good, the selection process is arbitrary and unscientific. They want a more rigid approach to representing decisions.

This is wrong. In life there is rarely one perfect way to make every management decision. Consequently, there will rarely be one perfect way to represent your decision. Your goal is to develop a fairly good way to do it.

The final form of a knowledge-based system will only be a reasonable replication of the way competent people would or could do a task or make a decision. In simple diagnostic situations there may be one best way, because that is the way the *actual situation* may work. However, if in an actual situation, a management decision situation for example, there are several good ways to reason to a solution, then any expert knowledge-based system for that situation could have several best ways to represent the actual situation. To insist on one best way in such situations would be naive and unrealistic. This helps explain statements such as: A knowledge-based system replicates *aspects* of human reasoning.

Interestingly, at times the expert knowledge-based system is an improvement over the way many experts do go about solving a specific problem consistently over an extended period of time.

## Technical Considerations Important

Technical computer considerations are not emphasized in this book because it is for nontechnicians and because it deals almost exclusively with prototype systems development, where technical computer considerations are not as important.

Technical considerations are nonetheless very important in knowledge-based systems development. First, they are important to make a system run at all. Second, they affect how the system runs, which in turn has an impact on user acceptance. Third, they affect how well a system runs, which affects the system's usefulness to a user. Fourth, they affect the cost efficiency of a system.

Some familiarity with the technical computer aspects of knowledge-based systems development is needed to shape the initial prototype system. A great deal more is needed to develop an effective and efficient larger operating knowledge-based system.

## Balancing Technical and Nontechnical Requirements

Knowledge-based systems represent a balanced reconciliation of many factors:

- □ Different ways different experts make decisions
- □ The theoretical "best" way to do it
- □ Limitations of the available computer programming tools
- □ Time and money constraints
- □ User interface requirements

A classic conflict between the technician (machine efficiency) and an expert (the way the situation works) can arise during systems development. When the technician distorts the actual expert situation to accommodate technical computer limitations, the system can become what is called a "technician's toy." In other words, it may be very useful in the lab, but of no use on the job. Constant reference to the situation scenarios and the expert are needed to keep this from happening. This can raise the cost of systems development, but it is a necessary cost to produce a good system.

In addition, as seen in the reworking of the user question earlier about appropriateness of proposed franchises, many problems will also arise when trying to make a system easier for a person to use. It takes time to make a system more accessible and friendly for the user. Surveys show that it takes some 40 percent of the systems development time on average to introduce user-accommodating refinements. In other words, it can almost double the cost of system development. If you do not plan for the time and expense to make a system that accommodates the user (that is, makes it user friendly), then you are risking having a system that is not accepted and used.

At the same time technical considerations cannot be ignored. Developing condensed rule structures can save processing time when a user is consulting a system. This will make the user more satisfied and save processing costs. Computer storage costs will also be less. Development costs can also become prohibitive if a nontechnician exercises too much control over a systems development project. Technical considerations will also dictate what is or is not possible within a knowledge-based system.

Systems engineering can seem an endless process. There always seems to be a way to make a system technically more efficient, more user friendly, and more accommodating to the nontechnician. The systems shown in this book are still being improved. The rule representations can all be made more condensed and more efficient. The questions can always be made more accommodating. The user interface can always be improved.

All these considerations are not as important for prototype systems development, however, where the objective is to get a system up and running quickly. For this reason, technical refinements not related to the situational accuracy of the system, while recognized as important in systems engineering, are beyond the scope of this book.

## A SITUATIONAL APPROACH TO KNOWLEDGE-BASED SYSTEM DEVELOPMENT

Although this chapter and the preceding chapter provide a general approach to knowledge-based system development, in practice there can be substantial variations from situation to situation in the application of this general approach.

For example, Dorothy Leonard-Barton [Leonard-Barton 1987] describes in some detail the development of the EXSEL expert system at Digital Equipment Corporation. This system was designed to support field sales personnel in originating computer configuration designs to meet customer needs.

The situation characteristics were:

- Development of a large and complex system for a large technological corporation by highly trained computer technicians using sophisticated computer hardware and software
- Use of the system by sales personnel at widely diversified geographic locations; the sales people had a wide range of experience in selling, from very little to over 20 years, and an equally wide range of computer literacy level
- A long development and introduction time span—measured in years
- Need for sophisticated computer hardware and software support designed specifically for users of the system after it was in place

As seen from Dr. Leonard-Barton's study, such a situation required attention to such things as:

- Cultivating users as co-developers, in a situation where users ranged widely in skills and interests, and where user turnover was frequent over the development period
- Taking steps to sell the system during development by creating a network of supporters among management and operating personnel involved
- Designing a delivery and support environment which accommodated the specific needs of the personnel and organization involved.

These organizational steps were all in addition to satisfying technical system requirements.

Several lessons were drawn from this experience. In order to take specific company factors affecting success into account, first it was necessary to study (or model) the organization for which the knowledge-based system was being developed. Next, it was necessary to create a development effort that took into account the many non-technical factors affecting the outcome in that particular company for that particular system.

Other types of development situations require different variations of the general approach to knowledge-based system development described in earlier sections. For example, DuPont focuses their development effort on creating hundreds of small systems each year [Mahler, 1986]. The company encourages operating managers to originate and participate in the design of the systems. To this end, the company provided PC expert system shells to enable the managers to do prototyping and, where appropriate, actual system development. The technical computer support organization is intended to function mainly to support the operating managers in the development effort, since it is clear that the major beneficiaries of the systems, the operating managers, are often expected to be the major initiators and developers of the systems.

In this situation, the technical manager in charge of the knowledge-based system development effort, Ed Mahler, played the role of salesman, selling the operating managers on the idea of expert systems. The technical group's role varied from assisting development in some instances to taking on more of the development work in other instances. Its role varied with the computer expertise of the operating manager and the complexity of the system under development. Throughout, the proprietors of the system remained the users, the operating managers who initiated and used the system, and to a greater or lesser degree participated in its actual development.

In these two examples, two different organizational approaches to knowledge-based system were used to meet the needs of two different business situations.

There are, of course, many other types of development situations that readers will encounter. Each requires adapting the general approach to knowledge-based system development to the specific company situation under study. Unfortunately, there is not yet a great deal of guidance for doing this.

The problem is that there are very few readily available examples of actual development situations, of the depth and sophistication of Dr. Leonard-Barton's. Until there are, it is difficult to develop a contingency framework of situational guidelines to provide managers with guidelines applicable to different types of situations they might encounter in their own businesses.

While there are general approaches to management, managers tend to think situationally in applying those general approaches. They must in order to get specific jobs done. Such a situational theory of management is fairly widely recognized and has been for a long time [for example, Mockler 1971]. Knowledge-based system development is in this sense another example of the situational or contingency character of management, which is sometimes referred to as the "It all depends . . ." theory of management.

Another major potential development problem is also raised in the two situations described above, at DuPont and Digital. In the first type of situation, such as that at Digital, special care needs to be taken to insure the system will not be so technologically driven that users resist it, both in the development and use phases. The second type of situation, such as that at DuPont, works only if the operating managers involved have the conceptual skills required not only to spot and model the decisions, tasks or problems for which the systems are being created. They also need the conceptual skills required to model their situations in such a way that these situations can be easily put onto computer.

This book focuses on ways to make expert system development efforts more user driven, not only in the larger system development efforts, but especially in systems developed by non-technical business managers using PC expert system shells. The more that non-technical operating managers are able to bridge the gap between the computer technician's and the manager's viewpoints, the more user-oriented and often more successful these efforts will be. To do this, however, managers need very special conceptual skills.

A manager, for example, needs to organize and explain (model) the decision, task, or problem situation under study in a way that not only reflects how the situation actually works, but also how it can be done in a way that works within the technical limitations of the computer hardware and software used to implement the application.

As an example, ask a manager to describe how they make a decision and draw a diagram of that decision flow. The model will generally focus on how the manager gets the job done. During this initial modelling phase, tools involved will be given secondary consideration. Any tool that helps get the job done is a good tool or the best tool.

A computer technician, on the other hand, thinks in terms of the constraints of the inferencing mechanisms available, whether on existing expert system shells or with existing software languages and environments or with existing AI and other hardware. This is natural, since that is their training and their mission is to make a system that will run on computers.

In training seminars run by the author, the computer technicians' model or drawing of a decision under study will most often differ substantially from that of the manager. These models will differ not only in where the decision process appears to each to start, but also in the major blocks of knowledge involved, how they interrelate, and the reasoning paths followed.

Such a difference is natural, since non-technical operating managers often do not initially know the limitations of computer tools. And, the computer technician very often initially knows much less than the manager about the management job under study.

The first goal is to gain a recognition and an acceptance of the conceptual difference between the manager's and technician's viewpoint as being a natural outgrowth of their different jobs. The technician's or the manager's viewpoint (or diagram or model of the situation under study) is not necessarily better than the other. They each serve a purpose, and each can be good or bad depending on the situation. "It all depends . . ." then is the guiding principle.

Once the difference is recognized, then the focus shifts to helping the operating manager understand the specific differences between the technical model and their own model. The non-technical manager tries to do two things:

- Attempts to make the initial model of the situation under study more closely emulate or replicate how the decision is actually made, the task done, or problem solved by the manager. There are incidentally many good ways to do it, in most situations.
- Attempts to reconceive or restructure the diagram in a way that makes putting the decision onto an expert system shell easy, while at the same time making sure the representation accurately reflects how the decision is actually made.

This two-pronged process of reconciliation is what is generally meant by maintaining the integrity of the model, while at the same time bridging the gap between the computer technician and non-technical manager in knowledge-based system development. While it is much more complex in situations involving expert systems written in original programming languages, than in those involving use of expert system shells, the principles involved are the same.

Learning how to effectively do the situation restructuring or reconceiving or reformulating helps non-technical managers:

□ Think more systematically on a conceptual level about their jobs
□ Understand the nature of the technological gap
□ Provide more competent assistance in bridging that gap, whether in a large or small knowledge-based system development effort

The degree of sophistication operating managers have in this conceptual area affects both the organization of a company's development effort and its outcome. It affects the amount and kind of technical computer support needed. It affects the degree and kind of user involvement possible and wanted, and the organizational steps needed to insure adequate user involvement. It affects the integrity of the system. It affects the eventual usefulness of the system.

It should be noted that where the two points of view cannot be reconciled, the system project should be reevaluated. If, in order for it to work on computers, the system has to be so modelled that it fails to accurately emulate management realities, it probably should be abandoned. The same is true if the management processes involved cannot be computerized.

The organization of the knowledge-based system development process then should be set up in a way that allows for equal weight to be given to input from management and technical sources. Otherwise, the risk of failure will increase.

Each project, then, should be treated from a situational viewpoint. The general approaches discussed in these chapters should be followed. But they should be followed selectively, and adapted to the specific requirements of the situation under study.

## SELECTING THE METHOD OF PUTTING THE KNOWLEDGE-BASED SYSTEM INTO A COMPUTER

Several ways to put a knowledge-based system into a computer are discussed here:

□ Knowledge-based system programming languages
□ Expert knowledge-based system shells
□ Other knowledge-based system development tools

Programming languages provide the most flexibility. At the same time they are more difficult to use than expert system shells, because the system developer is usually required to design from scratch both the knowledge base and the inference mechanism that accesses the knowledge base. For this reason using a programming language is normally more expensive and takes longer, but its use will usually lead to a system that will better match the specific requirements of the situation under study.

An expert system shell can be easier and quicker to use than either programming languages or development tools. Since the inference engine is preprogrammed in an expert system shell, a systems developer's main work is to create a knowledge base. The microcomputer versions of expert system shells are especially useful for doing smaller prototype systems. Shells have many limitations, however, so that they cannot be used in all situations.

In between expert system shells and programming languages, there is a wide range of development tools with a wide range of preprogrammed functions and routines. Some of these are Smalltalk, OPS5, INTERLISP, and Objective C. A variety of these expert knowledge-based system computer development tools are discussed in the following chapters.

The choice of a development environment is dictated largely by the situation. For example, if extensive forward chaining is used in actually making a decision, an expert system shell that can only backward chain will not do. If the decision situation makes little use of heuristics involving if-then rules, then expert system shells based on if-then rules would not be appropriate.

Besides being based on the situation, the selection of development software may also be influenced by the phase of the development process for which it is intended to be used. For example, it is possible that the prototype system can be developed on a small shell to get it out quickly, while the final system may have to be developed in a programming language.

Because it can save time and money, it is helpful to decide as early as possible in the development process what computer tools you will be using to put your system onto computer.

In addition to considering situational constraints, such as decision or user requirements and development-phase considerations, other technical factors are examined when choosing development software. These include product reliability (is it a proven product) and vendor reliability (does the company that developed the language, development tool or shell still support and maintain it).

Since this book is concerned only with prototype systems development by nontechnical business managers, expert system shells are used exclusively in the sample systems described in later chapters.


## CONCLUSION

This chapter has reviewed defining and documenting decisions, problems, and tasks for expert knowledge-based systems development. It has covered a number of basic documentation tools that might be used by a beginner or nontechnical manager to develop knowledge-based systems.  Many more are available, and many more will be developed by imaginative systems developers.

There are admittedly many other, and better ways, to do this phase of the systems engineering job in other types of situations.  The discussion here is only a short introduction to the subject for nontechnical business managers involved in developing prototype systems.

The next phase of developing or engineering the system—translating your documentation of the system into formal language for the computer and putting it onto the computer—is discussed in the following chapters.

## REVIEW QUESTIONS

1. What areas should be covered in a knowledge-based systems development proposal?

2. What topics are generally covered in knowledge-based systems descriptions?

3. Describe the major features of a knowledge-based system dependency diagram.  Discuss the function of a dependency diagram in the knowledge-based systems development process.

4. Discuss the ways in which typical expert situation scenarios can function to make the system a better replication of reality.  In what development situations are they especially useful?

5. Discuss what is meant by replicating how several pretty good experts work in a knowledge-based system.  Why can it be naive and unrealistic to insist on one best way in certain management decision situations?

6. Describe the relation between structured situation diagrams and both system knowledge segment diagrams and full system dependency diagrams?

7. Describe the ways in which structured situation analysis and documenting a knowledge-based system can be considered one continuous flowing process, and not two separate processes as might be inferred from their being treated in two separate chapters in this book?

8. What are decision charts?  Describe their role in the design of knowledge-based systems? At what point in the process are they developed?

9. What are the various knowledge representations forms that can be used?  What are the advantages and disadvantages of rule-based systems?

10. Describe some of the problems that can arise when writing out user questions.  Discuss some of the ways to resolve these problems.

11. Discuss some of the dangers that can arise from paying too much attention to the technical aspects of system development.

12. Describe some of the inefficiencies and costs that can result from paying too much attention to the nontechnician viewpoint in systems development.

13. Discuss some of the problems encountered when attempting to reconcile the technicians' and nontechnicians' viewpoints during systems development.

# REFERENCES

Leonard-Barton, D., "The Case for Innovative Integration: An Expert System at Digital," *Sloane Management Review*, Fall 1987, pp. 7–19.

Mahler, E., "The Business Needs Approach," *Knowledge-Based Systems: A Step-by-Step Guide to Getting Started* (The Second Artificial Intelligence Symposium). Austin, TX: Texas Instruments Company, 1986.

Mockler, R.J., "Situational Theory of Management," *Harvard Business Review*, May-June 1971, pp. 146–154.

# 5

# Putting Knowledge-Based Systems on Computer: Using M.1 and EXSYS

This chapter and the following ones give examples of the knowledge-based systems development phase that involves putting the system onto the computer. Once on the computer the system can be used for consultations by others.

Three of the most familiar tools for putting these systems on computer are

1. *Microcomputer expert system shells*, such as M.1, EXSYS, or GURU
2. *Development tools*, such as Smalltalk
3. *Programming languages*, such as LISP and PROLOG

This chapter discusses expert systems development shells for personal computers (or microcomputers). It shows how two of them, M.1 and EXSYS, are used to program small prototype systems. Another microcomputer expert system shell, GURU, is discussed in the following chapter. The following chapter also covers development tools and languages and expert system shells for mainframes. Information on where these software can be obtained is included in the software section of the Bibliography at the end of the book.

## MICROCOMPUTER EXPERT SYSTEM SHELLS

M.1, EXSYS, and GURU were selected for illustration because they represent the range of capabilities available in expert system shells for microcomputers. There are many other good microcomputer expert systems shells on the market today.

An expert system shell is most commonly used by knowledge-based systems developers who work on microcomputers and who do not know programming languages. Shells are also used by developers with a wide range of technical skills to prototype or create small systems, since shells are quicker and easier to use.

Expert system shells have built-in inferencing engines as well as routines for storing and editing knowledge bases. For this reason they require much less programming and are appropriate where the objective is to get a system up and running as quickly as possible. Shells have many limitations, however.

Instructions for using different expert shells follow. The small grass-cutting example discussed earlier is used here for ease of illustration and for comparisons between the shells disc  d.

## USING M.1

M.1 is capable of transferring your entire knowledge base into M.1 directly from your word processor, providing you use the correct syntax form. You use your word processor, therefore, to create the knowledge base for M.1. You may use any word processing package, so long as it is ASCII compatible.

Figure 4-12 in Chapter 4 provided a plain English language version and a condensed English version of the grass-cutting knowledge base. Figure 5-1 shows a somewhat modified version of that earlier condensed version. Several additions were made at the beginning and at the end as well as in the questions and rules. These additions and changes, which are discussed below, were made to adapt the knowledge base to run on M.1.

The following describes how the M.1 version of the knowledge base shown in Fig. 5-1 was constructed and put into M.1. Guidelines for using M.1 (version 2.1) are included in the discussion.

### Goals

The phrase "goal — cut." is the first item in Fig. 5-1. You should specify your goal near the beginning of the knowledge base, because the word *goal* activates M.1's inference engine. In this case the decision concerned grass cutting. The goal may be expressed in several ways, including:

```
goal = grasscut.
goal = cut-the-grass.
goal = cut.
```

Specific guidelines must be followed exactly in writing the goal.

- Every word on the right side of the equal sign (=) must be lower case. Uppercase words are variables in M.1. This goal is not a variable.
- The word "goal" is a restricted word, that is, it is a command word in M.1.

```
goal = cut.

            /* Introductory Materials */

initialdata = [intro_over,phase_over].
if display([nl,nl,nl,nl,nl,nl,nl,'

        ----------------------------------------------------------\r
        :                                                         :\r
        :                  WELCOME TO GRASSCUT                     :\r
        :                                                         :\r
        :                                                         :\r
        :            Copyright (c) 1988 by R.J. Mockler           :\r
        :                  All rights reserved.                   :\r
        :                                                         :\r
        :            Direct all inquiries for use to:             :\r
        :                  Robert J. Mockler                      :\r
        :                  114 East 90th Street                   :\r
        :              New York, New York 10128                   :\r
        :_____:\r


',nl,nl,nl,nl]) and
need_intro_1 = yes and
display([nl,nl,nl,nl,nl,nl,'

        **********************************************************\r
        *                                                        *\r
        *                  Welcome to Grasscut                   *\r
        *                                                        *\r
        *     In this system, you will be asked a series  of     *\r
        *     questions about your ability,   the ability of     *\r
        *     others, and the need to cut the grass, as well     *\r
        *     as about the condition of the equipment.   The     *\r
        *     computer will recommend whether or not  to cut     *\r
        *     the  grass  and, if  it  needs to be  cut, who     *\r
        *     should  cut it,  based on your   answers to the     *\r
        *     questions.                                         *\r
        *                                                        *\r
        **********************************************************\r
',nl,nl,nl,nl,nl]) and
need_intro_2 = yes
then intro_over.

question(need_intro_1) = 'Type "yes" or "1" to go on.'.
legalvals(need_intro_1) = [yes, 1].
question(need_intro_2) = 'Type "yes" or "1" to go on.'.
legalvals(need_intro_2) = [yes, 1].
automaticmenu(A1).
enumeratedanswers(Aii).
            /* Rule set one: the Final Decision */
rule-1:
    if need = no
    then cut = do-not.
```

*(continued)*

**FIGURE 5-1  Knowledge base—M.1 version of grass-cutting decision.**

```
rule-2:
    if need = yes and
       me-able = yes
    then cut = you.
rule-3:
    if need = yes and
       me-able = no and
       other-can = yes
    then cut = other-can.
rule-4:
    if me-able = no and
       other-can = no
    then cut = do-not.

              /* Rule set two: Determining the Need */
rule-5:
    if grass = long and
       season = growing
    then need = yes.
rule-6:
    if grass = short or
       season = non-growing
    then need = no.

              /* Rule set three: Determining User's Ability */
rule-7:
    if health = good and
       equip = ok and
       environ = ok
    then me-able = yes.
rule-8:
    if health = bad or
       equip = not-ok or
       environ = not-ok
    then me-able = no.

          /* Rule set four : Determining Others' Ability */
rule-9:
    if oth-avail = yes and
       environ = ok
    then other-can = yes.
rule-10:
    if oth-avail = no or
       environ = not-ok
    then other-can = no.

          /* Rule set five: Determining Condition of Equipment */
 rule-11:
    if good-eqp = yes and
       gas = yes
    then equip = ok.
 rule-12:
    if good-eqp = no or
       gas = no
    then equip = not-ok.
```

*(continued)*

**FIGURE 5-1** *(continued)*

```
        /* Rule set six: Determining Environmental Conditions */
rule-13:
      if weather = good and
         mowtime = midday
      then environ = ok.
rule-14:
      if weather = bad or
         mowtime = early or
         mowtime = late
      then environ = not-ok.

        /* Rule set seven: Making a conclusion */
rule-last:
      if cut is known and
         cut = A01 and
         display([nl,nl,nl,nl,nl,nl,nl,nl,nl,'

      ***************************************************************\r
      *                                                             *\r
      *                       Conclusion                            *\r
      *                                                             *\r
      *      Based on the answers you have given,  we               *\r
      *      recommend  ',A01,' cut at this time.                   *\r
      *                                                             *\r
      ***************************************************************\r
',nl,nl,nl,nl,nl,nl,nl])
      then phase_over = done.

                  /* User Questions */

question(season) = [nl,nl,nl,nl,nl,nl,nl,nl,nl,nl,nl,'
                        Is the present season the growing or
                        non-growing season?'
,nl,nl,nl,nl,nl,nl,nl,nl,nl,nl,nl].
legalvals(season) = [growing, non-growing].

question(grass) = [nl,nl,nl,nl,nl,nl,nl,nl,nl,nl,nl,'
                        Is the grass long or short now?'
,nl,nl,nl,nl,nl,nl,nl,nl,nl,nl].
legalvals(grass) = [long, short].

question(good-eqp) = [nl,nl,nl,nl,nl,nl,nl,nl,nl,nl,nl,'
                        Is the equipment available for mowing the
                        grass in good condition?'
,nl,nl,nl,nl,nl,nl,nl,nl,nl,nl,nl].
legalvals(good-eqp) = [yes, no].

question(gas) = [nl,nl,nl,nl,nl,nl,nl,nl,nl,nl,nl,'
                        Do you have enough gas to run the mower for
                        the entire cutting job?'
,nl,nl,nl,nl,nl,nl,nl,nl,nl,nl,nl].
legalvals(gas) = [yes, no].

question(weather) = [nl,nl,nl,nl,nl,nl,nl,nl,nl,nl,nl,nl,'
                        Is the weather good or bad?'
,nl,nl,nl,nl,nl,nl,nl,nl,nl,nl].
legalvals(weather) = [good, bad].
```

*(continued)*

**FIGURE 5-1** *(continued)*

```
question(mowtime) = [nl,nl,nl,nl,nl,nl,nl,nl,nl,nl,nl,nl,'
                        Is the time available for mowing the middle
                        of the day, or is it the early or late part
                        of the day?'
,nl,nl,nl,nl,nl,nl,nl,nl,nl,nl].
legalvals(mowtime) = [early, midday, late].

question(oth-avail) = [nl,nl,nl,nl,nl,nl,nl,nl,nl,nl,nl,'
                        Is someone else who has working equipment
                        available to cut the grass?'
,nl,nl,nl,nl,nl,nl,nl,nl,nl,nl,nl].
legalvals(oth-avail) = [yes, no].

question(health) = [nl,nl,nl,nl,nl,nl,nl,nl,nl,nl,nl,nl,'
                        Is the condition of your health good or
                        bad?'
,nl,nl,nl,nl,nl,nl,nl,nl,nl,nl,nl].
legalvals(health) = [good, bad].
```

**FIGURE 5-1** *(continued)*

The equal sign links the left and right side of the equation by assigning the value on the right side to the command word on the left side. Written with the blanks, "grasscut" becomes the end point of the M.1 consultation.

□ A goal must be a single word. Words joined by hyphens are read as a single word by M.1. There can be more than one goal. They would be written like the multiple values appearing after "initialdata" in the knowledge-base.

⊓ Completed statements must end with a period, to tell M.1 to start executing an inferencing routine.

□ There are many restricted words that are system commands, such as "multi-valued", "question", "initialdata", and "goal". Since these words trigger special built-in routines, or functions, their use is limited. You cannot use these words as a value and so cannot place those words in the right side of an equal sign. For example, the statement "goal = goal" is incorrect. The M.1 menu gives a list of restricted words and their meanings.

## Initialdata

The next word added to the knowledge base "initialdata" instructs M.1 to execute specific rules before searching for a value for "goal". Two values have been given to it in the example:

```
initialdata = [intro-over,phase-over].
```

Where there is more than one value square brackets are added, as in the example. M.1 will seek a value for "intro-over" first. Starting with "intro-over", M.1 will seek the first rule with the word "intro-over" in its then clause. This is M.1's normal backward chaining search routine. Since designing these initial rules requires special instructions, they will be discussed later under introductory and concluding panels.

## Rules

Rules must be written according to strict guidelines in any expert system shell. The first M.1 rule in this example is

```
rule-1:
          if need = no
          then cut = no.
```

The following guidelines are used in writing rules:

- □ A label should be assigned to each rule. Here, it is "Rule-1". M.1 uses these to process the knowledge base.
- □ A title should be given to each group of rules. For example, in Fig. 5-1 the first group is called "Rule set one: The Final Decision". Such notation titles, although not required, help locate rules later when you are making changes.
- □ All such programmer notations are placed between "/* . . . */" signs, as shown in Fig. 5-1. Anything between such marks is ignored by the M.1 shell program when it is processing a consultation.
- □ Key words like "need" and "cut" should be chosen carefully, because they are reused often in the knowledge base. They must always be spelled in exactly the same way, or M.1 will not be able to find and use them.
- □ An "or" or an "and" must be used to link multiple if clauses in a rule.

## Questions

As M.1's inference mechanism goes back up the reasoning chain, it eventually comes to if conditions that are not answered in another rule. At this point M.1 looks for questions that provide a meaning for the key word in an if clause. In this example, eight user questions were entered into the knowledge base. The first question in the example is:

```
question(season) = [nl,nl,nl,nl,nl,nl,nl,nl,nl,nl,nl,
                    'Is the present season the
                    growing or non-growing season?'
,nl,nl,nl,nl,nl,nl,nl,nl,nl,nl,nl].
legalvals(season) = [growing, non-growing].
```

The guidelines followed in preparing such questions are

- □ Put the key word being sought in parentheses directly after the word "question". There must be *no* space between the parentheses and either word. Spaces must be used before and after the equal sign, as elsewhere in M.1.
- □ Questions that you want to appear on a user's screen during a consultation must be placed within single apostrophe marks ('. . .'), as shown. The exact placement of the apostrophes may vary, depending on your word processor and the placement of the "nl's." The "nl's" indicate new or next lines; in

this case they specify the number of lines the question should be printed from the top and bottom of the screen when displayed for the user. In Fig. 5-1 the first apostrophe is at the end of the line above the question. It can be put on the next line, as in the example above.

□ So M.1 knows what answers to accept, each question must be followed with the phrase "legalvals(. . .) = [your designated alternative answers]" as shown in Fig. 5-1.

□ The alternate answers accepted from the user are often put between square brackets ([. . .]) at the end of the question, between the last word of the question and the question mark (?). This is not always necessary, since M.1 can be instructed to print out alternative acceptable answers automatically.

□ If you wish M.1 to print the acceptable answers after each question, then you have to enter the commands "automaticmenu" and "enumeratedanswers", as shown in Fig. 5-1 at the end of the introductory material.

□ The command "automaticmenu" tells M.1 to automatically list the acceptable answers on the screen. The command "enumeratedanswers" tells M.1 to put numbers next to the acceptable answers on the screen.

□ The "(A1)" and "(Aii)" after these two commands (the uppercase letters are variables) instructs M.1 to list and number *all* the acceptable answers after *all* the questions in the knowledge base in Fig. 5-1. If you omit "(A1)" or "(Aii)" you will get an error message when putting your knowledge base into M.1.

□ Do not use underlines anywhere in the knowledge base.

## Introductory and Concluding Panels

The following are guidelines for preparing the introductory and concluding panels. M.1 is programmed to carry out the "initialdata" instructions before it starts its search for the "goal". It, therefore, initially goes to the first rule with a then clause containing the first word written in the brackets after "initialdata = ". Here, it is "intro_over". In the sample knowledge base in Fig. 5-1 rules are used to instruct M.1 to print the introductory and concluding panels. The first if clause instructs M.1 to print the boxed panel on the user's computer screen through using the command word "display". The "nl" notations before and after the panel instruct M.1 to print the panel in the middle of the screen, just as they do for the questions. The next if clause "need_intro_1 = yes" tells M.1 to go to:

```
question(need_intro_1) = 'Type "yes" or "1" to go on'.
```

This will instruct a user to press "1" or type "yes" when finished reading the first panel, so that M.1 can go on to the next panel or rule.

The exact same procedure is followed in printing the second introductory display panel and the concluding display panel. The guidelines followed in preparing such panels are

□ First, type the text that you will be using in the panel to see how much space it takes. It is helpful to use paper lined with small boxes to do this. The text must be short enough to fit onto one computer screen. You can add a border around the text, as shown, at the same time you type the text. When you finish typing the text and border, measure how long each side is (lines and spaces). You should now be able to calculate where on the computer screen the text should be placed to be centered. Insert the number of "nl's" needed to correctly position the display panel on the screen.

☐ Use "\r" or "\r\n" within apostrophes to instruct M.1 to go to the next line, and "nl," or ",nl,nl," outside the apostrophes to do the same thing.

## Entering Your Knowledge Base into M.1 from Your Word Processor

Once the knowledge base is typed on your word processor, it should be saved as an ASCII file on a floppy disk. Here, the file is named GRASSCUT. You enter a knowledge-base file on M.1 by following these steps:

Place the M.1 disk in the left-hand drive (A), and your word processing disk with the GRASSCUT file on it in the right-hand drive (B) (after loading DOS):

```
disk drive :    --A--   --B--
disk        :    M1      your own program
```

Type the following when the "A⟩" prompt appears on the screen:

```
A⟩m1:⟨cr⟩
```

The "⟨cr⟩" symbol means that a carriage return key (also called an enter key) is pressed to end the entry and execute the instructions. When the M.1 application display panel appears on the screen, press the F9 key. When the "m1" prompt appears, type

```
m1⟩ load b:name-of-your-program⟨cr⟩
```

There are several alternate ways to load your program, which are given in the M.1 technical manual.

Once the file is loaded, in this case GRASSCUT, M.1 reviews the entire GRASS-CUT knowledge base as it is being loaded for use. If the machine stops, it is to note errors. Most errors are caused by using the wrong notation. Suggested ways to fix the error will be displayed on the screen, but they are not always helpful. Something as small as a misplaced period causes the program to stop, as is true in any other programming situation.

Although M.1 has a text editor, when a correction must be made during loading it is necessary to go back to your word processor, retrieve the GRASSCUT file, and make the corrections to the original file. Then the corrected file must be reloaded into M.1. This process may be repeated many times during this phase, which conventional programmers call "debugging a program."

## Running a Consultation

Once a knowledge base file has been loaded successfully, without any error messages, you can run a consultation using either a hypothetical or real decision situation test case. To run a consultation, first load your knowledge base, as instructed above. Then, type

```
M1)go⟨cr⟩
```

The consultation should then begin. During the initial runs of the consultation you will often find it necessary to make further corrections in the knowledge base. These can involve such things as rule logic and completeness, the position of questions and text on the screen, and the wording of questions.

It is possible to print out all the reasoning steps in your consultation as it runs. First, connect the printer and turn it on. Once you have loaded the knowledge-base file, the displayed prompt will be "M1)" as long as you are still in M.1. Then type

```
M1)log printer⟨cr⟩
M1)trace on⟨cr⟩
M1)go⟨cr⟩
```

Alternately, it is possible to print only the consultation, without the reasoning steps, by typing

```
M1)log printer⟨cr⟩
M1)go⟨cr⟩
```

It is also possible to display and print the knowledge base file from the shell by typing

```
M1)log printer⟨cr⟩
M1)list⟨cr⟩
```

During a consultation you can ask for a description of what constitutes a legal answer to a question by typing

```
⟩⟩options⟨cr⟩
```
*Note:* ⟩⟩ *is the prompt sign within a consultation.*

If an unacceptable answer is entered, a list of allowable answers, or a brief description of the criteria for an acceptable answer, will also be displayed

A user is free to ask why M.1 asked a question by typing

```
⟩⟩why⟨cr⟩
```

M1 displays the knowledge-base entries that are under consideration at the time of the request.

A user may also ask for help or to see a list of available commands by typing

```
M1)help list(cr)
M1)help [command-you-wish-to-be-explained](cr)
```

The following are some other helpful commands:

◻ During a consultation you may go back to the beginning by typing

```
))abort(cr)
```

The following will appear:

```
M1)
```

◻ To go from M.1 to the operating system environment, or the DOS A) prompt, requires typing

```
M1)quit(cr)
```

or

```
))quit(cr)
```

Either of these will take you back to the A) prompt, from which you can call back up your word processing program. The command "exit" is equivalent to "quit".


## Certainty Factors

Although they are not illustrated here, it is possible to use certainty factors with M.1. An example of how this is done in given at the end of Chapter 6.


## USING EXSYS

To use EXSYS, another microcomputer expert system shell, a knowledge base file must be prepared, as when working with M.1. With EXSYS, however, you cannot enter the knowledge base (rules, questions, and text panels) directly from a word processor. They must be entered one at a time, using the EXSYS rule editor.

Figure 5-2 gives the original plain English language version of the grass-cutting decision. As with M.1, the knowledge base has to be converted into a form useable by the expert system shell. Figure 5-3 gives the EXSYS version of the decision.

Notice that there are more rules in the EXSYS version than in the plain English version. That is because any rule with an "or" between two if clauses must be divided into two separate rules for EXSYS. For example, rule-6 in the plain English version in Fig. 5-2 is expanded into rule-6 and rule-7 in the EXSYS version in Fig. 5-3. Rule-

```
rule-1:
if the grass doesn't need to be cut
then we will not be cut

rule-2:
if the grass needs to be cut and
if I am able to cut it
then I will cut the grass

rule-3:
if the grass needs to be cut and
if I am not able to cut it and
if another person can cut it
then another person will cut it

rule-4:
if I am not able to cut it and
if another person can't cut it
then the grass will not be cut

rule-5:
If the grass is long and
if it is the growing season
then the grass needs to be cut

rule-6:
if the grass is short or
if it isn't the growing season
then the grass doesn't need to be cut

rule-7:
if my health is good and
if the equipment is working and
if the environment is favorable
then I am able to cut it

rule-8:
if my health is poor or
if the equipment isn't working or
if the environment is unfavorable
then I won't be able to cut it

rule-9:
if another is available to cut it and
if the environment is favorable
then another can cut it

rule-10:
if another is unavailable to cut or
if the environment is unfavorable
then another can't cut it

rule-11:
if the equipment is in good shape and
if gas is available
then equipment is working
```

*(continued)*

**FIGURE 5-2  Knowledge base—plain English version of grass-cutting decision.**

5:  Using M.1 and EXSYS

```
rule-12:
if equipment is not in good shape or
if gas is unavailable
then equipment isn't working

rule-13:
if the weather is good and
if midday mowing time is available
then the environment is favorable

rule-14:
if the weather is bad or
if midday mowing time is unavailable
then the environment is unfavorable
```

**FIGURE 5-2** *(continued)*

8, which has two "or's" between "if" clauses, is converted into three rules (rules 9, 10, and 11).

The following are instructions on how to put the grass-cutting decision knowledge base into EXSYS.

## Preliminary Steps

After the revised rules are prepared, the EXSYS programs must be loaded onto the computer. To do this, DOS must first be loaded. Then place the EXSYS DEMO DISK 1 in drive A and a blank disk in drive B. If you prefer, you can use the full version of the EXSYS program instead of the DEMO version, which is limited to systems of less than twenty-five rules. When the "A)" prompt appears on the screen, type "EDITXS ⟨cr⟩". The "⟨cr⟩" refers to pressing the carriage return key or enter key at the end of each entry. The screen looks like this:

```
A)EDITXS⟨cr⟩
```

After a few moments, a panel appears that indicates that the EDITXS system is active.

When the EXSYS editor program starts, it first asks for the name of the knowledge-base file that will be created or edited. In this case, a new file called GRASS-CUT will be created, so type "B:GRASSCUT⟨cr⟩". The screen looks like this:

```
Exsys System File name: B:GRASSCUT⟨cr⟩
```

When EXSYS cannot find the filename requested, it indicates that a new file must be started:

```
File GRASSCUT.TXT is not on the disk.
Do you wish to start a new file? (Y/N):
```

Pressing the Y key creates a new file. The ".TXT" file extension after "GRASSCUT" is added by EXSYS when it stores a file text.

*Note:* If EXSYS does not ask this question, it means that a GRASSCUT file

```
rule-1:
IF       The grass doesn't need cutting
THEN     The grass will not be cut

rule-2:
IF       The grass needs cutting
   and   I am able to cut it
THEN     I will cut the grass

rule-3:
IF       The grass needs cutting
   and   I am not able to cut it
   and   Another person can cut it
THEN     Another person will cut it

rule-4:
IF       I am not able to cut it
   and   Another person can't cut it
THEN     The grass will not be cut

rule-5:
IF       The grass is long
   and   It is the growing season
THEN     The grass needs cutting

rule-6:
IF       The grass is short
THEN     The grass doesn't need cutting

rule-7:
IF       It is not the growing season
THEN     The grass doesn't need cutting

rule-8:
IF       My health is good
   and   The equipment is ready to go
   and   The environment is favorable
THEN     I am able to cut it

rule-9:
IF       My health is bad
THEN     I am not able to cut it

rule-10:
IF       The equipment is not ready
THEN     I am not be able to cut it

rule-11:
IF       The environment is unfavorable
THEN     I am not able to cut it

rule-12:
IF       Another person is available to cut it
   and   The environment is favorable
THEN     Another person can cut it
```

*(continued)*

**FIGURE 5-3   Knowledge base—EXSYS version of grass-cutting decision.**

```
rule-13:
IF       Another person is unavailable to cut it
THEN     Another person cannot cut it

rule-14:
IF       The environment is unfavorable
THEN     Another person cannot cut it

rule-15:
IF       The equipment is in good shape
  and    Gas is available
THEN     The equipment is ready to go

rule-16:
IF       The equipment is not in good shape
THEN     The equipment is not ready

rule-17:
IF       Gas is not available
THEN     The equipment is not ready

rule-18:
IF       The weather is good
  and    The mowing time is mid day
THEN     The environment is favorable

rule-19:
IF       The weather is bad
THEN     The environment is unfavorable

rule-20:
IF       The mowing time is morning or evening
THEN     The environment is unfavorable
```

**Note:** EXSYS will automatically ask the questions about information needed from users consulting the system.

**FIGURE 5-3** *(continued)*

already exists in EXSYS. This indicates that you probably have inadvertently stored a GRASSCUT file on the blank B disk. Exit EXSYS (by pressing the control, alternate, and delete keys simultaneously with the DOS disk in the A drive) and check the blank disk in the B drive. If there is already a GRASSCUT file on the blank disk, either erase it or use a new file name, such as "GRASS-A", each time you practice entering a file. Now start over again.

Since the objective is to enter a new knowledge base, EXSYS asks for its subject. This subject will be displayed whenever a consultation is run by a user. Since this decision concerns grass cutting, type

```
GRASSCUT⟨cr⟩
```

Next, EXSYS asks for the system developer's name, as follows:

```
Author: your name⟨cr⟩
```

EXSYS then asks what kind of answers are wanted as responses to user questions. It displays the following options menu:

```
1. Simple Yes or No
2. A range of 0-10 where 0 indicates absolutely not &
   10 indicates absolutely certain. 1-9 indicate
   degrees of certainty.
3. A range of -100 to +100 indicating the degree of
   certainty
   Input number of selection or <H> for help:
```

Since this is your first time using EXSYS, you should keep it simple by just typing in "1" ⟨cr⟩. This yes or no (or true or false) mode is suitable for the grass-cutting situation. Use of the probability modes, which are used in several of the systems in Part 3, is explained in a separate user's instruction manual that accompanies the demo disk. Once either "2" or "3" is selected, it cannot be changed.

EXSYS next asks:

```
Number of rules to use in data derivation:
    1. Attempt to apply all possible rules
    2. Stop after first successful rule
Select 1 or 2 (Default = 1):
```

This means that when EXSYS needs information, it first tries to derive it from existing rules (before asking the user for it). EXSYS can test all appropriate rules to derive a piece of information. Alternately it can stop after it has found the first successful rule that allows it to derive the information needed. Using all rules, or option 1, is safest and is generally used whenever possible. Selecting option 2, to stop after the first successful rule, can save the user from being asked unnecessary questions, but it does not always yield the best solution. It is therefore advisable to start with option 1. So type in "1" or ⟨cr⟩.

## Introductory Panel and Concluding Text

The system developer is next asked to type in the text that will appear at the beginning of a consultation:

```
Input the text you wish to use to explain how to run
this file.
```

Any text that you type in here will be displayed at the start of an EXSYS consultation. It is possible to enter a full screen of text. This text would describe all the information that a user will need to run a consultation using your system. Type ⟨cr⟩ only at the end of all the text, as indicated. If you type ⟨cr⟩ at any point in the text (for example, after the WELCOME line), EXSYS will go directly to the next question. The following text should be entered:

```
                 WELCOME TO GRASSCUT
           [Copyright (c) 1988 by R.J. Mockler.
                 All rights reserved.]
  In this system, you will be asked a series of questions
  about your ability, the ability of others, and the need
  to cut the grass, as well as about the condition of the
  equipment. The system will recommend whether or not to
  cut the grass and, if it needs to be cut, who should cut
  it, based on your answers to the questions.⟨cr⟩
```

After typing the introductory text, it is necessary to type the text for the conclusion of a user consultation, as EXSYS asks the developer:

```
  Input the text you wish to use at end of the EXSYS run.
```

Like the introductory text, the ending text is optional. The ending text will be displayed during the consultation before EXSYS displays a recommendation for a user. The following is used for the concluding text in this example:

```
     Based on the answers you have given, the
     GRASSCUTTING system is making the recommendation
     shown on the following screen.⟨cr⟩
```

## Other Options

Once the beginning and ending text are entered, a question about rules is displayed:

```
     Do you wish the user running this expert system to
        have the rules displayed as the default condition?
```
*(The user will have the option of overriding this option)* **(Y_N) (Default = N):**

A developer has the option of having rules displayed as they are used, or not. Having the rules displayed enables a user to see which rules are being activated during a consultation. In the grass-cutting example, letting all rules display allows a user to see how they are used when running a system, so a "Y" is typed as the answer to this question.

The next question asked is:

```
     Do you wish to have an external program called
     at the start of a run to pass data back for
     multiple variables or qualifiers?
```
*(Other external programs may also be used to get data for single variables or qualifiers)* **(Y_N) (Default = N):**

As indicated, EXSYS can call external programs to get data during a consultation. In this example, an external program, such as a spreadsheet, is not needed, so press ⟨cr⟩.

## Entering Choices

EXSYS next asks for a list of all the possible choices or recommendations that can be made by the system at the end of a consultation. In this case there are three possible choices or recommendations, so type

```
1. The grass will not be cut⟨cr⟩
2. I will cut the grass⟨cr⟩
3. Another person will cut the grass⟨cr⟩
4. ⟨cr⟩
```

After all the choices or recommendations are entered, press ⟨cr⟩ twice, once after your last choice and again when the next number appears, just as shown above. The choices can be called back to edit (add to, change, or delete) later.

## A Final Question

The final preliminary question concerns checking previous rules:

```
The function that checks new rules against the
previous ones does NOT check the validity of
mathematical formulas. If you predominantly use
formulas it may be more convenient to switch
this option off.
Do you wish new rules checked against the previous
rules? Y/N (Default = Y):
```

In the grass-cutting example mathematics is not used, so press ⟨cr⟩ to leave the rule checker switched on.

At this point EXSYS is finished asking questions and rule entry begins.

## Entering the First Rule

An inverted "1" is now shown on the screen. It is the screen for rule entry. On the bottom of the screen, there is a main menu of command options. This menu changes after a command is selected.

The left side of the screen is for rules. Rules are built by using the right window, which is called a "qualifier" worksheet area, and then transferring the qualifier into the rules. To start building the first rule, press ⟨cr⟩ or "A". The menu line on the bottom of the screen changes.

When entering rules, it is necessary to refer to the knowledge base in Fig. 5-3.

Your objective is first to build the "if" clauses on the left hand side of the screen. The if clause is built by using the qualifier workspace on the right-hand side of the screen, where the blinking cursor is now located. To create a new qualifier, press "N". The cursor will move as you type.

A Qualifier has two parts:

□ Attributes (which are also sometimes called "qualifiers" in EXSYS)
□ Values

Qualifiers are built one at a time, as they are needed to build rules. To create the "if" clause in rule-1 "The grass doesn't need cutting" first type the attribute "The grass" in the upper right-hand corner of the screen and press ⟨cr⟩. Then type the value part next to 1 "doesn't need cutting" and press ⟨cr⟩. Next type in "needs cutting" after number 2, since you will be needing this value in rule-2. Press ⟨cr⟩ twice to end the value entries for this qualifier, once after typing the second value and once after number 3, as shown below:

```
The grass⟨cr⟩
1. doesn't need cutting.⟨cr⟩
2. does need cutting.⟨cr⟩
3. ⟨cr⟩
```

The completed qualifier (1) will appear in the workspace:

```
Qualifier #1
The grass
1. doesn't need cutting.
2. does need cutting.
```

With qualifier 1 in place, it is now possible to use part of it to create the "if" clause of rule 1. Do this by typing "1" and pressing ⟨cr⟩. This transfers the phrase "The grass doesn't need cutting" to the first if clause in the left window.

EXSYS now has qualifier 1 in its storage. Whenever this qualifier is needed for subsequent rules, it can be recalled by typing "1" and ⟨cr⟩, whenever the blinking light (the cursor) is in the right-hand window on the screen.

A list of all the qualifiers that will be entered in EXSYS for the grass-cutting decision are given in Fig. 5-4. The figure also lists the rules in which they are used.

To finish rule 1, next press ⟨cr⟩ to do its then clause, "The grass will not be cut." This is one of the three choices entered earlier. To retrieve the available choices, press "C". The three choices entered earlier will appear in the upper right-hand window where the qualifier entries had been earlier. Enter the number of the one you want transferred to the then clause. In this case it is "1", so press "1" and ⟨cr⟩. On the bottom of the screen, you will then be asked its value. Again press "1" and ⟨cr⟩, since you want only a yes or no answer. Now press ⟨cr⟩ to indicate the then clause is complete.

| Qualifier Number | Attributes With Values | Used in Rule(s) ( ) = use in THEN part of a rule |
|---|---|---|
| 1 | The grass<br>doesn't need cutting<br>needs cutting | 1  2  3  (5)  (6)  (7) |
| 2 | I am<br>able to cut it<br>not able to cut it | 2  3  4  (8)  (9)  (10)  (11) |
| 3 | Another person<br>can cut it<br>cannot cut it | 3  4  (12)  (13)  (14) |
| 4 | The grass is<br>long<br>short | 5  6 |
| 5 | It is<br>the growing season<br>not the growing season | 5  7 |
| 6 | My health is<br>good<br>bad | 8  9 |
| 7 | The environment is<br>favorable<br>unfavorable | 8  11  12  14  (18)  (19)  (20) |
| 8 | The equipment is<br>ready to go<br>not ready | 8  10  (15)  (16)  (17) |
| 9 | Another person is<br>available to cut it<br>unavailable to cut it | 12  13 |
| 10 | The equipment is<br>in good shape<br>not in good shape | 15  16 |
| 11 | Gas is<br>available<br>not available | 15  17 |
| 12 | The weather is<br>good<br>bad | 18  19 |
| 13 | The mowing time is<br>early day<br>mid day<br>late day | 18  20 |

**FIGURE 5-4  List of qualifiers for the EXSYS grasscut system.**

When "else" appears on the screen, just press ⟨cr⟩, since it is not used in this tutorial. When "note" and "reference" appear also press ⟨cr⟩. An explanation of how to use these functions is given in the user's instruction manual accompanying the demo disk.

Rule-1 will now appear in finished form. If it is correct, type "Y" or ⟨cr⟩ to go on to creating the next rule. If it is not correct, type "N". EXSYS will cancel the rule and let you create it over again.

## Making Corrections

Instead of cancelling an entire rule, it is possible to make corrections to mistakes. To do this, type "E" to select the "edit" routine from the options menu. Follow the instructions on the bottom of the screen to add to, change, or delete a partial or entire rule. If mistakes were made during the preliminary set up, they can be revised by typing "O" to select "options". Follow the screen instructions to retrieve and correct the items desired.

## Entering the Second Rule

To enter the second rule, press "A" (it means ADD) or ⟨cr⟩ when the inverted "T" appears again on the screen. If you want to recall a previous qualifier, as in this case, type "1" and ⟨cr⟩. It will show the entire contents of qualifier 1 in the right-hand window. It is a good idea to write down a list of qualifiers as you create them, as done in Fig. 5-4.

Since you wish to use the value "needs cutting" in the "if" clause of rule-2, simply press "2" and ⟨cr⟩.

To create the second part of the "if" clause in rule 2 "I am able to cut it" first type "N". It will create a new qualifier, qualifier 2. Then type "I am" ⟨cr⟩ for the attribute and the values "able to cut it" ⟨cr⟩ and "not able to cut it" ⟨cr⟩ ⟨cr⟩ next to "1" and "2" respectively.

Now type "1" ⟨cr⟩ to transfer "I am able to cut it" to the if clause in rule 2 in the left-hand window.

To create a "then" clause for rule-2, press ⟨cr⟩. "Then" will appear on the screen. Next, press "C" for choices. The second choice is used in rule-2, so press "2" and ⟨cr⟩. Type ⟨cr⟩ ⟨cr⟩ ⟨cr⟩ ⟨cr⟩ to complete rule 2 and see it in final form. Type "Y" ⟨cr⟩ if it is correct. Now the second rule is done.

## Entering the Remaining Rules

You should now proceed to enter all eighteen other rules into the knowledge base, one by one, as they are listed in Fig. 5-3.

When you get to rule-5, you will no longer be able to use "choices" to build the "then" clauses in your rules. At this point you are entering "then" clauses that do not contain choices or recommendations. Starting with rule 5, you enter the "then" clauses in the same way you build "if" clauses. You use the qualifier mode. You simply create a new qualifier for each "then" clause in the same way you do for the "if" clauses, and then transfer the appropriate item to the left window.

## Some Helpful Hints

The following are some helpful hints for entering rules into EXSYS:

- ☐ Remember to keep the same wording in the "then" clauses as in the "if" clauses to which they are linked. For example, rule 1 and rule 6 in Fig. 5-3 are so linked.
- ☐ In rule 20, two values are needed in one clause. Create the qualifier as follows:

```
The mowing time is
1. early day
2. mid day
3. late day
```

Press "1 3" or "1, 3" to link two values when EXSYS asks you to choose the number of the values. For example, in rule 20, it makes no difference whether the mowing time is early day or late day. The result will be the same. When you type "1 3" or "1, 3" ⟨cr⟩, EXSYS will create the if clause, "The mowing time is early day or late day".

- ☐ You can edit (add, change, or delete) a choice in the same way you edit a qualifier. Call the choices up in the right-hand window by pressing "C". Then press "T" (Type correction) and choose the number you desire to edit.
- ☐ To start over, leave the computer power on and press three keys simultaneously: CTRL, ALT, and DEL. This should be done with the DOS disk in drive A. Then start again with the introductory panel and concluding text step in the tutorial above.
- ☐ To get a printed copy of the rules, qualifiers, and choices press "P" when the inverted "T" rule editor is on the screen.
- ☐ To finish with an EDITXS session, press "S" to select the "store/exit" option from the menu on the bottom of the inverted "T" screen. The rules will be automatically saved in the file named at the beginning of the session.

## Questions

It is not necessary to create user questions in EXSYS. EXSYS automatically asks a user questions where necessary during a consultation.

## Consultations

To run a consultation, press "R" when the inverted "T" appears on the screen. Just follow the instructions on the screen.

## More Advanced Systems

It is possible to develop more advanced systems, using probabilities and user explanations. To learn to do this, place EXSYS DEMO Disk 1 in drive A and Demo Disk 2 in drive B, and at the "A" prompt type "demo b:⟨cr⟩":

```
A) demo b:⟨cr⟩
```

Alternately you may consult the user's instruction manual that accompanies the demo disks or a full version of EXSYS for more information.

## REVIEW QUESTIONS

1. Describe the major features of the M.1 expert system shell. Describe some of its limitations.

2. Why is it important to label each rule and rule set in M.1?

3. Describe the use of goal(s) and initialdata in M.1.

4. Describe the functions of questions in M.1.

5. What are the functions of legalvals in M.1?

6. Describe the major features of EXSYS expert system shell. Describe some of its limitations.

7. Identify the major differences between the two shells described in this chapter.

8. Describe several system development situations in which one or the other would be better to use. Explain the reasons for your choices.

# 6

# Putting Knowledge-Based Systems Onto the Computer: Using Level Five, 1st-CLASS, and VP-Expert

This chapter continues the discussion of computer software tools useful in knowledge-based systems development that began in Chapter 5. The topics covered here are

- □ Using Level Five (also called INSIGHT2+)
- □ Using 1st-CLASS
- □ Using VP-Expert

The grass-cutting decision example is again used in the following tutorials. This is done because the objective here is only to introduce the basic concept of the shells and to enable a quick overview comparison of their differences. Using a very brief, trivial example such as the grass-cutting decision was the easiest way to do this.

Those who wish a more comprehensive introduction to the shells should use the tutorials accompanying the demo or full disk versions of the shells.

## USING LEVEL FIVE (ALSO CALLED INSIGHT2+)

Level Five is a relatively easy to use expert system shell, which has built in editing facilities. In addition, you may transfer an entire knowledge base into Level Five from your word processor.

Figure 6-1, presented later in the chapter, contains a knowledge base designed for entry into Level Five. The plain English version of this knowledge base is shown in Fig. 5-2.

The following discussion covers

- Installing Level Five
- Using Level Five to create a knowledge base
- Alternative approach: loading an already created knowledge-base file
- Creating a small knowledge base for use with Level Five
- Creating display panels for your knowledge base file
- Running a consultation

## Installing Level Five

Level Five may be installed and used on a personal computer with either a hard disk or two floppy disk drives. The DOS operating system should be activated in either case.

**Installing the Level Five Expert System on a Hard Disk.** Put Level Five "DISK A" floppy disk into drive A and type "INSTALL":

```
A) INSTALL⟨Enter⟩
```

The "⟨Enter⟩" key is also known as the carriage return key "⟨cr⟩" on the keyboard. The following will appear on your screen:

```
INSIGHT2+ Installation
Copyright Level Five Research, Inc., 1986
For Yes or No answers just enter the letter Y or N.
To enter the defaults just press Enter. The defaults are in
  ( ).
To Exit at any time hold down the Ctrl key and C.
Your computer has a graphics card, does it have a color
  monitor ? (Y): YES
```

Always press ⟨Enter⟩ if you agree with the default answer within parentheses ( ) or type another answer (for example, "n" for no). After answering the first question, the following questions appear on the screen in sequence. Some typical answers are included in the example.

```
Do you want to install onto a hard disk ? (Y) : ⟨Enter⟩
From what disk drive are you going to install ? (A:) :
  ⟨Enter⟩
Do you want to install INSIGHT2+ ? (Y) : ⟨Enter⟩
Install onto what disk drive and/or directory? (C:\I2) :
  ⟨Enter⟩
Where are your knowledge bases going to reside ? (C:\PRL) :
  ⟨Enter⟩
```

When you have answered all the questions, the following will appear on the screen. Some typical answers are included in the example.

```
Do you want to install the sample knowledge bases ? (Y) :
   <Enter>
Put DISK A of the Level Five Program Master in the drive A:
Press any key when ready
Installing : C:\I2\I2.COM
Installing : C:\I2\I2.MSG
Installing : . . . . . .
```
> *(This is an example of a series of statements that will appear on the screen here and after the next two responses.)*

```
Put DISK B of the Level Five Program Master in the drive A:
Press any key when ready
Installing : C:\I2\I2.000
Installing : . . . . . .
Put DISK C of the Level Five Program Master in the drive A:
Press any key when ready
Installing : C:\PRL\JAS.PRL
Installing : C:\PRL\ . . . .
A)
```

Two directories (called I2 and PRL) have now been created on the hard disk. Directory I2 is the main Level Five shell that controls procedures and commands. Directory PRL is the place where files are stored.

To start using Level Five, first type

```
                     A)C:<Enter>
```

This puts you into the C drive on the hard disk. Then type

```
                     C)CD\I2<Enter>
```

This will take you to the main Level Five directory on the hard disk.

**Installing the Level Five Expert System with Two Floppy Disk Drives.**
If you are not using a hard disk, after installing DOS put the Level Five "DISK A" floppy disk into drive A and "DISK B" into drive B. Then begin with the "A)INSTALL" instructions given above, supplying the appropriate different answers:

```
Your computer has a graphics card, does it have a color
   monitor ? (Y): <Enter>
Do you want to install onto a hard disk ? (Y): N
From what disk drive are you going to install ? (A:):
   <Enter>
```

```
Do you want to install INSIGHT2+ ? (Y) : ⟨Enter⟩
Install onto what disk drive and/or directory ? (A:):
   ⟨Enter⟩
Where will the INSIGHT2+ overlays (I2.000-008) reside ?
   (B:): ⟨Enter⟩
Where are your knowledge bases going to reside ? (A:):
   ⟨Enter⟩
Press any key when ready ⟨Enter⟩
```

Level Five is now ready to be used.

## Using Level Five to Create a Knowledge Base

After Level Five has been installed on a personal computer, type

**IF INSTALLED ON HARDWARE DISK**

```
C)CD\I2⟨Enter⟩
C)I2⟨Enter⟩
```

**IF INSTALLED ON FLOPPY DISK**

```
A)I2⟨Enter⟩
```
After a menu appears, replace disk A with a blank formatted disk to store your knowledge base.

Level Five will then display the following menu, after the introductory panel:

```
          What would you like to do?
      ⇒   Run a knowledge base.
          Edit a knowledge base.
          Compile a knowledge base.
          Run a DBPAS program.
          Edit a DBPAS program.
          Compile a knowledge base.
          Edit a data base.
```

Since you are going to create a knowledge base, use the down arrow key on the keyboard to move the arrow key (⇒) to "Edit a knowledge base" and press ⟨Enter⟩. The title of the new screen is "Edit which knowledge base?"

You can use the labels at the bottom of the screen as a guide to command options. The option numbers refer to the numbered function keys located on the left side of the keyboard (for example: F1, F2, and so on).

Since you want to create a "new" file, press the F2 function key. Then type in the file name "grasscut" and press ⟨Enter⟩. For example:

```
     Enter the file name: grasscut⟨Enter⟩
```

The system will add ".prl" next to your file name automatically, as is shown on the next screen.

Now type in your file in the exact same form as shown in Fig. 6-1. After you

```
                                                      Page 1 of 2




                      WELCOME TO GRASSCUT


                 Copyright (c) 1988 by R.J. Mockler
                      All rights reserved.

                 Direct all inquiries for use to:
                      Robert J. Mockler
                      114 East 90th Street
                 New York, New York 10128




     Press PgDn Key to see the introductory explanation panel
     Press Function Key 3 to start the consultation
```

```
                                                      Page 2 of 2




                      Welcome to Grasscut

     In this system, you will be asked a series  of
     questions about your ability,   the ability of
     others, and the need to cut the grass, as well
     as about the condition of the equipment.   The
     computer will recommend whether or not  to cut
     the grass and,  if it needs  to be  cut,  who
     should cut it.




     Press Function Key 3 to start the consultation




     !
     !
     1. CUT IS WHAT
     !
     !
     !
     RULE 1
     IF     Need IS no
     THEN   Cut IS no
     AND    DISPLAY no cut
     !
```

*(continued)*

**FIGURE 6-1  Knowledge base to be used with Level Five—GRASS-CUT file.**

```
RULE 2
IF      Need IS yes
AND     I can cut the grass IS yes
THEN    Cut IS me
AND     DISPLAY I cut
!
RULE 3
IF      Need IS yes
AND     I can cut the grass IS no
AND     Other people can cut the grass IS yes
THEN    Cut IS other
AND     DISPLAY other cut
!
RULE 4
IF      I can cut the grass IS no
AND     Other people can cut the grass IS no
THEN    Cut IS no
        AND     DISPLAY no cut
!
RULE 5
IF      Grass IS long
AND     Season IS growing season
THEN    Need IS yes
!
RULE 6
IF      Grass IS short
OR      Season IS no growing season
THEN    Need IS no
!
!
RULE 7
IF      Health IS good
AND     Equipment IS ok
AND     Environment IS ok
THEN    I can cut the grass IS yes
!
RULE 8
IF      Health IS bad
OR      Equipment IS not ok
OR      Environment IS not ok
THEN    I can cut the grass IS no
!
!
RULE 9
IF      Others available IS yes
AND     Environment IS ok
THEN    Other can IS yes
!
!
RULE 10
IF      Others available IS no
OR      Environment IS not ok
THEN    Other can IS no
!
!
!
RULE 11
IF      Good equipment IS yes
AND     Gas IS yes
```

*(continued)*

**FIGURE 6-1** *(continued)*

```
THEN   Equipment IS ok
!
!
RULE 12
IF     Good equipment IS no
OR     Gas IS no
THEN Equipment IS not ok
!
!
RULE 13
IF     Weather IS good
AND    Mowtime IS middle
THEN   Environment IS ok
!
!
RULE 14
IF     Weather IS bad
OR     Mowtime IS early
OR     Mowtime IS late
THEN Environment IS not ok
!
!
TEXT Season
```

```
------------------------------------------------
                  Is the present season
              the growing or non-growing season?
------------------------------------------------
```

```
!
TEXT Grass
```

```
------------------------------------------------
                  Is the grass long or
                      short now?
------------------------------------------------
```

```
!
!
TEXT Good equipment
```

```
------------------------------------------------
              Is the equipment available for mowing the
                     grass in good condition?
------------------------------------------------
```

```
!
TEXT Gas
```

```
------------------------------------------------
              Do you have enough gas to turn the mower for
                     the entire cutting job?
------------------------------------------------
```

*(continued)*

**FIGURE 6-1** *(continued)*

```
!
TEXT Weather

------------------------------------------------------
              Is the weather good or bad?
------------------------------------------------------


!
TEXT Mowtime
------------------------------------------------------
         Is the time available for mowing the middle
         of the day, or is it the early or late part
                        of the day?
------------------------------------------------------


!
TEXT Others available

------------------------------------------------------
          Is someone else who has working equipment
                available to cut the grass?
------------------------------------------------------
!
!
!
TEXT Health


------------------------------------------------------
         Is the condition of your health good or bad?
------------------------------------------------------
!
DISPLAY no cut


                       CONCLUSION

              Based on the answers you have given,
          it is recommended that: no one cut the grass.

!
DISPLAY other cut


                       CONCLUSION

              Based on the answers you have given,
          it is recommended that: another person cut the grass.


!
DISPLAY I cut
```

*(continued)*

**FIGURE 6-1** *(continued)*

CONCLUSION

```
      Based on the answers you have given,
      it is recommended that: you cut the grass.

   !
   END
```

**FIGURE 6-1** *(continued)*

have finished typing in your file, press F3 to save and F4 to compile it, as indicated in the command menu at the bottom of the screen.

If the system displays an error message, press F3 to edit the file (fix the error). Then follow the same procedures again to save and compile the corrected file.

### An Alternative Approach: Using a Word Processor to Create a Knowledge Base

Instead of creating a knowledge base, such as the one shown in Fig. 6-1, from scratch using Level Five, as described in the preceding section, an alternative approach would be to use a word processor that you are familiar with. However, the knowledge base must be saved as an ASCII file with a ".prl" filename extension in your word processor. In this case, the filename would be "grasscut.prl". *Note:* The following procedure is for a two floppy disk drive system.

Using this approach, Level Five should be loaded as described in the previous sections until you come to a screen titled "What would you like to do?". Here, load into drive A your word processing disk with the file "grasscut.prl" on it in ASCII format. Move the arrow to the line "Edit a knowledge base" and press ⟨Enter⟩.

Your word processing files should appear on the next screen, "Edit which knowledge base?". Check to be sure the directory listed is "a:". If not, use F3 to change the directory to "a:".

Move the arrow to "grasscut" and press ⟨Enter⟩ to load the knowledge base. After it has been loaded (it will appear on the screen), press F4 to begin compiling. Any errors in the knowledge base will be listed as the knowledge base is compiled. After each error is detected, press F2 to continue until you get a complete list of errors or press F3 to edit the errors as you go along.

After correcting the errors, recompile the knowledge base by pressing F4 until it reads "Compilation complete, no errors detected." At this point, you may run a consultation using the knowledge base.

### Creating a Small Knowledge Base for Use with Level Five

The following section describes how to create such a knowledge base in your word processor. A sample file is given in Fig. 6-1.

To enter rules into a Level Five knowledge-base file, you use reserved words with special meanings that function as instructions. Reserved words are typed in upper case letters (for instance, TITLE, INIT, RULE. . .).   For example, when you type

```
TITLE Cut the grass DISPLAY
```

you use the reserved word TITLE to tell Level Five to start the program.

Creating the display panel shown next in the knowledge base in Fig. 6-1 is explained in a later section of these instructions.

As in other expert system shells you have to indicate your goal early in the knowledge base.   In Level Five you list the main goal after the number 1.   For example:

```
1. Cut IS WHAT
```

"IS WHAT" are reserved words and tell Level Five to seek a value for "Cut" during a consultation.   The Level Five system will investigate all rules based on the data a user provides in order to reach its goal.   It doesn't matter whether you type "cut" or "Cut" or "CUT" in the clauses you create in the knowledge base.   In general, however, it is best to use the upper case for the first letter of each clause (for example, "Cut IS no").

To create rules in a Level Five knowledge base, type in "RULE" and a number. For example:

```
RULE 2
IF     Need IS yes
AND    I can cut the grass IS yes
THEN   Cut IS me
AND    DISPLAY I cut
```

"IS" is a reserved word that combines an attribute and a value.   "ARE" also performs the same function where there is more than one value.   Where there is more than one "IF" clause, use "AND" or "OR" to connect each clause.   In the "THEN" and "ELSE" part of a rule, you can only use "AND" to connect clauses.

Between rules you can use blank lines or exclamation points (!) as separators, as shown in Fig. 6-1.   Next to the exclamation point you can type hints or comments to help anyone who works with the file to understand its content.   Level Five will ignore these comments when processing the knowledge base.

In Level Five you cannot use a dash (—) to connect or join two words.

You use the reserved word "TEXT" to instruct Level Five to ask a user running the consultation for information.   For example, type

```
TEXT Season
```

The question that is to generate the information response is typed next:

```
Is the present season the growing or
non-growing season?
```

Level Five will collect every possible permissible answer contained in the rules in the knowledge base and list them under the question as the program is consulted.

Use "END" to close the program.

## Creating Display Panels for Your Knowledge-Base File

To create a panel for display to users, type the message you want displayed in window:1. An example is the "Welcome to Grasscut" panel shown below.

```
*********************************************************************
*                                                  Page 1 of 2   *
*                                                                *
*                                                                *
*                                                                *
*                                                                *
*        -------------------------------------------------       *
*        ;                                              ;        *
*        ;          WELCOME TO GRASSCUT                 ;        *
*        ;                                              ;        *
*        ;                                              ;        *
*        ;       Copyright (c) 1988 by R.J. Mockler     ;        *
*        ;           All rights reserved.               ;        *
*        ;                                              ;        *
*        ;       Direct all inquiries for use to:       ;        *
*        ;            Robert J. Mockler                 ;        *
*        ;            114 East 90th Street              ;        *
*        ;          New York, New York 10128            ;        *
*        ;                                              ;        *
*        -------------------------------------------------       *
*                                                                *
*                                                                *
*        Press PgDn Key to see introductory explanation panel    *
*        Press Function Key 3 to start the consultation          *
*********************************************************************
```

## Running a Consultation

To run a consultation press ⟨Enter⟩ when the arrow in the Level Five Main Menu is at "Run a knowledge base" as shown below.

```
           What would you like to do?
       ⇒   Run a knowledge base.
           Edit a knowledge base.
           Compile a knowledge base.
           Run a DBPAS program.
           Edit a DBPAS program.
           Compile a DBPAS program.
           Edit a data base.
```

The next screen will ask you "Run Which Knowledge Base?" Press the space bar to move the arrow to the file you need (in this example your filename is GRASS-CUT) and press ⟨Enter⟩ to begin the consultation.

You will be shown the introductory panel. Press F1 to view an explanatory panel describing the purpose of the consultation. Next press F3 and begin answering the questions.

| | Factor 1 season | Factor 2 grass | Factor 3 health | Factor 4 good-equip | Factor 5 gas |
|---|---|---|---|---|---|
| 1: | non-growing | * | * | * | * |
| 2: | * | short | * | * | * |
| 3: | growing | tall | good | y | y |
| 4: | growing | tall | good | y | y |
| 5: | growing | tall | good | y | y |
| 6: | growing | tall | good | y | y |
| 7: | growing | tall | good | y | y |
| 8: | growing | tall | good | y | y |
| 9: | growing | tall | good | y | y |
| 10: | growing | tall | good | y | n |
| 11: | growing | tall | good | y | n |
| 12: | growing | tall | good | n | * |
| 13: | growing | tall | good | n | * |
| 14: | growing | tall | poor | * | * |
| 15: | growing | tall | poor | * | * |

| | Factor 6 weather | Factor 7 mow-time | Factor 8 other-avail | Goal or Result Cut | weight |
|---|---|---|---|---|---|
| 1: | * | * | * | no | 1.00 |
| 2: | * | * | * | no | 1.00 |
| 3: | good | mid-day | * | me | 1.00 |
| 4: | good | early | y | others | 1.00 |
| 5: | good | early | n | no | 1.00 |
| 6: | good | late | y | others | 1.00 |
| 7: | good | late | n | no | 1.00 |
| 8: | bad | * | y | others | 1.00 |
| 9: | bad | * | n | no | 1.00 |
| 10: | * | * | y | others | 1.00 |
| 11: | * | * | n | no | 1.00 |
| 12: | * | * | y | others | 1.00 |
| 13: | * | * | n | no | 1.00 |
| 14: | * | * | y | others | 1.00 |
| 15: | * | * | n | no | 1.00 |

**FIGURE 6-2   1st-CLASS example cases for the grass-cutting decision.**

When you have finished answering the questions, Level Five will give you a recommendation. Once you have been given a recommendation, press F10 to exit the system. You will be asked "Are you sure that you want to exit?" Press F1 to say yes and exit the system.

## USING 1st-CLASS

1st-CLASS, another PC expert system shell, differs somewhat from the others already described in this book. In addition to being able to enter a rule-based knowledge base, such as the one shown for the grass-cutting situation in Fig. 6-1, you may also generate a knowledge base from sample cases. The shell "induces" rules automatically from the collection of sample cases you supply. The sample cases used for the grass-cutting situation are shown in Fig. 6-2.

The following discussion covers

▫ Installing 1st-CLASS
▫ Creating a knowledge base in 1st-CLASS
▫ Running a consultation

Throughout the discussion the instructions ⟨cr⟩ and ⟨Enter⟩ are used interchangeably.

### Installing 1st-CLASS

To install 1st-CLASS, put the 1st-CLASS "Program" disk in drive A and type

```
A)1stclass⟨Enter⟩
```

You will see

```
1st-class by Programs in Motion Inc.       Release 3.09
             Welcome to 1st-CLASS
     (C) Copyright 1985,1986 William Hapgood
         your registration number is: . . .
             For support contact:
         . . . . . . . . . . . . .
     Is your computer IBM PC-compatible? [y/n]
```

Press "Y" or ⟨Enter⟩ if your computer is IBM PC-compatible, or press "N" if it is not. The next question then appears.

```
   Do you want to display in color like this? [y/n]
```

Press "Y" or ⟨Enter⟩ if your computer is a color system, "N" if not. 1st-CLASS is now installed.

## Creating a Knowledge-Base File in 1st-CLASS

There are six main screens in 1st-CLASS: FILES, DEFINITIONS, EXAMPLES, METHODS, RULE, and ADVISOR. These main screens are named on the second menu line of the next panel that appears on your screen. You will notice that there is a box around the word FILES. It indicates that the screen you are now viewing is FILES. This screen displays all the files that are on the disk in drive A.

Throughout 1st-CLASS you change screens by pressing F10 to go forward and F9 to go backward or to quit or leave 1st-CLASS.

The top menu line on the screen shows several commands: Get, Save, New, and so on. Since you wish to create a new file, press "N". Then 1st-CLASS will ask you:

```
New Knowledge Base Name:
```

Insert a blank formatted disk to store your knowledge base in the B drive and type

```
New Knowledge Base Name:B:grasscut⟨Enter⟩
```

If a file by that name already exists, press the escape key "⟨esc⟩", then press "N" again and type in a new, different name.

Once you have typed in the file name, 1st-CLASS takes you to the second screen, DEFINITIONS. You can tell you are in the DEFINITIONS screen because there is a box around the word DEFINITIONS. You enter or "define" the knowledge-base components on this screen. The first step in the DEFINITIONS screen is to enter your goal. You do this by pressing the up arrow key to move the highlight box over RESULT. You then enter the name of your goal by pressing "C" (Change). 1st-CLASS will ask you:

```
Changing name of "RESULT". Enter new name:
```

Type in the name of your goal, "CUT"⟨Enter⟩. It may be typed in either upper or lower case characters. Next, you need to fill in the values for the RESULT "cut", so press "V" (new-Value) and answer the questions.

```
            Enter a result:no⟨Enter⟩
            Enter a result:me⟨Enter⟩
            Enter a result:others⟨Enter⟩
```

As seen in the grass-cutting situation in Fig. 6-2, these are the only three goal choices for "CUT" in this situation. Now press ⟨Enter⟩ to conclude entering all the possible values for the goal or result.

The new screen that appears, DEFINITIONS again, has several functions or commands shown on the top of the screen. Since you next want to enter the factors affecting the result "CUT", you now press "F" (for new-Factor). These factors are the information the system asks users to supply during a consultation.

There are eight factors in this situation, as seen across the top of the matrix in Fig. 6-2. So a maximum of eight questions will be asked of the system user. When you press "F" to create a new factor, 1st-CLASS will ask you:

```
Enter name of factor to add:
```

Key in the factor name and ⟨Enter⟩, such as:

```
Enter name of factor to add:other-avail⟨Enter⟩
```

Then the system will ask you:

```
Enter a value for this factor:
```

Type in the values for this factor and press ⟨Enter⟩, as follows:

```
Enter a value for this factor:n⟨Enter⟩
Enter a value for this factor:y⟨Enter⟩
```

As you finish entering the values for each factor and want to move to the next factor, press ⟨Enter⟩ and then "F" again. Repeat the above procedure until all eight factors and their values are entered. The following is a list of the eight factors and their values that are entered for the grass-cutting situation:

```
other-avail  :  n         y
mow-time     :  early      mid day       late
weather      :  good       bad
gas          :  y          n
good-equip   :  y          n
health       :  good       poor
grass        :  tall       short
season       :  growing    non-growing
```

After you have entered the results or goals, all the factors, and all the values, press the F10 key on the left side of the keyboard to enter the EXAMPLES screen. The EXAMPLES screen is a large spreadsheet or matrix that is used to enter the example cases that cover the possible combinations of results, factors, and values. It is helpful, therefore, to first construct a spreadsheet or matrix on a separate sheet of paper containing all of the factor-value combinations that will give each result possible for "CUT", the goal. These fifteen example cases for the grass-cutting situation are shown in the spreadsheet in Fig. 6-2.

You must now enter the spreadsheet on the EXAMPLES screen. To type in the first example case (1) from Fig. 6-2, you press "E". When you press "E" (which means new-Example—to create a new example), the screen will then ask you to enter each factor-value one at a time. For example, in this instance the screen will show:

```
Select or type a value for season :
     growing      non-growing
```

Referring to Fig. 6-2, the value for season in example 1 is "non-growing". You, therefore, use the right arrow key to move the highlight onto the value you need "non-growing" and press ⟨Enter⟩ to select it.

The next factor then appears on the screen:

```
Select or type a value for grass :
     tall           short
```

Since you do not need this factor in example 1 in Fig. 6-2, just press the F10 key to move to the next factor. In example 1 you would keep pressing the F10 key until you reached the result of goal "cut" in the next to last column in Fig. 6-2.

```
Select or type a value for cut :
   me      others      no
```

You would then move the arrow key to the correct value, "no", and press ⟨Enter⟩. You would then press F10 again, and enter a value for "weight". In this case you would press ⟨Enter⟩ to accept the value of "1.00".

You are now ready to enter example 2 from the decision spreadsheet in Fig. 6-2. First, you press "E", to start creating your new (2) example. The screen will again show:

```
Select or type a value for season :
     growing        non-growing
```

Since this factor does not affect example 2, you press F10. You next are shown:

```
Select or type a value for grass :
     tall           short
```

Use the arrow key to move the highlight onto "short", and press ⟨Enter⟩. Enter the values of the remaining items in the same way you did for example 1.

Continue typing in each example line in the same way until you have typed in all the fifteen examples in the spreadsheet. If at any time you wish to correct errors, press the F1 key to get help for doing so.

Once you have entered all the examples on the spreadsheet, use the F10 key to enter the next screen, METHOD. In this screen you select the method by which rules are to be built by 1st-CLASS. There are four choices for the method:

```
1. O:
Optimize the rule
2. L:
Use the factors in order, Left-to-right
3. M:
Match the advisor responses against the examples
4. C:
Customize the rule with the rule editor
```

If you press the letter "O", 1st-CLASS will construct a rule set, based on the examples you entered, and will optimize the sequence of questions. So press the letter "O" (not the number zero) at this time. If this is your first time entering the file, 1st-CLASS will ask you if you wish to save your file. Press "S", type in the name of the file, and press ⟨cr⟩.

Press the F10 key to enter the next screen, RULE. The RULE screen displays the rules that have been induced by 1st-CLASS from your examples. It gives you the opportunity to review the rules, make changes where needed, and generally study the knowledge base. In the RULE screen, you will find all the rule situations diagrammed that were entered into the spreadsheet. Press the down (and up) arrow keys to scroll the screen to see all the rules, if they take up more than one screen.

You are now ready to consult the file, that is, run a consultation.

## Running a Consultation

Use the F10 key to enter the next screen, ADVISOR. You use the ADVISOR screen to run a consultation.

For example, on the ADVISOR screen press ⟨Enter⟩ if you agree with the answer where the highlight rests, or move the highlight to the choice you prefer and then press ⟨Enter⟩. When you finish the consultation, use the F9 key to move back through the RULE, METHOD, EXAMPLE, DEFINITIONS, and FILE screens. To save this knowledge base file on the B drive, press "S" (Save) and 1st-CLASS will ask you:

```
Save using file name:grasscut
```

Just press ⟨Enter⟩ to agree to it. At this point you should save the knowledge base again, even if you saved it earlier.

Then press the F9 key to escape the 1st-CLASS shell. You will be asked:

```
Quit 1st CLASS? [y/n]
```

Press "Y" to complete the consultation.

To start a consultation from the beginning, just follow the instructions given earlier for installing 1st-CLASS.

In the FILE screen, press "G" (which means GET) to get a file for consultation. 1st-CLASS will instruct you:

```
move cursor to file and press ⟨cr⟩, or type in name:
```

This means that if your file is in drive A on the program disk, then you can use the arrow keys to move the highlight onto the file name and press ⟨Enter⟩. Next, you can use the F10 key to go to the ADVISOR screen and run the consultation as directed above.

If earlier you stored your file on a hard disk or a separate floppy disk after you created it on 1st-CLASS, then you would retrieve the file from either the hard disk or floppy disk drive, and not from the program disk. In this case, you would type in the drive letter ("A:", "B:", or "C:") and the filename when asked on the FILE screen:

```
move cursor to file and press (cr), or type in name:
```

For example:

```
                              C:grasscut(cr)
```

or

```
                              B:grasscut(cr)
```

"C:" means that you want to load a file from the hard disk. "B:" means you want to load a file from the floppy disk in drive B. Do not add a subfilename extension (just type "grasscut") or you will not be able to load the file. The file that you create will be given the subfile name ".kbm" automatically (kbm means knowledge base module). You would then proceed to the ADVISOR screen and run the consultation as instructed above.

Unlike Level Five you cannot load a file from your word processor with 1st-CLASS.


## USING VP-EXPERT

VP-Expert is another expert system shell package that can be used to develop expert knowledge-based systems. One of its features is the ability to exchange data with existing spreadsheet and data base files. Another feature is the ability to use a pre-existing file, created with a word processor, data base, or spreadsheet program as a knowledge-base file.

This tutorial begins with instructions to install VP-Expert. Then it describes two alternative ways to create a VP-Expert knowledge-base file. Finally, it discusses how to run a consultation using VP-Expert.

### Installing VP-Expert

VP-Expert requires no special installation procedure to prepare it for use. The program is copy-protected and so prevents making a duplicate security copy before use. For an additional fee, however, a non-copy-protected version of the program can be obtained from the software vendor, Paperback Software International. If this version is used, a backup copy should be made of the program before it is used to develop expert systems.

If desired, VP-Expert can be installed on a hard disk by copying the program files to a hard disk. To do this, place the VP-Expert program disk in drive A and type "copy *.* C:(Enter)" at the "A)" (or DOS) prompt that appears on the screen.

To use VP-Expert to develop a new knowledge-base file or to run a consultation, proceed as follows:

<table>
<tr><td>

**IF VP-EXPERT IS ON A HARD DISK**

At the "C⟩" prompt type "VPX⟨Enter⟩". (Note: If the VP-Expert program disk used is copy-protected, then the program disk must be in drive A before typing "VPX.")

</td><td>

**IF VP-EXPERT IS ON A FLOPPY DISK**

At the "A⟩" prompt, type "VPX⟨Enter⟩" with the VP-Expert program disk in drive A and a formatted disk in drive B for storing knowledge-base files to be used.

</td></tr>
</table>

## Creating a Small VP-Expert Knowledge Base

Two methods of creating a knowledge-base file in VP-Expert will be covered in this tutorial. The first uses either the built-in text editor or an external word processing program. The second uses a process called "induction," where a knowledge-base file is automatically created, or "induced," from a table of example cases.

There are three basic elements in every VP-Expert knowledge base file. They are covered in detail in this tutorial and are

- The "ACTIONS" block—it controls the user consultation session.
- Rules—they contain the actual knowledge or expertise in the knowledge-base file.
- Questions—they allow a user to interact with the expert system during a consultation.

**ACTIONS Block.** Building the "GRASSCUT" knowledge-base file begins with the "ACTIONS" block. To activate the VP-Expert text-editor from the main menu, type "E". (There are four possible ways to select a command option: type the first letter of the command, type the command number, type the function key number, or use the arrow keys to scroll the cursor to the command and press the ⟨Enter⟩ key.)

Some commands are given below to facilitate building a knowledge-base file using the VP-Expert text editor:

| KEYS | DESCRIPTIONS |
|---|---|
| Right or Left arrows | Moves cursor right or left one character |
| Insert | Turns the insert mode on or off |
| Tab | Moves cursor to next tab stop |
| Ctrl-Enter | Adds a blank line |
| Del (or Ctrl-G) | Deletes character at cursor position |
| Backspace | Deletes character to left of cursor |
| Ctrl-T | Deletes from cursor to end of word |
| Ctrl-Y | Deletes line |
| Alt-F6 | Saves file and leaves editor |
| Alt-F8 | Abandons file without saving or changing |
| Alt-F5 | Updates file without leaving editor |

For a complete listing of other editing commands, consult the VP-Expert user's guide, *VP-Expert: Rule-Based Expert System Development Tool* (Berkeley, Calif.: Paperback Software International, 1987). Alternatively any favorite word processor can be used to create a VP-Expert knowledge-base file.

In answer to the prompt that asks for the name of the knowledge-base file to use, type "B:GRASSCUT⟨Enter⟩". This names a new file that will be saved on the B drive with the name, "GRASSCUT". (Note: For commands, VP-Expert is case-insensitive, which means that upper and lower case letters can be used interchangeably).

A blank screen appears, ready for typing the first part of the "GRASSCUT" knowledge-base file, which is the "ACTIONS" block. To duplicate the example shown in Fig. 6-3, type the following, but use upper and lower case letters for all text inside the quotation marks, which is not case-insensitive, as shown:

```
ACTIONS⟨Enter⟩
⟨Enter⟩
DISPLAY "⟨Enter⟩
GRASSCUT SYSTEM⟨Enter⟩
⟨Enter⟩
Copyright (c) 1988 by R.J. Mockler⟨Enter⟩
All rights reserved⟨Enter⟩
Direct all inquiries for use to:⟨Enter⟩
Robert J. Mockler⟨Enter⟩
114 East 90th Street⟨Enter⟩
New York, New York 10128⟨Enter⟩
⟨Enter⟩
Press any key to continue.¯"⟨Enter⟩
```

The lines just typed should be left-aligned, although those in Fig. 6-3 are not. In order to have the text display in the center of the screen during a consultation, two additional steps are necessary. The first is to activate the document option. Press the function key F9 to turn the "9Dcumnt" option on. Next use the arrow keys to move the cursor to the beginning of each line, starting with the "GRASSCUT SYSTEM" line. Then press the function key F5 for the "5Center" option, which centers each line.

Continue to type the "WELCOME" introductory screen and the remaining "ACTIONS" block information shown in Fig. 6-3. Remember to type ⟨Enter⟩ at the end of each line so that entries display exactly as shown in Fig. 6-3.

The VP-Expert keywords used in Fig. 6-3, "ACTIONS", "DISPLAY", "CLS", and "FIND", could be typed with lower case letters. They are entered as upper case letters only for tutorial emphasis.

The keyword "ACTIONS" appears only once in every knowledge-base file. Although not a requirement, it is advisable to place the "ACTIONS" block at the beginning of the file. It works like a mini-program that tells VP-Expert the order to follow when a user runs a consultation.

```
ACTIONS

DISPLAY "

                           GRASSCUT SYSTEM

                  Copyright (c) 1988 by R.J. Mockler
                       All rights reserved

                  Direct all inquires for use to:
                       Robert J. Mockler
                       114 East 90th Street
                  New York, New York 10128



Press any key to continue.~"

DISPLAY "



                        WELCOME TO GRASSCUT


        In this system, you will be asked a series of questions
        about your ability, the ability of others, the need to cut
        the grass, the condition of the equipment, and the condition
        of the environment.  The system will determine if the grass
        needs to be cut and who should cut it.

        In responding to user questions during a consultation, you
        may use the responses displayed after each question.




Press any key to begin.~"
CLS

FIND cut-grass

CLS

DISPLAY "Based on the answers you have just given, the Grasscut
System's recommendation on who should cut the grass is: {cut-grass}.



To continue with another consultation, select Go again.  If you
would like to see if the conclusion would be any different should
some of your responses be changed, select Whatif and follow the
instructions accordingly.

Otherwise, select Quit to exit from the Grasscut System.";
```

**FIGURE 6-3  VP-Expert—introductory screen, concluding screen, and goal statement of "GRASSCUT" knowledge-base file.**

"DISPLAY", unlike "ACTIONS", is an optional keyword. In this example, it is used to create screens to explain to a user what the "GRASSCUT SYSTEM" is about and what to expect during a consultation. Such enhancements can be used to make the expert system more user friendly to a nontechnician who runs a consultation.

All "DISPLAY" text appears in quotation marks. It appears on a user's screen during a consultation in the same order that it appears in the "ACTIONS" block. In this example, the "GRASSCUT SYSTEM" screen appears first, followed by the "WELCOME" screen when the consultation begins.

When the tilde symbol (˜) is included in "DISPLAY" text, as in this example, it causes the message within the quotation marks to pause at the point of the tilde. This allows a user to move on to the next screen whenever desired, by pressing any key to signal a move.

"CLS", or clear screen, is also an optional keyword. Depending on where it is placed in a knowledge-base file, "CLS" clears the screen of any text immediately preceding it. In this example, "CLS" clears the "WELCOME" screen before proceeding with the main part of the consultation.

The last keyword used in this example is "FIND". It must be present in every knowledge-base file for the system to work. "FIND" tells VP-Expert what value or values to find to reach a successful goal during a consultation.

In this example, the goal of the consultation is to find the value for the variable "cut-grass". The possible values for the variable "cut-grass" are "you, someone_ else, or no_one". As evident, multiword variables are joined by an underscore between words.

To conclude the consultation, the "DISPLAY" is used again. By placing the "DISPLAY" message after the keyword "FIND", VP-Expert displays the concluding screen only after the goal has been found.

In the final "DISPLAY" screen, "cut-grass" is placed in curly brackets. This instructs VP-Expert to substitute the goal value found in its place.

If the completed "ACTIONS" block is examined carefully, it is clear that the only absolutely critical keywords are "ACTIONS" and "FIND". But the "DISPLAY" and "CLS" keywords have an important role to make the knowledge base more user friendly.

Some additional considerations are

- Comment lines can be included in the "ACTIONS" block, or anywhere else in the knowledge-base file, as long as they begin with an exclamation mark (!) (not shown in the example).
- The "ACTIONS" block must end with a semicolon. There can be only one semicolon in the ACTIONS block.

**If-Then Rules.**    If-then rules are considered the heart of every knowledge base. In VP-Expert if-then rules are usually entered after the "ACTIONS" block as one continuous file. They are presented here as the separate Fig. 6-4 only to differentiate the rules section from the "ACTIONS" bock.

```
RULE 1
IF    season = growing AND
grass = long
THEN need = cut;

RULE 2
IF    season = non-growing OR
      grass = short
THEN need = not-cut;

RULE 3
IF    good-equip = yes AND
      gas = yes
THEN equip = OK;

RULE 4
IF    weather = good AND
      mow-time = midday
THEN environ = OK;

RULE 5
IF    health = good AND
      equip = OK AND
      environ = OK
THEN able = OK;

RULE 6
IF    others-available = yes
THEN other = OK;

RULE 7
IF    need = cut AND
      able = OK
THEN cut-grass = you;

RULE 8
IF    need = cut AND
      able = not-ok AND
      other = ok
THEN cut-grass = someone_else;

RULE 9
IF    need = not-cut
THEN cut-grass = no_one;

RULE 10
IF    good-equip = no OR
      gas = no
THEN equip = not-OK;

RULE 11
IF    weather = bad OR
      mow-time = earlyday OR
      mow-time = lateday
THEN environ = not-ok;
```

*(continued)*

**FIGURE 6-4   VP-Expert—if-then rules of "GRASSCUT" knowledge-base file.**

```
RULE 12
IF    health = bad OR
      equip = not-ok OR
      environ = not-ok
THEN able = not-ok;

RULE 13
IF    need = cut AND
      able = not-ok OR
      others-available = no
THEN cut-grass = no_one;
```

**FIGURE 6-4** *(continued)*

To enter the first two if-then rules, type

```
RULE  1⟨Enter⟩
IF    season = growing AND⟨Enter⟩
      grass = long⟨Enter⟩
THEN  need = cut;⟨Enter⟩
⟨Enter⟩
RULE  2⟨Enter⟩
IF    season = non-growing OR⟨Enter⟩
      grass = short⟨Enter⟩
THEN  need = not-cut;⟨Enter⟩
```

Notice that the rules begin with the keyword "RULE" followed by a space and a label that does not exceed twenty characters. In this case, the rules are labelled numerically from one to sixteen. Numbers are used as rule names in this example, but names could just as well be any twenty-character name desired. (The keywords "RULE", "IF", "THEN", "AND", and "OR" are shown here in upper case letters only for emphasis.)

After the keyword "IF", up to ten conditions can be stated. In rule 1 two conditions, "season = growing" and "grass = long", are combined with the logical operator "AND". Other logical operators include "OR" (as in rule 2) and "ELSE" (not used in this example).

A rule ends with the keyword "THEN" plus a variable phrase. In the case of rule 1, the variable "need" is assigned the value "cut" if the conditions in the if part of the rule are found to be true: if "season = growing" and "grass = long". The rule ends with a semicolon. Although rules can occur in any order in a knowledge-base file, their sequence affects the speed of a consultation session.

The remaining if-then rules found in Fig. 6-4 can be typed into the knowledge-base file using the same procedures described for entering the first two rules.

**Questions.** Questions, using the keywords "ASK" and "CHOICES", obtain information from a user during a consultation. For example, the first "ASK" statement shown in Fig. 6-5, asks a user what "season" it is. The question within the quotation marks is displayed during the consultation. To enter the first "ASK"

```
ASK season: "What is the present season?";
CHOICES season : Growing, Non-growing;

ASK grass: "What is the length of the grass?";
CHOICES grass : Long, Short;

ASK good-equip: "Is the equipment available for mowing the grass
in good condition?";
CHOICES good-equip : Yes, No;

ASK gas: "Do you have enough gas to power the mower for the
cutting job?";
CHOICES gas : Yes, No;

ASK weather: "Is the weather for mowing good or bad?";
CHOICES weather : Good, Bad;

ASK mow-time: "What part of the day is available for mowing the
grass?"; CHOICES mow-time : Earlyday, Midday, Lateday;

ASK health: "What is the condition of your health?"; CHOICES
health : Good, Bad;

ASK others-available: "Is someone else who has working equipment
available to cut the grass?";
CHOICES others-available : Yes, No;
```

**FIGURE 6-5   VP-Expert—user-questions of "GRASSCUT" knowl-
edge-base file.**

statement, type

```
ASK season : "What is the present season?";(Enter)
```

In order to create a menu of acceptable responses for each question in an "ASK" statement, the "CHOICES" keyword is used.   It defines acceptable values.   In this case, acceptable values for the variable "season" are: "growing" and "non-growing". To enter them, type

```
CHOICES season : Growing, Non-growing;(Enter)
```

In the same way, continue typing the remaining "ASK" and "CHOICES" combinations to complete building the user questions contained in the "GRASSCUT" knowledge-base file.   When you are done, save your file by pressing two keys together: ALT and F6.   At the prompt, "Save as "b:grasscut.kbs" (Y or N)?," type "Y".

### An Alternative Way to Build a VP-Expert Knowledge Base:
### The Induction Method

The first thing to do when developing a knowledge base using the induction method is to create a table of examples.   An example is a one-line scenario of one user's possible answers.   A collection of many users' answers provide many scenarios or

| Season | Grass | Health | Good-equip | Gas | Weather | Mow-time | Other-avail | Cut-grass |
|--------|-------|--------|------------|-----|---------|----------|-------------|-----------|
| non-growing | * | * | * | * | * | * | * | No_one |
| * | short | * | * | * | * | * | * | No_one |
| growing | tall | good | yes | yes | good | mid-day | * | you |
| growing | tall | good | yes | yes | good | early | yes | Someone_else |
| growing | tall | good | yes | yes | good | early | no | No_one |
| growing | tall | good | yes | yes | good | late | yes | Someone_else |
| growing | tall | good | yes | yes | good | late | no | No_one |
| growing | tall | good | yes | yes | bad | * | yes | Someone_else |
| growing | tall | good | yes | yes | bad | * | no | No_one |
| growing | tall | good | yes | no | * | * | yes | Someone_else |
| growing | tall | good | yes | no | * | * | no | No_one |
| growing | tall | good | no | * | * | * | yes | Someone_else |
| growing | tall | good | no | * | * | * | no | No_one |
| growing | tall | poor | * | * | * | * | yes | Someone_else |
| growing | tall | poor | * | * | * | * | no | No_one |

*Note*: * = value not required.

**FIGURE 6-6   VP-Expert—table of GRASSCUT system examples.**

examples, as shown in Fig. 6-6. They should, theoretically, cover all possible combinations of user responses to consultation questions. This collection of examples can be examined to induce rules that govern the conclusions, in the last column of Fig. 6-6.

A table of examples can be created with any word processor or text editor, with a data base management system program such as VP-Info or dBASE, or with spreadsheet programs such as VP-Planner or Lotus 1-2-3. In this example, the table is created using the VP-Expert text editor.

From the main menu, select "2Induce" by pressing the F2 function key. Next, press the F2 key again to select "2Create" to create a new file called "CUTTABLE", then type "B:CUTTABLE⟨Enter⟩". This will take you into the VP-Expert text editor.

To enter the first three rows of the examples table shown in Fig. 6-6, type

```
Season       Grass Health Good-equip Gas Weather Mow-time Other-avail Cut-grass⟨Enter⟩
non-growing  *     *      *              *   *       *        *           No_one⟨Enter⟩
*            short *      *              *   *       *        *           No_one⟨Enter⟩
```

Like any other table, the top row constitutes column headings. They define a set of variables called season, grass, health, and so on. The rightmost variable "cut-grass" is the goal variable and its value is determined by values entered in preceding columns.

An asterisk (*) appears in some columns. It tells VP-Expert that a value is not required for this column's variable. The conclusion (or goal) defined for the row can be obtained without the asterisked variables. As an example, as soon as "season" is found to be "non-growing", the conclusion is that "No_one" needs to cut the grass, regardless of what the values for the variables may be.

To complete constructing the examples table shown in Fig. 6-6, type in the values as they appear in the figure. Remember to end every row with an ⟨Enter⟩ key. When you are done, save the table by pressing two keys together: ALT and F6. At the prompt "Save as "b:cuttable.tbl" (Y or N)?" type "Y".

VP-Expert is now ready to generate, or induce, the knowledge-base file from the table of examples shown in Fig. 6-6. Select "2Induce" from the main menu by typing either "2" or F2. Next, select "4Text" to indicate that the table is stored as a text file.

In response to the screen prompt, "What is the name of the examples file?" type "b:cuttable⟨Enter⟩". This brings on the next screen prompt: "What is the name of the rules file to create?" The rules file, or knowledge-base file, will be given a default name "cuttable.kbs" if you press the ⟨Enter⟩ key here. Otherwise, you can give it a different name.

VP-Expert interrupts the induction process every time it recognizes values that occur more than once. In this case, ignore these messages by pressing the ⟨Enter⟩ key each time you see the interrupt message.

When the induction process is completed, VP-Expert returns to the "Induction Menu" screen. Press the function key F6 to select "6Quit" to exit into the "Main Menu" screen. Then, press the function key F6 again, this time to select "6FileName", and type "b:cuttable⟨Enter⟩" to select the knowledge-base file that was just created. Next, press function key F3 to select "3Edit" to view it. It looks like the example in Fig. 6-7.

The new, induced file looks similar to the one created with the text editor shown in Figs. 6-3, 6-4, and 6-5. But some details in the new "CUTTABLE" induction file are different from the first file because

□ The only keyword in the "ACTIONS" block of the "CUTTABLE" file is "FIND". No "DISPLAY" keywords are used to generate either introductory or concluding screens.
□ The rules in the "CUTTABLE" file are labelled with numbers starting from the number zero. Also, there are two more rules in the "CUTTABLE" file than in the first file.
□ Although the "ASK" statement is similar in both files, the "CUTTABLE" file version is written entirely in the generic form of "What is the value of . . . ?"

Both the "CUTTABLE" and "GRASSCUT" knowledge-base files will yield the same conclusions in a consultation when the same user responses are given. The "CUTTABLE" file, however, could use the manual addition of introductory and concluding screens. With these additions, it more closely resembles the first file when it is used in a consultation. Additions are easily inserted into an induction-generated knowledge-base file by using any word processor or the built-in VP-Expert text editor.

When ready, quit viewing the "CUTTABLE" file by pressing two keys together, the ALT and F6 keys. Then type "Y" to the "Save" file prompt.

```
ACTIONS
        FIND Cut;

RULE 0
IF      Season=non-growing
THEN    Cut=No_one;

RULE 1
IF      Grass=short
THEN    Cut=No_one;

RULE 2
IF      Season=growing AND
        Grass=tall AND
        Health=good AND
        Good-equip=yes AND
        Gas=yes AND
        Weather=good AND
        Mow-time=mid-day
THEN    Cut=you;

RULE 3
IF      Season=growing AND
        Grass=tall AND
        Health=good AND
        Good-equip=yes AND
        Gas=yes AND
        Weather=good AND
        Mow-time=early AND
        Other-avail=yes
THEN    Cut=Someone_else;

RULE 4
IF      Season=growing AND
        Grass=tall AND
        Health=good AND
        Good-equip=yes AND
        Gas=yes AND
        Weather=good AND
        Mow-time=early AND
        Other-avail=no
THEN    Cut=No_one;

RULE 5
IF      Season=growing AND
        Grass=tall AND
        Health=good AND
        Good-equip=yes AND
        Gas=yes AND
        Weather=good AND
        Mow-time=late AND
        Other-avail=yes
THEN    Cut=Someone_else;
```

*(continued)*

**FIGURE 6-7   VP-Expert—induction-generated "CUTTABLE" knowl-edge-base file.**

```
RULE 6
IF       Season=growing AND
         Grass=tall AND
         Health=good AND
         Good-equip=yes AND
         Gas=yes AND
         Weather=good AND
         Mow-time=late AND
         Other-avail=no
THEN     Cut=No_one;

RULE 7
IF       Season=growing AND
         Grass=tall AND
         Health=good AND
         Good-equip=yes AND
         Gas=yes AND
         Weather=bad AND
         Other-avail=yes
THEN     Cut=Someone_else;

RULE 8
IF       Season=growing AND
         Grass=tall AND
         Health=good AND
         Good-equip=yes AND
         Gas=yes AND
         Weather=bad AND
         Other-avail=no
THEN     Cut=No_one;

RULE 9
IF       Season=growing AND
         Grass=tall AND
         Health=good AND
         Good-equip=yes AND
         Gas=no AND
         Other-avail=yes
THEN     Cut=Someone_else;

RULE 10
IF       Season=growing AND
Grass=tall AND
Health=good AND
Good-equip=yes AND
Gas=no AND
Other-avail=no
THEN     Cut=No_one;

RULE 11
IF       Season=growing AND
         Grass=tall AND
         Health=good AND
         Good-equip=no AND
         Other-avail=yes
THEN     Cut=Someone_else;
```

*(continued)*

**FIGURE 6-7** *(continued)*

```
RULE 12
IF       Season=growing AND
         Grass=tall AND
         Health=good AND
         Good-equip=no AND
         Other-avail=no
THEN     Cut=No_one;

RULE 13
IF       Season=growing AND
Grass=tall AND
Health=poor AND
Other-avail=yes
THEN     Cut=Someone_else;

RULE 14
IF       Season=growing AND
         Grass=tall AND
         Health=poor AND
         Other-avail=no
THEN     Cut=No_one;

ASK Season: "What is the value of Season?";
CHOICES Season: non-growing,growing;

ASK Grass: "What is the value of Grass?";
CHOICES Grass: short,tall;

ASK Health: "What is the value of Health?";
CHOICES Health: good,poor;

ASK Good-equip: "What is the value of Good-equip?";
CHOICES Good-equip: yes,no;

ASK Gas: "What is the value of Gas?";
CHOICES Gas: yes,no;

ASK Weather: "What is the value of Weather?";
CHOICES Weather: good,bad;

ASK Mow-time: "What is the value of Mow-time?";
CHOICES Mow-time: mid-day,early,late;

ASK Other-avail: "What is the value of Other-avail?";
CHOICES Other-avail: yes,no;
```

**FIGURE 6-7** *(continued)*

## Consultation

To run a consultation using the first knowledge-base file created in this tutorial, select the option "6FileName" by pressing the function key F6. Next, type the name of the knowledge-base file to use: "B:GRASSCUT⟨Enter⟩". Then, from the main menu, select "4Consult" by pressing the F4 function key to activate the consultation process.

VP-Expert responds with a message "Loading File . . ." as it loads the desired knowledge-base file for the consultation. If VP-Expert detects syntactic errors in the knowledge-base file, the loading process stops. It then displays an error message to indicate what the error is and where the error is located in the knowledge-base file. For example, the following error message:

```
Syntax error in condition
(Press Any Key to go on)
Error in line 63
```

means that there is a syntax error in the "condition" part of an if-then rule in the sixty-third line from the first line of the knowledge-base file.

Pressing any key automatically switches VP-Expert into the "edit" mode where you may go to line 63, as indicated in the error message, to make the appropriate corrections. To save the corrected knowledge-base file, press the Alt key and F6 function key together. At the prompt, "Save as: "b:grasscut.kbs" (Y or N)?", type "Y". Then select "4Consult" by pressing the F4 function key at the main menu to restart the consultation process.

Otherwise, if there are no syntactic errors in the knowledge-base file, VP-Expert responds by indicating on the screen that the file is "loaded" and ready for a consultation session. The screen is split into three windows: a consultation window (in the top half), a rules window (in the lower left), and a results window (in the lower right). Select the option "2Go" to begin the session.

This split screen is helpful because it allows you to observe the "thinking" of the VP-Expert program as it interacts with the knowledge-base file and the user during a consultation. You can see how the intermediate and final conclusions are reached throughout the consultation session. The split screen is most useful when still in the development stage of testing the accuracy of your knowledge-base file.

You would, most likely, want to remove the split screen once you are satisfied with the file you developed. To remove the split screen, retrieve the "GRASSCUT" knowledge-base file by selecting "3Edit". Then insert a new line at the top of the file by pressing the Ctrl and Enter keys simultaneously. Then on the newly inserted line type "RUNTIME;(Enter)".

Running the consultation using the "RUNTIME" version of the knowledge-base file is exactly the same as the original file except for the absence of the split screen. You are greeted with the "GRASSCUT SYSTEM" introductory screen after selecting the "2Go" option. Then press any key, and the "WELCOME" screen appears.

The knowledge base proceeds to find the goal for "cut-grass". It asks a series of questions and displays a menu of acceptable responses. To answer a question, move the cursor to the desired response and press (Enter) followed by the "END" key (usually located on the numeric keypad).

Use the same procedure to answer each of the remaining questions until the "GRASSCUT" system arrives at a conclusion and displays the concluding screen. At this point you can choose to run the consultation again by selecting "2Go". You might want to change your responses to some of the questions to see how they affect the conclusion of the consultation.

In order to run a consultation using the "CUTTABLE" file, created with the induction method, first select "6FileName" from the main menu. Then type "B:CUTTABLE〈Enter〉" and follow the same procedures as described above.

Although the conclusion reached will be the same as with the other file, provided the same set of user responses to questions are given, differences are evident. This version lacks introductory and concluding screens. User questions are also characterized by the generic form of "What is the value of . . . ?" Also, this version asks fewer questions to obtain a value for the goal variable.

## REVIEW QUESTIONS

1. Describe the major features of Level Five (also called INSIGHT2+) and VP-Expert and how these expert system shells differ from the others described in this chapter and in Chapter 5.

2. Name and describe three ways in which the 1st-CLASS expert system shell differs from the other shells described in this chapter and in Chapter 5.

3. What does induction of rules from examples mean? How does it work to create rules in the 1st-CLASS system shell?

4. Describe the strengths and weaknesses of the three expert system shells described in this chapter. Describe several system development situations in which you would use one instead of the others? Explain the reasons for your choices.

5. In comparing the expert system shells described in this chapter and in Chapter 5, describe several systems development situations in which you would use either M.1 or EXSYS instead of either Level Five, 1st-CLASS, or VP-Expert. Explain the reasons for your choices.

# 7

# Putting Knowledge-Based Systems on Computer: Using GURU and Other Development Tools and Techniques

This chapter continues the discussion of computer software tools useful in knowledge-based systems development that began in the preceding chapters. The topics covered are

□ Another example of a microcomputer rule-based expert system shells: GURU
□ An object-oriented microcomputer knowledge-based system development tool: Smalltalk/V
□ Mainframe expert system development shells: KEE, ART, Knowledge Craft, and S.1
□ Knowledge-based systems programming languages: LISP and PROLOG
□ Using certainty factors in expert system shells

## USING GURU

GURU is a more advanced microcomputer expert system shell than either M.1 or EXSYS. It performs the functions that M.1 and EXSYS perform, however, it also allows access to built-in spreadsheet, data base, graphic, and telecommunication programs. It provides many programming options that enable the systems developer to tailor the shell's operation to specific knowledge-based systems requirements. It also has more modular development capabilities. These kinds of advanced features are needed when developing more advanced knowledge-based systems, such as the enhanced versions of STRATEGIC PLANNER I.

Because of its advanced features, GURU is more difficult to learn and use than other microcomputer shells. It also requires a hard disk computer. Instructions for installing GURU on your hard disk are in the GURU user manuals.

The following discussion covers how the grass-cutting knowledge-base system would be prepared and then entered into GURU.

## Structuring the Knowledge Base File for GURU

Preparing the knowledge base for GURU begins with the plain English version of the grass-cutting knowledge base given in Fig. 5-2. A version converted into a format usable with GURU is given in Fig. 7-1. The following are instructions for preparing the knowledge base file shown in Fig. 7-1.

**Goal.** In GURU, as in M.1 and EXSYS, a goal, which is the program's destination, is designated first. A user consultation will end when a value is found for the goal. The goal is typed

```
GOAL:     cut
```

**Initial.** The next section (called "INITIAL"), which is the "initialization" section of the knowledge-base file, gives both the known values and the unknown variable values to be sought during a consultation. The values of unknown variables come from the user or from the execution of rules. In the grass-cutting situation only unknown values are used. This section would include instructions to GURU for printing any introductory displays during a consultation.

Settings for environmental variables are also included in this section. GURU has over two hundred options (environmental variables) that enable the systems developer to tailor the shell's performance to the specific expert system needs. For example, the "e.lstr = 50" command in Fig. 7-1 limits the maximum length of any *display line* to fifty characters in the grass-cutting system.

**Do.** The heading "DO" contains instructions about what GURU is to do after a goal is found during a consultation. These instructions are called completion clauses. In the grass-cutting example GURU is instructed to print out the value of the goal by typing:

```
DO: output ^*goal
```

If you want to have concluding comments for a consultation, instructions for printing them would be given here.

**Rules.** The rules are printed in Fig. 7-1 in a condensed form. This form is used so that the rules can be inserted into GURU from the word processor, as is done with M.1. GURU also has a built-in text (or rule) editor so that the rules can also be inserted into GURU one by one by a systems developer or edited on the screen within GURU after having been inserted, just as in EXSYS.

```
GOAL:      cut

INITIAL:

cut = unknown
need = unknown
able = unknown
other = unknown
season = unknown
grass = unknown
health = unknown
equip = unknown
environ = unknown
othavail = unknown
goodequip = unknown
gas = unknown
weather = unknown
mowtime = unknown
e.lstr = 50

DO:      output ^#goal

RULE:    R1
 IF:      need="n"
 THEN:    cut="no"

RULE:    R2
 IF:      need="y" and able="y"
 THEN:    cut="me"

RULE     R3
 IF:      need="y" & able="n" & other="y"
 THEN:    cut="other"

RULE:    R4
 IF:      able="n" & other="n"
 THEN:    cut="no"

RULE:    R5
 IF:      grass="tall" and season="growing"
 THEN:    need="y"

RULE:    R6
 IF:      grass="short" or season="nongrowing"
 Then:    need="n"

RULE:    R7
 IF:      health="good" & equip="ok" & environ="ok"
 Then:    able="y"

RULE:    R8
 IF:      health="poor" or equip="notok" or environ="notok"
 Then:    able="n"

RULE:    R9
 IF:      othavail="y" and environ="ok"
 Then:    other="y"
```

*(continued)*

**FIGURE 7-1  Knowledge base—GURU version of grass-cutting decision.**

```
RULE:    R10
 IF:     othavail="n" or environ="notok"
 Then:   other="n"

RULE:    R11
 IF:     goodeqp="y" and gas="y"
 Then:   equip="ok"

RULE:    R12
 IF:     goodeqp="n" or gas="n"
 Then:   equip="notok"

RULE:    R13
 IF:     weather="good" and mowtime="middle"
 Then:   environ="ok"

RULE:    R14
 IF:     weather="bad" or mowtime <> "middle"
 Then:   environ="notok"


VAR:     GRASS
 FIND:   input grass with "Grass: tall or short?"

VAR:     SEASON
 FIND:   input season with "Season: growing or nongrowing?"

VAR:     HEALTH
 FIND:   input health with "Health: good or poor?"

VAR:     OTHAVAIL
 FIND:   input othavail with "Others Available: y or n?"

VAR:     GOODEQP
 FIND:   input goodeqp with "Good Equipment: y or n?"

VAR:     GAS
 FIND:   input gas with "Gas: y or n?"

VAR:     WEATHER
 FIND:   input weather with "Weather: good or bad?

VAR:     MOWTIME
 FIND:   input mowtime with "Mowtime: early, middle, or late?"

END
```

**FIGURE 7-1** *(continued)*

**Questions.**    The final section of the knowledge-base file in Fig. 7-1 (headed "VAR" for variables and "FIND") contains the questions asked a user by GURU during a consultation.   The variable to be sought is entered after the "VAR" heading, and the question to be asked the user follows the "FIND" heading.   These entries cover all the unknown items in the "INITIAL" section whose values will be sought from a user during a consultation.

The end of the text block, or rule set, is indicated by the word "END".   In this small example, it ends the entire program.

## Entering the Knowledge-Base File into GURU

After a knowledge-base file has been created, there are two ways to install it. You can transfer it from your word processor or GURU's built-in word processor into GURU; or you can type the knowledge-base entries one by one using GURU's built-in rule editor. The following instructions assume that the knowledge base file has been created on a word processor, as in Fig. 7-1, and that the file is saved under the name "GRASSCUT.RSS". You should consult GURU's user manuals for instructions on entering rules one by one. The following discussion assumes the reader is familiar with using a hard disk microcomputer and has installed GURU on one.

To prepare for loading the file into GURU, give your knowledge base a file name (no more than eight characters), if you have not done so already. Then add ".RSS" to that name. The "RSS" stands for "rule set source." Next, to start loading the knowledge base into GURU first type

```
c>md\guru\grasscut<cr>
```

This entry creates a subdirectory (with the command "md") for your knowledge base on the hard disk within the GURU directory. To get into the new subdirectory, type

```
c>cd\guru\grasscut<cr>
```

When in this subdirectory, to transfer the word processing file from, for example, a floppy disk into GURU type

```
c>copy a:grasscut.rss c: <cr>
```

The knowledge base file should now be loaded into the new subdirectory that is within the GURU directory. You may verify this by typing "dir" (for directory command) when in the GURU directory.

```
c>dir <cr>
```

Once it is verified that a knowledge-base file set is in an appropriate GURU subdirectory, then activate the GURU program by typing

```
c>cd\guru\grasscut<cr>
c>guru grasscut.rss<cr>
```

This will bring both GURU and your knowledge base into working memory. GURU now asks a number of questions.

1. When asked for "new session name", type in your last name.
2. When the "Expert Systems" command menu appears, with an expanded cursor highlighting "Expert Systems", press the return key ⟨cr⟩ or the first letter of the command "e" to go on.

3. When the next menu appears, type "b" for "Build an Expert System", or press ⟨cr⟩ if the highlighted cursor is on the command.

4. When the next menu appears, type "e" for "Existing Rule Set", which tells GURU a knowledge-base file already exists.

5. The name of your knowledge base automatically appears to the right with the cursor over it. Pressing the return key ⟨cr⟩ activates the file.

6. On the next menu type "e" for "Exit", since a rule set already exists.

7. The next menu that appears begins the actual knowledge-base file entry phase. During this phase, GURU "compiles" a knowledge-base file by adding coding needed to make it usable by GURU during a consultation. The compiled or converted file is stored in GURU under the name "GRASSCUT.RSC". The ".RSC" stands for "rule set compiled," and is the file version GURU will use during all consultations. Start this process by typing "c" for "Compile".

8. When the next screen appears, "Executable File Name: Grasscut.rsc", press the return key ⟨cr⟩.

9. Warning messages concerning the file may appear during the compiling process. The developer would make a note of any errors or print them out. Errors are usually typing, punctuation, or spacing errors. If these errors are not severe, the compile process produces only warnings. If these errors are major, like the use of "season" in the initialization section and "seasons" in the rule section, the compilation phase fails. GURU cannot resolve the problem. Fixing these major problems requires returning to the word processor to make corrections, and then redoing the compile process. If the changes are few, the built-in editor can be used to make corrections. When finished this phase, press the space bar to go on, as instructed on the screen.

10. On the next screen press "s" for "save". This saves the knowledge-base file for future use.

11. On the next screen press "q" for "quit". Then press the "escape" key several times until you are back to the original "Expert Systems" command menu.

## Running a Consultation

To run consultation, now that the compiled file is available, a user goes to the second menu, and instead of activating the "Build an Expert System" menu, activates the "Consult Expert System" one. On the next menu, move the cursor to the title of your knowledge base, which will be listed there, press the return key ⟨cr⟩, and then follow the instructions that appear on the screen. The consultation immediately begins by asking a user the questions necessary to resolve any unknown values. Since the GRASSCUT system is only a sample system, the session very quickly reaches a conclusion, advising the user to cut, not cut, or have someone else cut the grass.

After leaving GURU, the GRASSCUT subdirectory can be checked to see that it contains the following four files:

```
Grasscut.rss
Grasscut.rsc
Grasscut.wrn:
```
*(This is a warning file, and will appear only if there were compilation errors.)*

```
Grasscut.bak:
```
*(This backup file is automatically created.)*

This is only a brief introduction to creating a very simple knowledge-base file for use on GURU. Such an introduction cannot begin to fully explore the intricacies of using the external program or environmental control features that are available in GURU. If you wish to do advanced work with GURU, consult a copy of: Clyde W. Holsapple and Andrew B. Whinston, *Manager's Guide to Expert Systems Using GURU* (alternate title: *Business Expert Systems*) (Homewood, Ill.: Irwin, 1986). In addition, the *Reference Manuals* and *User Guides* that accompany the GURU software should be consulted.

## AN OBJECT-ORIENTED MICROCOMPUTER KNOWLEDGE-BASED SYSTEM DEVELOPMENT TOOL: SMALLTALK/V

The discussion so far in this book has concentrated on rule-based systems for several reasons. They are easier to understand, have wide applicability in management decision making situations, are easier to construct, and are widely used. In addition, most microcomputer expert system shells in common use today are largely rule-based, and most of the strategic planning systems described in this book are rule-based systems.

Object-oriented systems, which are also referred to as frame-based systems, are also used in expert system development. Object-oriented systems and structures appear to have potential usefulness in developing larger, more advanced management decision making systems. For this reason prototype strategic planning and management decision making systems using objects and frames are under development.

Smalltalk, one of the better known object-oriented development tools, was developed at Xerox's Palo Alto Research Center. Smalltalk is very versatile. It allows a programmer to switch among multiple windows. For example, the editor can be running in one window while the system code is on view in another, with a third showing a disk browser editing file. Text can be selected in one window and pasted into another. If an execution error occurs, a debugger window pops up, allowing the programmer to dynamically investigate and fix the error.

The Smalltalk language is based on a hierarchical collection of objects. Each subclass object inherits properties from its superclass ancestors. Each subclass is also capable of having new properties of its own. The concept is very much like the taxonomic classification of biology, where humans inherit certain properties by virtue of being mammals yet have unique properties by virtue of being human.

Each object has its own private variables and many also share variables with other members of its class. The objects respond to messages (requests) from other objects by executing methods or procedures. Smalltalk is capable of handling most conceivable operations, from arithmetic to text handling to graphics. In fact, the entire system from editor to compiler consists of objects that may be used or modified by the systems developer or programmer.

There is now available a microcomputer version of Smalltalk from Digitalk, which appears to have the feel of Xerox's original version of Smalltalk. It is called Smalltalk/V. Like most object-oriented development tools, Smalltalk/V makes use of both rules and objects (or frames).

Frames or objects are especially useful for organizing rules within large systems. As systems grow in size, it becomes increasingly difficult for systems designers to understand the interactions among rules, to debug them, and to control their behavior. Knowledge-based system rules, like conventional programs, need to be organized into small, easily managed modules according to their intended usage. This is especially true where several designers, some of them newly hired, work on a system over a long period of time.

For example, a systems developer might want to specify a collection of rules for diagnosing the behavior of a certain class of key industry factors, such as consumers. The intended purposes of the rules is well defined, analyzing potential consumer behavior under specified demographic and market conditions. Frame-based schemes provide a natural means of grouping the rules together into a class. This frame or object structure provides a basis for object-oriented programming. Frames or objects can be manipulated singly or as a group whenever the system is performing a reasoning task involving one of the frames, such as young-urban-professional consumers.

Smalltalk/V is an excellent tool for prototyping and small system development. It is also a tool with which to explore object-oriented programming, enjoy a powerful programming environment, and readily create software with well-designed user interfaces.

## MAINFRAME KNOWLEDGE-BASED SYSTEM DEVELOPMENT TOOLS

The four best-known mainframe expert system development shells, also called mainframe development environments or large-scale development tools, are discussed here:

- Knowledge Engineering Environment (KEE) from IntelliCorp
- Automated Reasoning Tool (ART) from Inference Corporation
- Knowledge Craft from Carnegie Group
- S.1 from Teknowledge

### KEE

KEE supports both rules and frames for knowledge representation, backward and forward chaining, object-oriented programming, an active-values mechanism, and viewpoints, which are called "worlds."

KEE's active-value mechanism provides a way to attach procedures to frame slots so that when these slots are accessed or changed, specified procedures are executed. For example, if the temperature represented in a frame slot is increased a procedure can be triggered that activates a thermostat or causes the temperature in an image of a thermometer to change accordingly.

Another KEE feature, "worlds," allows users to hypothesize various situations and reason about them in parallel. This enables the generation and evaluation of alternatives in such situations as determining alternate truck routes under varying dispatch conditions.

Babock & Wilcox has used KEE to build a factory welding scheduler. Lawrence Livermore Laboratories has used it to build an intelligent interface to instrumentation. The Electrical Power Research Institute has used KEE to build a crisis-management system for a nuclear power plant. Of the tools that support multiple knowledge representation and inferencing models (for example, rule-based and object-oriented), KEE is simplest to use.

## ART

In the past ART was considered a higher level—but more difficult to use—tool than KEE. ART's capabilities have been demonstrated through its use for developing the Hughes Radar Systems Group's circuit-board-diagnosis system, Composition System's electronic-typesetting and editorial-layout knowledge-based software, and Eastman Kodak's knowledge-based document-management and updating system for the F-14 aircraft documentation.

ART supports rules, frames, integrated backward and forward chaining, viewpoints for reasoning about hypothetical worlds, and object-oriented programming capabilities.

In object-oriented programming, procedures are called methods, and ART's version of methods is called "multimethods." Multimethods allow users to send a message—a procedure to be executed—to a generalized group of closely linked objects instead of to only a single object. This in turn allows for fewer procedures to be written because each one handles more objects.

For example, a factory system might be divided into groups of machines. During production certain groups of machines, such as a feeder, a milling machine, and a transporter must be periodically synchronized. With multimethods, a single generic synchronization procedure can be written for these machines. The message "synchronize" is then sent to the generalized class that contains the machines to be synchronized.

## Knowledge Craft

Knowledge Craft is an outgrowth of Schema Representation Language (SRL), a tool developed at Carnegie-Mellon University (CMU). In its precommercial days, Knowledge Craft was used to build ISIS—a CMU-Westinghouse Electric Company factory-scheduling system—and various other planning, factory-management, and monitoring systems for Westinghouse, Digital Equipment Corporation, the United States Air Force, and the Aluminum Company of America.

Knowledge Craft features rules and frames for representing knowledge. It supports three languages—OPS5, PROLOG, and CRL (a frame-based language). Another feature, an agenda mechanism, tracks multiple queues of events and manages scheduling of the events for execution. This feature is useful for such applications as simulation and scheduling. The agenda mechanism can also track multiple contexts (subdivisions of a problem) sprouted by rules, thus creating, in effect, a viewpoint mechanism.

A unique attraction of Knowledge Craft is a natural-language interface. It allows Knowledge Craft-based systems to obtain natural-language input. The ultimate goal is to allow knowledge engineers to use natural language to acquire domain knowledge and develop knowledge systems.

## S.1

Of these four tools, S.1 is the simplest to learn and use. It is primarily a rule-based, backward-chaining tool that also features a block-structure language. It has sometimes been accused of being limited in techniques and useful only for diagnostic applications, but S.1 users have revealed in interviews that they were never at a loss. Delco Products used S.1 to build its design systems for DC motor components. M.1 is, to a very limited degree, a microcomputer version of S.1.

## KNOWLEDGE-BASED SYSTEM PROGRAMMING LANGUAGES

The two most commonly used programming languages for knowledge-based systems development are LISP and PROLOG. One of the main differences among languages, development tools, and shells is that development tools and shells have many more, and different, varieties of preprogrammed (built-in) routines. For this reason languages are more flexible and so can handle more demanding problems. At the same time they require much more programming time and skill to use than do expert shells.

### PROLOG

PROLOG (which stands for PROgramming language for LOGic) was initially developed in 1972 by A. Colmerauer and P. Roussel at the University of Marseilles. PROLOG is a programming language that implements a simplified version of predicate calculus and is thus a true logical language.

PROLOG, like LISP, is designed for symbolic (word) manipulation, rather than simply numerical computation. PROLOG is very efficient at list processing. PROLOG is an interpreted language and so responds to any query by attempting to return an answer immediately, as is seen in the example below.

To program in PROLOG requires

1. Specifying some facts about objects and their relationships
2. Specifying rules about objects and their relationships

For example, the facts might be "Mary likes chocolates" and "Piquant is a well known brand of chocolates." These facts are entered in PROLOG as follows:

```
likes(mary, chocolates)
is(piquant, chocolates)
```

The format in which such statements are written is called a language's "syntax." Each sentence or line in this example, therefore, follows a formal structure dictated by the PROLOG language.

To ask the question "Does Mary like Piquant chocolates?" in PROLOG the following form could be used:

```
?-likes(mary, piquant)
```

PROLOG would respond to this question or query by printing

```
yes
```

In this small example, the word "likes" is the predicate that indicates that such a *relationship* exists between one *object*, Mary, and a second *object*, Piquant chocolates. The question, in effect, asks PROLOG to say whether it can establish the truth of the assertion that "Mary likes Piquant chocolates." In this case PROLOG says that it can, based on the facts it has been given.

A word starting with an upper case letter is used to create a variable in PROLOG. For example, if asked the question

```
?-likes(mary,X).
```

PROLOG would answer

```
X - chocolates.
```

The symbol for if, ":-", is used to establish an if-then rule in PROLOG. The rule in this case might read

```
buys(mary, piquant):-    is(piquant, chocolates).
```

Using the principles outlined so far, one can construct a simple prototype of a market product-customer matching system in PROLOG, such as is given in Fig. 7-2. The system took someone not very familiar with computers less than an hour to construct, and so is admittedly trivial. But it illustrates how a PROLOG knowledge base looks and works. For example, a user might ask the system outlined in Fig. 7-2 the question, "Is there a good chance the young-urban-professional (young adult) market would accept and buy Piquant chocolates?" as follows:

```
?-chance_buy(young_urban_professionals, piquant).
```

PROLOG would answer yes, based on the facts and rule-1 in the knowledge base in Fig. 7-2. A few minutes study of the relationships between the rule statements (and their variables) and the fact statements should give an understanding of the essence of how PROLOG works in logically manipulating lists of symbols.

Computation in PROLOG is controlled logical deduction. One states what one

Rule-1:

```
chance_buy(B,G) :-
    market(B),
    product(G),
    product_kind(A),                    Note: Uppercase letters
    is(G,C),                                  are the variables.
    is_well_educated(B),
    is_young_adult(B),
    is_affluent(B),
    likes(B,C),
    is_high_priced(G),
    is_high_quality(G),
    has_great_brand_image(G),
```

Facts:

```
product(piquant_chocolates).
is(piquant_chocolates, chocolate_candy).
product_kind(chocolate_candy).
is_high_priced(piquant_chocolates).
is_high_quality(piquant-chocolates).
has_great_brand_image(piquant_chocolates).
market(young_urban_professionals).
is_well_educated(young_urban_professionals).
is_young_adult(young_urban_professionals).
is_affluent(young_urban_professionals).
likes(young_urban_professionals,chocolate_candy).
```

**FIGURE 7-2  PROLOG knowledge base—product-market compatibility.**

knows, the facts, and the rules.  PROLOG is then prepared, when asked, to say whether or not any specific conclusion can be deduced from those facts and rules. In knowledge engineering terms, PROLOG's control structure is logical inference.

## LISP

LISP (which stands for LISt Processing language) was created by John McCarthy in 1958.  Of the major languages still in use, only FORTRAN is older than LISP.  Until recently it was the major AI language in this country.  There are many reasons for LISP's widespread popularity:

- □ Easy and flexible symbol manipulation
- □ Automatic memory management
- □ Sophisticated editing and debugging aids
- □ Uniform treatment of program code and data, which means a LISP can modify its own code as easily as its data.

This last feature lends itself to writing programs that learn new rules or modify existing ones in the knowledge base.

In LISP relations between objects are often represented as lists containing a relation followed by objects that the relation links.  For example, "the target market for Piquant chocolates is affluent young people" might be written in LISP-like notation as:

```
(MARKET(PIQUANT CHOCOLATES)(AFFLUENT YOUNG PEOPLE))
```

The term "MARKET" is a link that indicates a relation between the first argument "(PIQUANT CHOCOLATES)" and the second argument "(AFFLUENT YOUNG PEOPLE)". Using this same scheme one might write "If the target market for Piquant chocolates is high income people, then explore selling to young urban professionals (YUPS)" as follows:

```
(IF(MARKET CHOCOLATES AFFLUENT)
   THEN(EXPLORE SELLING-YUPS))
```

You would have to write an inference engine to match rule expressions like "(MARKET CHOCOLATES AFFLUENT)" against data expressions such as those found in the PROLOG example above about Piquant chocolates and young urban professionals. The expressions would be much more complex than those shown above, and considerably more lists would have to be constructed, as seen in Fig. 7-2.

Using LISP requires the translating of rules and facts into lists, such as those shown above between the parentheses. LISP then makes use of a variety of list processing functions. These functions enable similar kinds of information manipulation as was described in the discussions of knowledge-based systems, expert system shells, and other programming languages such as PROLOG.

The LISP notations shown above are not necessarily the correct or best way of representing the information in these situations. The illustrations are designed merely to give the reader a quick feeling for the list processing language LISP and how its syntax differs from PROLOG's.

## CERTAINTY FACTORS

A certainty factor is an informal measure or expression of certainty that a piece of evidence is true. Certainty factors are also called confidence factors and are abbreviated as cf. They deal with uncertain or unknown information. They are not, however, probabilities.

Human experts are not always 100 percent certain about assumptions or conclusions. For this reason most expert system shells have ways to handle or represent degrees of certainty or uncertainty.

A certainty factor is represented by a number within some predetermined range: for example, 0 to 100 in GURU, and $-100$ to $+100$ in M.1. In GURU a certainty factor of 100 is the highest possible certainty, while a 0 certainty factor represents the lowest possible certainty. In M.1 $+100$ represents the highest certainty, 0 represents neutrality, and $-100$ means that the value is definitely ruled out. If no cf is given, 100 percent certainty is assumed in both systems.

Certainty factors can be assigned to the value of a variable in premises, in answers to questions, or in conclusions. There are many ways to calculate and assign certainty factors. The following discusses some common ways that certainty factors are handled in the most popular knowledge-based system shells.

## User Input Information

A user may not be certain about a piece of information requested by an knowledge-based system during a consultation. For example, a system may ask a user:

```
What do you estimate the strength of the economy will be
over the next two years?
```

A user may answer

```
                          strong cf70
```

This answer indicates that the user is only 70 percent confident about the answer turning out to be true.

## A Premise cf Value Can Give a cf Value to the Then Clause

A cf value in premises can create a cf value in a then clause in a variety of ways:

1. Where a premise is given a cf value, for example, in a rule that reads

   ```
   If over the next two years the economy is expected
       to be strong,
   Then the likelihood of inflation is strong.
   ```

   If a user answers strong cf70 when questioned about the "economy" during a consultation, the conclusion about "inflation" would carry a value of strong cf70.

2. Where there is more than one premise and the premises are connected by an *and*, there are two commonly used ways to handle certainty factors. First, the then clause value could be given the *lowest cf value*. For example, a knowledge-based system might contain the following rule:

   ```
   If over the next two years the economy is expected to
       be strong and
       the availability of investment capital is expected
       to be low,
   Then the likelihood of inflation = strong.
   ```

   If during a consultation a user is asked questions about the first two premises and a user answers strong cf80 about the "economy" and low cf60 about the "availability of investment capital", the conclusion about "inflation" would carry a cf value of strong cf60.

Second, if a system developer feels the actual situation warrants it, the developer might choose to use *joint certainty* in this situation by multiplying 80 times 60 (divided by 100, since the figures represent a percentage) to get a "likelihood of inflation" of strong cf48.

3. Where there is more than one premise and the premises are connected by an *or*, there are again two common ways to handle certainty factors. First, the then clause value could be given the *highest cf value*. For example,

```
If over the next two years the growth outlook
      for the economy is poor or
    the unemployment outlook is poor,
Then the economic outlook is poor.
```

If during a consultation a user is asked questions about the first two premises and a user answers poor cf70 about the "growth outlook" and poor cf60 about the "employment outlook", the conclusion about "economic outlook" would carry a cf value of poor cf70.

Second, a systems developer may choose to *combine* the values in these premises if the developer feels that it better represents the situation and the expert system shell allows it to be done. For example, in the rule above for "economic outlook" the certainties could be combined using the formula: The sum of the certainty factors minus the product of the certainty factors (over 100) equals the combined certainty, or in this case:

$$60 + 70 - \frac{60 \times 70}{100} = 130 - 42 = \text{cf88}$$

## A Knowledge-Based System May Be Developed With a cf Factor Built into the Then Clauses

For example, a rule may be written:

```
If over the next two years the economy is expected
      to be strong
Then the likelihood of inflation is strong cf40.
```

If during a consultation a user is asked a question about the first premise and a user answers strong cf0 about the "economy", the conclusion about the "likelihood of inflation" would carry a cf value of strong cf28 (40 times 70 divided by 100 = 28).

## Some Systems Allow for Setting a Minimum Acceptable cf Value

A system may allow the developer to set a minimum acceptable cf value, for example 30, so that any resulting cf value in a then clause below 30 would yield a failed or negative answer, as in the rule in the example above.

## Incremental Certainty through Rule Firing

In the same way that premises can be combined to increase the certainty of a conclusion, then clauses may also be combined to yield a gradually increasing certainty for a goal conclusion. For example, in some systems each time a then clause fires with a cf factor, the ultimate goal becomes more certain. For example, if two different rules give the "likelihood of inflation" at cf28 and cf40 for different reasons, then the combined "likelihood of inflation" cf would be:

$$28 + 40 - \frac{28 \times 40}{100} = 68 - 11.2 = cf56.8$$

Here, as elsewhere, a developer would use the type of certainty factor calculation that best suited the real-world situation that was being replicated in the knowledge-based system.

## Fuzzy Variables

At times in decision situations variables can have more than one value. For example, two experts may have different ideas on the economic outlook—one may see growth ahead, another recession. Even the same expert can have differing ideas. For example, an expert may estimate that the economy over the next two years (outlook) will be strong with confidence factor of 70 and weak with a confidence factor of 40.

These are called "fuzzy variables" in an expert knowledge-based system. Most expert system shells are capable of simultaneously keeping track of different values for the same variable.

In M.1, for example, a system developer can give instruction to treat a variable as a fuzzy variable by writing "multivalued(. . .).", as in "multivalued(eoutlook)." in the knowledge base. With this instruction, when a user consults the system, the inference engine will not stop seeking other values for "eoutlook" after it finds the first value for it. The inference engine will simultaneously keep track of different values (for example, strong cf70 and weak cf40 for eoutlook) and independently carry out the subsequent inference for a fuzzy variables different values.

In GURU, fuzzy variable instructions are given, for example, as "eoutlook = { }" in the initial data. In the then clause of rules there could be "eoutlook + = strong cf70" and "eoutlook + = weak cf50" to assign values for it.

There are a variety of other ways that cf factors can be used in knowledge-based systems and expert system shells. The above discussion is designed to give only a brief introduction to this knowledge-based systems tool.

## REVIEW QUESTIONS

1. Describe the main features of GURU and how this expert system shell differs from the others described in preceding chapters.

2. Describe the nature and function of the "initial" section of a GURU knowledge base.

3. Describe how "VAR" and "FIND" are used in GURU.

4. Describe several knowledge-based systems development situations in which you could use GURU instead of one of the others. Describe situations in which you would not use GURU.

5. Describe the basic structure of the Smalltalk language.

6. Describe the key differences between rule-based expert system shells and object-oriented development tools.

7. Describe ART's multimethods.

8. What are some of the reasons for LISP's popularity?

9. Under what circumstances are programming languages, such as LISP and PROLOG, better than shells for knowledge-based systems development?

10. What are certainty factors?

# 8

# A Personal Investment Planning System

This chapter describes the development of a knowledge-based system designed to recommend a specific personal investment strategy. The discussion covers:

- The situation under study—understanding the experts' domain
- Studying the situation to be prototyped
- Documenting the prototype system

The strategy recommended by the prototype system will include a mix of financial investments designed to meet the goals and requirements of a particular investor.

## STUDYING THE OVERALL SITUATION: UNDERSTANDING THE EXPERT'S DOMAIN

The discussion in this section covers

- Selecting a decision area to work on
- Studying how the situation works and how decision are made
- Narrowing the focus under study

### Selecting a Decision Area to Work On

The general area under study is financial planning. Many areas of financial planning lend themselves to knowledge-based systems development, including personal investment planning, capital investment planning, cash management, merger and acquisition analysis, company by company investment analysis, and commercial and personal loan application screening.

Knowledge-based systems development activity is widespread in the financial planning area. Almost every financial services company and large industrial company has an active knowledge-based systems development program in finance.

There are also a number of commercial systems available. For example, *Financial Advisor*, now called *Management Advisor*, from Palladin Software assists in capital investment planning. The financial needs of self-employed professional and business owners can be assessed by another knowledge-based system with strategic planning components, *Businessplan*, from Sterling Wentworth Corporation. *Planpower* from the Applied Expert Systems Group assists in personal investment planning.

Personal investment planning was selected for study in the financial planning area for several reasons:

- There are recognized experts in the field.
- Expert decision skills are needed to do the job.
- The task is well understood.
- It is a manageable task from a knowledge-based systems viewpoint.
- The decisions can have a high payoff and practical value.
- Strategic planning plays a major role in decision making in this area.
- There are many existing systems in the area.

There are a wide range of decisions made within the personal investment planning area. It was recognized that, as the study progressed, eventually its focus would have to be narrowed. First, however, it was necessary to define the overall personal investment planning area.

## Studying How the Situation Works and How Decisions Are Made

As is seen in the structured situation diagram shown in Fig. 8-1, personal investment planning involves three critical areas of study: (1) investment instrument analysis, (2) investor analysis, and (3) analysis of the environment and its risks.

A wide range of investments are available to persons facing individual investment decisions. Each investment opportunity has major benefits and drawbacks dictated by their distinguishing characteristics. The list of potential *investment instruments* includes:

Money market funds          Certificate of deposit
T bills                     T notes
T bonds                     Corporate notes
Corporate bonds             Commercial paper
Banker's acceptance         Repurchase agreements
Municipal bonds             Municipal RANs, TANs, BANs

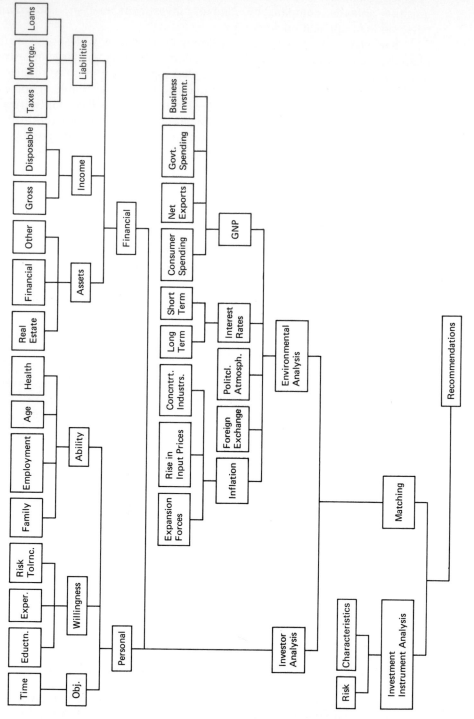

**FIGURE 8-1** An overview of the personal investment planning area.

| Preferred stock | Common stocks |
|---|---|
| Blue chip stocks | Growth stocks |
| Emerging growth stocks | Income stocks |
| Cyclical stocks | Defensive stocks |
| Speculative stocks | Options |
| Collectibles | Real estate |
| Precious metals | |

Figure 8-2 gives definitions of some of these investment instruments and their distinguishing characteristics.

As investments, these potential instruments have many advantages and disadvantages depending on the individual buying them. The individual factors affecting a personal investment decision, as outlined in Fig. 8-3, include: personal factors, such as ability, willingness, and objectives of investment, and individual financial factors, such as assets, liabilities, and income.

| Type | Description |
|---|---|
| Money Market Funds | Interest bearing checkbook deposits with no interest rate ceiling. The typical fund invests in United States T bills, bank certificates of deposit and commercial paper. All are the highest quality financial instruments with low or nonexistent risk of borrower default and limited fluctuations in price. |
| Certificate of Deposit | Time deposits that carry a fixed maturity and offer the highest interest rates a bank or nonbank institution can offer. Time deposits may be divided into non-negotiable certificates (CDs), which are usually small, consumer type accounts, and negotiable CDs that may be traded in the open market and are purchased mainly by corporations. |
| T Bills | Direct obligations of the United States government. Original maturity of one year or less. Minimum investment, $10,000. |
| T Notes and T Bonds | Direct obligations of the United States government. Original maturity greater than one year, but less than thirty. Minimum investment, $1,000. |
| Corporate Notes and Bonds | By convention, a note is a corporate debt contract whose original security is five years or less; a bond carries an original maturity of more than five years. Both securities promise the investor an amount equal to the security's par value (face value) plus interest payments at specified intervals until maturity is reached. Since both have similar characteristics other than maturity we will use bond to refer to both notes and bonds. |
| | Corporate bonds are generally issued in units of $1,000.00 and earn income that is, in most cases, fully taxable. Each bond is accompanied by an indenture, which is a contract listing the rights, privileges and obligations of the borrower and investor. Indentures usually contain at least some restrictive covenants designed to protect bondholders |

*(continued)*

**FIGURE 8-2  Available investment instruments and their distinguishing characteristics.**

| Type | Description |
|------|-------------|
| | against actions by a borrowing firm or its shareholders that might tend to weaken the value of the bonds.<br><br>One way to judge the quality of a bond is to examine the opinion of experts on the subject. Bond rating agencies, such as Moody's and Standard & Poor's, provide the investment community with an up-to-date record of their opinions on the quality of most large, publicly held corporate and government bond issues. Bond ratings rank issues mainly on the basis of the agency's judgment regarding the capacity and willingness of the issuers to meet their obligations.<br><br>Standard & Poor's has ten categories of bonds (AAA, AA, A, BBB, BB, B, CCC, CC, C, D). The first four ratings are considered investment grade "at least adequate capacity to pay principal and interest" or better. The others are considered as connoting a significant speculative element (also known as Junk Bonds) with respect to the issuers' capacity to pay interest and repay principal. |
| Commercial Paper | Short-term, unsecured promissory notes issued by well-known companies that are financially strong and carry high credit ratings. |
| Bankers' Acceptance | A time draft drawn on a bank by an exporter or an importer to pay for merchandise or to buy foreign currencies. When a bank honors the draft by stamping "accepted" on its face, the issuing bank has unconditionally guaranteed to pay the face value of the acceptance at maturity. Acceptances carry maturities ranging from 30 to 180 days. |
| Repurchase Agreements | An agreement whereby a dealer sells securities to a lender but makes a commitment to buy back the securities at a later date at a fixed price plus interest. |
| Municipal Bonds (Munis) | The most common type of municipal borrowing is through long-term bonds. There are two major types issued today—general obligation and revenue bonds. General obligation (GO) bonds are the safest and most secure form of municipal borrowing from the standpoint that they are backed by the "full faith and credit" of the issuing government and may be paid from any revenue source. The quality or level of risk of GO bonds depends, therefore, on the economic base of the municipality (state or local) and on the total amount of debt issued. Revenue bonds are payable only from a specified source of revenue such as toll road, toll bridge, or fees for usage of a plant or service like sewage. Revenue bonds depend for their value on the revenue generating capacity of the particular project they support. Most municipal bonds are rated in a similar fashion to the corporate bonds discussed earlier. |
| Municipal RANs, TANs, BANs | Revenue anticipation notes, tax anticipation notes, and bond anticipation notes are all short-term securities issued by state and local governments to smooth out cash flow. All municipal bonds and notes issued prior to 1987 are federally tax free and most are tax free on the state and local levels where issued. Bonds and notes issued in 1987 and after may or may not be tax free. For this project when we discuss municipal bonds and notes, we will only refer to tax free. |
| Preferred Stock | Is a hybrid form of investing, combining features of debt and common stock. It is an equity (ownership) investment, but it has no voting |

*(continued)*

**FIGURE 8-2** *(continued)*

| Type | Description |
|------|-------------|
| | privilege. Its claim on assets comes after creditors, but before that of common stockholders. It usually carries a stipulated dividend that is not an obligation of the company (though it does have a priority over the dividends paid to common stockholders). It has some features that protect its dividend rights-cumulative feature, unpaid dividends are carried forward and must be paid before common dividends. In addition it may have the right to convert into a fixed number of common shares, offering a possible chance for long-term growth. |
| Common Stock | Represents residual ownership; collectively the stockholders own the company. The common stock represents a residual claim against the assets of the issuing firm, entitling the owner to share in the net earnings of the firm when it is profitable and to share in the net market value (after all debts and preferred stockholders are paid) of the company's assets if liquidated. By owning common stock the investor is subject to the full risks of ownership—a business that may fail or whose earnings may fall to unacceptable levels. However, the risks of equity ownership are limited because the stockholder is liable only for the amount of his or her investment. There is a diversity in common stock that extends not only to industry and company, but to type of stock as well. |
| Blue Chip Stocks | Are high grade, investment quality issues of major companies that have long and unbroken records of earnings and dividend payments—for example, General Motors, Exxon, Dupont, and IBM. |
| Growth Stocks | A growth stock is one of a company whose sales, earnings, and share of market are expanding faster than the general economy and faster than the average for the industry. The company is usually aggressive, research minded, plowing back earnings to facilitate expansion. For this reason, growth companies, intent on financing their own expansion from retained earnings, pay relatively small dividends, and their yield is generally low. |
| Emerging Growth Stocks | A label often given to smaller companies that have survived the formative years and have entered a period of strong earnings gains—a result of expanding unit sales volume and widening profit margins. The stock prices are very volatile. |
| Income Stocks | Stocks that pay higher than average dividend yield. For the conservative investor, quality income stocks are to be found in the telephone and public utility fields. |
| Cyclical Stocks | Refer to stocks of companies whose earnings fluctuate with the business cycle and are accentuated by it. When business conditions improve, the company's profitability is restored and enhanced. The common stock price rises. When conditions deteriorate, business for the cyclical company falls off sharply, and its profits are greatly diminished. Industries that may be regarded as cyclical include steel, cement, paper, machinery, and airlines. |
| Defensive Stocks | Are stocks of companies that are "recession resistant." Such stocks lack glamour of market leaders, but are characterized by a degree of stability desirable when the economy faces a period of uncertainty and decline. Utility stocks are generally regarded as defensive issues, since |

*(continued)*

**FIGURE 8-2** *(continued)*

| Type | Description |
|---|---|
| | their slow but steady growth rate tends to hold up in recession years as well as in boom years. In addition to electric and gas utilities, the shares of gold mining companies have tended to be effective defensive issues. |
| Speculative Stocks | In a sense all common stocks are speculative. When you buy shares, you have no promises, no certainty that the funds you ultimately receive when you sell the stock will be more, less, or the same as the dollars you originally paid. Yet in the accepted parlance of Wall Street, speculative shares have a more limited meaning. High flying glamour stocks, "hot" issues, and penny mining stocks are speculative. |
| Options | A contract between one party, the seller (writer) who is said to be short the contract, and another party, the purchaser, who is said to be long the contract, which grants the long the right, but not the obligation to buy (in case of a call option) or sell (in case of the put option) a fixed number of units of some underlying asset at some specified price (strike or exercise price) for a defined period of time (the time to expiration). |

**FIGURE 8-2** *(continued)*

As outlined in Fig. 8-4, the investment choice can also depend on the economic and political environment, covering such factors as those discussed below.

**Foreign Exchange.** In times of unstable exchange rates investments overseas are more uncertain. When exchange rates are stable, foreign investments are more predictable.

**Political Atmosphere.** When foreign or domestic government policies and attitudes encourage investment, investments tend to be more secure.

**Inflation.** In times of high inflation, equities have proven over short periods of time to be poor hedges against inflation. Inflation reduces the value of returns on fixed investments, such as bonds. In times of low inflation financial assets (both stocks and bonds) have in recent years done better. Factors that tend to cause increased inflation are expansionary government actions, rising input prices, and increasing industrial concentrations.

- *Expansionary forces* are increased government spending, taxes (fiscal policy), and money supply (monetary policy).
- *Rising input prices* can occur in several areas. An increase in wages without an increase in productivity, for example, tends to increase inflation pressures. An increase in raw materials monopolies, such as the Organization of Petroleum Exporting Countries (OPEC), tends also to increase inflation because of the control of supplies. On the other hand, if the supply of commodities is plentiful, their costs are generally lower, thus lowering inflationary pressures.

| Personal Factors | Key Indicators |
|---|---|
| Ability | Age of Individual |
| | Marital Status |
| | Number of Children |
| | Age of Children |
| | Health |
| | Employment History |
| Objectives of Investment | Preservation of Capital Growth |
| | Total Return Income |
| | Holding Period |
| | Growth |
| | Income |
| Willingness | Risk Experience: History |
| | Experience |
| | Type |
| | Risk Tolerance |

Individual Financial Factors

| | |
|---|---|
| Assets | Financial |
| | Real Estate |
| | Insurance |
| | Other Assets |
| | — Real Estate Investments |
| | — Annuities |
| Liabilities | Taxes |
| | Loans |
| | Residential Mortgages |
| Income | Gross |
| | Disposable |

**FIGURE 8-3 Investor analysis—factors affecting a personal investment planning decision.**

☐ *In concentrated industries,* such as the automobile industry, if demand for goods increases, prices can be expected to rise and inflation increases.

**Interest Rates.** As interest rates rise, the value of all securities (other than the dollar) declines, particularly long-term bonds. Generally increasing interest rates favor short-term financial instrument investment. As interest rates decline, the value of securities rises, especially long-term bonds. Interest rates are generally determined by two factors, real interest rates and anticipated inflation. Real interest rates are determined by the amount of loanable money available (which is measured overall by the government figures [M1, M2, and the like] on money supply). If there is more money available for loans than is needed, real interest rates decline. When there is less money available, real interest rates will increase. The rate of inflation expected by investors in the market place is in theory added to the real interest rate to determine the current (nominal) interest rate.

| Factors | Key Indicator |
|---|---|
| Foreign Exchange | The Dollar |
| Political Atmosphere | Domestic |
| | Foreign |
| Inflation | Expansion Forces |
| | Rise in Input Prices |
| | Concentrated Industries |
| Interest Rates | Short Term |
| | Long Term |
| GNP | Consumer Spending |
| | Government Spending |
| | Net Exports |
| | Business Investments |

**FIGURE 8-4   Environmental analysis—factors affecting a personal investment planning decision.**

**GNP**   The gross national product (GNP) is determined by such factors as consumer spending, industrial investment, government spending, net exports, and taxes. As consumer spending, industrial investment, government spending, and net exports increase (which increases money circulation), GNP increases.   Increasing taxes and savings tend to decrease GNP by taking money out of circulation.   As GNP increases, financial instruments (particularly stocks) become more favorable, because profits generally rise and this increases a company's ability to pay interest, dividends, and return of principal.   Conversely, when the GNP decreases, financial instruments become less favorable because, as profits fall, a company's ability to pay interest, dividends, and return of principal decreases.

The risks associated with trying to anticipate the future economic environment, as reviewed in Fig. 8-5, include: purchasing power risk, business risk, market risk, political risk, and currency risk.

A personal investment planning decision involves a four phase process.   First, an understanding of the investment instruments and their distinguishing characteristics is necessary.   Second, an investor's situation is analyzed as to financial status, objectives, ability and willingness to assume risk, and term of investment.   Third, the investing environment is analyzed to determine the timeliness of the investments and the risks present in the environment.   Fourth, the investment instruments, investor situation, and environment are evaluated in matching the investor to the investment most appropriate for the investor given the economic and political environment and available investments.

### Narrowing the Focus

Several areas of personal investment planning were identified for possible prototype development:

□ Selecting a mix of different types of investments to have in an individual portfolio.

| | |
|---|---|
| Purchasing Power Risk (Inflation Risk) | Lenders of funds face the possibility that increases in the average level of prices for all goods and services will reduce the purchasing power of their income and principal when returned. Purchasing power risk must be faced even when equity is considered on the basis of total return. Based on the Dow Jones industrial average from 1900 to 1980, common stock prices over the long run have exceeded the growth of inflation. However, over shorter periods, inflation has often outrun common stock prices, and investors have often been disappointed in equities as a hedge against inflation. |
| Business Risk | A decline in earning power that reduces a company, federal, municipal, or governmental agency's ability to pay interest or dividends, or return principal, is also known as default risk. |
| Market Risk | The risk that the market price (value) of an asset will decline, resulting in a capital loss when sold. In the equity market a change in "market psychology" can cause a security's price to decline irrespective of any truly fundamental change in earning power of the company itself. A measure of a company's vulnerability to market psychology is measured quantitatively by beta analysis. |
| | Another aspect of market risk that affects all securities is interest rate risk. As interest rates rise, the value of all securities (except, of course the dollar) declines. A note here is necessary on debt instruments. Although a rise in interest rates will decrease the value of the instrument in the marketplace, at maturity it is redeemed at full value. Therefore, it must be recognized that the closer in time to maturity, the less the effect of a change in interest rates. Furthermore, interest rate risk can be eliminated if a desired maturity date is predetermined to coincide with planned use of the funds. |
| Political Risk | Refers to the possibility that changes in government laws or regulations will result in a diminished rate of return to the investor, or in extreme cases, a total loss of invested capital. |
| Currency Risk | The risk that adverse movements in the price of one national currency will reduce the net rate of return from a foreign investment. |

**FIGURE 8-5  Risks associated with the environment.**

□ Selecting a mix of individual bonds, stocks, or any other type of investment. For example, prototype systems have been developed as part of this project for selecting which individual stocks an investor should buy for the stock segment of that individual's portfolio.

□ Determining an individual's personal and financial willingness and ability to accept risks.

The first decision area was selected for further study during this phase of the project.

In this decision, the key individual factors are identified (investor finances and ability and willingness to take risks) and then matched with the opportunities (characteristics of each investment) and market and economic factors (the investment environment) to determine what kind of investment seems right for the individual answering the questions.

There were several reasons why this situation was chosen for prototype development:

- The prototype was part of a larger system, and the pattern of its decision was similar to other decisions made within the overall system. This enabled using this project to start doing background analyses for other parts of the system and to test the basic concept and structure of a larger system.
- By starting with specific test case decisions, and gradually building a general model on that base, the general model would have a much firmer foundation in reality.
- It provided a quick way to prototype, since the system developers were familiar with the investment analysis area under study.

## STUDYING THE SITUATION TO BE PROTOTYPED

Based on work related experience, as well as on interviews with several successful financial planning experts and on readings in the field, the following appears to be the way such decisions are made. The decision process analyzed here, as shown in Fig. 8-6, generally follows the overall financial planning process discussed in the preceding section. The description is structured in a way that provides models useful for later prototype system development.

Figure 8-6, a structured situation diagram or model, shows both the knowledge segments involved in the decision and the general way in which these factors affect the overall portfolio mix decision.

### Individual Factors

Questions about individual factors affecting a personal investment planning decision can be divided into two major categories and three subsections, as shown in Fig. 8-7.

**Financial.** The analysis of *individual investor finances* would include questions related to

- *Portfolio size*—the amount available for investment
- *Assets*—the amount of real estate, insurance, annuities, and other assets and investments owned
- *Liabilities*—the amount of taxes, loans, residential mortgages, and other debts outstanding
- *Income*—the amount of wages, rent, interest, dividends, profits, and other income

**Personal Investor Factors.** This analysis can be divided into three subsections: ability to take risks, willingness to take risks, and the objective of the investment.

There are four major factors that influence the investor's *ability to take risks*. As for employment status, if the employment is stable, more risks can generally be taken. As for age, the older the investors, the less risks they normally will be able to take. As for health, the better the health of the investors, the more risks they are generally able to take. As for family status, the more dependents the investor has, the less risks can usually be taken.

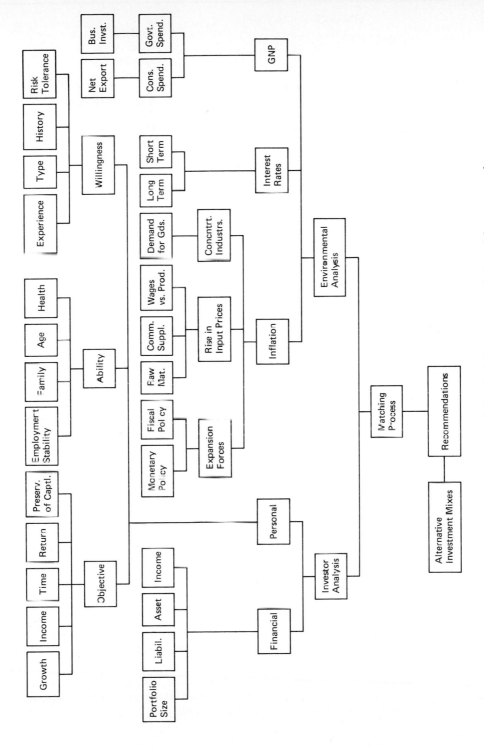

**FIGURE 8-6  An overview of the decision to be prototyped for personal investment planning.**

```
FINANCIAL FACTORS

                                        Portfolio Size
                                        Other Assets
                                        Liabilities
                                        Income
PERSONAL FACTORS
Ability                                 Employment Stability
                                        Age
                                        Health
                                        Family Status
Willingness                             Risk Experience
                                            — History
                                            — Type
                                            — Experience
                                        Risk Tolerance
Objectives of Investment                Preservation of Capital
                                        Growth
                                        Total Return
                                        Income
                                        Holding Period
```

**FIGURE 8-7  The decision situation to be prototyped for personal investment planning—investor analysis factors.**

Several key factors are examined in measuring the investor's *willingness to take risks*. Among them are current and past experiences of the investor in taking risks in investments or in other areas and the investor's risk tolerance, which can be measured by how the investor reacts to risk taking in other areas, such as games of chance or in career decisions.

In the situation under study, four options are specified for the *objective of the investment*. They are preservation of capital, income, total return, and growth. The major factor influencing total return or growth is time.

## Environmental Factors

As shown in Fig. 8-8, information is needed and assumptions made about the future economy in general, in several areas.

**Inflation.**  The following factors are known to influence inflation:

□ The future impact of *expansionary forces* on inflation can be measured by government spending (fiscal policy) and anticipated changes in money supply (monetary policy).
□ As discussed earlier, *rises in input prices*, which will affect future inflation, can be measured by three influencing factors: trends in wages, the power of raw material monopolies, and commodity supply trends.

| Factors | Key Indicator |
|---|---|
| Inflation | Expansion Forces |
| | — Fiscal Policy |
| | — Monetary Policy |
| | Rise in Input Prices |
| | — Union Wages Vs. Productivity |
| | — Raw Materials Monopolies |
| | — Commodity Supplies |
| | Concentrated Industries |
| | — Demand for Goods |
| Interest Rates | Long-Term Forecast |
| | Short-Term Forecast |
| GNP | Consumer Spending |
| | Government Spending |
| | Business Investments |
| | Net Exports |

**FIGURE 8-8  The decision situation to be prototyped for personal investment planning—environmental analysis factors.**

- In *concentrated industries*, if the demand for goods are expected to increase, prices will rise and inflation will increase.

In all cases these factors are studied in relation to the future trends anticipated. Most of the background information needed to determine the influencing factors affecting future inflation trends is available through financial publications such as the *Wall Street Journal.*

**Interest Rates.**   Although both short- and long-term interest rates are affected by the business cycle and inflation premium, as was noted earlier, they must be analyzed separately, because short-term rates are much more volatile than long-term rates.   Short-term interest rates, for example, can be affected by seasonal trends in money needs, which are not related to long-term inflation trends.   For investment purposes, the long-term interest rate trends anticipated will have a much greater impact on inflation projections used for investment planning purposes.

**GNP.**   The following factors affect GNP:

- *Consumer spending*—As consumer spending increases (as indicated by the movement in retail sales), the GNP increases.
- *Business investment*—As businesses increase their purchases of capital investments, the GNP increases.
- *Government spending*—Putting more money in the hands of business and consumers through government spending increases the GNP.
- *Net exports*—As exports increase relative to imports, domestic business generates a larger share of global sales, increasing the domestic GNP.

## Making Portfolio Decisions

For purposes of the initial phase of the study, the number of possible recommendations have been limited to four. Figure 8-9 shows the key characteristics of each. Whereas an investor might invest exclusively in one type of investment (for example common stocks), here the investor will also be able to consider investing in a combination (or mix) of several types. This is called the investment portfolio.

In arriving at a decision as to which (or what mix) of these four investment instruments to recommend, the key knowledge areas (investor analysis and environmental analysis) are manipulated in a variety of ways by an expert financial planner. This process is outlined in Fig. 8-10. The following describes two sample scenarios of this process at work.

In one of the typical personal investment planning decision situations studied while developing the prototype system, the financial planner first analyzed the *investor*.

As for the *personal* factors, the investor's health was good, he was married with two children, was between the age of thirty-six and fifty, and his employment history was stable. The conclusion was that the investor's *ability* to invest was moderate. The investor's investment *objective* was for total return (combination of growth and income) and the holding period was longer than one year (long term), so that his objective was also considered moderate. The investor had no experience in and little tolerance for risk taking, so that his *willingness* was classified as conservative. In total the personal factors affecting the investor's position were rated moderate overall.

Next the financial planner analyzed the individual's *financial* situation. The amount available for investment was under $20,000. The investor's other assets were valued at $21,000 and $125,000. His liabilities amounted to $21,000 and $125,000. His total annual income was $30,000 to $50,000. This led to a conclusion that the investor's financial position was moderate.

Based on a moderate financial and a moderate personal investor position, the conclusion of the financial planner was that the investor under study was a moderate investor.

| Type | Features |
|------|----------|
| Money Market Funds | Liquidity |
| | No Market Risk |
| | Little Business Risk |
| | Interest Income |
| T Notes & T Bonds | Federally Taxable Income |
| | Inflation Risk |
| | Interest Rate Risk |
| Common Stock | Dividends |
| | Business Risk |
| | Market Risk/Growth |

**FIGURE 8-9  The decision situation to be prototyped for personal investment planning—investment instrument analysis factors.**

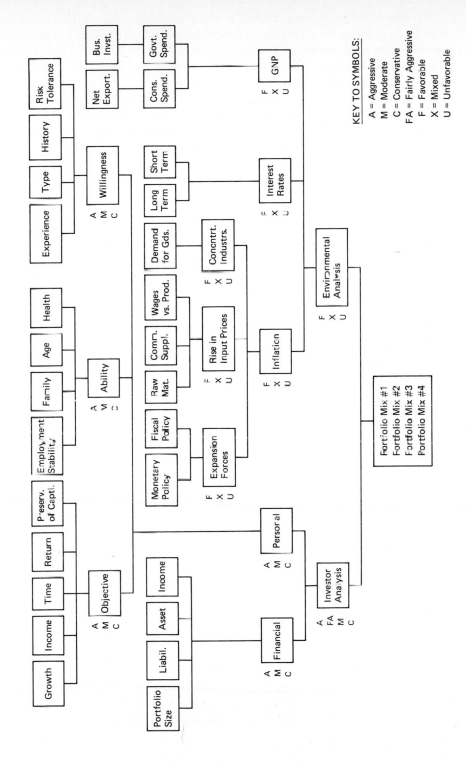

KEY TO SYMBOLS:

A = Aggressive
M = Moderate
C = Conservative
FA = Fairly Aggressive
F = Favorable
X = Mixed
U = Unfavorable

**FIGURE 8-10 Decision situation to be prototyped for personal investment planning analysis.**

The second key area studied was the *environmental analysis*. At the time of the study demand for goods in the concentrated industries were not increasing, which would have a favorable effect on *inflation*. With union wages stable, raw material monopolies decreasing, and commodity supplies in excess, the expected impact of input prices on inflation was also considered favorable. The government's fiscal policy was expansionary, as was monetary policy. This was expected to have an unfavorable impact on inflation. With expansionary forces being unfavorable, rise in input prices being favorable, and concentrated industries also having a favorable effect on inflation, the outlook for inflation was on balance considered moderate, at least over the near term.

At the time of the study, forecasts were for long- and short-term interest rates to decrease, so that the *interest rate* impact was judged to be favorable.

The financial planner examined projected consumer and government spending figures; business investment projections; and tax, export-import, and savings projections. At the time of the study, they all appeared to be favorable, so that the *GNP* forecast was favorable.

Because of the favorable conclusions drawn for the GNP, interest rates, and inflation, the overall environmental analysis conclusion was favorable.

Based on this key factor analysis, the financial planner recommended a portfolio mix consisting of 30 percent common stocks, 50 percent T bonds, and 20 percent money markets.

This portfolio is considered a moderate portfolio strategy. It allows for growth and income. Generally it fits an average investor. Given the environmental situation the investment in stocks and bonds is reinforced. With the limited recommendations available in this prototype, the financial planner could not recommend a portfolio mix that was any more aggressive. At the same time it was obvious that a more conservative portfolio mix was not judged appropriate in the current environment.

In the following prototypes, recommendations are limited to four choices, the one given in the above example and

- □ 100 percent common stocks
- □ 60 percent common stocks, 30 percent T bonds, and 10 percent money markets
- □ 10 percent T bonds and 90 percent money markets

In another typical situation studied, the investor's health was good, she was married with one child, was thirty-two years old, and her employment was stable, so that her *ability* to invest was moderate. Her investment objective was for growth and the holding period was longer than one year (long term), so that her objective was considered aggressive. She had no experience in investing, but had demonstrated a history of risk tolerance to attain her objectives, so that her *willingness* to invest was considered moderate. The conclusion about the personal analysis was, therefore, moderate overall.

As for the financial factors she had $43,000 to invest and had other assets valued at $62,000, liabilities of $71,000, and total annual income of $58,000. This led to a conclusion that the investor's financial position suggested an aggressive portfolio.

Based on an aggressive financial and moderate personal position, the conclusion of the financial planner was that the investor in the study was a fairly aggressive investor.

The second area studied was the *environmental analysis*. The three areas analyzed for the environment were inflation, interest rates, and GNP. This study was done at the same time as the one described above. Based on the conclusions given earlier for GNP, interest rates, and inflation, the environmental conclusion was favorable.

Since the investor was fairly aggressive and the environmental analysis was favorable, portfolio mix 2 was chosen. This portfolio of 60 percent common stock, 30 percent T bonds, and 10 percent money market funds is a fairly aggressive portfolio that suits the investor. The appropriateness of this portfolio was reinforced by the environmental analysis. The financial planner indicated that if the environmental analysis had been unfavorable, he would have suggested a less aggressive portfolio mix, even though this one best matched the investor's analysis.

In order to keep the initial prototype described in the following section manageable, several working assumptions were made. The number of recommendations have been limited to four. This number was expanded considerably in subsequent versions of the system. The individual using the system is expected to have already decided how much money is to be invested. Another area that will be simplified is in the environmental knowledge segment. The inflation and GNP forecast will be developed in detail, but interest rates projections have been given abbreviated treatment. Although limiting the system in this way created the danger that the system might be trivialized somewhat, such simplification was a necessary first step toward organizing and testing the soundness of the system's concept. Also, it was essential to developing a prototype within a reasonably short period of time.

## DOCUMENTING THE PROTOTYPE SYSTEM

The following discussion covers

- System proposal
- Description of the prototype system
- Dependency diagrams
- Decision charts
- Designing and constructing the knowledge base

### System Proposal

The general objective of the project is to develop a knowledge-based system that assists a financial planner or individual in making personal investment planning decisions. The system is designed to be used by a financial planner to aid a client or by an individual doing their own personal investment planning.

The first phase of the project is limited to a specific type of decision—choosing an investment strategy from the limited investments that have been selected. This phase is designed to help test and build a structure and concept for a much larger personal investment planning system. The prototype system will be a small version of the larger system, which will be more fully developed in subsequent phases of the project.

The system offers the financial planner and the individual the ability to do their personal investment planning in the most efficient and least time-consuming way. As a result a financial planner will be able to handle many more clients because of the time efficiency that the system brings to the job. The individual will also be able to work more efficiently and have the guidance of an expert.

There are a wealth of sources of information in this field. They include books, periodicals, daily papers, and journals, some examples of which are listed in the references at the end of this chapter. In addition, a large number of professionals who work in the field for a variety of institutions, from banks to brokerage houses to independent financial advisory consulting firms, were interviewed.

## Description of the System Proposal

**System Overview and Objective.** The prototype system is designed to help users decide on an investment strategy that is suited for themselves or clients. The system will ask users questions about a client's or their own individual finances, family situation, age, health, experience, and objective, as well as about present and anticipated economic and market conditions. The system uses if-then rules and backward chaining to reason about the information given by a user in order to reach its recommendation.

**Recommendations to Be Made by the System.** For prototyping purposes, the system is limited to making recommendations of portfolio mixes involving three different investment types—money market funds, T bills, and common stocks. These were selected because:

- □ They offer a diversified (though limited) choice of investment opportunities.
- □ They require considering all the relevant characteristics of the investor.
- □ Using only domestic investments eliminates considering currency and political risks in the prototype.
- □ This combination also allows for the inclusion in the decision of all the relevant economic factors.
- □ Overall, since this prototype uses all the same factors and decision process as the larger system, but on a smaller scale, it enables testing the basic concept and structure of the larger system.

The system is capable of recommending mixed strategies, that is combinations of different investments in different proportions. Figure 8-11 describes the range of portfolio mixes.

**Nature of User Interface, Including a Typical User Dialogue.** The typical user dialogue covers two knowledge areas:

| Number | Common Stocks | T Bonds | Money Markets | Return | Risk |
|--------|---------------|---------|---------------|--------|------|
| 1 | 100 | 0 | 0 | 18% | 19% |
| 2 | 60 | 30 | 10 | 15.85% | 11.82% |
| 3 | 30 | 50 | 20 | 14.20% | 6.99% |
| 4 | 0 | 10 | 90 | 11.65% | 2.12% |

**FIGURE 8-11  Prototype system for personal investment planning—possible recommendations.**

1. *Investor analysis.*
   a. *Financial.*  This information is obtained from the individual asking such questions as "What is the amount of money to be invested (under 20, 21–75, +75)?"  and "What is the value of your other assets, such as real estate, insurance, annuities, and cash (under 20, 21–125, +125)?"
   b. *Personal.*  This information is obtained from the individual by asking such questions as "How long has your employer been in business (under 1 year, 1–5 years, over 5 years)?" and "How long have you been employed in your present job (1 year, 2–5 years, over 5 years)?"
   c. *Willingness.*  This information is obtained from the individual by asking such questions as "When at school, did you ever take interesting courses that were hard and might have lowered your index (Yes, No)?" and "Late at night, when there is no traffic, do you ever go through traffic lights (Yes, No)?"
   d. *Objective.*  This information is obtained from the individual by asking such questions as "What is the purpose of your investment (1) preservation of capital, (2) income, (3) total return, (4) growth?" and "How long can the portfolio be left without taking the principal out (short term—under 1 year, long term—1 year or more)?"
2. *Environmental analysis.*  The *Wall Street Journal*, for example, continuously publishes surveys of leading economists on topics pertaining to the following questions.  The answers to these questions should be the average of those economists surveyed.  This information is directly available from the *Wall Street Journal* and other financial publications.
   a. *Inflation.*  This information is obtained from the individual by asking such questions as "Is the next projected budget expected to have a larger deficit (expansionary) or smaller deficit (contractionary)?" and "As measured by M2, is money supply growing faster than projected (expansionary) or below projected (contractionary)?"
   b. *Interest rates.*  This information is obtained from the individual by asking such questions as "Is the forecast for short-term interest rates increasing or decreasing?" and "Is the forecast for long-term interest rates increasing or decreasing?"
   c. *GNP.*  This information is obtained from the individual by asking such questions as "For the upcoming year is consumer spending forecasted to increase or decrease?"

**Description of the Knowledge Structure and Reasoning Processes.**  The recommendations made by the prototype system are based on two critical factors: the investor analysis, which is influenced by the individual's financial status and personal status, and the environmental analysis, which is influenced by inflation, interest rates, and GNP. In turn the values for each of these factors are determined by a number of other influencing factors:

- The *individual's financial status* is determined by portfolio size, income, assets, and liabilities.
- The *individual's personal status* is determined by the ability to take risks (which in turn is determined by employment stability, age, health, and family status), the willingness to take risks (which is measured by the risk experience, type of risk, history of risk taking, and risk tolerance), and the investor's objective (which is determined by the individual's need to preserve capital, the growth rate expected, the total return on investment required, and how long the investment is to be made).
- *Inflation* is determined by expansion forces (which in turn is determined by fiscal policy and monetary policy), rise in input prices (which is determined by wages versus productivity, raw material monopolies, and the commodity supply), concentrated industries (which is determined by demand for goods in industries that are dominated by a few large companies).
- *Interest rates* are determined by the supply and demand for money and available loans (which in turn is determined by the business cycle and savings), seasonality, and anticipated inflation.
- *GNP* is determined by consumer spending (which in turn is determined by personal income and credit availability), industry investment (which is determined by business cycle phase and interest rates), government spending (which is determined by fiscal policy), net exports (which is determined by the volume of exports and imports), taxes, and savings. The GNP is also monitored by analysis of retail sales and the unemployment rate.

Additional levels of influencing factors are needed as indicated in Fig. 8-12.

If-then rules are used to determine the values at each stage. The inference engine uses backward chaining. The values are measured for each of the factors in the reasoning chain either by aggressive, moderate, or conservative or by favorable, mixed, or unfavorable. This is indicated in Fig. 8-10.

## Dependency Diagram

Figure 8-12 shows the dependency diagram for the personal investment planning knowledge-based system. It is a complete summary outline of all questions, rules, knowledge segments and their interrelationships, values, and recommendations within the system.

## Decision Charts

Figure 8-13 shows a sample of decision charts for the personal investment knowledge-based system. The decision charts that are included are for every rule set triangle in the dependency diagram.

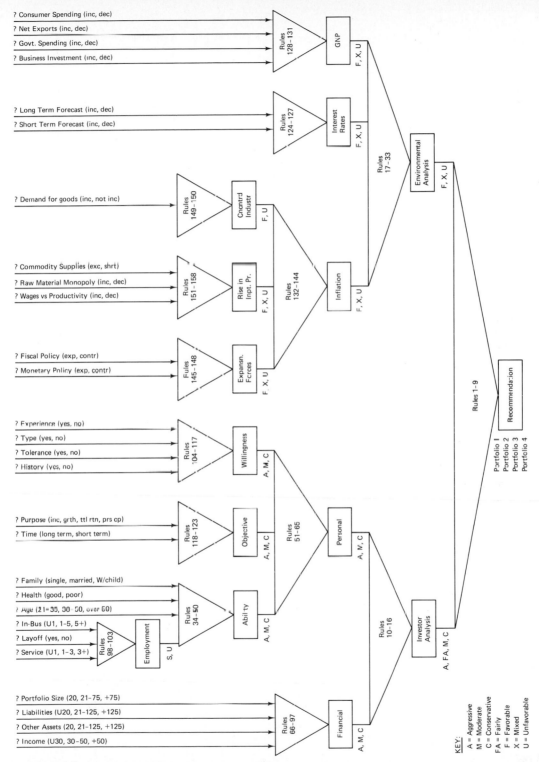

? Consumer Spending (inc, dec)
? Net Exports (inc, dec)
? Govt. Spending (inc, dec)
? Business Investment (inc, dec)

Rules 128–131

GNP

F, X, U

? Long Term Forecast (inc, dec)
? Short Term Forecast (inc, dec)

Rules 124–127

Interest Rates

F, X, U

? Demand for goods (inc, not inc)

Rules 149–150

Cnantrd Industr

F, U

? Commodity Supplies (exc, shrt)
? Raw Material Monopoly (inc, dec)
? Wages vs Productivity (inc, dec)

Rules 151–158

Rise in Inpt. Pr.

F, X, U

Rules 132–144

Inflation

F, X, U

? Fiscal Policy (exp, contr)
? Monetary Policy (exp, contr)

Rules 145–148

Expansn. Forces

F, X, U

Environmental Analysis

F, X, U

Rules 17–33

? Experience (yes, no)
? Type (yes, no)
? Tolerance (yes, no)
? History (yes, no)

Rules 104–117

Willingness

A, M, C

? Purpose (inc, grth, ttl rtn, prs cp)
? Time (long term, short term)

Rules 118–123

Objective

A, M, C

Rules 51–65

Personal

A, M, C

? Family (single, married, W/child)
? Health (good, poor)
? Age (21–35, 30–50, over 60)
? In-Bus (U1, 1–5, 5+)
? Layoff (yes, no)
? Service (U1, 1–3, 3+)

Rules 98–103

Employment

S, U

Rules 34–50

Ability

A, M, C

Investor Analysis

A, FA, M, C

Rules 10–16

Rules 1–9

Recommendation

Portfolio 1
Portfolio 2
Portfolio 3
Portfolio 4

? Portfolio Size (20, 21–75, +75)
? Liabilities (U20, 21–125, +125)
? Other Assets (20, 21–125, +125)
? Income (U30, 30–50, +50)

Rules 66–97

Financial

A, M, C

KEY:
A = Aggressive
M = Moderate
C = Conservative
FA = Fairly
F = Favorable
X = Mixed
U = Unfavorable

**FIGURE 8-12  Dependency diagram: personal investment planning.**

OBJECTIVE

| Holding Period | Presever. of Capita. | Growth | Total Return | Income |
|---|---|---|---|---|
| Long Term | C | A | M | M |
| Short Term | C | M | M | C |

Key for Objective:
A = Aggressive
M = Moderate
C = Conservative

PERSONAL ABILITY
Family and age

| Health & Employment | Single & Young | Single & Middle | Single & Older | Married & Young | Married & Middle | Married & Older | Married & Yng. & Child | Married & Mid. & Child | Married & Old & Child |
|---|---|---|---|---|---|---|---|---|---|
| Good & Stable | A | A | M | A | A | C | M | M | C |
| Poor & Stable | M | M | C | M | M | C | C | C | C |
| Good & Unstable | M | M | C | M | M | C | C | C | C |
| Poor & Unstable | C | C | C | C | C | C | C | C | C |

**FIGURE 8-13  Sample decision charts for personal investment planning system—personal factors (initial prototype).**

kb-50:
question(demand-for-goods) = 'Is the demand for goods in the
automobile industry expected to increase over the coming year?'.

kb-51:
legalvals(demand-for-goods) = [increasing, not-
increasing].

kb-52:
question(long-term-forecast) = 'What is the current forecast for
long term interest rates?'.

kb-53:
legalvals(long-term-forecast) = [increasing,decreasing].

kb-72:
question(type) = 'Have you ever or would you ever leave a job
without having another one lined up?'.

kb-73:
legalvals(type) = [yes,no].

kb-36:
question(object) = 'What is the purpose of your investment?'.

kb-37:
legalvals(object) = [preservation-capital,growth,income,
total-return].

kb-44:
question(union-wages) = 'As measured by the Department of
Commerce, are the percentage of wage increases in large union
contracts increasing or decreasing in comparison to worker
productivity?'.

kb-45:
legalvals(union-wages) = [decreasing,increasing].


RULES:

                    /* Rule Set Seven: Employment Analysis
rule-98:
if in-business = under-1-year and
          layoffs = no or
          layoffs = yes and
          length-service = under-1-year or
          length-service = 1-3-years or
          length-service = over-3-years
     then employment = unstable.
rule-99:
if in-business = 1-5-year and
          layoffs = no and

*(continued)*

**FIGURE 8-14  Sample segment of knowledge base for personal in-
vestment planning system—initial prototype.**

```
            length-service = under-1-year or
            length-service = 1-3-years or
            length-service = over-3-years
      then employment = stable.
rule-100:
if in-business = 1-5-year and
            layoffs = yes and
            length-service = under-1-year or
            length-service = 1-3-years or
            length-service = over-3-years
      then employment = unstable.
rule-101:
if in-business = over-5-year and
            layoffs = no and
            length-service = under-1-year or
            length-service = 1-3-years
      then employment = stable.
rule-102:
if in-business = over-5-year and
            layoffs = yes and
            length-service = under-1-year or
            length-service = 1-3-years
      then employment = unstable.
rule-103:
if in-business = over-5-year and
            layoffs = yes and
            length-service = over-3-years
      then employment = stable.


                /*  Rule Set Eight:  Willingness   */
rule-104:
if history = yes and
            tolerance = yes and
            type = yes and
            experience = yes or
            experience = no
      then willingness = aggressive.
rule-105:
if history = yes and
            tolerance = yes and
            type = no and
            experience = yes
      then willingness = aggressive.
rule-106:
if history = yes and
            tolerance = yes and
            type = no and
            experience = no
      then willingness = moderate.
```

**FIGURE 8-14** *(continued)*

## Designing and Constructing the Knowledge Base

Rules and questions were developed from the situation study. They were based on
the analysis of how a financial planner or individual might actually go about making
such decisions.

A segment of the prototype system's knowledge base is given in Fig. 8-14. The expert knowledge shell used is M1. The if-then rules in the knowledge base in Fig. 8-14 match those specified in the decision charts shown in Fig. 8-13. They were written to reflect the relationship shown in the dependency diagram in Fig. 8-12, and use the values shown there and in the decision charts. The questions in the knowledge base (Fig. 8-14) are those indicated in the dependency diagram.

## REVIEW QUESTIONS

1. Complete the knowledge-based system (or any segment of the system) partially documented in this chapter and enter it into the expert system shell you have.

2. Develop a knowledge-based system for recommending a portfolio consisting of a wider range of investment types, selected from the many listed in Figure 8-2.

3. Almost every expert system shell has a demonstration system involving personal investment planning. Compare the demonstration system accompanying your expert system shell (if it has one) with the prototype system described in this chapter, and describe the similarities and differences in structure and performance.

4. What three critical areas of study are involved in personal investment planning? Briefly describe them.

5. How are these three areas manipulated to choose an appropriate portfolio for an individual investor?

6. In general, who can afford to take more investment risk, a 65 year old with a wife and 5 grown children or a 24 year old with a wife and 1 young child? Should they assume greater risk?

7. What investment objective would you expect of a 21 year old just out of school with few responsibilities? Of a much older person?

8. What are some of the reasons that you would require a higher rate of return from an investment in a less developed country?

## REFERENCES

Burgauer, J., *The Do-It-Yourself Investor*, Chicago, IL: Probus Publishing Co., 1987.

Cohen, and J.B. Zinberg, *Investment Analysis and Portfolio Management*, 5th ed., Homewood, IL: Irwin, 1986.

Davidson, K., "Strategic Investment Theories," *Journal of Business Strategy*, vol. 6, 1985.

Evans, M.K., "Inflation's Return Changes Investment Strategy," *Industry Week*, vol. 230, Sept. 15, 1986.

Ibbotron, R.G., and G.P. Brinson, *Investment Markets: Gaining the Performance Advantage*, New York: McGraw-Hill, 1981.

Lamaute, D., "Building Up an Investment Portfolio," *Black Enterprise*, vol. 17, February 1987.

Nelson, C.R., *The Investor's Guide to Economic Indicators*, New York: John Wiley and Sons, 1987.

Ralo, C.J., and R. Klein, *Gaining on the Market: Your Complete Guide to Investment Strategy*, Boston, MA: Little, Brown, 1987.

Rose, P.S., *Money and Capital Markets*, 2nd ed., Business Publications, 1986.

Sherman, M.H., "Investments: An Enormous Shift in Investment Patterns,"*Across the Board*, vol. 23, September 1986.

Van Horne, J.C., *Financial Management and Policy*, 6th ed., Englewood Cliffs, NJ: Prentice Hall, 1983.

# 9

# A Commercial Loan
# Approval System

This chapter describes the development of a knowledge-based system for determining whether or not, and under what conditions, a bank loan officer should grant a business loan to a company.

The prototype system developed focuses on what is known as the strategic components of an overall commercial loan application screening system. The discussion covers

□ The situation under study: understanding the expert's domain
□ Studying the situation to be prototyped
□ Documenting the prototype system
□ Integrated knowledge-based and conventional computer systems

In developing the strategic or qualitative components of the system, many techniques are employed that were useful in developing the strategic planning systems described in Chapters 18 and 21.

## THE SITUATION UNDER STUDY: UNDERSTANDING
## THE EXPERT'S DOMAIN

The discussion in this section covers

□ Selecting a decision area to work on
□ Studying how the situation works and how decisions are made
□ Narrowing the focus of the study

## Selecting a Decision Area to Work On

The general area under study is financial planning and evaluation. Many areas of financial planning lend themselves to knowledge-based systems development, including personal investment planning, capital investment planning, cash management, merger and acquisition analysis, company-by-company investment analysis and evaluation, and commercial and personal loan application screening. Knowledge-based systems development activity is widespread and growing in the financial area.

The business or commercial loan application screening area was selected for prototype development for several reasons:

- There are recognized experts in the field.
- Expert decision skills are needed to do the job.
- It requires informed judgement.
- The task is well understood.
- It is a manageable task from a knowledge-based systems viewpoint—many major commercial banks already have such knowledge-based systems.
- The decisions have a high payoff and practical value, since many banks are now either developing these systems themselves or hiring consultants to do so.
- Strategic planning plays a major role in decision making in this area.

## Studying How the Situation Works and How Decisions Are Made

As shown in Fig. 9-1, banks offer a wide variety of services, including deposits; loans; and brokerage, investment, insurance and other services. The essence of banking is the management of liquidity.

Banks lend to many types of borrowers, for varying periods, on many bases, and for a variety of reasons. Loans therefore will vary in liquidity and risk. Concentrations must also be limited so that no single occurrence can have a significant adverse impact on a bank's financial health.

The loan screening process, based on a bank's credit policies, guides officers in balancing the quality and quantity of the loan portfolio to achieve earnings objectives, while also meeting other situation requirements. These requirements include maintaining proper credit standards, holding risk to reasonable limits, minimizing losses, providing adequate liquidity, and fulfilling community needs.

In order to ensure this acceptable credit quality, banks identify target markets. These target markets are established through a strategic analysis of the bank's business environment and the marketplace.

The screening or credit analysis process begins upon receipt by the bank of loan applications. These applications are either voluntarily submitted by a potential loan client, or result from a bank sales force's marketing efforts. The loan application normally contains the amount of money requested, the purpose of the loan, a repay-

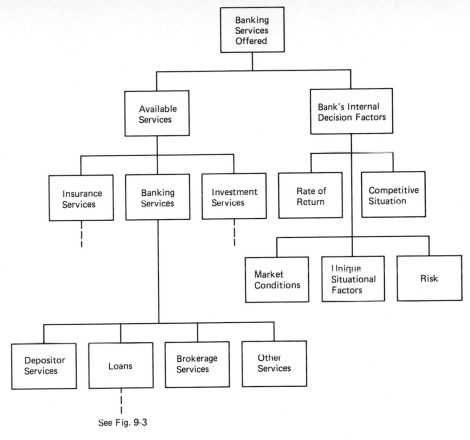

**FIGURE 9-1  Overview of banking services offered.**

ment proposal, and information relating to the applicant. An example of such an application is give in Fig. 9-2.

The application is assigned to a lending officer to perform a credit analysis. Before doing the detailed credit analysis, the lending officer *prescreens* the application, as shown in Fig. 9-3, to determine if the loan applicant matches the bank's target criteria, if the application is complete, if the applicant generally has acceptable characteristics, and if the purpose of the loan is reasonable and as claimed by the applicant. This phase is sometimes referred to as determining the *strategic fit* of the loan.

The *detailed credit analysis* entails gathering information through personal interviews, on-site visits, and document examination. The analysis includes reviews and evaluations of

- Information gathered on the applicant company's overall management character (willingness), to determine its likelihood to repay the loan
- The applicant's financial situation and capital situation to assess the company's financial strengths and weaknesses

# Partnership or Corporation

TO:

TO INDUCE THE BANK TO GRANT A LOAN
APPLICANT REPRESENTS THE FOLLOWING:

## Purpose

Applicant (Name of Partnership or Corporation)

Official Business Address — as stated in Certificate of Incorporation or Partnership Agreement

| City Town | County | State | | | Zip Code |
|---|---|---|---|---|---|

| Business Phone ( ) | Yrs. Estab. | Kind of Business | | Lease Expires |
|---|---|---|---|---|

| Names of Partners or Officers/Stockholders | Partnership Interest or Shrs. of Stock Owned | | Names of Partners or Officers/Stockholders | Partnership Interest or Shrs. of Stock Owned |
|---|---|---|---|---|
| | | | | |
| | | | | |
| | | | | |

| Date | |
|---|---|
| No. of Months | Proceeds to Borrower 1) |
| | Filing Fee 2) |
| Monthly Payment $ | Credit Life Insurance 3) |
| Tabular Rate A % | Amount Financed 4) |
| Impact of O.F. B | Prepaid Finance Charge (Origination Fee) 5) |
| Annual Percentage Rate on Note | Finance Charge (Interest to Maturity) 6) |
| A + B % | Total Finance Charge (5 + 6) 7) |
| | Total of Payments — Face of Note (4 + 6) 8) |
| If Corporation — No. of Shares No. Authorized | No. Issued |

## Business Bank Accounts

| Bank Name | Branch Address | Account No. |
|---|---|---|
| Checking | | |
| Savings | | |
| Time Deposits | | |

List All Judgements, legal proceedings and garnishments if any. Give particulars (attach statement if needed)

If none, state "NONE"

List All Debts — Installment loans, contracts, charge accounts, check credit, mortgages, equipment and motor vehicle leases, other obligations and credit applications. At this bank or elsewhere. (If none, state "NONE" (attach statement if needed))

| Name of Bank Company or Person | Address | Account Number | Date Made | Org. Amount | Unpaid Balance | Monthly Payments |
|---|---|---|---|---|---|---|

Name and Address of Three-Non-Bank Credit or Trade References of Partnership or Corporation

| Name | | Amount Owed |
|---|---|---|
| 1 | Address | $ |
| 2 | | $ |
| 3 | | $ |

Applicant affirms that the foregoing answers and any answers appearing on the accompanying statements are true and correct. The Bank and sources to which it may apply, or which may apply to it, are authorized to exchange credit information relative to the applicant and this application (which shall remain the bank's property), and loan. If the purpose of the loan is to pay for or purchase items indicated above or on the accompanying statements, no other credit in this connection has been or will be used, the proceeds will be held in trust until payment or purchase, and may be made payable to the Designee shown below or to the Seller, Agent or Broker.

The bank normally obtains Credit Reports for all loan applications, and for updates, renewals, or extensions of any credit granted. Upon request, the bank will inform you if a report has been obtained and will give you the name and address of the agency furnishing the report.

The applicant agrees to furnish the Bank: ( ) within 90 days after the close of each fiscal year a detailed report of audit prepared by independent public accountants satisfactory to the Bank; (ii) within 60 days after the close of each quarter, a balance sheet and income and expense statements, and (iii) such other information respecting the financial condition and operations of the Borrower as the Bank may from time to time reasonably request.

Designee:

Designee _____ Designee _____

Address _____ Address _____

**Credit Life Insurance** (Complete if Credit Life Insurance has been elected)

Name of Insured Individual _____ Relationship to Business (Complete if insured is not applicant) _____ Date of Birth _____

Applicant (Name of Partnership or Corporation) _____

X _____ Date _____
Signature of Partner or Corporate Official

X _____ Title _____
Signature of Partner or Corporate Official

| For Bank Use | | | | | |
|---|---|---|---|---|---|
| Date | Approval Signature | | Deduct Unpaid Balance of PL Number | | Special Instructions |
| By | | | | | |
| Branch No. | | | LAST PAYMENT RECEIVED | | |

| | Alpha Code | | Teller's No. & Date | Amount | Interviewer |
|---|---|---|---|---|---|

Signature of Partner or Corporate Official _____ Title _____

| Loan No. | Alpha Code | A | | $ | | C | $ |
|---|---|---|---|---|---|---|---|
| | | P | | | | O | |
| App. No. | | P | | | | M | |

**FIGURE 9-2   Sample application for monthly payment business loan.**

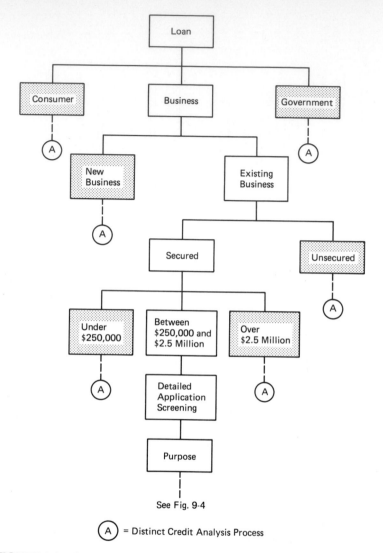

**FIGURE 9-3** **Decision situation diagram for prescreening of a commercial loan application.**

- The business' collateral and the personal collateral available to back any loan
- The applicant's marketing capabilities and operational characteristics, as well as the competitive environment and the company's future *strategic* position in the markets it serves

An overall outline of the credit analysis process is shown in Fig. 9-4.

Based upon the results of this analysis, utilizing the information gathered above to evaluate the applicant's credit risk, the lending officer decides whether to reject the loan request completely; approve the loan exactly as requested; or approve the

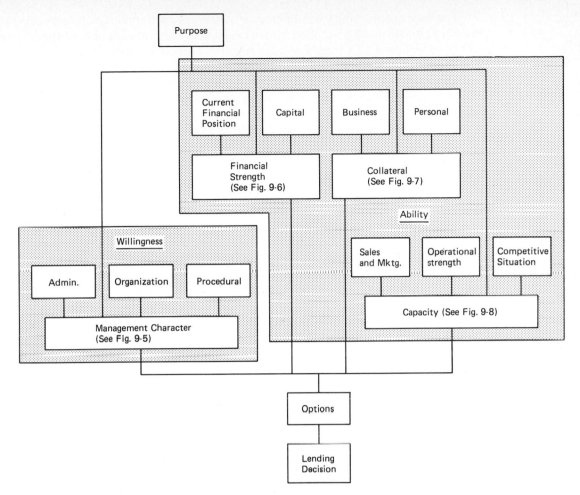

**FIGURE 9-4  Decision situation diagram for commercial loan screening—credit analysis.**

loan with modifications, such as reducing the amount of the loan, changing the term of the loan, modifying the collateral requirements, or increasing the interest rate.

**Narrowing the Focus**

There are several areas within the credit analysis process that were identified for possible prototype development in the commercial or business loan application screening area:

- □ New businesses, under three years old, that do not have a record of past performance
- □ Existing businesses
- □ Loans of varying amounts

The focus of the study was limited to a business or commercial loan request of between $250,000 and $2.5 million from a business in existence for at least three years and not in violation of a bank's policies regarding target markets.

The focus of this study was also further limited to concentration on nonfinancial considerations, since these considerations involve nonquantitative, more subjective, and more strategic factors and so are more appropriate for knowledge-based systems development.

Four possible systems development projects were planned:

□ The financial analysis and evaluation system, which is designed as a conventional computer program
□ A knowledge-based system for evaluating the management
□ A knowledge-based system for evaluating the strategic position of a company applying for a commercial loan
□ A knowledge-based system for determining the strategic fit of the loan, that is, how well the loan suited overall bank strategic objectives

Altogether they would provide an integrated commercial loan application screening system.

The following sections describe the development work done on an integrated prototype system that incorporated the results of traditional financial analysis done by conventional computer systems with more detailed strategic and qualitative analysis using knowledge-based systems.

The system was developed for use by a major commerical bank for whom several of the system developers worked. It is similar to other commercially available expert knowledge-based systems.

## STUDYING THE SITUATION TO BE PROTOTYPED

The following describes the structured situation analysis and structured models of the decision area to be prototyped developed from that analysis. The experts involved worked as commercial bank lending officers and so were able to base this structured situation study on typical decisions made on the job at their company.

### Prescreening

The loan application is first checked for accuracy and completeness. It is also prescreened to see that it conforms to bank lending policies, or strategic guidelines, for

□ Loan type
□ Business type
□ Secured or unsecured status
□ Loan size
□ Target market fit

During this phase loan officers may do a preliminary credit analysis to familiarize themselves with the applicant and the applicant company. This would involve not only review of the application, but also interviews, background checks, on-site visits, and other actions designed to gather information and formulate a plan for the detailed analysis.

Financial statement ratio analyses and comparisons are developed and financial projections made, usually by a specialist in financial analysis. Asset valuations are checked and verified, as are other financial aspects of the application.

The prescreening phase ends and the detailed credit analysis begins as the general purpose of the loan is examined in more detail and as each area of the application is subjected to closer scrutiny.

Many questions are explored to determine the specific need for the loan and the underlying causes for that need. For example, the application might state the loan purpose as "working capital." The applicant knows that the company needs cash for working capital, but the lending officer's analysis focuses on the real underlying causes for the need to use outside funds. For instance, the circumstances creating the need might be initial undercapitalization of the business, cash management difficulties, unprofitable operations, or excessive sales growth. This analysis is done to uncover the long-term strengths and weaknesses of the applicant.

At any point in the prescreening process, the application may be found sufficiently deficient to turn the loan down without further study.

## The Detailed Credit Analysis

The following is a more detailed examination of the overall decision situation structured in Fig. 9-4. The structured situation models described below are based on typical decision situations encountered by the bank lending officers participating in the prototype system development study.

**Management Willingness (Character).** There are many ways to judge management character. For example, the stated purpose of the loan application might be "take advantage of trade discounts." The actual intended use of proceeds, however, is subsequently found to be to repay personal loans from the officer or owners to the business, loans that should be subordinated to the bank's position and left in the business. This and other intentionally misleading statements would result in the lending officer's questioning the honesty, integrity, and character of the applicant's management as well as the credibility of the information supplied by them.

The lending officer could identify other trouble signs while conducting an investigation of the company's trade and bank references. The investigation could indicate sudden or excessive borrowing, late payment of bills, borrowing continuing after seasonal need is over, excessive overdrafts or withdrawals against uncollected funds in business checking accounts, deposited checks being returned, excessive cash balance declines, extensive and sudden changes in management, diversification into an unfamiliar business, unusual or unrealistic plans for the future, poor plant or

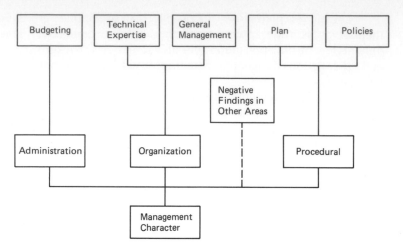

**FIGURE 9-5  Decision situation diagram for commercial loan screening—management character analysis.**

company appearance, poor employee attitude and morale, or increase in speculative assets or outside investments.  Many of these factors raise questions that involve qualitative judgments by a bank's loan officer.

After gaining answers to the questions above and identifying any *negative findings*, the lending officer will investigate the specific areas of concern, primarily *administration*, *organization*, and *procedural* aspects of the applicant, as shown in the structured situation model in Fig. 9-5.  Specific questions, examples of which are given in the systems documentation later, are asked in each of these areas as well as in the area of general character assessment.

As seen in Fig. 9-4, the *ability* of the loan applicant to repay a loan is measured by three critical factors: financial strength, collateral, and capacity.

**Financial Strength.**    Financial strength is a measure of the applicant's financial ability to meet its loan commitment.  At the company under study, the financial statements for the last three years were analyzed.  As shown in the situation model in Fig. 9-6, these statements ideally should have an *unqualified audit opinion* by an independent certified public accountant (CPA).  However, depending on circumstances (for example, first time the client has sought a bank loan, reputation of applicant, bank's past dealings with applicant, and the like) *unaudited* or *qualified audited* financial statements may also be acceptable.  If no acceptable financial statements are presently available, the lending officer will still analyze the loan application, but with more emphasis placed on the other areas for which information is available.

The *current financial position* is a composite of the applicant's strength in three different areas.  The lending officer analyzes the applicant's *cash flow*, as well as reported earnings and assets, by examining such questions as whether sales are final, accounts receivables are collectible and not excessively aged, any unrecorded payables exist, inventory is saleable, recorded assets exist and are productive, recorded intangible amounts seem reasonable, and all debts are recorded.  Cash projections are examined in light of this analysis to determine if they are consistent with historical amounts and will produce enough excess cash to cover loan payments.

The applicant's *liquidity* is also analyzed. Similar detailed questions are examined in this area. The *leverage* of the applicant is analyzed through comparing company financial ratios to industry ratios, such as debt to net worth, total debt to assets, debt to net worth, and net worth to assets. Leverage is also judged through identifying negative or positive trends in these ratios.

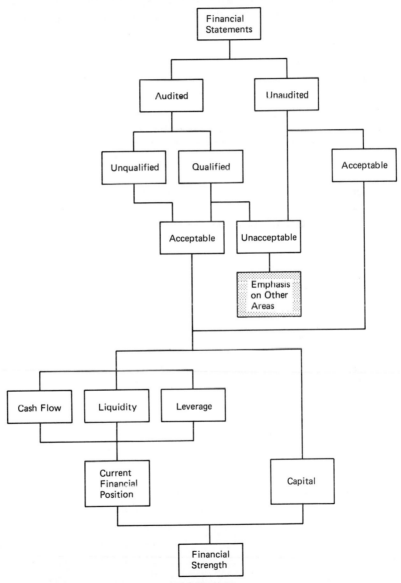

**FIGURE 9-6 Decision situation diagram for commercial loan screening—financial strength analysis.**

The next step in analyzing the applicant's financial strength is to investigate the owner's or owners' *capital* investment in the company. A good measure of a business' future prospects is the amount of faith (measured by invested and retained capital or equity) the owners themselves have placed in it. This review covers questions about such factors as the company's debt to equity ratio in relation to the industry, the one- to three-year trend of the company's equity balance, and the owners' plans to further invest in the business over the near term.

Both the financial strength at present and that anticipated over the term of the loan are studied, based on the implications of the financial analysis and their relation to subsequent findings during the credit screening.

**Collateral.** Collateral, defined as an asset in which the bank takes a security interest, entitles a bank to cash derived from the sale of the asset or assets in the event that the borrower defaults on the loan. Collateral may consist of *personal assets* and *business assets*, as shown in the situation model in Fig. 9-7. The pledge of collateral normally adds safety to the loan, since the lender can sell the *security* to obtain repayment if the debtor fails to pay. The lending officer, when examining the financial statements and/or while visiting the applicant's facility, will typically look for the existence (identification and location) of collateral, generally in the form of tangible assets (for example, stock certificates, bonds, certificates of deposit, buildings, land, equipment, inventory, and receivables).

Further questions asked include the collateral's *marketability* (is it really saleable for the entire term of the loan, can it be protected from deterioration, can the bank take possession of it), *appraised value* (can it be sold for the stated value), and *availability* (is it free from encumbrances).

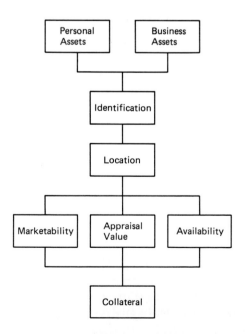

FIGURE 9-7 Decision situation diagram for commercial loan screening—collateral analysis.

**Capacity.**     Capacity, which is outlined in the situation model in Fig. 9-8, is another measure of the present and future health of the applicant company. It tells how successful a business has been in the past and will possibly be in the future. As such, it involves subjective strategic-planning questions.

At the company under study, the determinants of a business' future capacity to survive and succeed were its sales and marketing capability, its operational strength, and its position in the competitive environment.

The investigation of sales and marketing capabilities involves studying the *target market characteristics* by asking such questions as who purchases the company's products or service, who uses the product or service, who influences the purchase decision, is the market stable, where are the future opportunities, and what are the critical success factors. The objective here and in subsequent stages of this analysis is to identify not only the structure of the market (how it works) but also the opportunities (where the money will be made) and keys to success (how money will be made). In addition, a determination is made of the relation (ability to succeed) of the company to its target market and the keys to success, now and in the future.

An assessment is also made of the market for the company's *product or service*. Typical strategic market questions asked here are what product characteristics contribute to sales, how important is quality to the purchase decision, and how important is reputation to sales. How well the product matches the target market now and in the future provides key clues to future success.

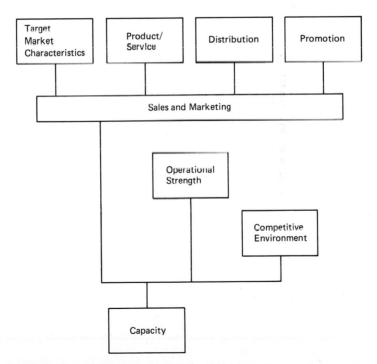

**FIGURE 9-8  Decision situation diagram for commercial loan screening—capacity analysis.**

Questions are also asked in key *promotion* and *distribution* areas, again in order to determine key opportunities and critical success factors as well as to determine the company's ability to meet these keys to success.

An analysis of the *operational* strengths of a company is designed to identify key present and anticipated company resources. These in turn can be matched with the opportunity areas and key-to-success factors to determine the likelihood of a company's future success.

The analysis of the *competitive situation* provides indications of how well a company can do in relation to the competition. This analysis involves answering typical strategic-planning questions about the kind and nature of the competition and the company's and competition's comparative strengths and weaknesses in opportunity and key-to-success areas.

From this analysis should emerge a picture of the company's strategic direction, its strategic position in the market place, and its strategic relation to the competition. This information is necessary to assess the potential of the applicant to handle the loan requirements. It also provides a perspective with which to view the company's present financial position in relation to further competitive market requirements.

A lending decision is based on the analysis of the critical factors described above. The individual factors are weighed one against the other, and in total, in order to come to a conclusion about the overall credit risk of the applicant. Typical decisions that might be reached are

1. *Acceptable credit risk, approve the loan as requested.* This recommendation indicates that the business has the willingness and ability to repay the loan in accordance with its terms.
2. *Poor credit risk, reject the loan request.* This recommendation indicates that the business' willingness and ability to repay the proposed loan is inadequate, and therefore the loan request should be rejected.
3. *Questionable credit risk, reduce amount of the loan requested.* This recommendation indicates that although the business' willingness is present, its ability to repay is questionable. It indicates that there is moderate credit risk, primarily due to the business' lack of financial strength and capacity.
4. *Questionable credit risk, change the term of the loan requested.* For the most part this recommendation indicates that although the business' willingness is present, the appropriateness of the requested loan's structure is weak (for example, the loan's term does not correlate with its purpose), and so the loan term should be reduced. It indicates that there is moderate credit risk, primarily due to a combination of the business' capacity and collateral not matching the requested loan structure. However, this recommendation would also be applicable if the term of the loan is to be extended due to an above average willingness and collateral but inadequate financial strength.
5. *Questionable credit risk, modify the collateral requirements.* This recommendation indicates that although the business' willingness is present, its ability to repay is slightly questionable. It indicates that there is a fairly moderate credit risk due mainly to an inadequacy of both the collateral originally proposed and the company's financial strength.
6. *Questionable credit risk, increase the interest rate.* This recommendation indicates that the business' willingness and ability to repay is slightly questionable,

and so the bank should be compensated for this above-average risk. It indicates that there is moderate credit risk primarily due, for example, to a lack of confidence in the management character.

A lending officer makes many subjective judgments as to the applicant's relative strength in the various areas. There is no strict formula that can be followed in arriving at the final lending decision. The human element, as relates to both the lending officer and the applicant, plays a key role in the analysis of all the pertinent facts. A complete credit analysis involves not only a careful study and understanding of the basic business conditions, therefore, but also the capacity to gauge the applicant's ability to handle the obligation over a long period of time.

The above six recommendations are only a sampling of the many ways in which a loan officer might go about making a lending decision. The list has been deliberately simplified in order to facilitate the prototype system development that is described in the following section. In addition, since the system is a proprietary one, and of considerable value, the full menu of recommendations could not be given here.

The objective of this phase of the study is to create structured models of the decision situation based on typical decision situations encountered by an expert, a bank lending officer. These models function not only as a guideline (or expert guidance) that could assist someone making these kinds of decisions. These structured models also serve as a definition of the structure of the knowledge-based system to be prototyped.

## DOCUMENTING THE PROTOTYPE SYSTEM

The following discussion covers

- System proposal
- Description of the prototype system
- Dependency diagrams
- Decision charts
- Designing and constructing the knowledge base

### System Proposal

The general objective of the project is to develop a knowledge-based system to assist a bank lending officer in making a decision about commercial loan applications.

Approving business loans requires extensive participation of senior lending officers in a bank. A knowledge-based system would make the expert knowledge of these senior officers permanently available to all lending officers in a bank, now and in the future. At the same time it would help standardize the bank's commercial credit approval process. This shared knowledge and greater standardization of the loan screening process would likely result in better loan decisions and a strengthening of the quality of a bank's loan portfolio.

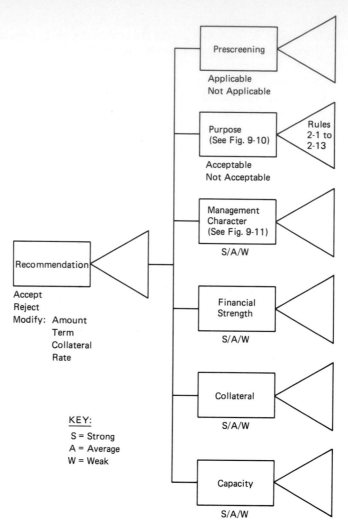

**FIGURE 9-9  Overall dependency diagram for commercial loan screening system—initial prototype.**

The system is segmented into seven major components, as shown in the overall dependency diagram of the system in Fig. 9-9. The first phase of the project is limited to a generalized prototype of the entire decision, for limited types of loans, with some detailed development of selected strategic and qualitative decision components. This phase is designed to help test and build a structure and concept for the complete system for commercial loan screening and to test its potential for expansion. The system will be more fully developed in subsequent phases of the project.

The knowledge sources used to develop the prototype included expert bank lending officers; books, periodicals, bank and industry manuals, forms, credit agency reports, and conventional financial analysis computer systems; and experienced knowledge engineers and system developers.

## Description of the Prototype System

**System Overview and Objective.**   The prototype system is designed to assist both junior and senior loan officers in a bank screen commercial loan applications. The system is limited to decisions on requests for a business loan of between $250,000 and $2.5 million from a business in existence for at least three years that is operating within the bank's policies regarding geographic or industry concentrations.

The system asks users questions about the applicant's management character, competitive situation, operational strength, marketing and sales situation, collateral, and financial strength as well as questions relating to the prescreening and purpose of the loan.

The system uses if-then rules and backward chaining to reason about the information given by a user in order to reach its recommendations.

**Recommendations to Be Made by the System.**   For prototyping purposes, the system is limited to making one of six possible credit determination recommendations:

- ☐ *Acceptable credit risk, approve the loan as requested.*
- ☐ *Poor credit risk, reject the loan request.*
- ☐ *Questionable credit risk, reduce the amount of loan requested.*
- ☐ *Questionable credit risk, change the term of the loan requested.*
- ☐ *Questionable credit risk, modify the collateral requirements.*
- ☐ *Questionable credit risk, increase the interest rate.*

In addition, the system will indicate if the loan request does not satisfy one of the prototype's preconditions and, therefore, that the knowledge-based system should not be used by printing *"This knowledge-based system is not applicable."*

The heuristics used in arriving at these recommendations have been somewhat simplified to enable prototype development and concept testing and to protect the system's proprietary aspects.

**Nature of User Interface, Including a Typical User Dialogue.**   The user is asked questions about the applicant and its environment that generally require yes or no answers or one of three possible estimates: strong, average, and weak.   The typical user dialogue covers the following key knowledge areas:

*Prescreening.*   This information is obtained from the loan application and interviews with the loan applicant.   A sample question would be "What type of loan is this (consumer, business, government)?"

*Purpose.*   This information is obtained from the loan application, the company's business plan, and interviews with the loan applicant.   A sample question would be "Have repairs and maintenance expenses been increasing rapidly during the past six months?"

*Management Character.*   This information is obtained from interviews with the loan applicant, on-site visits, and review of references. Sample questions are "How would you rate the professional reputation, integrity and experience of the owner and officers of the company?" and "Is there management continuity?"

*Financial Strength.* This information is obtained from interviews with the loan applicant and the review of the company's business plan, specifically the financial statements. Sample questions are "Are the financial statements audited?" and "Is there an excess of revenue after expenses in the cash flow projections that is sufficient to repay the loan and make interest payments over the future period?"

*Collateral.* This information is obtained from a review of the company's business plan and on-site visits to appraise the existence and condition of available collateral. Sample questions are "Is there any property in the business that could be pledged as security for the loan?" and "Does the term of the loan match the purpose of the loan (for example, purchase of inventory, machinery, and equipment)?"

*Capacity.* This information is obtained from reviewing the company's business plan, on-site visits, and a strategic appraisal of the market and industry in which the loan applicant company operates. Sample questions are "What is your estimate of the growth potential for the market in which the loan applicant company operates?" and "How would you rate the business' ability to meet key success requirements in the market, as compared to the competition's?"

**Description of the Knowledge Structure and Reasoning Processes.** After the prescreening and loan purpose review, the recommendations are derived from four critical factors: management character and willingness, financial strength, collateral, and capacity. In turn the values for each of these factors are determined by a limited number of other factors:

- *Management character and willingness* is determined by administration, organization, and procedural factors.
- *Financial strength* is determined by financial position (cash flow, liquidity, and leverage) and capital factors.
- *Collateral* is determined by marketability, availability, and appraisal value.
- *Capacity* is determined by sales and marketing, operational, and competitive characteristics.

Additional levels of influencing factors are needed as indicated in Figs. 9-10 and 9-11. Other components of the system have similar additional influencing factors. If-then rules are used to determine the values at each stage. The inference engine uses backward chaining. The values are measured for each of the factors in the reasoning chain as "yes, no"; "strong, average, weak"; or an "either, or" answer, as indicated in Figs. 9-9, 9-10, and 9-11.

Later versions of the system made use of certainty factors and were capable of accessing on-line data bases and financial simulation models for financial analysis information.

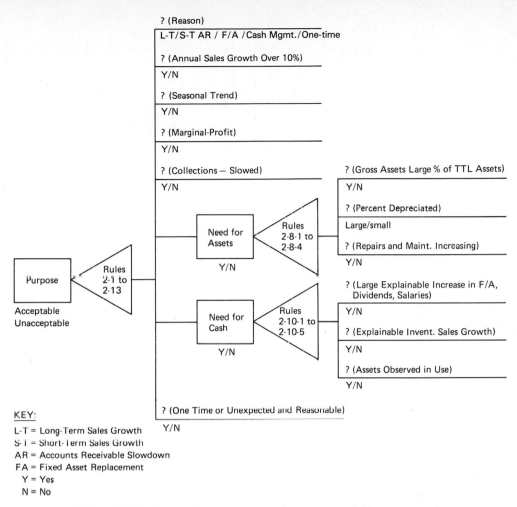

**FIGURE 9-10  Dependency diagram for commercial loan screening system—loan purpose segment (initial prototype).**

## Dependency Diagrams

Figure 9-9 gives the overall dependency diagram for the system.   Figures 9-10 and 9-11 show dependency diagrams for two segments of the system—loan purpose and management character or willingness.

## Decision Charts

Figure 9-12 shows a sample decision chart for a segment of the final rule set of the system.   There is a decision chart for every rule-set triangle in the decision chart.

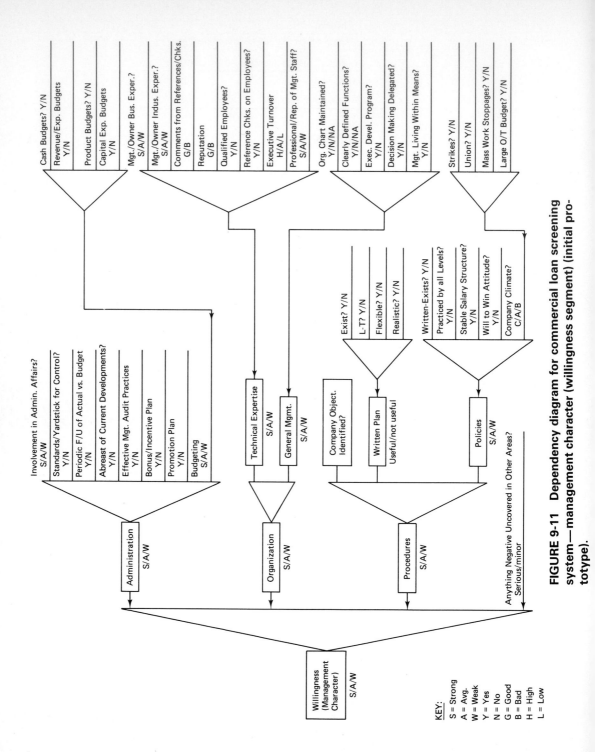

**FIGURE 9-11 Dependency diagram for commercial loan screening system—management character (willingness segment) (initial prototype).**

KEY:

S = Strong
A = Avg.
W = Weak
Y = Yes
N = No
G = Good
B = Bad
H = High
L = Low

206

If

| Screening | 1 | 2 | 3 | 4 | 5 | 6 | 7 | 8 | 9 | 10 | 11 | 12 | 13 | 14 | 15 | 16 | 17 | 18 | 19 | 20 | 21 | 22 | 23 | 24 |
|---|---|---|---|---|---|---|---|---|---|---|---|---|---|---|---|---|---|---|---|---|---|---|---|---|
| | ap | ap | ap | ap | ap | ap | ap | ap | ap | ap | ap | ap | ap | ap | ap | ap | ap | ap | ap | ap | ap | ap | ap | ap |
| Purpose | ac | ac | ac | ac | ac | ac | ac | ac | ac | ac | ac | ac | ac | ac | ac | ac | ac | ac | ac | ac | ac | ac | ac | ac |
| Management Character | S | S | S | S | A | A | A | A | W | A | A | A | W | W | W | W | W | W | S | S | S | W | W | W |
| Financial Strength | S | A | S | S | S | A | A | A | S | W | A | A | A | A | W | W | S | S | W | W | W | A | S | W |
| Collateral | S | S | A | A | S | S | S | A | S | S | W | A | S | S | A | S | W | S | S | A | W | A | A | A |
| Capacity | S | S | S | S | A | S | S | S | S | S | S | W | S | S | A | S | A | A | A | A | A | W | A | W |
| Recommendation | 1 | 1 | 1 | 1 | 1 | 1 | 6 | 5 | 6 | 3 | 5 | 3 | 4 | 2 | 2 | 2 | 2 | 2 | 4 | 5 | 3 | 2 | 3 | 2 |

Then

Key:

S = strong
A = average
W = weak
ac = acceptable
ap = applicable

Recommendations:

1. Acceptable credit risk, approve the loan as requested.
2. Poor credit risk, reject loan request.
3. Questionable credit risk, reduce amount of loan requested.
4. Questionable credit risk, change the term of the loan requested.
5. Questionable credit risk, modify collateral requirements.
6. Questionable credit risk, increase the interest rate.

**FIGURE 9-12  Decision chart for sample final rule set (partial) of commercial loan screening system.**

```
                    /*  Rule Set One: Screening  */

rule-1-1:if loan-type = consumer or
            loan-type = government or
            business-type = new or
            secured = no or
            loan size = over or
            loan size = under or
            target market = unacceptable
         then screening = not-applicable

rule-1-2:if loan-type = business and
            business-type = existing and
            secured = yes and
            loan-size = between and
            target-market = acceptable
         then screening = applicable


                /*  Rule Set Two:  Purpose (selections)  */

rule-2-1:if reason = long-term-sales-growth and
            annual-sales-growth = no
         then purpose = unacceptable

rule-2-2:if reason = long-term-sales-growth and
            annual-sales-growth = yes
         then purpose = acceptable

rule-2-4:if reason = short-term-sales-growth and
            seasonal-trend = yes and
            marginal-profit = no
         then purpose = unacceptable

rule-2-5:if reason = short-term-sales-growth and
            seasonal-trend = yes and
            marginal-profit = yes
         then purpose = acceptable

rule-2-8-2:if percent-of-total = yes and
              percent-depreciated = small and
              increased-repairs = no
           then need-for-assets = no

rule-2-8-3:if percent-of-total = yes and
              percent-depreciated = small and
              increased-repairs = yes
           then need-for-assets = yes

rule-2-9:if reason = fixed-assets and
            need-for-assets = yes
         then purpose = acceptable

rule-2-10:if reason = cash-management and
             need-for-cash = no
          then purpose = unacceptable
```

*(continued)*

**FIGURE 9-13  Sample of knowledge-base rules and questions.**

```
rule-2-10-3:if assets-dividends-salary = no and
             inventory-sales-growth = yes and
             assets-in-use = no
         then need-for-cash = no

rule-2-10-4:if assets-dividends-salary = no and
             inventory-sales-growth = yes and
             assets-in-use = yes
         then need-for-cash = yes


    /*  Rule Set One: Screening - Questions (selections)  */

question(loan-type) =
  'What type of loan request is this? (consumer/business/
  government)'.

legalvals(loan-type) = [consumer, business, government].

question(business-type) =
  'Is the loan applicant a new or existing business? (new/
  existing)'.

legalvals(business-type) = [new, existing].

question(loan-size) =
  'Is the amount of the loan under $250,000, between $250,000 and
  $2.5 million or over $2.5 million? (under/between/over)'.

legalvals(loan-size) = [under, between, over].

question(target-market) =
  'Is the loan applicant a business in an acceptable or
  unacceptable market in relation to the bank's lending policy?
  (acceptable/unacceptable).'

legalvals(target-market) = [acceptable, unacceptable].

    /*  Rule Set Two: Purpose - Questions (selection)  */

question(reason) =
  'As a result of your investigation of the loan applicant, what
  have you determined to be the purpose of the loan? (long-term-
  sales-growth/short-term-sales-growth/ accounts-receivable/
  fixed-assets/ cash-management/ one-time).'

legalvals(reason) = [long-term-sales-growth, short-term-sales-
  growth, accounts-receivable, fixed-assets, cash-management,
  one-time].

question(annual-sales-growth) =
  'Has the applicant experienced annual sales growth of over 10%
  for each of the last three years? (yes/no)'.

legalvals(annual-sales-growth) = [yes, no].
```

**FIGURE 9-13** *(continued)*

## Designing and Constructing the Knowledge Base

Rules and questions were developed from the situation study. They were based on the system developer's analysis of how an expert commercial loan officer might actually go about making such decisions.

A segment of the prototype system's knowledge base is given in Fig. 9-13. The expert system shell used is M.1. As with the other systems discussed in this book, subsequent prototypes within the system were done on GURU.

Two very simple introductory and concluding panels were created for the prototype system.

## THE FUTURE: INTEGRATED KNOWLEDGE-BASED AND CONVENTIONAL COMPUTER SYSTEMS

Like strategic planning in business, strategic planning knowledge-based systems have their most useful, practical, and immediate applications as segments of *integrated* systems.

Strategic planning is an integrated decision process. Planners weigh qualitative factors and come to decisions based on judgment. These judgments are not made in a vacuum, however. They are integrated decisions, involving economic data bases and financial planning simulations that support these qualitative judgments.

Many knowledge-based systems for strategic company planning replicate these actual planning experiences. As might be expected, the most successful practical applications of knowledge-based strategic planning systems technology so far have been as so-called "strategic components" to conventional computer systems.

For example, the system described in this chapter has a component for evaluating the anticipated strategic position and strength of companies applying for commercial bank loans. A second module evaluates management character, and a third studies the strategic fit of specific loan applications to overall bank strategic objectives and policies. All of these strategic decision modules are integrated with conventional (procedural) computerized financial planning and quantitative analysis software applications. The *integrated* system can make reasonably sophisticated loan decisions consistently.

Similar commercially available integrated systems have been developed for capital investment planning (Management Advisor), personal investment planning (PlanPower), and company financial planning and analysis (Alacrity). Many other knowledge-based systems, including ones developed by the author, exist today in these areas.

Knowledge-based strategic planning systems have also been integrated into decision support systems for marketing. In these systems decisions involving determining target market, product and media appropriate for a specific company, market, and competitive environments are supported by knowledge-based systems that are integrated with conventional computerized data bases.

The *stand-alone* knowledge-based systems described elsewhere in this book do not seem to have economical applications to overall strategic planning in large companies. Although much expanded versions of these systems can assist in doing such work at large companies, their costs exceed their benefits. The *stand-alone* strategic-planning applications described in this book seem to be most useful for smaller company planning, especially in the new venture and market analysis areas.

Based on the systems development research work and actual applications developed thus far, it is fair to conclude that the greatest areas for future applications of knowledge-based systems technology to strategic company planning will be

- As limited scope *stand-alone* systems designed for overall strategy development and planning for smaller companies or for strategic business units of larger companies, such as those described in Chapters 18 and 21, and
- As segments, modules, or "strategic front ends" of a wide range of *integrated* conventional financial, marketing, and operations computer systems, such as the ones described in this chapter.

## REVIEW QUESTIONS

1. Finish the knowledge base for the system (or any segment of the system) partially documented in this chapter and enter it into the expert system shell you have.

2. Reformulate a decision situation for one of the potential areas for knowledge-based systems development given in the "Narrowing the Focus" section and elsewhere in this chapter.

3. Describe ways in which you might integrate this system with conventional financial analysis computer systems.

4. Describe the qualitative and strategic components of the system described in this chapter. In what ways do they differ from conventional computer systems?

5. Why is it important to investigate a loan applicant's ability to take advantage of opportunities and meet key market success requirements when considering their loan applications?

6. What are the main factors affecting the loan decision? Describe the importance of each in making the decision.

## REFERENCES

*A Banker's Guide to Commercial Loan Analysis*, Washington, DC: American Bankers Assoc., 1977.

Behrens, R.H., *Commercial Loan Officer's Handbook: From Basic Concepts to Advanced Techniques*, Boston, MA: Banker's Publishing, 1985.

Bosma, A.R., "Lending: Determining Quality in the Loan Portfolio," *The Bankers Magazine*, vol. 170, March-April 1987.

Conlin, P.G. *Commercial Loan Review Procedures*, Philadelphia, PA: Robert Morris, 1978.

Fitch, T.P., "The Computer That Will End the Bank Loan Officer's Job," *Bankers Monthly*, vol. 104, March 1987.

Glassman, C.A., "Measuring and Managing Small Business Risk," *Magazine of Bank Administration*, vol. 63, January 1987.

Hillman, W.C., *Commercial Loan Documentation*, 2nd ed., New York: Practicing Law Institute, 1986.

Sihler, W.W., ed., *Classics in Commercial Bank Lending*, Philadelphia, PA: Robert Morris, 1981.

Sihler, W.W., and C. Meibery, *Casebook in Commercial Lending*, Englewood Cliffs, NJ: Reston Publishing, 1985.

# 10

# A Capital Investment Planning System

This chapter describes the development of a knowledge-based system for capital investment planning for manufacturing. The discussion is divided into four sections:

- The overall situation under study: understanding the expert's domain
- Studying the decision to be prototyped
- Documenting the prototype system
- Enhancements and extensions of the prototype system

The early sections of this report describe the overall situation for which the system is being developed. The later sections describe the situation analysis and situation model development and the development of a prototype system.

## THE OVERALL SITUATION UNDER STUDY: UNDERSTANDING THE EXPERT'S DOMAIN

The discussion in this section covers

- Selecting a decision area to work on
- Probing how the situation works and how decisions are made
- Narrowing the focus

## Selecting a Decision Area to Work on

The general area under study is capital investment planning in the manufacturing area. Manufacturing includes all the operations required to produce a product, including facilities, equipment, production, materials, and manpower.

Capital investment planning was selected as the subject for knowledge-based systems development for several reasons:

- Capital investment decisions are made by a few selected experts in a company. This expertise is, therefore, expensive and scarce.
- Capital investment planning decisions involve informed judgment.
- These decisions can be made in a reasonable amount of time and are fully understood.
- The expertise can be needed in several locations.

## Probing How the Situation Works and How Decisions Are Made

Capital investment planning is the process of determining how to allocate a firm's capital to investment projects that will support future business operations. There are several reasons why capital investment planning is considered to be so important:

- The magnitude of a single investment
- The complexity of choices
- Uncertainty of the future
- Irreversibility of decisions
- The high cost of mistakes

Because of its scope and importance to top management, capital investment planning involves more than just financial analysis decisions. Capital investment planning also involves qualitative considerations needed to assure that each capital investment decision is consistent with overall manufacturing and corporate strategies. Manufacturing decisions can be divided into five areas, as shown in Fig. 10-1.

- *Facility* decisions concern whether or not to build or purchase new plants as well as decisions regarding the product or products that will be produced in the facility and the facility location and size.
- *Equipment* decisions affect the type of machinery and tooling that will be used in the production process.
- *Production capacity* decisions link product demand requirements to equipment and facility decisions. Product demand defines the type and timing of production capacity needed, which in turn determines equipment and facility purchases required.
- *Vertical integration* decisions determine the number of production and distribution stages a firm will engage in.

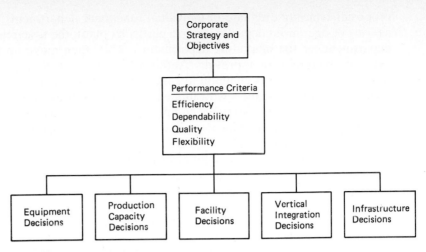

FIGURE 10-1 Situation overview—types of manufacturing decisions made within the framework of corporate strategy.

- *Manufacturing infrastructure* decisions determine the specific policies for production planning and control, quality control, inventory, and logistic systems required for manufacturing to function as a coordinated unit.

Individual capital investment decisions are evaluated in terms of established performance criteria, such as

- *Efficiency*, which includes both cost efficiency and capital efficiency, is generally measured by return on sales, return on assets, and return on investment.
- *Dependability* includes the consistency of the products produced as well as delivery and price factors.
- *Quality* concerns the product quality level standard.
- *Flexibility* includes flexibility in product and volume output.

Making capital investment decisions requires the balancing of many of these strategic performance criteria. For example, a proposal to invest in an automated high speed production line may increase efficiency both by decreasing downtime arising from breakdowns and by increasing the number of units produced per minute. In addition to reducing production costs per unit, it will also increase production capacity. However, the faster production process may also result in a lower product *quality standard* as well as a greater *inconsistency* in the manufacturing process. In addition, the highly automated line may also decrease *flexibility* due to difficulties in changing over the line to handle different products. The investment decision to increase efficiency may, therefore, result in a reduction in dependability, quality, and flexibility. For these reasons capital investment planning decisions require strategic judgment.

In large, diversified corporations, such as the one under study here, capital proposals typically originate in individual functional departments, such as the engineering or operations departments in a particular plant, the research and development department, or the marketing department. They then move up the organization's executive hierarchy for approval. Authorization of all projects that meet a minimum return on investment is common in companies with strong cash flows. However, it is important for companies with limited capital to approve only those projects that are necessary to further strategic company plans or cut costs significantly.

Capital investment planning in a manufacturing operation involves feasibility studies of marketing, technical, and financial factors, as seen in Fig. 10-2. These analyses allow problems and solutions to surface.

Marketing studies and technical analyses are performed within the context of enterprise-wide company strategy. These strategic factors include

- □ *Objectives,* such as strategic marketing, technical, and financial standards of performance. Objectives are often expressed as increasing new market penetration or positions, increasing productivity in different areas, or increasing the overall rate of return on capital.
- □ *Needs*, such as strategic requirements for survival, growth, or simply for continuity of operations. Needs may be defined as sustaining a market share for existing products, maintaining the competitive edge in technological innovation, or establishing a consistent cash flow.

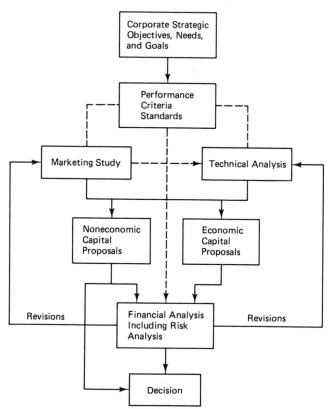

**FIGURE 10-2 Preliminary decision situation diagram for capital investment planning.**

□ *Goals*, such as overall concrete targets that in total represent the financial impact of a firm's strategies. Goals are usually expressed in quantitative terms such as a designated market share percentage, a desired number of units produced per period, or a required rate of investment return.

Investment proposals are evaluated as to their strategic, operational, and financial impacts. For instance, investments in new product development are evaluated in terms of forecasted market penetrations and position objectives. A decision to build a new plant is evaluated in terms of maintaining a technological edge and increasing productivity as well as reducing costs and increasing anticipated overall forecasted return on investment.

The *marketing study* defines the anticipated future size of the market and makes sales forecasts. It establishes if there is a viable market for the product and that the product can successfully compete. It involves

□ *Defining the market*—The market segment to be served is identified and defined by geographic, demographic, and other related strategic factors.

□ *Estimating market potential*—Competitive market data is analyzed in order to forecast the potential size of the market and the anticipated company share of that market.

□ *Analyzing competition and pricing*—Information on the competition is analyzed, and a competitive pricing policy is determined.

□ *Estimating sales*—Alternative distribution and sales systems, and their effect on sales volume, are analyzed. The overall sales volume and the market share are estimated. Unit sales and sales revenue by product and by geographic area are estimated.

□ *Estimating costs*—Sales (advertising, promotion, selling, and aftersales services) and distribution costs are estimated.

The marketing study provides a necessary input for the technical analysis, since it identifies future demand and cost requirements that must be met by the manufacturing function.

The *technical analysis* is performed by the engineering and operations divisions of a company and involves

□ *Determining capacity requirements*—The production schedule to meet the market demands is determined. The schedule is developed based on a one, two, or three shift operation.

□ *Specifying the production system*—All purchased input materials needed for production are specified as are the quantities needed and the sources of supply. The production process that converts purchased materials into finished products is defined. Equipment for each stage of the process is specified. Labor requirements are determined and an organizational plan detailing staff and supervisory needs is compiled.

□ *Determining space needs*—Space requirements for storage of raw materials, for other inputs, and for the finished products is determined. Space for each work station is also estimated, by considering physical equipment, worker and work space, and in-process material storage.

□ *Selecting location*—Special structural (for example, high ceilings, flooring, or controlled atmosphere) and site (for example, fuel storage, rail and/or highway access, or waste storage) requirements are determined. Location alternatives are selected based on a variety of factors (for example, taxes, governmental controls, labor factors, utilities, waste disposal, market factors, transportation, and the like) and analyzed for their effects on costs.

□ *Estimating costs*—Costs for fixed investments, preproduction capital expenditures, and factory costs are estimated.

It is during the technical analysis that present manufacturing operations are reviewed to determine if they are able to support the company's marketing objectives with existing production operations. In addition, other production methods and logistic (for example, management and flow of materials) areas are continually analyzed to determine where improvements could possibly be made.

Once it has been determined that a capital investment is needed to meet corporate and marketing objectives, that investment is subjected to financial analysis. *Financial analysis* represents the culmination of capital investment planning efforts. During this analysis

□ *Costs are estimated*—The market study provides estimates of sales income and of selling and distribution costs. The technical analysis provides cost estimates for fixed assets and operating costs. Remaining cost elements, such as general and administrative overhead costs, are estimated. The project financing is determined and the cost of this financing is estimated.

□ *Financial statements are prepared*—Cash flows are estimated and organized into cash flow tables. Other projected financial statements are constructed.

□ *Profitability is evaluated*—Projects are evaluated based on selected financial criteria. Each investment proposal attempts to meet a minimum return on investment criteria. Several financial indicators are used to evaluate investment proposals, the more common methods being discounted cash flow yield, net present value, and payback period.

□ *Risk analysis is performed*—Each investment proposal is subjected to risk analysis, since virtually all investment decisions are made under conditions of uncertainty. For each investment proposal assumptions that are considered crucial to the proposal are identified, the likelihood of them changing is assessed, and the resulting effect of changes on profitability is evaluated.

It is in the financial analysis stage that the final decision on a capital investment proposal is made. The proposal is either rejected or accepted based on a minimum rate of return, or it is returned to the marketing or technical people for reassessment and revision.

## Narrowing the Focus

Each company has its own method of classifying capital investment proposals. One common method is to distinguish between economic proposals and noneconomic proposals, as shown in Fig. 10-2.

*Noneconomic capital projects* are compulsory investments with little or no direct financial return. These projects typically are required for the continuity of operations, such as when funds are allocated to replace a collapsed roof or a burned-out engine. They may also involve compliance objectives, such as internal policy (product quality or working conditions) or environmental policies (product formulation or production process changes). Noneconomic projects may or may not be subjected to strict financial analysis techniques, depending on their importance to the continuity of operations. These decisions are typically simpler, involving the fastest and cheapest method available for completing the project.

*Economic capital investment proposals,* those projects whose costs and benefits are primarily economic, usually involve short- and long-term revenue-enhancing or cost-reducing investments. Economic proposals require more judgmental reasoning. These investment decisions may involve improving operations, such as replacement of obsolete assets; purchasing new innovative equipment; building an entirely new plant; or reducing quality control costs or overhead costs.

For purposes of developing a knowledge-based prototype system, the focus will be narrowed to economically based capital investment proposals for new process equipment that will expand production capacity. These decisions involve strategic, operational, and financial analysis.


## STUDYING THE DECISION TO BE PROTOTYPED

The specific situation under study is whether or not to invest capital in new process equipment in order to expand current production capacity. The situation analysis that follows is structured in a way that provides models useful for later prototype systems development. It is based on observations of financial planners at work in typical decision situations.

There were several reasons why this situation was chosen for prototype development: (1) It provides a quick way to prototype, since the rules are clearly defined. (2) The prototype is part of a larger system and the pattern of its decision is similar to other decisions made within the overall system. (3) The system developer intended to use the system at the company under study.

Based on related work experience in addition to discussions with several capital planning experts, the following appeared to be the general approach to making decisions in this area at the company for which the prototype system was being developed.


### Defining the Knowledge Needed

An outline of the kinds of information required (and so gathered) to make this decision is given in the structured situation diagram in Fig. 10-3. They were

- □ Capacity demand requirements
- □ Primary facility's potential for new equipment investment

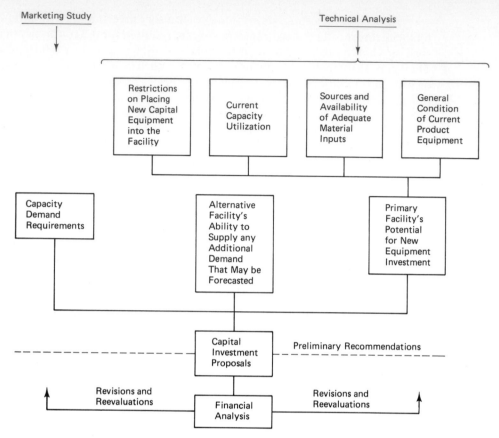

**FIGURE 10-3  An overview of a new equipment investment to expand capacity.**

□ Alternative facility's ability to supply any additional demand that may be forecasted

**Capacity demand requirements.**   Capacity requirements are determined by an in-depth marketing study.   The purpose of the market study is to establish the change in future demand requirements that is expected to be met by the facility being evaluated for new equipment investment.

Through consideration of factors such as market projections, competitive information, and the company's anticipated market share and market share strategy, the marketing division develops a marketing plan to be met by the manufacturing division.   The marketing plan is segmented geographically and is matched against the nearest production facility that produces the product being studied.

These studies are a key link between strategic marketing objectives and manufacturing capital investment decisions.   Since the market study can be extensive, during this initial phase of the prototype development study, input from the marketing analysis was limited to the key required information.

**Primary facility's potential for new equipment investment.**   Technical analysis is performed to

- Determine the current capacity utilization of existing production equipment
- Assess the availability and sources of adequate material inputs to supply proposed new equipment production capacity
- Analyze the general condition of current production equipment
- Assess the restrictions on placing new capital equipment into the facility

For example, based on this analysis the primary facility's potential for new equipment investment is strong if the current capacity of the production equipment is fully used, if raw and packing material inputs are available to supply the capacity of proposed new equipment, and if the general condition of existing equipment is determined to be only good to poor.   The primary facility's potential for investment is weak if the current capacity of production equipment is not fully used and the general condition of that equipment is determined to be excellent.   There is no potential for investment if there is substantial current idle capacity and the equipment's general condition is excellent.   In all situations, if there are site restrictions prohibiting the placement of new equipment in the facility, there is no potential for investment.

The general condition of current production equipment is analyzed through questions concerning the technological state of this equipment relative to the rest of the industry and the remaining useful life of this equipment.

Restrictions on placing new production equipment into the facility is determined by questioning the ability to place new equipment into the physical site.   In addition, environmental and health-safety restrictions are questioned.

**Alternative facility's ability to supply any additional demand that may be forecasted.**   A large manufacturing company often has several facilities serving different geographic regions.   Informed judgment is necessary to evaluate the possibility of allocating production volume to an alternative facility located outside the geographic region served by the primary facility.

In this study an alternative facility is *not* being evaluated for capital investment. Technical analysis is performed *only* to determine the alternative facility's ability to supply any additional demand that may be forecasted with *existing* production equipment.   Questions are specifically concerned with

- The facility's production capacity—Is there significant capacity that is not being utilized?
- Material inputs—The sources and availability of additional raw and packing material inputs must be analyzed.
- Transfer costs—The cost of delivering the product to distribution points normally supplied by the primary facility are identified and studied.

For example, based on this analysis the alternative facility will be able to supply additional demand if it has significant capacity that is not being used, if it has the raw and packing material inputs to raise production capacity to full, and if the estimated transfer costs are not prohibitive (that is, unit transfer costs are less than 6 percent of unit sales revenue).   If transfer costs are excessive (greater than 6 percent of unit sales revenue in this situation), the alternative facility's ability would be limited.

Under other conditions the alternative facility's availability would be limited if it has significant capacity not being used and if transfer costs are low, but the availability of material inputs to fully raise capacity are limited.   The alternative facility would also not have the ability to supply any demand if it does not have significant unused capacity and/or input materials are not available to raise capacity enough to meet anticipated demand.

## Decision Processes Involved in Making the Final Recommendation

Figure 10-4 gives a situation model of how decisions are made in this area at the company under study.   For example, an expert will propose investing in new equipment if the following conditions are met:

- Demand requirements are expected to be significantly higher.
- Current production capacity in the primary facility is limited or is unable to meet a higher demand requirement.
- There are no restrictions on placing new equipment into the facility.

In this situation if demand is expected to grow and production capacity in the primary facility is unable to meet a greater demand, then significant sales revenue may be lost, or additional costs may be incurred in using alternative facilities.   In all situations, in order to recommend an investment, there must not be any site restrictions preventing the placement of new equipment in the facility.

In another frequently encountered decision situation, if existing equipment is old or obsolete and a higher demand is expected, then it will usually become necessary to replace that equipment, either because of the higher probability of mechanical failures or because of the incremental cost of operating inefficient operating equipment.

An expert is less inclined to recommend investing large amounts of capital in equipment if

- Demand requirements are expected to stabilize or fall.
- The production capacity of the primary facility is able to meet expected demand.
- Existing production equipment is new.
- Restrictions make it impossible to place new equipment into the primary facility.

In this situation if demand is expected to be lower, then existing equipment can meet expected demand requirements.   It is not necessary to replace equipment unless it is old and obsolete.   If the equipment is new and technologically advanced, it is

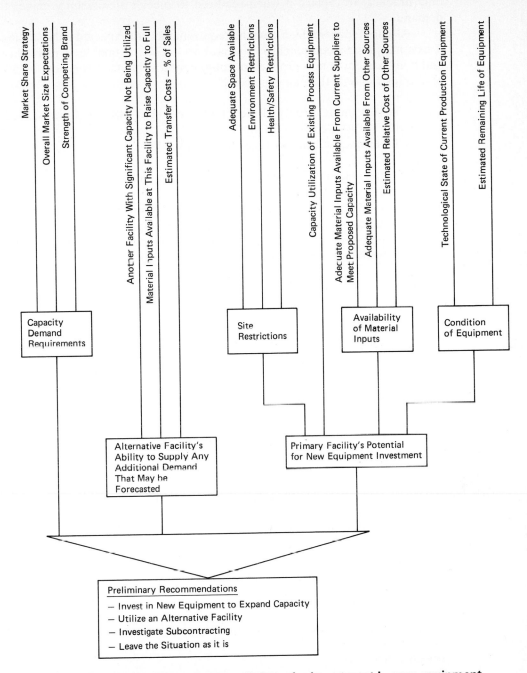

**FIGURE 10-4** Decision situation diagram for investment in new equipment to expand capacity.

only practical to replace it when required to meet a significantly higher forecasted demand.

As another example, if demand requirements are expected to be stable or higher, if existing process equipment in the primary facility is unable to meet this demand, and if investment in new production equipment for that facility is not possible because of site restrictions, then an expert will

□ Assess the feasibility of meeting the demand with an alternate facility within the corporation
□ Investigate subcontracting production

The financial implications of these recommendations are analyzed before the final decision is made, as seen earlier in Fig. 10-3. Financial analysis is not covered during this initial phase of the knowledge-based prototype development study. *Integrated* financial and strategic systems were developed later in the project.

The objective in drawing the decision model in Fig. 10-4 is to create a general model of the decisions made prior to the financial analysis. This is sometimes referred to as the "strategic front end" or "strategic component" of a computerized capital investment decision support system.

At this point the critical information or knowledge and the reasoning paths to be included in the system were deliberately limited to some of the more important ones. For example, the market analysis segment of the decision is a major, complex decision area for which an extensive knowledge-based system was developed during later stages of the project. In this initial system, however, only three input questions were included about the results of the market analysis.

Although limiting the system in this way created the danger that the system might be trivialized somewhat, such simplification was a necessary step toward testing the concept and structure of the system and developing a prototype system, within a reasonably short period of time.

## DOCUMENTING THE PROTOTYPE SYSTEM

The discussion in this section covers

□ System proposal
□ Description of the prototype system
□ Dependency diagrams
□ Decision charts
□ Designing and constructing the knowledge base

### System Proposal

The general objective of the project is to develop a knowledge-based system that assists in making a capital investment planning decision for manufacturing. The full system is designed for large manufacturing companies.

Capital investment requests are constantly submitted to corporate management for approval from various manufacturing facilities, located nationwide, at the company under study. A knowledge-based system will be beneficial in this area to enable deciding on these capital proposals more quickly and consistently.

The first phase of the project is limited to a specific situation, capital investment planning for new production equipment that will expand capacity. This first phase of the project is designed to test the feasibility of developing a larger expert knowledge-based system for capital planning and to provide a basis for further development work.

The knowledge sources used to develop the prototype system include

- On the job experience
- Management experts involved in capital planning
- Books and articles that deal with the linking of overall company strategic objectives to capital investment decisions
- Experienced knowledge engineers and system developers

### Description of the Prototype System

**System overview and objective.** The prototype system is designed to help users decide whether to invest in new equipment that will expand production capacity in a primary facility under study or to meet changing demand requirements by using other alternatives. The system asks users questions about future demand requirements, the primary facility's potential for new equipment investment, and the ability of an alternative facility to meet any additional demand requirements. The system uses if-then rules and backward chaining to reason about the information given by a user in order to reach its recommendations.

**Recommendations to be made by the system.** For prototyping purposes, the system is limited to making one of four recommendations:

- Invest in new production equipment that will expand production capacity in the so-called primary facility.
- Utilize another facility in the organization.
- Investigate subcontracting production.
- Do not invest in the new equipment.

**Nature of the user interface, including typical user dialogue.** The typical user dialogue covers three key knowledge areas.

*Capacity Demand Requirements.* This information is obtained from marketing managers and from published sales forecasts. Some typical questions might be "Based on strategic marketing studies, is the overall market for this type of product expected to grow, stabilize, or decline?" and "In your estimate, what percentage of the market is the major competitive brand expected to hold in the near future?"

*Primary Facility's Potential for New Equipment Investment.* This information may be obtained from consulting with engineers and operations people who have analyzed the facility's production operation. Sample questions include "Is the capacity utilization of existing production equipment full, limited (70 to 80 percent being utilized) or idle (less than 70 percent being used)?", "What is the remaining useful life of current production equipment?", and "Is there a health or safety Occupational Safety and Health Administration (OSHA) restriction that will prevent placing new process equipment into the facility?"

*Alternate Facility's Ability to Supply Any Additional Demand That May Be Forecasted.* This information can be obtained from published manufacturing performance reports or from discussions with manufacturing people in the alternative facility. Typical questions include "Will raw and packing material inputs be available from suppliers of the alternative facility under study to raise capacity to full utilization?" and "What are the estimated transfer costs per unit as a percentage of sales per unit?"

**Description of the knowledge structure and reasoning process.** The recommendations made by the prototype system are based upon three critical factors: expected capacity demand requirements, the primary facility's potential for new equipment investment, and an alternate facility's ability to supply any additional demand that may be forecasted. In turn, the values for each of these factors is based upon a limited number of other factors:

- □ The expected *capacity demand requirements* are determined by the forecasted size of the overall market for this type of product, company market share objectives, and the expected strength of the major competitive brands in this market.
- □ The *primary facility's potential for investment* is determined by the facility's current capacity utilization, the availability of material inputs to meet the proposed new capacity, the condition of existing production equipment, and any restrictions on placing new equipment in the facility.
- □ The *alternate facility's ability* to supply any additional demand is determined by current excess production capacity, transfer costs, and material inputs.

If-then rules are used to determine the values at each stage. The inference engine uses backward chaining. The values are measured for each of the factors in the reasoning chain as "significantly higher, a little higher, similar, or lower"; "strong, average, weak"; or "yes, limited, no"; or "aggressive, stable, nonaggressive"; or "available or unavailable."

## Dependency Diagrams

Figure 10-5 shows the dependency diagram for the prototype knowledge-based system for capital investment planning for manufacturing equipment to expand capacity. It is a summary outline of the questions, rules, knowledge segments and their interrelationships, values, and recommendations within the system.

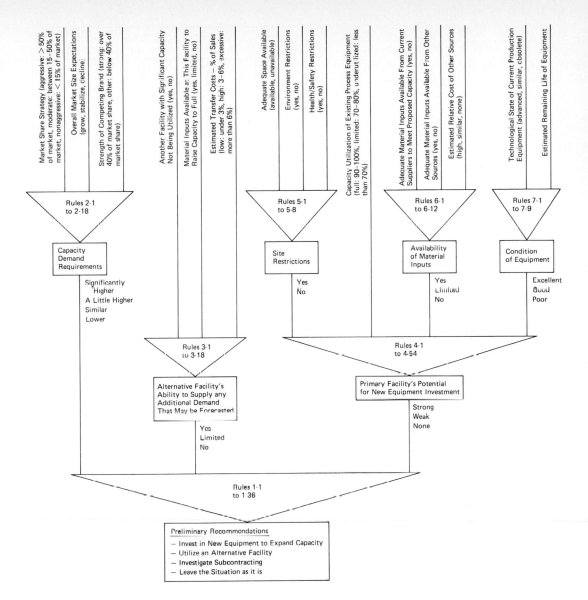

**FIGURE 10-5 Dependency diagram for investment in new equipment to expand capacity—initial prototype.**

## Decision Charts

Figure 10-6 shows a sample decision chart from the prototype system. There is a decision chart for every rule-set triangle in the dependency diagram.

| | RULES | | | | | | | | | | | | | | | | | |
|---|---|---|---|---|---|---|---|---|---|---|---|---|---|---|---|---|---|---|
| | 1 | 2 | 3 | 4 | 5 | 6 | 7 | 8 | 9 | 10 | 11 | 12 | 13 | 14 | 15 | 16 | 17 | 18 |
| **IF** Significant Capacity Not Being Utilized | Y | Y | Y | N | N | N | Y | Y | Y | N | N | N | Y | Y | Y | N | N | N |
| Availability of Material Inputs | Y | L | N | Y | L | N | Y | L | N | Y | L | N | Y | L | N | Y | L | N |
| Level of Transfer Costs | E | E | E | E | E | E | H | H | H | H | H | H | L | L | L | L | L | L |
| **THEN** The Facility's Ability to Supply Additional Demand is | | | | | | | | | | | | | | | | | | |
| Yes | | | | | | | X | | | | | | X | | | | | |
| Limited | X | | | | | | | X | | | | | | X | | | | |
| No | | X | X | X | X | X | | | X | X | X | X | | | X | X | X | X |

RECOMMENDATIONS

KEY:
Y = Yes
N = No
E = Excessive
H = High
L = Low

FIGURE 10-6  Sample decision chart for third rule set.  Determining the alternative facility's ability to supply any additional demand—initial prototype.

## Designing and Constructing the Knowledge Base

Rules and questions were developed from the situation study—from the system developer's analysis of how a capital planning expert might go about making such a decision.  A sample segment of the prototype system's knowledge base is given in Fig. 10-7.  The expert system shell used is M.1.

The if-then rules in the knowledge base in Fig. 10-7 match those specified in the decision charts shown.  The rules were written to show the relationships outlined in the dependency diagram in Fig. 10-5.  They use the values shown there and in the decision chart.  The questions are those indicated in the dependency diagram.

RULES:

```
                        /* rule set four */
              /* primary facility reason for investmnt */


rule-4-1:
      if current-capacity = full and
         input-materials = yes and
         equip-cond = excellent and
         site-restrictions = no
      then invest-potential = weak.

rule-4-2:
      if current-capacity = limited and
         input-materials = yes and
         equip-cond = excellent and
         site-restrictions = no
      then invest-potential = weak.

rule-4-3:
      if current-capacity = idle and
         input-materials = yes and
         equip-cond = excellent and
         site-restrictions = no
      then invest-potential = none.

rule-4-4:
      if current-capacity = full and
         input-materials = limited and
         equip-cond = excellent and
         site-restrictions = no
      then invest-potential = weak.

rule-4-5:
      if current-capacity = limited and
         input-materials = limited and
         equip-cond = excellent and
         site-restrictions = no
      then invest-potential = weak.

rule-4-6:
      if current-capacity = idle and
         input-materials = limited and
         equip-cond = excellent and
         site-restrictions = no
      then invest-potential = none.

rule-4-7:
      if current-capacity = full and
         input-materials = no and
         equip-cond = excellent and
         site-restrictions = no
      then invest-potential = none.
```

*(continued)*

FIGURE 10-7 Sample knowledge base segment: rules and questions for capital investment planning system—equipment (initial prototype).

```
rule-4-8:
    if current-capacity = limited and
       input-materials = no and
       equip-cond = excellent and
       site-restrictions = no
    then invest-potential = none.

rule-4-9:
    if current-capacity = idle and
       input-materials = no and
       equip-cond = excellent and
       site-restrictions = no
    then invest-potential = none.

rule-4-10:
    if current-capacity = full and
       input-materials = yes and
       equip-cond = good and
       site-restrictions = no
    then invest-potential = strong.

rule-4-11:
    if current-capacity = limited and
       input-materials = yes and
       equip-cond = good and
       site-restrictions = no
    then invest-potential = weak.

QUESTIONS:

question(space) = [nl,nl,nl,nl,nl,nl,nl,nl,nl,
'Does the facility being evaluated for new equipment
investment have adequate space readily available to install
the proposed new process equipment?',nl,nl,nl,nl,nl,nl].

legalvals(space) = [available, unavailable].

question(environ-restrict) = [nl,nl,nl,nl,nl,nl,nl,
'Is there any environmental restriction, such as waste
disposal regulations or pollution controls, which will
prevent the installation of new production equipment being
proposed to expand capacity?',nl,nl,nl,nl,nl,nl].

legalvals(environ-restrict) = [yes, no].

question(health-restrict) = [nl,nl,nl,nl,nl,nl,nl,nl,
'Is there any health and/or safety restriction (OSHA) which
will prevent the installation of new production equipment
being proposed to expand capacity?',nl,nl,nl,nl,nl,nl].

legalvals(health-restrict) = [yes, no].
```

**FIGURE 10-7** *(continued)*

## ENHANCEMENTS AND EXTENSIONS OF THE PROTOTYPE SYSTEM

The prototype system was intentionally limited in order to test the basic concept of the system in a reasonable period of time. During prototype development several areas were identified for possible extension and enhancement of the system.

The marketing planning segment was expanded substantially, to incorporate strategic planning and forecasting capabilities.

Alternative reasoning paths were developed. For example, as for site restrictions, alternative ways to overcome specific site restrictions are evaluated in subsequent versions of the system, as are mixed solutions, where demand is partially supplied by subcontracting or alternative facilities.

In the capital investment planning area, as in the commercial loan approval and personal investment planning areas, there are a number of commercially available *integrated* financial (quantitative) and strategic (qualitative) computer decision support systems. They combine knowledge-based systems technology with conventional computer technology. Similar financial analysis capabilities were added in later phases of this project.

## REVIEW QUESTIONS

1. Complete the knowledge-based system (or any segment of the system) partially documented in this chapter and enter it into the expert system shell you have.

2. Develop a knowledge-based system for any other area of capital investment planning, either within the equipment acquisition area or within other capital investment planning areas, such as facilities acquisition. Be sure to pay particular attention to developing detailed structured scenarios of typical decisions as well as detailed diagrams of the decision situation for the project of your choosing.

3. Describe the ways in which the structured situation analysis was and was not similar in the two system development situations described thus far in PART TWO.

4. Why is capital investment planning important? What are some of its qualitative considerations?

5. What are some of the performance criteria evaluated for individual capital investment decisions?

6. What is the purpose of the *Marketing Study*? What does it involve?

7. What is involved in the *Technical Analysis*?

8. Describe *Financial Analysis* and the areas involved in it for capital investment decisions.

9. What are non-economic capital proposals? Why do they usually require less analysis than economic capital investment proposals?

10. Describe economic capital investment proposals and what they involve.

11. What conditions would lead to the recommendation of investing in new equipment?

## REFERENCES

Bhandari, S.B., "Discounted Payback: A Criterion for Capital Investment Decisions," *Journal of Small Business Management*, vol. 24, April 1986.

Bierman, H., and S. Smidt, *The Capital Budgeting Decision—Economic Analysis of Investment Projects.* New York: MacMillan, 1984.

Brigham, E.F., *Fundamentals of Financial Management,* Hinsdale, IL: The Dryden Press, 1984.

Campanella, F.W., "Spending To Make It: Heavy Capital Spending Aids Fortunes of Culp, Fabric Maker," *Barrons,* vol. 67, Feb. 9, 1987.

Clifton, D., and D. Fyffe, *Project Feasibility Analysis: A Guide to Profitable New Ventures,* New York: John Wiley and Sons, 1977.

Coulthurst, N.J., "The Application of the Incremental Principle in Capital Investment Project Evaluation," *Accounting and Business Research,* vol. 16, 1986.

Cowen, S.S., "Five Flaws in Evaluating Capital Expenditures," *Business Horizons,* vol. 30, March-April 1987.

Finlay, M., "Guide to Corporate Facility Planners and Major Investments," *Site Selection Handbook,* vol. 32, February 1987.

Hodgetts, R.M., *Introduction to Business,* Reading, MA: Addison-Wesley, 1984.

Kaufman, M., ed., *The Capital Budgeting Handbook,* Homewood, IL: Dow Jones-Irwin, 1986.

Smith, G.W., *Engineering Economy: Analysis of Capital Expenditures,* 4th ed. Iowa City, IA: Iowa State University Press, 1987.

Wallace, W.A., and J.J. Wallace, *Practise Case for Auditing,* New York: MacMillan, 1986.

Woolf, E., *Advanced Auditing and Investigations,* Philadelphia, PA: Trans-Atlantic Publications, 1985.

# 11

# An External Auditing System

This chapter describes the development of a knowledge-based system to assist in auditing a firm's financial statements for compliance. The topics covered are

- The situation under study: understanding the expert's domain
- Studying the decision to be prototyped
- Documenting the prototype system

The viewpoint in this chapter is that of an external auditing firm or an individual certified public accountant (CPA).

## THE SITUATION UNDER STUDY: UNDERSTANDING THE EXPERT'S DOMAIN

The discussion in this section covers

- Selecting a decision area to work on
- Probing how the situation works and how decisions are made
- Narrowing the focus

### Selecting a Decision Area to Work On

The general area under study is auditing. For purposes of this study an *audit* is defined as an objective evaluation of the financial condition of a company. An auditor obtains and evaluates evidence to issue an unbiased opinion on the fairness with which a company presents their financial condition.

## Probing How the Situation Works and How Decisions Are Made

The audit process, as outlined in Fig. 11-1, is governed by generally accepted auditing standards (GAAS). Each segment of the audit must be performed in accordance to these standards.

The audit process ideally begins before year end with *planning the audit*. This phase covers the screening process that includes

- □ *Client selection*, which involves obtaining general information about the industry and specific information about the client. At this point, a client company's management integrity is assessed by an auditor to determine the risks involved in undertaking the audit.
- □ *Auditor competence*, which involves determining an auditor's ability to handle the assignment. Staffing, competence, timing, auditor independence, and scope of the assignment are considered here.

A *preliminary written audit program* is developed after an auditor accepts an engagement. This program outlines the procedures that are to be followed throughout the audit. It is modified as the audit progresses, depending on the findings at different stages of the audit. It also aids an auditor to supervise assistants, if any are involved in the audit.

*Preliminary review procedures* are also specified. These procedures would ideally be completed by fiscal year end. They involve

- □ *Client considerations*—In general, are accounting policies and procedures followed in compliance with generally accepted accounting principles (GAAP)? Are there any related party transactions? Are there items in the financial statements likely to need adjustments? Is the client providing assistance in the collection of necessary data?
- □ *Audit considerations*—Is the type, scope, and timing of the audit adequate to enable issuing a timely audit opinion? What is your preliminary assessment of the existing internal controls? Is an audit report to be given?
- □ *Detailed planning*—Is there a need for specialists, consultants, or assistance from the client's internal auditors? Can you meet the staff requirements necessary to complete the audit in a timely manner? Did you question the client about any significant current developments?
- □ *Documentation review*—Have you reviewed significant correspondence, prior year work papers and financial statements, and current interim statements?

After considering these questions, the auditor determines if the original audit plan needs to be revised, based on the auditor's assessment of materiality and risk. *Materiality and risk* are valuated at this point and continually throughout the audit. Materiality is the degree of omission or misstatement that would influence the judg-

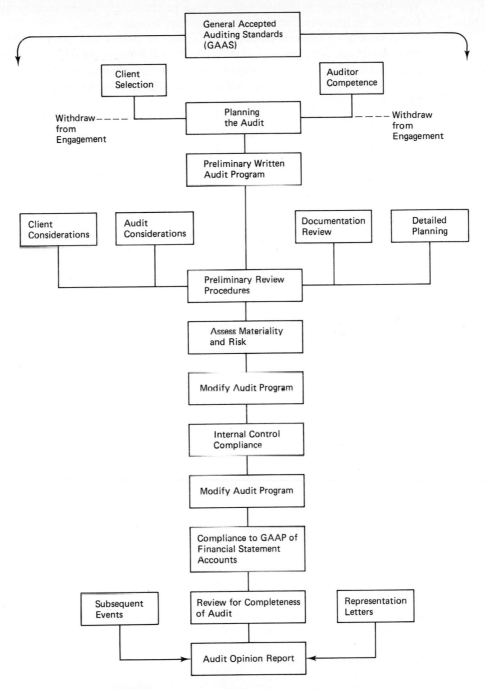

**FIGURE 11-1 Overview of the audit process.**

ment of a reasonable person relying on the information in the financial statements. The risk involved is that an auditor may unknowingly fail to modify the opinion on financial statements that contain materiality misstatement.

*Review of internal control compliance* is performed after preliminary review procedures are completed. This determines if internal control procedures are being followed as prescribed by management. A client's internal control procedures should be designed to prevent intentional or unintentional mistakes from entering the client's financial records.

After testing for compliance to internal controls, and determining materiality and risk, an auditor may again *modify the original audit program*, depending on the auditor's estimate of the reliance that can be placed on internal control procedures. That estimate of reliance would dictate whether and how the substantive tests are either expanded or reduced.

An audit of the financial statement accounts involves considerable *substantive testing*. Substantive testing involves verifying account balances. Substantive tests are designed to help determine the accuracy and fairness of a company's presentation of its financial condition. They involve sampling specific transactions, comparing data relationships, and examining documented evidence of the transactions and data.

Sampling techniques are also used to determine if the financial statement accounts are presented in compliance with GAAP. Accounts such as pension, lease, inventory, investments, and plant and equipment are examined. If any departures from GAAP are discovered during this part of the audit, GAAS require that the materiality of the departure or departures, either alone or together, be determined. The degree of materiality of the departure or departures determines the type of opinion the auditor can issue.

*Subsequent events* are any developments after the balance sheet date, but prior to issuing an opinion, that come to an auditor's attention that may have a material effect on the company's financial statements.

*Representation letters* must be obtained by an auditor from management and all client lawyers, both internal and external. Management's letter attests to the integrity and completeness (especially the inclusion of all liabilities) of the preparation of the financial statements. The lawyers' letters inform an auditor of any pending material contingent liabilities.

After all audit procedures are completed, they are reviewed by the auditor for completeness to ensure that all necessary tests have been performed to support the audit opinion.

An *audit opinion report* is issued based on the findings of an audit. This is the final outcome of the audit. It is how an auditor communicates to users of the financial statements the findings of the audit examination.

A more detailed structured diagram of the audit process, as described in this section, is given in Fig. 11-2.

## Narrowing the Focus

The audit process has many aspects that can be prototyped. Each block of the outline of the audit process represents a potential decision area to be prototyped, including

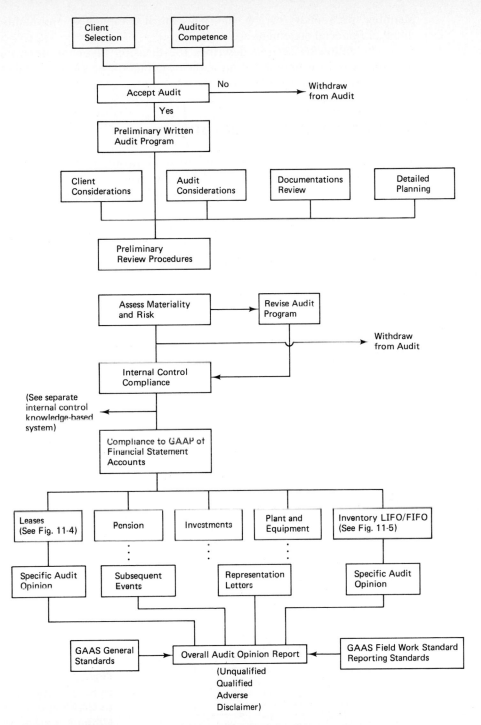

**FIGURE 11-2  More detailed outline of the audit process.**

planning, preliminary review, internal control compliance, and audits of all the individual financial statement accounts.

The following section describes the decision involving determining an audit opinion, based on findings of an audit examination of the financial statements and on their compliance with GAAP.

## STUDYING THE DECISION TO BE PROTOTYPED

The following description of the situation to be prototyped is structured in a way that provides models, like the structured diagram in Fig. 11-3, useful for later prototype system development. These structured models are based on descriptions or scenarios of typical decision situations faced by auditors working in the field.

The decision to be prototyped, as shown in Fig. 11-3, involves examining auditing statements for compliance to GAAP and auditing procedures for their compliance with GAAS. Both are studied to determine their impact on an audit opinion.

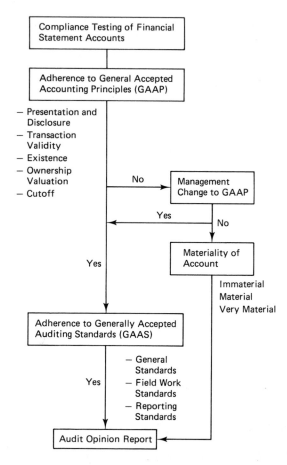

**FIGURE 11-3   Decision situation to be prototyped—compliance to GAAP and GAAS of financial statement accounts.**

GAAP are policies, procedures, and rules that a business should follow in accounting for its income, expenses, assets, liabilities, and ownership interests. No single reference exists for all GAAP, but accountants generally agree on what is considered acceptable at a particular time. An example of this is the way a business should account for an asset that is leased. Its accounting treatment is covered by the Financial Accounting Standards Board (FASB) statement number 13, which is considered part of GAAP.

The following are some of the more important factors an auditor might consider in determining whether financial statements accounts are in conformity with GAAP:

□ *Presentation and disclosure*—that is, whether particular components of the financial statements are properly classified, described, and disclosed in accordance with GAAP.

□ *Existence*—that is, whether recorded assets and equity capital claims actually exist.

□ *Transaction validity*—that is, whether all transactions recorded during the period are valid reflections of the changes in the company's resources and obligations during the period.

□ *Ownership*—that is, whether recorded assets are in fact owned by the client.

□ *Valuation*—that is, whether assets and liabilities are valued at proper amounts. Assets are valued at historical cost and liabilities are valued at the number of dollars needed to liquidate them at the balance sheet date.

□ *Cutoff*—that is, whether revenues and costs have been properly allocated among the appropriate accounting periods.

GAAS govern an auditor's conduct of the audit. These standards both govern the ethical conduct of an auditor, and guide an auditor during the field work and rendering of the audit opinion report. They cover

□ *General standards*—These standards relate to the auditor's ability to perform the audit in a professional manner. If they cannot be met, the auditor must either not accept the engagement or issue a disclaimer of opinion.

□ *Field standards*—These standards guide an auditor during the entire audit process. For example, the conduct of the internal control evaluation is a major area of field standards and is an area that is appropriate for knowledge-based systems development.

□ *Reporting standards*—These standards, which are uniform throughout the accounting profession, guide an auditor in writing the audit opinion report. The audit opinion report is an expression of opinion of the financial statements that are presented in accordance to GAAP and consistently observed from period to period, with reasonably adequate disclosure (explanations given in the financial statements where necessary for clarification), unless otherwise stated.

Questions of *materiality* arise when GAAP are not followed in the preparation of the financial statements by a client company. Once the degree of materiality is determined, an auditor is required to adjust the opinion report to reflect these departures, if the item is in fact material or significant.

The following are examples (scenarios) of some typical situations illustrating how the auditing process outlined in Fig. 11-3 is actually carried out in specific situations.

An auditor on a recent engagement came across an item in the financial statements that was recorded as a lease expense. The auditor proceeded to see if the expense was accounted for properly, as shown in Fig. 11-4.

According to FASB statement number 13, part of GAAP, leased property must be accounted for as an asset acquisition, that is, a capital item, if all the benefits and risks of ownership are transferred to the lessee. To determine this, the auditor reviews the lease agreement, asking the following questions:

- Does title of the asset pass to the lessee at the end of the lease period?
- Is the term of the lease equal to or greater than 75 percent of the life of the asset?
- Does the present value of the total of the minimum lease payments equal or exceed 90 percent of the present fair market value of the asset?
- During the term of the lease, does the lessee guarantee (ensure) the future value of the asset after the lease agreement expires?

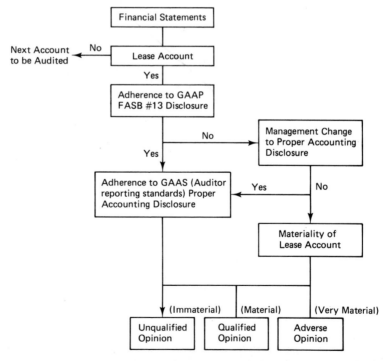

FIGURE 11-4 Decision situation to be prototyped—lease account audit.

     □ Is there an option to purchase the asset at a bargain price after the expiration of the lease?

    If the answers to any of the above five questions is yes, the leased item must be classified as a capital asset. Title of the asset did pass to the lessee in this situation, so the item was improperly recorded as an expense. The auditor brought this to the attention of the company's management, who decided not to change the accounting treatment for the lease.

    Since the item as stated was a departure from GAAP, the auditor next had to determine the materiality or importance of the item. After studying the materiality of this item, the auditor determined in this instance the departure was material (important). So, the auditor issued a qualified opinion.

    If management had agreed to change the accounting treatment for the lease and recorded it as a capital item, the auditor would have asked additional questions about compliance. Informative disclosure of lease agreements is required by GAAP. If disclosure is included in the statements, GAAS dictates that an unqualified opinion can be issued. If disclosure is not included in the financial statements, the auditor would determine the materiality of the entry. If the auditor determines that it is material and not disclosed, GAAS requires a qualified opinion be issued.

    In another situation, as shown in Fig. 11-5, an auditor in the course of the examination found that the company's management changed its method of pricing inventory from last in, first out (LIFO) to first in, first out (FIFO) from last year to this year. This is an example of an allowable change in accounting methods.

    The auditor consulted Accounting Principles Board statement number 20 (APB 20), another GAAP, which concerns the reporting requirements of these changes. The auditor then asked the following question, in order to determine if management had followed GAAP in the financial statements:

Were last year's figures restated to conform with the inventory valuations used this year?

    The retroactive restatement of the figures was not included by company's management in this year's financial statements being audited. The auditor requested management to include this statement, in order to fully comply with APB 20 and so to have financial statements that are in compliance with GAAP. Management was unwilling to do this—to include the restatement of prior periods. The auditor then had to determine if the new FIFO inventory valuation method was a material change. In this case, the auditor determined it to be a material item, since management was changing its method of inventory pricing for all of its inventory. In this situation, GAAS required the auditor to issue a qualified opinion because of the departure from GAAP.

    If management had agreed to include the retroactive restatement, the auditor would still have had to issue an opinion with a qualification as to consistency, that is, a statement explaining the different inventory valuation method used last year and this year, and why it was changed. This is because the accounting principle is no longer applied on a consistent basis from one period to the next, and the item was material.

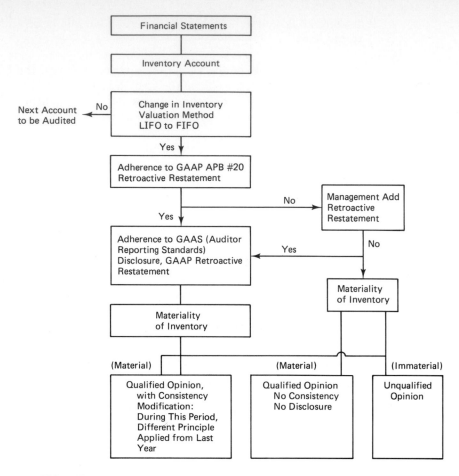

**FIGURE 11-5   Decision situation diagram for audit of inventory account change from LIFO to FIFO.**

If the new FIFO inventory valuation method were not a material change, the auditor would have issued an unqualified opinion.

The first phase of this prototype system development project is limited to the two auditing compliance decisions described above:

□ Lease agreements (covered by FASB 13)
□ LIFO-FIFO inventory valuation changes (covered by APB 20).

Later versions of the knowledge-based system cover auditing of additional financial statement accounts, internal control compliance review, and detailed preliminary review procedures.

At this point the critical information or knowledge and the reasoning paths to be included in the prototype were deliberately limited to some of the more important ones. For example, the first parts of the prototype system cover only a limited number of preliminary audit review questions. Although limiting the system in this way created the danger that the system might be trivialized somewhat, such simplification was a necessary first step toward organizing and testing the soundness of the system's concept and structure and developing a prototype within a reasonable period of time.

## DOCUMENTING THE PROTOTYPE SYSTEM

The following discussion consists of:

- □ System proposal
- □ Description of the prototype system
- □ Dependency diagram
- □ Decision charts
- □ Designing and constructing the knowledge base

### System Proposal

The general project objective is to develop a knowledge-based system that recommends an audit opinion based on findings of audit examinations of the financial statements. The audit would be made in accordance with GAAP, GAAS, and such other tests as considered necessary in the circumstances.

The system will evaluate compliance to GAAP and GAAS and the materiality of any noncompliance and render the appropriate audit opinion. This system can provide small auditing firms with necessary expertise that they may now lack as well as help in the training of inexperienced auditors both in school or at firms of all types. This system will also be portable for use on a client's premises.

The prototype system is limited to two small segments of the whole system, auditing lease accounts and inventory accounts, within the context of preliminary review procedures.

The sources of expertise used were interviews with auditors and auditing consultants, work in the field, publications containing auditing standards, and accounting texts and periodicals.

### Description of the Prototype System

**System overview and objective.** The prototype is designed to help users perform an audit examination. The system asks users questions relating to the initial client screening, preliminary review procedures, review of internal control compliance, audit of financial statement accounts, assessment of materiality, and issuance of the audit opinion report. The prototype will concentrate on two examples of financial statement accounts, lease accounts and inventory (LIFO or FIFO valuation method).

The system described here is the prototype of a much larger system for auditing, covering many other financial statement and auditing areas, such as pension, plant and equipment, and financial investment accounts, as well as internal control compliance.

**Recommendations to be made by the system.**    The following are possible audit opinions that can be recommended in the overall system:

- *Unqualified opinion* is commonly found in corporate annual reports. This opinion can be given only if the following are present: (1) enough competent evidence has been gathered to assure that the audit field work standards (GAAS) have been met, (2) no significant uncorrected departures from GAAP have been found, (3) no significant accounting changes affecting comparability of the financial statements from period to period have been found, and (4) no material uncertainties exist that cannot be estimated or satisfactorily resolved as of the report date.
- *Qualified opinion* is issued if one or more of the circumstances above are not present and it has an important effect on the financial statements.
- *Adverse opinion* is issued if one or more of the circumstances above are not present and it has an extremely misleading effect on the financial statements.
- *Disclaimer of opinion* is issued if financial statements are unaudited, if the auditor is not independent, or if the client withholds necessary information from the auditor.

The overall audit opinion is rendered based on the cumulative results of the individual account audits. The initial prototype system is limited to determining compliance with GAAP and GAAS and to recommending a qualified opinion with modifications, an unqualified opinion with a consistency modification, an unqualified opinion, or an adverse opinion for the lease account and the LIFO-FIFO inventory valuation account only.

These opinions would be incorporated by the system user into the standard audit opinion letter. For example, the standard short-form unqualified opinion, which is issued by an auditor and which is given below, would be modified whenever an opinion other than unqualified is issued.

To the Board of Directors (Shareholders):

We have examined the balance sheets of ABC Company as of December 31, 19XX and 19XX, and the related statements of income, retained earnings, and changes in the financial position for the years then ended. Our examinations were made with generally accepted auditing standards and accordingly, included such tests of the accounting records and such other tests as we considered necessary in the circumstances.

In our opinion, the financial statements referred to above present fairly the financial position of ABC Company as of December 31, 19XX and 19XX, and the results of operations and changes in its financial position for the years then ended, in conformity with generally accepted accounting principles applied on a consistent basis.

Signature

Date (last day of field work)

The first paragraph above is referred to as the scope paragraph and the second paragraph is referred to as the opinion paragraph.

**Nature of user interface, including typical user dialogue.**   The typical user dialogue covers a number of key knowledge areas, including

- □ *Accept audit*—This information is obtained by asking such questions as "Do you consider yourself independent?   A CPA is not independent if there exists: direct or indirect financial relationships with the client, a management or employee relationship, threatened or actual litigation involving the client and the CPA."
- □ *Preliminary review procedures*—This information is obtained by asking such questions as "After discussing the proposed audit with management and what management expects from the auditor, do you feel that the type, scope, and timing of the audit as defined is reasonably sufficient for you to issue an opinion?"
- □ *Internal control*—This information is obtained by asking "Are client internal control procedures followed by employees as prescribed by management?"
- □ *Lease agreement*—This information is obtained by asking such questions as "Is there a lease account in the financial statements?" and "Has the lease agreement been properly disclosed?"
- □ *LIFO-FIFO*—This information is obtained by asking such questions as "Has there been a change from LIFO to FIFO inventory valuation?"

**Description of the knowledge structure and reasoning process.**   The recommendations made by the prototype system are based on two factors involving compliance with GAAP and GAAS and materiality.   These factors are in turn based on other factors, such as audit acceptance review, preliminary review procedures, internal control review, and account existence determination (lease agreement, LIFO-FIFO).

If-then rules and backward chaining are used.   The values used at each level in the reasoning chain are indicated in Figs. 11-7A, 11-7B, and 11-7C.

### Dependency Diagrams

Figures 11-6, 11-7A, 11-7B, and 11-7C show the dependency diagrams for the audit opinion reports prototype knowledge-based system.   They give a summary outline of all the questions, rules, knowledge segments and their interrelationships, values, and recommendations within the system.

The dependency diagrams show the initial prototype stage, before substantial rule condensation and consolidation have been done.   The versions of the system are shown to give the reader a better feel for the specific reasoning steps involved in the decision and so underlying the system.   The system therefore illustrates some of the early steps a nontechnician might go through in developing such a system.

Substantial improvements, such as faster consultation running time, resulted

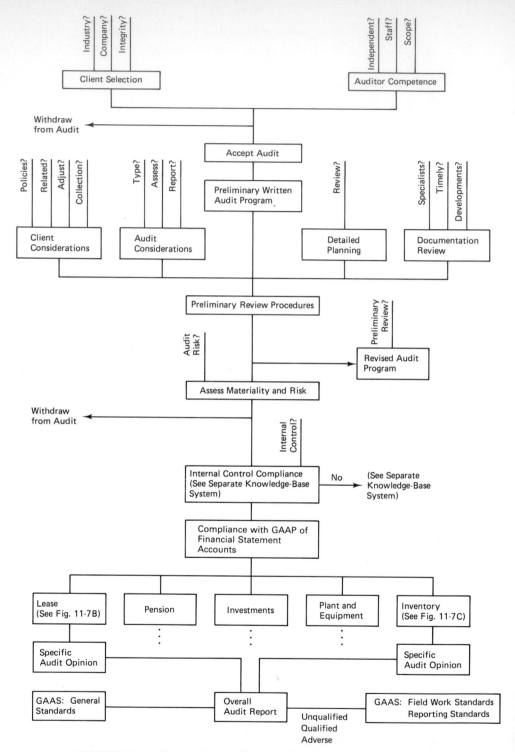

**FIGURE 11-6  Dependency diagram for overall audit process.**

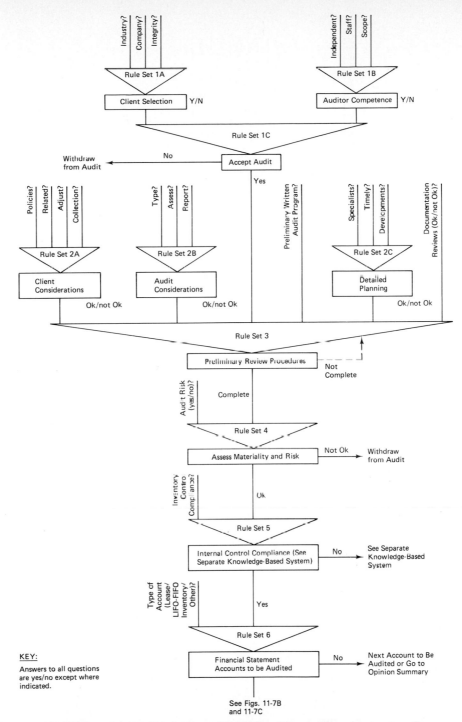

**FIGURE 11-7A Dependency diagram for auditing system—first stage—initial prototype.**

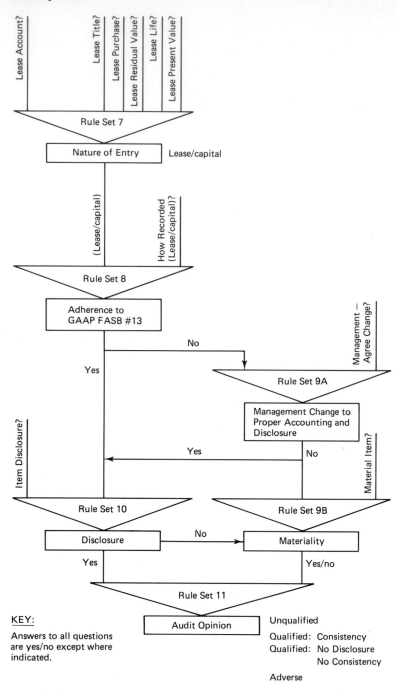

**FIGURE 11-7B  Dependency diagram for lease account audit sub-segment—initial prototype.**

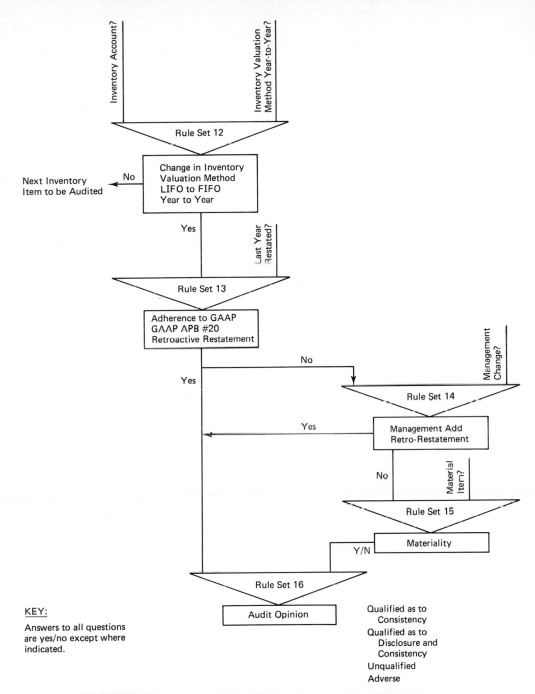

From Fig. 11-7A

Inventory Account?

Inventory Valuation Method Year-to-Year?

Rule Set 12

Change in Inventory Valuation Method LIFO to FIFO Year to Year

No → Next Inventory Item to be Audited

Yes

Last Year Restated?

Rule Set 13

Adherence to GAAP GAAP APB #20 Retroactive Restatement

Yes

No

Management Change?

Rule Set 14

Yes → Management Add Retro-Restatement

No

Material Item?

Rule Set 15

Materiality

Y/N

Rule Set 16

Audit Opinion

Qualified as to Consistency
Qualified as to Disclosure and Consistency
Unqualified
Adverse

KEY:

Answers to all questions are yes/no except where indicated.

**FIGURE 11-7C Dependency diagram for auditing system—audit of inventory account. Method of inventory valuation (LIFO-FIFO) sub-segment—initial prototype.**

11: An External Auditing System

249

Rule Set 7: Nature of Expense

|  | | 7-1 | 7-2 |
|---|---|---|---|
| IF: | Lease-Account | Y and | Y and |
|  | Lease-Title | Y or | N and |
|  | Lease-Purchase | Y or | N and |
|  | Lease-Life | $\geq$ 75% or | < 75% and |
|  | Lease-Present Value | $\geq$ 90% or | < 90% and |
|  | Lease-Residual Value | Y | Y |
| THEN: | Nature of entry | C | E |

Key: Y = Yes
    N = No
    < = Less than
    $\geq$ = More than or equal to
    C = Capitalize
    E = Expense

**FIGURE 11-8   Sample decision chart for auditing system—lease account audit subsegment (initial prototype).**

from the refinements introduced by the technical computer group that subsequently worked on the project.

## Decision Charts

Figure 11-8 shows a sample decision chart from the audit opinion reports of the prototype system.

## Designing and Constructing the Knowledge Base

Rules and questions were developed from the situation study. They were based on the system developers' analysis of how an auditor might actually go about making such decisions. Scenarios for these decisions are given in the structured situation analysis section of this chapter.

A segment of the prototype system's knowledge base is given in Fig. 11-9. The expert system shell used is M-1. The knowledge base in subsequent versions of the system was considerably more compact.

## REVIEW QUESTIONS

1. Complete the knowledge-based system (or any segment of the system) partially documented in this chapter and enter it into the expert system shell you have.

2. Describe a key difference between the system described in this chapter and the three described in the preceding chapters.

<u>Rules</u>

```
Rule
7-1: if lease-account = yes and
        lease-title = yes or
        lease-purchase = yes or
        lease-life = more-than-or-equal-to-75-percent or
        lease-present-value = more-than-or-equal-to-90-percent or
        lease-residual-value = yes
     then item = capitalize.

Rule
7-2: if lease-account = yes and
        lease-title = no and
        lease-purchase = no and
        lease-life = less-than-75-percent and
        lease-present-value = less-than-90-percent and
        lease-residual-value = no
     then item = expense.
```

<u>Questions</u>

```
question(lease-title) = 'answers to the following questions are
based on your review of the lease agreement.  Does title to the
asset pass to the leasee at the end of the lease period?'.
legalvals(lease-title) = [yes,no].

question(lease-purchase) = 'Is there an option to purchase the
asset at a bargain price after the expiration of the lease?'.
legalvals(lease-purchase) = [yes,no].

question(lease-residual-value) = 'During the term of the lease,
does the leasee guarantee the future of the asset after the lease
expires?'.
legalvals(lease-residual-value) = [yes,no].
```

**FIGURE 11-9 Sample segment of knowledge base—rules and questions for auditing system—initial prototype.**

3. In what ways is the incremental building of this system different from the ways that the earlier three systems would be enhanced and extended?

4. Describe the ways in which the system described in this chapter is more procedural in parts than the three earlier ones.

5. Identify other financial accounts for which knowledge-based systems might be developed. Draw a structured decision situation diagram for any one of them. Then design and document a prototype system for it.

6. What is an audit?  Describe the function of the auditor.

7. List the different aspects of the auditing process that can be prototyped.  Develop the concept of a knowledge-based system in one of these areas.

8. What are GAAP?  Describe them.

9. What are some of the important factors an auditor might consider in determining whether financial statement accounts are in conformity with GAAP?

10. Describe one cause of an auditor issuing a qualified opinion. Give an example.

11. What must be present for an auditor to issue an unqualified opinion?

## REFERENCES

American Institute of Certified Public Accountants, *Codification of Statements on Auditing Standards*, Chicago, IL: Commerce Clearing House, 1986.

Barr, B., et al., *Short Audit Case: The Valley Publishing Co.*, 5th ed., Homewood, IL: Richard D. Irwin, 1985.

Barrett, M.J., and V.Z. Brinks, *Internal-External Audit Services and Relationships*, Altamont Springs, FL: Institute of Internal Auditors, 1981.

Bority, J.E., et al., "Managing Audit Risk," *C A Magazine*, vol. 12, January 1987.

Carmichael, D.R., and J.J. Willingham, *Auditing Concepts and Methods*, 4th ed., New York: McGraw-Hill, 1983.

Chambers, A.D., et al., *Internal Auditing*, Philadelphia, PA: Trans-Atlantic Publications, 1987.

Gleim, I.N., and P.R. Delaney, *CPA Examination Review, Vol. 1, Outlines and Study Guides*, 13th ed., New York: John Wiley and Sons, 1986.

Henke, T., *Auditing Theory and Practice*, 2nd ed., Boston, MA: Kent Publishing, 1986.

Hubbard, T.D., and J.R. Johnson, *Auditing: Concepts, Standards, Procedures*, Houston, TX: Dame Pub., 1983.

Johnson, A.P., *Auditing Judgment: A Book of Cases*, Homewood, IL: Richard D. Irwin, 1980.

Kell, W.G., et al., *Modern Auditing*, 3rd ed., New York: John Wiley and Sons, 1986.

Kropatkin, P., *Audit Logic: A Guide to Successful Audits*, New York: John Wiley and Sons, 1984.

Munter, P., and T.A. Ratcliffe, *Applying GAAP and GAAS*, New York: Mathew Bender, 1985.

Sperber, W.H., "Developing an Automated Approach to Auditing," *Magazine of Bank Administration*, vol. 63, March 1987.

Thomas, C.W., and E.O. Henke, *Auditing: Theory and Practice*, 2nd ed., Boston: Kent Publishing, 1986.

Welsch, G.A., C.T. Zlatkovich, and W.T. Harrison, *Intermediate Accounting*, 6th ed., Homewood, IL: Richard D. Irwin, 1982.

# 12

# An Account Assignment System

This chapter describes the development of a knowledge-based system that assists accounting clerks in assigning invoices to proper accounts. The topics covered in this report are

- The situation under study: understanding the expert's domain
- Studying the situation to be prototyped
- Documenting the prototype system

The discussion begins with a decision situation analysis and model development for the decision situation under study for prototyping. The design and documentation of the actual prototype knowledge-based system is then described.

## THE SITUATION UNDER STUDY: UNDERSTANDING THE EXPERT'S DOMAIN

The discussions in this section covers

- Selecting a decision area to work on
- Probing how the situation works and how decisions are made
- Narrowing the focus

## Selecting a Decision Area to Work On

Accounting is concerned with the process of recording, sorting, and summarizing data related to business transactions and events, as shown in Fig. 12-1. In general terms the recording function deals with transferring information about a transaction (event) into a specific format that can be used for analysis and reporting.

*Recording* decisions usually deal with determining either the appropriate account to which to assign an invoice or other accounting transaction, or the appropriate amount to record. This study concerns the account assignment (sometimes called distributions) decisions.

Once transactions have been recorded, the data needs to be *sorted*. The data can be sorted by the type of financial statement account, the type of transaction (all cash disbursements, cash receipts, and the like shown together), or the transaction date. In most systems, the data is entered into a data base and can be sorted in any way needed to meet reporting and decision-making requirements.

Once the accounting entries have been sorted, the *summarization* procedure depends upon the external and internal reporting requirements of the company. The external summarization requirements are governed by outside authorities, such as the Financial Accounting Standards Board (FASB) and the Securities and Exchange Commission (SEC). The internal requirements are usually decided by senior management and are dictated by management decision-making needs throughout a company.

## Probing How the Situation Works and How Decisions Are Made

The account distribution decision, the focus of this study, involves the determination of which account or accounts to debit and which to credit for a particular transaction. Figure 12-2 gives a rough structured diagram of the general account assignment (or distribution) decision area.

As seen in Fig. 12-2, accounting transactions can be divided into the following four broad categories:

1. Cash disbursement and accounts payable entries
2. Cash receipt entries
3. Credit sales and accounts receivable entries
4. General journal entries

*Cash disbursement* entries all involve a reduction in the cash balance. These reductions are recorded as a credit to the cash account. *Accounts payable entries* occur when a cash disbursement is legally due to be paid, but payment is delayed. The delay could be the result of a vendor's payment terms, a dispute about the amount owed, or the unavailability of company funds. This increase in the amounts owed is recorded as a credit to accounts payable.

The recording of each transaction involves an entry to at least two accounts.

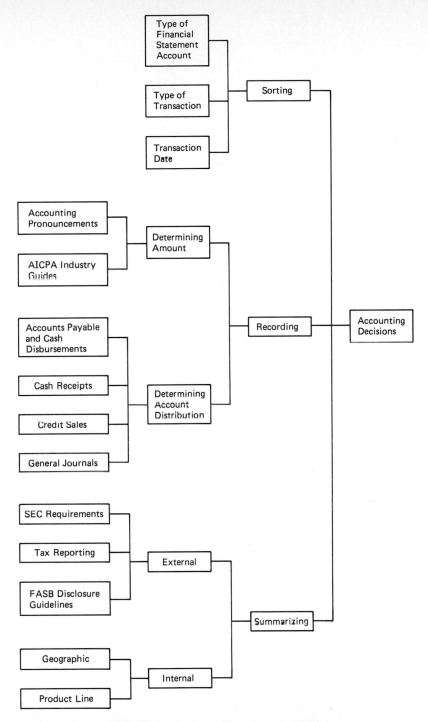

**FIGURE 12-1   Overview of accounting.**

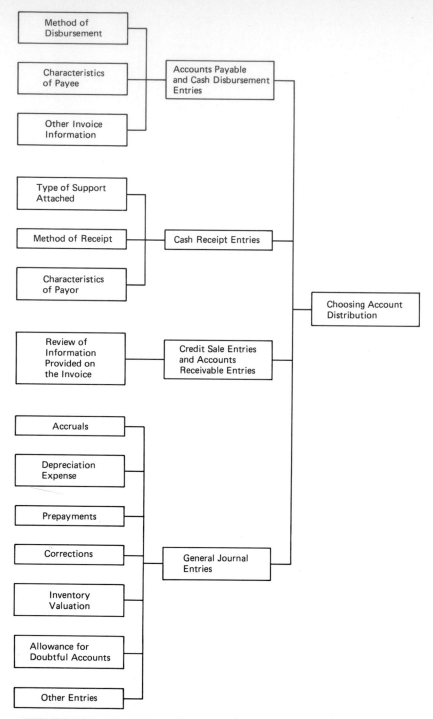

**FIGURE 12-2  Overview of account assignment or distribution decision area.**

For example, if you spend cash to purchase equipment, your bank balance will be lowered (credit to cash), whereas you will have an increase in equipment on hand (debit to equipment). This debit to equipment and credit to cash is considered a "balanced accounting entry," also referred to as double entry bookkeeping. When recording a cash disbursement or accounts payable entry, the decision to credit cash or accounts payable is straightforward, as explained above.

The debit side of these entries, however, is not always straightforward. For example, all invoices may show just a name of a company and an unclear indication of exactly what was purchased. A piece of equipment purchased might be debited to plant inventory or to supplies, because similar products are kept in both areas. A service charge might be debited to either professional services or repairs and maintenance. Such a transaction, therefore, can result in a debit to

- One or more asset accounts
- One or more expense accounts
- A combination of asset and expense accounts

Since these account assignment (or distribution) decisions require some judgment, they lend themselves to knowledge-based systems applications. An accounting expert's judgment is needed to ensure that the correct assignment (or distribution) decisions are made.

*Cash receipt entries* all result in an increase in one's cash balance. This increase is recorded as a debit to cash (opposite of a cash disbursement). The credit side of the entry needed to balance the transaction varies, since the cash received could be from a

- Bank loan (credit to long-term debt)
- From a cash sale (credit to sales)
- Collection of a customer's balance (credit to accounts receivable)

Since the volume of cash receipts is usually lower than cash disbursements and most receipt entries are straightforward, few companies would benefit from a knowledge-based system for account coding of cash receipts. There are some businesses, such as banks or finance companies, however, where the coding of cash receipts becomes more complex and a knowledge-based system has proved beneficial.

*Credit sales entries* involve the billing of customers for their purchase of a company's goods or services for payment at a later date. The payments to be received in the future (in exchange for the goods or services sold) are accumulated in an account called *accounts receivable*. Credit sales result in an increase in the amount of accounts receivable and are recorded as debits. The other side of the entry needed to balance the transaction is a credit to sales. The only complication could result from billing adjustments for freight, discounts, prepayments, and the like. These items are usually clearly indicated by the billing department on the sales invoice and the account distribution decision is straightforward. Few companies would need a knowledge-based system for determining the account distribution for credit sales.

The final major transaction type involves *general journal entries*. These transactions could result in debits or credits to any account. Typical uses are for recording accruals, depreciation expense, prepaid expenses, correcting entries, inventory valuation, allowance for doubtful accounts receivable, and the like. In this type of transaction decisions are voluminous and can require considerable judgment, so that there are many potential knowledge-based systems applications in this area. A review of the company's transactions in each subcategory of general journal entries would be needed to determine which ones would benefit most from a knowledge-based system.

## Narrowing the Focus

The company this initial system was developed for utilizes a centralized accounting department of fourteen clerks and four supervisors who code and input all accounting transactions for the divisions in the New York office. One of the constant complaints by division personnel is that the account assignment by these accounting clerks for cash disbursements is often incorrect. The major cause of the problem is that the clerks do not have accounting or finance backgrounds. Most of the clerks have only a high school education. A simple solution would be to hire college graduates with accounting or finance degrees. This solution is not feasible for two reasons. First, the job is fairly monotonous and hiring college graduates would result in constant turnover. Second, the Corporate Controller has already considered hiring more experienced clerks, but ruled against it due to budget constraints.

An alternative is to create a knowledge-based system that would assist a high school graduate, with little or no accounting expertise, to properly assign the correct account coding for cash disbursements. This type of situation is in fact, a very appropriate and cost effective knowledge-based systems application, and so a common one. Figure 12-3 provides a structured diagram or model of the account assignment (or distribution) decision for cash disbursements in general.

The number of cash disbursements recorded by a typical large company's centralized accounting department in a year is approximately 35,000. Figure 12-4 shows a list of a typical company's chart of accounts. Since cash disbursements could result in a debit to most of the accounts listed, creating a knowledge-based system to handle all 35,000 accounting decisions would be beyond the scope of this initial phase of this project. It was decided, therefore, to focus on the disbursement transactions that provided clerks with the most difficulty.

Interviews with accounting clerks, their supervisors, and certain department heads revealed that the following types of disbursements caused the clerks the most problems:

1. Professional fees
2. Repairs and maintenance
3. Membership fees and subscriptions
4. Temporary help expense

Professional fees was chosen for this prototype, since it deals with invoices for higher dollar amounts than the other areas. In addition, a detailed review of approximately two hundred and fifty disbursements over $1,000 charged to professional

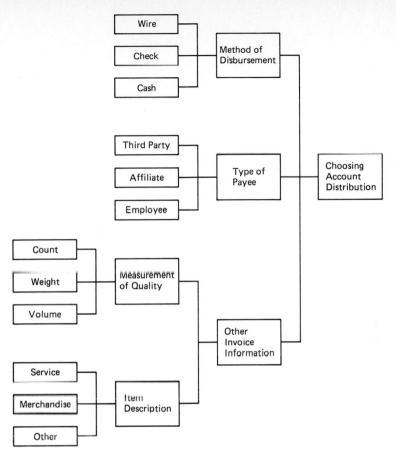

**FIGURE 12-3  Knowledge domain model for cash disbursement account distribution decision.**

fee accounts revealed thirty-eight instances where the vouchers should have been charged to a different type of account.   The scope of this prototype will also be limited to cash disbursements under $50,000.

## STUDYING THE DECISION TO BE PROTOTYPED

The factors considered in deciding which account to assign (or debit) a professional fee expense to when accounting for professional fees transactions are

1. The individual in the company requesting the payment
2. The description on the invoice
3. The dollar amount of the invoice
4. The payee's name
5. The service offered by the payee as indicated on the letterhead
6. The unit of measure

| ACCOUNT NUMBER | ACCOUNT NAME |
|---|---|
| | BALANCE SHEET ACCOUNTS |
| 1110101 | CASH—CHASE MANHATTAN |
| 1110102 | CASH—CHEMICAL BANK |
| 1110103 | CASH—CITIBANK |
| 1110104 | CASH—MANUFACTURERS HANOVER |
| 1110105 | CASH—IRVING TRUST |
| 1130100 | PETTY CASH |
| 1150100 | TIME DEPOSITS |
| 1160100 | SHORT TERM INVESTMENTS |
| 1190100 | MARGIN DEPOSITS |
| 1190500 | DUE FROM BROKERS |
| 1251011 | TRADE RECEIVABLES |
| 1251022 | DEMURRAGE/DESPATCH RECEIVABLES |
| 1251033 | CARRYING CHARGES RECEIVABLES |
| 1251044 | CLAIMS RECEIVABLES |
| 1251055 | OTHER RECEIVABLES |
| 1251100 | ACCRUED RECEIVABLES |
| 1251260 | ACCRUED INTEREST INCOME |
| 1251400 | OUTTURN RECEIVABLE |
| 1251800 | CONTRACT DEFAULT RECEIVABLE |
| 1251850 | RESERVE—CONTRACT DEFAULT RECEIVABLE |
| 1258100 | ALLOWANCE FOR DOUBTFUL ACCOUNTS |
| 1258150 | RESERVE—CARRYING CHARGES RECEIVABLES |
| 1258160 | RESERVE—CLAIMS RECEIVABLES |
| 1310001 | INTERCOMPANY RECEIVABLES |
| 1311001 | INTERCOMPANY LOAN RECEIVABLE |
| 1320001 | RECEIVABLES FROM AFFILIATES |
| 1321001 | LOANS TO AFFILIATES |
| 1410100 | COMMODITY INVENTORIES |
| 1410120 | BUNKER INVENTORY |
| 1411100 | ACCRUED MARKET DIFFERENCE |
| 1430100 | ADVANCE ON PURCHASES |
| 1451100 | PREPAID INSURANCE |
| 1455100 | PREPAID INTEREST |
| 1457100 | PREPAID RENT |
| 1457150 | PREPAID CHARTER HIRE |
| 1457200 | OTHER PREPAID EXPENSES |
| 1471150 | EMPLOYEE TRAVEL ADVANCES |
| 1471160 | OTHER EMPLOYEE ADVANCES |
| 1471200 | LOANS TO EMPLOYEES |

| ACCOUNT NUMBER | ACCOUNT NAME |
|---|---|
| | BALANCE SHEET ACCOUNTS (CONTINUED) |
| 1942510 | MISCELLANEOUS EXPENSE |
| 2011100 | NOTES PAYABLE |
| 2020100 | BANK OVERDRAFTS |
| 2100100 | ACCOUNTS PAYABLE |
| 2100200 | DEMURRAGE PAYABLE |
| 2210100 | ACCRUED INTEREST |
| 2220100 | STATE AND CITY WITHHOLDING TAXES |
| 2220200 | FEDERAL WITHHOLDING TAXES |
| 2220300 | F.I.C.A. |
| 2220400 | S.U.I. |
| 2220500 | F.U.I. |
| 2220600 | LONG-TERM DISABILITY WITHHELD |
| 2220700 | GROUP LIFE INSURANCE WITHHELD |
| 2220800 | ACCRUED RETIREMENT PLAN |
| 2250100 | ACCRUED BONUSES |
| 2260100 | ACCRUED PROFESSIONAL FEES |
| 2260150 | ACCRUED AUDIT FEES |
| 2260160 | ACCRUED VACATION |
| 2260200 | OTHER ACCRUED EXPENSES |
| 2400100 | ADVANCES ON SALES |
| 2451100 | ACCRUED FEDERAL INCOME TAX |
| 2460100 | ACCRUED STATE & LOCAL TAXES |
| 2490200 | EMPLOYEE LOAN PAYABLE |
| 2621100 | DEFERRED INCOME |
| 2630100 | DEFERRED INCOME TAXES |
| 2710100 | LONG-TERM DEBT DUE WITHIN ONE YEAR |
| 3100100 | PREFERRED STOCK |
| 3200100 | COMMON STOCK |
| 3300100 | EXCESS OF EQUITY OVER COST |
| 3500100 | TREASURY STOCK |
| 3710100 | RETAINED EARNINGS |
| 3730100 | DIVIDENDS PAID |
| | INCOME STATEMENT ACCOUNTS |
| 4100100 | INTERCOMPANY SALES |
| 4100500 | THIRD-PARTY SALES |
| 4150100 | INTERCOMPANY SALES ADJUSTMENTS |
| 4150500 | THIRD-PARTY SALES ADJUSTMENTS |
| 4500100 | COMMISSION INCOME |

1471250 EQUITY ADVANCES
1472500 OTHER CURRENT ASSETS
1510200 INVESTMENT IN CONSOLIDATED COMPANIES
1510300 INVESTMENT IN UNCONSOLIDATED FOREIGN SUBSIDIARIES
1540100 OTHER INVESTMENTS
1610100 LAND
1611100 ELEVATORS AND BUILDINGS
1612400 OCEAN VESSELS
1613100 MACHINERY AND EQUIPMENT
1615100 OFFICE FURNITURE AND FIXTURES
1616100 OFFICE EQUIPMENT
1616550 PERSONAL COMPUTERS AND COMPUTER SOFTWARE
1617100 AUTOMOBILES AND TRUCKS
1618100 AIRCRAFT
1619100 BARGES
1640100 LEASEHOLD IMPROVEMENTS
1645100 CONSTRUCTION IN PROGRESS
1645102 CAPITALIZED INTEREST
1651100 ACCUMULATED DEPRECIATION—ELEVATORS AND BUILDINGS
1652400 ACCUMULATED DEPRECIATION—OCEAN VESSELS
1653100 ACCUMULATED DEPRECIATION—MACHINERY AND EQUIPMENT
1655100 ACCUMULATED DEPRECIATION—OFFICE FURNITURE AND FIXTURES
1656100 ACCUMULATED DEPRECIATION—OFFICE EQUIPMENT
1656550 ACCUMULATED DEPRECIATION—PERSONAL COMPUTERS AND SOFTWARE
1657100 ACCUMULATED DEPRECIATION—AUTOMOBILES AND TRUCKS
1658100 ACCUMULATED DEPRECIATION—AIRCRAFT
1659100 ACCUMULATED DEPRECIATION—BARGES
1690100 AMORTIZATION OF LEASEHOLD IMPROVEMENTS
1910100 COMMODITY MEMBERSHIPS
1920200 LONG-TERM RECEIVABLES—OUTSIDE
1920300 LONG-TERM RECEIVABLES—INTERCOMPANY
1920400 LONG-TERM RECEIVABLES—AFFILIATES
1920500 OTHER NON-CURRENT ASSETS

4500200 CLAIMS INCOME
5100100 INTERCOMPANY PURCHASES
5100500 THIRD-PARTY PURCHASES
5150100 INTERCOMPANY PURCHASE ADJUSTMENTS
5150500 THIRD-PARTY PURCHASE ADJUSTMENTS
5160100 CONTRACT CANCELLATION EXPENSE
5200700 BEGINNING INVENTORY
5200800 ENDING INVENTORY
5300700 GAIN/LOSS ON OPEN CONTRACTS—BEGINNING
5300800 GAIN/LOSS ON OPEN CONTRACTS—ENDING
5400100 INTERCOMPANY HEDGES
5400200 GAIN/LOSS ON OPTIONS
5400500 THIRD-PARTY HEDGES
5450100 INTERCOMPANY COMMISSION EXPENSE
5450500 THIRD-PARTY COMMISSION EXPENSE
5512000 FREIGHT PURCHASES
5511100 VESSEL DEMURRAGE
5513100 STOWING AND TRIMMING
5515100 OTHER OCEAN FREIGHT EXPENSE
5515700 TIME CHARTER RENTAL
5516600 PORT CHARGES
5520200 BARGE FREIGHT
5520300 BARGE DEMURRAGE
5520500 OTHER BARGE EXPENSES
5530100 RAIL FREIGHT
5531500 RAIL DEMURRAGE
5540500 TRUCK FREIGHT
5600500 ELEVATION COSTS
5610500 STORAGE EXPENSE
5611100 INSPECTION & WEIGHING
5630300 STEVEDORING EXPENSE
5650500 FUMIGATION COSTS
5800100 INTERCOMPANY INTEREST EXPENSE INCLUDED IN COST OF SALES
5800500 THIRD-PARTY INTEREST EXPENSE INCLUDED IN COST OF SALES
5800700 CARRYING CHARGES
5920500 INSURANCE INCLUDED IN COST OF SALES
5990500 COMMODITY RESERVES

*(continued)*

**FIGURE 12-4 Sample chart of accounts.**

| ACCOUNT NUMBER | ACCOUNT NAME | ACCOUNT NUMBER | ACCOUNT NAME |
|---|---|---|---|
| | INCOME STATEMENT ACCOUNTS (CONTINUED) | | INCOME STATEMENT ACCOUNTS (CONTINUED) |
| 6600100 | RECOVERY OF BAD DEBTS | 7544150 | COMPUTER SOFTWARE |
| 6700100 | PROVISION FOR BAD DEBTS | 7550100 | POSTAGE |
| 6800100 | MISCELLANEOUS OPERATING INCOME | 7551100 | OFFICE SUPPLIES |
| 6810500 | MISCELLANEOUS OPERATING EXPENSE | 7551110 | MESSENGER SERVICE |
| 7400100 | ADVERTISING & PROMOTION | 7552100 | BUILDING MAINTENANCE & SERVICES |
| 7521100 | SALARIES—REGULAR TIME | 7553100 | UTILITIES |
| 7521200 | SALARIES—OVERTIME | 7554100 | REPAIRS & MAINTENANCE |
| 7522000 | SUPPLEMENTAL BENEFITS | 7554110 | MOVING & ALTERATIONS |
| 7522100 | FRINGE BENEFITS | 7556110 | LEGAL EXPENSES |
| 7522130 | SUPPER MONEY | 7556120 | ACCOUNTING FEES |
| 7522140 | FOOD SERVICES | 7556130 | OUTSIDE MISC EXPENSE |
| 7522160 | EMPLOYEE GIFTS | 7556140 | CONSULTING FEES |
| 7522170 | TUITION REFUNDS | 7556150 | OTHER PROFESSIONAL FEES |
| 7523100 | TEMPORARY HELP | 7561100 | OFFICE RENTAL |
| 7531100 | TRAVEL & ENTERTAINMENT | 7562100 | REAL ESTATE TAXES |
| 7531110 | TRANSPORTATION | 7664100 | EQUIPMENT RENTAL |
| 7531120 | OTHER TRAVEL | 7565100 | DEPRECIATION EXPENSE |
| 7531130 | LOCAL ENTERTAINMENT | 7566100 | INSURANCE |
| 7531140 | CONVENTIONS & MEETINGS | 7580100 | DONATIONS |
| 7531150 | REIMBURSED MILEAGE | 7580300 | BANK CHARGES |
| 7531160 | AUTOMOBILE EXPENSES | 7620300 | MISCELLANEOUS EXPENSES |
| 7532000 | SUBSCRIPTIONS | 8100500 | RENTAL INCOME |
| 7532100 | MEMBERSHIP DUES AND FEES | 8190100 | INTERCOMPANY INTEREST INCOME |
| 7532110 | OUTSIDE SEMINARS | 8190500 | THIRD-PARTY INTEREST INCOME |
| 7532120 | BOOKS & NON-SUBSCRIPTION PUBLICATIONS | 8200500 | RENTAL EXPENSE |
| 7533000 | RELOCATION EXPENSES | 8290100 | INTERCOMPANY INTEREST EXPENSE |
| 7533100 | OTHER EMPLOYMENT EXPENSES | 8290500 | THIRD-PARTY INTEREST EXPENSE |
| 7534000 | EMPLOYMENT ADVERTISING | 8320500 | DIVIDEND INCOME |
| 7534100 | AGENCY FEES | 8330100 | GAIN/LOSS ON SALE OF FIXED ASSETS |
| 7534120 | APPLICANT TRAVEL | 8330300 | GAIN/LOSS ON SALE OF MARKETABLE SECURITIES |
| 7534130 | PRE-EMPLOYMENT PHYSICAL | 8330600 | GAIN/LOSS ON SALE OF INVESTMENTS |
| 7535100 | INTERNAL SEMINARS | 8440500 | EQUITY IN NON-CONSOLIDATED SUBSIDIARIES |
| 7541100 | TELEPHONE EXPENSES | 8600500 | FOREIGN EXCHANGE GAIN/LOSS |
| 7542100 | COMMUNICATIONS EXPENSE | 9100410 | CORPORATE OVERHEAD ALLOCATION |
| 7543100 | QUOTATION EQUIPMENT & NEWS SERVICES | 9211100 | FEDERAL TAX EXPENSE |
| 7544100 | COMPUTER PERIPHERALS | 9214100 | STATE AND LOCAL TAX EXPENSE |

**FIGURE 12-4** *(continued)*

These factors can be seen in the first level of the knowledge domain model in Fig. 12-5. This is a decision model based on the structured situation analysis described here.

Approximately 250 professional fee transactions were reviewed and the characteristics of each transaction recorded. This information was an important source of rules and questions for the knowledge-based system.

The discussion of the interrelationships of the six key characteristics is best understood by reviewing a few examples. If a cash disbursement request for a legal fee were presented for account distribution, the first characteristic to look for is the requestor's department. Certain departments primarily request certain types of payments. In this example, over 80 percent of the cash disbursements initiated by the legal department are for legal fees. Therefore, if the requestor is from the legal department, one would immediately lean toward legal fees expense. Second, one would look at the invoice description. If the request is coming from the legal department and the invoice description is legal-related, the proper account distribution is almost definitely legal fees expense.

If the disbursement request is initiated by the legal department but the invoice description is general in nature (for example, professional fees), one would look to the name of the payee and the invoice letterhead to determine if the payment is being made to a law firm. If so the proper account distribution is almost definitely legal fees expense.

In another situation, the legal fee invoice may not have been initiated by the legal department, but the invoice description contains legal-related terms. In this case one would look at the dollar amount, expecting the amount to be under $30,000, since the legal department is supposed to initiate all payments for legal expenses over $30,000. Next, the payee's name would be examined to see if the payment is being made to a law firm. If the payment is for over $30,000, and is being made to a legal firm, the proper account assignment is again almost definitely legal fees expense.

Note that in these three examples the unit-of-measure characteristic did not enter into the decision process. This is because over 80 percent of legal invoices do not indicate the unit of measure on the invoice (for the other 20 percent, the unit of measure is usually hours). Therefore, the unit of measure is not a key characteristic in determining legal fees account assignment. When determining other professional fee expense account assignment, such as outside management information systems (MIS) expense and consulting expense, the unit of measure enters into the decision process.

## Two Typical Scenarios

To provide a clearer understanding of the process involved in making an account assignment in distribution decisions, two typical decision situation scenarios are described, one of which involves an accounting fees expense and another that involves an outside MIS expense.

**Accounting fees expense.** In the company under study, experience has shown that only two departments request disbursements resulting in a charge to this account,

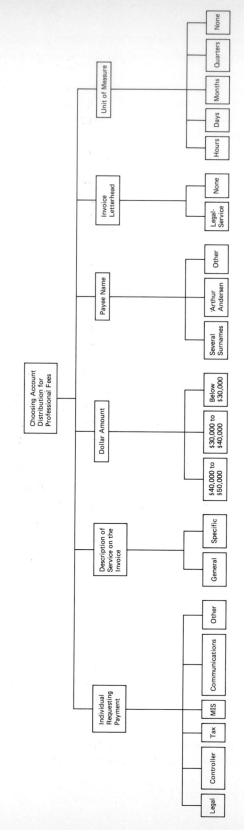

**FIGURE 12-5  Diagram of decision situation to be prototyped—professional fees account distribution decision.**

the corporate controller and corporate tax departments. Therefore, if any other department is the requestor, accounting fees expense would be immediately ruled out. Once the requestor is determined to be either from the controller or tax department, one would look at the invoice for the word *audit*, since accounting fee expense is an account used exclusively for recording audit fees. The final characteristic one reviews is the payee name, since each company has one primary auditing firm. In summation, if the department requesting the payment is controller or tax, the invoice mentions the word *audit*, and the payee's name is the company's independent auditing firm, then the proper account assignment is to accounting fees expense.

**Outside MIS expense.** In the company under study, experience has shown that 60 percent of the disbursements charged to outside MIS expense are initiated by the MIS or communications departments. Therefore, if the requestor is from a department other than MIS or communications, more information will be requested.

In either case the invoice will be reviewed for key words that indicate outside MIS expense, such as *on-line inquiries* or *computer interface*. In addition, experience indicates that charges to this account are always below $30,000. These two factors would be sufficient to determine account distribution, if the initiator was from the MIS or communications department.

If the initiator was from another department (40 percent of the time), one would also determine whether the invoice indicated an hourly or a monthly service, since 50 percent are billed hourly and 30 percent are billed monthly. The remaining 20 percent do not indicate the unit of measure. Therefore, the knowledge-based system will be unable to provide the account distribution approximately 8 percent of the time (20 percent times 40 percent) due to the lack of a unit of measure.

## The Initial Prototype

The initial prototype system does not handle these exceptional cases, but merely identifies them for manual review. The purpose of the initial system is only to provide consistency across the majority of cases and to isolate those for handling by a most experienced clerk.

The initial prototype also does not make use of certainty factors, since in the area of professional fees there were not a large number of exceptional cases. Subsequent versions of the system did include certainty factors, and so reduced considerably the number of decisions that had to be handled manually.

Experienced programmers have noted that the decision described in Fig. 12-5 could be programmed for a conventional computer system. However, the situation is evolving and changing as new accounts are added, new types of services are purchased, and new types of invoices are covered by the system, and conventional computer systems do not have the flexibility to allow such changes to be made quickly, easily and inexpensively. It was, therefore, decided to develop a knowledge-based system.

The development of a small prototype system for one limited professional services area is described in the following section. It is designed both to be used by clerks and to enable testing the concept and structure of a larger knowledge-based system.

## DOCUMENTING THE PROTOTYPE SYSTEM

The following discussion covers the system documentation phase, including

- □ System proposal
- □ Description of the system
- □ Dependency diagrams
- □ Decision charts
- □ Designing and constructing the knowledge base

### System Proposal

The purpose of this project is to design a prototype knowledge-based system to help individuals with limited accounting background to properly choose the account assignment for invoices. The system described here is a prototype of a larger system that would cover other types of disbursements as well as other accounting areas. The system will be developed using an M.1 expert system programming shell.

The next phase of the project system, containing other types of disbursements, would be put on a GURU expert system shell to take advantage of its color and graphics and to allow for interface with spreadsheets and data bases. Allowing interface with a vendor data base, for example, would give ready access to historical vendor information that could prove useful in the account assignment decision.

Two areas of knowledge were needed to develop the knowledge-based system. First, this system is largely based on experience. Many of the rules and questions are determined from an examination of hundreds of actual transactions in the prototype area. Reviewing these transactions and recording key information provided necessary knowledge to build a tailor-made system for the company under study.

In addition, formal training in accounting was also needed to determine which types of invoices should be categorized in the various accounts in the chart of accounts, as shown in Fig. 12-4.

### Description of the System

This section covers

- □ System overview and objective
- □ Recommendations to be made by the system
- □ Typical user dialogue
- □ Structure of the system's knowledge domain model and reasoning processes

**System overview and objective.** The purpose of the prototype system is to enable clerks, with limited accounting background, to properly determine the account assignment (or distribution) for professional fee invoices.

The major benefit of this system is that it will provide a cost-efficient means of ensuring the consistency and accuracy of accounting information. It also reduces clerk training time and enables effectively employing clerks with less advanced educational skills. In addition, a direct benefit will be the reduced need for correcting entries, which is a significant cost in terms of both computer time and wasted labor.

**Recommendations to be made by the system.** The prototype system is able to make one of the following recommendations:

1. Debit legal expense (account number 7556110)
2. Debit accounting fees expense (account number 7556120)
3. Debit outside MIS expense (account number 7556130)
4. Debit consulting fees expense (account number 7556140)
5. Debit other professional fees expense (account number 7556150)
6. This cash disbursement does not fit the system specifications for professional fees

**Typical user dialogue.** In the prototype system the user will be asked questions about the cash disbursement request and supporting invoice. The user will obtain this information from an examination of the invoice under study. For example, several questions are

□ *Individual requesting payments*—"What department does the employee who is requesting the payment work for?"
□ *Description of service on the invoice*—"Based upon the invoice description, which *specific* term is used to describe the service performed?" and "Based upon the invoice description, which *general* term is used to describe the service performed?"
□ *Dollar amount*—"What is the dollar amount of the disbursement request?"
□ *Payee name*—"How would you categorize the payee name?"
□ *Invoice letterhead*—"What description of the payee is indicated on the letterhead?"
□ *Unit of measure*—"How would you describe the unit of measure on the invoice?"

Typical permissible answers are given in the questions listed in the knowledge base in Fig. 12-8 (presented later in the chapter).

**Description of the knowledge structure and reasoning processes.** The knowledge structure is very simple, as seen in the diagram in Fig. 12-5. The reasoning processes involved in the prototype system are also fairly simple. The prototype system will always ask the same two questions first (requesting department and invoice description). These two are the most important. Based upon the answers to these questions, the knowledge-based system will either determine the account distribution immediately or decide which question or questions to ask next. If the characteristics of the transaction, as determined by the answers to all the questions, do not fit any of the first-level rules, the user will be told that the invoice is in all likelihood not a professional fees invoice. These exceptions are accumulated and screened once a day by a more experienced clerk.

The system is designed to provide reasons why the questions are being asked should the user desire such information.

## Dependency Diagram

Figure 12-6 is the dependency diagram for the prototype system. It is a complete summary outline of all the questions, rules, knowledge segments and their interrelationships, values, and recommendations within the system.

## Decision Chart

Figure 12-7 gives a decision chart from the prototype system. It covers all the if-then rules for the final system stage. There is a decision chart for every rule set in the system.

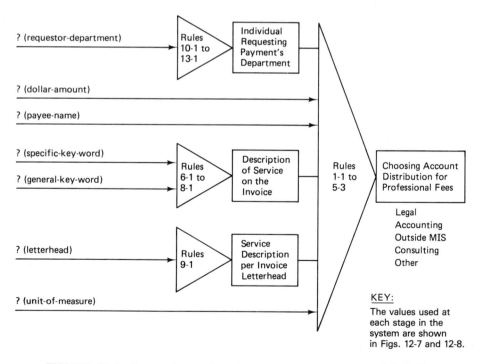

**FIGURE 12-6 Dependency diagram for knowledge-based system for account distribution—professional fees (initial prototype).**

RULES

| PREMISES | 1-1 | 1-2 | 1-3 | 2-1 | 3-1 | 3-2 | 4-1 | 4-2 | 4-3 | 5-1 | 5-2 | 5-3 |
|---|---|---|---|---|---|---|---|---|---|---|---|---|
| requestor-department | legal | legal | non-legal | Controller or Tax | MIS or Communications | non-MIS | MIS | Personnel | non-MIS and non-personnel | Loss Prevention | Office Services | (any) |
| invoice-description | legal-related | general | legal-related | audit | computer-related | computer-related | consulting | consulting | consulting | security service | food service | general |
| dollar-amount | (any) | (any) | Below $30,000 | (any) | Below $30,000 | Below $30,000 | Below $30,000 | $30,000 to $40,000 | Below $30,000 | Below $30,000 | $30,000 to $40,000 | Below $30,000 |
| payee-name | (any) | several surnames | several surnames | Arthur Andersen | other | other | (any) | other | other | (any) | (any) | (any) |
| invoice-letterhead | (any) | legal-service | (any) | (any) | (any) | (any) | (any) | (any) | (any) | (any) | (any) | (any) |
| unit-of-measure | (any) | (any) | (any) | (any) | (any) | Months or Hours | (any) | quarters | (any) | (any) | none | (any) |
| ACCOUNT DISTRIBUTION | Legal | Legal | Legal | Accounting | Outside MIS | Outside MIS | Consulting | Consulting | Consulting | Other Professional fees | Other Professional fees | Other Professional fees |

**FIGURE 12-7** Sample decision chart for professional fees account distribution—initial prototype.

goal—account-distribution.

rule-1-1:
   if requestor-department = legal and
      invoice-description = legal-related
   then account-distribution = legal.

rule-1-2:
   if requestor-department = legal and
      invoice-description = general and
      payee-name = several-surnames and
      invoice-letterhead = legal-service
   then account-distribution = legal.

rule-1-3:
   if requestor-nl = non-legal and
      invoice-description = legal-related and
      dollar-amount = below-30000 and
      payee-name = several-surnames
   then account-distribution = legal.


/\*Description of the Service on the Invoice\*/

rule-6-1:
   if specific-key-word = appeal or
      specific-key-word = arbitration or
      specific-key-word = claim or
      specific-key-word = court or
      specific-key-word = taxes or
      specific-key-word = legal or
      specific-key-word = litigation or
      specific-key-word = visa
   then invoice-description = legal-related.

rule-8-1:
   if general-key-word = professional-services or
      general-key-word = study or
      general-key-word = research
   then invoice-description = general.

rule-9-1:
   if letterhead = attorneys-at-law or
      letterhead = law-offices or
      letterhead = counselors-at-law or
      letterhead = barristers-and-solicitors
   then invoice-letterhead = legal-service.

*(continued)*

**FIGURE 12-8  Example of if-then rules, questions and legalvals for
EKBS for professional fees account distribution.**

question (requestor-department) = 'What department does the employee who is requesting the payment work for? [controller, communications, legal, loss-prevention, mis, office-services, personnel, tax, or other]'.

legalvals (requestor-department) = [controller, communications, legal, loss-prevention, mis, office-services, personnel, tax, other].

question (specific-key-word) = 'Based upon the invoice description, which specific term is used to describe the service performed? [actuarial, appeal, arbitration, audit, claim, computer-interface, computer-service, computer-storage, computer-usage, consulting, court, food-service, information-service, legal, litigation, on-line, taxes, security-service, translation, visa, or other]'.

legalvals (specific-key-word) = [actuarial, appeal, arbitration, audit, claim, computer-interface, computer-service, computer-storage, computer-usage, consulting, court, food-service, information-service, legal, litigation, on-line, taxes, security-service, translation, visa, or other].

question (general-key-word) = 'Based upon the invoice description which general term is used to describe the service performed? [professional-services, research, study, or other]'.

legalvals (general-key-word) = [professional-services, research, study, other].

question (payee-name) = 'How would you categorize the payee name? [several-surnames, arthur-andersen, or other]'.

legalvals (payee-name) = [several-surnames, arthur-andersen, other].

question (letterhead) = 'What description of the payee is indicated on the letterhead? [attorney-at-law, law-offices, counselors-at-law, barristers-and-solicitors, other, or none]'.

legalvals (letterhead) = [attorney-at-law, law-offices, counselors-at-law, barristers-and-solicitors, other, none].

question (dollar-amount) = 'What is the dollar amount of the disbursement request? [40000–50000, 30000–40000, or below-30000]'.

legalvals (dollar-amount) = [40000–50000, 30000–40000, below-30000].

**FIGURE 12-8** *(continued)*

## Designing and Constructing the Knowledge Base

Rules and questions were developed from the situation study. They were based on the system developer's analysis of how an accountant makes such decisions. Figure 12-8 contains a sample of the knowledge base for the prototype system. The final rule-set sample (rules 1-1 to 1-3) matches the rules specified in the decision chart in Fig. 12-7. In addition, the questions match those specified in the dependency diagram in Fig. 12-6.

Two very simple introductory and concluding panels were created for the system. The if-then rules in the knowledge base in Fig. 12-8 match those specified in the decision charts. They were written to reflect the relationships shown in the dependency diagram in Fig. 12-6. They use the values shown in the decision charts and in the knowledge base (Figs. 12-7 and 12-8). The questions in the knowledge base (Fig. 12-8) are those indicated in the dependency diagram.

## Testing the System

To test the knowledge-based system and to determine if its interrelationships were valid, over one hundred consultations were performed. The system was able to recommend the account distribution in over 90 percent of the cases and all recommendations were correct. The remaining cases, which the knowledge-based system could not handle, resulted in a message to the user that the "account assignment was sought but no value was concluded." Since no incorrect results were found in the test, confidence factors were deemed unnecessary for the prototype system.

## REVIEW QUESTIONS

1. Complete the knowledge-based system (or any segment of the system) partially documented in this chapter and enter it into the expert system shell you have.

2. Describe the major differences between the system described in this chapter and the other four accounting and finance systems described in the preceding chapters.

3. Describe the circumstances in business which make systems such as the one described in this chapter have such high payoffs in business, in spite of their relative simplicity.

4. Discuss the ways in which the system described in this chapter would or would not be considered an "expert" system.

5. Develop a list of other accounting/record keeping areas in which knowledge-based systems might have cost effective and efficient applications. Briefly outline the structure of one of these systems.

6. Describe the process of structured situation analysis and decision situation model development in the situation described in this chapter.

7. Describe the way in which structured situation analysis is used to provide a basis for prototype system design and documentation in the system described in this chapter.

8. It is clear that there may be as many ways to describe decision situations as there are people describing them. Describe some of the ways you have developed for structuring situations in a way that facilitates prototype knowledge-based system development.

9. What are the four broad categories that accounting transactions can be divided into?

10. What factors are considered in deciding which account to assign (or debit) a professional fee expense to when accounting for professional fees and transactions?

# REFERENCES

Barton, A.D., *Anatomy of Accounting*, 3rd ed., New York: University of Queensland Press, 1984.

Behrenfeld, W.H., and A.R. Biebl, *Accountants Business Manual*, New York: American Institute of C.P.A.s, 1987.

Bost, P.J., "Do Cost Accounting Standards Fill A Gap In Cost Allocation," *Management Accounting*, vol. 68, November 1986.

Doyle, D.M., *Efficient Accounting and Record Keeping*, New York: John Wiley and Sons, 1978.

Dudick, T.S., "Why SG&A Doesn't Always Work," *Harvard Business Review*, vol. 65, January–February 1987.

Myer, J.N., *Accounting for Non-Accountants*, New York: E.P. Dutton, 1987.

Sannella, A.J., "An Application of Income Strategy to Cost Allocation and Segment Reporting," *Journal of Accounting, Auditing and Finance*, 1986.

Simini, J.P., *Accounting Made Simple*, New York: Doubleday & Co., 1987.

Vasarhelyi, M.A., *Artificial Intelligence in Accounting and Auditing—Using Expert Systems*, New York: Marcus Wiener, 1987.

# 13

# A Customer Service Representative System

This chapter describes the development of an expert knowledge-based system designed to guide a customer service representative (CSR) at a major metropolitan utility in answering billing complaints on commercial accounts that have demand metering. The discussion covers

- The overall situation under study: understanding the expert's domain
- Studying the situation to be prototyped
- Documenting the prototype system

The early sections of the report describe the broad situation for which the system is being developed and the responsibilities of the CSRs. The situation to be prototyped, a segment of the total CSR job, is then described. The final section describes the development of the prototype system within the framework of the overall situation.

## THE OVERALL SITUATION UNDER STUDY: UNDERSTANDING THE EXPERT'S DOMAIN

The discussion in this section covers:

- Selecting a decision area to work on
- Probing how the situation works and how decisions are made
- Narrowing the focus

## Selecting a Decision Area to Work On

The decision situation under study involves a major public utility in a large metropolitan area. As shown in Fig. 13-1, the company is divided into four major organizational areas:

- Administration
- Construction
- Division operations
- Power generation

This study involves the division operations area. Division operations is responsible for all customer service related activities within the company's operating area. Organizationally there are separate divisions covering each of the six major geographic areas within the company's operating area. Each separate division has four operating departments:

- Administration
- Branch operations
- Field operations
- Electric and gas operations

The customer service representative (CSR) works in branch operations. The area of branch operations was selected because

- There are recognized experts in the field.
- Expert decision skills are needed to do the job.
- The task is well understood.
- This project was consistent with the company's strategic goals of reducing training costs and staffing in the CSR area.
- Good decisions in this area result in much more efficient usage of qualified personnel time.
- Good customer service is important to the company's public image.

## Probing How the Situation Works and How Decisions Are Made

CSRs are employed in various geographic branches of the utility. Within each branch CSRs are assigned to a specific group of customer accounts, so as to maintain an even work flow through the month. These groupings are called sets. There are almost six hundred CSR positions throughout the entire company.

As shown in Fig. 13-2, every CSR is involved in a minimum of four major areas: (1) customer accounting, (2) credit and collection, (3) telephone service, and (4) customer correspondence.

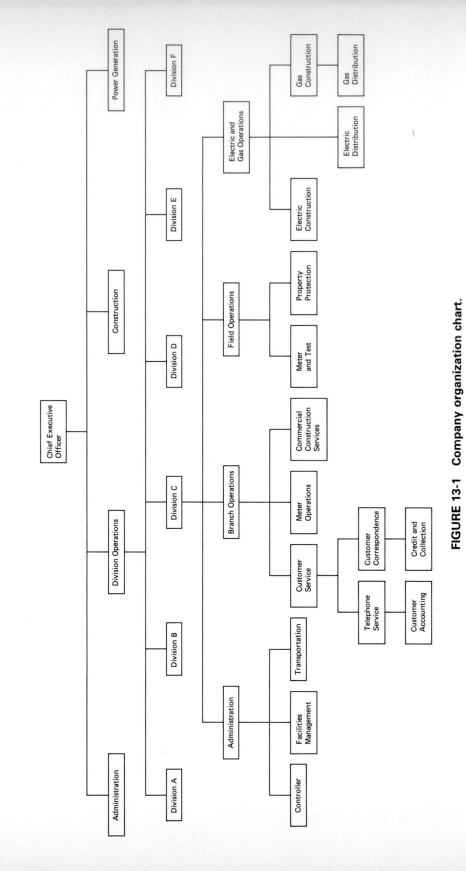

**FIGURE 13-1  Company organization chart.**

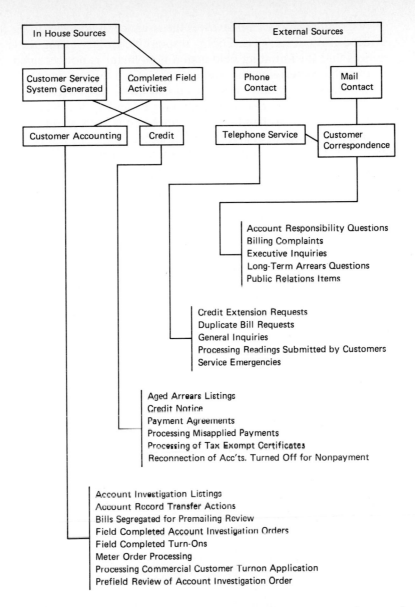

**FIGURE 13-2  Overview of customer service representative work functions.**

*Customer accounting* involves, among other tasks, reviewing a customer's account to determine whether a bill issued is correct. These accounts are obtained from listings generated by the mainframe customer account information system, which identifies and forwards to the CSRs questionable bill amounts or billing problems manually reported by a meter reader.

*Credit and collection* involves the issuance of notices for the collection of arrears or deposit requests. The CSR is responsible for reviewing these payment collection notices and for initiating field action if payment is not received. There are several factors that determine the appropriate actions to be taken. For example, shorter time frames are employed for high dollar accounts or accounts with prior difficulties.

*Telephone service* involves handling incoming customer telephone inquiries. Its main objective is to handle all customer phone calls as quickly as possible. Unfortunately an in-depth analysis of each inquiry may not always be possible. In these cases the CSR will generate a customer inquiry request that is sent to customer correspondence for subsequent investigation.

Telephone service also processes all routine turnon and turnoff requests, obtaining the necessary data and issuing these requests to meter operations for field completion. After field completion of turnons and turnoffs, the field completed documents are forwarded to customer accounting. The processing of turnons or turnoffs is the establishment and deletion of a customer on the company's computerized billing system. For example, if a person moves into an apartment that is individually metered, that person would call the company, tell them who they are, where they live, when they moved in, and some basic credit reference questions. The CSR puts this information into the customer account system. For a turnoff, a person calls and advises the CSR that they are moving on such and such a date and the CSR closes the account.

*Customer correspondence* involves the satisfactory completion of any phone generated customer inquiry request or any mail inquiry. This area requires a high level of experience or expertise to respond correctly and in a reasonable period of time.

Examples of the types of inquiries handled in this area are

- *Account responsibility*—This involves determining which customer is responsible for the bills at which location.
- *Billing complaints*—These can vary from high to low or no bill complaints.
- *Credit matters*—This includes investigating such matters as the status of unrefunded deposits.
- *Executive inquiries*—Those complaints directed to any company officer.
- *Public relations*—This includes handling matters such as crews making too much noise or failing to keep appointments.

In 1975, the company combined all four of the above activities under one job title, customer service representative. Prior to this each of these jobs were separate, and promotions to higher positions were given only after an employee passed required tests and training.

The most demanding functions were customer accounting and customer correspondence. These jobs required mathematical, writing, and analytical skills. The training for a customer account analyst, for example, began with thirteen weeks of formal schooling and several years working in a support position to improve analytical skills.

The company's decision to combine all customer service functions under one title resulted in many senior employees with no previous experience working in customer accounting. To rectify this, the company first attempted to formally train each individual. However, the large number of employees requiring training necessitated reducing the formal classroom training period, and more on-the-job training was conducted. With attrition more poorly trained, underqualified representatives took over. Because these employees were unable to analyze accounts properly, they often took the easy way out. They would make no decision and estimate the bill or request additional information or unnecessary physical inspections of meters. These requests placed additional burdens on field organizations.

The company has developed an extensive library of publications concerning customer service rules and guidelines, most of which are designed to show how to go about handling typical problems encountered. The publications fail, however, to deal with the interpretative decision processes involved in handling specific day-to-day problems quickly in specific situations. These technical publications do not provide this kind of situational help. The CSR must know what to look for, where to look for it, and how the various factors relate.

The purpose of a customer service representative assistance knowledge-based system is to help resolve these problems. It is designed to improve the decision skills of those CSRs, improve responsiveness to the customer, and reduce field costs.

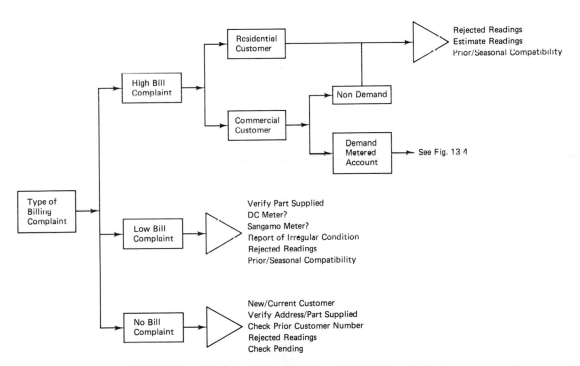

**FIGURE 13-3   Overview of billing complaint decision process.**

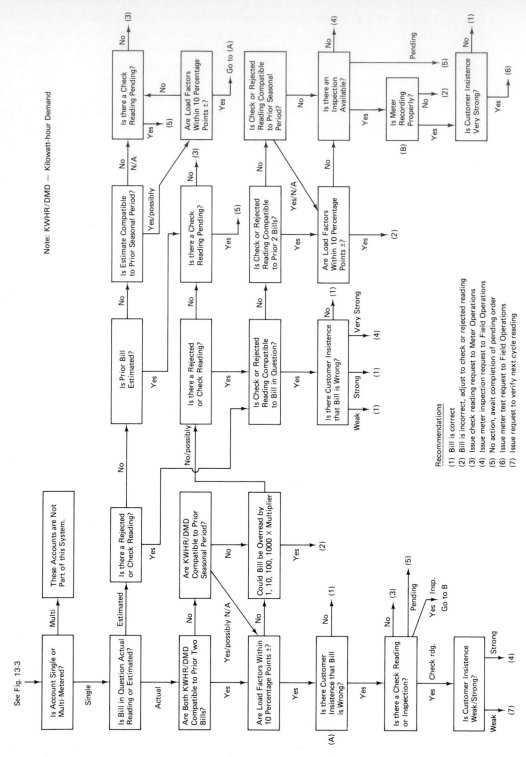

Note: KWHR/DMD — Kilowatt-hour Demand

Recommendations

(1) Bill is correct
(2) Bill is incorrect, adjust to check or rejected reading
(3) Issue check reading request to Meter Operations
(4) Issue meter inspection request to Field Operations
(5) No action, await completion of pending order
(6) Issue meter test request to Field Operations
(7) Issue request to verify next cycle reading

**FIGURE 13-4 Overview of system for commercial high bill complaint—demand metered account.**

### Narrowing the Focus of the Study

The broad range of functions shown in Fig. 13-2 is too large to be developed into a knowledge-based system during this initial prototype phase. Therefore, it was decided to select what appears to be the most difficult area for a CSR to understand and efficiently handle without assistance—billing complaints arising from customer correspondence or customer complaints generated by the telephone service area. The customer correspondence sector can be divided into three parts: high bill complaint, low bill complaint, and no bill complaint.

Figure 13-3 shows a simplified overview of the decision process involved in handling billing complaints. It is apparent from this flowchart that developing an expert knowledge-based system for even one of these three categories of customer correspondence would be too large an undertaking for the initial prototype development phase. Therefore, it was decided to narrow the focus of the first phase of the project to processing high bill complaints on commercial accounts that have demand metering devices, as described in Fig. 13-4.

## STUDYING THE SITUATION TO BE PROTOTYPED

This section first describes demand metering and demand billing and then the step-by-step handling of an actual billing complaint case by an expert CSR, using the reference screens that give customer account information stored on the mainframe computer.

A demand meter calculates the highest kilowatt-hour (kwh) usage average over two consecutive fifteen minute periods. For example, if a customer uses 15 kwh in a fifteen minute period and 25 kwh in the next fifteen minute period, the demand usage would be 20 kwh. If 10 kwh and 30 kwh were used in two consecutive fifteen minute periods, the demand usage would still be 20 kwh. This averaging continues throughout the billing cycle—the demand register showing only the highest of these averages—until the meter reader resets the demand register back to zero when the meter is read (at the monthly cycle), and the process begins again.

Demand billing is a surcharge for monthly peak usage of commercial customers whose kilowatt-hour consumption exceeds 3,000 kwh per month on average or 6,000 kwh in any two consecutive months. The reason for this surcharge is that the company must maintain adequate generating capacity to meet the highest peak usage requirements of its customers. Since electricity cannot be saved or stored, and these large commercial customers are the primary cause of this peaking, they are the ones charged for the maintenance of these extra generating plants. Demand is billed at a cost of $20 per kilowatt-hour.

In order to properly analyze these accounts when a complaint is received, a review of the reference screens available on the mainframe customer service system is necessary. Each of the screens listed below supplies specific data pertaining to the customer's account and would be utilized in conjunction with the flowchart in Fig. 13-4. The information available on the reference screen and the answers to the questions in Fig. 13-4 would help the CSR in determining the correct course of action.

The reference screens available are

- *Billing history*—a list of the dates, readings, usage and bill amounts
- *Rejected reading history*—a list of rejected (cycle) or check (off-cycle) readings that were not initially used to bill an account
- *Meter constant*—a number by which the difference between the present and previous readings is multiplied in order to calculate the customer's total usage
- *Inquiry history*—a list of prior customer contacts and pending and completed field requests
- *Load factor history*—a list of the demand meter readings and their percentage relationship to the kilowatt-hour usage
- *Pending history*—a list of specific information on pending or completed investigations

Figure 13-4 outlines how an expert CSR goes about handling a high bill complaint efficiently and accurately. This outline of the CSR decision process (see Fig. 13-4) will be used as a model for developing a knowledge-based system to assist with handling such complaints.

Figure 13-5 shows an example of how the process in Fig. 13-4 is applied to an actual situation. The shaded areas show the reasoning path followed by a CSR in handling a specific high bill complaint and making an appropriate recommendation.

The following discussion traces the handling of this specific high bill complaint from the initial customer contact to its disposition. The appropriate customer reference screens are shown in Fig. 13-6.

For example, on March 12, 1987, a CSR received a high bill complaint, which is indicated by an A in Fig. 13-6. Upon receiving this complaint the CSR accessed the customer's account using the computerized retrieval terminal (CRT) on his desk. The initial action was to determine which bill the customer was complaining about. In this complaint the bill in question was the January 28, 1987, to February 20, 1987, bill for 3,492 kwh with 8.46 points of demand usage and a dollar value of $549.90 (B in Fig. 13-6).

The steps followed by the CSR, as shown in Fig. 13-5, are

- *Step 1:* In addressing this complaint the CSR first determines whether the bill in question was an actual reading or an estimate. The CV notation (C in Fig. 13-6) indicates it was an actual reading.
- *Step 2:* Next, the bill in question was compared to the prior two bills (D in Fig. 13-6). Both these were again actual readings (CV). Since both of these bills were significantly less than the $549.90 bill the answer was *no* to compatibility.
- *Step 3:* The bill in question's compatibility with the prior seasonal period (E in Fig. 13-6) was checked. Again, the current and past bills were not totally compatible, but the prior seasonal period was closer. Therefore, the answer could be *possibly*.
- *Step 4:* The load factor relationships were studied to determine whether the February 20, 1987, load factor (F in Fig. 13-6) was within ten percentage points of the prior two bills' load factors (G in Fig. 13-6) and the prior seasonal bill's

Note: KWHR/DMD – Kilowatt-hour Demand

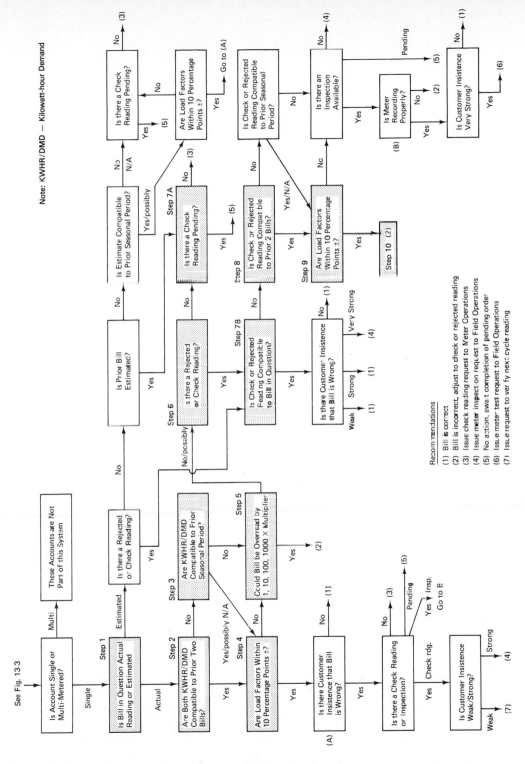

Recommendations

(1) Bill is correct
(2) Bill is incorrect, adjust to check or rejected reading
(3) Issue check reading request to Meter Operations
(4) Issue meter inspect on request to Field Operations
(5) No action, await completion of pending order
(6) Issue meter test request to Field Operations
(7) Issue request to verify next cycle reading

FIGURE 13-5  Overview of decision situation to be prototyped: high bill complaint—demand metered account.

283

## REFERENCE SCREEN: INQUIRY HISTORY

```
MPP4940010082        10 07 87105
437213 1432 2000 4   FURNITURE SYSTEMS FOR
85 10                AV 1FLC    E   2 G
MANHATTAN            10011
DATE-SRC TYPE  EMPL#  REFERL DISP  DATE
3/12/7 T  APP  58423  MOP    READ  3/17/7
3/12/7 T  HBE  55702         COMP  3/12/7   ←(A)
3/12/7 T  APP  55702  MOP    INPT  3/12/7
3/05/6 M  NFA  05944  ACC    REML  3/07/6
2/13/6 M  NFA  05944  ACC    REML  2/18/6
9/18/5 C  GEN  39275         COMP  9/18/5
9/12/5 A  TON  41263         COMP  9/12/5
                A/R BAL            -118.46
```

ACCESS CODE: INQ1

## REFERENCE SCREEN: BILLING HISTORY

```
MPP4940010083        10 08 87105
437213 1432 2000 4   FURNITURE SYSTEMS FOR
T-DATE M-DATE  CONS    CD DEMAND  AMOUNT
2/20/7 2/23/7  3492CV ←(C) 8.46   549.90   ←(B)
1/21/7 1/22/7  2106CV      7.02   327.53   ←(D)
D/19/6 D/22/7  1656CV      6.66   257.17
N/19/6 N/20/6  1386CV      7.20   223.99
O/20/6 0/21/6  1278CV      5.58   219.08
9/18/6 9/19/6  1332CV      5.22   241.06
8/19/6 8/20/6  1188CV      5.04   215.47
8/21/6 7/22/6  1566CV      4.86   287.23
8/19/6 6/20/6  2034CV      5.76   364.80
                LAR    1662 3/23/7
```

ACCESS CODE: EBL3

## REFERENCE SCREEN: BILLING HISTORY

```
MPP4940010084        10 08 87105
437213 1432 2000 4   FURNITURE SYSTEMS FOR
T-DATE M-DATE  CONS    CD DEMAND  AMOUNT
5/20/6 5/21/6  1764CV      6.30   294.80
4/21/6 4/22/6  1656CV      6.66   281.19
3/21/6 3/24/6  2538CV      7.20   435.01
2/20/6 2/21/6  2376CV      7.02   415.80   ←(E)
1/21/6 1/22/6  1944CV      7.38   332.52
D/19/5 D/20/5  1350CV      5.76   232.63
N/19/5 N/20/5  1026CV      4.86   187.45
O/18/5 0/21/5  1206CV      4.32   228.20
9/18/5 9/19/5  540CV       5.40   109.34
                LAR    1662 3/23/7
```

ACCESS CODE: EBL4

(continued)

```
MPP4940010085        10 08 87105
437213 1432 2000 4  FURNITURE SYSTEMS FOR
  DATE  DMD RDG CD CONST  DEMAND REG  PCT
3/23/7  06.89  CV  0018    7.56      00
3/16/7  06.47  SK           5.76      23
2/20/7  06.15  CV           8.46      00
1/21/7  05.68  VC                     00
1/20/7  06.15  CV           8.46      57   ←(F)
1/21/7  05.68  CV           7.02      37  ⎤
D/19/6  05.29  CV           6.66      34  ⎦ ←(G)
N/19/6  04.52  CV           7.20      26
D/20/6  04.52  CV           5.58      29
```

REFERENCE SCREEN:
LOAD FACTOR HISTORY

ACCESS CODE:  DMRD

```
MPP4940010086        10 08 87105
437213 1432 2000 4  FURNITURE SYSTEMS FOR
  DATE  DMD RDG CD CONST  DEMAND REG  PCT
9/18/6  04.21  CV  0018    5.22      35
8/19/6  03.92  CV           5.04      33
7/21/6  03.64  CV           4.86      41
6/19/6  03.37  CV           5.76      49
5/20/6  03.05  CV           6.30      40
4/21/6  02.70  CV           6.66      33
3/21/6  02.33  CV           7.20      50
2/20/6  01.93  CV           7.02      47   ←(H)
1/21/6  01.54  CV           7.38      33
```

REFERENCE SCREEN:
LOAD FACTOR HISTORY

ACCESS CODE:  DMR1

```
MPP4940010087        10 08 87105
437213 1432 2000 4  FURNITURE SYSTEMS FOR
71HT 5152'27 T3/D4  LOC 1FL  PROFAIL
K (I)→18 STATUS  ON PRES RDG 001662 06.89
ACTIVE SC  2       PREV RDG 001645 06.47
TAX F REJC Y AIDS N   T/L SIG    TENS L
60DAY 0C02900
T-DATE M-DATE   CONS  CD  DEMAND   AMOUNT
3/23/7          306CV     7.56
3/16/7 3/19/7  26105K     5.76     431.44
2/20/7           0CV      8.46
2/21/7         3492VC              549.90
                      LAR  1662 3/23/7
```

REFERENCE SCREEN:
BILLING HISTORY

ACCESS CODE:  EBL2

FIGURE 13-6  Reference screens for typical decision for h gh bill complaint—demand metered account.

285

```
MPP4940010088          10 09 87105
437213 1432 2000 4   FURNITURE SYSTEMS FOR
85 10                AV 1FLCE  2 ACTIVE
MANHATTAN          10011  G
ID TYPE EMP # APPROVAL CUTO    T 47071002220
01 REFD 58423 READ

              COMPLETE
```
←(J)

REFERENCE SCREEN: **PENDING HISTORY**

ACCESS CODE: **PEND**

```
MPP4940010089          10 09 87105
437213 1432 2000 4   FURNITURE SYSTEMS FOR
85 10                AV 1FLC   E  2 G
MANHATTAN          10011
DATE-SRC TYPE  EMPL#  REFERL DISP  DATE
3/12/7 T  APP  58423  MOP    READ  3/17/7
3/12/7 T  HBE  55702         COMP  3/12/7
3/12/7 T  APP  55702  MOP    INPT  3/12/7
3/05/6 M  NFA  05944  ACC    REML  3/07/6
2/13/6 M  NFA  05944  ACC    REML  2/18/6
9/18/5 C  GEN  39275         COMP  9/18/5
9/12/5 A  TON  41263         COMP  9/12/5
          A/R BAL           -118.46
```
←(K)

REFERENCE SCREEN: **INQUIRY HISTORY**

ACCESS CODE: **INQ1**

```
MPP4940010090          10 09 87105
437213 1432 2000 4   FURNITURE SYSTEMS FOR
MP M RESCINITI EMP# 55702 T
REFD TYPE APP DEPT MOP TEL# 2126863818
PLOC 3 REMARKS APPT TO READ * CRANK ELEC
MTR MON 3/16 BET 8 12 SEE J. STUART OR
JOSIE DOOR OPEN
   EMPL# 58423 DISP    READ DATE 031787
FCFR 10981            ACTION KW-1645 DF-
0615 DL-0647 K-18 VRFD 031687.
```
←(L)

REFERENCE SCREEN: **PENDING HISTORY**

ACCESS CODE: **PEND 01**

```
MPP4940010091        10 09 87105
437213 1432 2000  4  FURNITURE SYSTEMS FOR
T-DATE M-DATE  CONS  CD  DEMAND  AMOUNT
2/20/7 2/23/7  3492CV   8.46   549.90
1/21/7 1/22/7  2106CV   7.02   327.53
D/19/6 D/22/6  1656CV   6.65   257.17
N/19/6 N/20/6  1386CV   7.20   223.99
0/20/6 0/21/6  1278CV   5.56   219.08
9/18/6 9/19/6  1332CV   5.22   241.06
8/19/6 8/20/6  1188CV   5.04   215.47
7/21/6 7/22/6  1566CV   4.86   287.23  ┐
6/19/6 6/20/6  2034CV   5.76   364.80  ┘ (M)
                 LAR  1662  3/23/7
```

REFERENCE SCREEN:
        BILLING HISTORY

ACCESS CODE:  EBL3
          DIFF MULTIPLIER CONS

KWH RDG 2/20/87 1694   194 × 18 = 3492
KWH RDG 1/21/87 1500

DEMAND RDG 2/20/87 06.15   .47 × 18 = 8.46
DEMAND RDG 1/21/87 05.68

```
MPP4940010092        10 09 8710E
437213 1432 2000  4  FURNITURE SYSTEMS FOR
DATE  DMD RDG CD CONST  DEMAND REG  PCT
3/23/7  06.89  CV  0018   7.56   00
3/16/7  06.47  SK         5.76   23   ←(N)
2/20/7  06.15  CV         8.46   00
1/21/7  05.68  VC                00
2/20/7  06.15  CV         8.46   57
1/21/7  05.68  CV         7.02   37  ┐
D/19/6  05.29  CV         6.66   34  ┘ (G)
N/19/6  04.92  CV         7.20   26
0/20/6  04.52  CV         5.58   29
```

REFERENCE SCREEN:
        LOAD FACTOR HISTORY

ACCESS CODE:  DMRD

```
MPP4940010093        10 10 87105
437213 1432 2000  4  FURNITURE SYSTEMS FOR
   71HT 5152127 T3/D4  LOC 1FL  PRO-AIL
K   18 STATUS    ON PRES RDG 001662 06.89
ACTIVE SC  2        PREV RDG 001645 06.47
TAX F REJC Y AIDS N   H/L SIG   TENS L
60DAY 0002900
T-DATE M-DATE  CONS  CD  DEMAND  AMOUNT
3/23/7         306CV      7.56
3/16/7 3/19/7  2610SK     5.76   431.44  ←(O)
2/20/7          0CV       8.46
1/21/7         3492VC            549.90
                 LAR  1662  3/23/7
```

REFERENCE SCREEN:
        BILLING HISTORY

ACCESS CODE:  EBL2

**FIGURE 13-6** (continued)

load factor (H in Fig. 13-6). Since they were not (fifty-seven versus thirty-seven, thirty-four), the answer was *no*.

- *Step 5:* The CSR then considered if the February 20, 1987, reading (B) could be wrong. This required checking the meter multiplier (I in Fig. 13-6). The multiplier is the factor applied to the actual meter reading. On this account it was an eighteen. Therefore, for example, an overreading of ten (a common error) would be a difference of 180 in the billing kilowatt-hours and an overreading of 100 (another common error) would be a difference of 1,800. The consumption of the February 20, 1987, bill was 3,492 kwh, as previously stated. The CSR would deduct the 1,800 kwh—as a test of a possible overreading error—from 3,492 kwh (C in Fig. 13-6), leaving 1,692 kwh as the usage comparison. Returning to points D and E, the CSR determined whether this 1,692 kwh usage was compatible. It was compatible for the December 19, 1986, usage of 1,656 kwh, but low for both the January 21, 1987, usage of 2,106 kwh and the February 20, 1987, usage of 2,176 kwh. Therefore, the CSR determined that the reading was *possibly* overread.

- *Step 6:* The CSR then determined if there was any supporting information in the form of a rejected reading or a check reading. A rejected reading is a reading obtained at the scheduled meter reading day but not used because it failed one of the several billing checks that are built into the mainframe customer service system. A check reading is one obtained in order to verify a rejected reading or any other prior reading. This information was available on the "Pending History" reference screen shown as J in Fig. 13-6.

- *Step 7A:* At the initial review there were none, so the CSR issued a request to meter operations to check the reading. This is recommendation 3. At that point the CSR would await the return of the check reading information (L in Fig. 13-6). Now, the answer to "is there a rejected or check reading" was *yes*.

- *Step 7B:* The CSR then determined the compatibility of this rejected or check reading to the bill in question. The check reading on March 17, 1987, showed the reading to be 1,645 as opposed to the adjusted reading (3,492 minus 1,800 in step 5) of 1,694 on February 20, 1987 (M in Fig. 13-6).

- *Steps 8 and 9:* Since it was now apparent that the February 20, 1987, reading was wrong, a quick check of the compatibility of this reading's usage with the prior two bills and the prior seasonal period and of their respective load factors (D, N, and G in Fig. 13-5) was made.

- *Step 10:* Since both were *yes*, the recommended action was "bill is incorrect, adjust to check reading." The adjusted bill is shown as O in Fig. 13-5.

The steps described above outline a high bill complaint where the bill in question had an actual reading. If the bill in question had been estimated (at Step 1), the CSR would first check to see if there is a rejected or check reading. If there was, the CSR would go directly to Step 7B. If there was no check ready, the CSR would check the two prior readings (at Step 2). If the customer's account had two consecutive estimated bills, the CSR would immediately ask for a check reading, since a series of estimates can cause significant billing adjustments in the future. If the past bill was not estimated, the CSR would proceed to Step 3.

PART 2: DEVELOPING MANAGEMENT DECISION SYSTEMS

The final point that requires clarification in Fig. 13-4 is the area of customer insistence that the bill is wrong. Very often the CSR will make a decision that the bill in question is correct, but have difficulty in convincing the customer. At that point the CSR will review the account to determine what supportive data, such as check readings or inspection, have previously been obtained.

As indicated in Fig. 13-4, if the insistence is weak and there was a prior check reading, the CSR would take the action of only issuing a request to verify the next cycle reading. This recommendation is the least possible action, other than doing nothing. However, if the customer's insistence is strong, there was a prior check reading, and the CSR is unable to determine if the bill is correct, the CSR would issue a request for a meter inspection. Under the same circumstances, if the CSR determines the bill is correct, the CSR would issue a meter test request. Both these recommendations are a much greater response to the customer and are much more costly ones for the company.

In order to summarize the possible outcomes of a high bill complaint on a demand metered commercial account, the following section briefly describes the possible recommendations as shown at the bottom of Fig. 13-4.

- *Recommendation 1:* Bill is correct. The CSR has determined through a series of comparisons to other customer account information that the bill is right.
- *Recommendation 2:* Bill is incorrect, adjust to check or rejected reading. The CSR has determined through a series of comparisons to other customer account information that the bill is wrong.
- *Recommendation 3:* Issue check reading request to meter operations. The CSR was unable to determine whether the bill was correct or not, and requests an additional reading.
- *Recommendation 4:* Issue meter inspection request to field operations. The CSR was unable to determine whether the bill was correct or not, even after receiving a check reading, or there was strong customer insistence that the bill was still incorrect.
- *Recommendation 5:* No action, await completion of pending order. The CSR, in his review of the account, finds that a check reading or an inspection was previously requested but not yet completed by the responsible field organization.
- *Recommendation 6:* Issue meter test request to field operations. The CSR has determined that the bill is correct, has supportive data such as a check reading or an inspection, but there is a very strong insistence by the customer that the bill is still wrong.
- *Recommendation 7:* Issue request to verify next reading. The CSR has determined that the bill is correct, but the customer is slightly insistent that the bill is still wrong. This request notes the next month's meter reading document "verify," whereby the meter reader will simply double check the reading on that date.

The prototype system developed and described below is designed to assist company CSRs in handling the kinds of billing complaints described in this section.

# DOCUMENTING THE SYSTEM

The following discussion covers

- System proposal
- Description of the system
- Dependency diagram
- Decision charts
- Designing and constructing the knowledge base

## System Proposal

The general objective of the project is to develop a knowledge-based system that assists a CSR in determining the correct reply to make to customer billing inquiries (complaints).

The first phase of the project is limited to a specific type of decision, answering high bill complaints on commercial accounts that have demand metering devices. It is a prototype system that will be fully developed in subsequent phases of the project. The benefits of this project are

- *Improved CSR performance*—The system is designed to guide less experienced CSRs in handling commercial demand-metered billing complaints.
- *Training*—As CSRs observe the steps and logic of this system, they will also be gaining the knowledge necessary to make the correct decision themselves on their own eventually.
- *Reduced costs*—It is anticipated that this system will reduce wasted field time caused by incorrect or redundant requests.
- *Improved capability of evaluating CSR performance*—Since the system is designed for an individual with limited knowledge and experience. Use of this system by division or corporate auditors will allow them to monitor CSR performance more accurately.
- *Improved service to the customer*—Prompt and efficient processing of customer complaints will benefit the customer, as well as the company's public image.

Information needed to develop this system was obtained from experts in the customer service field, customer service manuals and procedures, information bulletins, customer service ready reference guides, and reviews of prior customer correspondence.

## Description of the Prototype System

**System overview and objective.** The prototype system is designed to help CSRs decide which kind of action should be taken about a high bill complaint on a commercial account that has a demand metering device. The system asks on-screen questions about the bill itself, the history of the account, and field checks and readings. These questions guide a CSR through a review of the customer's billing records (on-screen) in handling the complaint. The system uses if-then rules and backward chaining to reason about the information given by a user in order to reach its recommendation.

**Recommendations to be made by the system.** The system is able to make one of the following recommendations:

1. Billing is correct, advise customer.
2. Billing is incorrect, cancel and adjust.
3. Issue check reading request to meter operations.
4. Issue meter inspection request to field operations.
5. No action at this time, field action pending.
6. Issue meter test request to field operations.
7. Verify next cycle.

**Nature of user interface, including a typical user dialog.** The knowledge-based system developed is designed for users with a knowledge of the mainframe customer accounts record system. Using the many information histories available in that mainframe system, the CSR reviews the screens relevant to the complaint under study. For example, after the telephone service received a request for a payment extension from a customer, the CSR would review the credit history "CRED" for prior extensions and payment history "STAT" for prior timeliness. Then, depending on the period and reasons for the request they would grant, deny, or request supervisory approval.

The user of this expert knowledge-based system gets all the information asked by the system by examining the appropriate account and billing information computer reference screens, such as those shown in Fig. 13-6. This information is maintained in the company's customer account record system mainframe computer.

Depending on the type of high bill complaint, the user dialog covers up to four key knowledge areas.

*Status of Bill in Question.* The status is determined by the compatibility of the bill with preceding readings. The compatibility is obtained from the comparison by the user of various readings to the bill in question. A typical question is "Is the bill in question compatible with the prior seasonal bill for usage (kwh), as well as for demand (DMD)?" The status is also determined by the answer to the question "Could the bill in question be overread by 1, 10, 100, or 1,000 times the multiplier?"

*Compatibility of Supplementary Readings (Check and Rejected Readings) with Preceding Readings.* Having ascertained the existence of such a supplementary reading, this information is obtained from the comparison by the user of various readings to the supplementary reading in question. A typical question is "Is the available check reading compatible with the prior seasonal bill for usage (kwh), as well as for demand (DMD)?"

*Miscellaneous Information.* In certain cases the system has to ask for customer insistence by asking "What is the degree of customer insistence? [none, weak, strong, very strong]" and for the availability of check readings and of inspection readings by asking such questions as "Is there a check reading available?"

*Compatibility of an Estimated Bill.* In the special case when the bill in question is an estimate (which is determined under "status of bill") and there are no supplementary readings available (which is handled under "compatibility of supplementary readings"), the compatibility of the bill in question is determined by the following questions "Is prior bill an estimate?", "Is the estimate bill in question compatible with the prior seasonal bill for usage (kwh), as well as for demand (DMD)?" and "Are load factors within 10 percentage points $+/-$?"

**Description of the knowledge structure and reasoning process.** The recommendations made by the prototype system are based on the four key factors presented above. These factors are in turn determined by other influencing factors, or answers to user questions.

If-then rules are used to determine values at each stage. The inference engine uses backward chaining to determine these values.

The possible values for *status of bill* are

e = bill is an estimate
c = bill is an actual and compatible with preceding readings
o = bill is an actual and overread
n = bill is an actual, but noncompatible and not overread

The possible values for *compatibility of the bill in question with preceding readings*, are

y = bill is an actual and is compatible
n = bill is an actual and is not compatible
e = bill is an estimate (In that special case the system has to first check whether there is any supplementary reading available and then follow a different logic path, rule 10, to determine the compatibility of the estimated bill.)

The possible values for *compatibility of supplementary readings*, are

yb  = available reading is compatible to bill
ynb = available reading is compatible to preceding readings but not to bill
n   = available reading not compatible with any other reading
na  = there is no such reading available

The possible values for "inspection," which is part of *miscellaneous information*, are:

n   = no inspection report
p   = inspection pending
yp  = inspection done and meter found correct
ynp = inspection done and meter found incorrect

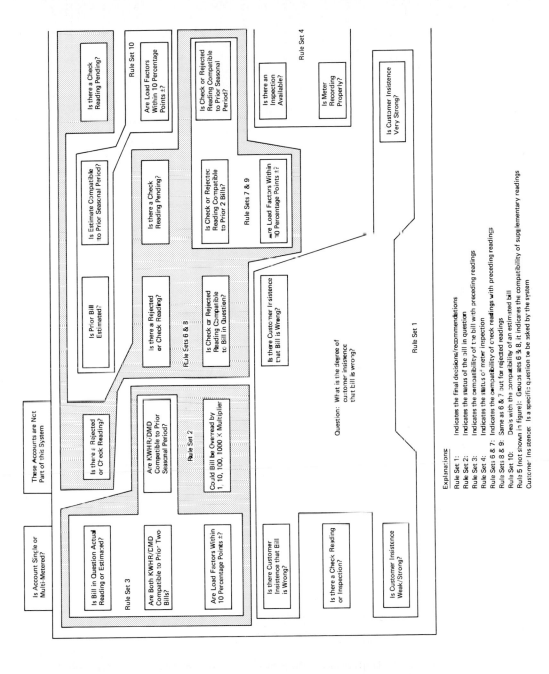

The boxes in the figure contain the following text:

**These Accounts are Not Part of this System**

**Is Account Single or Multi-Metered?**

**Is there a Rejected or Check Reading?**

**Is Bill in Question Actual Reading or Estimated?**

Rule Set 3

**Are Both KWHR/DMD Compatible to Prior Two Bills?**

Rule Set 2

**Are Load Factors Within 10 Percentage Points ±?**

**Could Bill be Overread by 1, 10, 100, 1000 × Multiplier?**

**Is Prior Bill Estimated?**

**Is there a Check Reading Pending?**

Rule Set 10

**Are Load Factors Within 10 Percentage Points ±?**

**Is Estimate Compatible to Prior Seasonal Period?**

**Is there a Rejected or Check Reading?**

Rule Sets 6 & 8

**Is Check or Rejected Reading Compatible to Bill in Question?**

**Is there a Check Reading Pending?**

**Is Check or Rejected Reading Compatible to Prior Seasonal Period?**

**Is Check or Rejected Reading Compatible to Prior 2 Bills?**

Rule Sets 7 & 9

**Are Load Factors Within 10 Percentage Points ±?**

**Is there an Inspection Available?**

Rule Set 4

**Is Meter Recording Properly?**

**Is there Customer Insistence that Bill is Wrong?**

**Is there Customer Insistence that Bill is Wrong?**

Question: What is the degree of customer insistence that bill is wrong?

**Is there a Check Reading or Inspection?**

**Is Customer Insistence Weak/Strong?**

Rule Set 1

**Is Customer Insistence Very Strong?**

Explanations:
Rule Set 1: Indicates the final decisions/recommendations
Rule Set 2: Indicates the status of the bill in question
Rule Set 3: Indicates the compatibility of the bill with preceding readings
Rule Set 4: Indicates the status of meter inspection
Rule Sets 6 & 7: Indicates the compatibility of check readings with preceding reading
Rule Sets 8 & 9: Same as 6 & 7 but for rejected readings
Rule Set 10: Deals with the compatibility of an estimated bill
Rule 5 (not shown in figure): Groups sets 6 & 8, it indicates the compatibility of supplementary readings
Customer Insistence: Is a specific question to be asked by the system

**FIGURE 13-7 Reformulating decisions process into rule sets prototype system for high bill complaint—demand metered account.**

293

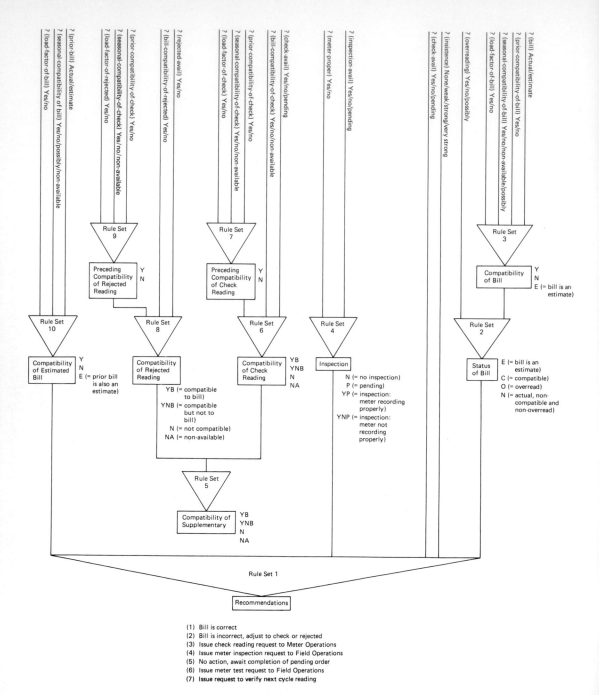

**FIGURE 13-8 Dependency diagram of prototype system for high bill complaint—demand metered account.**

| status e/c/o/n | e | e | e | e | e | e | e | e |
|---|---|---|---|---|---|---|---|---|
| insistence n/w/s/vs | not n | w | s or vs | s | w or s | w or s | vs | vs |
| compatibility-of-estimated-bill e/y/n | y | y | y | y | y | y | y | y |
| compatibility-of-suppl yb/ynb/n/na | na | na | na | na | na | na | na | na |
| check-avail y/n/p | — | y | y | y | n | n | not p | not p |
| inspection n/p/yp/ynp | p | — | n | yp or ynp | yp | ynp | yp | ynp |
| recommendation | 5 | 7 | 4 | 4 | 1 | 2 | 6 | 2 |

possible recommendations are:

1. billing is correct, advice customer
2. billing is incorrect, cancel and adjust
3. issue check reading request to Meter Operations
4. issue meter inspection request to Field Operations
5. no action at this time
6. issue meter test request to Field Operations
7. verify next cycle.

**FIGURE 13-9  Segment of final decision chart for high bill complaint—demand metered account (prototype system).**

The possible values for *compatibility of the estimated bill in question with preceding readings* are

y = estimated bill is compatible
n = estimated bill is not compatible
e = prior bill is an estimate

## Dependency Diagram

Figure 13-7 shows how the reasoning steps in Fig. 13-4 were grouped into rule sets in structuring the knowledge base system. This reformulation is shown in the dependency diagram of the knowledge-based system for high bill complaints coming from demand metered commercial customers shown in Fig. 13-8. It is a complete summary outline of all the questions, rules, knowledge segments and their interrelationships, values, and recommendations within the system.

## Decision Charts

A sample decision chart is shown in Fig. 13-9. There is a decision chart for each triangle in Fig. 13-8.

```
/*      7th set of rules: compatibility of check readings       */
/*                          with preceding data                 */

    rule-7-1:
if prior-compatibility-of-check = yes and
   load-factor-of-check = yes
then preceding-compatibility-of-check = y.

    rule-7-2:
if prior-compatibility-of-check = yes and
   load-factor-of-check = no
then preceding-compatibility-of-check = n.

    rule-7-3:
if prior-compatibility-of-check = no and
   not(seasonal-compatibility-of-check = no) and
   load-factor-of-check = yes
then preceding-compatibility-of-check = y.

    rule-7-4:
if prior-compatibility-of-check = no and
   not(seasonal-compatibility-of-check = no) and
   load-factor-of-check = no
   then preceding-compatibility-of-check = n.

    rule-7-5:
 if prior-compatibility-of-check = no and
   seasonal-compatibility-of-check = no
   then preceding-compatibility-of-check = n.



    /*      Questions to users                                  */
    /*      and legal values for answers                        */

    automaticmenu(ALL).

    question(bill) = '       Is the bill in question an actual or an
estimate?'.

    legalvals(bill) = [actual,estimate].

    question(prior-compatibility-of-bill) = '     Is the bill in
question compatible with the prior two bills for usage (kWh), as
well as for demand (DMD)?'.

    legalvals(prior-compatibility-of-bill) = [yes,no].

    question(seasonal-compatibility-of-bill) = '     Is the bill
in question compatible with the prior seasonal bill for usage
(kWh), as well as for demand (DMD)?'.

    legalvals(seasonal-compatibility-of-bill) =
  [yes,possibly,no,non-available].
```

**FIGURE 13-10  Segment of knowledge base: rules and questions for high bill complaint—demand metered account—prototype system.**

## Designing and Constructing the Knowledge Base

Rules and questions are developed from the situation under study. A sample of the prototype system's knowledge base is shown in Fig. 13-10. The system shell used is M.1.

The if-then rules in the knowledge base (see Fig. 13-10) match those specified in the decision charts. They were written to reflect the relationships shown in the dependency diagram in Fig. 13-8. They use the values shown there and in the decision charts. The questions in the knowledge base (see Fig. 13-10) are those indicated in the dependency diagram.

## REVIEW QUESTIONS

1. Complete the knowledge-based system (or any segment of the system) partially documented in this chapter and enter it into the expert system shell you have.

2. Describe the way this system differs from and is similar to those described in the financial and accounting system sections.

3. Make a list of similar applications in other operating areas, especially in the clerical area.

4. In the prototype system for customer service representatives, what are the four key knowledge areas covered by the user dialogue?

5. What are some of the benefits brought about by the C.S.R. system described in this chapter?

6. Describe the differences between the prototype knowledge-based system and the information in the customer service system mainframe. How do they help the C.S.R.?

7. In the knowledge-based system described in the chapter, what factors would bring forth a recommendation for a meter inspection?

8. Why is it beneficial to avoid, if possible, meter inspections and tests?

9. Why was "bill complaints" the area chosen for prototype development?

10. A bill in question is compared to the previous two bills. What other bills might it be compared to? Why?

## REFERENCES

"Field Execs Tell How Computerization Improves Customer Service," *Store*, vol. 69, Feb. 2, 1987.

Franco, J.J., "Proper Training of Customer Service Representatives Enhances Marketing Performance," *Marketing News*, vol. 18, Sept. 14, 1984.

"Information Systems Helps Shed Light on Customer Questions," *Data Management*, vol. 23, April 1985.

Kiefer, M., and R. Grosse, "Why Utility Customers Don't Pay Their Bills," *Public Utilities Fortnightly*, vol. 113, June 21, 1984.

McAlleer, L.J., and T. Dukich, "Customer Satisfaction: Key to Improved Service Planning," *Public Utilities Fortnightly*, vol. 115, June 13, 1985.

"Modern Technology Aids Utility in Providing Customer Service," *Public Utilities Fortnightly*, vol. 119, March 19, 1987.

Schauger, R.F., "Final Bill Collection System Automation Productivity and Performance," *Public Utilities Fortnightly*, vol. 114, Sept. 13, 1984.

Smarrt, L.E., "Whose the Responsibility When a Customer is Billed at the Wrong Rate," *Public Utilities Fortnightly*, vol. 116, July 11, 1985.

Smith, D.M., "Electronic Fund Transfer Customer Payment Plan Employed by Gas Distribution Company," *Public Utilities Fortnightly*, vol. 115, Jan. 10, 1985.

"Virginia: Utilities Bill Payment Procedures Under Study," *Public Utilities Fortnightly*, vol. 15, March 21, 1985.

# 14

# A Computer Configuration System

This chapter describes the development of a system for configuring computer system solutions. The report covers the following sections:

- □ The situation under study: understanding the expert's domain
- □ Studying the situation to be prototyped
- □ Documenting the prototype system

The overall context and structure of the situation is described first in general terms. The situation to be prototyped is studied next. The documentation of the actual prototype knowledge based system is then described.

## THE SITUATION UNDER STUDY: UNDERSTANDING THE EXPERT'S DOMAIN

The discussion in this section covers

- □ Selecting a decision area to work on
- □ Probing how the situation works and how decisions are made
- □ Narrowing the focus

### Selecting a Decision Area to Work On

The general area under study is computer system configurations, specifically the configuration of "turnkey" computer system solutions. A turnkey computer system solution is one that includes all computer hardware, software, applications, maintenance, installation, and training that would be required by a customer (or user of the computer system) to successfully use it. This turnkey solution covers every conceivable aspect of a product. It is an all encompassing solution.

Computer system solutions are found in situations ranging from adding a memory chip in an automatic coffee maker timer to the configuration of a network of supercomputers and of the communications needed to interconnect them for a consortium of New York State educational and research institutions located within the boundaries of the state.

Figure 14-1 gives an overview of the steps involved in creating and selling a turnkey computer solution. The overall goal is to provide a system configuration that is complete and meets the user requirements. The vendor that supplies a computer system solution must have experts available to configure the components of each solution to meet the specific needs of each customer. These requirements are unique for every customer.

Each proposal must include all of the necessary parts to totally implement the solution. The objective is to identify all costs (both monetary and time) and components that would be required by a customer to implement a computer system solution. Any missing components mean lost revenue to the company. Many times proposals are presented to customers and accepted by them before these proposals are approved by a trained analyst due to time scheduling and customer imposed deadlines.

A knowledge-based system to assist in computer system configuration would allow sales people with little technical knowledge to verify that all of the components required to meet the customer needs are included in the solution presented. This would lead to lower cost and more efficient and effective solutions than could be obtained by the hiring and training of additional analysts.

### Probing how the Situation Works and how Decisions are Made

The following discussion covers the individual components of the computer system configuration process shown in Fig. 14-1 at the company under study.

**Identifying the potential customer.** The first step is always to identify a customer that has the basic need for automation of a business function and the money to implement it. There is no need to spend time on a prospect that does not have money available. This initial step is usually known as *prospect screening*.

**Determining customer needs and characteristics.** Once it has been determined that a qualified prospect exists, a salesperson (assisted by a systems-marketing analyst) determines the customer's needs using a variety of methods, such as plant walk-throughs, customer interviews, and analysis of previous computer installations at similar types of sites. If the customer has previously purchased a computer system, its characteristics and functions will be noted in the event that some type of interfacing with this existing equipment must be accomplished.

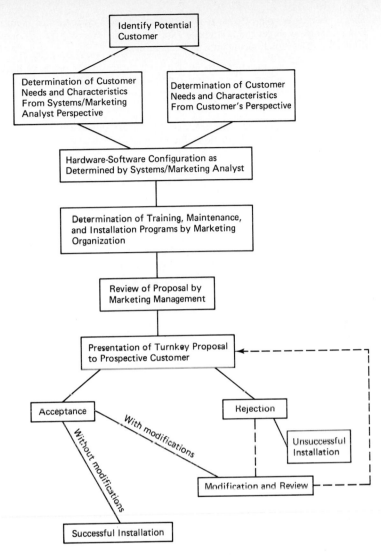

**FIGURE 14-1 Turnkey computer solutions—overview of the process.**

The customer also fills out an extensive questionnaire (usually done by more than one person in the customer organization) that will present the customer needs and characteristics as they are perceived by the customer. This customer questionnaire, a sample segment of which is shown in Fig. 14-2, helps eliminate the necessity for a salesperson interpreting the customer needs and characteristics. The goal is to determine as accurately as possible what the customer's real needs are.

**Hardware and software configuration.** Configuring the hardware and software that is needed to meet the customer requirements is done by one or more systems-

This figure is a sample of what is given to the potential customer for them to complete. It allows the vendor company to get the customer's ideas in writing directly. This is only a sample of the real questionnaire. The actual document is more extensive.

The purpose of this questionnaire is to record the customer needs without any interpretation by the marketing organization. (Note: There is no formal document for the vendor sales force to complete when collecting information regarding a potential customer's needs. This is presently being addressed by the company.)

The following questions are only a subset of the actual questionnaire and are intended to give the reader only an overview of the information collected from the customer.

1. What is the total number of users that will be on the system (include directly connected terminals, printers, and devices accessed via telecommunication venues)?
2. What is the average number of simultaneous users on the system during daily operation?
3. What application(s) will be on the system? Please list specific packages and/or functionality requested.
4. Is a specific operating system required? (Unix, Primos, etc.) If more than one operating system is required, do they need to be concurrently available.
5. Are any specific utilities required? (If yes, please specify name and functionality expected.)
6. By what percentage will your organization (as it relates to this automation project) increase in the next year? in the next three years?
7. Please list any other computer systems that this configuration will communicate with. Specify computer hardware, communication access method, and purpose of communication connection(s).
8. How often will the system be backed up (i.e.: daily, weekly, incrementally, etc.)?
9. Will computer tapes be exchanged with other computer systems? If yes, please specify the make and model of the computer system and the corresponding tape drive.
10. Please specify the hours during which the computer system will be accessed (i.e.: normal business, 24 hours, etc.)?
11. How many people in your organization will be trained as system administrators? operators? data base managers?
12. Is hardware training required? Is application training required? If yes, will it be on-site, off-site, or both?
13. Is transactional processing required? If yes, please list the appropriate applications.
14. Do you have files/information that are/is presently automated and need(s) to be converted and transferred? If yes, please include description of files and appropriate volume levels.

**FIGURE 14-2   Sample customer questionnaire.**

marketing analysts. The software needed is determined before the hardware can be specified, since the software is what the end user uses, and the hardware provides the platform to utilize the software.

Software involves an operating system, utilities, languages, and application programs. The operating system is the "hardware supervisor" that manages the computer resources such as the central processing unit, memory, controllers, and peripheral devices. Utilities are tools that reside on the computer and do functions such as copying files and setting up communication links. Examples of languages are BASIC, COBOL, and FORTRAN. The application programs are what the user of the computer works with to automate a business function. Examples of application programs are financial spreadsheets, word processing, drafting (computer-aided design and computer-aided manufacturing, frequently abbreviated CAD/CAM), and facilities management.

Figure 14-3 describes in detail how a systems-marketing analyst configures the hardware portion of a turnkey computer system solution.

Figure 14-4 diagrams the logic flows among the various steps involved in configuring the computer software and hardware. The configuration process requires knowledge of product functionality, cross-product conflicts, and interproduct dependencies. The analyst refers to configuration guides, product bulletins, technical bulletins, and previous experience during this process.

**Training, maintenance, and installation programs.** Training is important to get the maximum benefits out of a turnkey computer solution. It should be included as part of the total package presented to the customer, because it involves a sizable investment in both money and personnel time and because it impacts on the success of the system.

Maintenance is necessary to ensure that the computer system is reliable and will be available when needed after it is installed. There are different levels of maintenance for both hardware and software that should be presented to the customer, depending on how critical the computer system is to the customer's day-to-day business operations. For example, installation of the computer system might require special electrical and environmental conditions that must be planned for and set up before the computer system can be installed.

Training, maintenance, and installation policies and procedures are given in various types of literature available to the sales people and analysts. This literature is referenced for price and descriptions of specific programs. The training, maintenance, and installation programs that match the customer and system requirements are selected for inclusion in the turnkey computer solution.

**Review of proposal by marketing management.** Before any turnkey computer solution is presented to a prospective customer, it is reviewed by management to ensure that the solution has stayed within strategic marketing guidelines. There are many possible turnkey solutions that are correctly configured but are outside of specific marketing policies. This step ensures that marketing policies are adhered to by the sales organization and by the systems-marketing analyst.

**Presentation of turnkey proposal.** This is made to the customer by either the salesperson or both the salesperson and the systems-marketing analyst or analysts. Presentations, which are always done in person, can include visits to other manufacturer or vendor customer accounts, hardware and software demonstrations, and a review of how the final proposal meets the automation needs of this customer. At this point the customer will either accept (possibly with some minor modifications) or reject the proposal. If the proposal is rejected, it is possible that with some major modifications of the proposal the customer will again consider it.

A thorough and professional presentation is usually the key to success in getting a customer to accept the turnkey computer solution. Since the purchase and installation of a turnkey computer solution usually involves considerable money and time, it is not a decision taken lightly by the customer.

The following describes how the expert (known as the systems-marketing analyst) configures a turnkey computer solution. Figure 14-4 describes the logic flows among the following steps in the process as performed by a systems-marketing analyst in making each configuration decision. It should be noted that steps A, B, and C are preliminary steps that are necessary in order to properly address the hardware portion of the turnkey computer solution.

*Step A: Defining the Customer Needs*

The first step in developing a configuration is to ensure that the customer needs and requirements have been defined as clearly as possible by both the customer and the marketing representatives of the manu-facturer-vendor company. This involves reviewing both the notes of the marketing representatives and systems-marketing analysts, and the customer questionnaire (if one has been completed). Many times the analyst sets up a meeting with the customer to review the questionnaire and clarify any undefined or uncertain items.

It is very important that the analyst have a very clear idea what the customer is looking for in the way of the functionality of specific applications and the overall turnkey system. This definition is the foundation of the overall solution presented to the prospective customer for their review and approval later.

*Step B: Specifying the Software Needs*

From the overall customer requirements the analyst identifies exactly the complete software needs before any decisions are made regarding hardware specifications. The purpose of this step is to create a list of all software requirements covering:

- Operating systems
- Utilities and data bases
- Languages
- Applications

This list is placed in a logical order to be reviewed by an analyst. The term "logical order" refers to the sequence in which the analyst reviews the software requirements for their completeness. This logical order is dictated by each analyst's experience and might be different for each analyst. Whatever the actual order of the review, the end result is that the analyst can view the list of software items and determine that it is complete.

The analyst will examine the list for items that

- Are needed to complement each other
- Cannot be operational simultaneously
- Utilize the same hardwired memory resources and must be modified to run simultaneously
- Make the list complete to meet the customer's requirements

*Step C: Analyzing Volumes*

The third step is to review the customer questionnaire and marketing notes to ascertain maximum operational volumes that will be required by the system. This is a function of both the number of simultaneous users of the system and the total throughput that has been specified by the customer. The software and hardware will be configured to handle the peak volume of work that will be generated by the end users. The software must be able to perform the maximum number of transactions per minute, per hour, per day, etc. Each software module must be analyzed for the volume it will be required to handle. The analyst reviews the software for modules that will be operated in a stand-alone mode (when no other modules are active) or in multiuser mode.

*(continued)*

**FIGURE 14-3  Configuring the hardware portion of a turnkey computer system.**

During these early phases, the analyst defines exactly what software is required, how and when it will be used, and what volumes it must handle. To do this, the analyst has had to review the total number of system users and the total number of simultaneous users to get a good idea of system capacity requirements as they pertain to software.

*Step D: Start of Hardware Configuration—Central Processing Unit*

After the analyst has reviewed and identified the software requirements of the system, the analyst identifies hardware requirements and specifications.

The first piece of hardware to be examined is the central processing unit. This is the core of the system. To determine the model that will meet the user requirements, the analyst takes into account:

- Computational and connective capacity that peak activity will require
- Total number of users and devices that will be connected to the system
- Methods of connecting to the system (both local and remote)
- Volumes of data that need to be stored by the system
- Specific models of workstations that will be connected to the central processing unit
- Response time required by the end user during peak activity levels
- Environmental specifications are defined by the prospective customer and by the manufacturer-vendor
- Any redundancy specified by the end user, such as disk mirroring or dual central processing units
- Projected growth of processing needs
- Budgetary constraint

Once an analyst notes all of the known factors that affect the selection of a central processing unit, the analyst selects a unit that best meets the user requirements. The selection of the central processing unit automatically includes the selection of the appropriate memory required by that unit.

*Step E: Configuration of Disk Drives and Controllers*

After the preferred central processing unit has been identified, the analyst reviews the on-line data storage volume requirements as specified by the end user in the customer questionnaire and in the notes recorded by the marketing people. Once the on-line data storage volume is determined (this is a function of the total number of transactions stored on-line and the record size of each transaction added to the volume required by the operating system and by the programs), the analyst chooses one or more disk drives and the corresponding disk controller(s). If disk mirroring is required, additional items are configured. Once the total disk requirement is determined, the central processing unit selected is reviewed to ensure that it can support the configured disk drives. Cables for the disks and peripheral cabinet spaces are also reviewed at this time for availability. The central processing unit (CPU) selected *must* also support the disk models selected, since not all disks are supported by every CPU.

*Step F: Communications Controllers are Now Addressed*

To access the central processing unit (CPU), the workstations, modems, printers, etc. are connected to various types of communications controllers. Determining which controller(s) is (are) required is a function of

- Method of connection to CPU (local, remote, telecommunication link, ethernet, local area network, wide area network, etc.)
- Total number of users connected to the CPU
- Total number of CPU's networked together
- Number of slots available in CPU cabinet for communications controllers
- Speed of communications required to terminals and printers

*(continued)*

**FIGURE 14-3** *(continued)*

- Asynchronous or synchronous communications
- Government Tempest regulations to be met at this site, if any. (Tempest regulations refer to NACSIM 5100A, which are a set of government specifications for signal emissions from national security sensitive projects and installations. Military contractors are governed by these regulations depending on the sensitivity of the project they are working under.)
- Models of terminals, printers, and other user interface devices to be connected to the CPU

The major factor identified is the number of various connections to the CPU required.

Once the controllers needed to meet all communication requirements are configured, the CPU previously selected is then reviewed to ensure it will handle each type of controller and the absolute number of controllers configured.

The analyst also verifies that each controller selected can be coresident with all other controllers selected. If at any point, a situation is discovered that requires the changing of a controller, all communications requirements *must* be reviewed to ensure they have been properly addressed and the previously selected CPU *must* be reviewed again to ensure that it will handle all the configured controllers. The previously selected disk drives and their controllers must also be reviewed to ensure proper configuration in the event of any changes that might have taken place in the system configuration.

*Step G: Selection of Terminals, Printers, and any Other User Interface Devices*

User interface devices refer to any component of the computer system solution that an end user will directly interface with to input data into the system or output data already on the system. These are usually the final hardware components of the computer system solution to be selected. In most cases, any terminal, printer, or other user interface device can be connected to any central processing unit as long as the proper communications interface device is selected.

The interface functionality required by the end user will determine which devices are selected. The following is a list of factors that are considered when selecting these devices:

- Are computer punch cards required for input? If so, what volume is required?
- Is magnetic tape storage required? What volume is required? What density of data on the tape is required? Will be tapes be interchanged with other vendor equipment?
- What is the volume of printing to be done by the system? How many locations will require printers? What type of printing is to be done (i.e.: standard 132 column reports, graphics, desk top publishing, plotting of design drawings, laser printing)?
- Will user terminals require:
    self-contained intelligence,
    graphic displays,
    monotone or color displays,
    local printing capability,
    windowing application displays,
    local or remote connectivity, etc.

End user functionality determines the required number of cathode ray terminals (CRTs) and their specific functionality. The interface between the communications controllers and the terminals are reviewed to ensure that the proper communications controller in the proper quantity is already configured. The same is done for printers, tape drives, card readers, and any other user devices configured. If the proper controller has not been configured or is not available in the proper quantity, the communications controllers are reconfigured to meet the end user needs.

When any reconfiguration is done on the controllers, the analyst repeats the procedure of reviewing the controllers and the preferred central processing unit to ensure the viability of the configuration. If the

*(continued)*

**FIGURE 14-3** *(continued)*

central processing unit is changed at any time, all other controllers and devices that were subsequently configured *must* be reviewed.

*Step II: Selection of Interface Cabling and Cabinetry*

This step involves reviewing the components of the configuration and selecting the cables that will provide the interconnections between the various components (such as between a terminal and a communications controller). This step is very straightforward, since each type of interconnection will require a specific cable.

The importance of this step is to ensure that all interconnections are addressed and no cables are omitted from the configuration. A single cable that is improperly left out can render a configuration inoperable.

Each hardware component must reside in some type of cabinet according to Federal Communications Commission (FCC) regulations. There must be adequate cabinetry to house each component or the system cannot be installed. The analyst reviews each component of the system to ensure that the components either are purchased with a corresponding cabinet or that adequate cabinet space (slots) is available somewhere in the hardware configuration (i.e.: four disk drives can be configured in one office environment peripheral cabinet).

**FIGURE 14-3** *(continued)*

**Successful installation.** If a prospective customer has agreed to purchase a turnkey computer system solution, the successful installation of this solution is the final step of the process. Until the system has been installed, tested, and the users properly trained, the process has not been completed. When the system is installed, the customer signs a document stating that the system has been installed and meets the documented functionality specifications. At this point the solution is complete.

Figure 14-5 gives a summary overview of the process. The purpose of this overview is to facilitate the development of the knowledge-based system described later in this chapter by expanding on and reformulating somewhat the situation overview that was shown in Fig. 14-1. The diagram in Fig. 14-5 illustrates the factors that are involved with each step of this overall decision situation.

## Narrowing the Focus

There are hundreds of possible turnkey computer system solutions, ranging from single user PCs to mainframe systems with thousands of simultaneous users. Because of the potential for complexity this study will focus on only those solutions that function in office environment locations. *Office environment systems* refer to computers that do not require special air-conditioning or electrical connections to operate. Presently the manufacturer-vendor under study offers two central processing units with a minimal number of communication controllers, terminals, printers, and other computer components that can be configured for such an environment.

The first phase of the study is further narrowed to just the hardware portion of the computer system solution. This decision area was chosen for several reasons:

- A knowledge-based system speeds up the analysis and design and so increases the *timeliness* of the response.
- It assures more *consistency* in configurations.

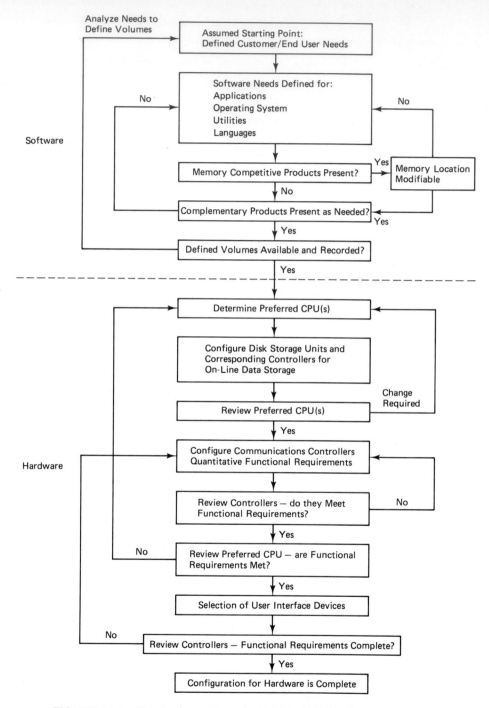

**FIGURE 14-4 Hardware segment of the configuration logic flow.**

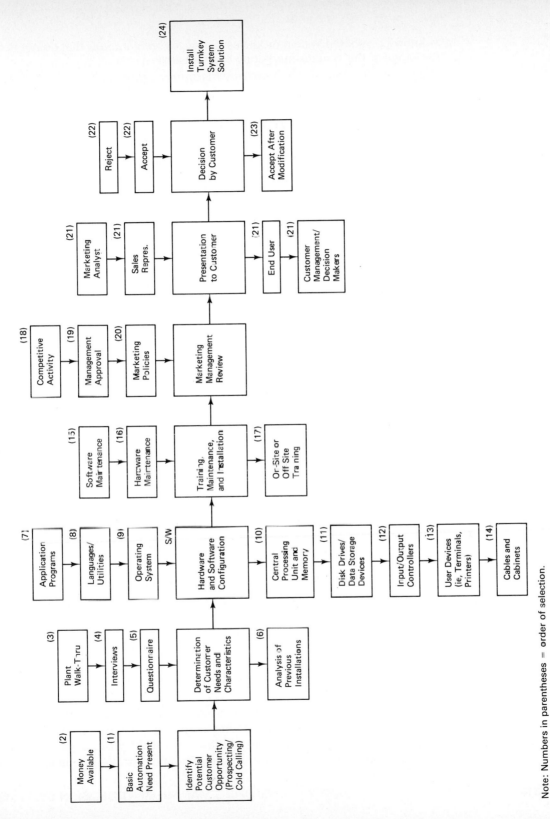

**FIGURE 14-5  Decision situation diagram for configuration of turnkey computer system solutions.**

Note: Numbers in parentheses = order of selection.

□ A knowledge-based system produces *complete configurations* that do not need the input of the systems-marketing support analyst.

□ It generates *cost savings* and *increased customer satisfaction*.

## STUDYING THE SITUATION TO BE PROTOTYPED

The situation to be prototyped is the configuration by a manufacturer-vendor's systems-marketing analyst of the hardware required to complete a turnkey computer solution that is installable in the standard office environment for a specific customer. In this situation the end user requirements will have previously been defined and noted, as will the software (operating systems, utilities, application programs, and programming languages) needed to meet these requirements.

Figure 14-1 defines the overall steps needed to create a turnkey computer system solution. The steps involved in carrying out the third phase shown in Fig. 14-1, the determination of the hardware and software configuration by the systems-marketing analyst, are described in Fig. 14-3.

The situation that will be the focus of this study is described in Fig. 14-3, step D through step H, where the steps involved and the knowledge used in making each decision are described in some detail.

The systems-marketing analyst's turnkey solution covers the following items:

□ Central processing unit with memory
□ Disk drives with disk controllers
□ Communications controllers
□ User interface devices such as terminals, printers, card readers, and tape drives
□ Cables and cabinets

The turnkey solution will be a hardware configuration that is complete and meets end user needs. As in many situations, however, there is often more than one solution that will satisfy a situation. Time does not permit an analyst to examine all possible solutions. Normally, therefore, an analyst will stop the search when an adequate solution has been found.

Figure 14-4 outlines the logic flow for configuring the hardware requirements of a turnkey computer system solution. It attempts to show the interrelationships among the various steps in the process and how the systems-marketing analyst manipulates the knowledge in analyzing the situation.

In this figure, for example, there are multiple points where the expert is required to review previous recommendations. Understanding these *loopback* points is central to understanding the reasoning processes of the expert and of the prototype system based on the expert's thinking.

As the experts are creating hardware configurations, they reach certain points where they need to review previous recommendations to ensure that they are still viable in the context of the new recommendations. In many cases changes to previously configured hardware will be made; all subsequent hardware recommendations are then reviewed again. Looping back more than once is not uncommon in actual configuration projects.

For example, a set of input-output controllers will be configured for a certain customer. The preferred central processing unit is then reviewed to ensure that all selected controllers will work simultaneously on the central processing unit. The central processing unit selected might have to be changed to meet the input-output needs of the customer. When the central processing unit is changed to match the input-output requirements, the previously selected disk drives and disk drive controllers must also be reviewed.

If this loopback reasoning does not occur, a decision that needs to be changed will not be reviewed and the final configuration, as a result, may not be viable from a functional point of view. Looping back, then, is critical to success in the expert's reasoning process.

In many situations more than one hardware component can be configured into the overall solution to meet a specific requirement. This is mostly applicable to the configuration of communications controllers and disk drives. The prototype system described in the following sections will be limited to recommending only one good solution.

Figure 14-5 diagramed the decision situation for configuration of the overall turnkey computer system solution. Figure 14-6 focuses on the hardware portion of the overall configuration decision situation shown in Fig. 14-5. The dotted lines in Fig. 14-6 refer to points where the logical process will loop back to a previous decision to reconcile any subsequent decisions that might have had an effect on a previous one.

The following is an example of what decision process the expert goes through when configuring an overall hardware configuration. For the purpose of this prototype system all decisions relating to applications, operating systems, utilities, and languages have been determined. In addition, it is assumed that the targeted hardware will be confined to the office environment products that will run under a given operating system. These limitations were necessary to keep this initial phase of the prototype manageable.

## Central Processing Unit and Memory

In reviewing the customer information provided in the situation under study, the systems-marketing analyst notes that a budget limit has been established. In addition, the system will be required to operate in an office environment. The office environment limits the expert to two possible central processing units, the 2350 and the 2450. The total number of system users is twenty-four and the application to run on the system, which was previously determined, is a medium overhead CPU application (that is, it will place a medium load on the CPU). The interactive response time is not a factor in this situation, since the solution is within an office environment and the maximum number of simultaneous users is twenty. The systems-marketing analyst did not consider future growth in this situation due to budgetary constraints. There was no need for disk or central processing unit redundancy. In addition, no synchronous terminals were required.

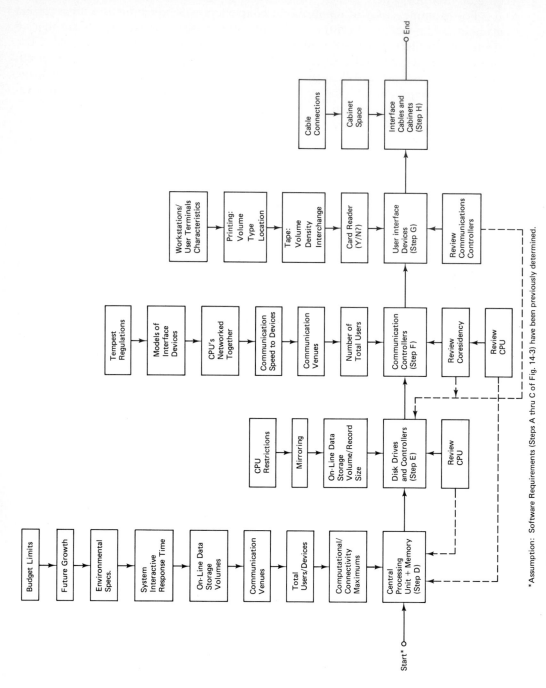

* Assumption: Software Requirements (Steps A thru C of Fig. 14-3) have been previously determined.

**FIGURE 14-6  Decision situation diagram for configuration of hardware segment of turnkey computer solution—situation to be prototyped.**

Based on knowledge and experience the systems-marketing analyst concluded that the above situational factors dictate that this situation would best be handled by the configuring of a 2450 model central processing unit with 4 megabytes (MB) of physical memory.

## Disk Drives and Controllers

A total of 400 MB of on-line disk storage is required by the customer, as determined by the application required and the volumes of data to be input to the system. Therefore, two 258 MB disk drives with the proper cables and disk controller are configured as part of the hardware solution. A separate cabinet is not required for these disk drives, since there is room for them in the CPU cabinet. At this point the CPU selected (the 2450) is reviewed to ensure that the preferred disk drives and controller will work properly with it. The review shows that it does. This is an example of a loopback point in the decision process.

## Communication Controllers

The systems-marketing analyst determines that the total number of communications connections to the CPU is twenty-six. This is the number of system users, plus two printers. There will be twenty-six asynchronous connections, none of which will be at a speed greater than 19.2 kilobaud. There will be no local-area network connections or wide-area network connection, according to information provided to the systems-marketing analyst by the customer. System Network Architect (SNA) and Ethernet protocols will not be required. This is also not a government Tempest site, so special Tempest communication connection cables are not required. Based on the analysis of the situation, therefore, the configuration will involve twenty-four asynchronous terminals, two serial printers, and no parallel printers.

The controller necessary to meet the above specifications is an ICS3 controller. There are no other communications controllers coresident, so there is no possibility of coresidency conflicts between multiple communications controllers. The ICS3-T model is selected, since it works with the 2450 central processing unit. There are many models of the ICS3 available, but only the ICS3-T will work with the 2450 central processing unit.

## User Interface Devices

A punch card reader will not be needed by this user. A ten-inch tape drive that can read and write tapes at 800 and 1,600 bits per inch is selected. This is a model 4660T tape drive. Two printers are required that will be able to print at least approximately two hundred pages per day per printer. The printers selected are model 3185s that are equipped with both tractor and cut-sheet paper feeders. The printers will reside in the same area as the 2450 central processing unit. Therefore, standard printer cables will be appropriate for this situation. Plotting is not required by this customer so no plotter will be configured as part of the overall hardware configuration.

According to information provided the systems-marketing analyst, desktop publishing capabilities are not required. If they were, a special laser printer and work-station terminal would be configured at this point. The user terminals that are needed are standard asynchronous monochrome terminals with no graphics capabilities or onboard intelligence. Twenty-four model PT200-p-us terminals with cables will be configured. There is no need for modems, since all terminals will be located on-site.

At this point the communications controller (the ICS3-T model) is reviewed to ensure that it can handle all of the user interface devices. All of the above devices will function with this communications controller. Had the controller selected needed to be changed or modified in any way, the central processing unit would be reviewed to ensure compatibility with the controller. This is another example of a loopback point in the decision process.

## Review Cables and Cabinets

The user interface devices are reviewed to ensure that there is adequate cabinet space for them to reside in, if necessary. Also each device is checked to see if it comes with the cables needed to connect it to the central processing unit or the communi-cations controller. In this case the model 4660T tape drive will require a model 7653-1 tape cabinet, which was not previously configured. All other devices do not need separately configured cabinets. They can either reside in the central processing unit cabinet or are manufactured with their own cabinets.

The following is a list of hardware components that can be configured using the prototype knowledge-based expert system. A brief description is given for each component.

2350—basic central processing unit (this is where "computing" occurs).

2450—same as 2350 but with 50% more processing power.

4 MB Memory—this is the physical memory that will be used by the 2350/2450.

8 MB Memory—same as above except in a larger capacity.

AMLC—communication controller with 8 asynchronous connections.

ICS1—same as above except with 1 additional connection for synchronous communications.

ICS3—communications controller with a capacity for 40 connections that can be either asynchronous or synchronous in any combination.

Disk Drives—these are available in the following capacities:
      60 MB
     120 MB
     258 MB
        They can be configured in any combination, up to a quantity of two per 2350 or 2450 system.

PT200—interactive terminal that can be either color or monochrome with or without graphics capabilities.

3185—letter quality printer.

LASER—refers to a laser printer.

Tape Drive—can be either used with cassette tapes or reel-to-reel tapes. Model numbers are 4660T and 4585F.

Cabinet—can be used to house tape drives. Model number is 7653-1.

Plotter—type of printer used for blueprint type drawings and special graphics printing.

Punch-card-reader—device used to read punch cards—usually only used for data conversion when installing one of the office environment type systems.

**FIGURE 14-7   Hardware components.**

Each device configured in this situation will automatically come with its own cable to connect to the central processing unit or the communications controller so there is no need to add any additional cables.

A list of the components previously determined is now put together to become part of the overall turnkey computer system solution. This list includes

- A 2450 CPU with 4 MB memory
- Two 258 MB drive with controller and cables
- An ICS3 model T communications controller with cable
- A 4660T tape drive with controller and cable
- A 7653-1 cabinet for tape drive
- Two 3185 printers with tractor and cut sheet feeders with cables
- Twenty-four PT200 terminals with cables

For purposes of the prototype system replicating this decision process, which is documented in the following section, the range of possible components that can be recommended by the prototype system have been limited to those shown in Fig. 14-7.

## DOCUMENTING THE SYSTEM

The discussion in this section covers

- System proposal
- Description of the system
- Dependency diagrams
- Decision charts
- Designing and constructing the knowledge base

### System Proposal

The objective of the project is to develop a knowledge-based system that assists in configuring a turnkey computer system solution. The system is designed for use specifically for the computer systems that are sold by a major computer manufacturer-vendor company. The prototype system is only for hardware installation in the office environment. The hardware encompasses all central and peripheral components and the connective cabling.

This prototype system will eventually become part of a larger system that will include the hardware, software, training, and maintenance that are part of a turnkey computer system solution. The larger system will also have applicability to wider range of customer situations.

The system will be useful to the sales force of the company for configuring proposals to be presented to prospective customers. These proposals prescribed by the system will be complete and functional even though they are not configured by the experts themselves—the systems-marketing analysts. It will also be useful to systems-marketing analysts who are both doing configurations and training others to do it.

The system will provide the ability to present higher quality proposals on a timely basis, to satisfy more customers, and the ability of the company to expand marketing volume without increasing the number of analysts. It will also provide a more cost effective way to train new analysts.

The knowledge for this system was acquired from experiences of systems analysts (also referred to as systems-marketing analysts) in the computer industry, from reference documents, and from consultations with other computer systems analysts from the company under study and from other companies in related industries.

## Description of the System

The discussion in this section covers

- □ System objective and overview
- □ Recommendations to be made by the system
- □ Nature of the user interface, including a typical user dialogue
- □ Description of the knowledge structure and reasoning process

**System objective and overview.** The objective of this prototype system is to assist system users in configuring the hardware component of a turnkey computer system solution. The system will be designed for use specifically with the computer hardware components of a particular manufacturer-vendor. These components are specifically designed to function in the climatic and physical limitations of the average office environment. The hardware encompasses central and peripheral components and their appropriate cabinetry and connective cabling.

**Recommendations to be made by the system.** The goal of the system is to be able to query the knowledge-based system user about specific characteristics of the end user (or prospective customer) of the turnkey computer system solution and then determine the hardware that will be needed to meet the user requirements. The system will recommend a hardware configuration that is complete and meets the end user needs. Figure 14-7 contains a list of hardware components that could be configured in the prototype system.

The prototype system will make only a configuration recommendation. Subsequent versions of the system will be able to recommend the most cost efficient configuration.

**Nature of the user interface, including a typical user dialogue.** The user interface is constructed so that the prototype system will query the user for the information that is needed to configure the hardware components for the computer system. In a fully implemented system many of these hardware questions will not have to be asked. Instead the system will be able to infer the answer to a hardware question from the response to a question about the application software or other user characteristic. (See Fig. 14-11 for sample user questions from the prototype system.)

**Description of the knowledge structure and the reasoning process.** The recommendations made by the prototype system are based on answers to questions posed by the prototype system to the user. The questions will give the prototype system the information it needs to reason which hardware components will best fit the situation.

The prototype system contains five main groupings of components. These are

□ Central processing unit and memory
□ Disk drives and controllers
□ Communications controllers
□ User interface devices
□ Review of cables and cabinets

If-then rules are used to determine the values of the components at each stage of the reasoning process. The inference engine will use backward chaining. At certain points in the reasoning process, the inference engine will loop back to a previous decision point to determine if a previously selected component is still viable.

There are situations that will occur during the execution of the prototype system that require the prototype to ask different questions. Some rule sets contain logical chains that branch a certain way to a subsequent question depending on the answer to a previous question. An example of this situation would be rule set 3 of the prototype. If the user answers the question "Will the number of asynchronous users be more than 8 (y/n)?" with a "y," then no further questions will be needed for this rule set. If the user responds to the question with an "n," the prototype system will ask an additional question to complete the rule set.

The system is designed to use both forward and backward driving.

## Dependency Diagrams

Figure 14-8 provides a dependency diagram that replicates how the expert views the configuration of a total turnkey computer system solution. This is an example of the larger systems to be developed in subsequent stages of the project.

Figure 14-9 is a dependency diagram of the hardware portion of the turnkey computer system solution. This is the initial prototype system that was developed. The diagram gives a complete summary outline of all the questions, rules, knowledge segments and their interrelationships, values, and recommendations within the system.

## Decision Charts

Figure 14-10 gives one of the decision charts from the prototype system. There is a decision chart for every rule set in the system.

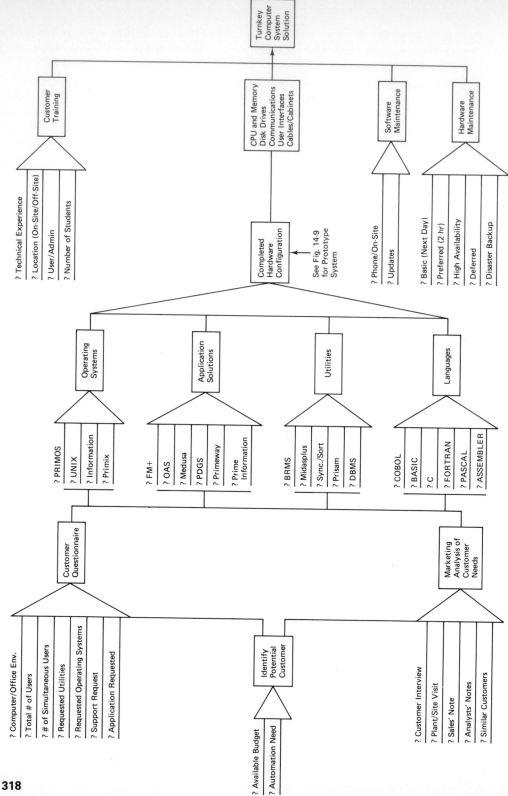

**FIGURE 14-8  Dependency diagram for configuration of turnkey computer system solution—overview of system.**

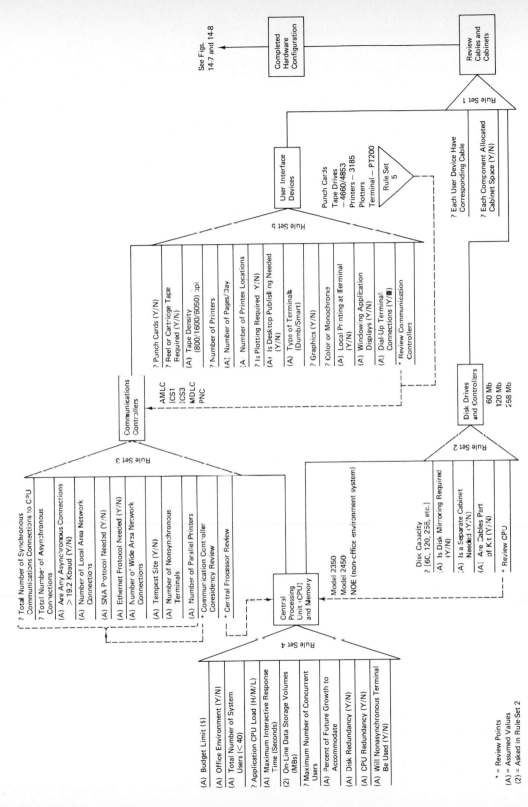

**FIGURE 14-9** Configuration of hardware segment of turnkey computer solutions—initial prototype system.

319

A. Decision Chart for Central Processing Unit Recommendation:

IF
Central Processing
Unit Application Load

| X = Concurrent # of Users | Light | Medium | Heavy |
|---|---|---|---|
| X ≤ 8 | 2350 | 2350 | 2350 |
| 8 < X ≤ 16 | 2350 | 2350 | 2450 |
| 16 < X ≤ 24 | 2350 | 2450 | NOE* |
| 24 < X ≤ 32 | 2350 | 2450 | NOE |
| 32 < X ≤ 40 | 2450 | NOE | NOE |
| X > 40 | NOE | NOE | NOE |

IF (brace on left)

*NOE = Non Office Environment System

THEN
Central Processing
Unit Recommended

B. Determining Communications Controller Needed: (Rule Set 3)

IF
Communications Protocols Supported

| Communications Controllers | Asynchronous | HDLC | Ringnet | Primenet | SNA | Ethernet |
|---|---|---|---|---|---|---|
| MDLC | N | Y | N | Y | N | Y |
| ICS1 | Y | Y | N | Y | N | N |
| ICS3 | Y | Y | N | Y | Y | Y |
| AMLC | Y | N | N | N | N | N |
| PNC | N | N | Y | N | N | N |

THEN (brace on left)

**FIGURE 14-10  Sample decision charts for configuration of hardware segment of turnkey computer solution—initial prototype.**

## Designing and Constructing the Knowledge Base

Rules and questions were developed from analysis done by the expert when configuring the hardware components of a turnkey computer solution. Sample rule sets and questions are shown in Fig. 14-11.

<u>Rules</u>:

```
/* rules 2 thru 10 are for cables and cabinets */

        rule-2:
        if cables = complete and
           cabinets = complete
        then cables-cabinets = complete.

        rule-3:
        if user-cables = complete and
           communication-cables = complete and
           disk-cables = complete
        then cables = complete.

        rule-4:
        if tape-cabinet = complete and
           ics3-cabinet = complete and
           disk-cabinet = complete
        then cabinets = complete.

/*      rule-5:
        if (card-punch-cable = 0 or
            card-punch-cable = 1) and
           tape-cables = complete and
           printer-cables = complete and
           terminal-cables = complete and
           modem-cables = complete
        then user-cables = complete.
*/


/* Cpu and memory section: This will be limited to the Models 2350 and */
/* 2450 office environment systems for the purpose of this prototype. */

        rule-4-1:
        if (cpu = 2350 or
            cpu = 2450 or
            cpu = out-of-range)
        then cpu-memory = complete.

        rule-4-1-1:
        if (cpu = 2350 or
            cpu = 2450 or
            cpu = out-of-range)
        then user-cables = complete.

        rule-4-2:
        if users = 8 and
          (application = light or
           application = medium or
           application = heavy)
        then cpu = 2350.

        rule-4-8:
        if users = 40 and
           application = light
        then cpu = 2450.
```

*(continued)*

**FIGURE 14-11    Knowledge base—sample rule set and questions (prototype system).**

```
rule-4-10:
if users = more
then cpu = out-of-range.
```

Questions:

```
question(users) = 'What is maximum number of users that will be
concurrently running on the system (8,16,24,32,40,more)?'.
legalvals(users) = [8,16,24,32,40,more].

question(application) = 'Is the main application that will be
run (light, medium, or heavy) in the way of cpu load?'.
legalvals(application) = [light,medium,heavy].
```

FIGURE 14-11 *(continued)*

## REVIEW QUESTIONS

1. Finish the knowledge-based system (or any segment of the system) partially documented in this chapter and enter it into the expert system shell you have.

2. The system described in this chapter is clearly distinct from all the systems described so far in this book. Describe these differences.

3. List other production tasks or decisions which appear to you to be good knowledge base applications. Develop the concept of a system for one of them, and draw a preliminary decision situation diagram of it.

4. There are two familiar types of operating knowledge-based systems not described in this book, production scheduling and process control. Describe some decision situations in those areas that appear to you to be good prospects for knowledge-based system development.

5. What is a turnkey computer system solution?

6. What are the individual components of the computer system configuration process?

7. What items are covered in the system/marketing analyst's turnkey solution?

8. What are some of the advantages of using a knowledge-based system in configuring the hardware portion of the computer system solution?

## REFERENCES

Allison, A., "RISC's Challenge Mini, Micro Suppliers," *Mini-Micro Systems*, vol. 19, November 1986.

Allison, A., "Varied Architectures Crowd Supermini Arena," *Mini-Micro Systems*, vol. 19, December 1986.

Becker, J.T., "Network Designers Face Shifting Industry Givens," *Data Communications*, vol. 15, December 1986.

Crabb, D.E., "Technical Topics for the IBM PC Family: An Annotated Bibliography," *Byte*, vol. 11, no. 11, 1986.

"Distributed SNA: A Network Architecture Gets On Track," *Data Communications*, vol. 16, February 1987.

Emmett, A., and Gabel, D., "Cases in Direct Microcomputer Connections: Nuts and Bolts," *Data Communications*, vol. 15, July 1986.

Hornstein, J.V., "Parallel Processing Attacks Real-Time World," *Mini-Micro Systems*, vol. 19, December 1986.

King, K.G., "Developments in Microcomputer Technology," *Journal of Accountancy*, vol. 162, September 1986.

Micossi, A., "Micro and Workstation Talents Converge," *Computer Decisions*, vol. 18, Sept. 9, 1986.

Purkiser, C., "Intel's 386 Unites UNIX and DOS Software," *Mini-Micro Systems*, vol. 20, April 1987.

Pryor, D., "NCR's PlatformStrategy Reaches to Multiprocessors," *Mini-Micro Systems*, vol. 20, March 1987.

Stevens, E.E., and B. Bernstein, "APPC: The Future of Microcomputer Communications within IBM's SNA," *Data Communications*, vol. 15, July 1986.

Taube, E.V., "Proper Modem Selection Ensures Free Flowing PC Communication," *Data Management*, vol. 24, September 1986.

Weadock, G.E., "Mini-Micro Hybrids Rival Local Networks," *Mini-Micro Systems*, vol. 19, September 1986.

# 15

# An Insurance Claim Evaluation System

This chapter describes the development of a knowledge-based system for an insurance company's handling of bodily injury claims. The discussion is in three parts:

- □ The situation under study: understanding the expert's domain
- □ Studying the situation to be prototyped
- □ Documenting the prototype system

The system is designed to help claims managers (adjustors) settle bodily injury claims more quickly, consistently, and effectively by providing a quick reference guide for more experienced claim managers and a step-by-step tutorial for inexperienced ones.

It has wide applicability because the knowledge base can be adjusted easily to meet local or regional factors that may affect claim evaluation.

This system may also be expanded into other claim decision areas, such as property damage to automobiles, damage to homes, and theft of personal property, all of which involve a similar decision process.

The discussion begins with a structured situation analysis and structured decision model development for the situation under study for prototyping. The design and documentation of the actual prototype system is then described.

# THE SITUATION UNDER STUDY: UNDERSTANDING
# THE EXPERT'S DOMAIN

The discussion in this section covers

- Selecting a decision area to work on
- Probing how the situation works and how decisions are made
- Narrowing the focus

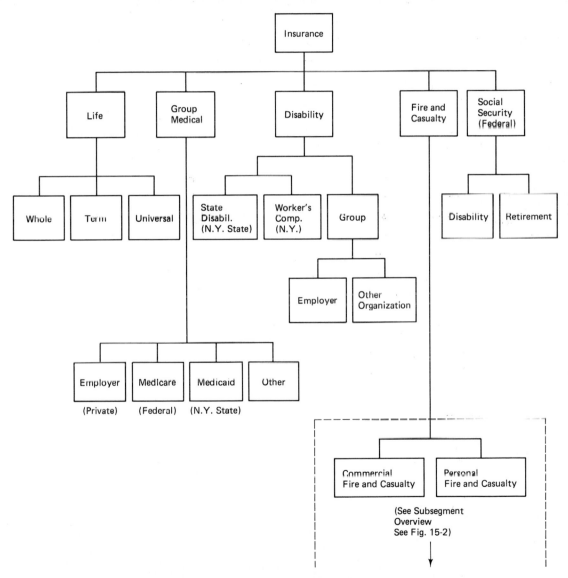

**FIGURE 15-1  Industry overview of types of insurance.**

## Selecting a Decision Area to Work On

The insurance industry offers specific kinds or "lines" of insurance, as seen in Fig. 15-1. Companies may specialize in one line only, handle multiple lines, or handle all lines. This study focuses on companies that handle the fire and casualty line, which is divided (with some crossover) into the commercial fire and casualty line and the personal fire and casualty line, as seen in Fig. 15-2. This chapter will focus on a segment of the personal fire and casualty line.

A *liability* claim is a claim for money damages that is filed by a *claimant* against

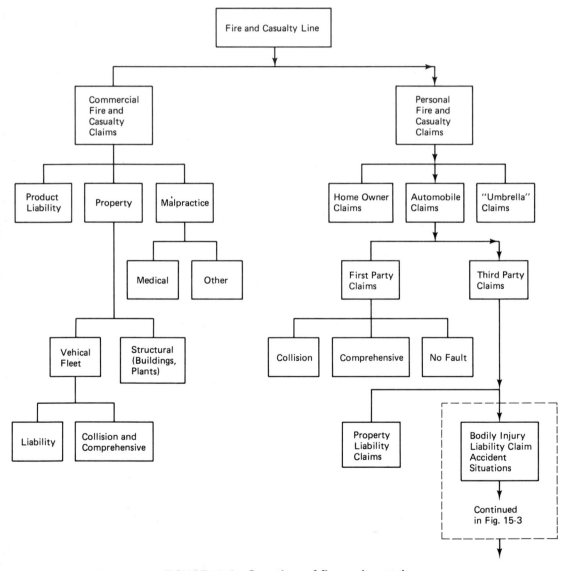

**FIGURE 15-2   Overview of fire and casualty area.**

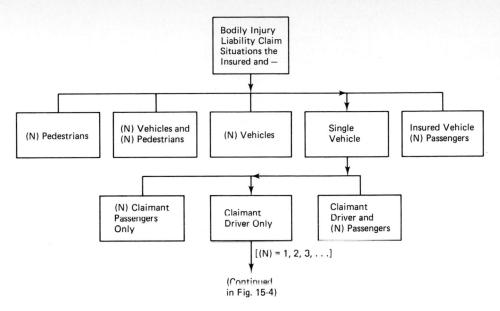

**FIGURE 15-3 Automobile bodily injury liability claims—types of accident situations.**

a person who is insured by a company. The claim is based on the fact that the *insured person* allegedly was to blame for an accident that injured the claimant.

The bodily injury claim segment of automobile liability, as shown in Fig 15-3, was selected for further study.

Technically a liability claim arises as a result of the insured person performing some physical *act* that may have resulted in creating a *hazard*.

In this study the situation is confined to automobile accidents. Automobile accidents could involve the insured person's vehicle and

- One or more claimant vehicles
- One or more claimant vehicles and one or more pedestrians
- One or more pedestrians alone
- One or more passengers in the insured's vehicle

The automobile accident situation selected for study is the most common one, that of an insured vehicle and a single claimant vehicle. A bodily injury claim is filed by the driver of the claimant vehicle, who is known as the claimant driver. It should be noted that the claimant driver may or may not own the vehicle being driven. The vehicle itself is not the concern of this study.

At the specific insurance company under study, when this type of accident is reported to the insurance company's claims department, a claim file is physically created and assigned to a claims adjustor in a bodily injury claim handling unit, as indicated in Fig. 15-4.

The adjustor handling the assigned bodily injury liability claim initiates an in-

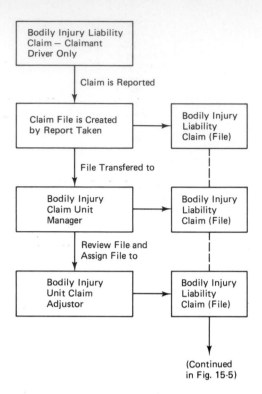

FIGURE 15-4 Overview of company claim department—accident report and file assignment system.

vestigation into the nature and validity of the claim. The adjustor gathers and verifies factual information concerning the injury claim. This process, the bodily injury claim evaluation, is outlined in Fig. 15-5, where an overview of the decision area under study is shown.

## Probing How the Situation Works and How Decisions Are Made

As seen in Fig. 15-5, a bodily injury liability claim investigation is broken down into three key segments:

- Policy or Policies
- Liability
- Damages

Each area must be investigated, although the extent of the investigation in each segment may vary, depending on several key factors:

- The information (or lack of it) available from the onset of the claim
- The existence of a *verified policy* with the company covering the insured for the accident claim
- The severity of the injury claim and any accompanying factors

PART 2: DEVELOPING MANAGEMENT DECISION SYSTEMS

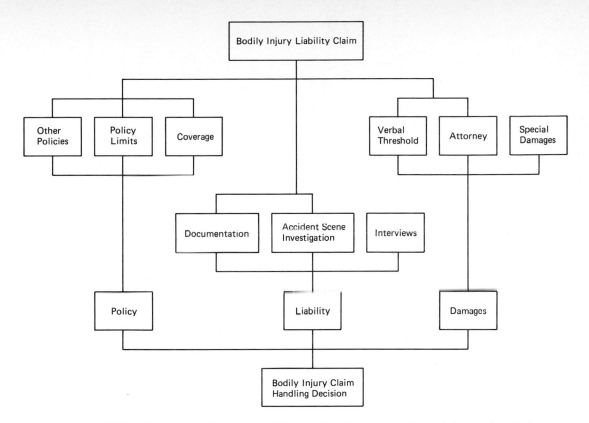

**FIGURE 15-5  Bodily injury claim evaluation—overview of the entire decision area.**

These factors are shown in Fig. 15-6, a more detailed view of the bodily injury claim evaluation situation.

The process described here is the one followed at the company under study. It is fairly typical of the industry in general. The process begins in the *policy* segment, where a new injury claim file is opened—that is, a manila file for printed and written documents is physically created. At that point a question may arise as to whether or not a policy was written for the insured prior to the occurrence of the injury claim. If the policy was written the day before the accident occurred but the policy had not yet been entered into the computer file, for example, the adjustor would verify that an automobile policy covering this accident had been in force prior to the accident. If it is found during this phase that no insurance policy existed, then no insurance coverage was in force and the investigation of the claim would stop. During this phase the adjustor would also determine *policy limits* and *other policies* in effect covering the insured.

As seen in Fig. 15-6, once coverage is verified, a *reserve* is set aside by the company. A reserve is an amount of money that reflects the *potential value* of the claim being made. The amount of the reserve is determined by an adjustor, based on an estimate of the ultimate value of the claim and the policy limits. Setting a

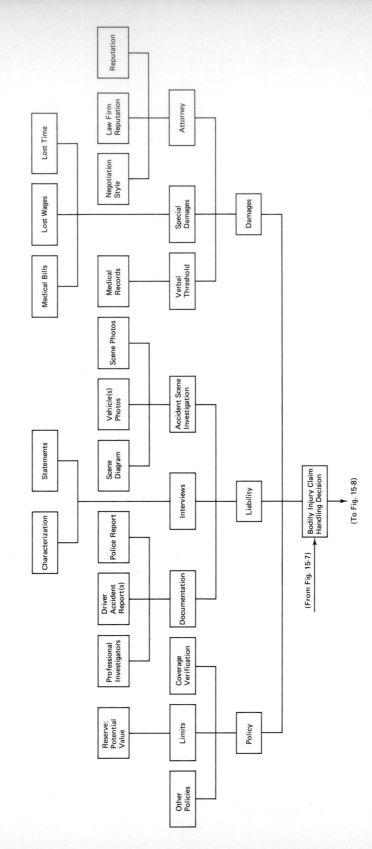

**FIGURE 15-6  More detailed view of the bodily injury claim evaluation situation.**

reserve amount is required by law. An insurance company must have adequate reserves for all of its claim files so that, in the event of company bankruptcy, outstanding claims against it would be covered.

During the *liability* phase, an adjustor weighs all factors involved in the accident's occurrence. Then an adjustor decides on a scale of 0 percent to 100 percent the extent to which the cause of the accident lies with the insured. If there is *no* liability or fault on the part of the insured, the adjustor normally would not pay any settlement money to the claimant. However, this does not necessarily end the process. For example, other pressures may be brought to bear on an insurance company and cause an adjustor (the claim manager) to reconsider the decision not to pay any settlement money. For instance, a trial jury might be so moved at the sight of someone missing a limb that it returns an unfavorable verdict against the insurance company.

During the *damages* phase an adjustor weighs all factors involved in deciding whether or not the injury warrants settlement, and if so, how much such damages are worth. This area also covers out-of-pocket expenses that a claimant may seek, such as lost wages from employment or medical expenses.

The damages area is important because the adjustor must verify that the injuries are at least sufficient enough to allow a claimant to qualify under one of the verbal threshold categories. A verbal threshold is defined as a nonmonetary or *verbal* condition, or *threshold*, of injury that a claimant must meet in order to qualify for a right to make an injury claim. For example, if the claimant's death results from an automobile accident, the estate of the claimant has a right to make an auto accident injury claim in New York state, because death is considered a *verbal threshold* category.

There are eight verbal threshold categories. They are discussed in detail in the section "Studying the Situation to Be Prototyped."

If there is no verifiable information to confirm that an injury is related to the auto accident, or that the injury exists, an adjustor may decide to deny payment of any settlement money.

Liability and damages are usually areas of considerable disagreement between an insurance company and an attorney representing a claimant. In practice most claims are decided in the insurance claim office, with very few ever going to full trial and court verdict.

Once an adjustor has completed the bodily injury claim evaluation process, shown in Fig. 15-6, an adjustor verifies the amount of settlement authorization. The *settlement authorization limit* is the predetermined amount of money a company will allow its representative (a claim adjustor, claim manager, or attorney) to offer in settling claims. It is common practice in the industry to grant a predetermined authorization limit, on a *per claimant* basis, to a claim adjustor based on an adjustor's experience and past performance.

If an adjustor wishes to settle a bodily injury claim for a dollar amount greater than the adjustor's assigned authorization limit, then the claim must be submitted to the adjustor's unit claim manager for the amount exceeding the adjustor's limit of authority in the company under study. If the dollar amount exceeds the unit claim manager's authorization limit, then that manager must bring it to the next authorization level, as is shown in Fig. 15-7.

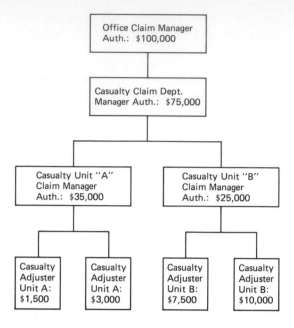

FIGURE 15-7 Overview diagram of a possible settlement authorization structure and amounts for approval to negotiate bodily injury claims.

An overview diagram of the possible results following from an adjustor's recommendations and subsequent negotiating of the claim is shown in Fig. 15-8.

Once the injury claim decision has been made (Fig. 15-6), the adjustor must either negotiate the claim (if a settlement amount has been recommended), or prepare to defend nonpayment against further legal action by the claimant.

For example, in Fig. 15-8 the path marked by the arrows traces the outcomes in a situation that an adjustor negotiated, but was unable to settle with the claimant's attorney. This results in an impasse or inability on the part of the company and the claimant's attorney to settle the claim without a lawsuit and possible trial.

In this example the claim was not settled and led to a trial by jury. Two other choices at this level were settlement at court prior to any trial taking place (which is a common occurrence) or trial without a jury in which the judge alone hears the injury claim (which is a rare occurrence).

A *jury trial* is a civil court trial, involving the insured, the claimant, their respective attorneys, the judge, and the jury. The burden of proof is on the claimant. This means that it is the claimant's responsibility to show that the injuries are worth more than the insurance company (representing the insured party who is liable for the accident) has offered.

An *unfavorable verdict* is the amount of money awarded by a jury exceeding the company's recommended settlement amount and can be very costly.

As seen from the above discussion, an adjustor needs considerable judgment to carry out the claim evaluation and subsequent negotiations, because of the amounts of money involved and the difficulties involved in obtaining and evaluating information.

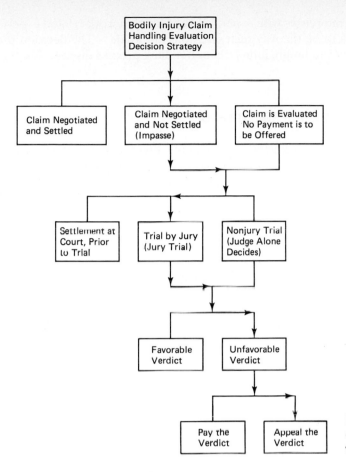

**FIGURE 15-8  Possible outcomes of the bodily injury claim evaluation decision.**

## Narrowing The Focus

Two areas of the decision situation were identified for possible prototype development. First, it seemed possible to develop a small prototype system of the overall bodily injury claim handling evaluation decision, as shown earlier in Fig. 15-6. Second, it seemed possible to develop a prototype system for each of the three key factor areas shown in Fig. 15-6.

The following describes the development of a prototype system for making a recommendation in one of the key factor areas, damages. There were several reasons this situation was chosen for prototype development:

1. It provided a quick way to prototype.
2. The prototype system was representative of the overall system and so enabled testing of the basic concept and structure of the overall system.
3. By using test cases with the smaller prototype, the general model would be produced gradually and more efficiently, and would replicate actual situations in a more realistic way.

On the basis of interviews with experts in the field and work related experience, the following appears to be the way such decisions are made. The decision process described here follows the bodily injury claim handling process discussed in the preceding section.

## STUDYING THE SITUATION TO BE PROTOTYPED

Each of the specific factors or knowledge segments affecting the damages decision is examined in detail in the following discussion. The description of the situation is structured in a way that provides models, like the one shown in Fig. 15-9, useful for later prototype systems development. These structured models are based on descriptions or scenarios of typical decision situations faced by experts working at the company under study.

The *verbal threshold* categories are the most important factor. An adjustor will consider the type of injury or injuries sustained, the severity of the injuries, and whether the injuries are temporary or permanent. Claimant's hospital records and doctor reports, as well as the company's doctor's report, are reviewed during this phase of the study to confirm the seriousness of the injury or injuries.

The adjustor selects at least one of eight verbal threshold categories under the damages decision. *Verbal thresholds* specify eight categories that allow a claimant the right to make a claim for pain and suffering from injuries related to the auto

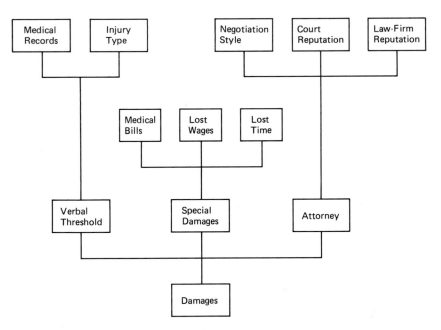

**FIGURE 15-9  Outline of the decision to be prototyped—bodily injury claim handling.**

accident in New York state. They are

1. Death
2. Permanent disability to a bodily member, organ, or function
3. Permanent partial disability to a bodily member, organ, or function
4. Permanent disfigurement (scarring)
5. Loss of limb, organ, or bodily function
6. Fracture
7. Significant limitation of a bodily member or function
8. (90) day disability within a (180) day period after date of the accident

Each of these has been given a dollar value limit by the company under study. This maximum dollar value limit is based on an industry average. For example, the maximum average dollar value for verbal threshold two, permanent disability, is $200,000. The value of permanent disfigurement, the fourth verbal threshold, is set at $100,000. These figures serve as a benchmark that can be adjusted upward or downward, depending on the situation circumstances.

*Special damages* refer to those damages suffered by the claimant, both monetary (for example, hospital and doctor bills and lost wages) and physical (for example, disability requiring physical therapy). Lost wages is usually examined separately when the adjustor is evaluating the damages area and then incorporated into the overall special damages portion. The claimant's occupation, lost time, and disability time are included in this category.

The decision is also affected by the *attorney* representing the claimant's interests. Knowing the abilities of the attorney representing the claimant is important in determining which negotiation strategies will be effective. The attorney's reputation among his associates on injury claims, his court reputation, and his negotiation abilities will influence the adjustor's evaluation decision.

An adjustor weighs all of the above factors in coming to a decision about the settlement dollar value and about the negotiating strategies to settle the claim or a defense strategy should the adjustor decide not to pay the claim. The following briefly describes a typical decision scenario illustrating that decision-making process at work.

The first step an adjustor takes upon receipt of an injury claim is to review the reported injury information to get some idea as to how serious the injury claim might be. The adjustor must then set out to gather and verify all information on the injuries claimed, to prove or disprove them.

For instance, an adjustor would secure all hospital, doctor, and medical exam reports. As an example, an adjustor might be assigned a facial scar injury claim of a twenty-seven-year-old woman. The medical records confirm the cause, nature, and extent of the injury as well as subsequent care such as surgical repair of the injury, hospital stay, X rays, and follow-up visits. Because the records confirm the reported injury, the claimant qualifies under verbal threshold category number four—permanent disfigurement or scarring. If the records had not confirmed the injury, then an adjustor would consider not paying any money on the claim as presented.

In this situation involving the twenty-seven-year-old woman, the adjustor simultaneously examined special damages to verify any lost time claimed from the woman's occupation. She was a teacher and had lost sixty days time from teaching. Such loses can involve gainful employment, such as for a lawyer, doctor, or teacher, or nongainful employment, such as for a mother-housewife. If lost wages due to the injury are claimed, records must be secured and verified as well. In this case lost wages amounted to $5,000. The claimant's medical bills must also be secured and verified. In this case the amount was $7,500.

An adjustor weighs each of these areas separately. In this case all of them were high, reaching almost to the policy limits. The adjustor concluded that the total special damages were verifiably very high.

During these early phases of the investigation, an adjustor is usually in constant communication (by letter and/or phone) with the claimant's attorney. The claimant's attorney may be a seasoned courthouse veteran. If so the attorney may be held in high regard by the courts, other attorneys, and other insurance carriers. Or the attorney might be considered as a steady, capable attorney, with only a fair court reputation. Or the attorney may be unknown to an adjustor.

An adjustor also considers the law firm's reputation among fellow adjustors, adjustors with other insurance companies, and other attorneys. The firm may be a well-known entity, but not that forceful, or little known, or an unknown quantity.

The attorney's negotiating style is also sized up in a similar fashion.

An adjustor then weights these factors (court reputation, law firm reputation, and negotiating style). In the case of the twenty-seven-year-old woman, the attorney was considered to have a highly regarded court reputation, with a well-known law firm, and to be uncompromising in negotiations. The adjustor concluded that this attorney would be a particularly dangerous adversary, and so rated the attorney as very strong.

All three key factors (verbal threshold, special damages, and attorney) are weighed in making the decision. In this situation, for example, the injury was confirmed to come under the verbal threshold four, permanent disfigurement, which had a maximum average dollar value of $100,000. The special damages were considered to be high, that is, they were significant enough to warrant offering the claimant a relatively large settlement. The attorney was considered to be strong, and so likely to be able to get the maximum dollar settlement figure for the claimant.

Weighing all three factors the adjustor arrived at a figure of $100,000. This figure is the maximum average dollar amount for such an injury, and was recommended because in this situation the attorney's reputation was very strong and the special damages were very high. Had the attorney been rated weaker, or the special damages less, the recommended dollar settlement amount would have been proportionately lower.

At times the special damages can be so large that the adjustor may adjust the maximum average dollar amount for an injury substantially upward. For example, the medical damages can climb to over $50,000 in hospital and surgical care in some cases, lost wages can exceed the same amount, or both events can occur simultaneously. Such exceptional amounts would impact significantly, as in the scar injury case described above, and would lead the adjustor to exceed the benchmark amounts by substantial dollar amounts. Although not common, settlement amounts can at times exceed many times $500,000. These are exceptional situations, however, and so are not included in the initial prototyping study, which covered only the most typical situations.

After the settlement value based on damages is calculated, then that figure is adjusted for policy limits. The lower of two will be selected. That figure is then adjusted for the company's percent of liability. Where damages are greater than the policy limits, the final settlement figure is normally the policy limit. Where the damages figure is less than the policy limit, the final settlement figure is more likely to be correspondingly below the policy limit. In each case additional adjustments can be made for the percent of liability, depending on the amounts involved.

The following section describes the knowledge-based prototype system that replicates these kinds of expert decisions.

## DOCUMENTING THE PROTOTYPE SYSTEM

The following discussion covers

- ☐ System proposal
- ☐ Description of the prototype system
- ☐ Dependency diagrams
- ☐ Decision charts
- ☐ Designing and constructing the knowledge base

### System Proposal

The general objective of the project is to develop an expert knowledge-based system that assists insurance company claim personnel to make a decision regarding a bodily injury claim at the company under study. It would be used by claims adjustors and by managers in a claim department of that company.

The first phase of the project is limited to a specific decision—whether or not a claim qualifies under the damages area and, if so, the dollar settlement value of the claim. If the claim decision recommends against paying a claim, then a zero dollar amount will be recommended by the prototype. This initial prototype phase is designed to test and build a larger knowledge-based system for handling bodily injury claims.

In later versions of the system the decision in the damages area is combined with the policy and liability decision areas to create an overall bodily injury claim evaluation decision system. This system is shown in the dependency diagram in Fig. 15-10. In addition to recommending a dollar claim settlement figure, the larger overall system recommends either a negotiation strategy (or strategies) to settle the claim or a defense strategy to defend the recommendation of not paying any money on the claim.

The benefits of the system are that it

- ☐ Provides a quick reference guide for experienced managers confronted with complex issues concerning an injury claim

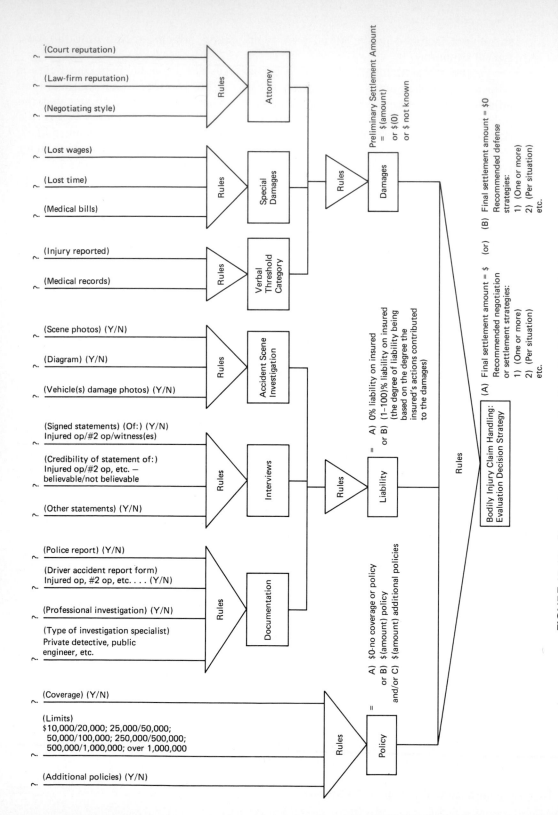

**FIGURE 15-10  Dependency diagram for New York State bodily injury claim handling evaluation system—subsequent prototype system.**

□ Supplements the company training programs by providing a tutorial for new employees

□ Incorporates the latest claim procedures, because modifications can be made without disturbing the system's reasoning process or knowledge base

□ Can be tailored to the particular claim needs of each regional claim territory

□ Fills the expertise gap left by the departure of experienced claim personnel to competitors in the industry

□ Provides recommendations that might be overlooked during manual evaluations by both experienced and inexperienced employees

The knowledge sources used to develop the prototype system included interviews with experts in the industry, actual work experience, and company-wide bodily injury procedural claim manuals.

## Description of the System

**System overview and objective.** The prototype system, which focuses on the damages area, is designed to assist claim department personnel to decide whether an injury claim will qualify for settlement money and, if so, the dollar amount range recommended for settling the claim.

The prototype system asks users questions about types of injuries reported, confirmation of injuries, medical bills, length of disability, occupational lost wages and lost time, and an assessment of the attorney or attorneys representing the claimant.

The system uses if-then rules and backward chaining to reason through the information provided by a user to reach its recommendation.

**Recommendations to be made by the system.** The prototype system will recommend either of two claim handling options: a scheduled *settlement value* (a figure ranging from $5,000 to $200,000) or *no payment* of the claim.

The larger system, shown in Fig. 15-10, makes the additional recommendations of various negotiating strategies for settling the claim, or a defense strategy to defend not paying the claim.

**Nature of the user interface, including typical user dialogue.** The typical user dialogue covers three knowledge areas:

□ *The claimant's injuries*—This information is obtained from a user by asking questions such as "What category does the reported injury fall under: (A list of the verbal threshold categories 1 through 8 appears on the screen, from which the user will select one)" and "Do all the available medical records, doctor reports, and exams confirm the injuries as reported, confirm them as moderate injuries, or confirm them as light, or none, or not-known injuries?"

□ *The claimant's special damages*—This information is obtained from a user by asking such questions as "What is the lost time from claimant's occupation due to the accident [0 to 90+ days, or not known]?" and "What is the dollar amount of the net lost income of the claimant [0 to $5,000+, or none]?"

□ *The claimant's attorney*—This information is obtained from a user by asking such questions as "Is the claimant attorney's reputation in court considered as highly regarded, capable, fair, or not known?" and "What type of negotiation style does the attorney seem to possess: uncompromising, compromising, settles-quickly, or not known?".

If-then rules are used to determine values at each stage. The inference engine uses backward chaining. The values are measured for each of the factors in the reasoning chain as "high, medium, low"; "strong, moderate, weak"; dollar amount; number of days; or type of verbal threshold.

**Description of the knowledge structure and reasoning process.** The recommendations made by the prototype system are based on three critical factors: the claimant's verbal threshold category; the claimant's special damages; and the claimant's attorney. In turn the values for each of these factors are determined by a number of other influencing factors:

□ *The claimant verbal threshold categories* are determined by such verification factors as hospital and doctor records and X rays, the findings of a medical examination by a doctor or panel of doctors of the insurance company, the type and length of disability, and the length of treatment or therapy or any surgery needed.

□ *The claimant's special damages* are determined by the dollar amounts of the claimant's medical bills and occupational lost wages. The total number of disability days related to the claimant's accident injuries is also considered.

□ *The claimant's attorney (or attorneys)* is also considered to assess the amount of influence the attorney may possess in the attorney's profession, in court, and in the style the attorney might use in negotiating an injury claim with an adjustor.

The system's reasoning processes are similar to those of the claims adjustor described earlier. First, the value of the injury, special damages, and attorney are determined. The maximum average dollar value of the injury (for example, $50,000 for a fracture—verbal threshold six) is then used as a benchmark value, which is then adjusted for the value of special damages and attorney. For example, if both attorney and special damages are strong or high, then the maximum average dollar value of the injury will be recommended as the settlement value. If the special damages and attorney are rated weaker, then the average dollar amount base is adjusted downward proportionately.

The initial prototype system has been simplified somewhat, since it deals with only the most typical situations. For example, cases can arise where special damages are so large that they are added to the maximum average dollar value of the injury. The initial prototype system does not deal with exceptional cases.

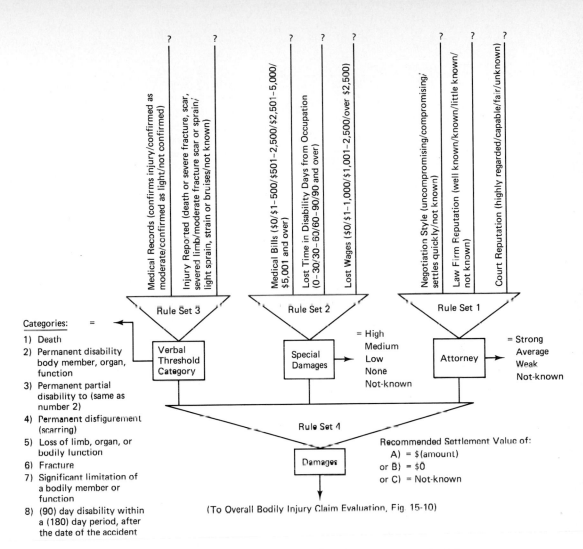

**FIGURE 15-11** Dependency diagram for damages area decision system—initial prototype.

## Dependency Diagrams

Figure 15-10 shows the dependency diagram for the overall system, combining the policy, liability, and damages areas. The overall decision strategy will recommend either negotiating the injury claim for the amount of money suggested for settlement by the system or not paying the claim. It also recommends appropriate negotiating or defending strategies.

Figure 15-11 shows the dependency diagram for the prototype system covering the damages area. It summarizes all the questions, rules, knowledge segments and their interrelationships, values, and recommendations within the system. The dam-

Rules

| | | 1-1 | 1-2 | 1-3 | 1-4 | 1-5 | 1-6 | 1-7 | 1-8 | 1-9 | 1-10 | 1-11 | 1-12 | 1-13 | 1-14 | 1-15 | 1-16 | 1-... |
|---|---|---|---|---|---|---|---|---|---|---|---|---|---|---|---|---|---|---|
| IF | LAW FIRM = | W-K | W-K | W-K | W-K | K | K | K | K | L-K | L-K | L-K | L-K | N-K | N-K | N-K | N-K | |
| | COURT REPUTATION = | H-R | CA | F | N-K | H-R | CA | F | NK | H-R | CA | F | NK | H-R | CA | F | NK | |
| | NEGOTIATION STYLE = | U | U | U | U | U | U | U | U | U | U | U | U | U | U | U | U | |
| THEN { | ATTORNEY = | S | S | A | A | S | A | A | A | S | A | A | W | S | A | W | A | |

Key:

Attorney
S = Strong
A = Average
W = Weak
N-K = Not-known

Law firm
W-K = Well-known
K = Known
L-K = Little-known
N-K = Not-known

Court reputation
H-R = Highly regarded
CA = Capable
F = Fair
N-K = Not-known

Negotiation style
U = Uncompromising
C = Compromising
S-Q = Settles quickly
N-K = Not-known

**FIGURE 15-12    Sample segment of decision chart for "attorney" in insurance claim evaluation system—damages (initial prototype).**

```
/*---------------Rules for the Attorney Segment----------------*/

        rule-1-1: if law-firm = well-known and
                court-reputation = capable and
                negotiation-style = uncompromising
              then attorney = strong.

        rule-1-2: if court-reputation = highly-regarded
              then attorney = strong.

        rule-1-3: if (law-firm = well-known and
                 court-reputation = fair) or
                 (law-firm = well-known and
                 court-reputation = not-known and
                 negotiation-style = uncompromising)
              then attorney = strong.

        rule-1-4: if law-firm = well-known and
                court-reputation = capable and
                negotiation-style = compromising
              then attorney = average.

        rule-1-6: if law-firm = well-known and
                court-reputation = capable and
                negotiation-style = not-known
              then attorney = average.

        rule-1-7: if law-firm = well-known and
                court-reputation = not-known and
                negotiation-style = not-known
              then attorney = average.
              then attorney = average.

        rule-1-12: if (law-firm = not-known and
                 court-reputation = capable and
                 negotiation-style = uncompromising) or
                 (law-firm = not-known and
                 court-reputation = not-known and
                 negotiation-style = uncompromising)
              then attorney = average.


/*---------------Questions for the Attorney Segment-------------*/

question(law-firm) = 'What reputation does the claimant attorney
law firm have in handling injury claims with insurance companies?
(Chose one from the following)

          - well-known.

          - known

          - little-known
```

*(continued)*

**FIGURE 15-13 Sample segment from knowledge base. Rules and
questions for insurance claim evaluation system—damages (initial
prototype).**

```
                        - not-known'.

legalvals(law-firm) = [well-known,known,little-known,not-known].


/*----------Questions for the Special Damages Segment--------*/

question(medical-bills) = 'What category do the medical-bills
qualify under? (choose one from the following list)

        - none($0)

        - low($1-1000)

        - medium($501-2500)

        - high($2501-5000 +)

        - not-known'.


legalvals(medical-bills) = [none,low,medium,high,not-known].
```

**FIGURE 15-13** *(continued)*

ages area recommend a specific dollar amount, or nonpayment of the claim. Both Fig. 15-10 and Fig. 15-11 are based on the structured situation models illustrated earlier.

### Decision Charts

Figure 15-12 shows a sample decision chart from the prototype system. There is a decision chart for every rule-set triangle in this dependency diagram.

### Designing and Constructing the Knowledge Base

A segment of the prototype system knowledge base, giving rules and questions, is shown in Fig. 15-13. The expert system shell used is M.1.

## REVIEW QUESTIONS

1. Complete the knowledge base for the system (or any segment of the system) partially documented in this chapter and enter it into the expert system shell you use.

2. Describe situations in other insurance areas you are familiar with that involve decisions, tasks or problems that lend themselves to knowledge-based system development.

3. Describe the process of structured situation analysis and decision situation model development in the situation described in this chapter. In what ways is it similar to or different from what was involved in the other operations systems described in Chapters 13 and 14?

4. Describe the ways in which structured situation analysis is used to provide a basis for prototype system design and documentation in the situation described in this chapter.

5. Describe some of the ways you have developed for structuring decision situations in a way that facilitates prototype knowledge-based system development.

6. What are the three key segments of a bodily injury liability claim investigation? Describe their importance.

7. What are the three critical factors used to determine the proper level of damages in the prototype system described in this chapter?

8. What is a "verbal threshold" category? List three examples.

## REFERENCES

Allison, A., "RISC's Challenge Mini, Micro Suppliers," *Mini-Micro Systems,* vol. 19, November 1986.

Allison, A., "Varied Architectures Crowd Supermini Arena," *Mini-Micro Systems,* vol. 19, December 1986.

Decker, J.T., "Network Designers Face Shifting Industry Givens," *Data Communications,* vol. 15, December 1986.

Best, A.M., *Best's Insurance Report,* Oldwick, NJ: A.M. Best, 1987.

Bradford, M., "Texas Claims Study Identifies Non-Economic Damage Costs," *Business Insurance,* vol. 21, March 2, 1987.

Brostoff, S., "Insurers Could've Saved Millions by Going To Court, JVR Contends," *National Underwriter,* vol. 90, Aug. 15, 1986.

Bundy, D., and S. Day, *Total Coverage: The Complete Insurance Guide,* New York: Harper & Row, 1987.

Cerone, J.F., "Claim Payments: Is Waiting Wiser?," *Best's Review,* vol. 87, September 1986.

Clarke, A.G., "Eastern Claims Conference—Curiosity Can Kill The Claim," *Best's Review,* vol. 87, April 1987.

Crabb, D.E., "Technical Topics for the IBM PC Family: An Annotated Bibliography," *Byte,* vol. 11, no. 11, 1986.

"Distributed SNA: A Network Architecture Gets On Track," *Data Communications,* vol. 16, February 1987.

Emmett, A., and Gabel, D., "Cases in Direct Microcomputer Connections: Nuts and Bolts," *Data Communications,* vol. 15, July 1986.

Herrmann, P.J., "Lawyer Urges Insurers To Contest Bad Claims," *National Underwriter,* vol. 90, Sept. 19, 1986.

Hoffman, P.A., "Structured Settlements in Auto Injury Cases," *National Underwriters,* vol. 90, May 2, 1986.

Hornstein, J.V., "Parallel Processing Attacks Real-Time World," *Mini-Micro Systems,* vol. 19, December 1986.

King, K.G., "Developments in Microcomputer Technology," *Journal of Accountancy,* vol. 162, September 1986.

Magarick, P., *Casualty Investigation Checklists,* 3rd ed., New York: Clark Boardman, 1985.

Margolis, H.R., "Loss Claims: Looking Beneath the Surface," *Best's Review,* vol. 87, January 1987.

Martin, F.H., "Claims Investigation: A Cost-Cutting Casualty?" *Risk Management,* vol. 33, June 1986.

Micossi, A., "Micro and Workstation Talents Converge," *Computer Decisions,* vol. 18, Sept. 9, 1986.

Narod, S., "Claims: Key To Winning," *National Underwriters,* vol. 91, March 23, 1987.

"Ontario Insurers Set Up Computer Claims Systems," *Best's Review,* vol. 87, May 1986.

Purkiser, C., "Intel's 386 Unites UNIX and DOS Software," *Mini-Micro Systems,* vol. 20, April 1987.

Pryor, D., "NCR's PlatformStrategy Reaches to Multiprocessors," *Mini-Micro Systems,* vol. 20, March 1987.

Stevens, E.E., and B. Bernstein, "APPC: The Future of Microcomputer Communications within IBM's SNA," *Data Communications,* vol. 15, July 1986.

Taube, E.V., "Proper Modem Selection Ensures Free-Flowing PC Communication," *Data Management,* vol. 24, September 1986.

Weadock, G.E., "Mini-Micro Hybrids Rival Local Networks," *Mini-Micro Systems,* vol. 19, September 1986.

# 16

# An Inventory Planning System

This chapter describes the development of a knowledge-based system for inventory planning. The topics covered are

- The situation under study: understanding the expert's domain
- Studying the situation to be prototyped
- Documenting the prototype system

## THE SITUATION UNDER STUDY: UNDERSTANDING THE EXPERT'S DOMAIN

The discussion in this section covers

- Selecting a decision area to work on
- Narrowing the focus of the study
- Studying how the situation works and how decisions are made

### Selecting a Decision Area to Work On

The general area under study is operations management. As shown in Fig. 16-1, operations management can be divided into five areas: design, production control, capital investment planning, forecasting, and materials management.

- *Design* involves decisions concerning product layouts; facility or capacity plan-

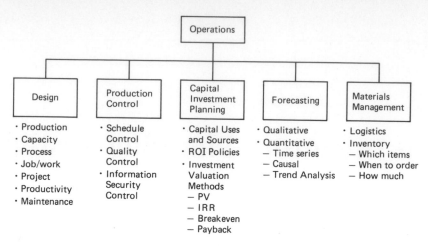

**FIGURE 16-1  Overall situation diagram.**

ning; process, job or work, and project control; productivity measurement; and maintenance and safety.

□ *Production control* involves decisions concerning schedule, quality, and information and security control.

□ *Capital investment planning* involves decisions about capital sources and uses, within company return-on-investment (ROI) policy guidelines, using such investment evaluation methods as present value (PV), internal rate of return (IRR), and breakeven and payback analysis.

□ *Forecasting* involves anticipating what might happen in the future. Forecasts are made using qualitative methods (judgment) and quantitative methods (for example, time-series, causal, and trend analysis).

□ *Materials management* involves decisions concerning inventory management and logistics.

These areas require expertise in fields ranging from engineering to psychology. They involve decisions that are both operational and strategic, and so lend themselves to knowledge-based systems applications.

## Narrowing the Focus of the Study

Due to the size and scope of the operations management area, the focus of the study was narrowed to materials management. Materials management can be divided into two areas: inventory and logistics. *Inventory* is idle material resources held for future use. Inventory planning concerns ensuring that what is required is available in sufficient quantities to satisfy demand. *Logistics* is concerned with the goods after they have left the production plant and before they have arrived at the warehouse or point of sale. Normally, some goods will be enroute all the time.

The study was further narrowed to inventory management in order to provide an opportunity for an in-depth analysis of a specific decision situation. There are several reasons why the inventory management area lends itself to knowledge-based systems applications:

- There are experts in the field.
- The field involves acquired skills that can be articulated and taught to others.
- Sound reasoning and judgment are involved.
- There seems to be agreement on how an expert goes about doing the job well.

## Studying How the Situation Works and How Decisions Are Made

Figure 16-2 diagrams the situation under study. Both qualitative and quantitative analyses are used when making inventory decisions. Five critical *qualitative* factors can influence these decisions: suppliers, competitors, customers, market demand, and company. The *quantitative* aspects of inventory management decisions may include using several well-known techniques such as inventory classifications (the ABC method), Min Max, and economic order quantity (EOQ).

The ABC method involves segregating the inventory into classifications based on an item's percentage of total inventory costs or the percentage of total profit contribution. Class A may consist, for example, of approximately 20 percent of the items and may represent 60 to 90 percent of the total costs or profits. Class B and class C would then consist of 30 percent and 50 percent of the items, respectively. The purpose of the ABC classification method is to set priorities regarding *which* items to pay most attention to.

Min-max is a method that sets the minimum and maximum level of inventory that is to be held at any given time. These minimum and maximum levels are generally set using statistical analysis of the average demand and the degree of variation in demand. *When* the inventory of the item drops to its designated minimum level, it is time to reorder an amount not to exceed the specified maximum level.

The economic order quantity (EOQ) specifies *how much* inventory is the most economical amount to order when demand, holding costs, and order costs are considered.

The three types of inventory management decisions are

- *Which material(s) or item(s) to order*—This can cover all the company's inventory items, the most profitable items, the most unevenly demanded items, the items in season, the least or most expensive items, the items needed for production, or items in demand. These recommendations are not necessarily mutually exclusive.
- *When to order an item*. This may be at the *reorder level* (which allows the suppliers an average lead time to supply the goods); at the *safety order level* (which specifies the minimum level of inventory that is to be held); as the materials resource plan (MRP) or the production plan specifies; or, when a certain percent of a forecasted item remains (Min-Max).
- *How much inventory to order*. This would be the optimum amount based on

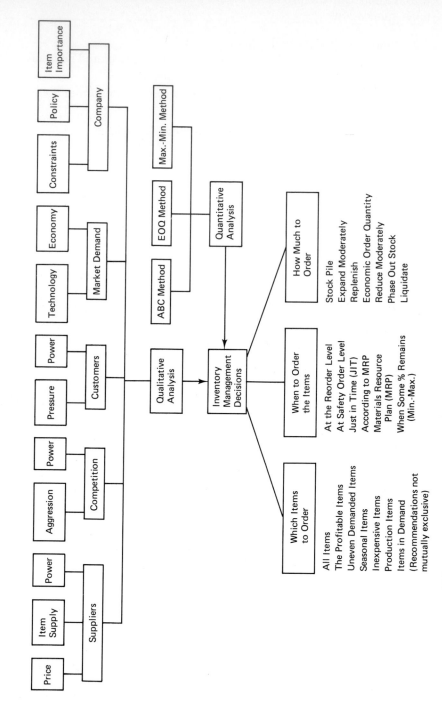

**FIGURE 16-2  Overview of the inventory management decision situation.**

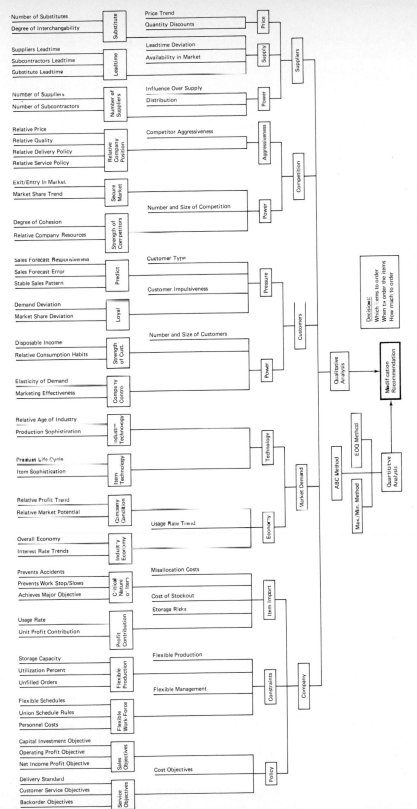

**FIGURE 16-3 Inventory management decisions—detailed situation diagram.**

a quantitative analysis, for example, using the EOQ method, adjusted for the qualitative factors affecting the decision. These adjustments might be categorized as: build substantially or stock pile, expand inventory moderately, replenish to meet the planning period's requirements only, use the EOQ base making no adjustments, reduce inventory moderately, or phase out or liquidate the inventory.

Figure 16-3 is a detailed structured diagram or model of the qualitative information needed for, and the quantitative methods used in, making these three inventory management decisions.

Although the quantitative recommendations are useful in making these decisions, they often have to be adjusted for qualitative, judgmental factors. For example, critical factors that create risks and uncertainties may have to be taken into account when making the final decisions. These decisions sometimes require considerable judgment.

Because of the complexities involved in these decisions, this phase of the study was narrowed to only one inventory management decision—how much inventory to order. This narrowing enabled studying in more detail how the qualitative factors influence the final decision.

## STUDYING THE DECISION TO BE PROTOTYPED

The situation analysis in this section covers

- □ The critical factors affecting the decision
- □ Tracing the reasoning process
- □ Assumptions made for prototyping

### Critical Factors Affecting the Decision

For discussion purposes the critical factors affecting the inventory acquisition decision can be divided into five categories.

**Suppliers.** This area concerns price trends, supply availability, and the power structure of suppliers. The trend in *price* is evaluated because it is less costly to hold more inventory during periods when prices are increasing and more costly during periods when prices are decreasing. Studying the *supply* helps to determine the difficulty the inventory manager will have in obtaining supplies in an emergency. The *power* structure of the suppliers is evaluated to determine the ability of the suppliers to manipulate supply to their best advantage. An example of this would be the buying power held by a cartel.

**Competition.** This area involves the competition's aggressiveness and the power structure of the market. The *aggressiveness* exhibited by the competition is evaluated because the more aggressive the competition is relative to the company, the more important it is to have ample inventory stocks at all times to keep from losing sales. Analyzing the *power* structure of the market includes studying the size and strength of the competition relative to the company's, as well as structural entry barriers, to determine how competitive the company has to be to maintain and increase its position.

**Customers.** This area deals with the degree of pressure customers can bring to bear and the customers' power structures. The *pressure* the customers can exert on the company is studied to determine if the customers as a group are placing increasing or unusual demands on the company. An example might be customers threatening to switch suppliers if the company's delivery service or price does not match that of its competitors. The customer *power* structure is examined to determine the inherent power held by customers because of the way the industry is structured. If a company depends on a limited number of customers for a large portion of its business, the power of the customers (and the risks associated with losing those customers) can potentially be great. In these situations a company has to pay particular attention to these customers' needs.

**Market demand.** This area relates to product technology levels and the economy of the industry. The level of product *technology* helps determine the relative demand for the item. For example, a technologically advanced or superior item has a greater and more certain immediate market potential due to the lack of currently competitive alternatives. On the other hand rapidly changing technology shortens the life cycle of a product and may create risks in holding an item. The *economy* of the industry helps determine the present overall demand and market potential for the kind of inventory product under study. The economic outlook then can affect the likelihood of an item being sold if held.

**Company.** This area is influenced by how important an individual item is to the company as well as the company's constraints and policies. The *importance of the item* to the company can influence inventory decisions. For example, an item that is so crucial to production that its shortage could stop the production line has to be given special attention. Company *constraints* can also affect inventory decisions. For example, if the work force schedule is flexible, overtime may be used in place of increasing inventories to meet possible changes in demand. If production lines are not very flexible, planning for an uncertain demand may require increased inventories. In addition, the *policies* of a company can have an impact on how much inventory to carry. For example, a company might wish to have a reputation for reliability by making it a policy never to have stockouts in certain items. Or a company may want to implement strict cost cutting measures to increase profitability and so have a policy of carrying the least amount of inventory possible.

It should be noted that in addition to examining the impact of trends within each critical area, the relative importance of each area to success in the industry should also be studied. For example, in some industries, such as the petroleum industry, supply availability and source dictate the relative importance suppliers have to a company's success.

**Quantitative analysis tools.** In addition to these qualitative or more judgmental factors, an inventory manager also uses quantitative analysis tools. For example, a major quantitative tool used in making a decision about how much inventory to acquire is the EOQ formula. This formula provides a quantitative order base that in turn can be adjusted to take into account the impact of the five critical qualitative factors affecting the decision.

The EOQ model specifies the optimum amount of inventory to order. Figure 16-4, the EOQ model, gives the formulas for calculating the EOQ and the *safety stock* (SS)—the minimum amount of inventory to be kept in inventory.

To calculate the EOQ, one needs to know the demand for the next period (the forecasted demand), the order cost or cost to set up the production line, the holding cost or the cost of carrying the item in inventory, the supplier's lead time (the time the supplier needs to deliver the goods), and the standard deviation (degree of variance) of the suppliers lead time.

Equation 1 in Fig. 16-4 is used to calculate the value of the EOQ (sometimes referred to as just Q), which designates how much should be ordered when the individual orders are placed throughout the planning period. At the point when just enough stock exists to last through the time needed to receive a delivery (the reorder level), another order must be placed.

Equation 2 in Fig. 16-4 is used to calculate the value of SS, which designates how much of a buffer (or safety) stock should be maintained to protect a company from variations experienced in the time a supplier takes to deliver goods.

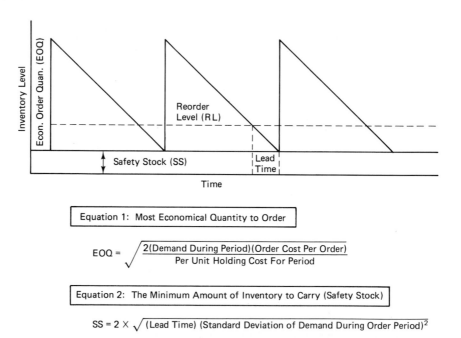

Equation 1: Most Economical Quantity to Order

$$EOQ = \sqrt{\frac{2(\text{Demand During Period})(\text{Order Cost Per Order})}{\text{Per Unit Holding Cost For Period}}}$$

Equation 2: The Minimum Amount of Inventory to Carry (Safety Stock)

$$SS = 2 \times \sqrt{(\text{Lead Time})(\text{Standard Deviation of Demand During Order Period})^2}$$

**FIGURE 16-4  Inventory management decision—how much to order (EOQ model).**

To use the EOQ model, the following conditions must be present in an inventory situation:

- Demand is constant.
- No quantity discounts are offered.
- No back order possibilities exist.
- Variations in lead time have an equal chance of being late or early.
- Ordering costs are not dependent on the quantity ordered.
- Holding costs are fixed per unit.
- Expected costs of stockouts are known in advance.
- The number of times stockouts might occur (how many times per period inventory is likely to drop to zero) is already factored into the safety stock level requirements.

Even if a company does not operate in such an ideal environment, the EOQ model can still provide a useful benchmark or quantitative base from which adjustments can be made.

The EOQ model, or other quantitative inventory management tools, are only one aspect of the inventory management decision, however. Other critical factors are taken into account when making a decision about how much inventory to acquire.

## Tracing the Reasoning Process

The following is a typical decision situation scenario of how an experienced inventory manager might go about determining how much inventory to order of a specific item.

In this situation the company is a strong competitor among personal computer (PC) firms. It manufactures and distributes a relatively competitive PC. The time is the spring of 1988. The item under study is a finished lap-top PC. The company plans its inventory needs one month prior to each quarter. It takes approximately one month from the time the inventory manager orders the finished PC from the manufacturing plant to the time it is received. No beginning inventory balance is anticipated, the cost to place an order and set up the production line is $1,000, and the cost to hold a PC for one quarter is $3.00.

The sales forecast projects 6,000 lap-top PCs will be needed during the next quarter with demand increasing approximately 12.5 percent per month over the period. Using equation 1 in Fig. 16-4, the EOQ model specifies an EOQ of 2,000:

$$2,000 = \sqrt{\frac{2(6,000)(1,000)}{3.00}}$$

This means the 6,000 forecasted PCs should be ordered in lots of 2,000, three times during the quarter. In this situation the reorder date is fixed at every thirty days prior to the first of the month for the three months of the quarter, because the objective is to determine how much, not when to reorder.

The forecast specified a 12.5 percent monthly increase in demand and the EOQ model assumes demand to be constant. The EOQ result is, therefore, revised to reflect this forecasted trend in demand.

The revised EOQ (adjusted 12.5 percent down in the first month and 12.5 percent up in the third month) specifies that 1,750, 2,000, and 2,250 PCs should be ordered during the three months of the next quarter. At first this might seem to be a straight forward decision. Order what is needed as specified by the revised economical order quantity.

The decision is not that simple, however, as is seen in the following discussion of the qualitative factors affecting the decision. The discussion generally follows the structured diagram or model of the decision situation given in Fig. 16-3.

**Suppliers.** In this situation the company is the supplier of the PC. It controls the supply and to some extent the price of the item. The lead time is stable and fairly predictable. The status of the company's manufacturing raw materials and work in process do not indicate that any difficulty will be encountered with shipment. Suppliers will be a neutral factor, therefore, when making the decision.

**Competition.** Even though the company's competitive position is strong, because its PC has a moderate competitive edge over other brands, the competitions' price and recent delivery policies are aggressive enough to consider increasing inventory to avoid potential lost sales.

The power of the competitors has also increased. Smaller, weaker competitors are dropping out of the market, leaving the well-financed companies that are able to devote substantial resources to maintain and increase their market share. This would suggest holding more inventory than normal to meet competitive threats.

**Customers.** Another influencing factor, customer pressure, indicates inventory should be increased. The increasing consumer sophistication and familiarity with the competing PC models in the market and the standardized compatibility of different brands of PCs has decreased brand loyalty. The changing customer base of lap-top computers has also increased the difficulty of predicting demand, as seen by sales forecast errors during recent periods.

On the other hand, the power and strength of the customers suggest decreasing inventory. The number of customers the company serves is increasing, but the amount of business each customer gives the company is decreasing. Although the customer power structure is weakening, it is outweighed by current customer pressures, indicating inventory should be increased.

**Market demand.** The company's PC is more technologically advanced than most other PCs. This implies that over the short term customers may wait a while for deliveries due to a current lack of comparable alternatives. However, the preferred status of the company's PCs is not expected to last due to the rapidly changing technology of the industry.

The overall industry seems to be entering a period of renewed accelerated economic growth. The company's sales generally follow the industry trend. This would suggest increasing inventories to take advantage of this increasing market potential.

**Company.**   The company has a rather flexible production operation that enables surges in demand to be met on relatively short notice.   This factor, therefore, does not indicate any additional inventory is necessary.

The importance of the lap-top PC to the company has been falling as price pressures have reduced the profitability of the product.   To date volume increases have offset declining margins somewhat, but it is uncertain how long this will continue.

Company policies emphasize maintaining and increasing market share, so inventory carrying costs are less important from a policy viewpoint.

**Relative impact of key factors.**   In addition to studying trends within each critical factor area, the inventory manager studied the relative impact of each key factor on success in the industry.   After examining the five critical nonquantitative factors affecting the decision, the inventory manager felt that, given the situation the company faces at present, competitive forces pose the greatest threat to the company's future.   Shifting customer buying patterns and the company's relatively small position in the market make customer factors the second most important force influencing success.   Market demand and company factors appear to have less of an impact on success in this market.   This is because the market is not erratic or declining and because the company is in a position to do what is necessary to succeed as it is not limited by either unusual financial or operating restraints.   The supplier factor is the least important, because the company controls the source of supply.

After balancing the different trends within each key factor area, which are summarized in Fig. 16-5, and also weighing the relative importance of each area to future success, the inventory manager decides that the original EOQ was insufficient Existing market conditions, including competitive pressure, potential changes in technology, and eroding profit margins in areas critical to success dictated changing the initial EOQ.   On the one hand more inventory was needed to meet competitive conditions; on the other there were great uncertainties in the market creating greater risks for holding excess inventory.   After balancing the opposing forces at work in

| FACTORS | IMPLY INCREASING | IMPLY DECREASING |
|---|---|---|
| COMPETITION: | aggressiveness and power structure | |
| CUSTOMERS: | pressure | power structure |
| MARKET DEMAND: | economy | technology |
| COMPANY: | policies | importance of item |
| SUPPLIERS: | (neutral) | |

**FIGURE 16-5   Inventory management decision—how much to order.   Factors influencing the decision—initial prototype.**

the marketplace, the decision was to replenish at a slightly higher level, that is, order 1,975, 2,200, and 2,475 for the three months of the next quarter. In the opinion of the inventory manager this would provide the buffer needed to meet changing competitive and buyer conditions while minimizing the risk of overstocking.

## Assumptions Made for Prototyping

For purposes of the initial prototype system seven alternative recommendations are possible. They are shown in Fig. 16-6.

An inventory manager could order the EOQ base, everything else being equal. However, as in the typical decision scenarios above, other factors may dictate adjusting this quantitative base. These adjustments could include *increasing* the quantitative order base in three ways:

- □ *Replenish*—Plan to order an additional 10 percent more inventory than the EOQ base specified. This is an amount that makes a stockout unlikely.
- □ *Expand*—Plan to order an additional 20 percent more than the EOQ base specifies. This is an amount that would make a stockout very improbable.
- □ *Stock pile*—Plan to order an additional 30 percent more than the EOQ base specifies. This is the largest quantity of inventory the company can reasonably afford to order. This amount decreases the risk of a stockout to the lowest possible economical level.

| FORECAST: | 0 beginning balance | 1,750 units | 2,000 units | 2,250 units |
|---|---|---|---|---|
| Options: | % of Base | Month 1 | Month 2 | Month 3 |
| Stock Pile: | 1.3% | 2,275 units | 2,600 units | 2,925 units |
| Expand: | 1.2% | 2,100 units | 2,400 units | 2,700 units |
| Replenish: | 1.1% | 1,925 units | 2,200 units | 2,475 units |
| EOQ: | 1% | 1,750 units | 2,000 units | 2,250 units |
| Reduce: | 0.9% | 1,575 units | 1,800 units | 2,025 units |
| Phase out: | 0.8% | 1,400 units | 1,600 units | 1,800 units |
| Liquidate: | 0.7% | 1,225 units | 1,400 units | 1,575 units |

FIGURE 16-6  Inventory management decision—how much to order. Acquisition alternatives—initial prototype.

PART 2:  DEVELOPING MANAGEMENT DECISION SYSTEMS

These adjustments might also include *decreasing* the quantitative ordering base in three different ways:

- □ *Reduce*—Plan to order 10 percent less than the EOQ base specifies. This is an amount that makes the chance of ending with unsold inventory balance unlikely.
- □ *Phase out*—Plan to order 20 percent less than the EOQ base specifies. This is an amount that makes the chance of ending with unsold inventory balance very improbable.
- □ *Liquidate*—Plan to order 30 percent less than the EOQ specifies. This is an amount of inventory that reduces the risk of unsold inventory at the end of the period to the lowest possible level.

Other types of inventory recommendations were made in later versions of the system.

In developing a prototype system of the decision situation described above, it is assumed that data exists from which the EOQ can be calculated; forecasted demand can be projected; suppliers lead time and lead time deviations can be obtained; and order or set up costs per order, holding costs per unit, and the beginning inventory balances of stock on hand are known.

It is also assumed that a user of this knowledge-based system has (or can obtain) a working knowledge of the technology of the item; the state of the economy; the policies of the company; the importance of the item to the company; the power of the customers, competition, and suppliers; and other related factors. A user consulting this system will need to know enough about the situation to provide most, but not all, of the information specified in Fig. 16-3.

The prototype is designed for a specific company operating in a specific industry, since it will contain the weights assigned to key success factors in the situation. Subsequent versions of the system allow a user to change these weights to match the specific company and industry the user is operating in.

## DOCUMENTING THE PROTOTYPE SYSTEM

The following discussion covers

- □ System proposal
- □ Description of the prototype system
- □ Dependency diagrams
- □ Decision charts
- □ Designing and constructing the knowledge base

## System Proposal

The general project objective is to develop a knowledge-based system that recommends an inventory acquisition strategy. The system is production, not service, oriented. Since a company makes repeated inventory decisions concerning every item it stocks and these decisions involve extensive dollar outlays, the project was considered both feasible and worthwhile.

The first phase of the project is limited to only one segment of the larger system, the decision about how much inventory to order. This prototype will be used to test the concept and structure of a larger knowledge-based system for recommending stock acquisition strategies and provide a basis for further development.

The information sources used in developing the system are personnel at the company under study, including warehouse managers and purchasing agents; company records, including inventory reports and data bases; and outside sources, including consultants, books, and periodicals. A list of useful reference sources is listed at the end of this chapter.

## Description of the Prototype System

**System overview and objective.** The initial prototype system developed is designed for use in situations where a company in a specific industry is deciding on the amount of inventory to order for a particular item. Based on the many company and market factors affecting the decision, the system would recommend how much of the EOQ base should be adjusted.

The system asks a user questions about suppliers, competitors, customers, market demand, and the company. The system uses if-then rules, numerical weighted average computations, and backward chaining to reason the information given by a user in order to reach the recommendation.

The initial prototype is designed for use by a competitive company in the PC manufacturing industry.

**Recommendations to be made by the system.** The seven possible recommendations are

- Stock pile
- Expand
- Replenish
- EOQ
- Reduce
- Phase out
- Liquidate

**Nature of the user interface and typical user dialogue.** Information sources that can be used to answer user questions are company managers at various levels, purchasing agents, marketing staff, company records and data bases, suppliers, and industry journals. A typical user dialogue covers the following key areas:

- *Suppliers.* Typical questions asked in this area are "Relative to other items in inventory, what is the expected trend in price for the item, or its components, over the next forecasted period (0 = most decrease, 5 = most increase)?" and "Relative to other items in stock, what is the length of time the company must wait to receive, or produce, the ordered item (0 = shortest time of all items, 5 = longest time of all items)?"

- *Competition.* A typical question asked in this area is "Of all the areas the company competes in, how aggressive is the competition with respect to this item or its eventual end product (0 = not at all aggressive, 5 = the most aggressive)?"

- *Customers.* A typical question asked in this area is "Relative to the other customers of the company, how willing are the customers of this item, or its eventual end product, to wait for the item to be delivered (0 = the most patient, 5 = the most impatient)?"

- *Market demand.* Typical questions asked in this area are "Relative to other similar products on the market, how advanced is the technology of the item (0 = most sophisticated, 5 = least sophisticated)?" and "What is the stage in the business cycle which the company's industry expects to be in during the next period (0 = recession, 5 = rapid expansion)?"

- *Company.* A typical question asked in this area is "Relative to the other items in inventory, what is the percentage of total profit contribution of the item, or its eventual end product (0 = least profit contribution, 5 = greatest profit contribution)?"

The answers are then weighted and combined to produce the final recommendation of how to adjust the EOQ base.

**Description of the knowledge structure and reasoning process.** Since not all factors have the same impact on the final success of the company, different factors are given different weights. As shown in Fig. 16-7, weights are assigned to the user questions as well as to each reasoning level in the system. For example, the weights of the five critical factors are competition (0.3), customer (0.25), market demand (0.2), company (0.15), and suppliers (0.1).

- *Competition.* This factor was considered most important, because changing and increasingly concentrated competitive forces pose the greatest risk to the company's long term success.

- *Customer.* This factor was considered the next most important, because the company is not the dominant player in the industry and shifting customer preferences thus present a major threat to the company's future.

- *Market demand.* This factor was somewhat less important, because a period of overall stable and growing demand for this type of product is anticipated.

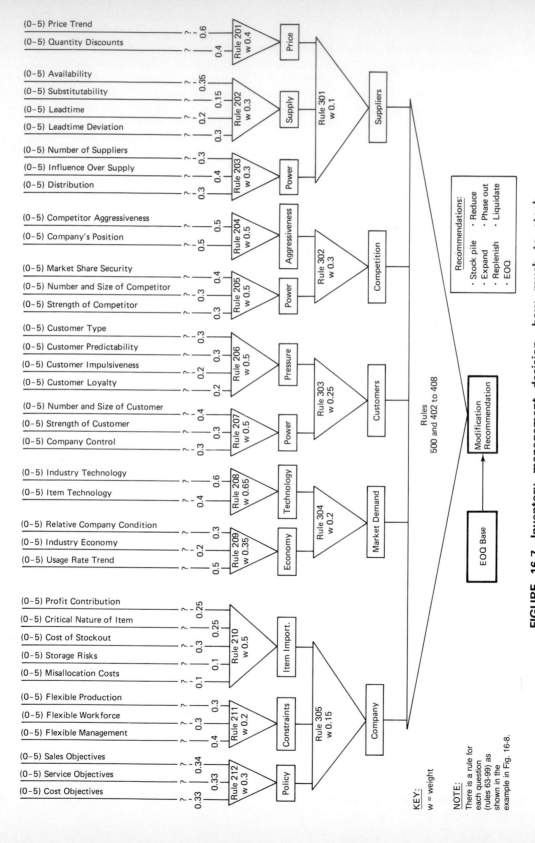

**FIGURE 16-7 Inventory management decision—how much to stock. Dependency diagram—initial prototype.**

□ *Company*. The company considerations were next to last in importance, because at present no specific company restraints, such as limited financial resources or product technology and inflexible production processes, posed any threat to the company's future.

□ *Suppliers*. This factor was given the least weight, because the company controlled the facility that made the product.

Weights were also assigned to other components, as shown in Fig. 16-7, in a similar way. In the initial prototype system these weights were built into the system to reflect the situation the company faces at present. In subsequent versions of the system, weights can be assigned to each factor by a system user before each consultation to reflect the user's own company and market situation.

The system reasoning process begins with the user's answers to the questions. Numbers between 0 and 5 are given for answers, as shown in the sample questions above. The answers to the questions are then weighted, combined, and calculated at each of the various reasoning levels to eventually come to a value for the final recommendation.

For example, if prices are expected to increase moderately, a user could enter the number 3 in response to the price trend question (the first sample question given above). Following in Fig. 16-7, the answer 3 given for price trend is then weighted by the question weight (0.6). Then the weighted question, price trend, is combined with the weighted quantity discount response to give a value to price. The values of price, supply, and power are then combined and weighted to give a value to supplier. The value of supplier is then in turn weighted (0.1) and combined with the other five critical factors to provide a value for the final recommendation. Each recommendation has a value range equal to 0.714 units on a zero to five recommendation scale. For example, the range 0 to 0.714 indicates a "liquidate" recommendation and the range 4.286 to 5.0 indicates "stock pile."

If the value of the total computation yields a value above 2.857, the final recommendation will be to increase the EOQ base order amount. If the computation yields a value less than 2.144, then the final recommendation is to decrease the base amount.

## Dependency Diagram

Figure 16-7 shows the dependency diagram for the inventory decision knowledge-based system. It is a complete summary outline of all questions, factors, rules, interrelationships, weights, and recommendations within the system.

## Decision Charts

Figure 16-8 shows sample decision charts from the prototype system. This set of charts traces the question, price trend, from the rule that weights the question to the rule that makes the final recommendation. Except for the recommendation rule, every conclusion made by a rule is used as input to another rule.

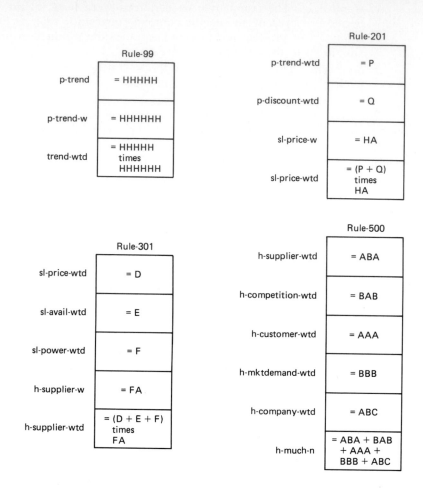

| | Rule-402 | Rule-403 | Rule-404 | Rule-405 | Rule-406 | Rule-407 | Rule-408 |
|---|---|---|---|---|---|---|---|
| Numeric Result | 0.000–0.714 | 0.715–1.428 | 1.429–2.143 | 2.144–2.857 | 2.858–3.571 | 3.572–4.285 | 4.286–5.000 |
| Implied Recommendation | Liquidate | Phase Out | Reduce | EOQ | Replenish | Expand | Stock Pile |

This valuation method holds for all questions,
factors, and the final recommendation

Key Facts:

p-trend-w = HHHHH = 0.6
sl-price-w = HA = 0.4
h-supplier-w = FA = 0.1

**FIGURE 16-8  Inventory management decision—how much to order.  Sample decision charts—initial prototype.**

**Price Trend Rule:**

```
rule-99:
      if itemno = ITEMNO and
      p-trend(ITEMNO) = HHHHH and
      p-trend-w = HHHHHH
   then p-trend-wtd = HHHHH*HHHHHH.
```

**Price Rule:**

```
rule-201:
    if p-trend-wtd = P and
       p-discount-wtd = Q and
       sl-price-w = HA
    then sl-price-wtd = (P+Q)*HA.
```

**Supplier Rule:**

```
rule-301:
    if sl-price-wtd = D and
       sl-avail-wtd = E and
       sl-power-wtd = F and
       h-supplier-w = FA
    then h-supplier-wtd = (D+E+F)*FA.
```

**Numerical Recommendation Rule:**

```
rule-500:  if h-supplier-wtd = ABA and
       h-competition-wtd = BAB and
       h-customer-wtd = AAA and
       h-mktdemand-wtd = BBB and
       h-company-wtd = ABC
    then how-much-n = ABA+BAB+AAA+BBB+ABC.
```

**Recommendation Rules:**

```
rule-402:
    if how-much-n = C and
       C>= 0 and
       C<0.7143
    then how-much = liquidate.
```

```
rule-403:
    if how-much-n = C and
       C>= 0.7143 and
       C<1.428
    then how-much = phase-out.
```

```
rule-404:
    if how-much-n = C and
       C>= 1.428 and
       C<2.143
    then how-much = reduce.
```

*(continued)*

**FIGURE 16-9  Inventory management decision—how much to order.  Segment of knowledge-base rule set—initial prototype.**

```
rule-405:
    if how-much-n = C and
       C>= 2.143 and
       C<2.857
    then how-much = eoq.

rule-406:
    if how-much-n = C and
       C>= 2.857 and
       C<3.5714
    then how-much = replenish.

rule-407:
    if how-much-n = C and
       C>= 3.5714 and
       C<4.2857
    then how-much = expand.

rule-408:
    if how-much-n = C and
       C>= 4.2857 and
       C =<5
    then how-much = stock-pile.
```

**FIGURE 16-9** *(continued)*

## Designing and Constructing the Knowledge Base

Rules and questions were developed from the situation analysis and structured decision models. They were based on how an inventory manager might actually go about making such decisions, through recreating actual typical decision scenarios. A segment of the system's knowledge base is given in Fig. 16-9. The expert system shell used is M.1.

The if-then rules in the knowledge base in Fig. 16-9 match those specified in the decision charts shown in Fig. 16-8. They were written to reflect the relationships shown in the prototype dependency diagram in Fig. 16-7.

The weights that pertain to the price trend calculation are shown in Fig. 16-10. These are the weights assigned by the system developers to price trend, price, and suppliers, based on their situation analysis. These weights can be changed from situation to situation, company to company, and industry to industry by a user. This system allows a user to adapt to a particular problem when using the system.

Figure 16-11 is the question about price trend, as it appears in the knowledge base.

```
fact-1:
    h-supplier-w = 0.1.

fact-6:
    sl-price-w = 0.4.

fact-18:
    p-trend-w = 0.6.
```

**FIGURE 16-10** **Inventory management decision—how much to order. Segment of knowledge-base weights—initial prototype.**

```
question(p-trend(ITEMNO)) = ['
```

Realitive to all items in inventory, what will the trend in price
of the item be (if item ', ITEMNO, ' is manufactured by the
company compare the expected trend in cost of production with the
other manufactured items).
```
0----------1-----------2------------3-------------4-------------5
```
the greatest                    the most stable         the most increase
of all items                    of all items            of all items
', nl].

```
legalvals(p-trend(ITEMNO)) = number(0,5).
```

**FIGURE 16-11   Inventory management decision—how much to order.   Segment of knowledge-base questions—initial prototype.**

## REVIEW QUESTIONS

1. Describe the ways in which the system described in this chapter differs from the other operating systems described in the preceding three chapters.

2. It is possible to develop a more conventional computerized version of this system. Discuss some of the reasons for using knowledge-based system technology for an inventory management system such as the one described in this chapter.

3. Under what circumstances would you use more conventional computer technology for developing a system for the inventory management situation described in this chapter?

4. Describe the ways in which the system described in this chapter might be enhanced and expanded.

5. In what ways does the knowledge-based system described in this chapter illustrate how knowledge-based system and conventional computer system technology might be integrated to develop more realistic and useful computerized management decision support systems.

6. What five areas can operating management be divided into?

7. What are the qualitative and quantitative aspects of inventory management decisions?

8. What are the three types of inventory management decisions?

## REFERENCES

Alcide, P. E., "The ABC's of Inventory Management," *The Practical Accountant*, vol. 19, August 1986.

Allison, A., "RISC's Challenge Mini, Micro Suppliers," *Mini-Micro Systems*, vol. 19, November 1986.

Allison, A., "Varied Architectures Crowd Supermini Arena," *Mini-Micro Systems*, vol. 19, December 1986.

Becker, J. T., "Network Designers Face Shifting Industry Givens," *Data Communications*, vol. 15, December 1986.

Crabb, D. E., "Technical Topics for the IBM PC Family: An Annotated Bibliography," *Byte*, vol. 11, no. 11, 1986.

Del Mar, D., *Operations and Industrial Management*, New York: McGraw-Hill, 1985.

Dilworth, J. B., *Production and Operations Management*, New York: Random House, 1986.

"Distributed SNA: A Network Architecture Gets On Track," *Data Communications*, vol. 16, February 1987.

Dudick, T. S., and R. Cornell, *Inventory Control for the Financial Executive*, New York: Wiley, 1979.

Emmett, A., and Gabel, D., "Cases in Direct Microcomputer Connections: Nuts and Bolts," *Data Communications*, vol. 15, July 1986.

Hohenstein, C. L., *Practical Stock and Inventory Techniques*, New York: Van Nostrand Reinhold, 1982.

Hornstein, J. V., "Parallel Processing Attacks Real-Time World," *Mini-Micro Systems*, vol. 19, December 1986.

King, K. G., "Developments in Microcomputer Technology," *Journal of Accountancy*, vol. 162, September 1986.

Kobert, N., "Using Turnover Analysis in Setting Inventory Policy," *Purchasing*, vol. 101, July 24, 1986.

Micossi, A., "Micro and Workstation Talents Converge," *Computer Decisions*, vol. 18, Sept. 9, 1986.

Plossl, G. W., and W. E. Welsh, *The Role of Top Management in the Control of Inventory*, Reston, VA: Reston Publishing, 1979.

Purkiser, C., "Intel's 386 Unites UNIX and DOS Software," *Mini-Micro Systems*, vol. 20, April 1987.

Pryor, D., "NCR's PlatformStrategy Reaches to Microprocessors," *Mini-Micro Systems*, vol. 20, March 1987.

Romano, P. L., "Techniques in Inventory Management and Control," *Management Accounting*, vol. 68, February 1987.

Shanis, M. J., *Operations Manager's Desk Book: A Guide with Forms, Labels and Other Aides*, Englewood Cliffs, NJ: Prentice-Hall, 1982.

"Squeezing Profits Out of Stores," *Management Today*, August 1986.

Stevens, E. E., and B. Bernstein, "APPC: The Future of Microcomputer Communications within IBM's SNA," *Data Communications*, vol. 15, July 1986.

Taube, E. V., "Proper Modem Selection Ensures Free-Flowing PC Communication," *Data Management*, vol. 24, September 1986.

Weadock, G. E., "Mini-Micro Hybrids Rival Local Networks," *Mini-Micro Systems*, vol. 19, September 1986.

# 17

# An Entrepreneurial New Venture Planning System

This chapter describes the development of an entrepreneurial new venture planning system. The topics covered are

- [ ] The situation under study: understanding the expert's domain
- [ ] Studying the situation to be prototyped
- [ ] Documenting the prototype system
- [ ] The role of financial planning and analysis

The early sections of the chapter describe the overall situation for which the system is being developed, new venture planning. The next sections describe the situation analysis and situation model development and the development of a prototype system for franchise selection. The chapter concludes with a discussion of the uses of financial planning and analysis in these types of systems.

## THE SITUATION UNDER STUDY: UNDERSTANDING THE EXPERT'S DOMAIN

The discussion in this section covers

- [ ] Selecting a decision area to work on
- [ ] Probing how the situation works and how decisions are made
- [ ] Narrowing the focus

## Selecting a Decision Area to Work On

Entrepreneurial new venture planning was selected for knowledge-based systems development because of the generally widespread and growing interest in the area. It is of interest to venture capital firms, established companies, and to individuals so that any knowledge-based systems development involving entrepreneurial new venture planning would benefit a wide audience.

In addition, new venture planning fits the guidelines for selecting knowledge-based systems development projects:

- There are recognized experts in the field.
- Expert decision skills are needed to do the job.
- New venture planning requires informed judgment.
- The task is well understood and manageable.
- The decisions can lead to high payoffs and have practical value, according to the business clients and individual entrepreneurs interested in having the system developed.

It was decided to concentrate initially on new venture decisions made by an individual entrepreneur. This would provide a model for all types of entrepreneurial decisions and at the same time enable working within well-defined parameters.

An *initial list* of questions such an individual might want answers to was drawn up:

- Whether or not to be an entrepreneur
- What kind of a new venture would be best to undertake
- Whether or not to go into business with partners or on one's own
- Whether or not to use franchising
- Whether or not to accept a specific new venture deal offered

## Probing How the Situation Works and How Decisions Are Made

An effort was made to define this *initial list* of decisions in more detail, as shown in Fig. 17-1. Contrary to what some might think, the outline in Fig. 17-1 and the figures that follow did not fall out of thin air, or appear in the proverbial light bulb over the developer's head. Instead they are the result of experimentation, interviews with experts, reading books and periodicals, time spent exploring possibilities that were later rejected, and many pieces of paper thrown away.

Nor should Fig. 17-1 and the following ones be considered the final word. The ideas there are not necessarily the best ones, or the only right ones. They are just useful ideas—an effort to get something down on paper and keep the project moving along. Expect such rough sketches to evolve. For example, Fig. 17-2 attempts to identify the reasoning requirements involved in each decision in the original list.

Before making a final selection of a knowledge-based systems development

1. Deciding whether or not the individual *really* wants to be an entrepreneur, if the individual has not made a firm commitment yet.
2. Deciding whether to go it alone, and essentially focus on a controlled personal services type operation, or to go into a venture with others and build capital through establishing a self-sustaining company.
3. Deciding what kind of venture to pursue on different levels:
   — retail, manufacturing, wholesale, mail order, consulting, professional services and the like.
   — if retailing is chosen, strategic profiles of the generic kind of retail store, such as local or national, large or small inventory, heavy personal involvement, all cash, etc.
   — specific kind of retail, such as nail salon, auto service, home furnishings, fast food, and the like.
   — franchising or on my own.
   — if franchising association, kind of franchising, both as to specific product or service, or franchising arrangement.
4. Deciding on the specific deal, once the decision restraints had been determined in phase 3. It is possible, for instance, to not care what the store will sell, but to focus on what stores are available within a specific category within your neighborhood, in making the decision. A strategic profile might be enough to narrow down the choices to be financially analyzed.

**FIGURE 17-1  New venture planning decision—preliminary ideas about specific decisions involved.**

project, however, the overall situation was examined in more detail. Both Fig. 17-1 and the general reasoning requirements described in Fig. 17-2 were reexamined, and rough sketches were drawn of the decision. For example, an early idea of how the decision looked to one of the system developers is represented by the diagram in Fig. 17-3. The diagram is deliberately a rough and simplified representation in order to give a realistic feel for how these projects evolve from very tentative ideas through many stages of development. Some of these initial drawings can be embarrassingly bad.

Figures 17-1, 17-2, and 17-3 are worksheets. Remember, most people go through many stages of such rough approximations, especially when only starting to learn knowledge-based systems development. Early efforts are usually filled with errors and misconceptions and often are totally off the mark, as is the diagram in Fig. 17-3. Such tedious explorations are especially common in broader management decision areas, such as strategic planning.

Through such steps the system developer gradually gets a clearer idea of the

1. Deciding on whether or not to become an entrepreneur requires matching an individual's profile (personality, skills, preferences, and resources) with the requirements for being a successful entrepreneur. This of course is the model for the career strategy selection decision.
2. All the levels of deciding on what kind of venture to pursue require matching the individual's profile against opportunities, keys to success, and competitive market factors to determine if the individual has a chance of being successful and if sufficient money can be made at it. This, of course, is a variation on the strategic planning model discussed earlier, with the addition of a financial analysis of the venture.
3. Deciding on the specific opportunity (the specific store being offered for sale, for example) requires matching an individual's profile, as well as the individual's other business restraints (such as other investments and businesses) with the market factors to determine if the specific project might be successful and profitable. This is a decision model similar to #2 above.

**FIGURE 17-2  New venture planning decision—preliminary idea of how decisions are made.**

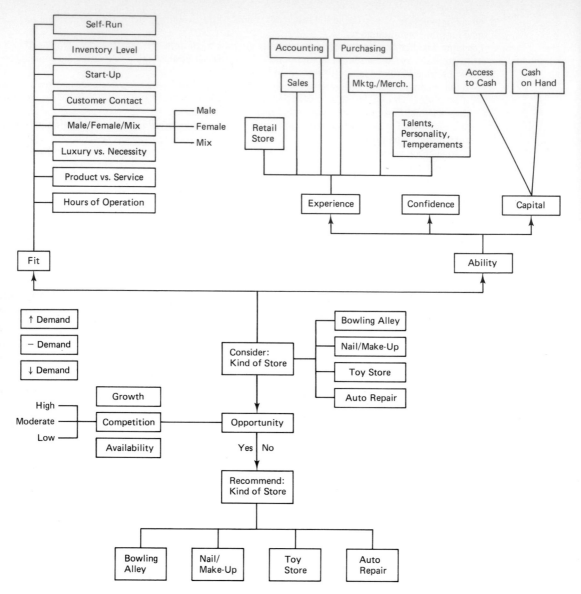

**FIGURE 17-3  Preliminary decision situation diagram for new venture decision.**

general situation, its different segments, and how they all work. The search, remember, is not for *the one single right answer*, but only for a *pretty good representation* for this point in the project.

Further analysis showed that the reasoning process was not as first shown in Fig. 17-3. Rather the decisions appeared to be made more in stages, as described in Figs. 17-1 and 17-2. The core reasoning pattern seemed to be similar to the general pattern of making strategy planning decisions, as shown in Fig. 17-4. However, it

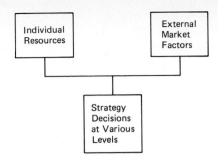

**FIGURE 17-4 Company strategy development decisions—general pattern.**

seemed to be repeated over and over again as the entrepreneur narrowed the available options. For this reason Fig. 17-5 seemed to come closer to showing in a more structured decision model what an expert goes through in making these decisions.

During the early phases an individual's choice about whether or not to go into business for oneself is basically a personal one. As shown in Fig. 17-5, all the relevant *individual resources and capabilities* are examined to determine whether an individual has the temperament, personality, aptitudes, skills, resources, and other characteristics needed to succeed in a *career* as an *entrepreneur*. At this point opportunities are of secondary importance.

The decision to go out *on your own* or with someone is similar, initially.

As the process continues, and questions raised about what *kind of new venture* to undertake as an entrepreneur, available market opportunity and key-to-success factors become more important. For example, the choice as to whether or not to open a retail store or a small manufacturing or a consulting firm would hinge on both the qualifications of the individual to meet success requirements and the opportunities and keys to success in the market area under study.

Choosing a *type (strategic profile) of retail store*, or other kind of venture picked for further investigation, would be another decision. For example, the opportunities and keys to success in fast foods and specialty food ventures might be considerably different from those for video movie rentals, printing services, or cosmetics and nail care for women.

The decision process continues on through *kind of food store*, for example, to *kind of fast food or specialty food store* to the *actual food store itself*, or through whatever area you have chosen to investigate for a possible new venture.

Deciding on whether or not to use *franchising* as a means of entering the retail area of your choice involves further considerations. In addition to considering opportunities in the franchise area and one's qualifications for entering it, consideration also has to be given to the franchise offering. This includes looking at the franchisor's financial requirements, the initial and continuing support provided, the strength of the franchise name, and similar factors.

All these detailed studies of new venture decision making eventually led to revised definitions and diagrams of the decision situation. The diagram or model in Fig. 17-5 was the result of many such studies. It shows the details of the different components and levels of new venture planning decisions from an individual entrepreneur's viewpoint.

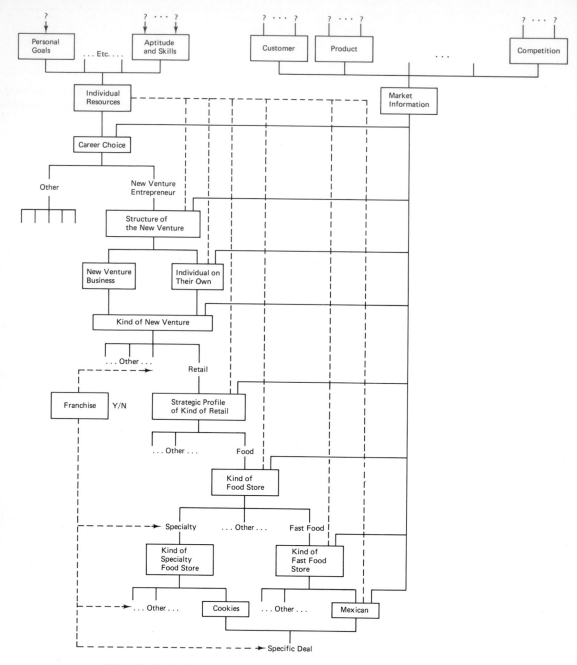

**FIGURE 17-5  Revised rough outline of decision situation for new venture decision.**

## Narrowing the Focus

Because the new venture decision area is so broad and complex, it was decided to select a segment of the overall system shown in Fig. 17-5 for prototype development. Several projects were identified as being worthwhile to pursue:

1. A system for career strategy selection
2. A system for deciding whether or not to go into business on one's own or with others
3. A system for choosing the kind of retail store
4. A system for deciding about whether or not to use franchising

The fourth area, franchise selection, was chosen for further study and eventual prototype system development. It is a decision frequently faced by individual entrepreneurs, both because of their lack of capital and because of their unfamiliarity with the particular business involved.

The focus of the study was further limited to the fast food and specialty food areas. Of the many possible retail ventures considered, fast foods and specialty food stores are recognized as strong *opportunity* areas, both because of population demographics (increasing numbers of working mothers and so dependence on convenience foods; an increase in working teenagers and young, affluent, childless couples; geographic population shifts; and shifts in shopping and eating habits) and because of local conditions (large groups of these people are concentrated in the selected area).

It was also assumed that the individuals involved in the study had already made the decision to be entrepreneurs, and to go into business on their own.

There were several reasons why this situation was chosen for prototype development:

1. It provided a quick way to prototype, since the system developer had access to an expert in the area and the area was narrowly defined.
2. The prototype was part of a larger system, as shown in Fig. 17-5, and the pattern of its decision was similar to other decisions made within the overall system. This enabled the developers to use this project to start doing background analyses for other parts of the system.
3. By starting with specific test case decisions, and gradually building a general model on that base, the general model would have a much firmer foundation in reality.

The following section traces how an expert might go about making a decision about whether or not to use franchising in opening a store in the retail fast food area.

## STUDYING THE SITUATION TO BE PROTOTYPED

Figure 17-6 gives an overview model of what is involved in making decisions in this decision area. This diagram, and the structured decision situation models given in

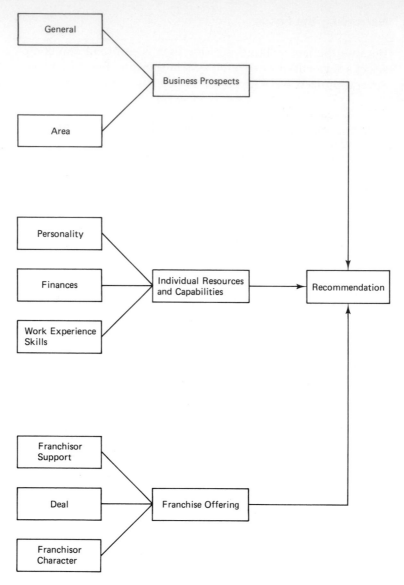

**FIGURE 17-6 Preliminary decision situation diagram for new venture using franchising.**

the five figures that follow, are based on analyses of typical decision situations in this area, such as the one described at the end of this section.

Three critical knowledge areas are examined in making these decisions:

□ General and local business prospects, including opportunities, success factors, and general market structure

□ The individual's resources and capabilities to meet success criteria
□ The franchisor's offering

The following discussion traces how a decision about whether or not to open a retail fast food store using franchising is made.

Once the *opportunity* is identified in general terms (for example, fast food retailing), and an individual has made a decision to be an entrepreneur, strategic planning questions about *what it takes to succeed* (in this case in fast food retailing) are considered.

Long hours of work are required, as is some knowledge of the specific kind of business under consideration. Skills in selling and in managing people are also needed. Adequate capital must be raised, either through borrowing or through savings. An individual would also need any specialized knowledge, skills, and training required by the business.

Since fast foods are generally classified as a staple food item, the target market has a very broad profile. Because of this factor the competitive environment becomes a very important consideration. The store location has to have high traffic potential and visibility, since the product can be both a convenience and an impulse item as well as a planned purchase. In addition, there has to be an ample supply of cheap labor in the neighborhood.

What to look for in a franchise offering must also be defined. Strong start-up and continuing support, reasonable contract fees, control and other contract terms, and a strong reputation are all keys to a successful franchise relationship.

These and other strategic planning factors are explored during this initial phase. For example, such questions are examined as:

□ What groups of consumers buy and eat these foods and what motivates the buying decision?
□ What will they pay for them?
□ What are the different ways in which these foods can be sold?
□ Who are the competitors, where are they located, how many are there, and what are their relative strengths and weaknesses?
□ What are the specific machinery and other facility requirements?
□ How much money is needed to open and sustain such a store until it is successful?
□ What are the advantages and disadvantages of franchising?

In addition, one reviews the history and structure of the market in an effort to get additional clues as to what the future prospects are and what it will take to succeed in the future competitive environment.

All this information helps develop a strategic success profile for retail fast food stores. Within the framework of the strategic success requirements, decisions about the ability of the individual, the market and competition factors, and the franchising offer are studied in an effort to determine what the individual's chances of success are.

## Business Prospects

As is seen in Fig. 17-7, this phase of the study can be divided into two segments: general and local business.

**General.** A number of factors are considered during this phase of the study:

□ *Product growth trends*, including the potential for growth in your product and the target market group, the reasonableness of the estimates of future growth, and the potential for developing complementary products in the line
□ *Staying power*, including how long the product has been in existence, how faddish it might turn out to be, and whether it can be modified or adapted to changing tastes
□ *Competitive market*, including the general competitive environment, the degree of product differentiation of your product or service from the competitors', and the likelihood of new entrants into the market

**Local.** Many questions are also answered in studying the local market. The *strength of the local target market* for the retail venture under study is examined. This requires answering such questions as "Is the product appropriate for a significant

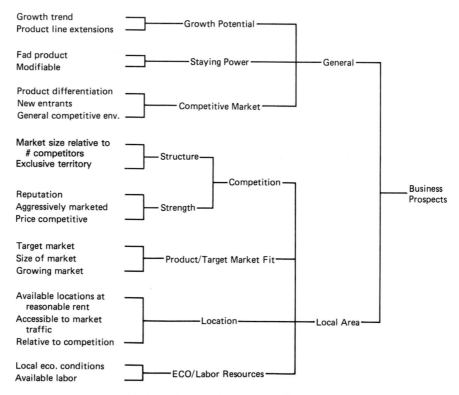

**FIGURE 17-7  Business prospects area.**

PART 2:  DEVELOPING MANAGEMENT DECISION SYSTEMS

portion of the local market?", "What are the average household incomes, buying habits, work locations, and tastes of the local population?", "How many potential customers are in the area and how concentrated are they?", "Is the market growing and, if so, how fast?", and "How accessible is the market?"

Questions about *local competition* are also studied. Some relate to the competitive structure of the market, such as "Who are the competitors?" and "How many are there in relation to the market?" Some relate to the strength of the competitors, such as "Where are they located?", "How well are they run?", "How well are they known?", and "How aggressive are they, including their pricing policies and product offerings?"

Questions about the availability, size, location, and rent of the *store sites* in the area are critical. The location should be in a high enough traffic area to attract convenience and impulse buyers, and it should be accessible to a large potential customer base. It should also be well situated relative to the competition.

Another factor to consider is the *available employee market*. Teenagers are an important source of cheap labor. Special skills are not required, so willingness to learn and work hard are more important employee success criteria. When the owner is not working at the store, someone trustworthy, with managerial experience or competence, will also be needed. The longer term *local economy's condition* is also relevant.

### Individual Resources and Capabilities

Questions about an individual's personal, financial, and business capabilities to meet the success criteria need answering, as is seen in Fig. 17-8.

**Personal.** Primarily, one would need the *individual capabilities required to succeed as an entrepreneur*. These are covered in detail in Chapter 22. They range from the ability to work well independently to the capacity to handle risk and failure.

The *ability to work well with people*, another important personal requirement in retailing, can mean doing so under stressful situations (handling customer complaints and difficult employees), for long hours, and under less than ideal working conditions.

*Physical stamina* is required to handle the long hours and stress, especially when working as a single proprietor. Long hours are also needed because employees (even relatives) handling cash have to be closely monitored. Close monitoring of the quality of product and service is also essential to getting and keeping customers. The long hours also mean extensive time away from family, so a very *supportive family environment* is critical to success.

Because the business is a franchise, one must also be willing to *work within other people's rules and regulations*. This is an important consideration, because frequently entrepreneurs have trouble working under someone else's control.

**Financial resources.** Financial resources are needed to buy the franchise, to obtain machinery and fixtures, to assume lease obligations, and to keep operating until the store builds a customer base. This initial investment can come from *available*

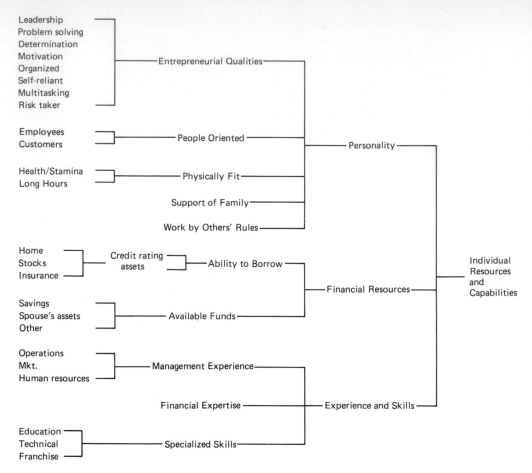

**FIGURE 17-8   Individual resources and capabilities.**

*funds*, such as savings, or from *borrowing*, which depends on an individual's credit standing and other available assets.

**Business experience and skills.**   One needs some *management experience* not only to handle people, but also to deal with advertising, marketing, purchasing, legal, and all the other daily business problems.   *Financial skills* are also needed to manage cash, business accounts, banking relations, and the like.   In addition, the business may have special *technical and educational requirements*.

### The Franchise Offer

A franchise is a method of distribution in which by contract the franchisor grants an individual the right to carry on a business in a prescribed way in a particular location for a specified period of time.   As described in Fig. 17-9, the franchisor provides some *assistance*.   In turn an individual (the franchisee) agrees to abide by certain

| FRANCHISE ASSISTANCE | FRANCHISOR CONTROLS | FRANCHISEE OBLIGATIONS |
|---|---|---|
| * merchandising | * product: quality, | * advertising |
| * management | ingredients | * financial reporting |
| * site selection and layout | * pricing | * adequate working capital |
| * advertising and promotion | * sales volume | * fee payment |
| * financial control procedures | * inventory | * product purchase |
| * financing | * advertising | * construction, repair, |
| * planning and operating | * accounting procedures | maintenance |
| guidelines | * hours | * proper use of trademark |
| * supplies | * architectural design | |
| * training | and layout | |
| | * equipment | |

| ADVANTAGES | DISADVANTAGES |
|---|---|
| * lack of specialized knowledge overcome by training, guidelines, etc. | * may pay for more services than needed |
| * benefit of franchisor's name, reputation, goodwill | * could cost as much as 10% of revenue or even half the profit for franchisor's name and support |
| * often less commitment of capital | |
| * less trial and error | * may not achieve estimated profit |
| * benefit of advertising, bulk purchasing, experience, R & D, etc. | * limited participation in discretionary actions and decision making |

**FIGURE 17-9 Factors considered when evaluating franchise.**

rules, guidelines, and terms and to make certain payments, as specified in the contract. It is important for an individual to be fully aware of these *obligations and controls*, which along with franchisor assistance to a large extent determine the venture's success.

The *advantages* of franchising can be many, for example, the company name, reputation, goodwill, and services provided by the franchisor. The *disadvantages* include limited participation in discretionary actions and decision making. Potential problems may be posed by extremely stringent or unreasonable controls on the franchise.

Most often the franchisor tries to contribute to the success of the franchisee. Some franchisors, however, are merely interested in a "fast buck." They may charge an exorbitant initial fee and more money for additional service requests, demand profit participation in exchange for providing financing, and require burdensome tie-in purchase arrangements.

In evaluating a franchise offering, an expert can assist an individual to assess the basic franchise considerations, as shown in Fig. 17-10. At this point in this study the assumption is made that the prescreening has been done and that the offering is worthwhile to consider.

**Franchisor support.** *Initially*, a franchisor should supply assistance with site selection and layout and adequate initial training of the franchisee and the managers.

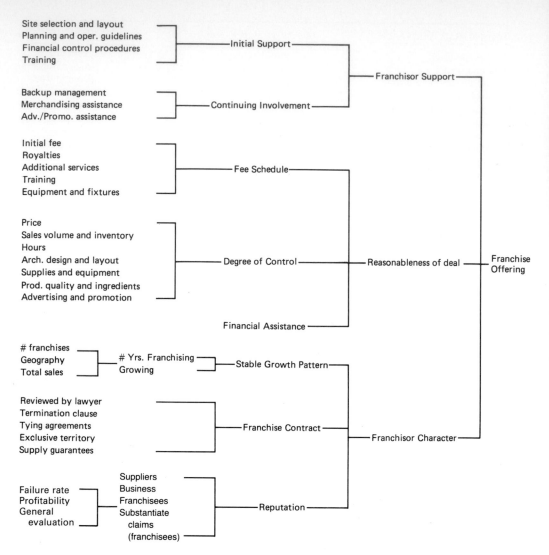

**FIGURE 17-10   Franchise offering area.**

Financial control procedures and planning and operating guidelines are also needed to ensure smooth day-to-day operation of a business. *Continuing involvement* on the part of the franchisor, consisting of back-up management, merchandising, advertising, training and retraining, and promotional assistance are all key success factors in franchising.

**Reasonableness of deal.**   The franchise contract defines all aspects of the *fee schedule*, including the initial fee, continuing royalties or percent of gross sales payments, equipment charges, and fees for other services.   A franchisee often needs *assistance in obtaining financing* as well as assurance of exclusivity of territory.   *Other contract terms*, such as supply guarantees, as well as the degree of control a franchisor has in the areas of hours of operation, amount of inventory, sales volume, and product and price composition, are also examined.

**Franchisor character.** It is necessary to study a franchisor's *stability and growth potential*. A franchisor should have been in existence for a while and should have grown at a steady rate. Newly established franchisors require additional analysis and so are beyond the scope of this study.

A number of *contract clauses* also provide insights into the character of the franchisor. One example is the contract termination clause. A franchisor should not be able to terminate the contract on the grounds of just cause nor forbid the franchisee from selling back an unprofitable franchise without at least a partial refund of the investment. The contract should not contain any tie-in purchasing agreements; and it should be reviewed by a lawyer familiar with small businesses and franchising.

A franchisor should have an established *reputation* with suppliers, present and former franchisees, and generally all business contacts. In addition to reviewing available literature on the franchisor, therefore, it is mandatory to interview as many present and former franchisees as possible.

Another important area examined by an expert is the *substantiation of claims* made by the franchisor. Probably the best test of a franchisor's character is their *dealings with other franchisees*. Present franchisees can tell you about why they are staying or why they are thinking of quitting. Former franchisees can also tell you the good and bad points of having this particular franchise. They are also the best source of information on actual profitability. The overall failure rate of franchisees would also be determined.

**A typical decision scenario.** In addition to determining the kinds of information or knowledge needed, the system developers explored the ways in which information is manipulated or reasoned about in coming to a decision. The following is a summary description of one of the typical decision situations they studied. A number of typical decision scenarios, such as the one described here, were developed for use later in the prototype development study.

Robert London, age forty-two, is a single male interested in a retail fast food franchise. He has worked in investment banking for the last ten years and prior to that, worked in a branch of a suburban bank. He holds a bachelor's and master's degree in business and lives in a rented apartment in a middle-class suburban area near a major city. Rob engaged a consultant (expert) in the field to assist him in deciding whether or not to purchase a Burger King franchise near his home.

The consultant first collected background information. In terms of general business prospects, the product was examined for growth potential and staying power. Since fast food products are common ones, ample demographic and market studies were available that showed the overall prospects were favorable. However, analysis of the local area revealed several weak points. The consultant found that the location Rob was looking at was already saturated with competition, including a McDonald's, a Wendy's and a Roy Rogers, all within a mile radius of each other. In addition, the franchise would be located near an exit ramp to a major highway, but would be the last eating place that travelers would reach coming off the highway.

Although the franchise's target market matched the demographic profile of the local area, the market area was not expected to grow significantly in the future. The consultant talked with other small business owners in the area and found that general indicators called for only modest overall growth. Although the other franchises in the area seemed busy, the consultant's research indicated that competitors' sales had been fairly flat over the prior three years.

The consultant interviewed Rob to see if he was cut out to be an entrepreneur. Based on experiences Rob described from his past, he seemed capable of taking charge, organizing and handling multiple jobs, and dealing effectively with people. He had demonstrated determination and self-reliance to a high degree. Rob generally seemed competent enough to run his own business but lacked the willingness to take big risks.

Next, the consultant examined the franchise offering. Burger King provides substantial initial and on-going assistance at no additional cost in the areas of operations, equipment maintenance, and training. However, they have a relatively high annual franchise payment, provide no assistance with financing, and subject franchisees to a wide variety of controls. Burger King, in business since 1954, has maintained excellent relations with its franchisees and business contacts. The company is predicted to increase its 3,000 units substantially in the next decade. Although a very reputable franchisor, Burger King's contract gives no guarantee of exclusivity of territory, and contains some tie-in purchasing agreements with suppliers.

The consultant summarized his evaluation as follows:

- □ *Business prospects*—The general prospects were favorable. However, because of a stagnating local market and poor location, the local factors were considered unfavorable. The business prospects were, therefore, rated unfavorable overall.
- □ *Individual resources and capabilities*—Because Rob had favorable personal, financial, and business skills the overall individual rating was favorable.
- □ *Franchisor offering*—Franchisor support was very favorable. However, due to the lack of financing assistance and an only fair fee schedule, the reasonableness of the deal was rated average. Although Burger King's reputation is excellent, lack of exclusivity of territory and tie-in agreements yielded an average rating for the contract. The overall rating for the franchise offering was average.

Based on this analysis and evaluation, the consultant's overall rating was only fair. Knowing that the local area was not well suited to the particular franchise, because of heavy competition, and that Rob would need assistance with financing, the expert recommended looking for a more generously financed offering, with a similar product but in a better location.

**The prototype system.** The system described in the next section attempts to replicate this somewhat condensed overview of how decisions are made in this area. Clearly it would be possible to explore these decisions in more depth. This was done subsequently, and more sophisticated versions of the initial prototype system have been developed based on these more detailed explorations. During this initial phase of the study, however, the project was limited to prototyping this condensed overview of the decision situation.

The objective in defining how experts make decisions, and in drawing diagrams of these decisions, such as those shown in Figs. 17-4 to 17-10, is to create a general model of the decision situation. The models in a sense function as a guideline (or expert guidance) that can help someone making this kind of decision. The models also serve as a definition of the structure of the knowledge-based system to be prototyped and a reference point for checking its validity.

Although they are models of how the decision is made, the diagrams in Figs. 17-4 to 17-10 are not necessarily *prescriptions* for how such a decision should be made. They are rather *descriptions* of the general approach a fairly competent expert might use in making these decisions. They were reviewed with both individual entrepreneurs and strategic planners associated with the study. They are the result of refining and revising many earlier rough drafts until they were, in the judgment of the experts, *pretty good* reformulations or replications of the approach a fairly competent decision maker might use. In this way the structured situation analysis, based on typical expert decision scenarios, provided models for prototype systems development.

The developers always kept in mind that this was to be only a first pass at the problem, so perfection was not insisted on. In most cases the first prototype system will be changed, or perhaps thrown out entirely, later in the study.

At this point the critical information or knowledge and the reasoning paths to be included in the system *were deliberately limited to some of the more important ones.* Although limiting the system in this way created the danger that the system might be trivialized somewhat, such simplification was a necessary first step toward organizing and testing the soundness of the system's concept. Also it was essential to developing a prototype within a reasonably short period of time.


## DOCUMENTING THE PROTOTYPE SYSTEM

The following discussion covers

- System proposal
- Description of the system
- Dependency diagrams
- Decision charts
- Designing and constructing the knowledge base


### System Proposal

The general objective of the project is to develop a knowledge-based system to assist in making decisions about starting a new venture using franchising. Since the system is designed to be used by anyone considering entering a new business, it can benefit potential and experienced entrepreneurs, whether they are individuals or new venture firms.

The first phase of the project is limited to a specific type of decision, evaluating franchise offerings in the fast food retailing area. This first phase of the project is designed to help test and build a structure and concept for the much larger system based on the decision situation model shown in Fig. 17-5. Therefore, the first system will be a prototype system, which will be more fully developed in subsequent phases of the project.

Several sources were used to acquire an understanding of the new venture planning area. Interviews were conducted with entrepreneurs, new venture consultants, franchise consultants, members of the small business administration and strategic planners, as well as with people who were exploring going into business for themselves.

## Description of the System

**System overview and objective.** The prototype system is designed to help users in deciding whether or not to take a particular franchise offering. The system asks users questions about the business prospects, potential competition, their individual capabilities, and the franchise's offering. The system uses if-then rules and backward chaining to reason the information given by a user in order to reach its recommendations.

**Recommendations to be made by the system.** For prototyping purposes, the system is limited to making the following recommendations:

- *Superior*—Actively pursue the offering.
- *Very good*—Pursue the offering, but commit to it only after further analyses and evaluations are completed.
- *Fair*—If the local business prospects are weak, examine a similar proposal in another location; if the franchise offering is the weak factor, look for another offering with a similar product and location, but through a different franchisor; should the general business prospects be unfavorable, abandon the proposal.
- *Poor*—Abandon the proposal.

**Nature of user interface, including a typical user dialogue.** The typical user dialogue covers three key knowledge areas:

- *Business prospects*—This information has to be obtained from a variety of sources: business publications; visiting competitors' stores; walking the area; researching local census and other demographic data; talking with equipment vendors, real estate brokers, employment agencies, the local chamber of commerce, local business people who run retail stores in the area, present and former franchisees in this or similar businesses, and potential customers. A typical question is "After examining demographic characteristics such as age, income, and size of the target market, what is your estimate of the potential growth in the market in general?"
- *The individual's capabilities*—This information is obtained from the individual's knowledge of their own personality, family environment, financial con-

dition, experience and skills. A typical question is "What amount of money
are you able to borrow?"

□ *The franchise offering*—This information is obtained from brochures and pam-
phlets, talking with present and former franchisees, reading about the company
and getting its Dun & Bradstreet rating, and examining the actual franchise
contract. Some typical questions might be "What has been the average failure
rate of former franchisees?" and "Has the general evaluation of former and
current franchisees been favorable?"

**Description of the knowledge structure and reasoning processes.** The
recommendations made by the system are based on three critical factors: business
prospects, individual capabilities, and the franchise offering. In turn the values for
each of these factors are determined by a limited number of other influencing factors:

□ The *business prospects* are determined by general and local area business
factors.
□ The *individual capabilities* are determined by personal, financial, and business
experience factors.
□ The *franchise offering* is determined by the franchisor support offered, the
reasonableness of the deal, and the franchisor character.

Additional levels of factors are needed as indicated in Fig. 17-11 in the next section.
If-then rules are used to determine the values at each stage. The inference

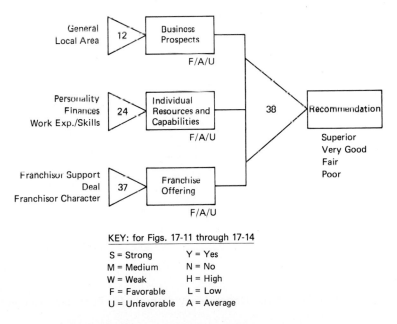

**FIGURE 17-11   Dependency diagram overview.**

engine uses backward chaining. The values are measured for each of the factors in the reasoning chain as indicated in the dependency diagrams that follow.

## Dependency Diagrams

Figures 17-11 through 17-14 show the dependency diagrams for the franchising decision knowledge-based system. These diagrams present a complete summary outline of all the questions, rules, knowledge segments and their interrelationships, values, and recommendations within the system.

## Decision Charts

Figure 17-15 shows a sample decision chart from the prototype knowledge-based system. There is a decision chart for every rule set in the system.

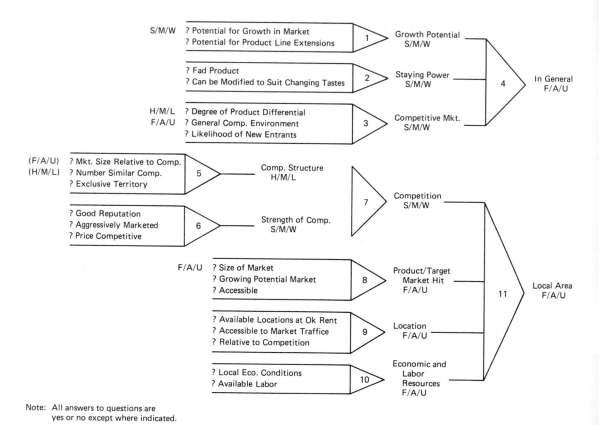

Note: All answers to questions are
yes or no except where indicated.

**FIGURE 17-12  Dependency diagram for business prospects area segment.**

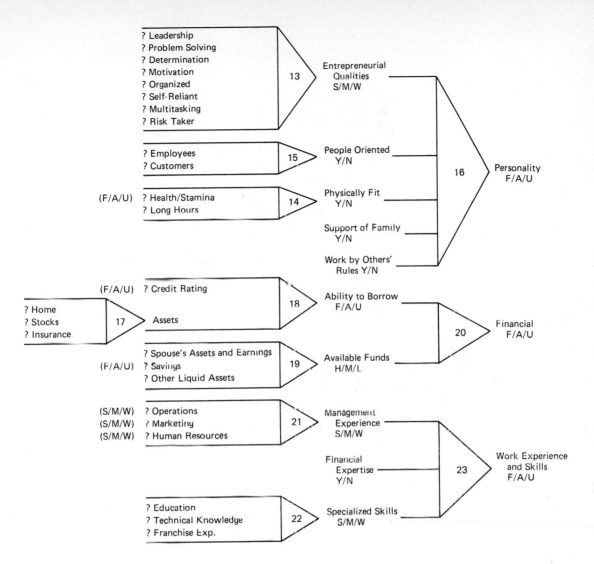

Note: All answers to questions are
yes or no except where indicated.

**FIGURE 17-13  Dependency diagram for individual resources and capabilities segment**

## Designing and Constructing the Knowledge Base

Rules and questions were developed from the situation study.  They were based on the system developer's analysis of how entrepreneurs actually go about making such decisions.

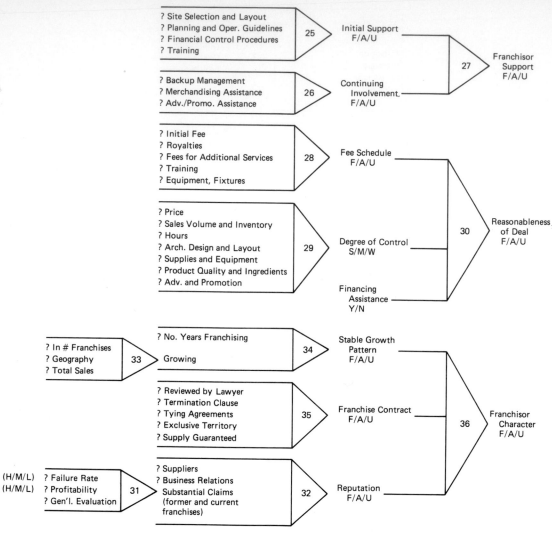

Note: All answers to questions are
yes or no except where indicated.

**FIGURE 17-14    Dependency diagram for franchise offering segment.**

A segment of the prototype system's knowledge base is given in Fig. 17-16. The expert system shell used is M.1. As with the other systems discussed in this book, subsequent prototypes within the system were done on GURU.

The if-then rules in the knowledge base in Fig. 17-16 match those specified in the decision charts. They were written to reflect the relationships shown in the dependency diagrams in Figs. 17-11 through 17-14. They use the values shown there and in the decision charts. The questions in the knowledge base (Fig. 17-16) are those indicated in the dependency diagrams.

| IF | | 108–110 | 111–113 | 114–116 | 117–119 | 120–122 | 123–125 | 126–128 | 129–131 | 132–134 |
|---|---|---|---|---|---|---|---|---|---|---|
| | Business | FFF | AAA | UUU | FFF | AAA | UUU | FFF | AAA | UUU |
| | Res-cap | FFF | FFF | FFF | AAA | AAA | AAA | UUU | UUU | UUU |
| | Offering | FAU | FAU | FAU | FAU | FAU | FAU | FAU | FAU | FAU |
| THEN | Superior | x | | | | x | | | | |
| | Very good | x | x | | | | | | | |
| | Fair | | x x | | | x x | x x | | | |
| | Poor | x | | x x x | | | x | x x x | x x x | x x x |

Key:

F—Favorable
A—Average
U—Very good
S—Strong
V—Very weak
FA—Fair
P—Poor

**FIGURE 17-15  Decision chart for new venture using franchising (initial prototype).**

## THE ROLE OF FINANCIAL PLANNING AND ANALYSIS

Financial projections are always necessary in new venture planning and can be integrated into more advanced knowledge-based systems, as shown in Chapter 9. The following traces some of the steps taken in making these projections in the kind of decision situations described in this chapter.

It is usually fairly easy to determine the total investment required. Equipment costs, leasehold and lease deposit outlays, and carrying costs required until the store operates profitably are factors that are examined. Reasonably accurate information is normally available about each cost factor.

The objective is to keep the cash outlay or investment as low as possible, consistent with borrowing costs. There are many ways to do this, including machinery vendor financing, borrowing from relatives, and bartering. These factors can be incorporated into the system's financial analysis.

Projecting operating costs is also relatively straightforward, since most of the cost factors are known (rent, salaries, utilities, and the like). These factors can also be incorporated into the system.

Projecting revenues is more difficult. They can be based on the experience of others or on expert's judgments. At best such projections are very uncertain estimates, since so much depends on strategic assumptions, such as

□ What the competition will be doing.
□ What changes will be occurring in the market.
□ What plans the individual can make to overcome some of the anticipated

```
/*  Questions: Franchise Contract  */

question(reviewed) = ['Has your contract been carefully
reviewed and approved by a lawyer?'].
legalvals(reviewed) = [yes, no].

question(term) = ['Does your termination clause prohibit your
franchisor from termination for just cause and allow you to
get a partial refund if the arrangement proves very
unprofitable?'].
legalvals(term) = [yes, no].

question(tying) = ['Does your contract contain tying
agreements?'].
legalvals(tying) = [yes, no].

question(exclusive) = ['Does your contract guarantee you
exclusivity of territory?'].
legalvals(exclusive) = [yes, no].

question(supp-guar) = ['Does your contract provide you with
supply guarantees?'].
legalvals(supp-guar) = [yes, no].

question(family) = ['Do you have the full support of your
family in your venture?'].
legalvals(family) = [yes, no].


/*  Rule set twenty seven:  Franchisor Support  */

rule-76:
    if in-supp = favorable and
       cont-involv = favorable
    then fran-supp = favorable.

rule-77:
    if in-supp = average and
        cont-involv = average or
        cont-involv = favorable
    then fran-supp = average.

rule-78:
    if in-supp = unfavorable and
       cont-involv = average or
       cont-involv = unfavorable
    then fran-supp = unfavorable.


/*  Rule set thirty:  Reasonableness of Deal  */
rule-85:
    if schedule = favorable and
       degree = weak and
       ass = yes
    then deal = favorable.
```

*(continued)*

**FIGURE 17-16  Sample segment knowledge base for new venture
using franchising.**

```
rule -86:
    if schedule = average and
       (degree = medium or
        degree = strong) and
        ass = yes
    then deal = average.

rule-87:
    if schedule = average or
       schedule = unfavorable and
       (degree = strong or
        degree = medium) and
        ass = no
    then deal = unfavorable.
```

**FIGURE 17-16**  *(continued)*

problems, to change the strategic focus, and to create a market niche or competitive advantage.

There are, however, ways to handle this uncertainty. First, determine what it will *cost* to go into the venture and survive until it can reasonably be expected to make money. Then calculate if a potential entrepreneur has or can get the money. If not, then the project is not feasible. Next, to determine the *risk*, calculate how much of that investment someone would lose if the venture does not work out. Can the potential entrepreneur financially and psychologically afford to take that loss under this worst case scenario? If not, then the entrepreneur should probably not go into the project.

To estimate *how long* the potential entrepreneur could hold out if things did not go too well at first, calculate anticipated monthly cash outlays and match them against available resources and anticipated monthly revenues. If one could not hold out for a fairly long period of time, using conservative revenue assumptions, then it could be a high risk venture. The *minimum revenue levels* needed to survive would also be calculated. If they could not conservatively be reached and sustained (within a reasonable period of time), then it is probably a high risk venture.

If there is a chance of doing better than just surviving, calculate how much potential marginal income is possible. If it is fairly high and reasonably achievable, then the venture has a potentially high payoff.

The reasoning involved in making these risk estimates, and the recommendations based on them, can be incorporated into enhanced versions of a knowledge-based system. These enhancements would be in addition to traditional financial planning and projecting capabilities.

Systems that *integrate* conventional financial planning computer applications with more qualitative knowledge-based systems are fairly common today. An example of such an *integrated system* is described in some detail in Chapter 9.

## REVIEW QUESTIONS

1. Finish the knowledge base for the system (or any segment of that system) partially documented in this chapter and enter it into the expert system shell you have.

2. Reformulate a decision situation for one of the potential areas for knowledge-based systems development given in the "Narrowing the Focus" section of this chapter. For an example refer to the career strategy planning prototype system described in Chapter 22, which is a subsystem of the overall new venture planning system described in this chapter.

3. What three critical knowledge areas are examined in decisions concerning the use of franchising in opening a store in the retail fast food area?

4. What are some of the local business factors that may be considered in determining a venture's prospects?

5. Discuss the role of individual factors in assessing a new venture's chances of success.

6. In what ways does the system described in this chapter resemble the strategic planning system described in Chapter 13? In what ways does it differ from it?

7. Describe some of the ways in which you might enhance or extend the prototype system described in this chapter.

## REFERENCES

Allison, A., "RISC's Challenge Mini, Micro Suppliers," *Mini-Micro Systems*, vol. 19, November 1986.

Allison, A., "Varied Architectures Crowd Supermini Arena," *Mini-Micro Systems*, vol. 19, December 1986.

Bard, R., and S. Henderson, *Own Your Own Franchise: Everything You Need to Know About the 160 Best Opportunities in America*, Reading, MA: Addison-Wesley, 1987.

Becker, J. T., "Network Designers Face Shifting Industry Givens," *Data Communications*, vol. 15, December 1986.

Brown, H., *Franchising: Realities and Remedies*, New York: New York Law Publishing, 1981.

Coltman, M. M., *Franchising in the U. S.*, Vancouver: International Self-Counsel Press, 1982.

Crabb, D. E., "Technical Topics for the IBM PC Family: An Annotated Bibliography," *Byte*, vol. 11, no. 11, 1986.

"Distributed SNA: A Network Architecture Gets On Track," *Data Communications*, vol. 16, February 1987.

Emmett, A., and Gabel, D., "Cases in Direct Microcomputer Connections: Nuts and Bolts," *Data Communications*, vol. 15, July 1986.

Foster, D. L., *The Complete Franchise Book: Everything You Ever Wanted to Know About Buying or Starting Your Own Franchise*, New York: Prima Publishing and Communication, distributed by St. Martin's Press, 1987.

"The Franchise Route," *Nation's Business*, March 1987.

Gross, H., and R. S. Levy, *Franchise Investigation and Contract Negotiations*, Babylon, NY: Pilot Books, 1985.

Henderson, S., and T. Schlade, "Deciphering and Dissecting Franchise Offering Circulars," *Hotel and Motel Management*, Feb. 2, 1987.

Hicks, T. G., *Franchise Riches Success Kit*, 3rd ed., Rockville Center, NY: International Wealth Success, 1987.

Hornstein, J. V., "Parallel Processing Attacks Real-Time World," *Mini-Micro Systems*, vol. 19, December 1986.

King, K. G., "Developments in Microcomputer Technology," *Journal of Accountancy*, vol. 162, September 1986.

Lipper, A., et al., *Venture's Guide to Investing in Private Companies*, Homewood, IL: Dow Jones-Irwin, 1984.

Mendelsohn, M., *The Guide to Franchising*, Oxford, England: Pergamon Press, 1982.

Micossi, A., "Micro and Workstation Talents Converge," *Computer Decisions*, vol. 18, Sept. 9, 1986.

Purkiser, C., "Intel's 386 Unites UNIX and DOS Software," *Mini-Micro Systems*, vol. 20, April 1987.

Pryor, D., "NCR's PlatformStrategy Reaches to Mutiprocessors," *Mini-Micro Systems*, vol. 20, March 1987.

Siegel, W. I., *Franchising*, New York: John Wiley and Sons, 1983.

Stevens, E. E., and B. Bernstein, "APPC: The Future of Microcomputer Communications within IBM's SNA," *Data Communications*, vol. 15, July 1986.

Taube, E. V., "Proper Modem Selection Ensures Free-Flowing PC Communication," *Data Management*, vol. 24, September 1986.

Webster, B., *The Insider's Guide to Franchising*, New York: AMACOM, 1986.

Weadock, G. E., "Mini-Micro Hybrids Rival Local Networks," *Mini-Micro Systems*, vol. 19, September 1986.

# 18

# A System for Determining Marketing Strategy: International Affiliates

This chapter describes the development of a knowledge-based system designed to assist in making marketing strategy decisions.  The specific prototype system developed involves determining marketing strategy for managers in local foreign affiliate offices of a multinational company.  The discussion covers

- □ The situation under study: understanding the expert's domain
- □ Studying the situation to be prototyped
- □ Documenting the prototype system

The discussion begins with a structured decision analysis and structured decision model development for the situation under study for prototyping.  The design and documentation of the actual prototype knowledge-based system is then described.

## THE SITUATION UNDER STUDY: UNDERSTANDING THE EXPERT'S DOMAIN

The general area under study is marketing planning and strategy development.  It involves determining the overall market thrust of the entire business, and so is a critical element of any overall strategic company plan.  The discussion in this section covers

- □ Selecting a decision area to work on
- □ Studying how the situation works and how decisions are made

□ The international marketing environment
□ Narrowing the focus

## Selecting a Decision Area to Work On

Developing a marketing strategy involves making decisions about product, distribution, promotion, and price in light of company factors as well as customer, competitive, and other market factors.

Marketing strategy decisions are only one segment of marketing planning. An overview of the marketing planning process is shown in Fig. 18-1.

Ultimately all marketing planning is based on the *customer*, sometimes referred to as the target market. Opportunities are defined in terms of size, growth rate, demographic profiles, and geographic and other "factual" characteristics of existing and potential customer markets. In addition, characteristics of the customer (or buyer) are defined in terms of motivation, buying habits, perceptions, and other similar "concept" characteristics in order to identify the keys to success in selling to each customer market identified.

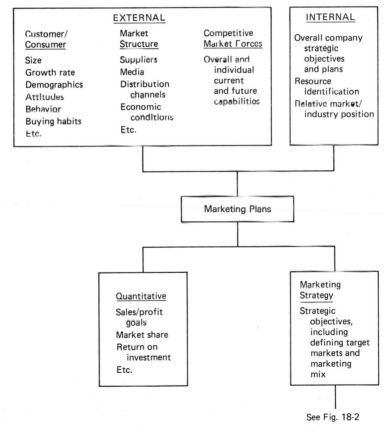

**FIGURE 18-1   Marketing planning—a general overview.**

Even though planning may start with a product in hand, final product decisions are usually not made until the product's appropriateness for the target market is studied and, where appropriate, adjustments made to the product.

*Structural* characteristics of the marketplace are also studied to determine the realistic limits of any marketing plans as well as to identify additional potential opportunities and threats. Areas examined include suppliers, distribution channels, new product threats, media, barriers to entry, economic and political factors, and technology.

Opportunities and threats are examined in relation to the *competitive environment*. Overall competitive factors as well as individual competitor strengths and weaknesses in critical areas affecting success in major opportunity areas are studied. Both the present position and anticipated future situation are studied.

*Company resources*, and potential company resources, are examined to define a company's strengths and weaknesses affecting success in identified opportunity areas. All company resource areas are studied, including financial, production, marketing, manpower, and image. A company's marketplace position is also identified, as are the company's enterprise-wide plans and strategies.

*Marketing plans* are developed within the context of all these situational factors. There are the familiar *quantitative* plans covering income, investment, return on investment, sales, and market share. In addition, marketing *strategies* are developed.

The development of marketing strategies is the focus of this study. The following discussion of this decision area is necessarily selective, because it is intended to provide a basis for knowledge-based systems development. It is not a comprehensive review of the entire field.

## Studying How the Situation Works and How Decisions Are Made

Marketing strategy development defines overall marketing strategy, target markets and the marketing mix of product, promotion media, distribution channels, and price for a company. These strategy decisions are made within the limitations of the marketplace and company resources, and within the context of the enterprise-wide strategic objectives and plans.

Specific strategies and programs are developed within each of the areas defined as important in the marketing strategy, as shown in Fig. 18-2 and discussed briefly below.

- □ *Product* decisions involve developing the right product for a target market, or at times finding the best target market for a product already developed. Product variables may include quality, features, options, style, brand name, packaging, sizes, services, warranties, and returns.
- □ *Distribution* decisions involve channels, levels of penetration and coverage, geographic locations, inventory levels, and transportation. Structural market factors, as well as competitive factors, have major impacts on decisions in this area.
- □ *Promotion* decisions, which are concerned with effective communication of

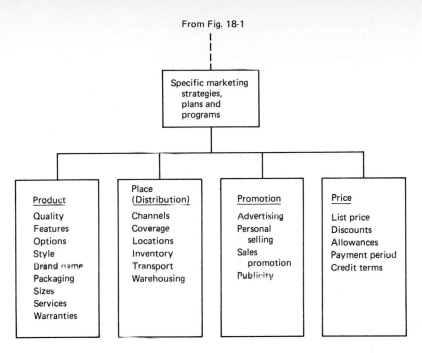

From Fig. 18-1

Specific marketing
strategies,
plans and
programs

| Product | Place (Distribution) | Promotion | Price |
|---|---|---|---|
| Quality | Channels | Advertising | List price |
| Features | Coverage | Personal selling | Discounts |
| Options | Locations | Sales promotion | Allowances |
| Style | Inventory | Publicity | Payment period |
| Brand name | Transport | | Credit terms |
| Packaging | Warehousing | | |
| Sizes | | | |
| Services | | | |
| Warranties | | | |

**FIGURE 18-2  Marketing strategy development—a general overview.**

product messages (benefits) to the target market, cover personal selling, advertising, sales promotion, and publicity.
- *Price* decisions (including mark-ups, discounts, allowances, and terms of sale and service) depend on such factors as the nature of the competition, existing market practices, production costs, demand levels, and strategic marketing objectives.

Marketing planning and strategy development, as outlined in Figs. 18-1 and 18-2, provides a rich potential for knowledge-based systems development. Systems in this area now under development include those for

- Selecting a media appropriate to both product and customer
- Designing a product development strategy to meet customer and other market requirements
- Selecting target markets for existing products
- Developing packaging strategies for higher-priced luxury consumer products
- Determining marketing strategies for local foreign affiliates of a multinational company

The last area, developing local affiliate strategies at a multinational company (in this case in the health-care products industry), was selected for further study during this phase of the project.

## The International Marketing Environment

Strategic planning in the international marketing environment follows patterns similar to those discussed in the preceding section. The key differences are found in the specific internal and external factors affecting a particular situation. These factors are shown in Fig. 18-3.

In the area of company factors, strategy decisions are made within the context of both the local affiliate's relative strengths and weaknesses, existing product range, sales and profit targets and available resources as well as within the context of the goals, strategies, and resources of the parent organization.

Market factors, both the local market's size, structure, legal environment, and future, as well as the market for the same product or segment of the product line in neighboring, similar, or highly influential countries, or worldwide, are considered.

Competitive factors, such as number and size, strengths and weaknesses, resources, and projected actions, at both the international and the local level also influence local strategy decisions. Customer factors, including attitudes and buying habits, product and brand awareness, and demographics, are a final consideration.

The international marketing planning is done at both the corporate and local level. Enterprise-wide strategic planning can cover a wide range of international areas. For example, corporate strategy decisions can involve deciding on whether to follow a *global* (for example, Coca Cola's same product and marketing strategies in all countries) or *multinational* (for example, varying strategies by country) or *combination global and multinational* strategy.

Local managers in individual countries where a company markets its products are involved in the development of marketing strategies for their markets. Although this planning is done within the context of overall (enterprise-wide) company planning, the corporate level plans often need to be adapted to the local environment. The degree to which a local strategy can deviate from the overall corporate strategic plans depends upon such factors as the management style of the overall organization (centralized or decentralized) and its international marketing philosophy (global or multinational).

Local marketing strategy development, as shown in Fig. 18-4, focuses mainly on developing strategies in the four marketing mix areas in light of the local and international market conditions outlined in Fig. 18-3.

In the health care field, for example, *product* decisions for nonprescription drugs are often limited by what the local laws and medical customs recognize as safe and effective use. Products such as Advil and Nuprin, which contain the pain-killing ingredient ibuprofen, are sold over the counter in consumer outlets in the United States, England, and Japan. In many other countries, such as Canada and Australia, products containing ibuprofen are restricted to sale by prescription only.

Because the media are heavily controlled by the government in many countries, *promotion* decisions can be limited by what is available or what is allowed. In some countries, such as Belgium and Saudi Arabia, for example, no medical advertising at all is allowed on broadcast media. In many other countries, including Venezuela, all medicine advertising must be approved by the government before airing—a process that can take from a few weeks to a few years for a single commercial.

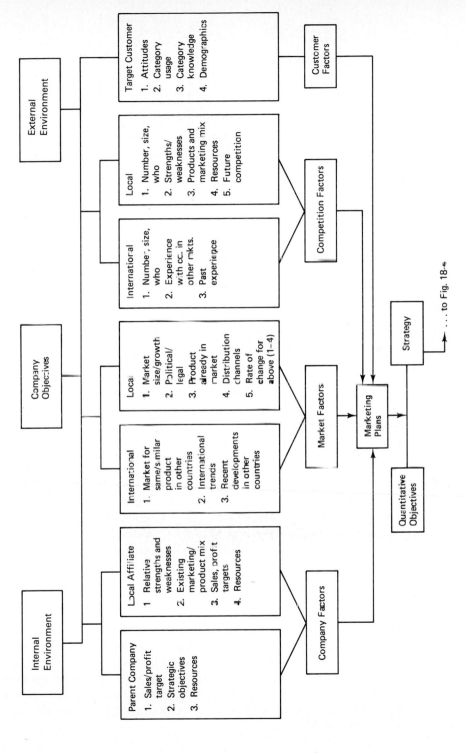

**FIGURE 18-3  Decision situation overview diagram for international marketing strategy development.**

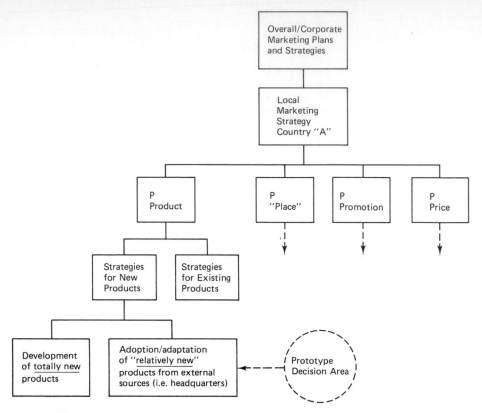

**FIGURE 18-4    Diagram of situation under study—international local affiliates marketing strategy.**

In some countries *distribution (place)* methods may be controlled as to where nonprescription products can be sold.   For example, in many countries pharmaceuticals can not be sold anywhere but in pharmacies.

*Pricing* decisions are also subject to a variety of local constraints.   In India, for example, the government sets prices for a given drug product based on what is charged by the lowest priced local producer.   All others wishing to sell that product must charge at or below this price—effectively removing pricing decisions from the control of the local manager.

**Narrowing the Focus of the Study**

Two major levels of strategic decisions made in international marketing can be identified as *corporate-level decisions* covering marketing strategies on a worldwide or international scale, and *local, foreign affiliate level decisions* covering marketing strategy and implementation for a single country or market.   The local decisions were chosen as the focus for further study.   The specific company under study is an international health care company seeking to market selected categories of nonprescription drugs on a global level.

Although many companies have top talent in their headquarters marketing staff, few managers at the local level, especially in smaller markets, have the experience or resources needed to develop comprehensive strategic plans. A knowledge-based system to help managers to do this planning would significantly improve the quality and financial results of local decisions.

Of all marketing strategy decisions faced by the local manager, the ones of greatest strategic importance involve new product introduction. New products, for a local affiliate of an international corporation, are often defined as "those products that are new to that particular country." In other words, they can be either *totally new*, that is, the product is so new that it has not yet been sold regularly elsewhere, or *relatively new*, that is, it has already been developed and sold outside of the specific country under study.

Most totally new products, at least in the health care industry, are developed in the major industrial countries of the world—for example, the United States, Japan, and the United Kingdom. For the most part products considered as new products in smaller, local country markets are in the relatively new category.

Decisions are made on a particular product by local managers after receiving basic information on it from headquarters or a sister country operation. This information is received either *at the request of the local manager*, who has identified an opportunity for a specific type of new product in his market and wishes to launch it or who has requested information on whether headquarters has a product "in house" that can be used to counter a specific competitive threat, or as part of *a specific worldwide new product project* in which identical product information is sent to each international market for evaluation and action.

The second of these, a local manager evaluating and developing strategies for the possible introduction of a corporation's worldwide new product proposal, was selected for further study and for possible prototype development for several reasons:

□ It is a useful decision area, with high long-term potential payoff in dozens of individual markets in the company under study.

□ It is narrow enough in scope and well defined enough to enable prototyping within a reasonable period of time.

□ It has good potential for further expansion and development.


## STUDYING THE SITUATION TO BE PROTOTYPED

The following describes how expert managers at a local foreign affiliate of an international health care products company might strategically evaluate new product proposals from company headquarters. The description of the situation is structured in a way that provides models useful for later prototype system development. These structured models are based on descriptions or scenarios of typical decision situations faced by experts working at the company under study.

In this study it is assumed that corporate management has already developed the product formula and recommended marketing strategies for the product. These strategies are based on preliminary research in major countries where the product has demonstrated significant international sales potential. Company headquarters has requested input from the local manager as to the feasibility and fit of the new product in their country.

It is also assumed that the new product proposal received from headquarters includes complete information on

- The product, its formula, and manufacturing (or import) specifications
- Full details (and necessary support documentation) of its medical purpose—that is, what it is designed to do
- The basic costs of raw materials and manufacturing or of importing the product
- The product's proposed consumer promise, brand name, and suggested promotional strategy (for local adaptation), an identification of the suggested target market segment or segments for whom the product was designed, and the product's recommended positioning versus competitive products
- Summaries of experiences (both positive and negative) to date in other international markets, such as consumer, competitive and trade reactions, initial levels of trial and purchase, likelihood of "me too" copies or generic competition, and regulatory barriers to entry
- Other information pertinent to local product decisions, such as the strategic importance to the parent company of introducing the new product in as many countries as possible as soon as possible to preempt competition

The product proposal is evaluated in the context of key customer, market, competitor, and company factors, as shown in Fig. 18-5.

## Customer Factors

To evaluate customer factors in the local country it is first determined if there is a sufficiently large, definable, and potentially viable market or market segment to which the product can be sold. Determining this involves comparing the target market defined in the proposal with local demographics and conditions. In evaluating the *viability of a target market segment*, such factors as income and appropriateness of the product are considered. A general evaluation of the *market size*, including estimates of total country population and per capita income, is also required.

## Market Factors

Market factors involve conditions a company faces in marketing products to customers in a given country, and include product factors, the general marketing environment, and entry barriers.

*Product factors* require judgments based on market research of such factors as awareness, usage frequency, brand loyalty, purchase frequency, and overall consumer involvement levels.

Evaluating the *marketing environment* involves determining the strengths and weaknesses of the existing marketing structure in a local country. Key considerations here are the available distribution channels and advertising media.

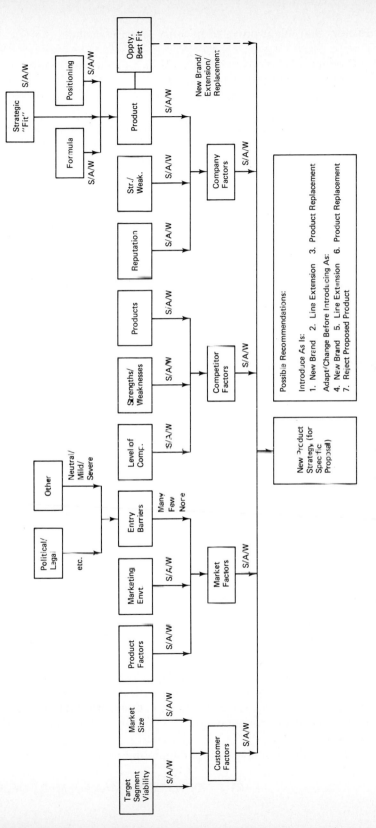

**FIGURE 18-5  Diagram of decision area to be prototyped—new product strategy for local country product proposal.**

Factors that might prove to be *entry barriers* include

- *Product* regulations, which can hinder a company's ability to register or distribute a given product or formula
- *Price* regulations in the form of either price freezes or direct profit constraints on manufacturers or retailers
- *Promotion* and advertising regulations, which can hinder a company's ability to communicate about a new product to a specific target population
- *Place and distribution* regulations, such as those restricting nonprescription drug sales to pharmacies
- *Foreign exchange controls*, which can hinder the efficient purchase of raw materials or finished products from international sources
- *Cultural factors*, such as those in Middle Eastern countries on women's dress and behavior, that could prohibit the introduction of such products as jewelry or bikini bathing suits
- *Inflation*, which in some Latin American markets can exceed 100 percent a year
- *Market saturation levels*, which could indicate diminishing returns for investment in new products

## Competitor Factors

Analyzing competitor factors involves examining the level of competition, the specific strengths and weaknesses of competitors in the industry, and the competing products. *Level of competition* measures how many competitors there are and how big and effective they are. *Competitor strengths and weaknesses* measures the overall strength of competitors' financial, distribution, manufacturing, promotional, and pricing resources. *Competing products*, their similarity to the product under consideration, their market position, their brand strength and the likelihood of "me-too" products, are also examined.

## Company Factors

To assess company factors, a firm's reputation or standing in that country is considered along with its operating strengths and weaknesses. The evaluation also weighs the specific attributes of the proposed new product and the way the product would best fit into the company's existing product range. *Reputation* is measured by examining the company's relations with three key groups (the trade, the medical community, and consumers) and by assessing the strength of the company's sales force.

The *company strengths and weaknesses* examined include the firm's distribution, manufacturing, and promotion capabilities; its competitive flexibility in pricing; and the resources available to support a new product introduction. Direct comparisons are made between the company and competitors, identifying relative strengths and weaknesses.

*Product* evaluation involves examining the proposed product's formula and positioning, as described in the new product proposal, and weighing its strategic fit both in terms of the local company and its international parent.

In evaluating the product, the degree to which the proposed *formula* conforms to local accepted medical practice as well as whether or not some aspect of the formula (for example, an ingredient) needs to be changed before the product is introduced is determined. The need for change can arise from regulations, accepted local norms for self-medication treatment, availability of raw materials, and other factors. Whether or not the product can be made in the country or imported is also studied. Formula considerations also include estimates of the new product's value to the market. Is it unique? Does it present a significant and valuable improvement over existing product offerings to consumers in the market? The absence of any such advantages would mean that the company is dealing with a "me-too" product—usually a weak position to be in.

Judging *strategic fit* requires evaluating how well the proposed new product would blend in with or improve a company's existing product mix. It also involves studying a company's worldwide strategy to determine if this introduction is part of broader company strategy of market penetration or positioning.

Three separate, although related, evaluations need to be made of a proposed *product's positioning*. These determine whether the positioning, or consumer promise, is

- □ *Clear and understandable* to the consumers in a local country
- □ *Relevant* to their wants, needs, and lifestyles
- □ *Believable* to people who will be asked to buy the product

## Opportunity: Best Fit

A number of other strategic factors are considered. For purposes of this study, these have been classified under the heading "Opportunity: Best Fit." For example, if a company has no existing brand in the proposed product category, the product would be introduced as a new brand if other factors are favorable. If the company already has a strong brand in the category, it is advisable in most cases not to introduce a new brand, but instead to incorporate the new product into the existing product family as a line extension. An example of this was Sterling Drug's introduction of Midol 200, a new pain-killing product introduced as a line extension to the existing Midol line, rather than as a new brand. This was a strategically sound move because the company did not have the resources to compete head-on with similar products of other companies, products such as Tylenol and Medipren.

When a company has a strong existing brand in the new product's category, but which is in the declining stage of its life cycle, it is often advisable to inject the new product into the market as a new, improved (replacement) version of the existing brand, rather than as a totally new brand. Where existing brands are weak and declining, introduction as a new brand would be preferable.

As seen from this discussion of the best opportunity fit, all these strategic opportunity and key-to-success factors have a significant impact on the final recommendation about whether or not, and how, to introduce the proposed new product.

## Possible Recommendations

After evaluating the impact of these major factors, seven possible strategic recommendations can be identified as possible responses a local manager might make to the new product proposal.

These decisions can be grouped into three basic categories, the first two of which have three different alternatives. The first and second groups of recommendations differ only in whether or not changes are needed in the formula.

1. Introduce the product (without change to formula)
   a. As a new brand
   b. As a line extension* to an existing brand
   c. As a replacement† for an existing brand
2. Change one or more elements of the proposed product
   a. As a new brand
   b. As a line extension* to an existing brand
   c. As a replacement† for an existing brand
3. Reject the proposed new product.

The ideal situation is one in which customer, market, and company factors strongly favor the company, and competitor factors are weak. In this case the final strategy choice is made by combining the appropriate "best opportunity fit" values—new brand, line extension, or replacement—with information on whether or not changes are needed.

For example, if the best opportunity fit is to introduce the proposed product as a new brand, and changes in the product are not needed, then the recommendation would be to *introduce the proposed product, as is, as a new brand*. If changes are indicated in the formula, the recommendation would change to *adapt or change the proposed product before introducing as a new brand*.

If the best opportunity fit indicates that the product would be best as a *line extension*, this would be the recommended strategy, depending on whether or not changes were needed. A similar pattern of recommendations occurs when best opportunity fit indicates product replacement.

Conditions are, however, rarely so totally favorable. Much more judgment is required in most situations. For example, where customer and market factors are either average or strong (indicating the market could support a new product introduction), but competitor factors are stronger than company factors (strong competitor and average company factors, or average competitor and weak company factors), a new brand introduction under any circumstances would not be recommended. Instead, assuming the company has a strong existing brand in the category, the only

---

*A line extension is an additional product, related to an existing one by function and name, but yet different in form, flavor, etc.—such as the Children's Tylenol line extensions of tablets, liquids, drops, and syrups.

†A replacement or product improvement example would be the replacement (improvement) of a new, alcohol- and sugar-free formula for the syrup version of the same Children's Tylenol product, replacing the old one that contained these two ingredients.

positive recommendations that could be made would be to introduce the new product as a *line extension or replacement*. This strategy relies on the existing brand strength in otherwise impossible circumstances. If there is no strong existing brand and no other special strategic corporate considerations, the proposed product would be rejected.

If competitor factors are strong, while customer, market, and company factors are weak, the recommendation would be to *reject the proposed product* and not introduce it—at least until conditions changed.

Other factors that would also trigger an automatic rejection include the presence of severe political, legal, or other entry barriers; weak formula and positioning (in combination); and weak customer and marketing environment factors.

The following section describes a prototype knowledge-based system designed to replicate the above decision processes.

## DOCUMENTING THE PROTOTYPE SYSTEM

The following discussion describes the documentation for the prototype system. It covers

- System proposal
- Description of the prototype system
- Dependency diagrams
- Decision charts
- Design and construction of the knowledge base

### System Proposal

The general project objective is to develop a knowledge-based system that can be used to recommend marketing strategies for local foreign affiliate offices of international corporations in the health care industry, especially in smaller countries where marketing expertise is not as prevalent as in major countries.

The first phase of the project is limited to a single strategy development situation. The prototype system would be used to test the feasibility and practical value of developing a larger expert knowledge-based system for product and marketing strategy selection for both new and existing product lines in a given country market.

Benefits the system can provide include

- Aiding local managers to make better new product decisions by enabling the use of more complete and organized evaluation methods
- Providing corporate or regional management with a tool to help enable more consistent and timely product decisions in many countries
- Providing faster, more complete feedback to corporate new product development, acquisitions, and licensing departments about trends and product opportunities in specific markets and market segments
- Serving as an additional strategic high tech tool that can help marketing and

business development managers at all levels gain experience and proficiency in both strategic planning and in marketing decision situations

Two problems to be faced in field-testing the system are (1) convincing management to support the test and purchase or license the necessary software (for use in six to twelve countries), and (2) convincing local managers that such a system can actually work, and getting them to sit down and try it in an actual situation (most have little, if any, computer experience or time to experiment with new systems). Additional problems encountered in some countries are those of language and computer availability.

These problems were resolved by limiting the scope of the initial prototype to make it easier to understand and use, and by limiting the initial tests to countries that had English speaking managers and access to microcomputers.

## Description of the System

**System overview and objective.** The prototype system is designed for use by local managers of foreign affiliate offices in international health care companies. The specific situation addressed by the system is evaluating and making strategic decisions relative to the introduction, in that country, of new nonprescription drug products proposed by the firm's headquarters product development or business development departments.

The system's objective is to assist a manager to strategically evaluate the proposed product's potential in the local market, and—after considering all relevant external and internal factors—to reach a well-reasoned decision as to whether a specific product should be introduced, and if so, how.

Knowledge sources used as expert references included international marketing and business development managers, job experience of the system developers, textbooks and periodical articles, and business documents actually used by the international company for which the system was developed. A knowledge engineer was also frequently consulted during the development phase. Among the published sources consulted were Cateora (1983), Channon and Jalland (1978), Hill and Still (1984), Keegan (1981), Kothari (1979), and Wiechman and Pringle (1979).

**Recommendations made by the system.** The system recommends one of seven possible alternatives about whether a proposed new product should be introduced in the user's market, and if so, how.

1. Introduce the product as is, without alteration, as a new brand (using the brand name proposed).
2. Introduce the product as is, without alteration, as an extension to an existing product line.
3. Introduce the product as is, without alteration, as a replacement for an existing product (while phasing out the old product or formula).
4. Adapt or change one or more elements of the product (such as strength, form, or key active ingredients), and then introduce as a new brand (using the brand name proposed).

5. Adapt one or more elements of the product (as in recommendation 4), and then introduce as a line extension.
6. Adapt one or more elements of the product (as in recommendation 4), and then introduce as a replacement for an existing product.
7. Reject the proposed product and do not introduce.

For prototype purposes, the system does not recommend which elements to adapt or change for recommendations 4, 5, and 6. Also it does not provide a rationale for why a particular strategy recommendation was chosen. These enhancements are seen as critical to making the system real with practical use in the field, and will be added in enhanced versions of the system.

**Nature of the user interface.** The typical user dialogue covers five key knowledge areas.

- *Customer factors* include judgments about the viability of the target market and an evaluation of the market size. A typical question is "For the target segment for the proposed product, what is the relative average income level of the typical consumer: high (top third of population), medium (middle third), low (bottom third)?" Answering these questions would require some market research.
- *Market factors* include product (category) factors, marketing environment, and entry barriers. Answering product (category) questions requires some fairly sophisticated market research or reliance by the user on extensive experience with consumers in the specific country. Marketing environment and entry barrier questions require knowledge of the marketing restrictions and conditions existing in the country. Some typical questions are "Within the product category of the proposed product, what is the current level of brand loyalty among consumers: high, medium, low?" and "What is the current or anticipated level of regulatory controls on prices in the category of the one proposed: neutral (no price controls), mild (low degree of controls, not expected to be a problem), severe (heavy controls, major problems)?"
- *Competitor factors* include an evaluation of competitive products currently or potentially on the market and the size, number, and relative strengths and weaknesses of key competitors in the market. Some typical questions are "What is the general level of financial strength of the major competitors in the proposed product's category: strong, average, weak?" and "What is the general level of market share strength of competing products in the category: strong, average, weak?"
- *Company (internal) factors* include specific evaluations of the company's reputation (with trade, consumers, and the medical community) and its specific strengths and weaknesses in key areas (that is, distribution and manufacturing), as well as the strength of the proposed product. Typical questions include "How strong are the company's manufacturing capabilities, in comparison to the major competition: stronger, equal, weaker?" and "How closely does the medical rationale for the proposed product conform to medical practice and consumer self-medication habits and customs in your country: closely, approximately, not closely?"

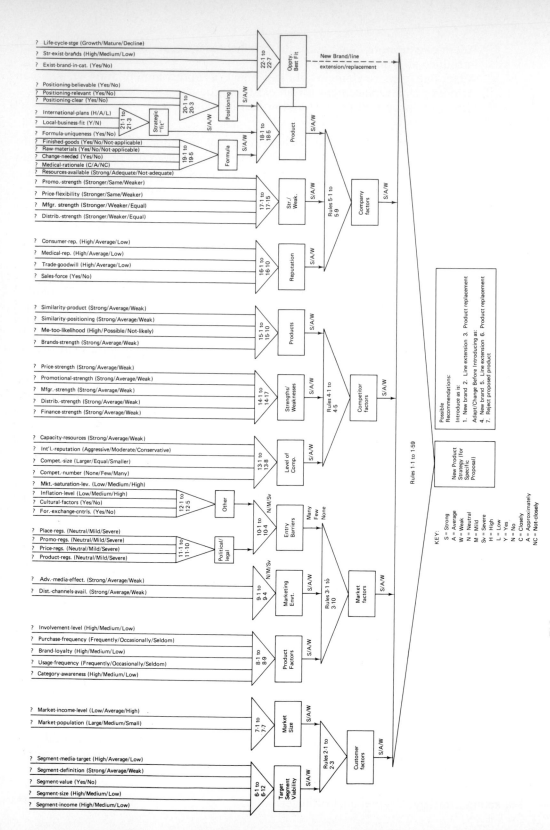

**FIGURE 18-6 Dependency diagram for new product strategy selection for local country product proposal—initial prototype.**

□ *Best opportunity fit* includes an evaluation of where the proposed product best fits into the existing product mix of the company. This is dependent upon whether or not the company already markets a product in the same category as the proposed new product. Typical questions include "If you currently market a brand in the same category, what is the relative market share strength of the existing brand: high (market leader), moderate (among top four), low (also-ran)?" and "How would you describe the product life cycle stage of the existing brand: growth, maturity, decline?"

**Description of the knowledge domain structure and reasoning process.** The recommendations made by the prototype system are based on five critical factors—customers, the market, competitors, the company, and best opportunity fit with strategic plans—as well as on the description of the proposed product in the evaluation proposal received from headquarters. The overall relationships and reasoning process are outlined in Fig. 18-6.

## Dependency Diagram

Figure 18-6 shows the dependency diagram for the new product strategy selection for local country decisions on a proposed new nonprescription drug product. It is a complete outline of all the questions, rules, knowledge segments and their interrelationships, values, and recommendations within the system.

## Decision Charts

A sample decision chart is given in Fig. 18-7. There is a decision chart for every rule set in the system.

## Design and Construction of the Knowledge Base

Sample rules and questions selected from the prototype system's knowledge base are given in Fig. 18-8.

| Rule No. | Trgt. Seg. | Mkt. Size | Outcome (Strong/Avg./Weak) |
|---|---|---|---|
| 1 | S | S | S |
| 2 | S | A | A |
| 3 | S | W | W |
| 4 | A | S | S |
| 5 | A | A | A |
| 6 | A | W | W |
| 7 | W | S | W |
| 8 | W | A | W |
| 9 | W | W | W |

**FIGURE 18-7 Sample decision chart—competition factors rule set— initial prototype.**

<u>Rules</u>.
```
rule-19-3:
    if change-needed = no and
       formula-uniqueness = yes and
       formula-medical-rationale = closely or
       formula-medical-rationale = approximately and
       not (formula-raw-materials = yes and
            formula-finished-goods = yes)
    then formula = strong.
rule-19-4:
    if change-needed = yes and
       formula-uniqueness = yes and
       formula-medical-rationale = closely or
       formula-medical-rationale = approximately and
       not (formula-raw-materials = yes and
            formula-finished-goods = yes)
    then formula = average.
rule-19-5:
    if formula-raw-materials = yes or
       formula-finished-goods = yes
    then formula = weak.


    /* Rule set twenty: Determining Positioning Factors */
rule-20-1:
    if positioning-believable = no or
       positioning-relevant = no
    then positioning = weak.
rule-20-2:
    if positioning-clear = no and
       positioning-relevant = yes and
       positioning-believable = yes
    then positioning = average.
rule-20-3:
    if positioning-clear = yes and
       positioning-relevant = yes and
       positioning-believable = yes
    then positioning = strong.
rule-17-12:
    if company-resources-available = strong or
       company-resources-available = adequate and
       company-manufacturing-strength = stronger and
       company-distribution-strength = stronger
    then co-sw = equal.
rule-17-13:
    if company-resources-available = strong and
       company-manufacturing-strength = stronger and
       company-distribution-strength = equal and
       company-price-flexibility = weaker or
       company-promotion-strength = weaker
    then co-sw = equal.
rule-17-14:
    if company-resources-available = strong and
       company-manufacturing-strength = stronger and
       company-distribution-strength = equal and
       company-price-flexibility = stronger and
       company-promotion-strength = weaker
    then co-sw = stronger.
```

*(continued)*

**FIGURE 18-8  Sample questions and rules from segment of knowledge base—initial prototype.**

```
rule-17-15:
     if company-resources-available = strong or
        company-resources-available = adequate and
        company-manufacturing-strength = stronger and
        company-distribution-strength = weaker and
        company-price-flexibility = weaker or
        company-promotion-strength = weaker
     then co-sw = weaker.
```

<u>Questions</u>.

```
              /* MARKET FACTORS - ENTRY BARRIERS - OTHER */

     question(foreign-exchange-controls) =
     [nl,nl,nl,nl,nl,nl,nl,nl,nl,'
     Are there any controls on foreign exchange that would present
     major problems to successfully obtaining the required raw
     materials or finished goods for the proposed product?'
     ,nl,nl,nl,nl,nl,nl,nl,nl].
     legalvals(foreign-exchange-controls) = [no, yes].

     question(cultural factors) = [nl,nl,nl,nl,nl,nl,nl,nl,nl,'
     Are there any specific cultural factors that would present
     serious problems to the successful introduction of the proposed
     product?'
     ,nl,nl,nl,nl,nl,nl,nl].
     legalvals(cultural-factors) = [no, yes].

     question(inflation-level) = [nl,nl,nl,nl,nl,nl,nl,nl,nl,'
     What is the current or anticipated relative level of inflation in
     the coming 2 years?
     [low (not a problem), mild (minor but manageable problem) high (
     major problem)] '
     ,nl,nl,nl,nl,nl,nl,nl,nl].
     legalvals(inflation-level) = [low, mild, high].

     question(market-saturation-level) = [nl,nl,nl,nl,nl,nl,nl,nl,nl,'
     To what degree is the market for the proposed product saturated?
     [low (room for major growth), mild (room for growth and market
     share competition), high (vary saturated, high entry cost)] '
     ,nl,nl,nl,nl,nl,nl,nl,nl].
     legalvals(market-saturation-level) = [low, mild, high].
```

**FIGURE 18-8** *(continued)*

## REVIEW QUESTIONS

1. Finish the knowledge base for the system (or any segment of the system) partially documented in this chapter and enter it into the expert system shell you have.

2. Reformulate a decision situation for one of the potential areas for knowledge-based systems development given in the "Narrowing the Focus" section and elsewhere in this chapter.

3. Create versions of this system that might be useful in different industries and markets in the United States.

4. Discuss the ways in which the system described in this chapter is similar to and different from the ones described in the chapter on enterprise-wide strategic planning knowledge-based systems.

5. Using the outline of the general marketing planning process given in the initial sections of this chapter, develop outlines or models of possible prototype knowledge-based systems for other marketing planning areas, such as media selection, target customer analysis and selection, distribution planning, and the like.

6. What is involved in developing a marketing strategy? In what ways is it similar to, and related to, enterprise-wide strategic planning?

7. What are the main factors that determine new product strategy recommendations in this chapter's prototype system?

8. What is "strategic fit"?

# REFERENCES

Cady, J., and R. Buzzell. *Strategic Marketing*, Boston, MA: Little, Brown, 1986.

Cateora, P. R., *International Marketing*, 5th ed., Homewood, IL: Richard D. Irwin, 1983.

Channon, D. F., and M. Jalland, eds., *Multinational Strategic Planning*, New York: AMACOM Division of American Management Association, 1978.

Hill, J. S., and R. R. Still, "Adapting Products to LDC Tastes," *Harvest Business Review*, March/April 1984, pp. 92–101.

Keegan, W. J., "Multinational Marketing Management," in Rothberg, R. R., ed., *Corporate Strategy and Product Innovation*, Detroit: The Free Press Division of MacMillan, 1981, pp. 491–499.

Kothari, V., "Strengthening Foreign Marketing Programs," in Berkman, H. W., and I. R. Vernon, eds., *Contemporary Perspectives in International Business*, New York: Houghton Mifflin, 1979.

Reeder, R. R., et al., *Industrial Marketing: Analysis, Planning and Control*, Englewood Cliffs, NJ: Prentice-Hall, 1987.

Scheive, C. D., *Marketing: Principles and Strategies*, New York: Random House, 1987.

Sethi, S. P., and H. Etemad, *International Context of Marketing Strategy: Designing and Implementing Strategies for Competition at Home and Abroad*, Cambridge, MA: Ballinger Publishing, 1987.

Twinbull, P. W., and J. P. Valla, eds., *Strategies for International Industrial Marketing: The Management of Customer Relationships in European Industrial Markets*, Wolfeboro, NH: Longwood Publishing Group, 1986.

Wiechmann, U. E., and L. G. Pringle, "Problems That Plague Multinational Marketers," *Harvard Business Review*, July/August 1979, pp. 118–124.

# 19

# A Media Strategy Selection System

This chapter describes the development of another knowledge-based system designed to assist in making marketing strategy decisions. The prototype system developed involves selecting appropriate types of media for specific customer markets and products. The discussion is divided into four parts:

- □ The situation under study: understanding the expert's domain
- □ Studying the situation to be prototyped
- □ Documenting the prototype system
- □ A multi-model system: integrating object-oriented, data base, and rule-based system structures

The prototype system described here makes use of if-then rules, and was developed using an expert system programming shell. Subsequent versions were developed using both data base management and object-oriented (frame-based) development tools. Marketing planning experts often approach strategy decisions by first breaking the decision situation into frame or data base concepts before manipulating them in making a decision.

## THE SITUATION UNDER STUDY: UNDERSTANDING THE EXPERT'S DOMAIN

The general area under study is marketing planning and strategy development. It involves determining the overall market thrust of an entire business, and so is a critical element of any overall strategic company plan. The discussion in this section covers

- Selecting a decision area to work on
- Narrowing the focus
- Studying how the situation works and how decisions are made

## Selecting a Decision Area to Work on

Developing a marketing strategy involves making decisions about distribution, product, promotion, and price in light of company factors, consumer requirements, competition, and other market factors.

Marketing strategy decisions are only one segment of marketing planning. An overview of the various factors involved in the marketing planning process is shown in Fig. 19-1.

Marketing strategy development defines overall marketing strategies, target markets, and the marketing mix. Determining the appropriate marketing mix involves decisions about product, promotion, distribution channels, and product price for a

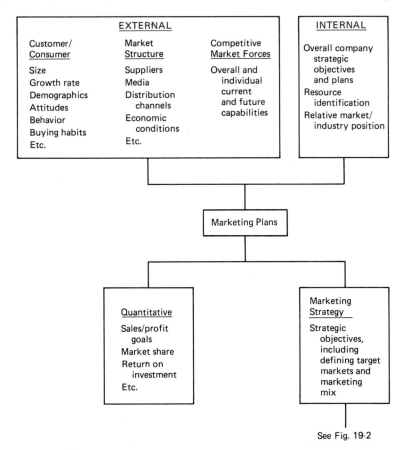

**FIGURE 19-1   Marketing planning—a general overview.**

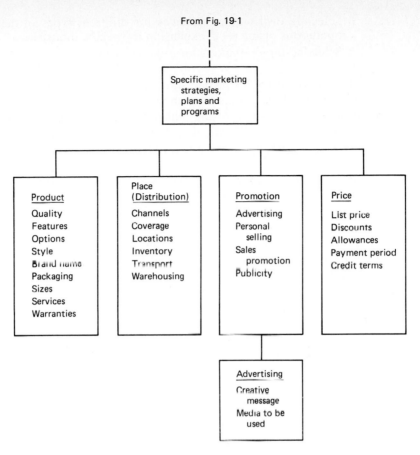

FIGURE 19-2  **Marketing strategy development—a general over-view.**

company.  These strategy decisions are made within the limitations of the marketplace and company resources, and within the context of enterprise-wide strategic objectives and plans.

Specific strategies and programs are developed within each of the areas defined as important in the marketing strategy, as shown in Fig. 19-2.

## Narrowing the Focus of the Study

Marketing planning and strategy development, as outlined in Figs. 19-1 and 19-2, provides a good potential for knowledge-based systems development.  Systems in this area now under development include those for

- Selecting a media appropriate to both product and customer
- Designing a product development strategy to meet customer and other market requirements

□ Selecting distribution strategies for different types of mail-order marketing operations or for retail expansion in specific industries
□ Selecting target markets for existing products

The area selected for further study during this phase of the development project was strategy development decisions in the promotion area. From the segments within the promotion area—advertising, publicity, sales promotion, and personal selling— the decision about media strategy, that is, the mix of media to use for a specific product and customer market, was selected for further study.

## Studying How the Situation Works and How Decisions Are Made

Media selection involves the efficient and effective use of time and space in the selected media by matching media audiences and delivery environment with consumer and product factors. The decision situation analyzed here assumes the product already exists and that the demographic profile of the target market is already known.

Figure 19-3 outlines the general process involved in media selection. Three key knowledge areas affect the media decision.

**Media.** The available media and their audience, and other distinguishing characteristics, affect the mix decision. Figure 19-4 gives a summary of such an impact study for four selected media categories. Other media studies define specific demographic audience profiles, using such factors as age, income, sex, and occupation. Some studies combine demographic and other characteristics, including media costs.

Media are evaluated in terms of their cost efficiency in reaching target audiences

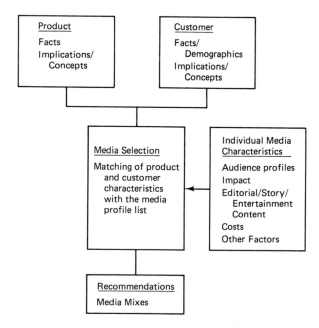

**FIGURE 19-3 General media selection process—overview.**

| Audience Reach: | TV | RADIO | MAGAZINE | NEWSPAPER |
|---|---|---|---|---|
| Total population reach | high | average | low | average |
| Selective upscale reach | low | average | high | average |
| Young adult selectivity | low | high | high | low |
| Local market selectivity | average | average | low | high |
| *Creative Requirements:* Opportunity to exploit editorial content | low | average | high | average |
| Emotional stimulation | high | average | average | low |
| Ability to demonstrate product | high | low | low | low |
| Attention getting device | high | low | high | average |
| Ability to convey detail and information | low | average | high | high |
| Package identification | average | average | high | average |
| Ability to talk to audience (person-to-person) | average | high | low | low |
| Ability to be used as a shopping medium | poor | average | average | high |
| Ability to advertise high involvement products | low | low | high | average |

*(continued)*

FIGURE 19-4   **Media characteristics—overview summary.**

| Creative Requirements: | TV | RADIO | MAGAZINE | NEWSPAPER |
|---|---|---|---|---|
| Ability to advertise low involvement products | high | high | low | average |
| Ability to appeal to rational customer | low | low | high | high |
| Ability to control frequency | average | average | average | high |
| Audience involvement with medium | low | average | high | average |
| Cost/Budget: | | | | |
| Budget required | high | low | high | average/ high |
| Cost per 1,000 ratio | low | high | high | average |
| Audience: | | | | |
| Ability to service seasonal audience | low | high | average | average |
| Predictability of audience level | low | average | average | high |
| Pass along cost per 1,000/audience | none | none | high | average |
| Depth of demographic audience survey | low | low | high | average |
| Other Characteristics: | | | | |
| Selective ad positioning | low | average | average | high |
| Ad intrusiveness | high | average | low | low |
| Ad clutter | high | high | low | low |
| Prestige and respectability of medium | average | average | high | high |

An explanation of the key characteristics of the major media used in this study follows.

*(continued)*

**FIGURE 19-4** *(continued)*

PRINT MEDIA

*Magazines.* Magazines enable media planners to segment audiences by interests and life styles. Magazine content appeals to consumers' need for information, instruction, and problem solving. Readers are actively involved in seeking information. The decision to select magazines as a media choice would be based on the following:

> Target market is selective
> Consumers are high-motivation seekers
> The product is high involvement
> The consumer is a rational buyer
> Need to convey information and detail
> Product requires use of a shopping medium

*Newspapers.* Newspapers are a shopping medium, which can be used as an aid for price comparisons since a wide variety of products can be offered to consumers in a single advertisement. Newspapers are an effective medium for products and services of local advertisers. The decision to select newspapers would be based on the following:

> Target market is selective and local market coverage is needed
> Customers are information seekers
> Product can be high or low involvement
> The customer is a rational buyer
> Need for media to be used as a shopping guide for price comparisons

BROADCASTING

*Television.* Television is a low-involvement medium that tends to ask little of the viewer. It is generally, therefore, better suited to low-involvement items where less information is needed. Television is a good medium for products requiring demonstration and those that would be based on the following:

> Target market is broad audience
> Customers are low-information seekers
> Product is low involvement
> Product requires audio and visual demonstration

*Radio.* Radio is very effective in reaching select markets, such as local markets and the teenage market. Radio commercials serve as reminders, with high frequency and repetition. The decision to select radio would be based on the following:

> Target market is selective:
> (a) local market
> (b) teenage market
> Product is a summertime product
> Information sought is low
> Product is low involvement
> Product requires repetition and advertising serves as a reminder through high frequency

The underlying logic of a media selection decision is not to simply reach prospects or target groups. The idea is to reach them efficiently, or at a relatively low unit cost. One commonly used measure of efficiency is the cost per thousand calculation referred to as CPM. It shows the cost of a thousand members of each audience figured at cost $\times$ 1,000/audience. When advertising carriers are compared on this yardstick, all other things being equal, those with the lowest CPMs are judged most efficient.

The above section provides a general overview of the strengths and characteristics of the four major media types used in this study.

**FIGURE 19-4** *(continued)*

as well as in terms of their effectiveness in delivering creative messages appropriate to the product and target customer involved.

**Product.**    As shown in Fig. 19-5, product characteristics can initially be defined in terms of the type of product, such as refrigerators and computer-related products or consumer and industrial products.    They may also be defined in terms of their intended uses and users, such as products made for children.

The characteristics of products and product groups can be identified, covering such factors as quality and price level, brand and packaging, level of technological sophistication, and the like.    Inferred product concepts, such as image, degree of involvement, psychological benefits and appeals, and the like, also need definition. These product concepts might include "high involvement" or "functional."

**Consumer.**    As shown in Fig. 19-5, the potential buyer (target market) can be initially defined in factual demographic terms, such as age, income, education, occupation, sex, location, household, and the like.    These can usually be grouped in terms of categories of consumers, such as "middle-income married couples with no children" or "young, affluent, single, upwardly mobile professionals."    In addition, inferences about the buying habits, motivation, interests, life-style, goals, and other more conceptual customer factors that might affect the buying decision need to be defined.

**Media selection decisions.**    The media mix decision involves finding effective and efficient combinations of these three factors.    A common way to do so is to match a product's customer profile with the media's audience profile or its "reach." For example, television is a very strong media for reaching the total population, and is effective for low-involvement, standard, functional products.    Some magazines can be more effective for reaching more educated, higher income audiences and for selling products requiring more informed buying decisions and so the communication of more product information.

The media at other times may be chosen because of image identification, editorial orientation, or editorial coverage.    This happens where intangibles, such as image, prestige, and quality associations will affect a buying decision.

The product under study can also affect the media selection decision.    This sometimes occurs where the product (for example, skis) can be matched with the editorial content of a publication.    Or it can occur where the complexity of the product requires substantial information conveyance.

In addition to the effectiveness of media environment in delivering advertising messages, the media decision will also be affected by cost or efficiency considerations. Media realistically deliver varying amounts of useful target readers for any single product.    The total cost of a media buy has to be evaluated in light of the percentage of the total audience useful to a particular product advertiser as well as in light of the power of the media under consideration to involve and move their audience.

Very often no single factor dominates in making the selection decision.    Instead the decision is based on a combination of factors and considerable judgment is involved.    For these reasons knowledge-based systems technology appears to have many

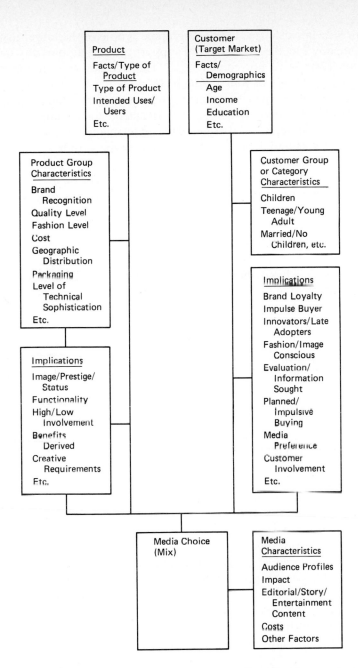

**FIGURE 19-5  Media selection process—more detailed view.**

potential applications in the media selection and marketing strategy area.  Considerable work is now being done on developing such applications.

The media selection decision can vary considerably by audience, media, product, company, and market conditions.  Because of the vast array of different media strategy decisions possible, the focus of the study was limited during the initial prototyping phase to four media—radio, television, newspapers, and magazines.  It was assumed that the product is already in existence, the demographic profile of the target market is known, and the company's media budget could support the selection of any media type. For this reason costs were not considered. The decision was limited to a strategy decision involving the mix of four media to be used.

Although limiting the prototype system in this way created the danger that the knowledge-based system's first prototype might be trivialized somewhat, such simplification was a necessary first step toward organizing and testing the system's concept and structure. Also it was essential to developing a prototype within a reasonably short period of time.

Later phases of the study were designed to expand the focus of the study and develop more comprehensive and sophisticated expert knowledge-based systems.

## STUDYING THE SITUATION TO BE PROTOTYPED

The product and customer data bases shown in Fig. 19-5 and described in more detail in Figs. 19-6 and 19-7, can serve many decision-making purposes. They can be used, for example, to make decisions about what customers might be the best prospects for existing products. A mail-order marketing company makes such decisions when it reviews which mailing lists to use to promote their products. Such data bases can also be used to make decisions about whether products are appropriate for designated target markets, and whether and how they might be better designed or configured to improve chances of success. In addition, media selection decisions can make use of these data bases in a variety of ways.

Because of the many factors and subjective judgments involved, there is not total agreement on how media decisions are made—the science of media selection is still developing. Even though there are these variations, however, there are many competent experts who accomplish the selection well. There is also sufficient agreement on some very good fundamental approaches to enable defining the processes involved and developing prototype knowledge-based systems replicating those processes.

The following describes the way a representative group of media experts might go about making media selection decisions, within the limited situation described above—four media choices, product in existence and definable, and demographic profile of target market known. Since the focus of this study is on the strategic aspects of the decision, costs are not considered during this initial study phase.

In addition, because of the wide range of media decisions and because of their complexity, the focus of the study was further limited to the following nine influencing factors selected from the many shown in Figs. 19-6 and 19-7:

| PRODUCT DATA BASE | CUSTOMER DATA BASE |
|---|---|
| Product type | Customer type |
| Product involvement | Customer media preference |
| Target market | Customer buying decision |
| Geographic reach | |

The last two influencing factors were *special requirements* and *specific advertising requirements*.

Media decisions do not always involve the same influencing factors. The specific combination of product and customer variables within the situation under study determine which influencing factors will affect that specific media decision. For example, customer media preference may be used as a factor to determine appropriate media if a product is a specialty item. However, if the product under study is a shopping goods item, then media preference may not be considered as important in making the media decision.

The wide range of product and customer situations encountered makes it necessary to include a large number of influencing factors in the media decision model in Fig. 19-8. By including a broad range of these factors, the model is applicable in a wider variety of situations and is a more accurate representation of how experts might make these decisions.

The structured decision diagram in Fig. 19-8 of the limited decision situation under study is based on the decision situation analysis described in these sections. The following sections discuss the underlying situational basis for this model.

## Product Data Base

The decision situation under study here is limited to four categories of consumer products:

- Convenience
- Impulsive
- Shopping
- Specialty

The following are the relevant factors selected from the product data base shown in Fig. 19-6 that are used in the situation under study.

**Product type.** Product type can be defined by five key influencing variables:

- Product involvement
- Target market
- Product decision making
- Geographic distribution
- Brand loyalty

These factors are in turn inferred from and influenced by many other factors.

**Product involvement.** This can be inferred from two factors: *product information required* and *performance risk*. The amount of product information required to make a purchase is inferred from the degree of explanation needed to make the

| Type of Product: | Impulsive Goods | Type of Product: | Shopping Goods |
|---|---|---|---|
| Brief Description: | Goods bought without planning | Brief Description: | Items that are subject to price and style comparisons |
| Examples: | Toys, inexpensive clothing, and food | Examples: Two types of Shopping Goods: | Fashion clothes, television sets |
| | | Heterogeneous | Customers compare style and quality for suitability with price relatively unimportant Example: high-priced clothes |
| | | Homogeneous | Customer comparisons of competing merchandise is limited to price Example: television set |

**Product Characteristics:**

| | | Product Characteristics: | |
|---|---|---|---|
| Brand Loyalty: | Brand loyalty is low | Brand Loyalty: | Brand loyalty is low |
| Product Info.: | Low information | Product Info.: | Requires much shopping time and information search |
| Quality Level: | Low | | |
| Distribution: | Wide Geographic Distribution/Mass merchandisers | Distribution: | Specialty/Mass Merchandisers |
| Performance Risk: | Low | Performance Risk: | High/Medium |
| Price: | Generally low-priced items | Price: | Medium/High-priced items |

**Implications:**

| | | Implications: | |
|---|---|---|---|
| Involvement = | Low-involvement product | Involvement = | High-Involvement Products |
| Benefit Sought = | Convenience | Benefit Sought = | a) Fashion/Style & Prestige/Status = Heterogeneous goods b) Economy or Fashion/Style = Homogeneous goods |
| Product Info. Required = | Low info. search | Product Info. Required = | High |
| Advertising Requirements = | Short duration messages, emphasizing a few key points, visual and sound components are important | Creative Requirements = | Media to be used as a shopping medium to compare prices and product offerings |
| Media Implications = | Requires massive advertising, large media budget | | |
| Target Market = | General | Target Market = | Selective/General |

*(continued)*

**FIGURE 19-6  Selected product data base—consumer goods.**

| Type of Product: | Convenience Goods | Type of Product: | Specialty Goods |
|---|---|---|---|
| Brief Description: | Nondurable, quickly used up, and frequently purchased | Brief Description: | Goods for which a customer is willing to make a special purchasing effort |
| Examples: | Cigarettes, candy, magazines | Examples: | Gourmet foods, Rolls Royce |

| Product Characteristics: | | Product Characteristics: | |
|---|---|---|---|
| Brand Loyalty:<br>Product Info.: | Brand loyalty is high<br>Goods bought with a minimum amount of shopping effort, low-information search | Brand Loyalty:<br>Product Info.: | Brand loyalty is high<br>Product information required is high but customers do not generally compare brands |
| Distribution: | Wide Geographic Distribution/Mass merchandisers | Distribution: | High image retail outlets/Specialty stores |
| Performance Risk:<br>Price: | Low<br>Generally low-priced items | Performance Risk:<br>Price: | High<br>High price but customer is usually relatively disinterested in price |

| Implications: | | Implications: | |
|---|---|---|---|
| Involvement = | Low-involvement product | Involvement = | High-involvement product |
| Benefit Sought =<br>Product Info.<br>Required =<br>Advertising<br>Requirements = | Convenience<br><br>Low<br>Promotion is aimed at brand identification packaging is important, to differentiate product through advertising. Short duration messages, focusing on a few key points. | Benefit Sought =<br>Product Info.<br>Required =<br>Advertising<br>Requirements = | Prestige/fashion<br><br>High<br>Selling image and prestige to a market, reinforcing brand name. May need national campaign to reinforce brand name, but use local advertising to inform the public where products can be purchased.<br>Editorial content geared toward an upscale market would be a good place to advertise |
| Media Implications = | Convenience goods require massive selling and large advertising budgets | | |
| Target Market = | Broad/General | Target Market = | Selective |

**FIGURE 19-6** *(continued)*

| Customer Category | Customer Category | Customer Category |
|---|---|---|
| Family Life cycle = teenager/young adult | Family Life cycle = young/single | Family Life cycle = married no children |

**Fact/Demographics**

| | | | | | | |
|---|---|---|---|---|---|---|
| Age: | 12–17 | Age: | 25–34 | Age: | 25–34 |
| Income: | | Income: | $21,000–49,000 | Income: | $50,000 or more |
| Education: | high school | Education: | college grad | Education: | college or higher |
| Sex: | M/F | Sex: | M/F | Sex: | M/F (household) |
| Social Status: | | Social Status: | upper middle | Social Status: | upper middle |

**Implied Customer Characteristics**

| | | |
|---|---|---|
| flexible to change | socially oriented | affluent (dual income) |
| brand switchers | fashion opinion leaders | high purchase rate of durables |
| generally buy impulsively | well educated | fashion/style conscious |
| shop in mass merchandisers | appreciate product quality | well educated |
| | seek product information/evaluate brands | career-oriented |
| | shop in specialty/department stores | |
| media habits = radio, magazine | media habits = read magazines more than watch television | media habits = read magazines more than watch television |
| innovators | innovators | innovators |
| other directed | inner directed | inner directed |
| degree of brand loyalty = low impulsive buying habits | brand loyalty = medium/low | brand loyalty = medium |
| dist. outlets frequently used = mass merchandisers | planned buying habits | planned buying habits |
| benefit sought = fashion/style | dist. outlets frequently used = dept./specialty stores | dist. outlets frequently used = dept./specialty stores |
| buyer = irrational buyer | benefit sought = fashion/style | benefit sought = status/prestige |
| | buyer = rational | buyer = rational |

*(continued)*

**FIGURE 19-7   Selected customer data base—prototype situation.**

purchase.   Performance risk is inferred from two variables: product price and product quality.   In general, high-priced, high quality products are high performance risk items, with the reverse being true of low-quality, low-priced items.

In addition to its impact on determining product type, as seen in Fig. 19-8, product involvement is also an important direct influencing factor in the media selection decision.   This is because specific media types (such as broadcast media) are better suited for low-involvement products, while others (such as print media) are better suited for high-involvement products.

**Target market.**   For purposes of this initial phase of the study the target market or audience for a product is classified as either selective or general.   It can be inferred from three factors:

□ Product involvement

| Customer Category | Customer Category |
|---|---|
| Family Life cycle = married/with children | Family Life cycle = elderly |

| Fact/Demographics | | Fact/Demographics | |
|---|---|---|---|
| Age: | 35–44 | Age: | over 65 |
| Income: | $20,000 or less | Income: | $20,000 or less |
| Education: | high school grad | Education: | high school grad |
| Sex: | M/F (household) | Sex: | M/F (household) |
| Social Status: | upper lower class | Social Status: | lower middle |

Implied Customer Characteristics

working class/wage earners

generally do not search for product info.
buy standard well-known products
tend to buy lower quality products

media habits = television is an important media for this group

late adopters
other directed
brand loyalty = high
impulsive buying habits

dist. outlets frequently used = discount stores or mass/merch.
buyer = irrational

Implied Customer Characteristics

group will pay higher prices to receive service
seek product information

tend to shop in specialty stores
flexibility to change is low
tend to be brand loyal
media habits = television is important

late adopters
other directed
rational buyers
information search is high/low (high services, low/products)
dist. outlets frequently used = specialty stores
buyer = rational

**FIGURE 19-7** *(continued)*

⊓ Distribution outlets
⊔ Benefit sought

Information about *benefits sought* and *distribution outlets* is determined from information available about the product and customer. *Product involvement* determination was discussed earlier.

The inference about target audience can be drawn in the following way. High-involvement products, which provide a benefit of status and prestige or fashion and style and are distributed to speciality or department stores, generally have a selective market. Low-involvement items offering convenience or economy are geared toward a more general market. These products are generally distributed through chain stores and mass merchandisers.

In addition to its impact on determining product type, the target market can also affect the media decision directly, because certain media have the capability of reaching general audiences, while other media are capable of reaching selective audiences.

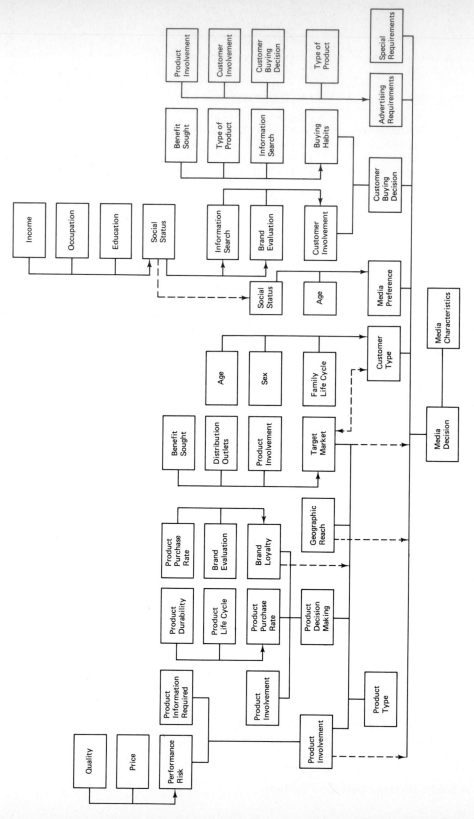

**FIGURE 19-8  Critical factors affecting media decisions.**

**Product decision making.**  This variable involves determining if a product requires a complex or a limited decision-making process or is simply bought out of habit.  Inferences about this factor are drawn from *product purchase rate*, *brand loyalty*, and *product involvement*.

Product purchase rate is derived from information about whether the product is durable or nondurable.  Durable products tend to be bought less frequently, for example, a television.  Nondurable products are generally high-turnover, low-margin items and are quickly used up and so are frequently purchased, for example, packaged food products.  Durability, then, can be determined by the physical characteristics of the product and the purchase cycle and frequency.

Brand loyalty is inferred from two factors: *product purchase rate* and *brand evaluation*.  Products that are purchased frequently provide the opportunity for a brand loyal relationship to develop.  If products are frequently purchased, repeat purchasing of the same brand is likely and brand evaluation tends to be low; therefore, brand loyalty tends to be high.  If the purchase rate is infrequent, brand loyalty is unlikely to occur, because where product purchases are at longer time intervals new preferences and choices are likely to occur between purchases.  With high-involvement items, where much evaluation occurs and more information searching is done, brand loyalty also tends to be lower.

The product decision-making factor is inferred or determined from product purchase rate, brand loyalty, and product involvement in the following way:

- When product is high involvement, purchase rate is infrequent, and brand loyalty is low decision making is usually inferred to be complex.
- When product is low involvement, purchase rate is frequent, and brand loyalty is high decision making is inferred to be minimal and products usually bought out of habit.
- When product involvement is low and the purchase rate infrequent, decision making tends to be limited.


**Geographic reach.**  Geographic reach comes from information known about the product and its market.  For purposes of this study it can be categorized as national, regional, or local.  Sometimes, although not always, like so many of the other influencing factors discussed in this chapter and included in the decision diagram, geographic factors will have a major direct impact on a media decision.  For example, such situations might involve both select and local appeal products, piecemeal region-by-region introduction of new products, and coordination with specific sales-support activities.

All these analyses of product involvement, target market, product decision making, geographic distribution, and brand loyalty can be used to infer the overall product type in various ways.

- *Convenience goods* are low-involvement products with a general target audience.  Decision making is usually minimal, products are generally bought out of habit, and brand loyalty is high.

□ *Impulsive goods* are low-involvement products with a general target audience. Decision making is limited and brand loyalty is low.

□ *Shopping goods* are generally high-involvement items with a selective or a general market. Decision making is complex and brand loyalty is low.

□ *Specialty goods* are high-involvement items with a selective audience. Decision making is complex and brand loyalty is high.

Product type affects every media decision. It can influence the decision directly, as for example when advertising skis in a ski magazine, and indirectly through an analysis of a product's advertising requirements.

## The Customer Data Base

The following are the relevant factors selected from the customer data base shown in Fig. 19-7 that are used in the decision situation study.

**Customer type.** Customer type is a factor directly inferred from the customer demographic characteristics, such as family life cycle and age. The customer types used in the limited situation under study in this chapter include: teenager or young adult, young and single, married with no children, married with children, and elderly. The profiles of each of these customer types is shown in Fig. 19-7. Similar, but much more specific, subgroup data bases have been developed for forty such customer subgroups.

Customer type can have an impact on media choice, since some (but not all) customer types (or groups) are known to use certain media more. For example, teenagers frequently listen to radio.

**Media preference.** Media preference can, for example, be determined by *age* and, in some instance, by *social status*. Social status is inferred from the customer demographic information: education, occupation, and income. Social status can be generally categorized for purposes of this initial prototype study as upper, middle, and lower.

Media preference, like other key factors listed in Fig. 19-7, is critical in only some situations. For example, media preference is significant with some specialty products aimed at select audiences. In contrast customer media preference is not as critical a factor with low-involvement, mass-marketed products, since the dominant influencing factors there are often geographic and total population penetration.

The varying impact of different influencing factors, such as media preference and social status, on the media selection decision is one reason a large data base is used.

**Customer buying decision.** For purposes of this study, the customer buying decision is classified as either rational or irrational. The customer buying decision is influenced by *customer involvement* and *customer buying habits*.

Customer buying habits may vary, depending on the particular type of product and benefit sought and on the degree of information search. They can be classified as planned or impulsive.

Customer involvement, which for purposes of this study is classified as either active or passive, can be measured by both information search and brand evaluation characteristics of the target consumer group, both of which are in turn influenced by social status. For instance, upper- and middle-class consumers tend to be information seekers and brand evaluators, with the reverse being true of the lower-class consumer.

When consumer involvement is active and buying habits are planned, the buying decision tends to be rational. When consumer involvement is passive and buying habits are impulsive, then the buying decision tends to be irrational.

The customer buying decision is one of the main factors considered in determining the media selection. For example, rational consumers tend to be information seekers, and so they require media that can deliver information in detail. On the other hand, irrational consumers are low-information seekers, and so require media that can help create awareness and stimulate purchasing behavior when trying to reach that audience.

As seen from these discussions, a considerable amount of inferencing is involved in media decisions. For this reason there will be exceptions and variations, depending on both the situation and the expert involved. For example, high-income and educated customers will, in some instances, make the final decision impulsively (fashion and fads in clothing, for example). These variations are recognized and incorporated into later versions of the system. The larger data bases enable such extensions and enhancements.

For prototype purposes, however, some limitations and simplifications were needed. This was necessary in order to test the concept and structure of knowledge-based systems for market planning before developing larger, more complex systems.

## Advertising Requirements

Advertising requirements are determined by specific product and customer advertising characteristics. These requirements can be classified in terms of

- *Audiovisual presentation*—Audiovisual components enable advertisements to demonstrate products through "slice of life" approaches. This involves elements such as music, characters, and scenery.
- *Shopping medium*—Some products require a medium that can be used as a shopping guide to compare product offerings and price. Some products also frequently require the use of coupons.
- *Convey information and detail.*—Some products require information or an explanation of how the product works. Advertisers may also want to highlight special features or characteristics that convey or show the product's benefits.
- *Create awareness.*—Some products may be highly competitive or price sensitive and use advertising as a means of differentiating product and creating awareness of brands. This requirement is usually necessary for products that are homogeneous in nature.
- *High repetition, short messages.*—Some products require frequent messages,

emphasizing a few key points. This is done to ensure brand familiarity by keeping the product name in front of the consumer.

Product advertising requirements can be inferred from the *type of product* and *product involvement*. Low-involvement products, with a high incidence of habitual purchasing, such as convenience goods and impulse goods, are more likely to use advertising as a reminder. In such cases frequent advertising is important. Advertising for low-involvement products requires creating awareness and familiarity through repetition. Nonmessage elements, such as music, characters, and scenery are important in stimulating purchasing behavior. Emphasis is placed on a few key points. Low-involvement products tend to lend themselves to broadcasting media for an audiovisual presentation. On occasion convenience goods may also require the use of a shopping medium, such as newspapers, if the product requires use of coupons.

High-involvement products, such as speciality or shopping goods, are characterized by complex decision making and are more likely to use advertising selectively to convey information and detail to specific audiences. These products therefore require a medium that has the ability to convey information and detail. Print media are better suited for high-involvement products, because the pace of exposure is within the reader's control and the reader has the opportunity to reflect on the advertisement. The content of the message is the key for high-involvement items.

Shopping goods, which are defined as product compared for style, quality, and price, also lend themselves to use of a shopping medium. This medium provides the opportunity to make price and quality comparisons. Specialty goods require a medium that has the ability to reach a selective market. Magazines provide this capability.

One newer medium, TV shopping channels, is capable of providing close to the same message content as newspapers. Local TV, when longer commercials are used in special time slots, sometimes also serves the same function. These are exceptions to the way TV is normally used. Although such exceptions are recognized, they are not included in the initial prototype system.

Customer advertising requirements are influenced by the *customer buying decision* and *customer involvement*. For example, when consumer involvement is active, customers are information seekers and processors. These consumers compare brands to see which provides the more benefits and buy based on multi-attribute comparisons of brands. The media selected therefore should enable advertisements to convey information and detail to these rational buyers.

On the other hand when consumer involvement is passive, consumers learn information at random. Consumers buy first and evaluate later. The job of the media selected is to help advertising to create awareness and familiarity.

## Special Requirements

Special requirements are unusual customer and product factors that override recommendations that would normally be made. Some of these are

     □ *Direct mail merchandise.* Merchandise sold exclusively through direct mail (direct response) ads would be limited to newspapers and/or magazines, or to longer, very selective TV spots.

- □ *Shopping channel.* Television is not generally considered a good shopping medium. However, with the growth of cable television, shopping channels have been started that enable customers to shop in the convenience of their own home. Shopping channels are changing the way television normally is used.
- □ *Seasonal products.* If products are seasonal, for example a summertime product, radio may be used as a high percentage of the advertising budget, since radio provides a strong audience for summertime exposure.
- □ *New products.* These may require a broader than normal media mix in order to create awareness and acceptance of new products.

## A Typical Scenario

The following is a very abbreviated version of how one media planner dealt with a fairly typical advertising media selection situation. The scenario description has been restructured and condensed considerably to highlight its relationship to the decision situation model given in Fig. 19-8.

This sample situation involves the automobile industry. The planner had to decide which type of media would be most appropriate to promote a sports car. The situation was analyzed as follows.

After analyzing product involvement, target market, product decision making, brand loyalty, and geographic distribution, the *product type* was determined to be a shopping good. *Product involvement* was determined to be high, because performance risk (high quality, high-priced product) and product information required were high. The *target market* for this automobile was defined as selective, after examining product involvement (high), distribution outlets (select auto dealerships), and benefits sought (style and prestige). Product decision making was reasoned to be complex in this particular situation, because of the purchase rate (infrequent), product involvement (high), and brand loyalty (low). *Geographic distribution* was national. Based on this analysis, the particular sports automobile under study was determined to be a high-involvement shopping type product.

The product was designed for specific *customer types*, young single consumers and young married couples without children. This customer group is defined as fairly affluent, well educated, and professionally employed. From this information, social status was determined to be upper- or middle-class.

*Media preference* was considered, because this particular consumer market has a generally high magazine readership profile. Advertisements could effectively be placed in magazines that catered to the young relatively affluent professional, if this media was also appropriate for the product under study.

Both brand evaluation and information search were generally high, because fairly well-educated, well-off customers are more likely to be information seekers. High information search and brand evaluation indicated that the customer would likely be actively involved in making the purchase. Customer buying habits were determined to be planned, because information search was high, customer benefits sought was prestige and style, and type of product was a shopping good. The *customer buying decision* was, therefore, determined to be rational, because customer involvement was active and buying habits were planned.

*Advertising requirements* were to convey information and detail. The product required a high information level to explain the automobile's qualities and benefits. The type of consumer that this automobile was targeted toward are information seekers, and require a medium that can satisfy their need for explanation and knowledge of products. Although television is not a medium that is frequently used by this group, the expert felt that this product required some visual demonstration to highlight the qualities, benefits, and performance standards of the product, and to create awareness for the new product. Selective position of commercials to tie in with editorial programming of interest to this market could, therefore, provide effective advertising exposure.

Advertising in magazines was selected as 75 percent of the advertising budget, because it was felt that magazines could best convey information and detail to satisfy customer buying decision and product requirements. Also magazines have the ability to reach a selective target market and customer type, which for this particular case was necessary. Select magazines would also reinforce the quality image of the product. Targeted, selective television was allocated 25 percent of the advertising budget, because the product was new and also required demonstration to visually show the performance features of the automobile. In addition, the market was national and TV covers a national market.

The above description is probably more detailed than required by the level of decision made, *type of media*. Such an analysis is, however, necessary to understand the decision process involved, since its application to more complex situations is not so simple. There is clearly some overlapping and reconfirmation in the process, and this can create complexities as the scope of the decision expands.

In practice the process described here and in Fig. 19-8 is in fact a simplification of the actual process involved in evaluating customer and product characteristics when selecting an appropriate media mix. This simplification was necessary, however, in order to develop and test the basic concept and structure of the media selection decision process.

The prototype system described in the following section attempts to replicate the basic media selection decision process analyzed and modelled in this section.


## DOCUMENTING THE PROTOTYPE SYSTEM

The following areas are covered in this section:

- □ System proposal
- □ Description of the system including
- □ Dependency diagram
- □ Decision chart
- □ Designing and constructing the knowledge base

## System Proposal

The general objective of this project is to develop a knowledge-based system to assist media selection decisions. This system is intended to be used by media planners in consumer product companies. In its final form it should cover a wide range of decision situations (product, customer, and media) and be able to make specific media recommendations. It should be of benefit to both experienced and beginning media planners, when searching for how to invest advertising dollars in those media that more effectively and efficiently match the product and customer requirements with media characteristics and audience.

The first phase of this project is limited to a small system for selecting among four media types. This initial prototype phase is designed to help test and build the structure and concept of much larger system. The system's critical data base core will enable substantial expansion of the system within the original design structure.

The knowledge sources to be used in the development of this system will include interviews with media planning experts; books and articles on consumer behavior, marketing planning, strategy development, and media planning and selection; and the actual work experience of the system developers.

## Description of the System

**System overview and objective.** The initial prototype system is designed to be used by individuals involved in selecting media to be used in advertising consumer products. Since this initial system focuses on strategy decisions, costs and cost efficiency are not considered.

This system is a data base oriented system, with information grouped in two main data bases: the customer data base, and the product data base. The prototype system asks the user a limited number of questions about customer and product and then uses if-then rules to reason about information given by the user in order to reach its recommendations.

**Recommendations to be made by the system.** The initial prototype system is limited to recommending one of, or some combination of, four media types—newspaper, magazines, television, and radio.

**Nature of user interface, including a typical user dialogue.** The typical user dialogue covers two key knowledge areas.

□ *Customer* demographic information is obtained by asking the user such questions as "What is the education level of the target customer for the product under study [high is college or beyond, medium is some college or technical training, low is grade school or less, and any]?" and "What benefits are sought by the customer when considering purchasing the product under study [economy, convenience, prestige-status, fashion-style]?"

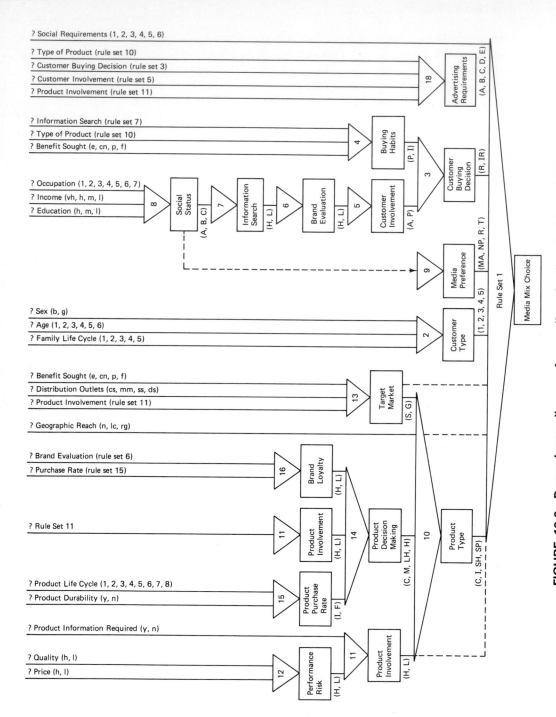

**FIGURE 19-9 Dependency diagram for media selection decision—initial prototype.**

440

Family Life Cycle:

1 = Teenager
2 = Young/Single
3 = Married/No Children
4 = Married With
    Children
5 = Elderly

Sex:

B = Male
G = Female

Income:

Low = Under $20,000
Medium = $21,000–
    49,000
High = Over $50,000
Very High = Over
    $100,000

Age:

1 = 12–17
2 = 18–24
3 = 25–34
4 = 35–44
5 = 45–54
6 = Over 65

Occupation:

1 = Professional
2 = White Collar
    (Managers)
3 = Small Business
    Owners
4 = High-Paid Blue Collar
    Workers
5 = Low-Paid Blue Collar
    Workers
6 = Unskilled Workers
7 = Student
8 = Housewife
9 = Retired

Education:

High = College Graduate
    or Beyond
Medium = Some College
    or Technical
    Training
Low = Grade School or
    High School
    Graduate

Social Status:

A = Upper
B = Middle
C = Lower

Customer Involvement:

AC = Active
  P = Passive

Buying Habits:

PL = Planned
IM = Impulsive

Buying Decision:

 R = Rational
IR = Irrational

Benefit Sought:

  E = Economy
CN = Convenience
  P = Prestige/Status
  F = Fashion/Style

Product Type:

  C = Convenience Good
  I = Impulsive Good
SH = Shopping Good
SP = Specialty Good

Product Decision Making:

CM = Complex
LM = Limited
HB = Habit

Product Purchase Rate:

  F = Frequent
IF = Infrequent

Product Durability:

  D = Durable
ND = Nondurable

Target Market:

G = General
S = Selective

Geographic Distribution:

  N = National
RG = Regional
LC = Local

Distribution Outlets:

CS = Chain Stores
MM = Mass Merchandisers
DS = Department Store
SS = Speciality Store

Advertising Requirements:

A = Audio/Visual
    Presentation
B = Convey Information
    and Detail
C = Shopping Medium
D = Create Awareness
E = Repetition/Short
    Messages

Special Requirements:

2 = Direct Mail Merchandise
3 = Shopping Channel
4 = Product is Banned from
    Broadcasting Media
5 = Seasonal Product
6 = New Product

Product Life Cycle

1 = Week
2 = Month
3 = Three Months
4 = Six Months
5 = 1 Year
6 = 2 Years
7 = 3–5 Years
8 = 10 Years

Y = Yes
N = No

H = High
L = Low

**FIGURE 19-9** *(continued)* **Codes for the dependency diagram.**

☐ *Product* information is obtained from asking the user such questions as "What is the life-cycle of the product under study [week, month, six months, one year, two years, over two years?]" and "What outlets are used to distribute the product under study [mass-merchandisers, specialty stores, department stores, all types]?"

**Description of the knowledge structure and reasoning process.** The recommendations made by the prototype system are based on nine critical customer, product, and other factors. The values for these factors are in turn inferred from other influencing factors. *Customer type* is determined by age, sex, and family life cycle, *media preference* by age and social status, and *customer buying decision* by customer involvement and buying habits.

*Product type* is influenced by such factors as product involvement, target market, and product decision making, *product involvement* by product risk and product information required, *target market* by product involvement, distribution outlets, and benefit sought, and *geographic reach* by product characteristics.

*Advertising requirements* are determined by customer involvement, customer buying decision, product type, and product involvement, and *Special requirements* are defined by the system user.

Additional levels of influencing factors are involved in the decisions as shown in the dependency diagram in Fig. 19-9. The values assigned all factors at all levels are given in the notes to Fig. 19-9.

As is evident from the interlocking patterns of the reasoning process, the system's rules draw many levels of inferences from the user's initial input information. This variety and flexibility of interrelationships reflects the actual decision processes of media experts.

Different products, customers, and media interact in different ways in different advertising situations. Not all factors affect each decision in the same way. Large data bases, interrelated by if-then rules to draw inferences and make decisions, provided the flexibility needed to expand the structure of the initial prototype system and enable it to handle an increasingly wider range of media selection decision situations. For example, in the sports automobile decision described earlier, detailed information about the customer in the data base can be used to specify the kinds of magazines or type of TV spots to use.

## Dependency Diagram

Figure 19-9 shows the dependency diagram for the media selection decision prototype system. It is a complete summary outline of all the questions, rules, knowledge segments and their interrelationships, values, and recommendations within the initial prototype system.

## Decision Charts

Figure 19-10 shows selections from several sample decision charts from the prototype system. There is a decision chart for every rule set in the system.

## Designing and Constructing the Knowledge Base

Rules and questions were developed from the situation study. They were based on the system developer's analysis of how an expert in media planning might actually go about making such decisions. A segment of the knowledge base is given in Fig. 19-11.

RULE SET 1: FINAL RULE SET MEDIA SELECTION

| IF: | RULE 1-1 | RULE 1-2 | RULE 1-3 | RULE 1-4 | RULE 1-5 |
|---|---|---|---|---|---|
| PRODUCT TYPE | C,I | C,I | SP | SH | SH |
| TARGET MARKET | S | G | S | G | S |
| PRODUCT INVOLVEMENT | L | L | H | L,H | H |
| GEOGRAPHIC REACH | LC,RG | N | RG,N | LC | N |
| CUSTOMER DEMOGRAPHIC TYPE | 1 | 2,3,4,5 | 2,3,4 | 2,3,4,5 | 2,3 |
| MEDIA PREFERENCE | RD | T | MA-NP | | MA |
| CUSTOMER BUYING DECISION | IR | IR | R | IR,R | R |
| ADVERTISING REQUIREMENTS | E | A,D | B | C | D,B |
| SPECIAL REQUIREMENTS | | | | | |
| THEN MEDIA = | | | | | |
| RADIO | 100% | | | | |
| TELEVISION | | 100% | | | 25% |
| MAGAZINE | | | 100% | | 75% |
| NEWSPAPER | | | | 100% | |

FIGURE 19-10   Sample decision charts for media selection decision—initial prototype.

## POSSIBLE EXTENSIONS AND ENHANCEMENTS OF THE PROTOTYPE SYSTEM

*Media recommendations* in the initial prototype system were limited to only four media types.   Recommendations in later versions of the system are designed to include

   □ More media types
   □ Different kinds of media within each media type

<u>Rules</u>

```
        /*  Rule Set 1:  Final Selection Decisions  */


Rule 1-1:
if   customer-type = 'teenager' and
     media-preference = 'radio' and
     buying-decision = 'irrational' and
     product-type = 'convenience' or
     product-type = 'impulsive' and
     target-market = 'selective' and
     product-involvement = 'low' and
     geographic-reach = 'local' or
     geographic-reach = 'regional' and
     advertising-requirements = 'repetition-short-duration-messages'
then media = 'radio'



        /*  Rule Set 3:  Customer Buying Decision  */


Rule 3-1:
if   customer-involvement = 'active' and
     buying-habits = 'planned'
then buying-decision = 'rational'

Rule 3-2:
if   customer-involvement = 'passive' and
     buying-habits = 'impulsive'
then buying-decision = 'rational'



        /*  Rule Set 4:  Customer Buying Habits  */


Rule 4-1:
if   benefit-sought = 'convenience' or
     benefit-sought = 'fashion-style' and
     product-type = 'convenience' or
     product-type = 'impulsive' and
     information-search = 'low'
then buying-habits = 'impulsive'



Rule 4-2:
if   benefit-sought = 'economy' or
     benefit-sought = 'prestige-status' or
     benefit-sought = 'fashion-style' and
     product-type = 'shopping' or
     product-type = 'specialty' and
     information-search = 'high' or
     information-search = 'low'
then buying-habits = 'planned'
```

*(continued)*

**FIGURE 19-11  Sample segment of knowledge base for media selection decision—initial prototype.**

```
question(age) = 'What is the age of the consumer?'
legalvals(age) = [12-17,18-24,25-34,35-44,45-54,over-65].

question(income) = 'What is the income of the consumer(very-high is
over $100,000, high is over $50,000, medium is $21-49,000, low is
under $20,000)?'
legalvals(income) = [very-high,high,medium,low].

question(primary-household-occupation) = 'What is the primary
   household occupation?'
legalvals(primary-household-occupation) = [professional,
   white-collar,small-business-owner,high-paid-blue-collar,low-paid-
   collar,unskilled-worker,retired].

question(education) = 'What is the education level of the consumer
   (high is college-graduate or post college, medium is some college
   or technical training, low is grade-school or high-school
   graduate)?'
legalvals(education) = [high,medium,low].

question(product-information) = 'What is the information or
   explanation level required of the product?'
legalvals(product-information) = [high,low].

question(distribution-outlets) - 'What are the distribution outlets
   used to distribute products?'
legalvals(distribution-outlets) = [chain-stores,mass-merchandisers,
   specialty-stores, department-stores].
```

**FIGURE 19-11** *(continued)*

□ Recommendations for specific magazines, newspapers, and radio and TV stations

The *customer data base* in later system versions is designed to cover forty customer demographic types. The *product data base* not only covers more products, but services as well.

In later versions of this system, the *product type* can be inferred by the system from product characteristics as a check on the user's input information.

Because there is a degree of uncertainty inherent in all inferences, later versions of the system included *certainty factors*.

Among the *new systems* under development using the data base structure of the prototype system are ones that

□ *Recommend appropriate customer prospects for products.* In this system a user inputs product information. The system then develops implications from the factual product information and based on them recommends good customer prospects for the product. This will prove useful in selecting mail order lists to promote products to.

□ *Recommend appropriate products for defined customer groups.* In this system a user inputs customer information and the system then recommend products likely to succeed when promoted to a specific customer group. This system will prove especially useful for developing product promotions to mail-order lists and lists of department store customers.

- □ *Recommend product changes (if any).* In this system the appropriateness for the target market is studied and changes needed to meet target requirements are specified.
- □ *Recommend whether or not to sell products to specific markets.* In this system the target market is studied to determine if a product should be introduced to a market.

## MULTIMODEL SYSTEM

Because of the use of data base information, these marketing strategy planning systems lend themselves to object or frame structures. Research was, therefore, done on the relative effectiveness and efficiency of using three system structures:

- □ Rule-based
- □ Data bases
- □ Object-oriented (frame-based)

The research suggests that integrated systems produce the best systems.

Data bases are used extensively, as shown in this chapter's discussion, in media decisions. Since the data bases are interrelated in making the decisions, many of the techniques of object-oriented systems that facilitate movement among the data bases, are useful. As also shown in this chapter, rule-based reasoning (heuristics) plays a key role in media and marketing planning decisions.

Tests so far indicate pure data-based systems are effective for smaller systems, rule-based systems for moderate size systems, and integrated object-oriented structures for the larger systems in the marketing planning and strategy development areas.

## REVIEW QUESTIONS

1. Complete the knowledge-based system (or any segment of the system) partially documented in this chapter and enter it into the expert system shell you have.

2. Develop a knowledge-based system for another area of media planning of your choosing.

3. Develop a knowledge-based system for another marketing planning area of your choosing.

4. Clearly, the situation models described in this chapter are much broader than most of those given earlier. Describe the ways in which this affects prototype knowledge-based system development.

5. Describe the ways in which the system described in this chapter differs from the ones described in the two preceding chapters, especially as regards the role of data bases and inferential reasoning.

6. If just the narrow problem media selection defined for prototype development were diagrammed, how would that condensed diagram compare to the larger one shown in Figure 19-8?

7. What three key knowledge areas affect the media selection decision? What is involved in the media mix decision?

8. What determines advertising requirements? List the five classifications described in this chapter.

## REFERENCES

Cohen, W. A., *Developing a Winning Marketing Plan*, New York: John Wiley and Sons, 1987.

David, B. E., *A Shoestring Approach to Profitable Advertising: A Handbook for Small Business*, 4th ed., Tucson, AZ: EJP Publishing, 1987.

Hayes, H., "How to Have More Fun Writing a Media Plan," *Marketing and Media Decisions*, vol. 21, December 1986.

"How Business Talks to Business—A Guide to Media Buying and Planning," *Marketing and Media Decisions*, vol. 21, June 1986.

Irving, J. H., "Creative Media—Creative What?" *Marketing and Media Decisions*, vol. 21, July 1986.

Kaatz, J., "Media Connections in a Changing Consumer Environment," *Journal of Advertising Research*, vol. 26, April-May 1986.

Link, G., "Impact of Fragmentation on Mass Media World Continues Unabatedly," *Television/Radio Age*, vol. 34, Sept. 1, 1986.

Rapp, S., and Collins, T. "Today's Media Market Offers Embarrassment of Riches," *Adweek's Marketing Week*, vol. 27, Nov. 10, 1986.

Roman, E., "Integrated Direct Marketing: Maximizing Media Mix," *Direct Marketing*, vol. 49, September 1986.

Rust, R. T., et al., "Estimating the Duplicated Audience of Media Vehicles in National Advertising," *Journal of Advertising*, vol. 15, no. 3, 1986.

Templeton, J. F., *Focus Groups: A Guide for Marketing & Advertising Professionals*, Chicago, IL: Probus Publishing, 1987.

Wolfson, L., "Media Cross Pollenization," *Marketing and Media Decisions*, vol. 22, March 1987.

# 20

# A Sales Quota Development System

This chapter describes the development of a knowledge-based system for determining sales quotas. The system provides assistance to sales managers in establishing sales quota for each salesperson in their territory. The discussion covers

- The situation under study: understanding the expert's domain
- Studying the situation to be prototyped
- Documenting the prototype system

The first section of this chapter describes the overall situation for which the system is being developed. The second section describes how an expert sales manager goes about making sales quota decisions in the specific situation under study for prototyping—a company manufacturing and distributing over-the-counter health products. The final section documents the prototype system.

## THE SITUATION UNDER STUDY: UNDERSTANDING THE EXPERT'S DOMAIN

The discussion in this section covers

- Selecting a decision area to work on
- Probing how the situation works and how decisions are made
- Narrowing the focus of the study

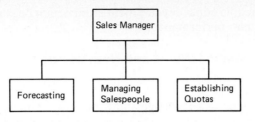

**FIGURE 20-1  Overview of sales management job.**

### Selecting a Decision Area to Work on

The general area under study, sales management, is outlined in Fig. 20-1.   A sales manager has many responsibilities, including forecasting demand (sales), managing the salespeople, and establishing quotas.

*Forecasting demand* involves such activities as estimating future company sales based upon historical trends, knowledge of present market and company conditions, experience, and estimates of future market trends.   These forecasts can cover both sales to the outlets that distribute a company's products and sales by the outlets to consumers.

*Managing salespeople* involves such activities as hiring and training the sales force, supporting the salespeople in their work, meeting with customers, establishing territories, and evaluating performance.

*Establishing sales quotas* involves studying a wide range of strategic and operational factors, including

- Past sales in the territory
- Company overall strategic, marketing, and advertising plans and objectives and plans for other sales activities, such as promotion discounts, increased sales training and incentives, and the like
- Competitive factors
- Local and national economic conditions
- Demographic trends
- Seasonal sales fluctuations

A sales manager studies anticipated changes in all these factors and weighs the importance of each to estimate potential future sales.   Based upon these estimates and other factors, quotas are established.   It is a time consuming, complicated process that relies heavily on the judgment, experience, and competency of the sales manager.

Quota development was selected as a topic because

- The task has to be repeated for every salesperson in every territory every year.
- The task is definable and manageable from a knowledge-based systems viewpoint.
- Quotas are judgmental in nature and require expertise to achieve fairness and reliability.

❑ Fair and reasonable quota development is important because it affects bonuses, commissions, and performance.

## Studying How the Situation Works and How Decisions Are Made

A sales manager uses general knowledge and experience, combined with information supplied by company records and outside research material, to establish new quotas. This information is formulated into six critical factors, as shown in Fig. 20-2. The following discusses these factors and their potential influence on sales quota decisions.

*Past sales of the territory* is the first factor used to establish a new sales quota base. The past sales record for the previous year is taken from company records and compared to the quota for last year to see both what last year's performance was and how it related to the quota set. The sales manager can do this by company, product, or territory.

*Company strategies, and advertising and other sales support*, especially important factors in quota establishment for consumer products, are determined by answering questions involving plans for new product additions (such as line extensions) and deletions, advertising expenditures, and other promotional activities scheduled for the coming year, as well as by considering the position of the product in its life cycle. For example, if a media blitz is scheduled for the coming year, this would likely be reflected in an increase in sales and, therefore, a larger quota.

*Competitive actions*, such as increased advertising expenditures and new product introductions, can affect market share, which in turn would have to be reflected in sales quotas. Competitive information is difficult to come by and so often requires judgments based on hearsay.

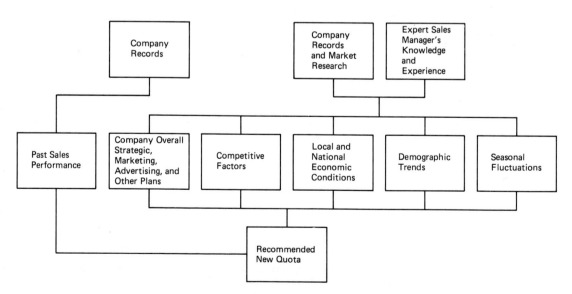

**FIGURE 20-2 Sales management quota-setting decisions—an overview.**

*Economic conditions* cover national, and local economies. Changes in economic conditions can affect consumer purchases. For example, when there are large layoffs in an area, consumers reduce their purchases of nonessential items. In these circumstances purchasers may change from a name brand to a generic one, even for necessities.

*Demographic conditions* can influence sales quotas in many ways. Population increases or decreases affect the number of people buying, changes in the average age of the population or its ethnic mix may influence buying habits, and changes in average available disposable income may affect the sales of the product. Although the impact of most of these changes is almost always long-term, some can on occasion affect year-to-year sales changes.

*Seasonality (fall, winter, spring, or summer)* is important for companies doing quarterly sales quota development for products whose sales are affected by seasonal changes.

In order to establish a new sales quota, sales managers must first establish a sales quota base. In the company under study the base for the quota is determined by adjusting last year's quotas in relation to the percentage that last year's actual sales were over- or underachieved. For example, when last year's actual sales are within 15 percent of last year's quota, then the new quota base for the coming year is made equal to last year's quota (if sales $\leq 1.15 \times$ quota, then last year's quota = base for new year quota). Where actual sales were more than 15 percent over quota, the new year's quota is adjusted upward proportionately.

Then a manager decides what effect each of the five other factors might have on the new quota base for the coming year. For example, if a company's overall strategy calls for increasing market penetration by reducing prices, quotas would be increased proportionately to reflect this.

The impact of individual factors may change depending upon the type of company, market, and product. In addition, the quota development process may vary in some ways with each company, product, and market situation. For this reason the focus of the study was narrowed, before starting prototype system development.

## Narrowing the Focus

The knowledge-based system described in this chapter was to be developed for a specific company, product, and territory. The following describes the specific situation and why it was chosen for study here.

**Type of company.** A large marketer of over-the-counter health care products was chosen both because it had a fairly typical sales operation and because of the availability of an expert familiar with such a company, its operations, and its strategies. All the necessary data and expert experience was, therefore, accessible.

**Type of product.** An oral health care product was chosen because it is a familiar product and is representative of a major segment of the consumer products market. One widely used product was selected in order to give focus to the study and provide a clear test of the concept and design of such a system.

**Type of territory.**   A large metropolitan sales territory was chosen for several reasons: it is a well defined territory, the data for it is readily available, and it provides a profile of all the major factors affecting the sales quota development and so will serve to test the concept and design of larger sales quota development knowledge-based systems.

## STUDYING THE SITUATION TO BE PROTOTYPED

The following section describes that specific situation in more detail.   This decision was chosen for prototype development because it is typical of many decisions made in this area and so provides a means of building a general model for the entire decision situation.

The quota-setting decision process at the company under study for the most part followed the general approach to sales quota development described in the earlier section of this chapter.   There were nonetheless variations arising from the specific company, product, and territory applications under study.

The specific product under study is a dental care product marketed by a producer-distributor of over-the-counter health care goods.   The prototype project involves developing sales quotas for salespersons selling this product in one of the company's larger territories.

Figure 20-3 gives a diagram of the situation under study.   The process described here is followed in developing sales quotas for each individual salesman.

The *past year's sales performance versus the past year's quota* is used by the sales manager to determine the base for next year's quota, using the formula: Last year's quota is increased by the amount that last year's sales exceeded 115 percent of last year's quota.   This new figure becomes the sales quota base for the coming year. This formula is described in more detail in the following section.

Upcoming overall and local *strategic* and *operational changes* in company product development, advertising, and promotion (including pricing) plans for oral health care products are studied.   The sales manager determines the importance and impact of their influence and incorporates this impact as a percentage change in the new quota base.

Determining the *competitive activity* and its impact on next year's sales depends even more on a sales manager's judgment, knowledge, and experience, because this information is often based on hearsay and partial knowledge.   Sales quotas may be significantly affected by this factor in some years and nominally in other years.

Anticipated *competitor* promotion, new product, and advertising plans are all influencing factors in this area.   The sales manager determines the importance and impact of their influence and incorporates this impact as a percentage change in the new quota base.

*Economic conditions*, although very important in some product situations, do not have a significant impact on the dental care product market.   For example, although mouthwash sales do best during times of economic booms, the decrease in sales in hard times is small.   Although small, however, the influence on the decision has to be considered.   The potential influence can be measured by projected or

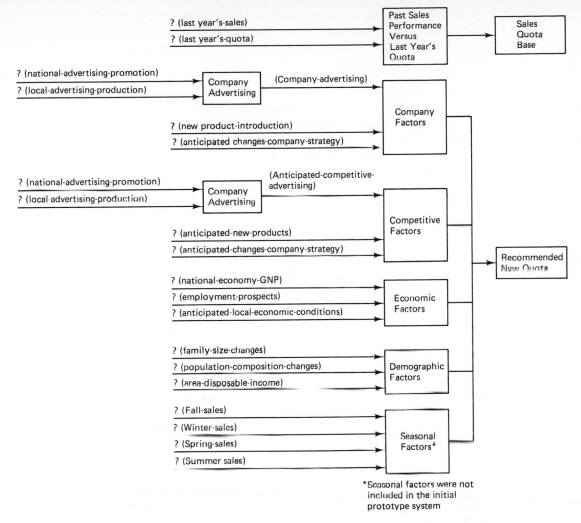

**FIGURE 20-3  Overview of the decision to be prototyped—sales management quota-setting decision.**

anticipated employment prospects and local and national economic conditions. The sales manager determines the importance and impact of their influence and incorporates this impact as a percentage change in the new quota base.

Although *demographic conditions* can affect sales quotas over the long run, they affected the situation under study only nominally. As a result the weight given demographic factors is slight in the situation under study. The sales manager determines the importance and impact of their influence and incorporates this impact as a percentage change in the new quota base.

*Seasonal fluctuations* (fall, winter, spring, and summer) have no impact on the decision under study since it involves annual sales quota development.

Recommendations are made by assigning *weights* and *values* to these critical factors. The *weights* are determined by the relative importance of the factor to the quota; for example, company strategy and competitive strategy would influence the quota heavily, while demographics have only a long-term effect on the quota and are assigned very light values.

These weights may vary by product, industry, and company. They are built into the initial prototype system described in the next section. Subsequent versions of the systems allow a user to input such weights to suit their own sales situations.

*Values* are then assigned each factor by a sales manager, according to the prevailing conditions in the situation under study. For example, the sales manager might learn that the company is planning a major advertising campaign for the coming year and would raise quotas proportionately. Next, the sales manager might hear the competition is also planning a major advertising campaign, which might cause the quota to be adjusted downward proportionately.

The final quota developed will be a balance of the *values* assigned each influencing factors, adjusted for the *weight* of importance of each.

The following is an example of how this process works in practice. When establishing the mouthwash sales quota base for his top salesman in the New York territory early in January 1988, the territory sales manager first obtained information on last year sales and quotas. He then determined if the actual sales exceeded the quota by more than 15 percent. It did. The salesman's sales in 1987 were $250,000 for the mouthwash and the quota was $200,000. The new *sales quota base* for the coming year was, therefore, set at $20,000 ($250,000 − [$200,000 × 1.15]) plus $200,000 (last year's sales quota).

The sales manager then considered the impact of the company's planned 5 percent increase in advertising and promotion in 1988, as well as of their not planning to introduce any new product line extensions in 1988. Several corporate policy changes were to be made, leading to increased sales force training. The sales manager estimated the cumulative effect of all these *company factors* on next year's sales as significant.

The sales manager next considered the impact of competitive actions. Based on a market study provided by corporate management and what he had heard about competitive plans, the sales manager concluded that major new product introductions or line extensions were not expected from the competition next year, nor were competition pricing policies expected to change. The competition was expected, however, to increase its national and local advertising somewhat. The manager estimated that the total of *competitive factors*, based on this analysis, would be no more than average.

As for local and national economic conditions, the manager anticipated the GNP would be rising strongly in 1988, based on what he had been reading in the *Wall Street Journal*. The employment prospects in his local area were expected to be equally strong, as were local economic conditions. The sales manager, therefore, estimated the total impact of *economic factors* as significant in 1988.

Few demographic changes had been occurring recently in the area, and seasonal variations did not affect the annual sales of the product.

He then adjusted the sales quota base for the importance of each factor. Company and competitive factors had a great impact on sales, but seasonal and demographic did not, in general. Since the most important factors were also the ones with the greatest change he looked at them more closely. In his opinion, the steps planned by the company were greater than those of the competition. As a result, he decided to increase the base sales quota by a medium amount of 5 percent to $231,000 ($220,000 × 1.05).

The prototype system described below replicates this sales manager's decision processes, with the following limitations:

- The system does not provide for quota establishment for products with no sales history or for sales people in a new territory.
- The system does not provide for reductions in the quota.

## DOCUMENTING THE PROTOTYPE SYSTEM

The discussion in this section covers

- System proposal
- Description of the prototype system
- Dependency diagrams
- Decision charts
- Designing and constructing the knowledge base

### System Proposal

The general objective of the project is to develop a sales quota-setting system. This initial phase, which is limited to an oral health care product and its sales quota-setting in one territory, is intended to help test and build the structure and concept for a much larger system, useful in all product areas throughout the company. The first system will be a prototype of the larger system.

There are several benefits to the system. It saves time and increases accuracy. In addition, it encourages greater consistency and so fairer treatment of all salespeople. Its more advanced versions also have direct access to computerized sales and quotas records by individual salespersons, which will save additional time.

The knowledge sources used to develop the prototype system include expert salespeople and expert sales managers.

### Description of the Prototype System

**System overview and objective.** The prototype system is designed to help users establish for each salesperson fair and reasonable sales quotas for a brand of mouthwash in a local sales territory. The system asks questions about individual past sales performance, changing demographics, economic conditions, seasonality, competition, and new product and company information, as shown in Fig. 20-3. The system uses if-then rules and backward chaining to reason about the information given by the user in order to reach its recommendations.

**Recommendations to be made by the system.**    Based upon the information given to the system by a user, it will recommend a percentage amount by which the sales quota based should be increased, by recommending a figure between zero and 8 percent.   The sales manager would then increase the sales quota base by a percentage equal to the figure recommended by the system.

**Nature of user interface, including a typical user dialogue.**    The typical user dialogue covers six key knowledge areas:

□ *The past sales performance.*   Information for determining this factor is obtained from company records.   Typical questions are "What was last year's sales for the salesperson under study?" and "By how much was last year's quotas exceeded?"

□ *The company objectives and strategies.*   The source of this information is the sales manager and company records.   Typical user questions might be "Are new products or sizes being added or deleted in the coming year and if so what is their expected impact on sales?" and "Are any promotional programs planned for the coming year and if so what is their expected impact on sales?"

□ *The competition.*   This information is obtained from the manager's knowledge of anticipated competitor activity in the area.   A question is "Estimate introduction of new products by the competition and their impact on your sales."

□ *The economic conditions.*   This information can be obtained from outside sources, such as newspapers and trade journals, or from company management.   A typical user question would be "What are local economic conditions expected to be next year?"

□ *The demographics of the target market area.*   This information can be obtained by outside records, such as census reports or relevant information provided by trade journals, or from company management.   A typical user question might be "Are any significant demographic changes, such as a major shift from families with children to young professional singles, occurring in your area, and if so, what is the expected impact on sales?"

□ *Seasonality.*   This information is obtained from past company records.   No questions about seasonality are asked in this prototype system because this factor does not apply to this product.

**Description of the knowledge structure and reasoning processes.**    The recommendations made by the system are based on five critical factors: past sales performance, company plans, competition plans, economic conditions, and demographic conditions.   These critical factors are in turn based on other influencing factors.

□ Past sales performance is based upon last year's performance by the salesperson under study.

□ Company objectives and advertising support is determined by studying planned product changes, deletions and additions, and by studying scheduled changes in local and national advertising, promotion, and overall strategy.

- Competitive factors are influenced by anticipated increases in local and national advertising expenditures, and changes in new product introductions and strategies by the competition.
- Economic conditions are influenced by increasing or decreasing employment levels and national and local economic trends.
- Demographic conditions are determined by changes occurring in average family size, disposable income, and overall family composition.
- Seasonal changes, which are determined from past sales records, were not included in this initial prototype system.

If-then rules are used to determine the values of each factor. The inference engine uses backward chaining. The values established for each of the five critical factors are based on the answers given to user questions, which are limited to: none (0), very weak (1), weak (2), average (3), strong (4), or very strong (5).

The answers to the questions (there are three questions in rules 3 to 7 and two questions in rules 1 and 2) are added together in rules 3 to 7 and averaged in rules 1 and 2. This gives a range of points for each of the four key factors (company, competition, economic, demographic) of zero to fifteen. These point totals are then weighted for their importance and translated into a percentage increase (or percentage decrease for competition) in the sales quota base.

For example, following the dependency diagram in Fig. 20-4, the sales manager might estimate employment prospects to be very strong, expected national economic growth to be average, and local economic conditions to be average. This would give a total of eleven points for economic factors. According to the table shown in Fig. 20-5, eleven points would be an above average rating.

The same is done for all influencing factors. Not all influencing factors are given equal weights, however, as is seen in Fig. 20-5. These weights are applied to each factor value. For example, the system would apply a percentage increase value of 2.4 percent to the eleven point value of the economic factor in the above example. If the point value for company factors is fourteen (5 percent), competition eight ($-3$ percent), and demographics six (0.2 percent), the total increase in the sales quota base would be 4.6 percent (2.4 percent + 5 percent $-$ 3 percent + 0.2 percent). Applying this percentage increase to the earlier sales quota base of $231,000 would give a new quota for the coming year of $241,626 ($231,000 $\times$ 1.046).

## Dependency Diagrams

Figure 20-4 shows the dependency diagrams for the sales quota knowledge-based system. It is a summary outline of the questions, rules, knowledge segments, and their interrelationship in creating new quotas.

## Decision Charts

Figure 20-6 shows a sample decision chart based on if-then rules from the knowledge-based system. There is a decision chart for every rule set in the system.

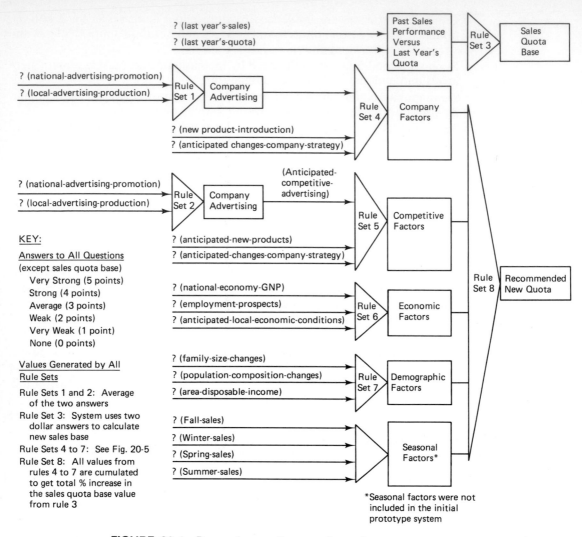

**FIGURE 20-4  Dependency diagram for sales management quota-setting decision—initial prototype.**

## Designing and Constructing the Knowledge Base

Rules and questions were developed from the situation study. They were based on the system developer's analysis of how sales managers actually go about making such decisions.

A segment of the prototype system's knowledge base is given in Fig. 20-7. The expert system shell used is M.1. As with the other systems discussed in this book, subsequent prototypes within the system were done on GURU.

Two very simple introductory and concluding panels were created for the system.

| | Weights for Company and Competitive Factors | Weights for Economic Factors | Weights for Demographic & Seasonal Factors |
|---|---|---|---|
| None (0 points) | 0 | 0 | 0 |
| Very little (1–3 points) | 1% | 2.1% | 0.01% |
| Somewhat (4–6 points) | 2% | 2.2% | 0.02% |
| Average (7–9 points) | 3% | 2.3% | 0.03% |
| Above average (10–12 points) | 4% | 2.4% | 0.04% |
| Significantly (13–15 points) | 5% | 2.5% | 0.05% |

**FIGURE 20-5   Relative weights given each key influencing factor.**

The if-then rules in the knowledge base in Fig. 20-7 match those specified in the decision chart shown in Fig. 20-6. They were written to reflect the relationships shown in the dependency diagram in Fig. 20-4. The rules use the values shown there and in the decision chart. The questions in the knowledge base (Fig. 20-7) are those indicated in the dependency diagram.

## ENHANCEMENTS AND EXTENSIONS OF THE SYSTEM

The reason a knowledge-based system was used instead of a conventional computer system was its flexibility. Influencing factors could be changed and added to, weights and values adjusted, and connections made to other software applications with relative ease. This enabled sales management to use the same basic system framework in a variety of different locations, and apply it to a variety of product situations, without technical computer assistance.

RULE SET 1

| RULE | 1-1 | 1-2 | 1-3 | 1-4 | 1-5 | 1-6 |
|---|---|---|---|---|---|---|
| IF    Company-national-advertising | very-strong | strong | average | weak | very-weak | none |
| THEN    Company-advertising-N | 5 | 4 | 3 | 2 | 1 | 0 |

| RULE | 1-7 | 1-8 | 1-9 | 1-10 | 1-11 | 1-12 |
|---|---|---|---|---|---|---|
| IF    Company-local-advertising | very-strong | strong | average | weak | very-weak | none |
| THEN    Company-advertising-L | 5 | 4 | 3 | 2 | 1 | 0 |

**FIGURE 20-6   Sample decision chart for sales management quota selling decisions—initial prototype.**

```
question(company-new-products) =
'Give your estimate of the impact of new product introductions
    on the quota.
    [very strong, strong, average, weak, very weak, none].'

legalvals(company-new-products) = [very-strong,strong,average,weak,very-weak,
none].

question(company-changes-strategies) =
'Give your estimate of the impact of changes in company policies
    on the new quota.
    [very strong, strong, average, weak, very weak, none].'

legalvals(company-changes-strategies) = [very-strong,strong,average,weak,
very-weak,none].
```

Rule Set 4:

```
rule-4-1:
    if company-factor-ad = AA and
       AA = 10
    then company-factor-a = 5.
rule-4-2:
    if company-factor-ad = AA and
       AA = 9
    then company-factor-a = 5.

rule-4-3:
    if company-factor-ad = AA and
       AA = 8
    then company-factor-a = 4.

rule-4-4:
    if company-factor-ad = AA and
       AA = 7
    then company-factor-a = 4.

rule-4-5:
    if company-factor-ad = AA and
       AA = 6
    then company-factor-a = 3.

rule-4-6:
    if company-factor-ad = AA and
       AA = 5
    then company-factor-a = 3.
```

Rule Set 3:

```
rule-1:
    if last-years-sales = SALES and
    last-years-quota = QUOTA and
    SALES <= 1.15*QUOTA
 then base = QUOTA.
```

*(continued)*

**FIGURE 20-7   Sample segment of knowledge base for sales management decision—initial prototype.**

```
rule-2:
    if last-years-sales = SALES and
       last-years-quota = QUOTA and
       SALES >1.15*QUOTA and
       QUOTA+(SALES - 1.15*QUOTA) = NEWBASE
    then base = NEWBASE.
```

**FIGURE 20-7**   *(continued)*

## REVIEW QUESTIONS

1. Complete the knowledge base for the system (or any segment of that system) partially documented in this chapter and enter it into the expert system shell you have.

2. Describe the major differences between the system described in this chapter and three other marketing systems described in this section.

3. Discuss the ways in which each of the four marketing systems described in this section would or would not be called an "expert" system.

4. List other sales management areas that might lend themselves to knowledge-based systems applications.   Briefly outline the structure of one of these systems.

5. Discuss the ways in which the structured situation analysis in the situation described in this chapter differs from that in the preceding three chapters.

6. Describe ways in which the system described in this chapter might be programmed using a data base management or spreadsheet or BASIC language application.   What in your opinion are the advantages and disadvantages of using a knowledge-base and expert system shell, instead of one of the other applications, for the sales quota development system.

7. What strategic and operational factors are considered in establishing sales quota?

8. Describe how the new sales quota base is arrived at.   Give an example.

## REFERENCES

Berry, D., "Index Series Finds the Truth in Sales Performance," *Marketing News*, vol. 20, Nov. 7, 1986.

Berry, D., "Sales Analysis Without the Guesswork," *Sales and Marketing Management*, vol. 137, December 1986.

Epstein, J., "Estimating and Sales Analysis with a PC," *Graphic Arts Monthly and the Printing Industry*, vol. 58, December 1986.

Green, H. L., "Retail Sales Forecasting Systems," *Journal of Retailing*, vol. 62, 1986.

Schnaars, S. P., "An Evaluation of Rules for Selecting an Extrapolation Model on Yearly Sales Forecasts," *Interfaces*, vol. 16, 1986.

Scott, G. G., *Effective Selling and Sales Management*, Andover, MA: Brick House Publishing, 1987.

Smith, D. C., and Prescott, J. E., "Couple Competitive Analysis to Sales Force Decisions," *Industrial Marketing Management*, vol. 16, February 1987.

# 21

# A System for Developing Strategic Company Objectives

Chapter 21 describes an expert knowledge-based system for developing enterprise-wide strategic objectives.  The chapter covers

- The situation study: understanding the expert's domain
- Studying the situation to be prototyped
- Documenting the system
- Putting the prototype systems onto computer using M.1 and GURU
- Extensions and enhancements of the prototype system

## THE SITUATION UNDER STUDY: UNDERSTANDING THE EXPERT'S DOMAIN

The following discussion covers

- Selecting a decision area to work on
- Narrowing the focus

### Selecting a Decision Area to Work On

The decision situation selected for study was developing enterprise-wide strategies. A general model of this decision area is given in Fig. 21-1.

The planning area was selected for study for two reasons.  First, the area has many *practical applications*.  For example, strategic planning systems are a major component of many currently available commercial expert knowledge-based systems,

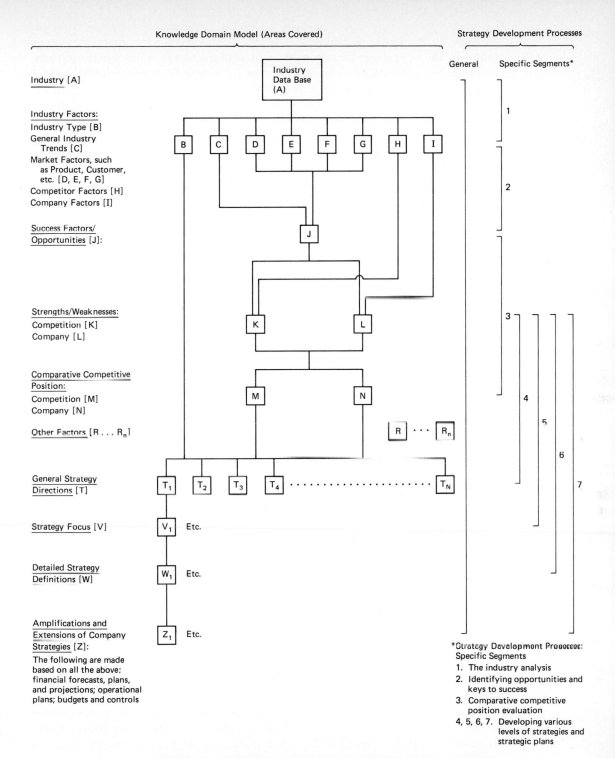

**FIGURE 21-1  Overview of strategy development processes.**

Industry [A]

Industry Factors:
Industry Type [B]
General Industry
  Trends [C]
Market Factors, such
  as Product, Customer,
  etc. [D, E, F, G]
Competitor Factors [H]
Company Factors [I]

Success Factors/
Opportunities [J]:

Strengths/Weaknesses:
Competition [K]
Company [L]

Comparative Competitive
Position:
Competition [M]
Company [N]

Other Factors [R . . . $R_n$]

General Strategy
Directions [T]

Strategy Focus [V]

Detailed Strategy
Definitions [W]

Amplifications and
Extensions of Company
Strategies [Z]:
The following are made
based on all the above;
financial forecasts, plans,
and projections; operational
plans; budgets and controls

*Strategy Development Processes:
Specific Segments
1. The industry analysis
2. Identifying opportunities and
   keys to success
3. Comparative competitive
   position evaluation
4, 5, 6, 7. Developing various
   levels of strategies and
   strategic plans

21:  Developing Strategic Company Objectives                                    **463**

involving such areas as personal investment, capital investment, marketing planning, auditing, and operations management. In addition to these immediate payoffs, the prototype systems discussed in this chapter provide a basis for building more comprehensive and advanced strategic planning systems. Second, a development project of this kind can provide insights into the more complex aspects of management decision making, because strategic planning is one of the least defined and most general of the management decision areas. As a *research project*, then, it focuses on solving major stumbling blocks to faster and more widespread development of management decision-making systems using expert knowledge-based systems technology.

Strategic planning knowledge-based systems are feasible, because

□ Expert decision skills are needed to do the strategic planning job.
□ There are recognized experts in the field.
□ The job requires informed judgment.
□ A number of specific company strategy development tasks, especially where small companies or strategic business units are concerned, involve manageable tasks that can be defined with sufficient precision to enable expert knowledge-based systems development.

### Narrowing the Focus

A number of well-defined components of the overall strategic planning process described in Fig. 21-1 were selected for prototype system development:

□ Company strategy direction and focus development
□ Opportunity and critical success factor identification
□ Comparative competitive position evaluation
□ Financial extensions of corporate strategies

The first area chosen was determining the overall strategy direction for a company. This area was chosen because it was narrowly definable, and so manageable. At the same time it provided a means of studying the process underlying the structure of the overall system, since it would provide a prototype test of an essential component of the system.

Further there existed some planning theories widely accepted by business managers that would provide a basis for the prototype system. The prototype itself would, therefore, be useful to business managers actually involved in doing strategy development for their companies.

## STUDYING THE SITUATION TO BE PROTOTYPED

A great deal of work has been done in analyzing general or generic types of company planning situations, and building structured models for developing general company strategy directions and focus in each type of situation (Porter 1980; Porter 1985; and Hamermesh 1986). Figure 21-2 gives a structured diagram or model of an overall approach to developing general strategy directions.

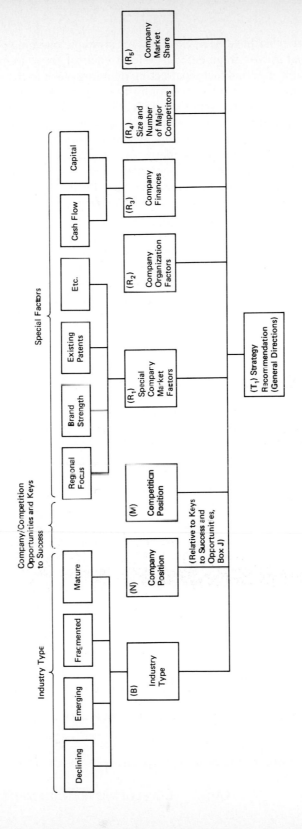

**FIGURE 21-2  Overview of the general strategy development decision situation.**

*Industry types* have been classified for strategic planning purposes as emerging, declining, mature, or fragmented. Within each of these industry types, there are various possible external factors affecting planning, such as the *comparative company and competitor position* relative to opportunities and keys to success (which can be affected by buyer and customer strength, the likelihood of substitute product introduction, and the threat of new entrants), special *company market, organizational, and financial* factors, and *competitors' size and number*. Different types of company positions, such as dominant company, low-market-share company, and regionally concentrated company have also been identified.

Based on a study of these characteristics, Porter and others (such as the Boston Consulting Group planners described by Hamermesh [1986]) have identified a variety of possible generic or general strategies. For example, some possible general or generic strategies for a declining industry might be liquidate, phased-withdrawal, hold position, selective- or niche-concentration, or aggressive investment, depending on the company and other key factors in the situation under study.

These studies have, in effect, developed a so-called contingency framework for dealing with strategy development situations. Contingency guidelines within this framework are often presented in a series of if-then type statements. For example, *if* specific industry type, company, competition, and market conditions are present in a situation, *then* a certain type of general strategy might be worthwhile to consider.

This general approach to developing strategies reflects the way many strategic planners work during the *initial stages* of a project. For example, in doing a preliminary analysis of a situation, planners often review their past experiences in a search for similar *patterns* that might be useful in solving the present situation. Such an approach helps in thinking about possible ways to approach the decision at hand.

In reviewing a situation, the planner might observe, for instance, that the present situation under study involves a mature industry, where several large competitors are dominant in the market, and where the company being planned for is a relatively small player. The planner would review any experiences with other mature industries to search for analogous situation factors that might suggest possible solution patterns useful to explore in the present situation.

There is obviously a good deal more to strategic company planning than just specifying a general strategic direction, such as "phased-withdrawal" or "selective-investment." Such a general approach is, however, a useful starting point to help a planner develop a focus and direction for the more detailed studies that follow.

This general approach also provides a useful starting point, and conceptual foundation, for developing a prototype knowledge-based system in the enterprise-wide strategy planning area.

## DOCUMENTING THE PROTOTYPE SYSTEM

This section covers the major areas of documentation:

□ System proposal
□ Description of the prototype system

- Dependency diagrams
- Decision charts
- Designing and constructing the knowledge base
- Selecting a computer development tool

## System Proposal

The purpose of this project is to design a knowledge-based system for enterprise-wide strategy development. The specific project was to design a system that recommended an overall strategic direction.

A diagram of the complete system to be eventually developed is shown in Fig. 21-1. The system described here, STRATEGIC PLANNER I, goes only as far as the first strategy level, general strategy direction. It is a prototype of one segment of the overall planning process (segment 4) in the figure.

The prototype itself would be developed in stages. The first or initial stage would be a kind of bare bones outline. It would be done using the M.1 expert system programming shell. The subsequent, enhanced versions would be done using the GURU expert system shell. They would have embellishments such as color and graphics, additional user questions and text explanations, and interfaces with other programs, such as spreadsheets and data bases.

The overall system not only will provide aid and guidance in strategy planning, but will also provide a basis for developing strategic planning components of a wide range of integrated systems involving such areas as marketing and financial planning.

The primary source of knowledge about strategic planning was experts in the field. It is necessary to have done strategic company planning to really know it. Although most of what is written on the subject tends to be very general and so not useful for knowledge-based systems development, some recent published research, which provides a more scientific framework for the field (for example, Porter [1980 and 1984], and Hammermesh [1986]), was useful. A wide selection of these knowledge sources is given in the reference list at the end of this chapter.

## Description of the Prototype System

**System overview and objective.** The objective of the prototype system is to provide users with assistance in determining what overall strategic direction they should choose for their company or enterprise.

Such planning decisions involve two major knowledge bases: (1) market factors, including opportunities and key factors that affect success for both the company and the competition, and (2) company strengths and weaknesses in relation to factors affecting success in the industry. These two major knowledge blocks are manipulated in coming to a decision in almost all types of enterprise-wide strategic-planning decision situations.

**Recommendations to be made by the system.** The system is able to make one of the following recommendations:

- *Get out of the business*—With this strategy a company would consider one of several options: liquidate the business (sell the assets), sell the business as a going entity, or harvest or milk the business (run the business without further investment to extract profits until it goes out of business).

- *Hold position*—With this strategy a company would consider investing only enough to produce some earnings to keep the business going.
- *Selective investment*—With this strategy a company has strength in an industry or industry segment that has growth potential. The company would concentrate its resources in that selective industry or industry segment.
- *Niche concentration*—With this strategy a company is not strong within the industry in general but has some special strength in a specific product or service area. It would focus its resources on the area of its strength.
- *Aggressive investment*—With this strategy a company has strength in a strong growth area, and so would aggressively invest in that area.

**Nature of user interface, including typical user dialogue.** In the initial prototype system the user is asked questions about their company, its market, the industry, and the competition. For example, several of the questions are:

- To what degree is your industry or industry segment dominated by relatively large major competitors?
- Assess the degree to which your company has a strong market position (almost a kind of monopoly) in some important area, such as distribution, brand name recognition, patent protection for a product or manufacturing process, and the like.
- Estimate the number of new companies expected to enter your industry over the next few years.

The subsequent, enhanced versions of the prototype system explore industry background information in greater depth with many more user questions. They also give users an opportunity to recheck and revise their initial answers, based on additional information provided by the system.

**Description of the system's knowledge structure and reasoning processes.** The description of the initial prototype's knowledge structure followed the general pattern outlined in Fig. 21-2.

In the initial prototype system basic information about the industry is gathered by a user from a study of the industry data base. In enhanced versions some information is drawn from existing computerized industry data bases.

In the initial prototype system the industry type, a key determining factor in strategy direction decisions, is identified early in the system, based on user answers to questions. Four types of industries are specified in the system: emerging, mature, declining, and fragmented.

Opportunities and keys to success are identified next as are company and competitor strengths and weaknesses in key-to-success areas. The initial prototype system requires a user to interrelate all these factors and draw their own conclusions as to the relative company and competitor positions in relation to key success factors. Only the overall results of this comparative evaluation are entered into the system by a user. The enhanced versions of the system are designed to interact with a user during the consultation, and in this way to guide and assist a user in doing these comparative evaluations.

The last step involves asking a user questions during the consultation about special market and company factors. The system then combines these answers with information built into the system to come up with an overall strategy direction recommendation.

## Dependency Diagrams

The prototype system's dependency diagram is shown Fig. 21-3. This diagram shows the interrelationships among the knowledge components or segments.

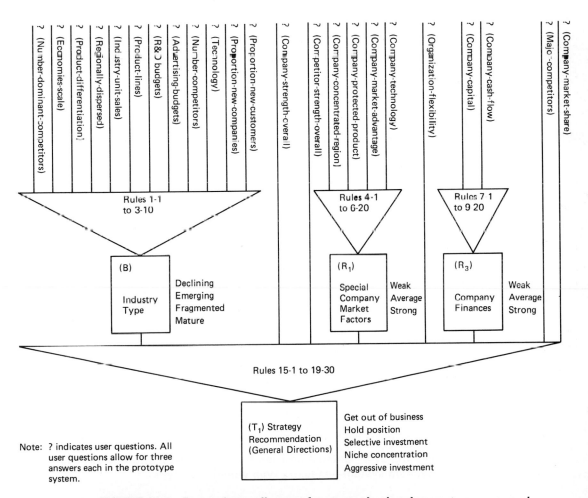

**FIGURE 21-3  Dependency diagram for strategic planning system—general strategy direction segment—initial prototype.**

| PREMISES | RULES | | | | |
|---|---|---|---|---|---|
| | 1 | 2 | 3 | 4 | 5 |
| number-dominant-competitors | high | med | | | |
| economies-scale | and high | and med | | | |
| product-differentiation | or high | or med | | | |
| regionally-dispersed | or high | or high | | | |
| industry-unit-sales | | | decreasing | stable | increasing |
| product-lines | | | decreasing | stable | increasing |
| r&d-budgets | | | decreasing | stable | increasing |
| advertising-budgets | | | decreasing | stable | increasing |
| number-competitors | | | decreasing | stable | increasing |
| technology | | | mature | mature | emerging |
| proportion-new companies | | | low | average | high |
| proportion-new customers | | | low | average | high |
| INDUSTRY TYPES | | | | | |
| Fragmented | x | x | | | |
| Declining | | | x | | |
| Mature | | | | x | |
| Emerging | | | | | x |

**FIGURE 21-4  Sample decision chart for general strategy direction decision system—industry type (initial prototype).**

## Decision Charts

Figure 21-4 is a sample decision chart from the initial prototype system.

## Designing and Constructing the Knowledge Base

Examples of the if-then rules and questions developed for the initial prototype system are given in Figs. 21-5 and 21-6. Rule-7 in Figure 21-5 is part of the final rule set.

The knowledge base was prepared in a format for use on the M.1 expert system shell, the shell to be used for the initial prototype. There are over three hundred rules in the knowledge base in the initial prototype system. Subsequent versions were done using the GURU expert system shell.

## Selecting a Computer Development Tool

The M.1 expert system shell was chosen for the initial prototype system development for several reasons:

- □ No hard disk is required, so a regular 640 K PC can be used.
- □ The knowledge base can be written on a word processor in reasonably clear English and transferred directly into the M.1 expert system shell.

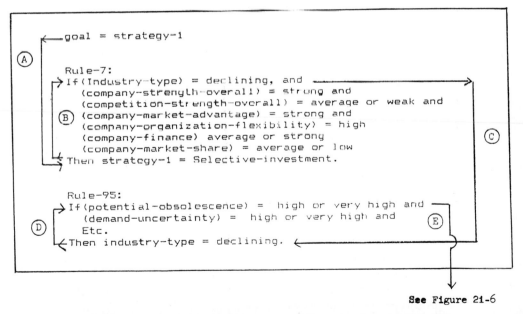

(Actual printed output of rules stored in an M.1 knowledge base.)

```
        goal = strategy-1
  A

        Rule-7:
      If(Industry-type) = declining, and
         (company-strength-overall) = strong and
         (competition-strength-overall) = average or weak and
      B  (company-market-advantage) = strong and
         (company-organization-flexibility) = high
         (company-finance) average or strong                        C
         (company-market-share) = average or low
      Then strategy-1 = Selective-investment.


        Rule-95:
      If(potential-obsolescence) = high or very high and
         (demand-uncertainty) = high or very high and
  D      Etc.                                               E
      Then industry-type = declining.
```

See Figure 21-6

**FIGURE 21-5** Sample segment of knowledge base for general strategy direction decision system—rules and the inference engine search process (initial prototype).

```
question(potential-obsolescence) = 'How would you characterize
                                    the potential for technological
                                    obsolescence in this industry
                                    segment [very low, low,
                                    average, high, very high]?'

question(demand-uncertainty) = 'How would you assess the
                                uncertainty of future demand in
                                this industry segment [very low,
                                low, average, high, very high]?'
```

The first question above, which is stored in the system's knowledge base, causes the system to print the following on a user's computer screen:

```
    How would you characterize the potential for technological
obsolescence in this industry segment [very low, low, average,
high, very high]?

    >> (A user types an answer in here.)
```

**FIGURE 21-6   Sample segment of knowledge base for general strategy direction decision system—questions and a user query (initial prototype).**

- ☐ The syntax required is not too complicated.
- ☐ M.1 has a built-in explanation facility.
- ☐ M.1 is generally very good for simple prototype systems development.
- ☐ M.1 version 2 has a limited on-screen editor.

There were drawbacks to using M.1 as well, however.  For example, if a standard (086 microprocessor) microcomputer is used, loading and reloading the knowledge base is a slow and tedious job.  In addition, because it is easy to use, M.1 also has fairly limited capabilities.  Finally, because of its major advantage, easy familiarity of English syntax, it is consequently cumbersome and time-consuming to prepare knowledge bases using M.1, and it is slow running.

The GURU expert system shell was selected for the enhanced versions of the prototype system for several reasons:

- ☐ The knowledge base can be written in English on a word processor and transferred directly into GURU, as with M.1.

- It has a built-in editing facility, so that changes can be made directly to segments of the knowledge base without exiting out of the expert shell to the word processor.
- It can have color and graphics capabilities, which are important for building attractive screens for user consultation runs.
- It has built-in spreadsheet and data base capabilities and so was necessary for the more sophisticated phases of the expert system development project.
- It has the ability to alter reasoning paths.
- It is generally more powerful and flexible than other available PC expert system shells in areas important to the project.

GURU also has several drawbacks. For example, GURU is more difficult to learn and use because it is more powerful and flexible. GURU also requires substantially more programming time and expertise and a great deal more computer storage space. Because it requires substantial computer technician time, GURU costs considerably more. Finally, the system could not be transported as easily when making presentations, because all the files have to be loaded into a hard disk to use GURU, and so it requires longer set up times.

Other good expert system shells are available. Each system developer should study their own situation requirements and select that shell which best suits them.

## PUTTING THE PROTOTYPE SYSTEMS ONTO A COMPUTER USING M.1 AND GURU

In the initial prototype system, twenty-three questions and about three hundred rules were developed, using the M.1 syntax and format. Samples of both of these were given in Figs. 21-5 and 21-6. Decision charts, such as the one shown in Fig. 21-4, were used to verify the completeness and accuracy of the rules, and to help develop them.

In addition, introductory panels, such as the one shown in Fig. 21-7, as well as concluding panels, were developed.

In converting the system to computer, the rules were further condensed in order to save time and space. Control rules were created for the final rule set, recommending a general strategy direction, as shown at the top of Fig. 21-8. This is a generalized version of the rule shown in Fig. 21-5. The first eight if clauses in the control rule establish variables for each if condition, and the ninth if clause,

```
and strategy_1 (CSO, CompSO, IT, CMF, COF, CF, MC, CMS) = S_1
```

puts these into a condensed format.

This control rule enabled the condensing of each individual rule, as shown at the bottom of Fig. 21-8:

```
strategy_1 (weak, Any_2, declining, Any_4, Any_5,
weak, Any_7, Any_8) = 'get out of business'.
```

```
initialdata = [intro_over,  phase_1_over].
```

```
if intro_1_over
   and intro_2_over
then intro_over.
```

```
if display([nl,nl,nl,nl,nl,nl,nl,
```

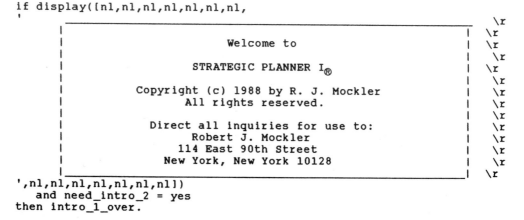

```
',nl,nl,nl,nl,nl,nl,nl])
   and need_intro_2 = yes
then intro_1_over.
```

**FIGURE 21-7  Introductory panel of M.1 version of strategy direction decision—initial prototype.**

Using this condensed format enabled writing each rule in two lines instead of ten lines.

Even using this condensed format, writing the rules for M.1 is a very time consuming task.  With larger systems, M.1 is very inefficient even though it is easier to understand and more familiar for the nontechnician.  This is especially true for the nontechnician who is unfamiliar with the many techniques and development tools available for shortening and speeding knowledge base construction.

Correcting syntax errors during the conversion is another tedious and time consuming job.  Frequently it is difficult to even determine precisely what is wrong, so one has to experiment, just as during the debugging phase in conventional programming.

The next phase, converting the initial (first) prototype system onto GURU, was not much more difficult.  The knowledge base first had to be adapted to the GURU syntax as shown in Chapter 7.  Loading the knowledge-base file into GURU was no more complicated than for M.1.  Since GURU has a more extensive built-in editing facility, making corrections was easier.

Creating an enhanced version of the initial prototype system, using GURU's advanced features, was much more difficult.  For example, the introductory panels were given color borders.  This involved learning the GURU graphics routines and

A. Control Rule

A. Control Rule:

```
/*            <<<<<<  strategy_1 >>>>>>            */

multivalued(strategy_1).
multivalued(strategy_1(CSO, CompSO, IT, CCR, CPP, CMA, CT,
         COF, CC, CCF, MC, CMS)).




rule-s-1:
if company-strength-overall =  CSO
   and competitors-strength-overall = CompSO
   and industry-type = IT
   and company-market-factors = CMF
   and company-organization-flexibility = COF
   and company-finance = CF
   and major-competitors = MC
   and company-market-share = CMS
   and strategy_1(CSO, CompSO, IT, CMF, COF, CF, MC, CMS) = S_1
   then strategy_1 = S_1.
```

B. Condensed Rule Form:

```
/*              get out of business       */

/*         rule-1      */

strategy_1( weak, Any_2, declining, Any_4, Any_5, weak, Any_7, Any_8) =
'get out of business'.

strategy_1( weak, Any_2, mature,   Any_4, Any_5, weak, Any_7, Any_8) =
'get out of business'.

strategy_1( weak, Any_2, fragmented,Any_4, Any_5, weak, Any_7, Any_8) =
'get out of business'.


strategy_1( weak, Any_2, declining, Any_4, Any_5, Any_6,Any_7, weak) =
'get out of business'.

strategy_1( weak, Any_2, mature,   Any_4, Any_5, Any_6,Any_7, weak) =
'get out of business'.

strategy_1( weak, Any_2, fragmented,Any_4, Any_5, Any_6,Any_7, weak) =
'get out of business'.
```

**FIGURE 21-8   Sample segment of knowledge base of M.1 version of strategy direction decision—initial prototype.**

creating several new files.   Figure 21-9, for example, shows the file for the first introductory panel.   This panel was similar to the M.1 version of the same panel given in Fig. 21-7.

Rules were also written somewhat differently in GURU, as seen in the top half of Fig. 21-10.   The questions in GURU also require an entirely different form, as is also shown in the bottom half of Fig. 21-10.

```
FORM LICENSE
        AT 7, 19 PUT "              Welcome to"
        AT 7, 23 PUT " "  USING "  "
        AT 9, 23 PUT "    STRATEGIC PLANNER I   "
        AT 11, 19 PUT "Copyright (c) 1988 by R.J. Mockler"
        AT 12, 26 PUT "All rights reserved."
        AT 14, 19 PUT "Direct all inquiries for use to:"
        AT 15, 26 PUT "Robert J. Mockler"
        AT 16, 24 PUT "114 East 90th Street"
        AT 17, 22 PUT "New York, New York 10128"
        AT 22, 19 PUT "-- Press any key to continue --"
        AT 4, 12 TO 5, 57 PUT "FCBU"
        AT 4, 58 TO 20, 60 PUT "FCBU"
        AT 6, 12 TO 20, 14 PUT "FCBU"
        AT 9, 15 TO 9, 26 PUT "FRBA"
        AT 9, 15 TO 9, 26 PUT "FRBA"
        AT 9, 24 TO 9, 46 PUT "FMBR"
        AT 19, 15 TO 20, 57 PUT "FCBU"
ENDFORM
```

**FIGURE 21-9   Sample segment of knowledge base of GURU version of strategy direction decision—license panel (second version of prototype).**

In all thirty-six files had to be created for the GURU version of the initial prototype system just to enhance user interface.   No additions were initially made to the content of the first prototype system, except for more detailed explanations of the recommendations at the end of the consultation.

So, although it was relatively easy to use GURU to create a working version of the initial prototype system, it took a substantial amount of time and a high level of computer expertise to create a more professional looking version.

Subsequent enhancements of the prototype are described in the following section.   These enhancements, which were needed to turn the prototype system into a more useful and expert knowledge-based system, also required a more sophisticated development environment.   GURU provided that.

## EXTENSIONS AND ENHANCEMENTS OF THE INITIAL PROTOTYPE SYSTEM

Although the initial prototype version of STRATEGIC PLANNER I functions as a useful decision support system, it was only a small segment of the larger system outlined in Fig. 21-1.   Several key expansion areas identified during its development were

1. *Comparative competitive position evaluation*—A subsystem to develop more precise estimates of company and competitor strengths and weaknesses relative to key success factors (identified as process 3 in Fig. 21-1)

A. Rules:

```
rule: s_1-9-2
if:        CSO = "average"
    and    CompSO = "strong"
    and    (IT = "fragmented" or IT = "mature")
    and    (CMF = "weak" or CMF = "average")
    and    (CFI = "average" or CFI = "strong")
then: S1 = "selective investment"

rule: s_1-9-3
if:        CSO = "average"
    and    CompSO = "strong"
    and    (IT = "fragmented" or IT = "mature")
    and    CMF = "strong"
    and    COF = "low"
    and    (CFI = "average" or CFI = "strong")
then: S1 = "selective investment"
```

B. Questions:

```
VAR: PD
    FIND: let #found = false
          while not(#found) do
          at 15,4 output \
          "Assess the degree of product differentiation in this industry,"
          at 16,4 output \
          "based on either brand recognition or product characteristics
           [high,"
          at 17,4 input pd using "llllllllll" with "medium, low]."
          obtain record from legalval for attribut = "pd" and lvalue = pd
          clear
          if not(# found) then
          putform warning
          endif
          endwhile
   LABEL: product differentiation
```

**FIGURE 21-10  Sample segment of knowledge base of GURU version of
strategy direction decision—second version of prototype.**

2. *Industry analyses*—A subsystem to access data bases directly to obtain more reliable and comprehensive information about specific industries than could be expected to be provided by a user (identified as process 1 in Fig. 21-1)
3. *More detailed strategy development*—Subsystems to provide recommendations at the next two strategy levels, strategy focus and detailed strategies (identified as processes 5 and 6 in Fig. 21-1)
4. *Financial projections*—Subsystems to perform meaningful financial projections of recommended strategies (identified as process 7 in Fig. 21-1)
5. *Opportunity and key-to-success identification*—A subsystem to guide and stimulate the opportunity and key-to-success identification process (identified as process 2 in Fig. 21-1)

The following sections briefly describe how these areas were developed and integrated into an expanded version of the initial prototype system.

## Enhancement 1: Comparative Competitive Position Evaluation

The first major addition was a subsystem for doing the comparative competitive position evaluation.

**The initial prototype system.** This comparative evaluation requires first examining a wide range of critical factors that potentially might affect success in an industry. This checklist included such factors as

- New technological developments
- Brand loyalty
- Raw material availability
- Manufacturing cost efficiency
- Pricing
- Distribution channel accessibility

Such factors were part of a list that initially contained over one hundred items. The preliminary list was subsequently reduced to the fifty most relevant items.

In the initial prototype system a user examined these factors and estimated their relative importance to success before the consultation. A user then rated the company's and competition's strengths and weaknesses in each area, first as relates to individual factors and then cumulatively. A user might use a manual form to do this, such as the one shown in Fig. 21-11. A user entered only the final results of this study into the initial prototype system, an estimate of the overall relative strength of their company and an estimate of the competition's strength in general. Although a user was encouraged to do a thorough situation study to prepare these estimates before the consultation, the quality of the estimates varied considerably.

**The enhanced prototype system.** A list of fifty questions were first developed to guide a user in estimating the importance of situation factors to success in a specific industry under consideration. Some sample questions are

- Assess the importance of brand loyalty to success in this industry [very low, low, average, high, very high].
- To what degree does the ability to be a technological leader affect success in this industry [very low, low, average, high, very high]?

The enhanced system was then expanded to ask the user these questions during a consultation. This enhancement gave the system the capability to reorder and sort the success factors in the order of importance assigned by a user. The final list is limited to the most important seven factors. This list of seven critical factors is then presented to a user on the screen for review, in much the same way as is shown in Fig. 21-11.

At this point in the system, a user is given the opportunity to revise the estimates of importance, reorder the list, and add to, modify, or eliminate individual key success

| (1) | (2) | (3) | (4) | (5) | (6) | (7) | (8) |
|-----|-----|-----|-----|-----|-----|-----|-----|
| Industry & Market: Keys to Success | Keys to Success Rethink, Reword, Reorder. Write Down Revised Version in Order of Importance | Give Weight to Each Area (Total = 100) | Our Company's Strengths in Key-to-Success Areas. Use Same Rating Scale as Used in Column (5) | Individual Competitor's or Competitor Group's Strength in Relation to Each Key-to-Success Area (Scale: 1 = Weak; 2 = Average; 3 = Strong) <br> C-1 C-2 C-3 C-4 C-5 C-5 | Competition's Overall Strength. Average of Individual Competitor's Strength in Section (5) | Rate Company's Strength Versus Competition's (3 = greater 2 = same 1 = weaker) | Weighted Value = Column (3) Times Column (7). (Highest Possible Value = 100 × 3 = 300) |
| 1. | 1. | | | | | | |
| 2. | 2. | | | | | | |
| 3. | 3. | | | | | | |
| 4. | 4. | | | | | | |
| 5. | 5. | | | | | | |
| 6. | 6. | | | | | | |
| 7. | 7. | | | | | | |
| 8. | 8. | | | | | | |
| 9. | 9. | | | | | | |
| | | Column (3) Total Should Equal 100 | | | Total Score of Column (8) = <br> Total Score of Column (8) As Percent of 300 = | | |

**FIGURE 21-11** Comparative competitive position evaluation of industry segment or opportunity area under study: _____.

factors. A user is then required to rate the company's and the competition's strength in relation to each of the listed critical success factors on screen.

The system then determines the cumulative weight given to both the company's and the competition's relative overall strength within an industry. These two overall values are then integrated and used in one segment of the decision rules, where the system weighs them with many other factors in reaching a decision and recommendation.

On average, in user tests of the system the *enhanced version* of the system improved the quality of responses by over 50 percent when compared with the judgments made by a user when consulting the *initial version*. The reason seems to be that it is not enough to just tell a person to study a situation in depth.

What the enhanced version seems to do is to structure a user's detailed analysis, evaluation, and synthesis of an industry, and then guide a user through the comparative industry study. It does not do the study. Rather it assists a user in doing it during this phase of the industry study. The specific advantages of the enhanced version seem to be

- □ It guides, encourages, and facilitates a more thorough study of industry success factors, and in this way improves the quality of the industry analysis.
- □ It provides a user with a method to verify and cross-check their initial estimates of importance by organizing and presenting (feeding back) a graphic summary of the initial estimates to the user.
- □ It provides an orderly and systematic way for a user to reexamine the cumulative effect of estimates made and, where necessary, revise them in light of their impact on each other when limited resources are taken into account.
- □ It enables the integration of these estimates into the strategy selection decision process automatically.

Manual aids, such as the one shown in Fig. 21-11, serve a similar function, but they require considerably more attention and work to use and manipulate. They are also much more limited in scope, liable to error, and so of not much value in dealing with major industries.

Another related enhancement to the initial prototype system involves a subsystem for doing structured competitive scenario analyses.

## Enhancement 2: Industry Analyses Using Existing Data Bases

Industry analyses can involve considerable work. Using the initial prototype system required a user to search out, evaluate, and organize this industry data on their own.

The next enhancement involved creating individual industry data bases. They were constructed in a way that

- □ The knowledge-based system could access them directly to avoid detailed and extensive questioning of a user about industry data.
- □ The data base could be updated periodically, as new industry data became available, without disturbing the knowledge base in the system.

□ The data base could be expanded as needed to support more advanced knowledge-based systems under development.

The idea of creating computer industry data bases designed to support strategic company planning is not new. Strategic Intelligence Systems (SIS), for example, has developed over thirty of them and sells access to them. They are reportedly updated every month. These services are used mostly by large companies. SIS is only one of many companies that provide access to such computerized data bases.

These services are expensive and are organized in way that would not be directly accessible by an expert knowledge-based system. For these reasons it was necessary to create new data bases to support the prototype knowledge-based systems for strategic planning under development. These industry data bases would be designed using key elements from STRATEGIC PLANNER I's knowledge base for its structure. The following was done to begin development of such an industry by industry data base file.

First, a test industry was selected, the computer software industry. Industry data was gathered and organized into categories corresponding to the key identification words used in the prototype knowledge-based system. This was necessary to enable the system to read the data directly into the system.

Second, data bases were developed and maintained in files separate from the system's knowledge-base file, so that they could be updated independently, without disturbing the prototype system's knowledge base. These data bases were designed to contain considerably more information than was needed in the current version of STRATEGIC PLANNER I, since they were expected to be used in later versions of the system.

Third, additions were made to the prototype system to enable it to access external data bases directly. For example, a menu option was introduced into the system:

```
1. Retrieve the Industry Information from an Existing
   Data Base.
2. The Industry Information will be Entered by the User.
```

If a user consulting the system chooses option 1, the system searches the external industry data base files. If it finds a data base for the industry being examined by a user, it obtains the answers to questions about the competition and industry under study that were formerly asked of a user in the initial prototype system. A user still answers questions about the company under study in the enhanced prototype.

The system then shows a user the answers obtained from the external data base, and the conclusions or inferences drawn from that information, to enable a user to verify and, if necessary, modify the information.

Graph and pie chart analyses were also added to the system during this enhancement phase.

Other industry data bases were developed. For example, one involves a family of data bases. These consist of information about local industries in a specific geographic area. They are designed to assist small and medium size companies, as well as individual entrepreneurs, in new venture strategy planning in that area.

## Enhancement 3: Recommending More Detailed Strategies

The initial prototype system, and all enhanced versions discussed so far, are limited to making general strategy direction recommendations.

A new subsystem, STRATEGIC PLANNER II, was developed to make more extensive recommendations, including:

- Recommend a strategy focus
- Recommend specific business areas that might be included in a detailed company strategy

This prototype system, which has a similar structure to STRATEGIC PLANNER I, first refines the overall strategy direction into what is referred to as a strategy focus. This focus might, for example, be a more specific recommendation for ways to "get-out-of-the-business" (a general strategy direction): liquidate, or divest, or withdraw gradually and harvest, and the like. Or it might suggest specific company strengths to build on in thinking about an overall niche-concentration strategy direction.

STRATEGIC PLANNER II first requires a user to analyze and evaluate ten key business areas:

- Product or service offered
- Manufacturing
- Advertising
- Retailing
- Distribution
- Customer service
- Sales force
- Research and development
- Human resources
- Finance and management

The system then requires a user to estimate the importance of factors critical to success in each area. For example, in the advertising and promotion area a user is asked to assess the importance of such factors as

- Word-of-mouth-advertising
- Point-of-sales-promotions
- Direct-response-advertising
- Customer-ties
- Computer-telecommunications
- Specific-media-selected
- Publicity
- Advertising-amount, in relation to other promotion media, such support services offered
- Any other factors the user thinks are important

Next, a user answers the following question for each critical factor in each of the ten business areas that have any relevance to the industry and company under study:

How will the company under study fare against the competition in the future in relation to each of these factors?

In this way a user is guided through a kind of in-depth, component-by-component industry analysis.

The information obtained from a user is then compiled and manipulated by the system. At the end of a consultation the system makes specific recommendations about areas that might be strategically emphasized by a company under study.

### Enhancement 4: Financial Projections

The initial prototype system made no financial projections. A new subsystem, STRA-TEGIC PLANNER III, provides guidance to help a user prepare five-year projections for a company or strategic business unit under study. These projections are broken down by

- Gross industry revenues, based on projected growth rates and present industry segment sales provided by a user
- Market shares, provided by a user
- Costs by each major cost category, provided by a user

The assumptions underlying these projections are based on the strategic-planning factors identified in the earlier phases of the study.

Based on these assumptions and the financial information provided by a user, the system then projects profitability and cash flows for the strategies recommended earlier by the system during a consultation.

In a final segment of the prototype system a user develops and enters capital investment figures, and the system calculates projected returns on investment for a company under study.

### Enhancement 5: Identifying Opportunities and Keys to Success

The initial prototype system provided little assistance in identifying opportunities or keys to success. Enhancement 1 provides some help by suggesting possible factors to consider and a method of rating their importance; enhancement 2 provides several data base sources for the information in a few specific industries.

A great deal more is involved in identifying opportunities and keys to success, however. Identifying opportunities, threats, and keys to success requires a large measure of conceptual and inferential reasoning skills. Thinking at the intuitive, associative, and creative level is also necessary. These processes and skills are less definable and so less adaptable to existing computer applications. At the same time they can have a significant impact on successful enterprise-wide strategy development at the expert level.

It is possible to develop knowledge-based systems that can assist in the inferential reasoning involved in strategic planning. Many of the techniques used to develop the media strategy system described in Chapter 19 are applicable here. As discussed there, these types of knowledge-based systems require the use of object or frame knowledge structures.

Significant basic research is being done that will enable further developments in this area. For example, Jaime Carbonell, a computer scientist at Carnegie-Mellon, is developing programs that allow a computer to access analogies from its memory, based on those that humans use, so that it can gain new insights and meanings. This in some ways replicates the kind of associative reasoning encountered in some areas of strategic corporate planning. Roger Schank, head of the computer science department at Yale, is doing research on developing language interpretation programs. These can provide ways to help computers deal with the context within which concepts appear, and so help with replicating some aspects of inferential reasoning—that is, the drawing implications from basic industry and company information (Rothfeder 1985, 12–13).

## REVIEW QUESTIONS

1. Finish the knowledge base for the system partially documented in this chapter and enter it into the expert system shell you have.

2. Do a structured situation analysis and develop structured situation diagrams or models for any of the potential areas for knowledge-based systems development given in the "Narrowing the Focus" section in this chapter. Samples of these are given in Chapters 17, 18, and 19 for your guidance.

3. Describe ways in which the strategic-planning models discussed in this chapter can be integrated into other types of knowledge-based systems. An example of such integration is given in Chapter 9.

4. Describe some of the problems encountered in putting the initial prototype system onto computer.

5. Discuss the differences between using the M.1 and GURU expert system shells for creating different prototype versions of the general strategy directions decision systems.

6. Do a situation analysis of the comparative competitive position evaluation described in the chapter, and construct a structured situation diagram or model of it. Construct a dependency diagram of this prototype subsystem based on your situation model.

7. Discuss some of the potential uses of object-oriented (frame-based) representation tools in future enterprise-wide strategy development knowledge-based systems.

# REFERENCES

Boseman, G., A. Phatak, and R. E. Schallenberger, *Strategic Management*, New York: Wiley, 1986.

Briggs, W., "Software Tools for Planning," *Planning Review*, September 1985, pp. 36ff.

David, F. R., *Fundamentals of Strategic Management*, Columbus, Ohio: Merrill, 1986.

Hammermesh, Richard G., *Making Strategy Work*, New York: Wiley, 1986.

Hohn, Siegfried, "How Information Technology is Transforming Corporate Planning," *Long Range Planning*, August 1986, pp. 18ff.

Luther, William, *Strategic Planning Model*, Stanford, Conn.: Luther Management, 1984.

Mockler, R. J., *Business Planning and Policy Development*, New York: D&G Publishers, 3rd ed., 1983 (originally published by Prentice-Hall).

Mockler, R. J., "Computer Aids for Strategic Corporate Planning," *Business Horizons*, March/April 1987.

Mockler, R. J., and D. G. Dologite, *Knowledge-based Systems and Strategic Corporate Planning*, Oxford, Ohio: The Planning Forum, 1987.

Mockler, R. J., "The Situational Theory of Management," *Harvard Business Review*, May–June 1971.

Mockler, R. J., "Theory and Practice of Planning," *Harvard Business Review*, March–April 1970.

Naylor, Thomas, and Michele H. Mann, eds, *Computer-Based Planning Systems*, Oxford, Ohio: The International Society for Planning and Strategic Management, 1982.

Orsini, Jean-Francois, "Artificial Intelligence: A Way Through the Strategic Planning Crisis?" *Long Range Planning*, August 1986, pp. 71ff.

Porter, Michael E., *Competitive Advantage*, New York: The Free Press, 1985.

Porter, Michael E., *Competitive Strategy*, New York: The Free Press, 1980.

Power, Daniel, Martin Gannon, Michael McGinnis, and David Schweiger, *Strategic Management Skills*, Reading, Mass.: Addison-Wesley, 1986.

Rothfeder, Jeffrey, *Minds over Matter: A New Look at Artificial Intelligence*, New York: Simon & Schuster/Computing Book Division, 1985.

Sawyer, George C., *Designing Strategy*, New York: Wiley, 1986.

Steiner, George A., *Strategic Planning*, New York: The Free Press, 1979.

Thompson, Arthur A., and A. J. Strickland, *Strategic Management*, 4th ed., Plano, Tex.: Business Publications, 1987.

# 22

# A Career Strategy Planning System

This chapter describes the development of a knowledge-based system for career strategy decisions. The topics covered are

- The situation study: understanding how the decision works
- Studying the situation to be prototyped
- Documenting the system
- System refinements

The early sections of the chapter describe the overall situation for which the system is being developed. The next sections describe the decision situation model development and the design and documentation of the prototype system based on the structured situation analysis. The chapter concludes with a discussion of special features of the system.

## THE SITUATION UNDER STUDY: UNDERSTANDING HOW THE DECISION WORKS

This section covers

- Selecting a decision area to work on
- Studying how the situation works and how decisions are made
- Narrowing the focus of the study

## Selecting a Decision Area to Work On

A career decision was selected for knowledge-base systems development for several reasons:

- It is relevant to many of the readers of this book, and so has practical value.
- It relates to an important component of the new venture system described in Chapter 17.
- It concerns a significant strategic decision choice.
- It is a well-defined area, at least in part, since there are several major conventional computer programs that function as decision assistants in making different kinds of career choices.
- There are experts in the field to whom people turn for advice.

One critical segment of the career strategy decision area, determining the entrepreneurial capabilities of an individual, will be the focus of prototype development in this chapter. This is the first decision to make when dealing with new venture decisions, such as those covered in Chapter 17, since if the answer is no, there is no need to continue the study. If you are not ready to be an entrepreneur, it is pointless to discuss what kind of venture to go into.

## Studying How the Situation Works and How Decisions Are Made

This section describes some of the key decisions that are made when selecting a career strategy.

First, there is the obvious decision about what profession or general kind of job to pursue. The possible career choices are many and can be classified in a variety of ways, including:

- Executives, administrators, and managers
- Engineers and architects
- Medical doctors and other health specialists
- Writer, artists, and entertainers
- Marketing and sales occupations
- Computer and mathematical scientists
- Production, manufacturing, and operations persons

Second, there are important potential specific occupational or job choices within the overall categories. For example, following are some of the choices within two career areas related to business. The *executives, administrators and managers* category includes accountants and auditors, managers in finance, managers of administrative services, government officials and administrators, and managers in medicine and health. *Marketing and sales occupations*, on the other hand, might be advertising and sales related occupations, financial service and sales occupations, sales representatives positions, insurance sales occupations, and supervisors of marketing and salespersons.

Third, in addition to career and occupation choices, one can choose between working for someone else or becoming a self-employed, independent business person.

Whether or not to go into business for oneself can be a difficult decision for persons of any age, unless they have been exposed to someone within their family or among close friends who has been on their own. Obviously, it takes the ability to work without direction from someone else and to take risks (as opposed to gambling), to initiate and self-motivate, and to live without the security of a steady job even when faced with continuing obligations, such as mortgage and family needs. Many other personal and professional considerations are also involved in the choice to go into business for oneself. But these are merely abstractions to someone who has not experienced them. Unless you have lived with it or close to it on a day-to-day basis, it is hard to develop an understanding or feel for what it is like to be on your own.

Professionals often face this choice. For example, lawyers have the option of going out on their own, of working for a professional firm with the hope of becoming a partner someday, or of working for a company or public institution. Accountants have similar options.

Fourth, your choice may be whether to go into business on your own as an individual—which is really just another kind of job—or to build your venture into a business, which will enable you both to have a job and to eventually realize a capital gain. The second choice usually involves working with partners.

Fifth, your choice may involve what kind of institution to work for: government, private business, a school, a large or small company, and the like.

For most people choosing a career path or strategy is a difficult decision, especially when it involves choices they are not familiar with. Trying out a variety of careers is one way to do your investigation, but that can be fairly limiting and time consuming. In place of this many people try indirect ways to identify what each career entails and the requirements of the jobs within the career field under consideration. These requirements are then matched against an individual's qualifications for that job.

*Identifying what is involved in a job or career* can come from observing others, asking questions, reading books and especially newspapers, attending seminars, taking part-time and regular jobs in the field, and the like. As in other planning studies, keys to success and opportunities in each career area can be identified, specifically and in writing, from such situation analyses.

*Specifying one's own individual qualifications* involves first deciding what is meant by qualifications. Major factors that are involved in defining qualifications include

- Intelligence, abilities, and skills—both amount and kind of
- Education and training—both amount and kind of
- Temperament and personal preferences
- Interests

□ Personal and financial goals
□ Physical limitations

A person then assesses their own strengths and weaknesses in each of these areas and matches them to the success criteria defined for each occupation. It is a strategic-planning decision that is in many ways similar to others discussed in this book.

Applying this theoretical strategic-planning approach to career strategy selection is not always a simple task. For example, the opportunities and requirements for success as accountants and auditors can be identified as follows:

□ Intelligence, aptitudes, and skills—requires learning, verbal, numerical, clerical, and some conceptual, but not much spatial, form, eye and hand coordination abilities
□ Education and training—requires specialized and sometimes graduate training, along with possible certification and apprenticeship
□ Temperament—requires assuming responsibility, making decisions based on concrete evidence, meeting rigid standards, and sometimes working under deadline pressures
□ Interests—requires working with things, numbers, or objects; business contact with people; and scientific or technical tasks
□ Work environment—requires working indoors, at a sedentary job for long hours
□ Opportunities    offers high salary and a growing field

Questions about an individual's qualifications to meet these success requirements need answering. Some of these will be *easy* to answer—for example, you know how much education and training you've had. Unfortunately some of these questions are *not so easy* to answer. For example, just what kinds of conceptual skills do you have? How good a problem solver are you? What kinds of problems do you like to solve, or solve well? How effective are you under pressure? Such questions do not always have *precise* answers.

One way to help find these answers is through the *incident* approach. This involves making, and then analyzing, a list of things you have done well, things you enjoy doing, and things you get great satisfaction from doing (if different from the above). Using this approach involves searching your memory for actual events, and writing down the events and their outcome. You then assess what in particular about each event made you like it or what caused it to turn out the way it did.

The first advantage of this approach is that it starts an individual thinking about concrete events, rather than abstractions. You focus on things you did. Second, this approach forces an individual to think in terms of outcomes, or results. Did the incident turn out well or poorly? Third, it requires evaluation or assessment, since you have to determine what led to good or bad outcomes and what led to your likes, dislikes, or satisfaction.

It is somewhat helpful to know what tasks we performed poorly or did not like to do.  But this only helps eliminate occupations.  It is more important to focus on events with successful outcomes.

Very quickly you can begin to isolate specific characteristics.  You may handle people very well, but only in certain situations.  Define these situations precisely.  For example, you may find that you can deal effectively with customers or people on a daily basis, as do salespeople.  Or you might realize that you can deal effectively with people at meetings and from time to time in a work environment, but prefer for the most part to work alone, as a market researcher might have to.

In the area of intelligence, aptitudes, and skills, everybody is smart or good at something.  Logic problems may intrigue you.  Precise figures about them, however, may bore you.  Manipulating shapes and forms, as required in architecture, may have kept you up long into the evening in the past.  You may like to design information systems, but hate to program them; or vice versa.  Anything to do with abstractions or concepts may make you uncomfortable.  Or you may prefer dealing with concepts.

With a little effort and good written discipline, it is possible to identify *patterns* about yourself, "profiles" of the *kinds of things* you like to do and do well.  This exercise is like the scenario or test case exercises done in other strategic-planning decision situations.  The scenarios are designed to help identify those characteristics that have to be matched against success requirements in opportunity areas.

Such an incident approach is needed because it does not work to simply ask a person such questions as "Are you good with people?" or "Are you a good problem solver?"  The answers would be clouded with ego perceptions.  For this reason the information has to be gotten indirectly in most instances, through studying reactions to incidents.  This is because it is a rare individual who has the capacity to identify their own character traits objectively, in terms that make it easy to match them with job and career requirements.

As the "decomposing" of the decision components continues, one begins to make rough sketches of the decision steps and interrelationships in order to get a clearer picture of the decision.  One of the many such rough sketches from early in this study of the total career decision is given in Fig. 22-1.

The agonies of self-analysis are familiar to all of us.  Most of us are also aware of the difficulties of getting accurate and useful information about working conditions and requirements in specific areas of each occupational field.  This complexity suggested that a narrower focus was needed to pinpoint a segment of the career strategy decision that would provide a useful area for developing a prototype knowledge-based system.

## Narrowing the Focus of the Study

An examination of the decisions involved in the career strategy area led to identifying a number of possible segments that might make useful prototyping systems.  These included

- Choosing a specific occupation or job
- Deciding what type of organization you would want to work for, if you are to look for a job

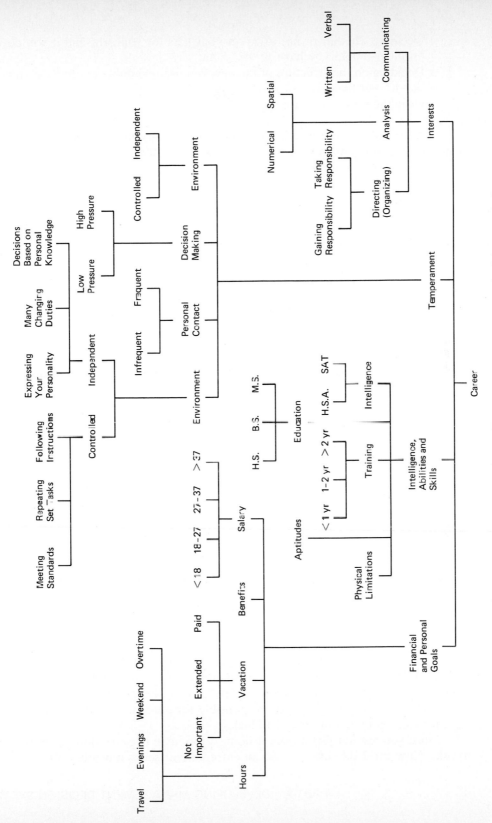

**FIGURE 22-1  Individual factors affecting a career strategy decision—rough sketch.**

- Deciding whether or not to go into business for yourself, and if you do what problems might you have to overcome
- Deciding on the structure of the new venture—should you do it on your own or with partners
- Deciding on the venture

The decisions about whether or not to be an entrepreneur, and if so, whether or not to do it on your own or with partners, were chosen for further study and for prototype system development.

## STUDYING THE SITUATION TO BE PROTOTYPED

It is necessary to analyze in a more structured way how the decision is made, and what working on your own involves, in order to build a structured model of the decision situation useful as a basis for knowledge-based systems development. The following discussion covers the major success requirements an individual considers when deciding to be an entrepreneur.

There is the problem of not having the organizational support that those working for existing companies have. When you are on your own, you have to establish working relationships with auditors, banks, suppliers, lawyers, distributors—everyone affecting your business. An existing company provides these. Operating without these existing company support services requires a lot of determination, perseverance, drive, and initiative. It requires those qualities normally associated with the term *self-starter*.

Since there are no bosses to please or displease when on your own, the measure of success shifts from a promotion or a raise to things like increased sales, more satisfied customers, meeting payrolls, and the like. An entrepreneur would, therefore, seem to be more goal or opportunity oriented.

On your own there is also no organization to hide behind when things do not work out. On the other hand, when things do work out it is pretty clear who should get the credit—you. An entrepreneur would seem to have to like being the one responsible for performance and outcomes of performance, whether successes or failures.

Things can get hectic at times when you are on your own. There is never enough time to do things right; there is always too much to do. These circumstances require a person who likes to solve problems quickly, not at a leisurely pace. Also that person would have to be someone who can tolerate ambiguity, stress, uncertainty, and in many instances lack of perfection.

When on your own there is great reliance on performance—meeting deadlines, keeping promises and commitments, avoiding shoddy services and products—in order to establish strong links with customers. Because of this entrepreneurs seem to have a great sense of believing they are responsible for outcomes, and not the victims of circumstances gone wrong or of bad luck.

Since you are not just a worker doing a job in an organization, there is no boss to ask "How can I do better?" So an entrepreneur seeks out other means of feedback—actual performance, other people, and advisors. Failure is another source of learning feedback. Interestingly entrepreneurs seem to look upon failure as the price of risk taking, a step along the way, something that can be learned from. They expect some failures and are not discouraged by them.

Since working on your own requires balancing many forces, entrepreneurs are usually good negotiators and have a sense of humor. They are also realistic about their own limitations and the limitations of others. They may be persistent, but they seem to know when to move away from unresolvable problems.

Being keenly aware of the consequences of success and failure, entrepreneurs are good risk takers. They are not gamblers. They seem to know not only how to measure the odds, but more important how to create more favorable odds. They take steps to reduce risks, rather than avoid risks entirely.

The ability to resolve contradictions is another characteristic of successful entrepreneurs. They seem to be able to resolve paradoxes, find new solutions, balance many conflicting factors in a situation, and negotiate for pragmatic solutions. They are above all realists. Their creative solutions are reached within the limits of available resources.

Where the situation involves new ventures with partners, an entrepreneur needs to be able to share—not only risks, but also responsibilities, credit, decision making, and rewards.

Although entrepreneurs seem to be driven by a desire for control over their own destinies, they do not seem driven by a need for control and power over others. They do not seem to primarily seek status symbols as the end of their effort, but just as by-products of their entrepreneurial activity. They are interested in a greater degree of control over their own future than can be provided by working for a company owned by someone else.

Unfortunately one of the major negative by-products of entrepreneurial pressures is an over-consuming dedication to the venture. This can often damage or even destroy personal relationships. For someone looking ahead to being an entrepreneur, this factor can set limits on how the venture will be formed and structured.

From this analysis of the types of situations within which entrepreneurs operate, it is possible to develop a *structure* of individual requirements for being a successful entrepreneur. This is the same type of definition that was needed earlier when studying occupations and their requirements for success. These individual requirements can be summarized as follows:

- □ Determination, commitment, perseverance, and initiative
- □ Great desire to grow and achieve something, but little desire for status
- □ Goal or opportunity orientation
- □ Responsibility for performance and outcome of performance
- □ Ability to solve problems quickly
- □ Reliability of performance
- □ Belief that outcomes are not based on luck or circumstances but on one's own performance
- □ Seeking out and using feedback

- Good negotiating skills, a sense of humor, and a realistic assessment of one's weaknesses
- Good risk taking skills and temperament
- Ability to reconcile conflicts and differences
- Capacity to share and work with a team
- Not much interest in power over others or status
- Ability to balance family commitments and commitments to work
- Tolerance for stress and ambiguity
- Belief that failure is a learning experience

In addition to these learnable attributes, there are several not so learnable ones that seem to characterize entrepreneurs. These include intelligence, at least of a pragmatic kind; excellent conceptual and inferential reasoning skills; and good associative reasoning skills and related creative skills. In addition, two other characteristics that seem to be needed are good health and high energy level and a capacity to get others to work for you.

A lot of thinking goes into devising ways to find out whether or not, and to what degree, a specific individual can meet these requirements. Again, as earlier, associated *incidents* or *test cases*, or indirect motivational questioning, are superior to direct questions, such as "Are you good under stress?"

Once an individual's characteristics are identified, the decision involves *pattern matching*. One tries to compare the kind of resources an individual possesses with the requirements for being a successful entrepreneur. The answer will rarely be 100 percent, but more often is an estimate of chances of success. Hopefully the answer will also contain some specifics about areas of weakness that will need to be strengthened.

Much more can be involved in starting and running a new venture. What has been isolated here, through a selective situation analysis, are those aspects that are relevant to the specific question of an individual's qualifications for undertaking a new venture as an entrepreneur.

This decision, which was chosen for prototype knowledge-based system development, was initially broken into three parts:

- The general decision about going into business for oneself. The answer here would be in terms of the chances of success as an entrepreneur, rated as high, medium, or low.
- Deciding on the scope and objective of the venture. Should the individual work alone or involve others in the venture? Working with others would lead to developing a larger venture, and so a greater possibility of capital gain—it is hard to sell a single proprietor business. It would also involve sharing ownership and responsibility.
- Recommendations of steps needed to improve chances of success. Hopefully, this third answer would provide a framework for structuring the actual new venture in a way that a person could live with and still be successful—for example, by setting more modest goals in order to reduce the personal (and family) sacrifices that might have to be made.

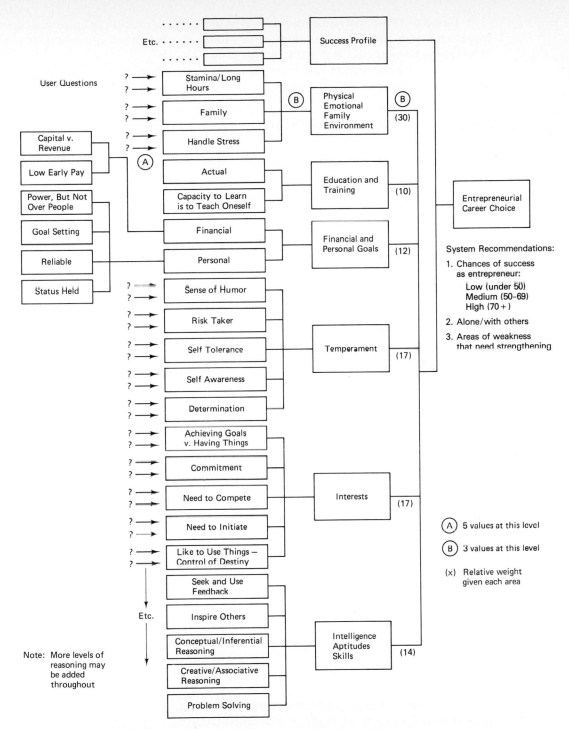

**FIGURE 22-2** **Rough sketch of individual career choice—entrepreneur.**

Based on these analyses of decisions typically faced in making an entrepreneurial career choice, a rough general diagram or model of what the decision appeared to involve was developed. It is given in Fig. 22-2.

The following section describes the prototype system that was developed to assist users in making such decisions.

## DOCUMENTING THE PROTOTYPE SYSTEM

The following discussion covers the system design and documentation phase:

- □ System proposal
- □ Description of the system
- □ Dependency diagrams
- □ Decision charts
- □ Designing and constructing the knowledge base

### System Proposal

The general objective of the project is to develop a knowledge-based system that gives an individual advice about deciding on a career. The specific project is to develop a system for making decisions about an individual's entrepreneurial capabilities. Since the system will not only assess the likelihood of success, but also advise on steps to take to improve the chances of success, it should be of benefit to anyone considering such a career choice.

The prototype system developed during the first phase of the project is limited to a narrower range of options in order to test the feasibility of developing a larger knowledge-based system for career strategy selection. The system can also be used as a prototype of an early segment of the new venture planning system described in Chapter 17 (see Fig. 17-6).

Examples of the sources of expertise used in developing the prototype system were books and journals, existing computer career and occupation selection advisory systems, and experts in the fields of guidance counselling and entrepreneurial decision making.

### Description of the Prototype System

**System overview and objective.** The prototype system is designed to help users determine how suited they are to a career as an entrepreneur and what they might do to increase their chances of succeeding as entrepreneurs. The system uses if-then rules and backward chaining to reason about the information given by a user in order to reach its recommendations.

**Recommendations to be made by the system.** The initial prototype system is limited to making three kinds of recommendations:

- How suitable an entrepreneurial career is for the user
- Areas of weaknesses that need strengthening
- If a new venture is undertaken, whether the user might be better off going it alone or with others

**Nature of the user interface.**    The typical user dialogue covers six key knowledge areas:

- *Interests*—In exploring a user's capabilities in this area, sample questions that might be asked include "When you are playing a game, such as football, tennis, or monopoly, do you get upset if the game is well played on all sides but you or your team loses?"   And if the answer to that question is negative, "Would you be upset if you had placed a bet on the game?"
- *Temperament*—In exploring a user's capabilities in this area, sample questions that might be asked include "Do you generally avoid taking on a job you are pretty sure you cannot handle?" or "Late at night when there is no traffic, does it bother you if the driver of the car you are in goes through a red light?"
- *Intelligence, aptitudes, and skills*—In exploring a user's capabilities in this area, sample questions that might be asked include "How frequently do you approach co-workers or fellow students to get their opinions of your ideas or work performance?" or "When you work with others, how often does the interaction of your group lead to creative solutions to problems that no individual alone would have developed?"
- *Financial and personal goals*—In exploring a user's capabilities in this area, sample questions that might be asked include "Is it more fun to make money than to spend it?", "Would you be willing or able to have an irregular paycheck, or no paycheck at all, until your new venture gets off the ground?", or "When you tell a friend or business associate you will do something by a certain time, do you do it as promised?"
- *Education and training*—In exploring a user's capabilities in this area, sample questions that might be asked include "Do you possess any valuable special training such as CPA certification, technical training, or unique job experience?" or "How often do you teach yourself how to do something new by doing it, making mistakes, yet sticking to it until you get it right?"
- *Physical, emotional, and family environment*—In exploring a user's capabilities in this area, sample questions that might be asked include "Would you be willing to work long hours and on weekends on a regular basis for several years to make a go of your own new venture?" or "Do you have family responsibilities that require you to have a steady work income?"

Although some general questions are asked, a great number of the questions involve an individual's reaction to specific incidents, or so-called test cases.

**Description of the knowledge structure and reasoning process.**    The recommendations made by the prototype system are based on six critical factors: intelligence, aptitudes, and skills; interests; temperament; financial and personal goals;

education and training; and the physical, emotional, and family environment. In turn, the values for each of these factors is based on a number of other factors:

- *Interests* are determined by the degree of competitiveness, commitment, need to initiate and control one's destiny, and kind of goal orientation.
- *Temperament* is determined by self-awareness, how one handles failure, ability to take risks, sense of humor, and strength of determination.
- *Intelligence, aptitudes, and skills* are determined by such factors as creative, conceptual, and problem solving abilities; inferential and associative reasoning skills; and the capability to use feedback and inspire others.
- *Financial and personal goals* are determined by such factors as available financial resources, family obligations, and personal values.
- *Education and training* are determined by the user's actual formal training and education and by their capacity to learn.
- *Physical, emotional, and family environment* are determined by health, family situation, and ability to handle stress.

Samples of additional levels of influencing factors are given in the dependency diagrams cited below.

If-then rules are used to determine the values at each stage. The inference engine uses backward chaining. The values are measured for each of the factors in the reasoning chain as high, medium, low; disagree, agree; salary-size, challenge-goal; sometimes, usually, always; money, accomplishment; yes, no, agree, disagree; certainty factors; and a variety of similar values.

## Dependency Diagrams

Figure 22-3 gives an abbreviated dependency diagram for the entire prototype system. Figure 22-4 gives one of the six detailed, complete segment dependency diagrams. They provide complete summary outlines of all the questions, rules, knowledge segments and their interrelationships, values, and recommendations within the system.

## Decision Charts

Figure 22-5 shows a sample decision chart from the prototype knowledge-based system. There is a decision chart for every rule-set triangle in the dependency diagram.

## Designing and Constructing the Knowledge Base

Rules and questions were developed from the situation study. They were based on the system developer's analysis of how expert career planners actually go about giving advice in such decisions.

A segment of the prototype system's knowledge base is given in Fig. 22-6. The expert system shell used is M.1. As with the other systems discussed in this book, subsequent prototypes within the system were done on GURU.

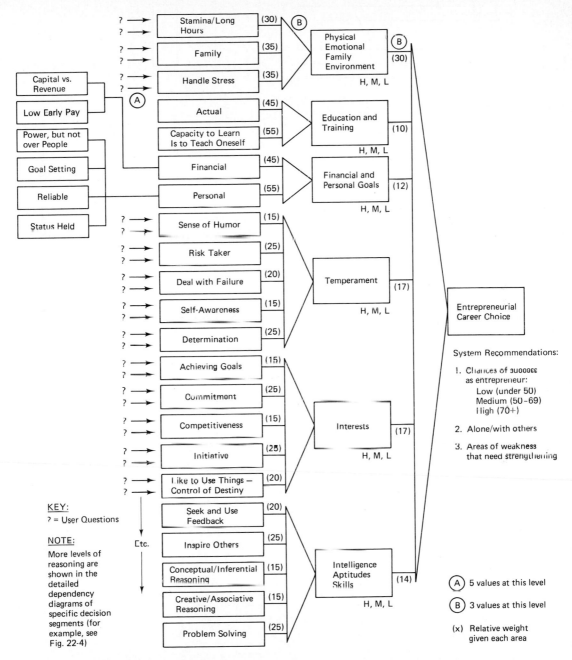

**FIGURE 22-3  Dependency diagram for individual career choice—entrepreneur.**

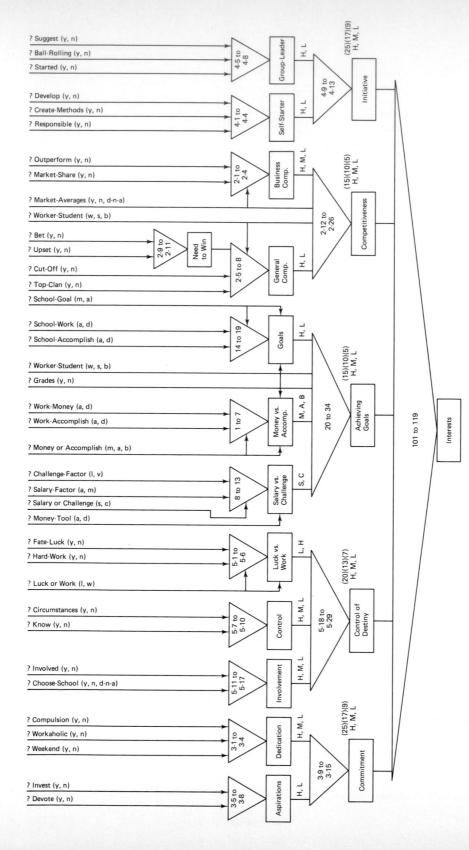

**FIGURE 22-4** Dependency diagram for individual career choice as entrepreneur (one segment—interests).

Rules

| Decision Chart: | 1 | 2 | 3 | 4 | 5 | 6 | 7 |
|---|---|---|---|---|---|---|---|
| **MONEY-V-ACCOMPLISHMENT** | | | | | | | |
| If: Work-money | Agree | Disagree | Agree | Disagree | | | |
| Work-accomplishment | Agree | Disagree | Disagree | Agree | | | |
| Contradiction | | | | | True | True | True |
| Money-or-Accomplishment | | | | | Money | Accomplishment | Both-same |
| Then: Contradiction | True | True | | | | | |
| Accomplishment | | | | X | | X | |
| Money | | | X | | X | | |
| Both-about-same | | | | | | | X |

Rules

| | 14 | 15 | 16 | 17 | 18 | 19 |
|---|---|---|---|---|---|---|
| **GOALS** | | | | | | |
| If: Schoolwork | Agree | Disagree | Agree | Disagree | Agree | Disagree |
| School-accomplishment | Agree | Disagree | Disagree | Agree | Agree | Disagree |
| School-goal | Money | Accomp. | | | Accomp. | Money |
| Then: Goals = High | | X | | X | X | |
| Goals = Low | X | | X | | | X |

**FIGURE 22-5  Decision charts for entrepreneurial career decision—prototype.**

Two very simple introductory and concluding panels (screens) were created for the prototype system to help the user to understand and use the system during a consultation.

The if-then rules in the knowledge base in Fig. 22-6 match those specified in the decision charts shown in Fig. 22-5. They were written to reflect the relationships shown in the dependency diagram in Fig. 22-4. They use the values shown there and in the decision charts. The questions in the knowledge base (Fig. 22-6) are those indicated in the dependency diagram.

```
/*------------------INTERESTS-------------------*/

/*----------------Achieving Goals--------------*/
automaticmenu(ALL).
enumeratedanswers(ALL).

question(work-student) = 'Do you consider yourself a menber of
the work force, a student, or both?'

legalvals(worker-student) = [work-force,student,both].

question(work-money) = 'You work primarily for money and what it
brings.'

legalvals(work-money) = [disagree,agree].

question(work-accomplishment) = 'You work hard primarily for the
sense of accomplishment it brings.'

legalvals(work-accomplishment) = [disagree,agree].

question(money-tool) = 'Money is a tool to measure your success
(keep score) and judge your performance compared to others.'

legalvals(money-tool) = [disagree,agree].

question(salary-factor) = 'When you accepted your most recent job
offer, of all the factors you considered in your decision to
take the job, how important a factor was the size of the salary?'

legalvals(salary-factor) = [of-average-importance,
the-most-important-factor].

question(challenge-factor) = 'When you accepted your most recent
job offer, in your decision to take the job, how important a
factor was the challenge of achieving new goals?'

legalvals(challenge-factor) = [little-importance,very-important].

question(money-or-accomplishment) = 'Do you work hard mainly for
the money, or do you work hard mainly for the sense of
accomplishment and the goals you achieve?'

legalvals(money-or-accomplishment) = [money,
both-about-same,accomplishment].

question(salary-or-challenge) = 'When you accepted your most
recent job offer, the size of the salary or the challenge of
achieving new goals, was most important in your decision to take
the job?'

legalvals(salary-or-challenge) = [salary-size,challenge-goals].

question(schoolwork) = 'You work hard at your schoolwork
primarily to get good grades so you can make money when you
graduate.'
```

*(continued)*

**FIGURE 22-6  Segments of knowledge base for entrepreneurial career decisions—prototype.**

```
legalvals(schoolwork) = [disagree,agree].

question(school-accomplishment) = 'You work hard at your
schoolwork primarily for the sense of accomplishment it brings.'

legalvals(school-accomplishment) = [disagree,agree].

question(grades) = "Do you often aim to get an "A" in courses you
are taking, and do you meet your goal of getting them?"

legalvals(grades) = [yes,no].

question(school-goal) = 'Do you work hard at your schoolwork
primarily to get good grades so you can make money when you
graduate or for the sense of accomplishment it brings?'

legalvals(school-goal) = [money,accomplishment].


/*----------Rules-Money-v-Accomplishment----------*/

rule-1:   if work-money = agree and
             work-accomplishment = agree
          then contradiction = true.

rule 2:   if work-money = disagree and
             work-accomplishment = disagree
          then contradiction = true.

rule-3:   if work-money = agree and
             work-accomplishment = disagree
          then money-v-accomplishment = money.

rule-4:   if work-accomplishment = agree and
             work-money = disagree
          then money-v-accomplishment = accomplishment.

rule-5:   if contradiction = true and
             money-or-accomplishment = money
          then money-v-accomplishment = money cf 80.

rule-6:   if contradiction = true and
             money-or-accomplishment = accomplishment
          then money-v-accomplishment = accomplishment cf 80.

rule-7:   if contradiction = true and
             money-or-accomplishment = both-same
          then money-v-accomplishment = both-about-same.


/*---------Rule-Salary-v-Challenge---------*/

rule-8:   if salary-factor = of-average-importance and
             challenge-factor = little-importance
          then contradiction-b = true.
```

*(continued)*

**FIGURE 22-6** *(continued)*

```
rule-9:   if salary-factor = the-most-important-factor and
             challenge-factor = very-important
          then contradiction-b = true.

rule-10:  if contradiction-b = true and
             salary-or-challenge = salary-size
          then salary-v-challenge = salary cf 80.

rule-11:  if contradiction-b = true and
             salary-or-challenge = challenge-goals
          then salary-v-challenge = challenge cf 80.

rule-12:  if salary-factor = of-average-importance and
             challenge-factor = very-important
          then salary-v-challenge = challenge.

rule-13:  if challenge-factor = little-importance and
             salary-factor = the-most-important-factor
          then salary-v-challenge = salary.


/*--------------------goals--------------------*/

rule-14:  if schoolwork = agree and
             school-accomplishment = agree and
             school-goal = money
          then goals = low.

rule-15:  if schoolwork = disagree and
             school-accomplishment = disagree and
             school-goal = accomplishment
          then goals = high.

rule-16:  if schoolwork = agree and
             school-accomplishment = disagree
          then goals = low.

rule-17:  if schoolwork = disagree and
             school-accomplishment = agree
          then goals = high.

rule-17:  if schoolwork = disagree and
             school-accomplishment = agree and
             school-goal = accomplishment
          then goals = high.

rule-19:  if schoolwork = disagree and
             school-accomplishment = disagree and
             school-goal = money
          then goals = low.
```

**FIGURE 22-6**  *(continued)*

## SYSTEM REFINEMENTS

The prototype system included several refinements found throughout other systems described in this book.

### Testing for Accuracy of Input Information

Multiple questions are often asked, for example, about a character trait such as self-awareness to verify the accuracy of a user's general initial self-assessments. The verification usually is in the form of asking for reactions to specific test situations.

### Resolving Contradictions

Where contradictions are found, for example, in stating personal goals, additional questions are generated by the system to resolve the conflict.

### Alternate Reasoning Paths

In many other instances, alternate lines of reasoning (and series of questions) will be followed depending on information provided by a user or conclusions drawn at different points in the inferential reasoning chain. For example, at times different questions are asked of professionals and of students.

### Confidence Factors

These are used in later versions of the system to replace value sets such as high-medium-low.

### Relative Impact of Different Factors

Since not all factors affect the assessment as to entrepreneurial potential, different weights are given different character traits.

### Reducing the Risks

Identifying one's weaknesses in relation to the demands of an undertaking serves to reduce risks. The process pinpoints strategic choices to avoid. For example, if we lack critical resources required to make a strategy work, we can decide not to pursue it. In addition, the process pinpoints steps that should be taken to make a strategic plan work. If we lack critical resources required to make a strategy work, for example, we can decide to get those resources, if the strategy otherwise is desirable. Either way the risk of failure is reduced. Identifying weaknesses is an enormous help in building a strategic plan. It indicates where additional resources will be needed to succeed. It enables taking anticipatory action to avoid problems and increase the chances of success.

Providing a knowledge-based system with the capability to recommend risk reducing steps to consider is another step toward introducing ways of taking advantage of the judgmental capabilities of knowledge-based systems.

## REVIEW QUESTIONS

1. Finish the knowledge-base for the system (or any segment of the system) partially documented in this chapter and enter it into the expert system shell you have.

2. Career planning choices involve a great deal more than just deciding on whether or not to be an entrepreneur. For example, one often faces a choice of what profession to go into, what type of institution or size of company to work for, what kind of work to do within a professional business area, and the like. Make a list of all the types of prototype knowledge-based systems that might be developed in the career planning area.

3. Design the concept and structure for a prototype knowledge-based system in one of the areas listed in your answer to question 2.

4. In what ways is the prototype system described in this chapter similar to and different from the ones discussed in earlier chapters? Do some of the techniques used to build this system come into play in building the earlier systems?

5. What is involved in the "incident" approach to individual factor analysis, and in what ways is it useful in career planning decisions?

6. In what ways might a knowledge-based system help reduce the risk of failure in a new venture?

7. Discuss the reasons why a perfectionist is not likely to make a good entrepreneur.

## REFERENCES

Ballas, George C., and Dave Holls, *The Making of an Entrepreneur: Keys to Your Success.* Englewood Cliffs, N.J.: Prentice-Hall, 1980.

Baumback, Clifford M., and Joseph R. Mancuso, *Entrepreneurship and Venture Management*, 2nd ed. Englewood Cliffs, N.J.: Prentice-Hall, 1987.

Cook, James R., *The Start Up Entrepreneur: How You Can Succeed in Building Your Own Company Into a Major Enterprise Starting from Scratch.* New York: Harper & Row, 1987.

"Inside the Mind of the Entrepreneur (and Intrapreneur)," *Marketing Communication* (vol. 12, February 1987).

Kirchhoff, Bruce A., et al., eds., *Frontier of Entrepreneurship Research.* Wellesby, Mass: Babron College, 1987.

Silver, A. David, *The Silver Prescription: The Eight-Step Action Plan for Entrepreneurial Success.* New York: John Wiley, 1987.

Stevenson, Howard H., Michael J. Roberts, and H. Irving Grossbeck, *New Business Ventures and the Entrepreneur*, 2nd ed. Homewood, Ill.: Irwin, 1985.

Timmons, Jeffrey A., *New Venture Creation*, 2nd ed. Homewood, Ill.: Irwin, 1985.

# Appendix A

## The Nature and Evaluation of Commercial Expert System Building Tools

*William B. Gevarter*
*NASA Ames Research Center*

The development of new expert systems is changing rapidly—in terms of both ease of construction and time required—because of improved expert system building tools (ESBTs). These tools are the commercialized derivatives of artificial intelligence systems developed by AI researchers at universities and research organizations. It has been reported that these tools make it possible to develop an expert system in an order of magnitude less time than would be required with the use of traditional development languages such as Lisp. In this article, I review the capabilities that make an ESBT such an asset and discuss current tools in terms of their incorporation of these capabilities.

## THE STRUCTURE OF AN EXPERT SYSTEM BUILDING TOOL

The core of an expert system consists of a knowledge base and an accompanying inference engine that operates on the knowledge base to develop a desired solution or response. If one is to use such a system, an end-user interface or an interface to an array of sensors and effectors is required for communication with the *relevant world*. (A "relevant world" is a system or situation operated on by or in contact with the expert system.) In addition, to facilitate the development of an expert system, an ESBT must also include an interface to the developer

□ so that the requisite knowledge base can be built for the particular application domain for which the system is intended,

□ so that the appropriate end-user interface can be developed, and

---

US Government work not protected by US copyright. This article originally appeared in *IEEE Computer*, May 1987, pp. 24–41.

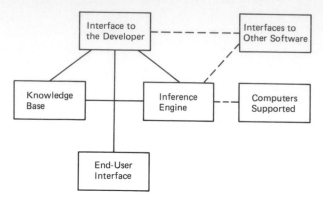

**FIGURE 1   The structure of an expert system building tool. (Solid lines represent basic relationships, and broken lines represent related aspects.)**

□ to incorporate any special instructions to the inference engine (reasoning system) that are required for the particular domain.

The character and quality of these interfaces are two of the main differentiations between commercial tools and ESBTs developed at universities and used in research.   Also important in the structure of ESBTs are

□ interfaces to other software and databases, and
□ the computers on which the ESBTs will run—not only the computers used for development of expert systems, but also those used for their delivery to an end user.

Figure 1 summarizes the structure of an ESBT.

## KNOWLEDGE REPRESENTATION

The knowledge that can be easily represented by the tool is a key consideration in choosing an ESBT.   As indicated by Figure 2, there are three aspects of knowledge representation that are fundamental to these tools—*object descriptions* (declarative knowledge such as facts), *certainties*, and *actions*.   One method of representing objects is by frames with or without *inheritance*.   (Inheritance allows knowledge bases to be organized as hierarchical collections of frames that inherit information from frames above them.   Thus, an inheritance mechanism provides a form of inference.)   *Frames* are tabular data structures for organizing representations of prototypical objects or situations.   A frame has slots that are filled with data on objects and relations appropriate to the situation.   One version of programming referred to as *object-oriented programming* utilizes objects that incorporate provisions for message passing between objects; attached to these objects are procedures that can be activated by the receipt of messages. Declarative knowledge can also be represented by parameter-value pairs, by use of logic notation, and, to some extent, by rules.

Actions change a situation and/or modify the relevant database.   Actions are most commonly represented by rules.   These rules may be grouped together in modules (usually as subparts of the problem) for easy maintenance and rapid access.   Actions may also be represented in terms of *examples*, which indicate the conclusions or decisions reached.   Examples are a particularly desirable form of representation for facilitating knowledge acquisition, and inductive systems capitalize on them.   Examples are much easier to elicit from experts than rules, and may often be a natural form of domain knowledge.   Actions can also be expressed

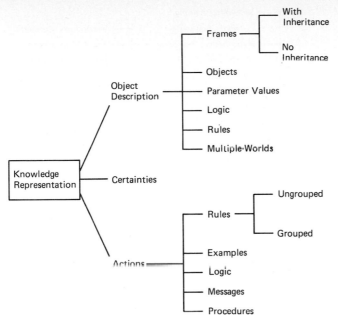

FIGURE 2   Different methods of knowledge representation.

in logic notation, which is a form of rule representation.   Finally, actions can be expressed as procedures elicited by either

- messages (in object-oriented programming) or
- changes in a global database that are observed by *demons*.   ("Demons" are procedures that monitor a situation and respond by performing an action when their activating conditions appear.)

In addition to the representation of objects and actions, one must consider the degree to which the knowledge or data is known to be correct.   Thus, most ESBTs have provisions for representing certainty.   The most common approach is to incorporate "confidence factors"; this approach is a derivative of the approach used in the Mycin expert system.[1]  Fuzzy logic and probability are also used.

An alternative way of handling uncertainties or tentative hypotheses is to consider multiple worlds in which different items are true or not true in these alternative worlds.   Another consideration is whether or not a *deep model* (which is a structural or causal model) of the system can readily be built with the tool in question as an aid in model-based reasoning.   (The same underlying model can often be employed for other uses, such as preservation of knowledge and training.)   Finally, system size (for example, as measured by the number of rules needed) can be of critical importance, as it can have an important effect on memory requirements, memory management, and runtimes.

## INFERENCE ENGINE

Figure 3 indicates the major alternative means by which an ESBT performs inferencing.   The most usual approach is *classification*, which is appropriate for situations in which there is a fixed number of possible solutions.   Hypothesized conclusions from this set are evaluated as

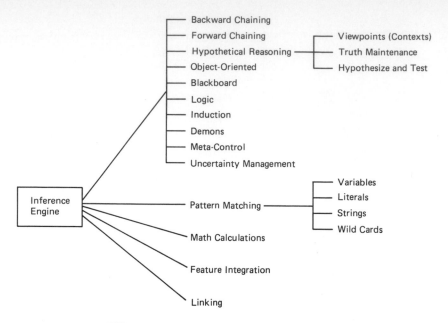

**FIGURE 3   Inference-engine possibilities.**

to whether they are supported by the evidence. This evaluation is usually done by *backward chaining* through *if-then* (that is, antecedent-consequent) rules, starting with rules that have the hypothesized conclusions as their *consequents*. Rules are then searched for those that have as their consequent the conditions that support the *antecedents* (input conditions) in the hypothesized conclusion rule. This process continues recursively until the hypothesis is fully supported or until either a negation or a dead-end is reached. If either of the latter two events happens, additional hypotheses may be tried until some conclusion is reached or the process is terminated. This depth-first, backward-chaining approach was popularized by the Mycin expert system. The corresponding Emycin ESBT shell[2] is the prototype of virtually all the hypothesis-driven (that is, *goal-driven*) commercial ESBTs currently available.

*Forward chaining* starts with data to be input or with the situation currently present in a global database. The data or the situation is then matched with the antecedent conditions in each of the relevant rules to determine the applicability of the rule to the current situation. (The current situation is usually represented in the global database by a set of attributes and their associated values.) One of the matching rules is then selected (for example, by the use of *meta-rules*, which help determine the order in which the rules are tried, or by *priorities*), and the rule's consequents are used to add information to the database or to actuate some procedure that changes the global situation. Forward chaining proceeds recursively (in a manner similar to that of backward chaining), terminating either when a desired result or conclusion is reached or when all relevant rules are exhausted. Combinations of forward and backward chaining have also been found useful in certain situations.

*Forward reasoning* (a more general form of forward chaining) can be done with data-driven procedures (demons).

*Hypothetical reasoning* refers to solution approaches in which assumptions may have to be made to enable the search procedure to proceed. However, later along the search path, it may be found that certain assumptions are invalid and therefore have to be retracted. This *nonmonotonic reasoning* (that is, reasoning in which facts or conclusions must be retracted in light of new information) can be handled in a variety of ways. One approach that reduces the difficulty of the computation is to carry along multiple solutions (these solutions represent different hypotheses) in parallel and to discard inappropriate ones as evidence that contradicts them is gathered. This approach is referred to as *viewpoints, contexts*, and *worlds* in different tools. Another approach is to keep track of the assumptions that support the current search path and to backtrack to the appropriate branch point when the current path is invalidated. This latter approach has been referred to by names like *nonchronological backtracking*. A related capability is *truth maintenance*, which removes derived beliefs when their conditions are no longer valid.

*Object-oriented programming* is an approach in which both information about an object and the procedures appropriate to that object are grouped together into a data structure such as a frame. These procedures are actuated by messages that are sent to the object from a central controller or another object. This approach is particularly useful for simulations involving a group of distinct objects and for real-time signal processing.

The *blackboard inference approach* is associated with a group of cooperating expert systems that communicate by sharing information on a common data structure that is referred to as a "blackboard." An agenda mechanism can be used to facilitate the control of solution development on the blackboard.

In the case of ESBTs, *logic* commonly refers to a theorem-proving approach involving *unification*. "Unification" refers to substitution of variables performed in such a way as to make two items match identically. The common logic implementations are versions of a logic-programming language, Prolog, that utilize a relatively exhaustive depth-first search approach.

An important inference approach found in some tools is the ability to generate rules or decision trees inductively from examples. Human experts are often able to articulate their expertise in the form of examples better than they are able to express it in the form of rules. Thus, inductive learning techniques (which are currently limited in their expressiveness) are frequently ideal methods of knowledge acquisition for rapid prototyping when examples can be simply expressed in the form of a conclusion associated with a simple collection of attributes. The human builders of the resultant expert system can then refine it iteratively by critiquing and modifying the results inductively produced. *Inductive inference* usually proceeds by starting with one of the input parameters and searching for a tree featuring the minimum number of decisions needed to reach a conclusion. This *minimum-depth tree* is found by cycling through all parameters as possible initial nodes and using an *information theoretic approach* to select the order of the parameters to be used for the remaining nodes and to determine which parameters are superfluous. An "information theoretic approach" is one that chooses the solution that requires the minimum amount of information to represent it. The depth of the tree is usually relatively shallow (often less than five decisions deep), so large numbers of examples usually result in broad, shallow trees.

Some tools incorporate demons that monitor local values and execute procedures when the actuation conditions of the demons appear. These tools are particularly appropriate for monitoring applications.

A number of tools offer a choice of several possible inference or search procedures. In systems built with such tools, means are usually made available to the system builder to control the choice of the inference strategy, which the builder causes to be dependent on the system state. Such control is referred to as *meta-control*. One form of meta-control is the use of *control blocks*, which are generic procedures that tell the system the next steps to take in a given situation so that the search will be reduced, enabling a large number of rules to be accommodated without the search space becoming combinatorially explosive.

As the certainty of data, rules, and procedures is usually less than 100 percent, most systems incorporate facilities for certainty management. Thus, they have various approaches for combining uncertain rules and information to determine a certainty value for the result.

*Pattern matching* is often required for mechanizing inference techniques, particularly for matching rule antecedents to the current system state. The sophistication of the pattern-matching approach affects the capabilities of the system. Types of pattern matching vary—from matched identical strings to variables, literals, and wildcards, and can even include partial and/or approximate matching that can serve as analogical reasoning.

Other ESBT capabilities vary from tool to tool. Some inference engines offer rapid and sophisticated math-calculation capabilities. One of the more valuable capabilities is supplied by inference engines that can manage modularized knowledge bases or modularized solution subproblems by accessing and linking these modules as needed.

Another important consideration in a tool is the degree of integration of its various features. Full integration is desirable so that all the tool features can be brought to bear, if needed, on the solution of a single problem. For example, in the case of ESBTs incorporating both object representations and forward and backward chaining rules, it is desirable that expert-system developers be able to mix forward and backward chaining rules freely and be able to reason about information stored in objects when these actions are appropriate.

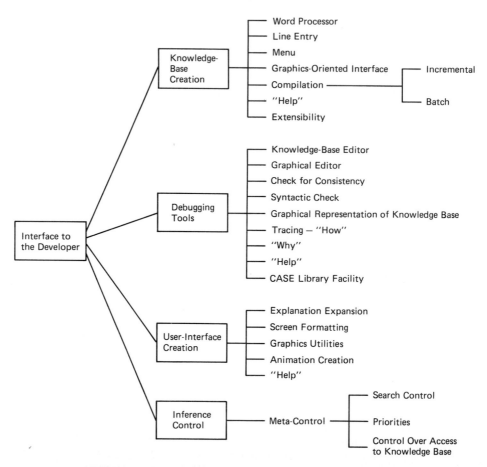

**FIGURE 4   Possibilities for the interface to the developer.**

## THE INTERFACE TO THE DEVELOPER

Various tools offer different levels of capabilities for the expert-system builder to use to mold the system. The simpler tools are shells into which knowledge is inserted in a specific, structured fashion. The more sophisticated tools are generally more difficult to learn, but allow the system developer a much wider choice of knowledge base representations, inference strategies, and the form of the end-user interface. Various levels of debugging assistance are also provided. Figure 4 provides an indication of the possible options (options are tool dependent) that are available for each aspect of the interface to the developer.

## END-USER INTERFACE

Once the expert system has been built, its usability depends in large part on the end-user interface. Figure 5 provides an indication of the range of end-user facilities found in ESBTs. Since most expert systems are really intelligent assistants, the end-user interface is often designed to allow interactive dialogue. This dialogue and/or the initial input most often appear to the user as structured data-input arrangements incorporating menu choices that allow the user to answer requests by the system for information. In some cases, to increase system flexibility, systems will accept multiple and uncertain user responses and still arrive at conclusions (though the certainty of the resultant conclusions is reduced). In sophisticated systems, graphics are often used to show the line of reasoning when the system responds to users' "how" questions; in simpler systems, a listing of the rules supporting the system's conclusions may be employed. ESBTs often answer a user's "Why do you need this information?" question by quoting the rule for which the information is required. The ability of the system to answer the user's "why" and "how" question is important, for it increases the end user's confidence in the system's decision-making ability.

Other capabilities often found in ESBTs are facilities that allow the end user to select alternative parameter values and observe the effect on the outcome (these facilities support "what if" queries), facilities to allow the user to perform an initial pruning of the line of

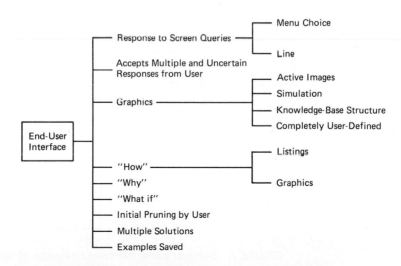

**FIGURE 5  Possibilities for the end-user interface.**

questioning so that the system need not pursue areas that the user feels are irrelevant or unnecessary, and the capability to save examples for future consideration or use.

Very sophisticated tools often include interactive graphics and simulation facilities that increase the end user's understanding and control of the system being represented. Above all, the end-user interface needs to be user friendly if the system is to be accepted.

## PROGRAMMING-LANGUAGE CONSIDERATIONS

In addition to the structure and the paradigms supported by a tool, the programming language in which the tool is written is of major importance. The language determines whether the expert system is compilable and, if it is, whether incrementally or in a batch mode. Compilability reduces the memory requirements and increases the speed of the expert system; incremental compilability speeds development. Figure 6 is illustrative of the aspects related to the tool-language choice.

In general, the more sophisticated tools have been written in Lisp. However, even these tools are now being rewritten in languages such as C to increase speed, reduce memory requirements, and to promote availability on a larger variety of computers. However, some new approaches to mechanizing Lisp may reduce the speed and memory advantages associated with C.

The user can usually extend tools written in Lisp by writing additional Lisp functions. This is also true of some of the other languages, for example, Prolog and Pascal. Similar extensibility is usually found in tools having language hooks for accessing other programs or database hooks for accessing other information. In some cases, the expert system generated

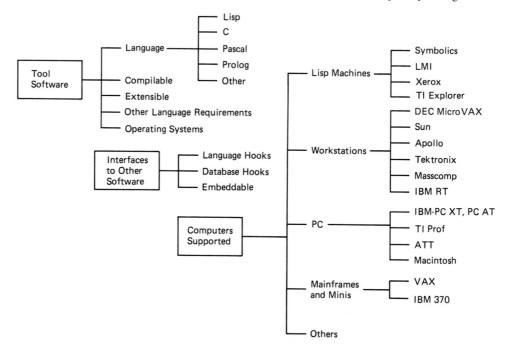

**FIGURE 6** **Software and hardware aspects of tools.**

by the tool is fully embeddable in other systems, which produces increased autonomy. Whether or not a system is fully embeddable in other systems and is therefore capable of autonomous operations is becoming increasingly important, now that expert systems are moving from prototypes to being fielded. Reliability and memory management (in Lisp, the latter takes the form of *garbage collection*) are often important considerations for fielded systems. "Garbage collection" is the collection of no-longer-used memory allocations; these allocations can slow the system operation.

The computers supported by the various tools are primarily a function of the language and operating system in which the tools are written, and the computer's memory, processing, and graphics-display capabilities. The trend toward making expert system shells available on personal computers (such as those made by IBM) results in part from the increasing capabilities of these computers. However, this trend is also partly owing to the writing of tools in faster languages, such as C, and to taking advantage of modularization in building the knowledge base. As mentioned earlier, such modularization involves decomposing the problem into subproblem modules and providing appropriate linking between these modules as required during operation.

## FUNCTION CAPABILITIES

Of primary consideration are the function applications that can readily be built with a particular ESBT. A review of the major function applications follows (see also Figure 7).

**Classification.** By far the most common function addressed by expert systems is *classification*. "Classification" refers to selecting an answer from a fixed set of alternatives on the basis of information that has been input.

Below are some subcategories of classification.

□ *Interpretation of measurements.* This refers to hypothesis selection performed on the basis of measurement data and corollary information.

□ *Diagnosis.* In *diagnosis*, the system not only interprets data to determine the difficulty, but also seeks additional data when such data is required to aid its line of reasoning.

□ *Debugging, treatment or repair.* These functions refer to taking actions or recommending measures to correct an adverse situation that has been diagnosed.

□ *Use advisor.* An expert system as a front end to a computer program or to a piece of machinery can be very helpful to the inexperienced user. Such systems depend both on the goals of the user and the current situation in suggesting what to do next. Thus, the advice evolves as the state of the world changes. Use advisors can also be helpful in guiding users through procedures in other domains (for example, auto repair and piloting aircraft).

Classification and other function applications can be considered to be of two types: *surface reasoning* and *deep reasoning*. In surface reasoning, no model of the system is employed; the approach taken is to write a collection of rules, each rule asserting that a certain situation warrants a certain response or conclusion. (These situation-response relationships are usually written as heuristic rules garnered from experience.) In deep reasoning, the system draws upon causal or structural models of the domain of interest to help arrive at the conclusion.

```
1. Classification
     a. Interpretation of measurements
          Hypothesis selection based on evidence
     b. Diagnosis
          Measurement selection and interpretation
          (often involves models of system organization and behavior)
2. Design and synthesis
     Provide constraints as well as guidance
3. Prediction
     Forecasting
4. Use advisor
     "How to" advice
5. Intelligent assistant
     Provide decision aids
6. Scheduling
     Time-ordering of tasks, given resource constraints
7. Planning
     Many complex choices affect each other
8. Monitoring
     Provide real-time, reliable operation
9. Control
     Process control
10. Information digest
     Situation assessment
11. Discovery
     Generate new relations or concepts
12. Debugging
     Provide corrective action
13. Example-based reasoning
     The source of most rules
```

**FIGURE 7   AI function capabilities.**

Thus, systems employing deep models are potentially more capable and may degrade more gracefully than those relying on surface reasoning.

**Design and synthesis.**   "Design and synthesis" refers to configuring a system on the basis of a set of alternative possibilities.   The expert system incorporates constraints that the system must meet as well as guidance for steps the system must take to meet the user's objectives.

**Intelligent assistant.**   Here the emphasis is on having a system that, depending on user needs, can give advice, furnish information, or perform various subtasks.

**Prediction.**   "Prediction" refers to forecasting what will happen in the future on the basis of current information.   This forecasting may depend upon experience alone, or it may involve the use of models and formulas.   The more dynamic systems may use simulation to aid in the forecasting.

**Scheduling.**   "Scheduling" refers to time-ordering a given set of tasks so that they can be done with the resources available and without interfering with each other.

**Planning.**   "Planning" is the selection of a series of actions from a complex set of alternatives to meet a user's goals.   It is more complex than scheduling in that tasks are chosen, not given. In many cases, time and resource constraints do not permit all goals to be met. In these cases, the most desirable outcome is sought.

**Monitoring.** "Monitoring" refers to observing an ongoing situation for its predicted or intended progress and alerting the user or system if there is a departure from the expected or usual. Typical applications are space flights, industrial processes, patients' conditions, and enemy actions.

**Control.** Control is a combination of monitoring a system and taking appropriate actions in response to the monitoring to achieve goals. In many cases, such as the operation of vehicles or machines, the tolerable response delay may be as small as milliseconds. In such a case, the system may be referred to as a *real-time system*. "Real-time" is defined as "responding within the permissible delay time" to the end that the system being controlled stays within its operating boundaries.

**Digest of information.** A system performing this function may take in information and return a new organization or synthesis. One application may be the inductive determination of a decision tree from examples. Others may be the assessment of military or stock market situations on the basis of input and corollary information.

**Discovery.** Discovery is similar to digest of information except that the emphasis is on finding new relations, order, or concepts. This is still a research area. Examples include finding new mathematical concepts and elementary laws of physics.

**Others.** There are other functions, such as learning, that are directly subsumable under the ones I have enumerated thus far. In many cases, these functions (and some of those already mentioned) can be ingeniously decomposed into functions discussed previously. Thus, for example, design and some other functions can often be separated into subtasks that can be solved by classification.

## IMPORTANCE OF VARIOUS ESBT ATTRIBUTES FOR PARTICULAR FUNCTION APPLICATIONS

Table 1* is an attempt to relate the various attributes that are found in different ESBTs to their importance in facilitating the building of expert systems that perform different functions. A solid circle indicates an attribute that is very worthwhile in helping to build that function. An open circle indicates that it is a lesser contributor. A dash (—) indicates an attribute that does not provide a significant contribution. As indicated earlier, the evaluation is subjective because, depending on the insight and ingenuity of the system developer, some of the functions can be decomposed into other functions. Thus, Table 1 reflects what I see as obvious and perhaps necessary attributes for straightforward construction of expert systems that perform the indicated functions.

---

*In the future, various ESBT approaches may be shown to be Turing Machine equivalents, which would mean that any computation could be performed by them. Therefore, it usually cannot be said definitively that ESBT *x* cannot perform function *y*. Thus, Table 1 in the sidebar is really an attempt to reflect my perception of which ESBT attributes simplify the programming of various expert-system functions.

**TABLE 1.** A Subjective View of the Importance of Various Expert System Tool Attributes for Particular Function Applications.

● VERY
○ SOMEWHAT
— LITTLE

| | DIAGNOSIS AND CLASSIFICATION | DATA ANALYSIS AND INTERPRETATION | DESIGN AND SYNTHESIS | PREDICTION AND SIMULATION | MONITORING | USE ADVISOR | INTELLIGENT ASSIST: | PLANNING AND SCHEDULING | CONTROL |
|---|---|---|---|---|---|---|---|---|---|
| **INFERENCE APPROACH** | | | | | | | | | |
| BC | ● | ○ | ○ | — | ○ | ○ | ○ | ○ | ○ |
| FC & FORWARD REASONING | ○ | ● | ● | ● | ● | ● | ○ | ● | ● |
| BC, FC, & FORWARD REASON. | ● | ● | ● | ○ | ○ | ○ | ● | ● | ○ |
| HYPOTHETICAL REASONING | ● | ● | ● | ○ | ○ | ○ | ○ | ● | — |
| OBJECT-ORIENTED | ○ | ○ | ○ | ● | ○ | ○ | ○ | ○ | ● |
| BLACKBOARD | ● | ● | ● | ○ | ○ | ○ | ○ | ● | — |
| INDUCTION | ● | ○ | ○ | — | — | ○ | ○ | — | ○ |
| **OBJECT DESCRIPTION** | | | | | | | | | |
| FRAMES | ● | ○ | ● | ○ | ○ | ○ | ○ | ● | ○ |
| FRAMES W/INHERITANCE | ● | ○ | ● | ○ | ○ | ○ | ○ | ● | ○ |
| OBJECTS | ○ | ○ | ○ | ● | ○ | ○ | ○ | ○ | ● |
| PARAMETER VALUES PAIRS | ○ | ○ | ○ | — | ○ | ○ | — | ○ | ○ |
| LOGIC | ○ | ○ | ○ | ○ | ○ | ○ | ○ | ○ | ○ |
| RULES | ○ | ○ | ○ | ○ | ○ | ○ | ○ | ○ | ○ |
| CERTAINTIES | ● | ● | ○ | ○ | ○ | ○ | ○ | ○ | ○ |
| **ACTIONS** | | | | | | | | | |
| RULES | ● | ● | ● | ● | ● | ● | ● | ● | ● |
| EXAMPLES | ● | ○ | ○ | ○ | — | ○ | ○ | — | ○ |
| LOGIC | ● | ● | ● | ● | ○ | ○ | ○ | ○ | ○ |
| MESSAGES | ○ | ● | ● | ● | ○ | ○ | ○ | ● | ● |
| PROCEDURES | ○ | ○ | ● | ● | ● | ○ | ○ | ● | ● |

# BRIEF DESCRIPTIONS OF COMMERCIAL ESBTs

The following are descriptions of some of the current commercial expert system building tools in common use. The attributes of these tools are summarized in Tables 2 and 3 for easy comparison. This sidebar is not intended to be an exhaustive survey. For example, VP-Expert, an inexpensive (under $100) but capable rule-based ESBT for PCs, has recently been introduced by Paperback Software in Berkeley, Calif. GEST, an evolving university-supported ESBT from Georgia Tech, provides high-order capabilities (such as multiple knowledge representations) at a fraction of the cost of commercial, more polished tools offering similar capabilities. GURU, from mdbs in Lafayette, Ind., a composite ESBT integrated with a database spreadsheet and natural-language front end, is also available.

## ART

ART is a versatile tool that incorporates a sophisticated programming workbench. It runs on advanced computers and workstations such as those produced by Symbolics, LMI, TI, Apollo, and VAX. ART's strong point is *viewpoints*, a technique that allows hypothetical *nonmonotonic reasoning*; in nonmonotonic reasoning, multiple solutions are carried along in parallel until constraints are violated or better solutions are found. At such points, inappropriate solutions are discarded. ART provides graphics-based interfaces for browsing both its viewpoint and *schema* (frame) networks. ART is primarily a forward-chaining system with sophisticated user-defined pattern matching; the pattern matching is based on an enhanced version of an indexing scheme derived from OPS5. (OPS5 is discussed below.) Object-oriented programming is made available by attaching *procedures* (active values) to objects (the objects are called *schemata*). ART has a flexible graphics workbench with which to create graphical interfaces and graphical simulations. ART was designed for near-real-time performance. To achieve this performance, ART compiles its frame-based as well as its relational knowledge into logic-like assertions (the latter are called *discrimination networks*). Applications particularly suited for ART are planning/scheduling, simulation, configuration generation, and design. Currently written in Lisp, ART employs a very efficient, unique memory management system that virtually eliminates garbage collection. A C-language version is now available. (Further information on ART is available from Inference Corp., 5300 W. Century Blvd., Los Angeles, CA 90045; (213) 417-7997.)

## KEE

KEE, which runs on advanced AI computers, is the most widely used programming environment for building sophisticated expert systems. Important aspects of KEE are its multifeature development environment and end-user interfaces, which incorporate windows, menus, and graphics. KEE contains a sophisticated frame system that allows the hierarchical modeling of objects and permits multiple forms of inheritance. KEE also offers a variety of reasoning and analysis methods, including object-oriented programming, forward and backward chaining of rules, hypothetical reasoning (which is incorporated as KEE Worlds), a predicate-logic language, and demons. It has an open architecture that supports user-defined inference methods, inheritance roles, logic operators, functions, and graphics. KEE has a large array of graphics-based interfaces that are developer/user controlled, including facilities for graphics-based simulation (the graphics-based simulation facility, Sim Kit, is available at extra cost). KEE has been used for applications in diagnosis, monitoring, real-time process control,

**TABLE 2.** Attributes of Some Commercial ESBTs.

| NAME | ART 3.0 | KEE 3.0 | KNOW-LEDGE CRAFT | PICON | S.1 | ES ENVIRON/ VM OR MVS |
|---|---|---|---|---|---|---|
| **FUNCTIONAL USES** | | | | | | |
| Classification | X | X | X | X | X | X |
| Design | X | X | X | | X | |
| Planning/Scheduling | X | X | X | | | |
| Process Control | X | X | X | X | | |
| **KB REPRESENTATION** | | | | | | |
| Rules | | | | | | |
| Structured Rules | X | X | X | X | X | X |
| Certainty Factors | | | | | X | X |
| Rule Limit | | | | | | |
| Frames w/Inherit. | X | X | X | X | No inherit. | |
| Object-Oriented | X | X | X | X | | |
| Logic | X | X | X | | X | |
| Examples | | | | | | |
| Structured Examples | | | | | | |
| Procedures | X | X | X | | X | X |
| **INFERENCE ENGINE** | | | | | | |
| Forward Chaining | X | X | X | X | FR | X |
| Backward Chaining | (goal rules) | X | X | X | X | X |
| Demons | X | X | X | X | X | |
| Blackboard-Like | X | | | | | |
| Time-Modeling | X | X | | X | | |
| Truth Maintenance | X | X | | | | |
| Meta Control | X | X | X | X | X | X |
| Logic | X | X | X | | X | |
| Induction | | | | | | |
| Math Calculations | X | X | X | X | X | |
| Context | X | X | X | | | |
|   (Viewpoints, Worlds) | | | | | | |
| **PATTERN MATCHING** | | | | | | |
| Variables | X | X | X | X | | |
| Literals | X | X | X | X | X | |
| Sequences | X | | X | X | | |
| Segments | X | | X | X | | |
| Wildcards | X | | X | | | |
| **DEVELOPER INTERFACE** | | | | | | |
| KB Creation | | | | | | |
|   Word Processor | X | | X | | X | X |
|   Line Entry | | X | X | X | X | |
|   KB Editor | X | X | X | X | X | X |
|   Menu | X | X | | X | X | |
| Check for Consistency | | X | | X | X | |
| Graphics Rep of KB | X | X | X | X | X | |
| Inference Tracing | X | X | X | X | X | X |
| Graphics Utilities | X | X | X | X | e | |
|   to build end-user interface | | | | | | |
| Screen Format Utilities | X | X | X | X | X | X |
| Graphics Simulation | X | Sim Kit (Extra cost) | Simulation-Craft (Extra cost) | X | e | |
|   Capabilities | | | | | | |
| Why | X | X | X | | X | X |
| How | X | X | X | X | X | X |
| Explanation Expansion | X | X | X | X | X | X |
| Online Help | X | X | X | | X | X |
| Syntax Help | X | X | X | X | X | |
| Tool Extensible | X | X | X | X | | |

*(continued)*

**TABLE 2.** *(continued)*

| ENVISAGE | KES | M.1 | NEXPERT OBJECT | PERSONAL CONSUL. + | EXSYS. 3.0 | EXPERT EDGE | ESP FRAME ENGINE |
|---|---|---|---|---|---|---|---|
| X | X | X | X | X | X | X | X |
|  |  |  | X |  |  |  | X |
|  |  |  | X |  |  |  |  |
|  |  |  | X |  |  |  |  |
|  | X | X |  |  | X |  |  |
| X |  |  | Cataloged | X |  | X | X |
| X | X | X 1000 | 2000 | X 800 | X 5000 | X |  |
|  |  |  | X | X |  |  | X |
|  |  |  |  |  |  |  | X |
|  |  |  |  |  |  |  |  |
| X | X |  | X | X |  |  | X |
| A |  | FR | X | X | X |  | X |
| X | X | X | X | X | X | X | X |
| X |  | X | X | X |  |  | X |
|  |  |  | X |  |  | X |  |
| X |  | X | X | X |  |  | X |
|  |  |  |  |  |  |  | X |
| X | X | X | X | X | X | X | X |
|  | X | X | X |  | Numeric | Numeric | Numeric & String |
|  |  |  | X |  |  |  |  |
| X |  |  |  |  | X |  |  |
|  | X |  |  |  |  |  |  |
|  |  |  |  |  |  | X |  |
| X | X | X |  |  | X | X | X |
|  | X |  | X | X | X | X |  |
|  |  | X | X | X | X | X |  |
|  |  | X | X | X | X | X |  |
|  |  | X | X |  | X | X | ESP |
|  |  |  | X | X |  |  | X |
| X | X |  | X | X | X | X | X |
|  |  |  | X |  |  |  |  |
|  |  | X | X | X | X | X |  |
|  |  |  | X |  |  |  |  |
| X | X | X | X | X | X | X | X |
| X | X | X | X | X | X | X | X |
| X | X | X | X | X | X | X | X |
| X |  | X | X | X | X | X | X |
| X |  | X | X | X |  | X |  |
| X |  |  | X | X |  | X | X |

**TABLE 2.** *(continued)*

| NAME | INSIGHT 2+ | TIMM | RULE-MASTER | KDS 3 | 1st CLASS |
|---|---|---|---|---|---|
| **FUNCTIONAL USES** | | | | | |
| Classification | X | X | X | X | X |
| Design | | | X | X | |
| Planning/Scheduling | | | | X | |
| Process Control | | X | X | X | |
| **KB REPRESENTATION** | | | | | |
| Rules | | | | | |
| Structured Rules | X | | X | | X |
| Certainty Factors | X | X | X | X | X |
| Rule Limit | 2000 | | | 16000 from 4000 examples | |
| Frames w/Inherit. | | | | | |
| Object-Oriented | | | | X | |
| Logic | | | | | X |
| Examples | | | | | |
| Structured Examples | | X | X | X | X |
| Procedures | | | | | |
| **INFERENCE ENGINE** | | | | | |
| Forward Chaining | X | X | X | X | X |
| Backward Chaining | X | | X | X | X |
| Demons | | | | | |
| Blackboard-Like | | | | X | X |
| Time-Modeling | | | | | |
| Truth Maintenance | | | | X | |
| Meta Control | | | | | |
| Logic | | | | | |
| Induction | | X | X | X | X |
| Math Calculations | X | | | X | |
| Context (Viewpoints, Worlds) | | | | | |
| **PATTERN MATCHING** | | | | | |
| Variables | Numeric | | X | | Numeric & Logical |
| Literals | | | | | |
| Sequences | | | | | |
| Segments | | | | | |
| Wildcards | | | | | X |
| **DEVELOPER INTERFACE** | | | | | |
| KB Creation | | | | | |
| Word Processor | | | | | X |
| Line Entry | X | X | X | X | X |
| KB Editor | X | | X | X | X |
| Menu | | X | | X | X |
| Check for Consistency | | X | X | X | X |
| Graphics Rep of KB | | | | | X |
| Inference Tracing | X | X | | X | X |
| Graphics Utilities to build end-user interface | | | | X | |
| Screen Format Utilities | X | X | | X | X |
| Graphics Simulation Capabilities | | | | | e |
| Why | X | | X | X | |
| How | X | | X | X | TREE |
| Explanation Expansion | X | X | X | X | X |
| Online Help | X | | X | X | X |
| Syntax Help | | | X | X | |
| Tool Extensible | | | X | X | X |

*(continued)*

**TABLE 2.**  *(continued)*

| NAME | ART 3.0 | KEE 3.0 | KNOW-LEDGE CRAFT | PICON | S.1 | ES ENVIRON/ VM OR MVS |
|---|---|---|---|---|---|---|
| **SOFTWARE** | | | | | | |
| Language of Tool | COMMON-LISP | COMMON-LISP | COMMON-LISP | ZETA-LISP.C | C | PASCAL |
| Compilable | Incremental | Incremental | Incremental | X | X | Incremental |
| Other Lang. Req. | COMMON-LISP | COMMON-LISP | COMMON-LISP | LISP | | CMS, GDDM, PASCAL/VS |
| Operating Sys. | VMS, UNIX | | | | UNIX VM/CMS VMS | VM/CMS or MVS |
| **COMPUTERS SUPPORTED** | | | | | | |
| Symbolics | X | X | X | | | |
| LMI | X | X | X | X | | |
| TI Explorer | X | X | X | X | | |
| VAX | X | | X | | VMS ULTRIX | |
| XEROX | | X | | | | |
| IBM PC | | | | | | |
| Macintosh | | | | | | |
| TI Prof. | | | | | | |
| APOLLO | | X | | | X | |
| SUN | X | X | | | X | |
| IBM 370 | | | | | X | X |
| Others | | X | X | | X | |
| **SYSTEMS INTERFACE** | | | | | | |
| Lang. Hooks | Via Host Computer | Via Host Computer | Via Host Mach | Via Host Mach | C, Others | X |
| DB Hooks | Via Host Computer | Via Host Computer | Via Host Mach | Via Host Mach | Via " | X |
| **END USER INTERFACE** | | | | | | |
| Screen Capabilities Line | | X | X | X | X | X |
| Menu | X | X | X | X | X | X |
| Graphics | X | X | X | X | e | |
| Simulation | X | Sim Kit | Simulation-Craft | X | e | |
| Why | X | X | X | X | X | X |
| How | X | X | X | X | X | X |
| Help | X | X | X | X | X | X |
| Initial Pruning | X | X | | | | |
| Multiple Solution | X | X | X | | | |
| Examples Saved | | | X | X | X | X |
| Mult. & Uncertain User Resp. OK | X | X | | | X | |
| What If | X | X | X | X | X | X |
| COMPANY | Inference | Intellicorp | Carnegie Group | LMI | Teknow-ledge | IBM |
| COST (1st unit) | $65K | $52K includes training | $50K includes training | $60K | $25K 1 user mach. $45K mult. user | $35K |
| Run Time Sys. Cost | $1–8K | PC Host + VAX $20K + 0.5K/PC | None Yet | | $9.5K | $25K |

*(continued)*

**TABLE 2.** *(continued)*

| NAME | ENVISAGE | KES | M.1 | NEXPERT OBJECT | PERSONAL CONSUL. + | EXSYS. 3.0 |
|---|---|---|---|---|---|---|
| **SOFTWARE** | | | | | | |
| Language of Tool | PASCAL | C | C | C | LISP | C |
| Compilable | X | X | X | Incremental | X | Incremental |
| Other Lang. Req. | | | | | | |
| Operating Sys. | VMS | MSDOS on PC | MSDOS | MSDOS VMS | MSDOS | MSDOS VMS |
| **COMPUTERS SUPPORTED** | | | | | | |
| Symbolics / LMI | | | | | | |
| TI Explorer / VAX | X | X | | | | VMS UNIX |
| XEROX / IBM PC | | X | X | AT | X | X |
| Macintosh / TI Prof. | | | | X | X | |
| APOLLO / SUN | | X / X | | | | |
| IBM 370 / Others | X | X | | X | | |
| **SYSTEMS INTERFACE** | | | | | | |
| Lang. Hooks | PASCAL etc. | C | X | C, PASCAL | LISP | X |
| DB Hooks | X | X | X | DBASE III | DBASE III | X |
| **END USER INTERFACE** | | | | | | |
| Screen Capabilities Line | X | X | | | X | |
| Menu | X | X | X | X | X | X |
| Graphics | | e | | X | e | e |
| Simulation | | | | X | | |
| Why | X | X | X | X | X | X |
| How | X | X | X | X | X | X |
| Help | X | X | X | X | X | X |
| Initial Pruning | | | | | X | |
| Multiple Solution | | X | | X | X | X |
| Examples Saved | X | X | | X | X | X |
| Mult. & Uncertain User Resp. OK | X | X | X | | X | X |
| What If | X | X | | X | X | X |
| COMPANY | Sys. Designers Software | S/W Arch. & Engr. | Teknow-ledge | Neuron Data | TI | Exsys, CA Intel |
| COST (1st unit) | $25K on VAX $15K on MicVAX | $4K PC $7K WkStns $25K VAX | $5K | $5K PC-AT $3K MAC | $3K | $395 PC $5K VAX |
| Run Time Sys. Cost | | 10% of Develop Sys. | ≈$50 | $1K | $75 First Unit | One Time Fee |

*(continued)*

| EXPERT EDGE | ESP FRAME ENGINE | INSIGHT 2+ | TIMM | RULE-MASTER | KDS 3 | 1st CLASS |
|---|---|---|---|---|---|---|
| C | Prolog 2 | Turbo-PASCAL | FORTRAN | C | 8086 Assembly | PASCAL |
| X | Incremental | X | X | X | | X |
| | | | | C Compiler | | |
| MSDOS | MSDOS | MSDOS | | DOS 3.0 UNIX, VMS | MSDOS | MSDOS |
| | | | X | X | | |
| X | X | X | X | AT | X | X |
| | | X | | | | X |
| | | | | X | | |
| | | | | X | | |
| | | X | X | X | | |
| X | Prolog 2 | X | X | Most | PASCAL, BASIC | ANY |
| X | Via " | DBASE II | | X | Reads Assem. Lang. | X |
| X | X | | X | | X | X |
| X | X | X | | X | X | X |
| | | | | | X | c |
| | | | | | X | |
| X | X | X | | X | X | |
| X | X | X | X | X | X | X |
| X | X | X | | X | X | X |
| X | | X | | | X | |
| X | X | | X | | X | X |
| X | | X | X | | X | |
| X | | X | X | | X | X |
| Human Edge | Exp Sys Inter | Level-5-R | GRC | Radian | KDS Dev Sys | Progr. in Motion |
| $2500 Adv $5000 Pro | $895 | $485 | $1.9K PC $19K others | $995 PC $5K Wkst $17.5K VAX | $1495 | $495 |
| $50 | By Agreement | Negoti. | No Fee | $100 PC $500 UNIX/VMS | Based on Quality | No Fee |

*(continued)*

**TABLE 3.** A Composite View of Some Commercial ESBTs.

| SYSTEM | OBJ. REP. | CERTAINTIES | ACTIONS | EXAMPLES | PATTERN MATCH. | BC | FC | OBJ.-ORIENTED | LOGIC | INDUCTION | HYPO. REASON. | CLASS. INTERPRETA. (SHALLOW) | ADVICE (SHALLOW) | CLASS. INTERPRETA. (DEEP) | ADVICE (DEEP) | DESIGN | PLANNING | MONITOR/CONTROL |
|---|---|---|---|---|---|---|---|---|---|---|---|---|---|---|---|---|---|---|
| | KNOW. REP. | | | | | | | INFERENCE ENGINE | | | | FUNCTIONAL CAPABIL. | | | | | | |
| ART | ● | □ | ● | | ● | ● | ● | ● | ● | | ● | ● | ● | ● | ● | ● | ● | ○ |
| KEE | ● | □ | ● | | ● | ● | ○ | ● | ● | | ● | ● | ● | ● | ● | ● | ● | ○ |
| KNOWLEDGE CRAFT | ● | □ | ● | | ● | ● | ● | ● | ● | | ● | ● | ● | ● | ● | ● | ● | ○ |
| PICON | ● | | ● | | ● | ● | ● | ● | | | ● | ● | | | | | | ● |
| S.1 | ○ | C | ● | | ○ | ● | FR | | ○ | | | ● | ● | ○ | | | | |
| ES ENVIRON/VM OR VMS | | C, F | ● | | ○ | ● | ○ | | | | | ● | | | | | ○ | |
| ENVISAGE (ADVISOR) | ○ | F, B | ● | | ○ | ● | ○ | | | | | ● | ○ | | | | | |
| KES | | C, B | ● | | ○ | ● | ○ | | | | ● | ● | ○ | | | | | |
| M.1 | | C | ● | | ○ | ● | FR | | ○ | | | ● | | ○ | | ○ | ○ | ○ |
| NEXPERT OBJECT | ● | □ | ● | | ○ | ● | ● | | | | | ● | | ○ | | ○ | ○ | ○ |
| PERSONAL CONSULTANT + | ○ | C | ● | | ● | ● | | | | | | ● | ○ | | | | | |
| EXSYS 3.0 | | C | ○ | | ○ | ● | ○ | | | | | | ○ | | | | | |
| EXPERT EDGE | | B | ○ | | ○ | ● | | | | | | ● | | | | | | |
| ESP FRAME ENGINE | ● | | ● | | ○ | ● | ○ | | ● | | | ● | | ● | | | | |
| INSIGHT 2 + | | C | ○ | | ○ | ● | ○ | | | | | ● | | | | | | |
| TIMM | | C, I | ○ | ● | | ● | | | | ● | | ● | ○ | | | | | ○ |
| RULEMASTER 3.0 | | F | ○ | ● | ○ | ● | ○ | | | ● | | ● | | | | ○ | | ○ |
| KDS 3 | ○ | C | ● | | ● | ● | ● | ○ | | | | | | ○ | | ○ | ○ | ○ |
| 1st CLASS | | C | ○ | ● | ○ | ○ | ○ | | | ● | | ● | | | | | | |
| OPS5 + | | | ● | | ● | | ● | | | | | ● | | ○ | | ○ | ○ | ○ |

● STRONG    FR—FORWARD REASONING
○ FAIR
□ USER PROG.

C—CONFID. FACTOR
F—FUZZY LOGIC
B—BAYSIAN LOGIC
I —INCOMPLETE INFO

*
L —LISP
PA—PASCAL
A —ASSEMBLY
F —FORTRAN
PR—PROLOG
O —OTHERS
C —C

**
@
D —DISCRIM. NET
R —RULES
IN —INCREMENTAL
Y —YES
DT—DECIS. TREE

*(continued)*

| KB CREATION | DEBUGGING | GRAPHICS | USER INT. CREA. | INFER. CONTROL | WHY/HOW | SCREEN INTER. | GRAPHICS | WHAT IF | TOOL LANG. ** | COMPILABLE @ | LANG/DB HOOKS | COMPUTERS @@ | 1st UNIT COST $K |
|---|---|---|---|---|---|---|---|---|---|---|---|---|---|
| • | • | • | • | ○ | • | • | • | • | L | D, IN | ○ | V, Su, S, L, T | 65 |
| • | • | • | • | • | • | • | • | • | L | IN | ○ | A, S, L, T, X, O | 52† + SIM KIT |
| • | • | • | • | □ | • | • | • | ○ | L | IN | ○ | L, S, T, V, O | 50† + SIM |
| • | • | • | • | ○ | • | • | • | • | L, C | Y | • | L, T | 60 |
| • | • | • | • | • | • | ○ | | • | C | Y | • | 370, V, Su, H, O | 25, 45 |
| • | ○ | • | ○ | • | • | ○ | | ○ | PA | IN | • | 370 | 60 |
| ○ | • | | ○ | ○ | • | ○ | | ○ | PA | Y | • | V, μV | 25, 15 |
| ○ | ○ | | ○ | | • | ○ | | • | C | Y | ○ | I, A, V, O, Su, μV | 4, 7?, 25† |
| • | • | | ○ | | • | ○ | | | C | Y | • | I | 5 |
| • | • | • | • | • | • | • | • | • | C | IN | • | I, M, O | 3, 5 |
| • | • | ○ | • | • | • | ○ | • | • | L | Y | • | I, TP, T | 3 |
| • | • | ○ | • | • | • | ○ | • | | C | IN | ○ | I, V | 0.4, 5 |
| • | • | | • | | • | • | ○ | | C | Y | ○ | I | 2.5, 5 |
| • | • | ○ | ○ | ○ | • | • | | | PR | IN | ○ | I | 0.9 |
| • | • | | ○ | | • | ○ | | • | PA | Y | • | I, O | 0.5 |
| • | • | ○ | | ○ | • | • | • | ○ | F | R | • | TP, I, V, O | 1.9, 19 |
| • | • | ○ | | ○ | ○ | | | | C | DT | • | I, A, Su, V | 1, 5, 17.5 |
| • | ○ | ○ | • | ○ | ○ | • | • | ○ | A | R | • | I, TP | 1.5 |
| • | • | ○ | ○ | | ○ | ○ | | ○ | PA | DT | • | I, TP | 0.5 |
| • | • | | ○ | | ○ | | | | C | Y | ○ | A, Su, I, M, O | 1.8, 3 |

@@

| | | |
|---|---|---|
| 370—IBM370 | T —TI EXPLORER | †—INCLUDES |
| M —MACINTOSH | X —XEROX | TRAINING |
| TP—TI PC | V —VAX | |
| I —IBM PCs | μV—MICROVAX | |
| S —SYMBOLICS | Su —SUN | |
| L —LMI | A —APOLLO | |
| | O —OTHERS | |

planning, design, and simulation. (Further information on KEE is available from IntelliCorp, 1975 El Camino Real West, Mountain View, CA 94040; (415) 965-5500.)

## KNOWLEDGE CRAFT

Knowledge Craft (KC) is a hybrid tool based on frames that have user-defined inheritance. It is an integration of the Carnegie Mellon version of OPS5 and of Prolog and the SRL frame-representation language. It is a high-productivity tool kit for experienced knowledge engineers and AI system builders. Frames are used for declarative knowledge; procedural knowledge is implemented by the attaching of demons. KC is capable of hypothetical (nonmonotonic) reasoning when Contexts (a facility offering alternative worlds) is employed. Search is user defined. A graphics-based simulation package (Simulation Craft) is available. Designed to be a real-time system, KC is particularly appropriate for planning/scheduling and, to an extent, is appropriate for process control, but it is something of an overkill where simple classification problems are concerned. (Further information on Knowledge Craft is available from Carnegie Group, Inc., 650 Commerce Court, Station Square, Pittsburgh, PA 15219; (412) 642-6900.)

## PICON

Picon is designed as an object-oriented expert system shell for developing real-time, on-line expert systems for industrial automation and other processes that are monitored with sensors during real time; such processes are found in some aerospace and financial applications. Picon operates on the LMI Lambda/Plus Lisp machine and the TI Explorer, which combine the intelligent processing power of a Lisp processor with the high-speed numeric processing and data-acquisition capabilities of an MC68010 processor. The two processors operate simultaneously, enabling Picon to monitor the system in real time, detect events of possible significance in process, diagnose problems, and decide on an appropriate course of action. Picon's icon editor and graphics-oriented display enable a developer with minimal AI training to construct and represent a deep model of the process being automated. Rules about the process are entered by means of a menu-based natural-language interface. Picon supports both forward and backward chaining. (Further information on Picon is available from Lisp Machine, Inc., 6 Tech Dr., Andover, MA 01810; (617) 669-3554.)

## S.1

S.1 is a powerful commercial ESBT aimed at structured classification problems. Facts are expressed in a frame representation; judgment-type knowledge is expressed as rules. Though ostensibly a backward-chaining system, S.1 performs forward reasoning by means of a patented *procedural control block technique*. Control blocks can be viewed as implementations of flow diagrams; they guide the system procedure by telling the system the next step to take in the current situation. Control blocks can invoke other control blocks or rules, or they can initiate interactive dialogue. Control blocks are a powerful, knowledge-based means of controlling the search, and thus they have made it possible for one to write programs containing thousands of rules without being overwhelmed by a combinatorial explosion (runtimes tend to be linear with the number of rules). S.1 is written in C and executes very rapidly. A major advantage of S.1 is that it can readily be integrated into existing software. A delivery version is available without the system-development portion of S.1; the delivery version can be completely embedded in applications. S.1 is not aimed at exploratory programming; it is aimed at commercial applications in which iterative development of solutions to solvable problems is desired. S.1 has an excellent user interface that features mouse-driven, graphical representations of both the knowledge bases and the inference traces. Problems can be solved in terms of subproblems, which can be linked to handle the complete problem (consistency checking is performed as part of linkage). All S.1 features are expressed in an integrated, strongly typed, block-structured language that facilities system development and long-term maintenance. (Further information on S.1 is available from Teknowledge, Inc., 1850 Embarcadero Rd., PO Box 10119, Palo Alto, CA 94303; (415) 424-0500.)

## ES ENVIRONMENT/VM OR MVS
## (ESE/VM OR ESE/MVS)

ESE is an improved version of Emycin; it is designed for classification problems, but does allow for forward chaining. It consists of two components: a development interface and a consultation interface. A Focus Control Block mechanism has been added to allow the developer to modify and control the flow of inference and, thus, to increase the system speed. ESE/VM and ESE/MVS have good utilities for enabling the developer to fashion the user interface and to incorporate graphics in the user interface when appropriate. ESE is particularly suitable for IBM mainframe users who must interface with existing software and databases. (Further information on ESE is available from IBM, Dept. M52, 2800 Sand Hill Rd., Menlo Park, CA 94025; (415) 858-3000.)

## ENVISAGE

Envisage is a Prolog-derived tool. Thus, instead of entering rules, one enters logical assertions. Non-Prolog features include demons, fuzzy logic, and Bayesian probabilities. Envisage is primarily aimed at classification problems. (Further information on Envisage is available from System Designers Software, Inc., 444 Washington St., Suite 407, Woburn, MA 01801; (617) 935-8009.)

## KES

KES is a three-paradigm system that supports production rules, hypothesize-and-test rules (hypothesize-and-test rules use the criterion of minimum set coverage to account for data), and Bayesian-type rules for domains in which knowledge can be represented probabilistically. KES is primarily geared to classification-type problems. KES can be embedded in other systems. The hypothesize-and-test approach starts with a knowledge base of diagnostic *conclusions* (that is, classifications) with their accompanying *symptoms* (also called "characteristics"). The session begins with the selection by the system of the set of all diagnoses that match the first symptom of the given problem; the system then reduces this set as the remaining problem symptoms are considered. If the initial set of diagnoses does not include all the remaining symptoms, new diagnoses are added to the set to cover these cases. (Further information on KES is available from Software Architecture and Engineering Inc., 1600 Wilson Blvd., Suite 500, Arlington, VA 22209-2403; (703) 276-7910.)

## M.1

M.1 is a PC-based ESBT targeted for solvable problems rather than for exploratory programming. It is basically a backward-chaining system designed for classification. It includes the capability for meta-level commands that direct forward reasoning. Written in C, it can readily be integrated into existing conventional software. Its main drawback is that it has no true object-description capability and therefore cannot readily support deep systems. However, M.1 does have a good set of development tools and developer- and user-friendly interfaces. (Further information on M.1 is available from

Teknowledge, Inc., 1850 Embarcardero Rd., PO Box 10119, Palo Alto, CA 94303; (415) 424-0500.)

## NEXPERT OBJECT

Nexpert Object is a powerful, rule-based tool coded in C to run on a Macintosh with 512K of RAM, the Mac Plus, or the IBM PC AT. It has editing facilities comparable with those found on a large tool designed to run on the more sophisticated AI machines. The system allows the developer to group rules into categories so that the rules need to be called up only when they are appropriate. Nexpert Object supports variable rules and combinations of forward and backward chaining. The system can automatically generate graphical representations of networks of rules; these representations of networks indicate how the rules relate to one another. Similar networks can be generated to show rule firings that take place in response to a particular consultation. Nexpert Object includes the capabilities of both frame representations that have multiple inheritance and of pattern-matching rules, so deep reasoning is facilitated. Nexpert Object is a sophisticated system with a focus on the graphical representation of both the knowledge bases and the reasoning process, which makes possible natural and comprehensible interfaces for both the developer and end user. (Further information on Nexpert Object is available from Neuron Data Corp., 444 High St., Palo Alto, CA 94301; (415) 321-4488.)

## PERSONAL CONSULTANT+ (PC+)

PC+ is an attempt to provide on a personal computer many of the advanced features found in more sophisticated tools; such tools include KEE. Thus, PC+ utilizes frames with attribute inheritance, and rules. PC+ supports the backward-chaining approach derived from Emycin. It also includes forward-chaining capabilities without variable bindings. PC+ has an extensive set of tools for both development and execution that incorporate user-friendly interfaces. The new 2.0 version supports up to 2M bytes of expanded or extended memory for increased knowledge-base capacity. It also supports the IBM Enhanced Graphics Adapter and access to the popular dBase II and III database packages on the IBM PC. A version of PC+ is also available for the TI Explorer Lisp Machine. PC Easy, a simplified version of PC+ without frames, is also offered. (Further information on PC+ is available from Texas Instruments, Inc., PO Box 209, MS 2151, Austin, TX 78769; (800) 527-3500.)

## EXSYS 3.0

Exsys 3.0 is written in C for PCs as an inexpensive, rule-based, backward-chaining system oriented toward classification-type problems. Rules are of the if-then-else type. Exsys includes a runtime module and a report generator. Exsys can interface to the California Intelligence company's after-market products: Frame (to provide frame-based knowledge representation) and Tablet (to provide a blackboard knowledge-sharing facility that incorporates tables). (Further information on Exsys 3.0 is available from Exsys, Inc., PO Box 75158, Contr. Sta. 14, Albuquerque, NM 87194; (505) 836-6676.)

## EXPERT EDGE

Expert Edge is basically a rule-based, backward-chaining system aimed at rapidly prototyping and delivering classification applications in the 50-to-500 rule range. It uses probabilities and Bayesian statistics to handle uncertainties and lack of information. Its outstanding features are its excellent developer and end-user interfaces, which feature pop-up windowing environments. These are accompanied by a natural-language interface and very good debugging facilities. The professional version interfaces with a video disk and is also able to do extended mathematical calculations. (Further information on Expert Edge is available from Human Edge Software Corp., 1875 S. Grant St., San Mateo, CA 94402-2669; (415) 573-1593.)

## ESP ADVISOR AND ESP FRAME-ENGINE

ESP is a Prolog-based system that is particularly appropriate for designing expert systems that guide an end user in performing a detailed operation involving technical skill and knowledge. The developer builds the system by programming in KRL (Knowledge Representation Language), a sophisticated and versatile language that supports numeric and string variables, including facts, numbers, categories, and phrases. Prolog's heritage is clearly apparent in the system's ability to support a full set of logic operators, which enables the developer to write efficient, complex rules. The ESP consultation shell offers a well-designed, multipanel display that makes good use of color. A *text-animation* feature allows the developer to insert text at any point in a consultation. Though ESP Advisor was designed as an introductory prototype tool, its extensibility makes expert systems of greater complexity possible. ESP Frame-Engine supports frames with inheritance, forward and backward chaining rules, and demons. (Further information on the ESP products is available from Expert Systems International, 1700 Walnut St., Philadelphia, PA 19103; (215) 735-8510.)

## INSIGHT 2+

Insight 2+ is primarily a rule-based, backward-chaining (that is, goal-driven) system, but it can support forward chaining as well. Facts are represented as elementary objects with single value or multivalue attributes. Rules are entered in PRL (Production Rule Language). The knowledge base is compiled prior to runtime. Uncertainty is handled by means of confidence factors and thresholds. Because Insight 2+ lacks methods for representing deep models, it is best used for heuristic problems, for which it is a useful tool. Its ability to access external programs and databases is a major enhancement. (Further information on Insight 2+ is available from Level Five Research, Inc., 503 Fifth Ave., Indialantic, FL 32903; (305) 729-9046.)

## TIMM

TIMM is an inductive system that builds rules from examples. Examples are first translated into rules, which are then used to build more powerful generalized rules. TIMM handles contradictory examples by arriving at a certainty that is based on averaging these examples' conclusions. Partial-match analogical inferencing is used to deal with incomplete or nonmatching data. TIMM indicates the reliability of its results. The expert systems that result from it can be embedded in other software programs. (Further information on TIMM is available from General Research Corp., 7655 Old Springhouse Rd., McLean, VA 22102; (703) 893-5900.)

## RULEMASTER 3.0

Though Rulemaster is capable of independent forward and backward chaining, its major distinguishing feature is its capability for inductively generating rules from examples. It also offers fuzzy logic. Interaction with the knowledge base is accomplished by means of a text editor. If they prefer, knowledge engineers can develop

Rulemaster applications by writing code directly in the high-level Radial language of Rulemaster instead of using examples. However, a strong programming background is required for easy usage. Rulemaster can generate C or Fortran source code for fast execution, compactness, and for creation of portable expert systems that can interface to other computer programs. (Further information on Rulemaster is available from Radian Corp., 8501 Mo-Pac Blvd., PO Box 9948, Austin, TX 78766; (512) 454-4797.)

## KDS3

KDS3 inductively generates rules from examples. Examples can be grouped to develop knowledge modules, which KDS calls *frames* and which can be chained together to form very large systems. Both forward and backward chaining are supported. KDS3 can take input from external programs and sensors and can drive external programs. Expert systems built with KDS3 can be made either (a) interactive or (b) fully automatic for intelligent process control. The entire system is written in assembly language for very rapid execution on PCs. Graphics can be incorporated automatically from picture files or, if one makes use of built-in KDS3 color graphics primitives, they can be drawn in real time. KDS3 incorporates a blackboard by means of which knowledge modules can communicate. KDS2 without the blackboard facility is also available. (Further information on KDS3 is available from KDS Corp., 934 Hunter Rd., Wilmette, IL 60091; (312) 251-2621.)

## 1ST-CLASS

This is an induction system that generates decision trees, which are elaborate rules, from examples given in spreadsheet form. Problems can be broken down into modules derived from sets of examples; the modules can be chained together with forward or backward chaining. Rules can also be individually built or edited in graphical form on the screen. Several algorithms are available for inferencing: The system can match queries to examples that exist in the database, or the system can utilize the rule trees either as generated or in the *preferred mode*, which employs optimized rule trees that ask questions in the best order. Because all the rules are compiled, the system is very fast. The 1st-Class induction system is designed to interface readily with other software. (Further information on 1st-Class is available from Programs in Motion, Inc., 10 Sycamore Rd., Wayland, MA 01778; (617) 653-5093.)

## OPS5

Various versions of the OPS5 expert-system-development language, developed at Carnegie Mellon University, are available. OPS5 is a forward-chaining, production-rule tool with which many famous expert systems used at DEC, such as R1/XCON, have been built. OPS5 pattern-matching language permits variable bindings. However, OPS5 does not have facilities for sophisticated object representations. In general, the development environment is unsophisticated, although some debugging-and-tracing capability is usually provided. The use of a sophisticated indexing scheme (the Rete algorithm) for finding rules that match the current database makes OPS5 one of the tools that executes the fastest. Unfortunately, it is not an easy tool for the nonprogrammer to use. Variations of a representative version, OPS5+, can be obtained for the IBM PC, Macintosh, and the Apollo Workstation. (Further information on OPS5 is available from Computer*Thought Corp., 1721 West Plano Pkwy., Suite 125, Plano, TX 75075; (214) 424-3511.)

## ATTRIBUTES OF PARTICULAR COMMERCIAL ESBTs

The sidebar entitled "Brief descriptions of commercial ESBTs" presents some of the better-known commercial ESBTs. Attributes of these ESBTs are listed in Table 1 of that sidebar. Inclusion of an ESBT in the sidebar in no way represents an endorsement of that product. The descriptions and listings have been constructed from company and noncompany literature, discussions with company representatives, demonstrations, exploratory use of the tools, and so on. However, some incompleteness, errors, and oversights are inevitable in such an endeavor, so it behooves the interested person to use this material as a guide to examine the systems directly. Direct examination is particularly important because increasing competition is forcing ESBT developers to make rapid improvements and changes in both their systems and their prices.

## A COMPARATIVE, COMPOSITE VIEW OF THE VARIOUS TOOLS

Table 2 of the sidebar provides a composite view of the various ESBTs. Many of the attributes have been integrated to provide a more easily understandable picture of the capability of the tools in each subcategory (for example, the rule and procedure attributes have been combined into "representation of actions"). A solid circle indicates that the tool appears to be strong in a subcategory, an open circle indicates that it appears to be fair, and an empty cell indicates little or no capability in this area. Note that by relating each tool's attributes to its functional importance, I have attempted to indicate each tool's suitability for developing various function applications. Also, note that the more expensive (and correspondingly more sophisticated) tools have the widest applicability. This is often because they are a collection of different paradigms incorporated into a single tool. As a result, they may often be regarded as higher order programming languages and environments, instead of as simple shells into which information is inserted to create an expert system directly. The shell model is more nearly true of the simpler induction systems; such systems can be considered as knowledge-acquisition and rapid prototyping tools from which more complex systems can be built by means of other tools by enlarging upon the simple rules inductively generated.

## OVERALL USABILITY OF A TOOL

Figure 8 summarizes some of the aspects that enter into the critical ESBT attribute "overall usability of a particular tool." In addition to obvious factors such as costs and function applicability (function applicability is a measure of which functions are easily accomplished with a tool and which are difficult to accomplish with it), tool choices should be guided by the size of the system to be built, how rapidly a system of the given size and complexity can be built with the tool, and the speed of operation of the tool both during development and, particularly, during end use. (During end use, sub-elements of the tool act as a software delivery vehicle for the developed expert system.) Perhaps the most important factor, however, is the degree of satisfaction of both the developer and the end user. This is related to how obvious the uses of the tool features are, how direct the lines of action to the user's or developer's goals are, the control the developer and end user sense that they have over the system, the nature of the interaction or display (for example, whether they take place by means of menu or graphics), how easy it is to recover from errors, the on-line help that is furnished, and the perceived esthetics, reasonableness, and transparency of the system. Also of major importance is how easy it is to learn the system. This often depends on many of the factors already

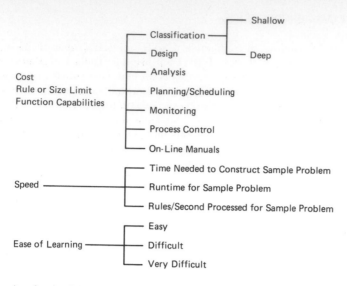

Cost
Rule or Size Limit
Function Capabilities

- Classification — Shallow / Deep
- Design
- Analysis
- Planning/Scheduling
- Monitoring
- Process Control
- On-Line Manuals

Speed
- Time Needed to Construct Sample Problem
- Runtime for Sample Problem
- Rules/Second Processed for Sample Problem

Ease of Learning
- Easy
- Difficult
- Very Difficult

Interfaces to Other Software
Portability
Documentation
Training
Company Support
User Satisfaction — Is System Poor, Fair, Good, or Excellent?

**FIGURE 8   Considerations for assessing the overall usability of a tool.**

discussed, but is also closely related to how apparent the choice is at each step (for example, the apparent choice when menus are used is different from the apparent choice when programming is required), the quality of the documentation and on-line help, and the ESBT's structure. Manufacturer-sponsored courses help; however, these are often expensive and inconvenient. A related factor is manufacturer support of the tool, particularly the availability of help over the telephone when it is required.

Finally, such factors as the system's portability, the computers it will run on, the delivery environment, the system's capability of interfacing with other programs and databases, and whether the developed system can be readily embedded in a larger system are all important in an evaluation of a tool. A more difficult factor to evaluate is the ease of prototyping versus life cycle cost. As prototypes are expanded into fielded systems and as they are iteratively further expanded and updated, difficulties are often encountered in system stability, runtime, and memory management.

Though many of these factors can be deduced from the tool's specifications and from system demonstrations, in many cases one can properly differentiate between two tools intended for the same application only if he or she learns both systems and attempts to build the same set of applications with each one. Nevertheless, the factors described in this article and the initial evaluation furnished in the sidebar should prove useful as initial guides to potential users.

To date, ESBTs have made possible productivity improvements of an order of magnitude or more in constructing expert systems. Current tools are only forerunners of ESBTs yet to come. The trend is toward less expensive, faster, more versatile, and more portable tools that will readily make possible development of expert systems that can directly communicate with existing conventional software such as databases and spreadsheets, and can also be embedded into larger systems, with resulting autonomous operations. Higher-end ESBTs are now moving from Lisp machines to more conventional workstations that are less expensive. Lower-end systems are becoming more capable and now appear on IBM PCs and Macintoshes. Delivery systems, which utilize a subset of the complete ESBTs (ESBTs with the development portion removed) are now allowing the completed expert system to be delivered on personal computers or workstations. In addition, versatility will be enhanced with increased choices of inference engines such as blackboard systems. Also in the works are modular ESBTs that will allow the developer to choose various knowledge representations and inference techniques as he or she desires and still be able to build an integrated system. Already appearing are ESBTs coupled to other software systems such as databases and spreadsheets. Also beginning to appear are expert systems that are specialized to specific functions such as scheduling, process control, and diagnosis.

Finally, the developer and end-user interfaces are getting friendlier and more capable. One of the things providing greater capability is the increased use of graphics and graphical simulations. It is expected that as these friendlier systems emerge, there will be increased development of expert systems directly by the experts themselves.

The rich and growing variety of ESBTs may make it more difficult to choose a tool, but if it is properly selected, the tool will be more closely matched to developer and end-user needs.

## References

1. E.H. Shortliffe, *Computer-Based Medical Consultations: Mycin,* Elsevier-North Holland, New York, 1976.
2. W. van Melle, "A Domain-Independent System that Aids in Constructing Knowledge-Based Consultation Programs," tech. report No. 820, 1980, Computer Science Dept., Stanford University, Stanford, Calif.

## Suggested Reading

Gevarter, W.B., *Intelligent Machines,* Prentice-Hall, Englewood Cliffs, N.J., 1985.

Gilmore, J.F., and K. Pulaski, "A Survey of Expert System Tools," *Proc. Second Conf. on Artificial Intelligence Applications*, Dec. 11–13, 1985, Computer Society Press, Los Alamitos, Calif., pp. 498–502.

Gilmore, J.F., K. Pulaski, and C. Howard, "A Comprehensive Evaluation of Expert System Tools," *Proc. SPIE Applications of Artificial Intelligence*, Apr. 1986, SPIE, Bellingham, Wash.

Harmon, P., and C.D. King, *Artificial Intelligence in Business*, John Wiley & Sons, New York, 1985.

Hayes-Roth, F., D.A. Waterman, and D.B. Lenat, *Building Expert Systems*, Addison-Wesley, Reading, Mass., 1983.

Karna, A., and A. Karna, "Evaluating Existing Tools for Developing Expert Systems in PC Environment," *Proc. Expert Systems in Government,* K.N. Karna, ed., Oct. 24–25, 1985, Computer Society Press, Los Alamitos, Calif., pp. 295–300.

Riley, G.D., "Timing Tests of Expert System Building Tools," NASA JSC Memorandum FM 7 (86-51), Apr. 3, 1986, FM7/Artificial Intelligence Section, Johnson Space Center, Houston, Tex.

Richer, M.H., "An Evaluation of Expert System Development Tools," *Expert Systems*, Vol. 3, No. 3, July 1986, pp. 166–183.

Waterman, D.A., *A Guide to Expert Systems*, 1986, Addison-Wesley, Reading, Mass., pp. 336–379.

"AI Development on the PC: A Review of Expert System Tools," *The Spang Robinson Report*, Vol. 1, No. 1, Nov. 1985, pp. 7–14.

"Expert Systems-Building Tools," *Expert Systems Strategies*, P. Harmon, ed., Vol. 2, No. 8, Aug. 1986, Cutter Information, Arlington, Mass., pp. 17–24.

"Small Expert Systems Building Tools," *Expert Systems Strategies*, P. Harmon, ed., Vol. 1, No. 1, Sept. 1985, Cahners Publishing, Newton, Mass., pp. 1–10.

*Catalogue of Artificial Intelligence Tools*, A. Bundy, ed., Springer-Verlag, New York, 1985.

*PC* (issue on expert systems), Vol. 4, No. 8, Apr. 16, 1985, pp. 108–189.

# Appendix B

Selecting A Shell

*Ronald Citrenbaum*
*James R. Geissman*
*Roger Schultz*

What are the most desirable features to look for in an expert system development environment? Some of the features discussed in this article are widely available in commercial products; others will undoubtedly appear in the future. So many different purposes and hardware environments exist that a single shell is unlikely to satisfy all of them.

Our observations are based on our experience designing and developing more than 20 expert systems over the past four years. We have utilized a wide range of software and hardware (such as symbolic computers, minicomputers, and PCs), AI languages (like LISP and PROLOG), specialized knowledge processing paradigm languages (OPSn), multifunction shells (such as Inference Corp 's ART), and simpler shells/rapid prototypers (for example, Insight 2+ from Level Five Research Inc.).

Our target audience consists of three groups: first-time buyers of expert system shells who need to know which features are most significant for their specific needs; persons with a major expert system responsibility (for example, at a corporate level) who are trying to establish high-level standards to help control the multiplicity of tools, languages, and even basic concepts to improve productivity; and future developers of expert system shells since some features we mention are not yet available in the marketplace.

---

Ronald Citrenbaum, Ph.D., is chair of the board of Abacus Programming Corp., Van Nuys, Calif., where he also heads the Abacus AI Group.

James R. Geissman is AI project manager at Abacus.

Roger Schultz, Ph.D., is principal scientist in the Abacus AI Group.

---

Reprinted with the kind permission of Ronald Citrenbaum, James R. Geissman, and Roger Schultz. Source: *AI Expert*, September 1987, pp. 30–39.

In the technical literature and common usage, expert system shells can lie anywhere on a continuum from interpreters of relatively simple languages to very elaborate development environments. Each has its own purposes and strengths and can complement other shells by being used at different times in a project's life cycle.

What shells have in common is the minimum feature set of a knowledge representation scheme, an inference or search mechanism, a means of describing a problem, and a way to determine the status of a problem while it is being solved (see W.B. Gevarter's "The Nature and Evaluation of Expert System Building Tools").

Although not everyone agrees on what the word "shell" should mean, products like LISP and PROLOG are frequently used to develop expert systems. This kind of product supports an expert system language specialized for the expression of knowledge processing statements and can result in programming productivity increases of approximately one order of magnitude; a program that is 1,000 lines long in FORTRAN can typically be written in less than 100 PROLOG statements.

Expert system language environments can be specialized to a single knowledge representation for maximum efficiency—such as OPS5 and OPS83 (Production Systems Technologies Inc.), which implement the forward-chaining, rule-based production system model—or more general (like LISP and PROLOG). The shell can be extended by tools that run the gamut from interpreters and compilers to symbolic debuggers.

A much different approach is taken by inductive products like ExpertEase (Expert Software International Ltd.) and its descendants, which build a system from a statement of knowledge and its relationships. With an inductive shell, the user states the knowledge used to arrive at conclusions. These shells take a set of discriminating examples, in tabular or other form, and the resultant conclusions and produce an optimized query tree, implicitly determining the intermediate nodes.

Other shells take an explicit set of rules and goals and interact with the user to determine the facts required to satisfy the goals. With Insight 2+, for example, the knowledge takes the form of *IF-THEN* rules. Some shells perform analysis to optimize the dialog and allow (or require) the user to exert control over operations.

The more elaborate systems available on symbolic computing hardware and powerful minicomputers, such as ART and IntelliCorp's KEE, are also called expert system shells, although some observers would say that this is too limited a name for these tools and that a term like "knowledge programming environment" should be used instead.

In this article, what we mean by "expert system shell" covers all of the previously mentioned concepts, although probably no single product can serve all possible purposes. The general notion is an environment for the development of an expert system containing the four basic functions of knowledge representation, inference mechanism, problem description, and status determination.

However, the specific requirements for selecting a shell as discussed here do not point to a single product because the activities performed during the expert system development cycle are carried out by people with varied interests and experience, and are targeted at different products.

## FOUR STAGES OF DEVELOPMENT

We identify four stages in expert system development: problem selection, initial prototype, expanded prototype, and delivery system. Each stage benefits from a shell, and each stage

**PROBLEM DETERMINATION AND SPECIFICATION**
Identify candidate opportunities
Build on analogous successes
Determine knowledge requirements
Specify system functions

**INITIAL PROTOTYPE**
Select inference mechanism
Select knowledge representation
Use existing advanced tools
Limit initial scope
Minimize initial use of experts
Determine feasibility

**EXPANDED PROTOTYPE**
Expand use of experts
Utilize rapid prototyping
Expand scope of system
Provide I/O interfaces
Add bells and whistles

**DELIVERY SYSTEM**
Optimize speed
Target to appropriate hardware
Customize user interface
Maintain system

**FIGURE 1 Four-stage expert system development methodology.**

stresses different features. An overview of the four-stage expert system development methodology is presented in Figure 1.

The problem selection stage, involving system specification and problem determination, corresponds to the requirements analysis stage in a conventional software development project. The major objective is to insure that the project will both satisfy a real need and be technically feasible. The main steps are to determine whether an expert system approach is most suitable for the problem, carefully select an initial prototype subset problem so a successful demonstration can occur relatively quickly, and discover the problem's underlying knowledge requirements so appropriate knowledge representations and tools (such as a shell) can be brought to bear.

The major objective of the initial prototype stage is to quickly demonstrate the technical and economic feasibility of the desired expert system. An early demonstration has several advantages, especially from a management perspective, where there may be reluctance to fund a major development in a risky or unknown technology—especially when there is no history of past success.

The initial prototype is typically concerned with only a central subset of the problem and does not provide the full range of ultimate functions. Functions such as data base interface, real-time performance, and superintelligent user interface may be missing, but an explanation facility should be present to validate the reasoning and promote user acceptance.

Development of the initial prototype consists of devising a suitable expert system architecture and knowledge representation. The strategy taken will depend on the depth and complexity of the problem, whether it is forward chaining or data driven, the anticipated strength of inferences possible (how certain the conclusions must be), and the extent to which subproblems are likely to interact. Obviously, the more flexible the tool(s) used, the more responsive the design can be to subtle details of the problem.

Two major problems usually encountered in this phase are the requirement of prompt project completion within a limited budget and the need for sufficient knowledge engineering to insure that all essential parameters are included. Depending on the tool, the initial prototype may be completed by the domain experts themselves, although the services of specialized knowledge engineers (expert system programmers) are often recommended to avoid becoming trapped in unsuitable representations.

Following an initial prototype demonstration of the concept and project approval, the major objective of the expanded prototype stage is to develop the full set of expert system functions required to deal with the complexity of the complete problem. The subset problem selected for the initial prototype is expanded to the full complexity of the domain area, and interactions with related systems such as data bases, measuring equipment, video, voice I/O, and so forth are included.

It may be reasonable to enhance the initial prototype iteratively or discard it (keeping the knowledge) and move to a different model; this often depends on the capabilities of the shell selected for the initial prototype. A quick-implementation shell with limited power often makes sense for the initial prototype, even though it cannot support eventual expansion. The major development problems encountered in this stage tend to be technical in nature, resulting from the complexity and sophistication of the features built into the system.

The expanded prototype may be suitable for deployment as a delivery system if only a few copies are needed and the prototype performance is sufficient for the target environment. However, in many cases, an operational environment based on different hardware (for example, a 68000 workstation or PC instead of a Symbolics machine) may be required, necessitating redeployment of the system.

The major objective at this stage is to port the expanded prototype system to the target environment. Typically, a delivery system differs from the expanded prototype in that it is widely deployed geographically and thus must run on inexpensive hardware such as a PC. Usually it must also satisfy more stringent performance and robustness requirements. The major development problems encountered in this phase typically result from design and function trade-offs required to make the system faster, smaller, and portable.

## USERS AND USES OF SHELLS

One group of requirements on an expert system shell results from its application in the stages of the expert system development cycle already discussed. Other requirements result from the users of expert system shells and the activities they perform. The thumbnail sketches that follow are profiles of personnel on an expert system development team. The end user who develops an expert system for his or her own use will adopt several of these roles (for example, domain expert, knowledge engineer, prototyper, and developer) during the course of system development.

**Students:** Students use a shell to learn about expert systems and knowledge-based programming. By definition, they cannot be expected to have any background in the subject and hence have to be supported by the shell, especially the user interface. Students will use a shell for knowledge engineering and initial prototyping but will probably not pursue development to enhanced prototypes of delivery systems.

**Domain experts:** Domain experts are involved in the activities of knowledge engineering and prototyping, both initial and expanded. They may be assisted or led by knowledge engineers or, with suitable tools or an agreeable shell, function on their own. One of the most important aspects of their contact with the expert system is in testing and extending prototypes to deal with progressively larger and more complete problems.

**Knowledge engineers:**    Knowledge engineers are concerned with defining the initial problem, knowledge engineering, and developing prototypes.   They can be presumed to have some familiarity and skill with the internals of the knowledge representation methodology and the expert system shell.

**Builders and programmers:**    Builders and programmers are concerned with implementation, especially the enhanced prototype and delivery system phases, and are likely to be involved earlier.   Their special skills relate to the computer and operating system being used, as well as the details of the expert system shell.   The correctness of the knowledge in the system remains the responsibility of the knowledge engineer and domain expert.

Because needed features differ at each stage of expert system development, a single expert system shell may not be capable of completing an entire project (unless it is a big, expensive one).   For development and deployment on PCs, an integrated set of tools may be a superior option, with each tool specializing in certain functions.

The following features are some of the most important, from the user's perspective. They are not an exclusive set of attributes that define the ideal shell; instead the list is organized in a way that is convenient for attaching our observations on how such a shell might be used.

## KNOWLEDGE REPRESENTATION AID

An expert system shell should not only accept one or more knowledge representations, it should help the user select the appropriate representation and develop it for the specific problem.   A shell that does this will have the following attributes:

- Utilize clear knowledge representations.   Representations that are relatively intuitive (or graphic) are advantageous in the initial stages when it may not be clear to the user whether or not the representation is correct.   After the user better understands and elaborates the representation, this requirement may cease to be important.
- Provide brainstorming aids for poorly structured or poorly understood problems.
- Compare alternative representations of a given set of knowledge in some relatively obvious format.
- Help users select the representation scheme.   This could be a tutorial function in which the shell takes the lead and actively participates in the knowledge representation selection process.   Alternatively, the shell might come with worked examples, which the user could take and transform into an expert system to deal with his or her own problem area.   A shell that required no programming background would be especially attractive to inexperienced users.
- Provide translation to a standard knowledge representation for portability, at least within a specific integrated set of tools.   Ideally, there would be an ANSI standard for knowledge import and export (like the Initial Graphics Exchange Specification (IGES) graphics standard), allowing a knowledge base to be ported widely between shells.   This standard would have one form for rules, another for schemata, and so forth.   For example, Abacus Programming Corp. developed the EXCABL Space Shuttle cabling system in OPS5, enhanced it in ART, and then automatically translated it to OPS83.   This was possible because a strict subset of ART dealing only with production system models was used.

    In the short term, one approach is to use a tool that has been implemented on a variety of systems, such as ART (on LISP machines, Digital Equipment Corp.'s

VAX, and C-based workstations), OPS83 (on C-based workstations, VAX, and PCs), or Common LISP.

- Provide a variety of interlinked representations that utilize ordinary knowledge forms as well as more sophisticated AI forms (for instance, a rule cites a cell in a spreadsheet that inherits properties from a frame in which a slot value comes from a rule or data base table). The transfer of knowledge from one representation to another should be relatively transparent. This implies support for a variety of low-level data types (symbols, integers, real numbers, record types, etc.) and the means to build up representations from primitive elements.

## KNOWLEDGE ENGINEERING

An expert system shell should provide knowledge engineering tools to assist users who do not have the assistance of expert knowledge engineers. Such tools would also be useful to knowledge engineers reviewing their own work. Relevant tools should:

- Allow the user to first gather and assert knowledge and then shape it while providing feedback regarding its structure and interrelationships.
- Provide knowledge consistency and completeness checking with a high-quality explanation facility to indicate the cause of any inconsistencies found.
- Develop rules and/or decision trees from a set of examples (inductive knowledge engineering).
- Optimize query sequences in rule-based systems. The user would only be required to enter rules; the shell would work out the needed dialog and optimum rule sequence.
- Allow users to change knowledge representations easily, with transformations between compatibile forms.
- Provide reasonable defaults for all options, slots, etc. Ideally, these defaults would be provided both at the system level (global defaults) and separately for different classes of frequently occurring problems. Problem classes with their own defaults could include the areas of diagnostics, classification, and configuration.
- Provide built-in, high-level domain expertise in certain basic areas to guide the user.
- Interpret a reasoning audit trail maintained by the inference engine and suggest ways to reach desired conclusions more quickly and/or surely.

## INFERENCE ENGINE FEATURES

The inference engine is the processor that uses the knowledge in the selected representations to solve problems. An effective inference engine must deal efficiently with the knowledge representations the shell can provide and offer a variety of problem-solving strategies.

Ideally, the inference engine should:

- Support multiple paradigms and search strategies. A flexible inference engine should be able to deal with a given knowledge representation in more than one way. For example, with a set of production rules and some asserted facts, forward chaining creates new facts; with the addition of a goal, backward chaining can operate on the same rules and facts.
- Allow user modification to modify or tune the basic control mechanisms.

- Allow dynamic user influence of hypothesis generation and search strategy; for example, by assigning priorities to rules or intermediate states.
- Allow variables as well as literals within rules.
- Provide belief maintenance, updating all related knowledge, conclusions, and reasoning strategies as individual facts become known or change.
- Support uncertain reasoning, dealing with less-than-certain conclusions and a multiplicity of possible reasoning paths. This should be done while maintaining knowledge of how certain each conclusion is, without irrevocably pruning off alternatives if their probabilities might later be improved.
- Provide explanation and audit trail. This involves giving a clear account of the path followed to arrive at conclusions and hypotheses in terms the user can understand. Exactly what the user wants to know in this regard and how much he or she can understand may vary widely.

## COMPATIBILITY/PORTABILITY

Compatibility and portability requirements mean that an expert system developed under one shell should not be left high and dry in one representation, running on only a small set of possible processors. If a problem grows or rehosting to new hardware is necessary for reasons not connected to the knowledge processing, it should be possible to transport the knowledge base to other environments and add additional standard features to the shell.

In this regard, shells should:

- Provide compatibility with other shells or tools that specialize in different phases of the expert system development cycle. This means that where different tools are used for different tasks (for example, knowledge engineering vs. delivery system), interfaces or hooks should go from one to the next. (Another approach is to have a single tool provide a full set of functions and operate on a wide range of hardware.)
- Fit into a logical tool migration path. For example, the shell could be both an interpreter and compiler for a knowledge representation.
- Provide links to widely used productivity products, including data bases and spreadsheets (for example, Microrim Inc.'s R:base, Ashton-Tate Inc.'s dBASE, and Lotus 1-2-3 on IBM PC; Digital Equipment Corp.'s RDB on VAX; SAS Institute's SAS on mainframes).
- Follow a standard interface between individual expert systems to facilitate distributed processing systems.
- Interface with algorithmic or procedural languages for specific performance-critical functions within an expert system.

## USER INTERFACE SPECIALIZATION

A shell's user interface is very important. If knowledge engineering is provided by a special tool, it may have its own interface that users should be able to customize with application-specific templates. A relatively fixed, structured, and easy-to-learn interface with a large number of standard or default features would be suitable for the initial prototype, while a highly programmable one should be available for delivery systems that are likely to require customization (such as company colors, type fonts, logos, and slogans).

An ideal user interface should:

□ Provide standard default features enabling plain vanilla expert systems to be constructed with minimum effort.

□ Provide guidance. A very simple user interface may be suitable for new users or domain experts with no expert system development experience (or interest). The interface should provide guidance, either explicitly or implicitly, through the model of the world and default values it presents. Essentially, the shell should put together an interesting expert system without requiring the user to make decisions that require knowledge of the internals of expert system operations.

□ Deal with graphics. Some user interfaces deal easily with graphics, especially image capture and display (for example, dialog such as "which picture looks most like the one you're thinking of?").

□ Aid in prototyping. The user interface may allow the prototype builder to dummy up unimplemented user interface features for demonstration purposes.

## PERFORMANCE/PRODUCTIVITY

A shell should include development tools and an environment to maximize programmer productivity and system performance. It should:

□ Provide access to system functions, data bases, etc.

□ Support modular design and independent development.

□ Provide strong debugging features.

□ Accommodate a large knowledge base work space.

□ Produce a high-performance, small-size delivery product by dropping unneeded (but available) features.

□ Produce versions that are portable to various delivery systems, including low-cost hardware like PCs.

□ Provide high-performance features for the delivery system (compiler, parallel rule evaluation).

## ADVANCED FEATURES

A number of improvements in expert system processing are being introduced in the laboratory and will probably be available soon in commercial tools. These include improvements in expert system performance through using optimization algorithms and taking advantage of improved hardware. Advanced features are frequently said to be required if expert systems are to function in critical real-time environments.

In this article we have not paid much attention to this dimension because hardware and software advances resulting in several orders of magnitude improvements are sure to occur in a few years without our requesting them. Also, we are principally concerned with how to make expert system technology easier to use and apply, however fast the programs work. Advanced features, nevertheless, should include taking advantage of parallel processing abilities in hardware and supporting distributed expert systems composed of a number of autonomous processes by incorporating some problem subdivision mechanisms and communication or blackboarding protocol.

Expert systems should be portable to a number of different environments, ranging from corporate mainframes to home-based PCs. If a given product is available both on the mainframe for a mainframe price and on the PC for a brown-bag price, cost-conscious users will of course purchase the PC version.

Incentive to develop shells for major computers can be maintained by providing modular shells. Different models of the same shell might be provided at different prices. The shell could be modular with plug-in functions or a number of shells could be provided, each offering a different subset of features. In this way, users could avoid purchasing unneeded features.

Another way to maintain incentive is to allow portability to low-cost hardware. It will generally be to the advantage of a shell if it can run on inexpensive hardware (PCs), although a trade-off of features is likely. A shell that is portable to various hardware is desirable, especially with extra features available on more powerful hardware.

## USER OBJECTIVES

A shell shouldn't be judged solely by whether it has a particular feature or representation scheme but whether it allows its users to effectively do what they need and want to do. An effective shell might have all the features but conceal them from most users. Gevarter's article (see references) indicates which shells are most useful for different functional uses (classification, design, planning/scheduling, and process control).

We view shells from a different perspective, deriving user objectives from the intersection of four user categories (student, domain expert, knowledge engineer, developer) and five possible uses (learning, knowledge engineering, initial prototype, expanded prototype, and delivery system). This cross-tabulation could result in 20 classes of user objectives, but in practice not all of them occur (for example, student users will by definition not be developing a delivery system).

## LEARNING EXPERT SYSTEMS

One important use for expert system shells is in education. Although undertaken principally by student users, these observations are relevant to all user categories. The student may be a software manager or a college student who wants to broaden his or her understanding by seeing how an expert system works.

What a shell should do to assist in learning depends on the student's technical background: a programmer may learn best from a close-up look at underlying inference mechanisms while someone less technical may prefer to see a number of carefully selected examples from an application area he or she understands. In either case, learning is likely to involve performing some knowledge engineering and building a small system similar to an initial prototype.

Figure 2 highlights the most significant features a shell can provide each user type in learning about expert systems. Depending on the amount the users want to learn about expert system concepts and knowledge engineering, the most important feature a shell can have is intuitiveness or transparency of knowledge representation. The expert system paradigm(s) and knowledge representation(s) supported by the shell should closely parallel the world of everyday knowledge and the user interface should provide an easy-to-grasp view of the structure of the knowledge the system uses (probably with graphics). Without a transparent representation and an interface that displays it clearly, users with little or no expert system background may not penetrate the subject far enough to grasp the basic processes.

Other important features for learning about expert systems include low software cost and PC hardware compatibility (especially for individuals), a user interface that spells out everything needed to make the system function so casual or infrequent users can use it, a useful set of default values, and an explanation facility that relates the shell's operation to both the shell's

**STUDENT USER**
**Most important features**
Intuitive knowledge representation(s)
Low-cost hardware/software platform
Casual user interface
Useful default values
**Other features**
Simple explanation facility
Examples

**DOMAIN EXPERT**
**Most important features**
Intuitive knowledge representation(s)
Domain expert interface
Knowledge base browsing
Examples
**Other features**
Useful default values
Inductive knowledge acquisition
Casual user interface
Low-cost hardware/software platform
Training and support

**KNOWLEDGE ENGINEER**
**Most important features**
Useful default values
Multiple representation schemes
Casual user interface
Integration of representation schemes
**Other features**
Good documentation
Appropriate examples
Training and support
Low-cost hardware/software platform

**EXPERT SYSTEM SOFTWARE DEVELOPER**
**Most important features**
Good documentation
Useful defaults
Casual user interface
Examples
**Other features**
Low-cost hardware/software platform
Access to source code
Multiple knowledge representations
Multiple reasoning paradigms
Training and support

**FIGURE 2   Significant features for learning about expert systems.**

documentation and everyday knowledge.   A shell with these features will simplify the student's task of building a demonstration system without requiring the problem to be oversimplified.

## KNOWLEDGE ENGINEERING

Knowledge engineering includes defining the appropriate representation scheme and collecting and organizing applicable knowledge under that scheme.   Knowledge engineering may be

**STUDENT USER**
  **Most important features**
    Intuitive knowledge representation(s)
    Low-cost hardware/software platform
    Casual user interface
  **Other features**
    Multiple knowledge representation schemes
    Integration of multiple schemes
    Useful default values

**DOMAIN EXPERT**
  **Most important features**
    Intuitive knowledge representation(s)
    Knowledge elicitation support
    Knowledge base browsing
  **Other features**
    Inductive knowledge/acquisition
    Useful default values
    Domain-specific expertise

**KNOWLEDGE ENGINEER**
  **Most important features**
    Multiple representation schemes
    Integration of representation schemes
    Representation selection aids
    Knowledge gathering aids
    Knowledge base browsing facility
  **Other features**
    Knowledge completeness and
        consistency checks
    Useful default values
    Explanation facility
    Logical tool migration path
    Brainstorming aids
    Inductive knowledge acquisition aids

**EXPERT SYSTEM SOFTWARE DEVELOPER**
  N/A

**FIGURE 3   Significant features for knowledge engineering.**

overlooked if it is thought of as merely a preliminary to the more important activity of programming the expert system.

Knowledge engineering (and developing the initial prototype) are just as related to requirements gathering as programming. To facilitate knowledge gathering, a shell should permit new knowledge to be added without upsetting existing knowledge. Knowledge engineering also involves representation, which, as an activity, seems to involve twisting the knowledge scheme this way and that until something obviously right and operationally useful for the problem at hand is found.

The most significant features a shell can provide each of the user types in knowledge engineering are listed in Figure 3. The most important shell features for use in knowledge engineering center on the knowledge representations supported and the knowledge-gathering and verification tools provided. For students and domain experts, these tools should use relatively transparent representations; the specialist knowledge engineer may be concerned with representations that are more sophisticated and less intuitive.

After a scheme is laid out and some knowledge has been collected, the tool can assist greatly by permitting browsing through the knowledge base and performing automatic con-

**STUDENT USER**
**Most important features**
Intuitive knowledge representation(s)
Low-cost hardware/software platform
Casual user interface
**Other features**
Useful default values
Examples

**DOMAIN EXPERT**
**Most important features**
Explanation facility
Consistency and completeness checking
Inductive knowledge acquisition aids
**Other features**
Built-in domain expertise
Knowledge base browsing
Useful default values

**KNOWLEDGE ENGINEER**
**Most important features**
Useful default values
Built-in domain expertise
Consistency and completeness checking
Knowledge gathering aids
Knowledge base browsing
**Other features**
Logical tool migration path
Explanation facility

**EXPERT SYSTEM SOFTWARE DEVELOPER**
**Most important features**
Interface simulation capability
Graphics support
**Other features**
Casual user interface
Friendly developer interface
Interface with popular productivity tools

**FIGURE 4   Significant features for initial prototype.**

sistency and completeness checks.  If the knowledge engineering user is not an expert, the other features mentioned in Figure 3 are important, too.

## INITIAL PROTOTYPE

The purpose of the initial prototype is proof of concept, not system production.  The user's needs at this stage, therefore, probably do not extend to complex structures and mechanisms but to speed of implementation and the ability to simulate specific user interface features where required for verisimilitude.  The goal is to take a knowledge representation and turn it into a functioning system simply and quickly.

The most important shell feature for developing an initial prototype center on knowledge engineering (it should be easy to set up the knowledge), the user interface (should be accessible to casual users and easy to make a complete-looking mock-up without a lot of tedious programming), and the explanation facility (for checking and debugging).  The most important aspect of user interface support appears to be a system's ability to develop dialogs and ask the user pertinent questions without the need to program the dialog explicitly. The expert system shell generates the dialog from an analysis of all of the unknowns in the knowledge base.

For student users, a lead-by-the-hand user interface, where the tool makes sure the developer provides it with all the information it needs for normal operation, is valuable (although the delivery system builder probably does not care for this). The most significant features a shell can provide each user type in initial prototyping are listed in Figure 4.

## EXPANDED PROTOTYPE

The expanded prototype is the stage most concerned with powerful inferencing and knowledge representation mechanisms. A key issue is the capability of dealing with the multitude of special cases and exceptions usually ignored in the simplified initial prototype; these may produce a large problem space. And it can be a system's ability to handle special cases that finally convinces experts and management that an expert system is not a toy.

Another important issue at this stage is the user interface, which should be easy to define and alter, particularly where special cases require fancy user interaction or access to special knowledge such as data bases or telemetry.

The most important shell features for developing an expanded prototype are the availability of sophisticated knowledge representations and a full range of inferencing approaches (Figure 5). Knowledge consistency checking, hypothetical reasoning, belief maintenance, and uncertainty support are some of the more specialized functions useful at this stage.

STUDENT USER
  N/A

DOMAIN EXPERT
  **Most important features**
    Explanation facility
    Consistency and completeness checking
  **Other features**
    Knowledge base browsing

KNOWLEDGE ENGINEER
  **Most important features**
    Consistency and completeness checking
    Large problem space
    Multiple integrated representation schemes
    Uncertainty support
    Belief maintenance
  **Other features**
    Logical tool migration path
    Explanation facility
    Modifiable inference engine

EXPERT SYSTEM SOFTWARE DEVELOPER
  **Most important features**
    Large problem space
    External product and language bridges
    Modular
    User interface development kit
    Graphic support
  **Other features**
    Friendly developer interface

**FIGURE 5   Significant features for expanded prototype.**

It can be important for the builder of the expanded prototype to be able to exercise close control over the reasoning process to achieve realistic results in difficult cases. To do this, the shell should be able to link with other systems specialized in data bases, graphics, or operating system functions. The student user would not by definition be doing this, so an easy-entry user interface is not as significant.

If the expanded prototype is to be followed by a delivery system, there should be a migration path to the delivery environment so the knowledge base and special programming to deal with special cases, user interface, and so forth can be ported to the delivery environment.

## DELIVERY SYSTEM

Developing a delivery system is more like conventional software engineering than the earlier steps (although most managers and budgeters would be happy if new programming could be avoided altogether by this point). Presumably, by this time the problem is well understood and the users have had opportunities to experiment with the earlier prototypes. Therefore the software engineering issues of performance, integration with other systems, portability, modularity, debugging support, and adherence to standards become more important, as op-

**STUDENT USER**
  N/A

**DOMAIN EXPERT**
  **Most important features**
    Explanation facility
    Consistency and completeness checking
    Knowledge maintenance interface
  **Other features**
    Knowledge base browsing

**KNOWLEDGE ENGINEER**
  **Most important features**
    Consistency and completeness checking
    Large problem space
    Multiple integrated representation schemes
    Uncertainty support
    Belief maintenance
  **Other features**
    Logical tool migration path
    Modifiable inference engine

**EXPERT SYSTEM SOFTWARE DEVELOPER**
  **Most important features**
    High speed
    Large problem space
    External product and language bridges
    Modular
    Strong debugging tools
    Drop unneeded features
    User interface development kit
    Graphics support
  **Other features**
    Friendly developer interface
    Portable to various hardware including PC

**FIGURE 6  Significant features for developing delivery system.**

posed to "gee-whiz" features that have already been displayed in the expanded prototype. Of course, the delivery system shell must support all of the sophisticated representations (such as uncertainty and belief maintenance) used in the expanded prototype.

The most important shell features for developing a delivery system are those related to high performance and programmer productivity. Examples of these features are source code provision or other ways to rewrite the inference engine, compilability, an operating system interface, and linkability of object code. Figure 6 lists the most significant features for delivery system support.


## WHAT IT ALL MEANS

Two main conclusions can be drawn from this complex set of desirable features. First, the requirements for an expert system shell do not exist a priori but are derived from the uses to which the shell will be put. These uses in turn depend on who the user is and at which stage in an expert system project he or she is working.

Second, because of the large number of attributes (some of which are contradictory), no single shell may have all the attributes needed for all purposes. Therefore, a shell should be compatible and portable in knowledge representation with other products so expert systems can be transported to the most appropriate tools for each user in each task.

**References**

Citrenbaum, R., and Geissman, J.R. "A Practical, Cost-Conscious Expert System Development Methodology," in *Proceedings of the Second Annual AI and Advanced Computer Technology Conference*. Wheaton, Ill.: Tower Conference Management, 1986.

Gevarter, W.B. "The Nature and Evaluation of Commercial Expert System Building Tools." *IEEE Computer* 20(5):24–41 (May 1987).

Gilmore, J.F., K. Pulaski, and C. Howard. "A Comprehensive Evaluation of Expert System Tools," in *Proceedings, SPIE Applications of Artificial Intelligence*. Bellingham, Wash.: SPIE, 1986.

Harmon, P., and C.D. King. *Artificial Intelligence in Business*. New York, N.Y.: John Wiley and Sons, 1985.

Hayes-Roth, F., D.A. Waterman, and D.B. Lenat. *Building Expert Systems*. Reading, Mass.: Addison-Wesley, 1983.

# Appendix C

## Knowledge Acquisition in the Development
## of a Large Expert System

*David S. Prerau*

*Knowledge acquisition* is the process by which expert system developers find the knowledge that domain experts use to perform the task of interest. This knowledge is then implemented to form an expert system. The essential part of an expert system is its knowledge, and therefore, knowledge acquisition is probably the most important task in the development of an expert system.

In this article, several effective techniques for expert system knowledge acquisition are discussed based on the techniques that were successfully used at GTE Laboratories to develop the COMPASS expert system. Knowledge acquisition for expert system development is still a new field and not (yet?) a science. Therefore, expert system developers and the experts they work with must tailor their knowledge-acquisition methodologies to fit their own particular situation and the people involved. As expert system developers define their own knowledge-acquisition procedures, they should find a description of proven knowledge-acquisition techniques and an account of the experience of the COMPASS developers in applying these techniques to be useful.

The next section of this article is a discussion of the COMPASS project. The major portion of the article follows, with over 30 points on knowledge acquisition that were found to be important during the work on COMPASS. Initial points cover the knowledge-acquisition considerations in selecting an expert and an appropriate domain for the expert system. The remaining points highlight techniques for getting started in knowledge acquisition, documenting the knowledge, and finally, actually acquiring and recording the knowledge. Each point is followed by a general discussion and then by a description of how the point specifically applied to the COMPASS project.

Reprinted with the kind permission of the American Association for Artificial Intelligence. Source: *AI Magazine,* Vol. 8, No. 2, Summer 1987, pp. 43–51.

## COMPASS

COMPASS is a multiparadigm expert system developed by GTE Laboratories for telephone switching-system maintenance (Prerau et al. 1985b; Goyal et al. 1985). COMPASS accepts maintenance printouts from telephone company central office switching equipment and suggests maintenance actions to be performed.

In particular, COMPASS accepts maintenance printout information from a GTE Number 2 Electronic Automatic Exchange (No. 2 EAX). A No. 2 EAX is a large, complex telephone call switching system ("switch") that can interconnect up to 40,000 telephone lines. Such a switch generates hundreds or thousands of maintenance messages daily. The current manual procedure of analyzing these messages to determine appropriate maintenance actions takes a significant amount of time and requires a high level of expertise. COMPASS uses expert techniques to analyze these messages and produce a prioritized list of suggested maintenance actions for a switch-maintenance technician.

COMPASS is implemented on Xerox 1108 Lisp machines using the KEE™ system (Fikes and Kehler 1985) from IntelliCorp. The COMPASS implementation utilizes multiple artificial intelligence paradigms: rules, frame hierarchies, demon mechanisms, object-oriented programming facilities, and Lisp code.

COMPASS is a large expert system: the COMPASS "knowledge document" (Prerau et al., 1986), which contains a succinct English-language record of the COMPASS expert knowledge, is approximately 200 pages long. The COMPASS implementation consists of about 500 Lisp functions, 400 KEE rules, and 1000 frames with a total of 15,000 slots. The system (COMPASS, KEE, and Interlisp-D) requires about 10 megabytes. COMPASS alone requires about 5 megabytes, and is growing larger as data are analyzed.

In its initial field uses, COMPASS has displayed performance comparable to (and, in some cases, better than) that of domain experts and significantly better than that of average No. 2 EAX maintenance personnel (Prerau et al., 1985a). COMPASS is probably one of the first major expert systems designed to be transferred completely from its developers to a separate organization for production use and maintenance. COMPASS has been put into extensive field use by GTE Data Services (GTEDS) of Tampa, Florida (Prerau et al., 1985d). It has been run on a daily basis for about a year to aid maintenance personnel at 12 No. 2 EAXs in four states. These switches service about 250,000 telephone subscribers. COMPASS is currently being put into production use by GTE telephone companies.

Because COMPASS is designed to be maintained by a group completely separate from its developers, major consideration during development was given to the potential maintainability of the final COMPASS system. The COMPASS project team developed a set of software engineering techniques for expert system implementation (Prerau et al., 1987). These techniques were utilized for COMPASS and are being used in other expert system developments.

## SELECTING AN EXPERT

A domain expert is the source of knowledge for the expert system. Therefore, even before the actual process of knowledge acquisition begins, a decision crucial to its success must be made: the choice of the project's expert (or experts). Because of the significance of this decision, among the important criteria for selecting an appropriate expert system domain are considerations related to the choice of a domain expert. These considerations primarily relate to the degree that the expert will function well in the role of knowledge source.

## IMPORTANCE OF EXPERT SELECTION

◻ Significant time and effort is needed to select an expert.

The selection of an expert is an important element in knowledge acquisition, and knowledge acquisition is critical to the overall expert system.

Early in the COMPASS project, an extensive set of criteria for selecting an expert system domain were developed (Prerau 1985). This set included criteria for selecting a project expert (of these criteria, only those related to knowledge acquisition are discussed here). We then spoke with several contacts in the domain area and explained our need for a project expert and our criteria for selecting one. The discussions yielded a small list of potential No. 2 EAX experts for our project. The most promising of these experts were asked to come separately to GTE Laboratories for two days of meetings. At these meetings, we discussed the project, expert systems in general, and the potential participation of the expert in our project. At the same time, we tried to see how the potential expert met our selection criteria. Based on these meetings, we selected the COMPASS expert.

## AN EXPERT'S CAPABILITIES

◻ Select an expert who has developed domain expertise by task performance over a long period of time.

The expert must have enough experience to be able to develop the domain insights that result in heuristics (rules of thumb). These heuristics most distinguish the knowledge in an expert system from that in a conventional program and are the main goal of the knowledge-acquisition process.

Our COMPASS expert, W. (Rick) Johnson, is a switching-services supervisor in the electronic operations staff at General Telephone of the Southwest (GTSW). He has been working in telephone switching for 16 years, including about 5 years specifically on the No. 2 EAX.

◻ Select an expert who is capable of communicating personal knowledge, judgment, and experience and the methods used to apply these elements to the particular task.

An expert should not only have the expertise but also the ability to impart this expertise to the project team, whose members probably know little or nothing about the subject area. Experts should be introspective, able to analyze their reasoning processes; and communicative, able to describe those reasoning processes clearly to the project team.

The COMPASS expert was an excellent communicator in teaching the COMPASS knowledge engineering team the basics of the No. 2 EAX and in discussing and explaining the methods he used to analyze No. 2 EAX maintenance messages.

◻ An expert should be cooperative.

An expert should be eager to work on the project or at worst be nonantagonistic. It is a hard job to be a project expert and to have to examine in detail the way you have been making decisions. If the expert is not interested or is even resentful about being on the project, then the expert might not put in the full effort required. One way to ensure a cooperative expert is to find a person who is interested in computers and in learning about expert systems (and possibly in becoming a local "expert" on expert systems and AI when the project is completed).  Also, an expert who sees a big potential payoff in the expert system being developed might want to be involved with it.

The COMPASS expert was very interested in, and enthusiastic about, the project, and the effort he put in was more than what was expected.  He learned a good deal about AI and expert systems during his work on the COMPASS project and became familiar with the Lisp machines being used.  Also, he received considerable visibility with his local management and eventually shared in a major award for COMPASS.

   □ Select an expert who is easy to work with.

A domain expert in an expert system project spends a lot of time with the project team. In COMPASS, we had an excellent working relationship with our expert.

## AN EXPERT'S AVAILABILITY AND SUPPORT

   □ Select an expert who is able to commit a substantial amount of time to the development of the system.

Because knowledge acquisition requires long hours, days, and weeks of discussions between experts and knowledge engineers, an expert for an expert system project must be willing and able to commit the significant time and effort required by the project.
One important factor in the COMPASS project was that our expert was willing and able to make a major commitment to the project.

   □ Strong managerial support is needed for an expert's commitment to the project.

Because knowledge acquisition for a major expert system can require many weeks or months of discussions with an expert, ample time should be set aside in the expert's schedule for meetings.  Available time is often a problem.  The best experts in the most important corporate areas are usually the ones who can least be spared from their usual position.
We were very fortunate in the COMPASS project to be able to obtain from GTSW management a commitment of one week per month of our expert's valuable time for the duration of the project (over two years).  Any smaller commitment of time would have significantly affected the speed of the project development, and a major cutback would have made it almost impossible to achieve the results that we did.

## SELECTING THE DOMAIN

In addition to the selection of the expert, criteria for the selection of an appropriate domain for expert system development (Prerau 1985) directly relate to the ease of knowledge acquisition.

   □ The domain should be such that the expert system does not have to perform the entire task to be useful: some degree of incomplete coverage can be tolerated (at least initially).

C:  Development of a Large Expert System       **555**

If this statement is true, the expert system development project can begin by developing a system to cover one subdomain and then expand by adding other subdomains. This method of development allows the knowledge acquisition for a large domain to be focused on one subdomain at a time.

For COMPASS, we spent almost the entire first year concentrating on one class of No. 2 EAX error messages (albeit the most important and most complex message class)—the "network recovery 20" messages. Our knowledge-acquisition sessions did not even consider the analysis of any other message types until our first system was completed. The subsequent expansion of COMPASS added the capability of handling every other No. 2 EAX message type that requires detailed expert analysis.

□ The task should be decomposable, allowing relatively rapid prototyping for a closed small subset of the complete task and then slow expansion to the complete task.

This approach allows knowledge acquisition to focus on a subset of the task rather than the entire task at once. Combined with the previous item, the knowledge acquisition can then be directed at any one time to one subtask for one subdomain.

In COMPASS, we (including our expert) did not know at first that the task was decomposable; so, we started by finding rules and procedures for the entire initial task (analysis of network recovery 20 messages). After some time, it became clear that the task could be decomposed into five major phases: Input, Identify, Analyze, Suggest, and Output (Prerau et al., 1985b). Then, we were able to concentrate our knowledge acquisition at any one time on one particular phase, thus focusing our attention.

□ The domain should be fairly stable.

An unstable domain can yield a situation where a large number of knowledge structures (for example, rules) found early in the knowledge acquisition are no longer valid but cannot easily be changed without redoing a major part of the knowledge-acquisition process.

For COMPASS, the No. 2 EAX domain that we selected was very stable. Through the entire development, no rule was ever altered because of a change in the No. 2 EAX architecture or control software.

## GETTING STARTED

Before discussing the major techniques for acquiring, recording, and documenting the expert knowledge (see the next two sections), let us consider some points related to getting started: how to set up the knowledge-acquisition meetings, what the first knowledge-acquisition meeting should cover, and what knowledge-acquisition techniques can be used at these initial meetings.

## KNOWLEDGE ACQUISITION MEETINGS

The planning and scheduling of knowledge-acquisition meetings are important practical concerns.

□ Organize knowledge-acquisition meetings so as to maximize access to the expert and to minimize interruptions.

As mentioned, the best experts often are the ones who can be least spared from their usual position. If an expert is consulted frequently for major and minor crises, knowledge-acquistion meetings held near the expert's location are likely to have many interruptions. It might be desirable to hold the meetings at a site remote from the expert's place of business. However, knowledge acquisition at the expert's site might allow observing the expert performing tasks in a usual environment, and this experience can be advantageous (see Starting Knowledge Acquisition).

We held our COMPASS knowledge-acquisition meetings at our Waltham, Massachusetts site, and our expert flew from San Angelo, Texas, to attend them. By having scheduled meetings in Massachusetts, we minimized—but did not completely eliminate—the times when our expert was called upon to help in crises, necessitating a rescheduling of our knowledge-acquisition meetings. However, once the expert was in Massachusetts, we could count on his availability except for occasional telephone calls.

> ▫ Knowledge-acquisition meeting attendees should have access to the implementation machines.

Several reasons exist for running the developing expert system program during a knowledge-acquisition session: to check parts of the developing program, to examine results of new knowledge that was acquired and implemented during the session, and to use the output of a part of the program as test input for knowledge acquisition of a succeeding part of the program. Thus, it is important to have access to the implementation during knowledge-acquisition. This access can be achieved by having the knowledge-acquisition meetings at the location of the knowledge engineering team. Meetings at this location might offer additional benefits, such as decreased travel expenses and better access to knowledge-acquisition aids, but it might also increase interruptions for other business.

Having COMPASS knowledge-acquisition meetings at our Waltham site gave us immediate access to the COMPASS program for the purposes described. We also minimized travel expenses because one expert, rather than two to four knowledge engineers, had to travel. Work at our site facilitated use of our knowledge-recording and documentation-updating mechanisms. A negative aspect was that the knowledge engineers were sometimes called away to attend various meetings, delaying knowledge acquisition. However, because our primary job was developing COMPASS (as opposed to the expert's primary job: his work at GTSW), we were able to schedule other meetings so that we were rarely called away for long periods.

## GETTING BACKGROUND DOMAIN KNOWLEDGE

The knowledge engineers developing an expert system are often completely unfamiliar with the domain of the system. Thus, as part of the knowledge acquisition, they must be provided with some background in the domain.

> ▫ An initial period of the knowledge acquisition should be devoted to the expert giving the knowledge engineers a tutorial on the domain and the domain terminology, without any actual knowledge acquisition going on.

Although there is a natural impatience to get right into the "real" knowledge acquisition, domain concepts and terms will occur over and over in the knowledge-acquisition meetings. Thus, it is useful to invest some time up front discussing the domain in general without focusing on the specific task to be performed by the system.

In COMPASS, we devoted the entire first week of knowledge-acquisition meetings with our expert to a tutorial on telephone switching in general and on the No. 2 EAX structure. During this week, no mention was made of the specific task of COMPASS—the analysis of maintenance messages. Instead, the knowledge engineers learned a lot of basic telephone-switching ideas and No. 2 EAX jargon that would prove very useful during the remainder of the knowledge acquisition.

□ Preparation of a tutorial document on the domain is useful.

This document can be used during the initial tutorial period and can then be available to knowledge engineers who join the project at later stages.

In COMPASS, the expert prepared a tutorial document that consisted of a package of pertinent excerpts of several existing No. 2 EAX reports and publications. This document provided the knowledge engineers with a useful reference during and after the tutorial week. Also, a copy of the document was given to each of the three new project members who eventually joined the COMPASS project. The expert also gave the new individuals private minitutorials as needed, based on the document.


## STARTING KNOWLEDGE ACQUISITION

Once the knowledge engineers have some basic background in the domain, it is time to start the actual knowledge acquisition.

□ References such as books or other written materials discussing the domain can form the basis of an initial knowledge base.

In a book, an expert has already extracted and organized some of the domain expertise. This organized knowledge might prove useful (at least initially) in building the system.

As mentioned, in COMPASS, we used the existing No. 2 EAX reports and publications to help us gain general knowledge about the No. 2 EAX. However, no written materials explained the kind of analysis our expert went through to find and repair problems in the switch; therefore, we could not get any initial rules directly from books or reports.

□ Begin the knowledge acquisition by having the expert go through the task, explaining each step in detail.

If possible, the expert should slowly work through the task for some test cases, explaining each step in detail. This task, however, is usually very difficult for the expert. An alternative is to have the expert perform the task at close to normal speed, verbalizing whenever possible, and record the process on audio or videotape. Another alternative is to record the expert on location [when] the expert actually performs the task. In either of these cases, the tape of the task performance can be played back one short segment at a time, with the knowledge engineers attempting to find out from the expert exactly what is being considered and what decisions are being made at each point. A briefly considered decision by the expert often actually involves a very large amount of information that must be put into the expert system.

We initially used audiotapes in COMPASS, with our expert going through the task at close to normal speed. We obtained some initial idea of his domain techniques using this method. However, after a brief time, it became clear that our expert was able to slowly step through his analysis while we interrupted him at each step to probe for his methodology. Thus, we stopped taping after just a few days and relied upon this alternative.

## DOCUMENTING THE KNOWLEDGE

In order to fully discuss the techniques that can be used to elicit the knowledge, it is important to describe first what this knowledge will look like and what techniques can be used to document it.

- ☐ Use some form of quasi-English if-then rules to document expert knowledge whenever possible; use quasi-English procedures when rules cannot reasonably be used.

Utilizing if-then rules for documenting the knowledge acquisition allows the knowledge to be acquired in independent chunks, in a way that might become a basis for implementation. An expert should be able to understand this method of knowledge representation more easily than other AI paradigms and after some exposure might be able to relate some of the knowledge to the knowledge engineers by utilizing this paradigm. Other experts should be able to read and understand the documentation in this form for verification or technology-transfer purposes.

In the COMPASS knowledge acquisition, we used quasi-English if-then rules almost always. Occasionally, other forms of knowledge documentation were used. For example, when a complicated looping procedure was found, a procedure in English was documented. Additionally, when a large amount of data was found related to some items, data in tabular form were utilized. Our expert could easily read and refer to the rules. Later in the development, other No. 2 EAX experts were asked to evaluate COMPASS. They were able to read the rules and procedures in the knowledge document and understand the knowledge inside the system. Also, we were often able to implement a knowledge-acquisition rule by one or more implementation rules in KEE (usually with associated Lisp functions). When this implementation could be done, it allowed a nice isomorphism between the knowledge and the implementation that would not have been possible if the documented knowledge were not in rule form.

- ☐ Keep rules and procedures in a "knowledge document."

As the rules and procedures are found, keep them in a knowledge document. The knowledge engineers and the expert will be using the knowledge document frequently. It can be given to other experts for system verification purposes. It can also be considered a "specification" for the knowledge implementation. Finally, the knowledge document should become part of the final documentation of the project (possibly part of, or generated from, the corresponding implementation). The COMPASS knowledge documents (Prerau et al. 1985b, 1986), were used extensively throughout the project for all these purposes.

- ☐ Develop conventions for documenting the knowledge-acquisition rules in order to add clarity.

Because the knowledge document can be used for many purposes, clarity is important.
A rule from the COMPASS system documentation (Prerau et al. 1986) is shown in Figure 1. Note the use of capitalization and indentation to make the rule readable. The four points that follow highlight some of the other conventions we used.

BC DUAL EXPANSION ONE PGA DOMINANT LARGE NUMBER
MESSAGES ANALYSIS RULE

IF     There exists a BC Dual Expansion One PGA Dominant Problem
       AND

          The number of messages is five or more

THEN

          The fault is in the PGA in the indicated expansion (.5)
       AND

          The fault is in the PGA in the silent expansion (.3)
       AND

          The fault is in the IGA (.1)
       AND

          The fault is in the Backplane (.1)

BECAUSE

          Most messages are in one expansion, so the problem is probably in that PGA.

**FIGURE 1   A COMPASS rule.**

□ The rules and procedures in the knowledge document should use standard domain jargon that the expert and other domain practitioners can understand; any special conventions should be clearly specified in the document.

This practice allows the document to be used for all the purposes mentioned.

The COMPASS rule shown in figure 1 uses No. 2 EAX domain jargon (for example, "PGA" and "expansion"). Also, the COMPASS knowledge document makes clear (though this point is not evident in the figure) that a number in parentheses in the rule represents the likelihood that the fault is in the cited location.

□ Group the documented rules in reasonable divisions.

Organizing the rules aids the user in finding them in the document. It also puts related rules together, which often facilitates document editing. If possible, the implementation should follow this grouping, but grouping the documented rules is a useful procedure to follow even if the implementation cannot correspond to the grouping.

In figure 1, NR 20 XY ANALYSIS RULES refers to a set of analysis rules (Analysis is one major phase of COMPASS) for network recovery 20 messages that deal with problems of the switch which the expert would group under the term "XY".

□ Give the knowledge-acquisition rules unique descriptive names (lengthy if necessary) rather than numbers.

The rule name should be descriptive enough to ensure that it is unique. If a rule name is descriptive, it can be utilized as part of the explanation facility of the expert system. If possible, it can also be used to identify the corresponding part of the implementation. Rule numbering should be avoided because of the problems it can cause. The set of rules changes continually during knowledge acquisition (and later in program maintenance). Rules are regrouped; new rules are added; and old rules are deleted, combined, or split. If rules are numbered, they must be renumbered continually. Lengthy names are cumbersome, but they clearly define the rule and remain constant as the rule set changes.

In Figure 1, the COMPASS rule name BC DUAL EXPANSION ONE PGA DOMINANT LARGE NUMBER MESSAGES ANALYSIS RULE identifies the expert rule to be applied in the analysis phase of the task under the following specific situation: the system has narrowed the problem to the BC portion of the switch, there are two expansions, the number of messages for one of the two PGAs is significantly more than (dominates) the number of messages for the second PGA, and the total number of messages is large (defined in this rule as "five or more"). The very long rule name can stay with the rule no matter how other rules change. In the COMPASS implementation, the KEE rule that implements this knowledge rule is given the same name (within allowable rule-name syntax).

    □ Include an explanatory clause as a part of each rule.

An explanatory clause (for example, a BECAUSE clause) appended to an if-then rule provides additional information on the expert's justification for a rule (Kyle 1985). Although this clause has no effect on the operation of the expert system, it can help the expert and the knowledge-acquisition team remember why they defined certain rules as they did and can clarify these decisions for other experts and the maintainers of the system. The explanatory clause might also be used in a justification part of the system.

The COMPASS rules originally did not have an explanatory clause. We found that occasionally when we examined a knowledge rule which we hadn't looked at in a while, we could not remember exactly why something was done one way rather than another. We wasted valuable time reconstructing the arguments that were used previously. Furthermore, we found related problems occurred when the COMPASS rules were read by persons outside the COMPASS development team (for example, an outside expert who is examining the COMPASS knowledge base or someone involved with COMPASS maintenance). These people sometimes found it difficult to understand the reasoning behind certain parts of COMPASS. The addition of BECAUSE clauses to COMPASS knowledge rules that were not self-explanatory minimized these problems and should help reduce future problems.

## ACQUIRING AND RECORDING THE KNOWLEDGE

The major work in the knowledge-acquisition process is the lengthy time spent with an expert eliciting, modifying, and recording the domain knowledge.

## ACQUIRING THE KNOWLEDGE

    □ Follow a basic cycle of elicit, document (or document and implement), and test.

An effective method of knowledge acquisition is to use the following basic cycle: (1) elicit knowledge from the expert; (2) document and, if possible, implement the knowledge; and (3) test the knowledge by comparing the expert's analysis against hand simulations of the documented knowledge or against the implementation (see Figures 2 and 3).

We used this method for the COMPASS knowledge acquisition. We found hand simulations best for examining each small step of reasoning, while comparisons against the implementation were most useful when a large section of knowledge had been completed.

    □ Use test cases to elicit expert techniques.

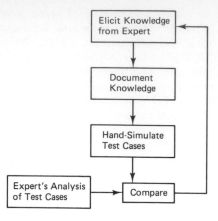

**FIGURE 2  Knowledge-acquisition cycle with hand stimulation.**

When initially considering a new area of the domain, go through several test cases. For each test case, formulate and document the rules and procedures the expert used to perform the task.

We went through each test case with the COMPASS expert. He tried to explain each substep in as much detail as he could, and we formulated knowledge-acquisition if-then rules or procedures to document each substep. We discussed each rule with the expert and modified it until he was satisfied. Because he knew each rule was to be considered just an initial version of the rule and would be subject to much change in the future, he did not feel that accepting a rule was a major decision requiring a great deal of thought.

&#9633; Use a large number of additional test cases to expand and modify the initial knowledge.

Go through numerous additional test cases. For each test case, attempt to use the existing rules and procedures to perform the task for the test case. Do this process by hand, or, if the pertinent rules and procedures have already been implemented, by machine. In each

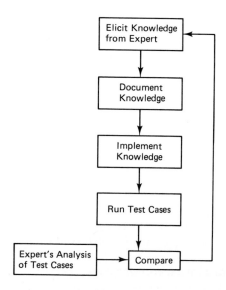

**FIGURE 3  Knowledge-acquisition cycle with program runs.**

case, have the expert examine the reasoning of the system step by step. Find all points of disagreement between the expert and the system, and modify and expand the existing rules and procedures so that they work correctly, that is, they agree with the expert. As the system gets bigger and the implementation grows, you can compare the expert's final results with those of the system and examine in detail only those cases where there is disagreement.

We went through numerous test cases with the COMPASS expert. Rules and procedures were continually changed. At some points fairly early in the process, we (including the expert) thought that we were almost finished. Subsequently, we would find test cases that opened up completely new areas which hadn't been considered, and we would find other test cases that pointed to major required changes and expansions to the existing rules and procedures. The expert made many subtle decisions and checks in his analysis that he did not realize he was making until a test pointed them out.

□ Have the expert define the domain reasoning in terms of knowledge-acquisition rules and procedures if possible.

Explain to the expert the ways the knowledge will be documented. As the knowledge-acquisition process continues, an interested expert will begin to understand the use of if-then rules and other AI concepts (just as the knowledge engineers will begin to understand some of the deeper concepts of the expert's domain). This understanding might help the expert describe the domain knowledge by directly using the knowledge-acquisition formalisms, thus speeding the knowledge-acquisition process. In addition, it helps the expert interpret the knowledge base being built and provides a foundation for the expert to eventually participate in the maintenance of the expert system implementation.

As the knowledge-acquisition process continued, the COMPASS expert became increasingly familiar with the rule formalism we used and often was able to formulate his domain expertise in this form. (At the same time, the COMPASS knowledge engineers slowly became No. 2 EAX miniexperts.)

□ As knowledge is acquired and updated, generate and continually update the knowledge document.

During the knowledge-acquisition sessions, each knowledge engineer and expert should have an up-to-date copy of the knowledge document. When knowledge is being acquired and modified rapidly, new versions of the document should be printed as soon as possible.

We had our COMPASS knowledge document in our word processor. We updated and reprinted it after every one-week knowledge-acquisition session—at the least. When knowledge acquisition was rapid, we updated and reprinted it daily or even more frequently. (The COMPASS knowledge document was time-stamped to the nearest second—only a slight exaggeration of what was required.)

□ Be general in wording, if necessary, when initially defining knowledge-acquisition rules and procedures.

Use general phrases in the rules each time the expert has trouble detailing or quantifying a specific knowledge item. This procedure avoids getting the knowledge-acquisition session bogged down in minor details before the important problems are solved. Later in the knowledge-acquisition process, the general phrase can be replaced by a specific quantity if possible, or techniques for dealing with uncertainty can be used.

During COMPASS development we used this technique several times. For example, the phrase "a sufficient number of messages" was used as a part of several rules for several months. A rule might state, "IF X is true AND there is a sufficient number of messages, THEN conclude Y." The phrase was given a working definition ($=5$) for a time to allow initial rule implementation and only after several months was the phrase replaced in the rules by a specific number. The number turned out to be different for different rules.

□ Use each test case to generate many additional test cases.

When a test case has $X = 5$ and a rule is formulated, ask the expert whether the rule would be the same if X were 1, X were 10, and so on. By going through this process in the middle of the discussion of the original test case, the entire context of the test case does not have to be rediscussed in order to come to the point at issue. Several new knowledge rules are often quickly generated in this manner.

This technique worked very well in COMPASS, frequently allowing us to examine several different situations based on a single test case.

□ Use the generated test cases to find the "edges" of each rule.

If a rule applies for $X = 10$ and another applies for $X = 20$, ask the expert which rule applies if X is 15, 17, and so on. Such questioning might make the expert uncomfortable because the rules of thumb often do not have sharp boundaries. However, after some thought, the expert might be able to pick a reasonable cutoff point. Note that if the expert is unsure which of two rules applies for a certain situation, the expert system might not be too far wrong if it uses either one; so, the expert's selection might not be critical. Again, this technique worked very well in COMPASS.

## RECORDING THE KNOWLEDGE

The final documentation of the knowledge was previously discussed. Here, let us consider techniques for initially recording the knowledge as it is acquired during the knowledge-acquisition sessions.

□ Record acquired knowledge in a flexible manner at the knowledge acquisition sessions.

The method in which the acquired knowledge is initially recorded at the knowledge-acquisition session should allow for frequent changes in rules while they are being discussed. It also should facilitate the transfer of the knowledge to the knowledge document when the discussion is completed. It would be efficient if the initial knowledge recording could be immediately and automatically transformed into the knowledge documentation (and even better if the documentation could then be transformed into the implementation). However, if this transformation cannot take place easily, it is wise to use the recording technique best suited to the knowledge acquisition rather than to delay the knowledge-acquisition sessions while the documentation and implementation are being produced.

In the COMPASS knowledge-acquisition sessions, we wrote the knowledge-acquisition rules and procedures on a whiteboard, and after a rule or procedure had been agreed on, we took an instant photograph of the board. The knowledge document was updated as soon as possible after a day's knowledge-acquisition session using the photographs (which were kept on file for reference). This technique proved very useful in COMPASS, but it did require that a project member spend a significant amount of time transcribing the information from the photographs.

□ Use suitable conventions for knowledge recording.

To speed the knowledge recording process, develop some reasonable recording conventions.

In COMPASS, we found that adopting a color code for different categories of information (for example, new rules, revisions of old rules, comments, and so on) was initially a help. After several months as we became familiar with our knowledge-recording and -transcribing process, we abandoned the color coding.

□ Use reminders to defer overly detailed or secondary items.

During knowledge acquisition, you sometimes come upon topics to discuss or actions to take that are beyond the scope of the current discussion. For example, one obscure case might be complicated enough to require a significant amount of knowledge acquisition. Rather than diverting the knowledge-acquisition session into a very detailed area or, alternatively, neglecting the topic, it is useful to have a formal mechanism to record "reminders" that can trigger a knowledge-acquisition session at a later date.

In the COMPASS knowledge-acquisition meetings, reminders were treated as an outcome of knowledge-acquisition, similar to the rules and procedures. These reminders were updated, deleted, or added to in the same manner as the other knowledge. Every so often, the group would go through the reminder list to see if any reminder should be treated immediately or if any could be deleted as no longer necessary.

## A RELATED IMPLEMENTATION CONVENTION

□ Implement knowledge acquisition rules by a corresponding implementation rule(s) with the same name if possible.

Using the same name for a knowledge-acquisition rule and its corresponding rule(s) in the implementation helps keep the knowledge acquirers from worrying about the details of the implementation, yet it preserves the correspondence between the acquired rules and the implemented rules. It greatly aids technology transfer and maintenance because it makes a clear correspondence between the knowledge document and the implementation. Use of this technique also facilitates implementation.

As mentioned earlier, COMPASS is implemented using multiple AI paradigms (rules, frames, demons, object-oriented programming, and Lisp), making use of all the facilities of KEE. However, to maximize the maintainability of COMPASS, we tried to use KEE rules to implement knowledge-acquisition rules whenever possible. Furthermore, when possible, we tried to have a one-to-one correspondence between the knowledge rules and the KEE rules. Although it might have been more efficient in many cases to use a different paradigm (for example, Lisp code), we feel that the use of KEE rules to implement knowledge-acquisition rules makes COMPASS much easier to understand and maintain, which was a priority for us (Prerau et al., 1987). Each KEE rule used was given the same name as the corresponding knowledge-acquisition rule. When a knowledge-acquisition rule was implemented by multiple KEE rules, then the implementation rules were given the same name as the knowledge rule but with a number added. Thus, the COMPASS knowledge rule F-SWITCH ANALYSIS RULE is implemented by two KEE implementation rules named F-SWITCH ANALYSIS RULE #1 and F-SWITCH ANALYSIS RULE #2.


## CONCLUSIONS

This article presented several effective techniques for knowledge acquisition and some of the details of a real expert system knowledge-acquisition process. It is doubtful that every point discussed will be usable or even pertinent to the knowledge-acquisition task for another project. However, until some general theories of knowledge-acquisition become accepted, it is important for expert system developers to describe successful techniques they have used in order to allow others to glean what they can. Some of the principal techniques that were found to be beneficial in knowledge-acquisition are: (1) considering knowledge-acquisition when selecting the domain, (2) considering knowledge acquisition when selecting an expert, (3) using test cases to elicit knowledge, (4) using generated test cases to multiply the effectiveness of test-case analysis, and (5) using good knowledge-recording and -documentation practices.


### Acknowledgments

I would like to thank Dr. Shri Goyal and members of the Knowledge-Based Systems Department at GTE Laboratories for their continuing support in this work. I especially acknowledge the excellent contributions of Dr. Alan Lemmon, Robert Reinke, Alan Gunderson, and Dr. Mark Adler to the COMPASS knowledge acquisition and the development of the knowledge-acquisition techniques described in this article. I'd like to thank Scott Schipper of GTE Data Services for his contribution to the knowledge acquisition and also his initial documentation of some of the COMPASS knowledge-acquisition techniques. Scott's work was a catalyst for this article. The knowledge acquisition would not have been successful without the fine job done by our expert, W. (Rick) Johnson of General Telephone of the Southwest. Finally, I'd like to thank Dr. Charles Rich of the Massachusetts Institute of Technology, who provided many useful suggestions throughout the course of the work that led to this article.

### References

Fikes, R., and Kehler, T. 1985. The Role of Frame-Based Representation in Reasoning. *Communications of the ACM* 28(9): 904–920.

Goyal, S., Prerau, D. S., Lemmon, A., Gunderson, A., and Reinke, R. 1985. COMPASS: An Expert System for Telephone Switch Maintenance. *Expert Systems: The International Journal of Knowledge Engineering* 2(3):112–126. Also published in Proceedings of the Expert Systems in Government Symposium, 112–122. New York: Institute of Electrical and Electronics Engineers.

Kyle, T. 1985. Expanding Expertise by Use of an Expert System. In Proceedings of the 1985 Conference on Intelligent Systems and Machines, 244–247. Rochester, Mich.: Oakland University.

Prerau, D. S. 1985. Selection of an Appropriate Domain for an Expert System. *AI Magazine* 4(2): 26–30.

Prerau, D. S., Gunderson, A., Reinke, R., and Goyal, S. 1985a. The COMPASS Expert System: Verification, Technology Transfer, and Expansion. In Proceedings of the Second International Conference of Artificial Intelligence Applications, 597–602. Washington, D.C.: IEEE Computer Society.

Prerau, D. S., Lemmon, A., Gunderson, A., and Reinke, R. 1985b. A Multi-Paradigm Expert System for Maintenance of an Electronic Telephone Exchange. In Proceedings of the Ninth International Computer Software and Applications Conference (COMPSAC-85), 280–286. Washington, D.C.: IEEE Computer Society.

Prerau, D. C., Lemmon, A., Gunderson, A., Reinke, R., and Johnson, W. 1985c. COMPASS-X Rules and Procedures, Technical Note, TN-85-176.2, Computer Science Laboratory, GTE Laboratories Incorporated.

Prerau, D. S., Schipper, S., and Janis, J. 1985d. Artificial Intelligence Technology Transfer Related to the COMPASS-X Expert System, Technical Note, TN-85-176.6, Computer Science Laboratory, GTE Laboratories Incorporated.

Prerau, D. S., Gunderson, A., Reinke, R., Adler, M., Johnson, W., and Schipper, S. 1986. COMPASS-II Knowledge Document, Vols. I to IV, Technical Notes, TN86-176.8 to TN86-176.11, Computer and Intelligent Systems Laboratory, GTE Laboratories Incorporated.

Prerau, D. S., Gunderson, A., Reinke, R., and Adler, M. 1987. Maintainability Techniques in Developing Large Expert Systems. Forthcoming.

# Appendix D

## The Problem of Extracting the Knowledge of Experts from the Perspective of Experimental Psychology

*Robert R. Hoffman*

For perceptual and conceptual problems requiring the skills of an expert, expertise is rare, the expert's knowledge is extremely detailed and interconnected, and our scientific understanding of the expert's perceptual and conceptual processes is limited. Research on the skills of experts in any domain affords an excellent opportunity for both basic and practical experimentation. My investigations fall on the experimental psychology side of expert system engineering, specifically the problem of generating methods for extracting the knowledge of experts. I do not review the relevant literature on the cognition of experts.[1] I want to share a few ideas about research methods that I found worthwhile as I worked with expert interpreters of aerial photographs and other remotely sensed data (Hoffman 1984) and on a project involving expert planners of airlift operations (Hoffman 1986). These ideas should be useful to knowledge engineers and others who might be interested in developing an expert system.

### THE BOTTLENECK

In generating expert systems, one must begin by characterizing the knowledge of an expert. As far as I can tell from the literature on expert systems, getting this characterization is the significant bottleneck in the system development process. For example, from their experience in the development of PROSPECTOR, Duda and Gashnig (1981) concluded that ". . . something must be done to shorten the time needed to interview experts and represent their special knowledge. . . [It] may take several months of the expert's time and even more of the system builder's" (p. 264). Three years later, Duda and Shortliffe (1983) echoed this lament: "The identification and encoding of knowledge is one of the most complex and arduous tasks encountered in the construction of an expert system" (p. 265).

Reprinted with the kind permission of the American Association of Artificial Intelligence. Source: *AI Magazine*, Vol. 8, No. 2, Summer 1987, pp 53–67.

**TABLE 1.** Types of Methods That Can Be Used to Extract the Knowledge of an Expert.

| METHOD CATEGORY | DESCRIPTION |
| --- | --- |
| METHOD OF "FAMILIAR" TASKS | Analysis of the tasks that the expert usually performs. |
| STRUCTURED AND UNSTRUCTURED INTERVIEWS | The expert is queried with regard to knowledge of facts and procedures. |
| LIMITED INFORMATION TASKS | A familiar task is performed, but the expert is not given certain information that is typically available. |
| CONSTRAINED PROCESSING TASKS | A familiar task is performed, but the expert must do so under time or other constraints. |
| METHOD OF "TOUGH CASES" | Analysis of a familiar task that is conducted for a set of data that presents a "tough case" for the expert. |

Some common phrases that occur in the literature are "knowledge acquisition is the time-critical component" (Freiling et al. 1985), and "extracting and articulating the knowledge is the most important phase" (Gevarter 1984), and "the process of extracting knowledge can be laborious" (Quinlan 1984). I encountered passages of this type in every major review article or textbook on expert systems that has come to my attention (for example, Bramer 1982; Denning 1986; Hayes-Roth, Waterman, and Lenat 1983; Mittal and Dym 1985; Raulefs 1985, Weiss and Kulikowski 1984). Such articles dutifully assert that "the first step is to get the knowledge" (Freiling et al. 1985, p. 152). What follows, however, is typically a discussion of abstract inference strategies, details of Lisp code, and descriptions of system architecture rather than an answer to the question of exactly how to get the knowledge.

Some papers have titles that explicitly suggest they deal with the nuts and bolts of how to extract an expert's knowledge (for example, "Acquisition of Knowledge from Domain Experts," Friedland 1981; see also Nii and Aiello 1979; Politakis and Weill 1984). However, such papers deal mostly with the representation of knowledge. In short, apparently little or no systematic research has been conducted on the question of how to elicit an expert's knowledge and inference strategies (Duda and Shortliffe 1983; Hartley 1981).[2] How can one find good tasks for extracting the knowledge of an expert? How can various tasks be compared? Can tasks be tailored to extract specific subdomains of knowledge within the expert's broader domains of knowledge? My research has addressed these questions.

Methods for extracting expert knowledge seem to fall neatly into a handful of categories, as shown in table 1. One obvious methodological category involves observing the performance of the expert at the kinds of tasks the expert is familiar with or usually engages in. A second category of methods is the interview. Artificial tasks can be devised that depart from what the expert usually does by limiting the information that is available to the expert or by constraining the problem the expert is to work on. Another type of method involves studying the expert's performance on the "tough cases" that sometimes occur. The categorization shown in table 1 forms the topical organization of this paper. Following a brief discussion of each of these method types is an examination of some ways in which the data they yield can be analyzed and the various methods compared.

## THE METHOD OF FAMILIAR TASKS

The method of familiar tasks involves studying the expert while he or she is engaged in the kinds of tasks that are usually or typically engaged in. Looking across a set of experts' specific tactics and procedures, one should see commonalities in terms of goals, the information the experts like to have available, and the data or records that are produced (Mittal and Dym

1985). In a number of reviews (for example, Duda and Shortliffe 1983; Stefik et al. 1982), the various tasks that experts engage in have been analyzed and categorized into basic types, such as diagnosing (interpretation of data), planning, designing, and explaining.

Psychologically, the tasks that an expert typically performs involve at least the following: (1) the analysis of complex stimuli into relevant features or cues based on a process psychologists call "perceptual learning," (2) the analysis of conceptual categories in terms of the relevant features (the perception of similarities and differences), (3) the analysis of the features and the categories in terms of relevant underlying causal laws (involving "concept-formation processes"), and (4) abilities to infer and test hypotheses.

Although these (and probably other) psychological factors are involved, the products that result from familiar tasks bear on these tasks and might not actually be very informative about the expert's reasoning. For example, the standard method of aerial-photo interpretation *(terrain analysis)* provides lots of information about the land that appears in an aerial photo but says precious little about how the expert arrived at the description (cf. Mintzer and Messmore 1984; Way 1978). Such is also probably true for the kinds of diagnostic notations made by radiologists when they interpret X rays (Feltovich 1981). Nevertheless, an analysis of familiar tasks can be very beneficial because it can give the knowledge engineer a feel for the kinds of knowledge and skill involved in the domain.

An analysis of familiar tasks (including an analysis of available texts and technical manuals) can be used to generate a "first pass" at a data base. What the expert knows is represented as a categorized listing of statements cast in some sort of formal language (such as propositions) using terms and categories that are meaningful and related to the domain at hand (Freiling et al. 1985). Such propositions can express observation statements or facts as well as implications or potential if-then rules of inference.[3] Table 2 presents example excerpts from the data base of the aerial-photo-interpretation project.

## THE UNSTRUCTURED INTERVIEW

As far as I can tell, the development of most existing expert systems started with unstructured interviews of the experts. Indeed, most system developers have apparently relied exclusively on the unstructured interview method. Some developers have even apparently taken it for granted that an unstructured interview is the only way to extract expert knowledge (for example, Weiss and Kulikowski 1984, p. 105).

In an unstructured interview, the knowledge engineer asks more-or-less spontaneous questions of the expert while the expert is performing (or talking about) a familiar task (see Freiling et al. 1985). For instance, the interviewer might ask the expert a question such as "How do you know that?" whenever the expert seems to tap into knowledge or make an inference, or "Do you want a cup of coffee?" whenever they get tired.

Presumably, the knowledge engineer's prior analysis of the familiar tasks has turned the engineer from a novice into an apprentice (or even a master). Thus, the engineer is trained in what to look for during the interview. Should the training or preparation proceed so far as to turn the knowledge engineer into an expert? I do not know if there can be any principled answer to this question. It has been claimed (Davis 1986) that the novice interviewer might be better able to ask questions about ideas or procedures which an expert tends to leave implicit or take for granted (see also Hartley 1981).

Table 3 presents an example excerpt from an unstructured interview conducted during the airlift-planning project (Hoffman 1986). This excerpt is prototypical in that there are inquiries from the interviewer, speech pauses and hesitations, ungrammatical segments, and

**TABLE 2.** An Example Set of Excerpts from the Aerial-Photo-Interpretation Data Base (Hoffman 1984). Within each category and subcategory there can appear potential if-then rules ("X implies Y"), as well as facts (observation statements). Stream gully shapes refer to their cross sections.

ROCK FORMS #3—DOME
   Raised circular, linear or ellipsoid rock
   Can be small, compound, or clustered
   Can have radiating fractures
   Can be salt, gypsum, or intrusive bedrock
   Radial drainage pattern, annular pattern at base of the slope

ROCK TYPE #1—FLAT SHALE
   Gently rolling, irregular plain
   Symmetrical finger ridges
   Branching rounded hills with saddle ridges
   Scalloped hill bases
   V- and U-shaped stream gullies
   Uniform slope gradients imply homogeneous rock
   Compound slope gradients imply thick bedding
   Escarpments, very sharp ridges, steep slopes, and steep pinnacles imply sandy soils

HUMID CLIMATE
   Implies rounded hills
   Implies find dendritic drainage pattern

ARID CLIMATE
   Implies steep, rounded hills and ridges with asymmetrical slopes
   Implies intermittent drainage
   Implies barren land or shrub land
   Implies light or mottled soil tones

FLUVIAL LANDFORMS #17—PLAYAS
   Dry, very low relief lakebeds in arid regions
   Can include beach ridges
   Few drainage features
   Irrigation and intense cultivation
   Scrabbled surface implies alkaline deposits

SOIL TYPE #2—SILT
   Light tones
   U-shaped stream gullies

DRAINAGE PATTERNS #5—THERMOKARST
   Stream gullies form polygons and hexagons, linked by meandering streams
   Implies permafrost

GULLY SHAPES #2—U SHAPED GULLIES
   Moderately steep slopes with curved channel bottom
   Implies loess soil type

AGRICULTURE TYPE #4—ORCHARDS
   Vegetation in lattice pattern or repeated uniform rows
   Porous, well-drained soils
   Level terrain plus trees in a rectangular pattern imply nuts or citrus
   Rolling, uneven terrain plus trees in a contoured pattern imply fruits

**TABLE 3.**   Example Excerpts from an Unstructured Interview.

*I:* What information are you given about airports?

*E:* Now, just some rudimentary information comes with it.  Common name, latitude and longitude, ah . . . no information comes with it about the ah . . . maximum number of airplanes on the ground or the port capability that is at the field.  None of that comes along with it.

*I:* What's the difference between MOG and airport capability?

*E:* Ah . . . MOG maximum on the ground is parking spots . . . on the ramp.  Airport capability is how many passengers and tons of cargo per day it can handle at the facilities.

*I:* Throughout . . . ah . . . throughout as a function of . . .

*E:* It all sorta goes together as throughput.  If you've only got . . . if you can only have ah . . . if you've only got one parking ramp with the ability to handle 10,000 tons a day, then your . . . throughput is gonna be limited by your parking ramp.  Or, the problem could be vice versa.

*I:* Yeah . . .

*E:* So it's a (unintelligible phrase).

*I:* What if you only had one loader, so that you could only unload one wide-body cargo airplane at a time?  You wouldn't want to schedule five airplanes on the ground simultaneously.  How would you restrict that?

*E:* We know we're not gonna get all the error out of it.  We're gonna try and minimize the error. And then we'll say that . . . ah . . . we'll say an arrival-departure interval of one hour, so that means that the probability of having two wide-bodies on the ground tryin' to get support from the loader is cut . . .

---

unintelligible segments.  The expert's monologues in this excerpt are brief.  Occasionally, they can be much longer.

Knowledge engineers sometimes make an audiotape of the expert's ruminations; this recording is called a *verbal protocol* (Ericcson and Simon 1984).  The trick is to train the expert into thinking out loud, which requires practice because the act of speaking one's thoughts can actually interfere with or inhibit trains of thought for some individuals.  Other individuals, those who habitually think out loud, might not actually leave a very good record of their reasoning.

Audiotapes are necessarily a partial representation of the key information.  An expert's facial expressions and gestures can also reveal inference-making processes (McNeill and Levy 1982).  For instance, in the analysis of 10 hours of unstructured interviews (Hoffman 1986), I found that a majority of the 957 questions asked by the interviewer were not marked by clearly rising intonation.  Typically, the interviewer was repeating some bit of knowledge that had just been asserted by the expert.  The intention was that the expert would either confirm, deny, or qualify the interviewer's statement.  The pragmatics of such utterances as "ah" and "um" (and their gestural counterparts) are only captured as ephemera on audiotape.[4]

The moral here is that the interviewer should always take copious notes and not rely passively on audiotapes.  Furthermore, it is prudent to distinguish between interviews, which are one-on-one, and discussion groups.  In general, discussion group sessions need not be recorded.  An important exception to this rule is the recording of the discussions of teams of experts who are working on tough cases (to be discussed later).

## THE STRUCTURED INTERVIEW

A powerful and yet conceptually simple alternative to unstructured interviews is the structured interview.  In a sense, the structured interview combines an analysis of familiar tasks with an unstructured interview.  In order to add structure to an interview, the knowledge engineer initially makes a first pass at a data base by analyzing the available texts and technical manuals, or by conducting an unstructured interview. The expert then goes over the first-pass data base one entry at a time, making comments on each one. Recording this process is not necessary because the knowledge engineer can write changes and notes on a copy of the printout of the first-pass data base.

A structured interview in one way or another forces the expert to systematically go back over the knowledge. Any given comment can have a number of effects on the data base. It can lead to (1) the addition or deletion of entries, (2) the qualification of entries, (3) the reorganization of the hierarchical or categorical structure of the data base, or (4) the addition or deletion of categories. The result is a second pass at the data base.

## LIMITED-INFORMATION TASKS

Limited-information tasks represent the application of basic scientific method: to understand how something works in nature, we tinker with it. Limited-information tasks are similar to the familiar tasks, but the amount or kind of information that is available to the expert is somehow restricted. For example, an expert radiologist might like to have available all sorts of information about a patient's medical history before interpreting an X ray. Many expert aerial-photo interpreters like to have all sorts of maps available during the interpretation of photos. In the limited-information task, such contextual information can be withheld, forcing the expert to rely heavily upon (and hence provide additional evidence about) their knowledge and reasoning skills.

In general, experts do not like it when you limit the information that is available to them. It is commonly assumed in familiar tasks that all the relevant information is available and that the expert's judgments are correct. Some experts would rather give no judgment at all than give one that is based on incomplete information. It is important when instructing the expert to drive home the point that the limited-information task is not a challenge of their ego or of their expertise: The goal of the task is not to determine how "clever" the expert is.

Once adapted to the task, experts can provide a wealth of information. The limited-information task is especially useful for revealing an expert's strategies (as opposed to factual knowledge). The incompleteness of the information affords the formulation of hypotheses (rather than final judgments), strategic thinking (What if . . . ?), and the use of heuristics (rules of thumb).

The limited-information task can be used to provide information about subdomains of the expert's knowledge, to fill in any gaps in the data base or a set of inference rules. For example, in the aerial-photo-interpretation project, the structured interview with one particular expert did not yield much information about certain geological forms. Hence, other experts could be run through a limited-information task that involved photos of precisely these geological forms.

## CONSTRAINED-PROCESSING TASKS

Constrained-processing tasks are like limited-information tasks in that both involve tinkering with the familiar task. Constrained-processing tasks involve deliberate attempts to constrain or alter the reasoning strategies that the expert uses. One simple way to achieve this goal is to limit the amount of time that the expert has in which to absorb information or make judgments. For example, the interpretation of aerial photos typically takes hours, but in a constrained-processing task the expert might be allowed, say, two minutes to inspect a photo and five minutes to make judgments about it.[5]

Another way to constrain the processing is to ask the expert a specific question rather than to require the full analysis that is conducted during the familiar task. Two subtypes of a constrained-processing task that involve this single-question processing are what can be called the method of simulated familiar tasks and the method of scenarios.

## THE METHOD OF SIMULATED FAMILIAR TASKS

Here, a familiar task is performed using archival data. The best example of this method I've seen is used in probing the knowledge of expert weather forecasters (Moninger and Stewart 1987). The experts have to do a forecast but in displaced real time. In this simulated familiar task, the clock can be stopped at any point and the expert queried with regard to reasoning strategies or subdomains of knowledge as incoming data are monitored and predictions are made.

## THE METHOD OF SCENARIOS

While analyzing cases, experts often draw analogies to previously encountered situations or cases. A given case is explored in terms of any relevant or salient similarities and differences (at either perceptual or conceptual levels) relative to a previously encountered case. For example, Klein (1987) examined how expert mechanical and electrical engineers design new components by analogy to other components that perform similar functions. Moninger and Stewart (1987) documented how expert weather forecasters make predictions about the growth of storms based on analogies to previously experienced storms.[6]

One type of constrained-processing task involves having the interviewer deliberately encourage the use of scenarios during the performance of a familiar task. Such a practice should evoke evidence about the expert's reasoning for the kinds of scenarios involved in the data at hand.

## COMBINED CONSTRAINTS

A task can involve combining limited-information constraints with processing constraints. For example, the expert aerial-photo interpreter could be asked to interpret a photograph without the benefit of maps and with only two minutes in which to view the photo (Hoffman 1984).

If an expert does not like limited-information tasks, chances are the opinion will be the same about constrained-processing tasks. In general, the more constrained the task—or the more altered it is relative to the familiar tasks—the more uncomfortable the expert is doing the task. However, in my experience, once an expert begins to open up and becomes less hesitant about giving uncertain or qualified judgments, the limited or constrained tasks can be good sources of information about the expert's reasoning strategies.

## THE METHOD OF TOUGH CASES

Research on an expert's reasoning encounters special difficulty during its later phases when some of the expert's knowledge and methods of reasoning have already been described. The task that now confronts the knowledge engineer is to get evidence about the subtle or refined aspects of the expert's reasoning. One needs to know something about the expert's reasoning that is not already known.

Subtle or refined aspects of an expert's reasoning are often manifested when an expert encounters a tough case, a case with unusual, unfamiliar, or challenging features. It is usually intuitively obvious to an expert when a case is a tough one. Almost by definition, such cases are rare. As a consequence, the knowledge engineer must adopt special methods of study. The limited-information and constrained-processing tasks work by making routine cases challenging; they do not turn routine cases into tough cases.

Methodologically, the method of tough cases is quite simple. The knowledge engineer is not likely to be present when an expert encounters a tough case; so, the expert is equipped with a small tape recorder and is instructed how to make a verbal protocol of personal ruminations when encountering a tough case.

It seems to me that for all important domains of expertise—those which take years of practice—all experts and teams of experts should routinely make recordings of their tough cases. Expertise should never be wasted. Although the analysis of protocols can be time consuming (more on this point later), benefits will no doubt accrue from recording the knowledge that took someone a lifetime to acquire. Ultimately, recording of knowledge might be the crowning achievement of the modern work on expert systems. As Doyle (1984) put it, "It may be fruitful to separate training in articulate apprenticeship from training in current computer systems, for the former will be useful today and tomorrow, while the latter will continually become obsolete" (p. 61).

## COMPARISON OF THE METHODS

For an independent example of how all these various methods crop up in work on expert systems, see the section "Step by Step" in a review article by Patton (1985). Looking through her discussion, one can ferret out an example of a structured interview, an analysis of tough cases, a simulated familiar task, and a constrained-processing task. Given all these various tasks, how can they be compared? One way to compare them is in terms of their relative advantages and disadvantages, some of which I have already alluded to for the various tasks. Table 4 summarizes these points.

**TABLE 4.** Some Salient Advantages and Disadvantages of the Various Methods for Extracting an Expert's Knowledge.

| METHOD | ADVANTAGES | DISADVANTAGES |
|---|---|---|
| ANALYSIS OF FAMILIAR TASKS | The expert feels comfortable | Can be fairly time-consuming |
| INTERVIEWS | For a first- and second-pass at a data base, it can generate much information | Typically very time-consuming |
| LIMITED INFORMATION TASKS | Can be tailored to extract information on selected subdomains of knowledge. | Expert feels uncomfortable and is hesitant to make judgments. |
| CONSTRAINED PROCESSING TASKS | Can be tailored to extract information on selected subdomains of knowledge, or on the expert's strategies | Expert feels uncomfortable and is hesitant to make judgments. |
| ANALYSIS OF "TOUGH CASES" | Can yield information about redefined reasoning | Occur predictably, the knowledge engineer may not be present. |

**TABLE 5.**  Some Criteria by Which Methods Can Be Analyzed and Compared.

| CRITERION | OPERATIONAL DEFINITION |
|---|---|
| SIMPLICITY OF THE TASK | Brevity of the industructions that are necessary to specify exactly what the expert is expected to do, and in what order. |
| SIMPLICITY OF MATERIALS | The number of stimuli or other materials that are needed, and their complexity, relative to the familiar task. |
| BREVITY OF TASK | Total time taken by the task, including the reading of the instructions and the analysis of the data. |
| FLEXIBILITY OF TASK | Is the task adaptable to different materials, to variations in the instructions, or to different experts? |
| ARTIFICIALITY OF TASK | Does the task depart much from the familiar task? |
| DATA FORMAT | Are the data in a format ready for inputting into a data base? |
| DATA VALIDITY | Do the data records provide correct evidence about important knowledge and reasoning strategies? |
| METHOD EFFICIENCY | How many informative propositions are produced per task minute? |

Apart from the qualitative advantages and disadvantages, the experimentalist would like to have some quantifiable criteria for use in a comparative analysis.  Some possible criteria are presented in table 5.

## TASK AND MATERIAL SIMPLICITY

The method of familiar tasks and the method of tough cases are essentially equal in terms of the simplicity of the tasks and the materials, as are the limited-information and constrained-processing tasks.  For all these methods, the instructions involved are about a page or so long, and the materials will be one or a few pages of information, displays, graphs, and so on.  The structured interview stands out because it requires a first-pass data base, which can itself consist of a relatively large and complex set of materials.

## TASK BREVITY

Ideally, one wants to disclose the expert's reasoning as quickly as possible.  Familiar tasks can take anywhere from a few minutes (X-ray diagnosis) to an hour (weather forecasting) to an entire day (aerial-photo interpretation).  Interviews take on the order of days or even weeks.  Although a time-consuming process, interviews can yield a great deal of information, especially when used in the initial phase of developing a data base.  Limited-information and constrained-processing tasks can be intensive and should be designed to take somewhere between 15 and 45 minutes.  Although they are not very time consuming, these tasks do require time for transcribing and coding the audiotapes (more on this point later).

## TASK FLEXIBILITY

Ideally, the task should be flexible: it should work with different sets of materials and with variations in instructions.  For some experts, abundant information about reasoning can be evoked by the simplest of questions.  For other experts, the verbalizations might be less discursive. For some experts, a tape recorder might be absolutely necessary; for others, shorthand notes might suffice.

## TASK ARTIFICIALITY

The task should not depart too much from the familiar tasks. After all, one does not want to build a model of reasoning based on research evidence gained from tasks that never occur in the expert's experience. The further the task departs from the usual problem-solving situation, the less it tells the knowledge engineer about the usual sequences of mental operations and judgments. However, deliberate violations of the constraints that are involved in the familiar tasks (that is, tinkering with the familiar tasks) can be used to systematically expose the expert's reasoning.

None of the tasks that I have described in this paper depart radically from the familiar tasks. They do differ in the degree to which they relax the constraints that are involved in the familiar tasks in order to evoke instances of reasoning.

## DATA FORMAT

Ideally, the data that result from any method should be in a format ready to be input into the data base. Only the structured interview has this characteristic. The other methods can result in verbal protocol data, which need to be transcribed and analyzed.[7]

## DATA VALIDITY

The data that result from any method should contain valid information, valid in that it discloses truths about the expert's perceptions and observations, the expert's knowledge and reasoning, and the methods of testing hypotheses. In addition to validity in the sense of truth value, one would like to feel that a data base is complete—that it covers all the relevant subdomains of knowledge. One would also like to know that different experts agree about the facts. This agreement is validity in the sense of reliability or consensus across experts. Finally, one would like to have some assurance that a set of facts includes the most important ones.

Without such valid information, an expert system cannot be built. How can one be sure that a data base represents valid information?

**Validity: the importance of the data.** Some of an expert's statements will obviously be irrelevant (Do you want a cup of coffee?). Excepting these statements, the knowledge engineer generally takes it for granted that a given statement by the expert is relevant to the domain of expertise being studied. However, just because a given statement (or datum) is relevant does not mean that it is at all important.

Validity in the sense of the relative importance of a given fact or rule can be assessed in a number of ways. One way is the direct approach—ask the experts some more-or-less structured questions to get their judgments of the relative importance of a data-base entry. Another way to assess importance is to see how early or how often a given fact crops up in the data from various experts.

**Validity: reliability or consensus.** The running of additional experts in a knowledge-extraction task presumably has as its major effect the generation of lots of information which is redundant in that it repeats data which are already in the data base (having come from earlier studies of some other expert). This redundancy can be taken as evidence of the validity of the data, validity in the sense of agreement or reliability across different experts.

How many experts is enough? I am not sure there can be a principled answer to this question. Some domains have only one expert, leaving one with little choice. At the other extreme is the "shotgun" approach of interviewing as many different experts as possible (for example, Mittal and Dym 1985) in order to get a complete data base.

**Validity: the completeness of the data base.** Having more than one expert perform various tasks can also help assure validity—in the sense of the completeness of the data base. Indeed, a good rule of thumb is to "pick the brains" of more than one expert for any domain in which different experts have widely different degrees of experience with different subdomains. In addition to their idiosyncratic knowledge, they might have idiosyncratic strategies (Mittal and Dym 1985). Thus, having more than one expert go through the various knowledge-extraction tasks should have the effect of "pushing" the data base toward completeness by filling in the gaps, which occurred in the aerial-photo-interpretation project. One expert knew a lot about desert forms, another expert knew a lot about glacial and arctic forms.

**Validity: the truth value of the data.** The question of how many experts is enough cuts two ways. The study of more than one expert is bound to generate some disagreements, and disagreements are indigestible contradictions as far as any logic-based machine system is concerned. Nevertheless, it might become inevitable that contradictions arise as one refines a data base, adds details, and fleshes out the experience-dependent subdomains of knowledge.

It has been proposed that expert system development projects should only use one expert precisely in order to avoid contradictions (for example, Prerau 1985). This strategy assumes that disagreements are pervasive, but it also seems to assume an underlying reason for the pervasiveness—it is the expert knowledge itself that is plagued by uncertainty. If this statement is true in a given domain, one obviously runs the risk of generating a system that is wholly idiosyncratic at best and based on trivial knowledge at worst. In any event, it could be that the domain at hand is not really well-suited to the application of expert system tools. The advice of trying to avoid contradictions seems to the experimental psychologist to miss the point of expert system work. Disagreements should be used as clues about the basic research that might be needed to fill in the knowledge gaps, perhaps even before any expert system work can be done.

Less extreme than the assumption of pervasive uncertainty and disagreement is the assumption that experts in a given domain agree about most of the basic facts and relevant causal laws, but might disagree about how to go about applying them. An example is the project on the effects of sunspots on the weather (McIntosh 1986). Although the relevant laws are known (that is, electromagnetism, particle physics, and so on), the dynamics of the sun's atmosphere are only partially understood. Thus, the solar weather experts sometimes disagree on how to go about predicting solar phenomena.

Another realistic possibility is the experts agreeing on the relevant laws and about how to go about applying these laws but disagreeing about hypotheses for some specific cases. Such occurrences routinely happen in knowledge-extraction tasks that involve more than one expert at a time. For example, weather forecasters can be paired in the simulated familiar task (Moniger and Stewart 1987) and they often enter into debates as hypotheses are hashed about. Aerial-photo interpreters sometimes work in teams of research groups. For cases such as these team efforts, the experts' discussions, debates, and exchanges of hypotheses can be very informative, especially when the team encounters a tough case.

Whether disagreements among experts are pervasive, are due to uncertainty in the application of relevant knowledge, or are due to uncertainty about specific hypotheses, it is ultimately the responsibility of the knowledge engineer to resolve any unreliable or contradictory rules or facts. Suppose that each of a set of expert aerial-photo interpreters produces a rule about the identification of limestone sinkholes but that the rules are somehow mutually incompatible. The knowledge engineer really has only two choices: either combine the rules into a new logically coherent rule, or select one of them for use. In any event, only one rule for identifying limestone sinkholes can appear in the expert system (that is, there can be no contradictions in its logic). Formally, the machine can only model one expert at a time.

## METHOD EFFICIENCY

Perhaps the most important criterion in a practical sense is overall efficiency. For the sake of people out there "in the trenches," I thought I'd try to apply some efficiency metrics to the various methods. In the case of knowledge acquisition, efficiency involves the number of propositions generated per unit of time. Time is expressed as total task time, that is, the time it takes the knowledge engineer to prepare to run the expert at the task plus the time it takes to run the task plus the time it takes to analyze the data.

One can assess the production rates of propositions of different types. One seeks not only facts (predications or observation statements), one also seeks information about potential if-then rules (the expert's inference strategies and heuristics). Furthermore, one seeks not just propositions of these types but new ones, informative ones because they are not already in the data base. Table 6 presents this classification of propositional data.

Table 7 presents some efficiency analyses for the projects I've been involved with. I present these analyses not to imply that knowledge engineers should routinely perform such analyses, but hopefully to save them the trouble. I suspect that the rate statistics presented here are representative of what people can expect in work on expertise systems.

Let me focus on unstructured interviews because this knowledge-acquisition method is the most commonly used. For unstructured interviews, one can assess efficiency in a number of ways. Total time can be divided into the number of propositions obtained (for both observation statements and potential if-then rules). Also, the number of propositions obtained can be divided into the number of questions asked by the interviewer (or the number of pages of transcript).

**TABLE 6.** A Matrix for Classifying the Data Generated by a Task That Is Intended to Extract the Knowledge of an Expert. The Frequency of propositions of each of two types (facts or observation statements, and inferences or potential if-then rules) can be used to assess the relative difficulty of extracting the two types of knowledge: "old" or "new" relative to the current data base.

TYPES OF PROPOSITIONS

| | OBSERVATION STATEMENTS | INFERENCES |
|---|---|---|
| OLD | Quite easy to obtain<br>Requires no special methods | Relatively easy to obtain<br>Requires no special methods |
| *STATUS* | | |
| | Relatively difficult to obtain | Relatively very difficult to obtain |
| NEW | Requires special methods | Requires special methods |

**TABLE 7.** A Comparison of the Results for Four Methods in Terms of Some Measures of Efficiency. The unstructured interview results are from the project on expert airlift planners (Hoffman 1986). The other results are from the aerial photo interpretation project (Hoffman 1984). The third task listed here is one that combined limited information with processing constraints. All rate computations are based on total task time.

| METHOD | RESULTS |
|---|---|
| UNSTRUCTURED INTERVIEW | For each question the interviewer asked, the method generated 0.8 propositions. The method generated 0.13 propositions per task minute. |
| STRUCTURED INTERVIEW | Of the 1,400 propositions in the first-pass data base, 30 percent were modified. The first-pass data base was increased in size by 15 percent.<br>The method generated about one new proposition per task minute. |
| LIMITED INFORMATION AND CONSTRAINED PROCESSING TASK | The method generated between one and two new observation-related propositions and between one and two inference-related propositions per task minute. |
| METHOD OF "TOUGH CASES" | The method generated between one and two new observation-related propositions and between one and two new inference-related propositions per task minute. |

For the project on expert airlift planners (Hoffman 1986), the analysis of the 10 hours of taped unstructured interviews yielded a total task time of 100 hours, a total of 957 questions asked by the interviewer, and a total of 753 propositions (including both observation statements and potential if-then rules). Thus, the unstructured interview generated only approximately 0.13 propositions per task minute and approximately 0.8 propositions for each question asked by the knowledge engineer.

The unstructured interview produced lots of propositions in the first hours of the interview (over 5 propositions per page of transcript or over 200 propositions per hour), but the rate trailed off rapidly (to less than 1 proposition per page of transcript or about 40 propositions per hour). In part, this result was due to the fact that in the later sessions, the interviewer and expert spent time sitting at a computer terminal and informally discussed user needs and system design. In just the first 5 of the 10 hours, the unstructured interview yielded approximately 1.6 propositions per task minute.

In general, if a knowledge engineer finds that knowledge is being extracted at a rate of about two new propositions per task minute, the engineer can be assured of probably being on the right track. If the rate is closer to one proposition per task minute, chances are there is some inefficiency somewhere. If the rate is closer to three per minute, the knowledge engineer is golden.

## RECOMMENDATIONS

Overall, the unstructured interview is not too terribly efficient. This finding deserves emphasis because most expert systems have apparently been developed using unstructured interviews. Preliminary unstructured interviews can be critical for obtaining information on three key questions: (1) Who are the experts? (2) Is this problem well-suited to the expert system approach? and (3) What are the needs of the people who will use the system? However, if the knowledge engineer needs to become familiar with the domain, then an analysis of familiar tasks should be conducted and a first pass data base gleaned from this analysis. Once a first-pass data base has been produced, then unstructured interviews (using note taking rather than tape recording) can be used to determine user needs. If the knowledge engineer wishes to build a refined or second-pass data base, structured interviews are more efficient. In fact, they can be many times more efficient overall, according to my results.

As data bases become very large, it becomes necessary to use special tasks. Limited-information or constrained-processing tasks or the method of tough cases can be used in order to focus on specific subdomains of knowledge or to disclose aspects of reasoning that the data base might lack. Otherwise, the knowledge engineer might spend hours working at an inefficient task, inefficient in that it produces lots of propositions which happen to already reside in the data base.

All experts differ, and all domains of expertise differ; so, too, will all expert system-development projects differ. Some methods for extracting an expert's knowledge will fit some projects and not others. For example, an analysis of familiar tasks might not be very fruitful for domains in which there are no texts or in which the available technical manuals provide little information about what the experts actually do. Such was the case for the airlift-planning project (Hoffman 1986). It made sense in that project to begin with an unstructured interview to learn not only about user needs but to simultaneously get some very basic information about what airlift planners actually do in their planning tasks (that is, the familiar task).

Despite such domain specificity, I can propose a generalized series of steps for extracting the knowledge of experts, as shown in table 8. Situations probably exist for which my recommended series of steps is not quite fitting. However, I'd wager that one or another slight variation on this theme would fit.

The figures in table 8 for "Effort Required" are approximate ranges based on my experience. According to my estimates, it can take at least three months to get to the point of having a refined or second-pass data base. How does this time frame compare with the experiences of other artificial intelligence (AI) researchers? Actually, it is impossible to tell from reading the expert system literature exactly how much effort went into building the data base in any expert system project. (It is for this reason that I feel compelled to present my own "ballpark" estimates.) Typically, authors do not even state how the knowledge was obtained—sometimes from texts and manuals, sometimes from archived data, and usually from unstructured interviews. Typically, research reports jump right into a discussion of system architecture.

Some reports on expert system projects state how long it took to develop a prototype, but one can only guess how long it took just to acquire (or extract) the data. The development of MYCIN (Davis, Buchanan, and Shortliffe 1977), a system for diagnosing infectious diseases, took many years. The development of INTERNIST, another medical-diagnosis system, took 10 years with the help of a full-time specialist in internal medicine (Buchanan 1982). R1, which configures the VAX computer (McDermott 1980), took two man-years to develop by a team of about a dozen researchers and is still being refined. In general, it takes one to two years to develop a prototype and about five years to develop a full-scale system (Duda and Shortliffe 1983; Gevarter 1984).

In contrast, the PUFF system for the diagnosis of pulmonary disorders was reported to have been developed in less than 10 weeks (Bramer 1982). The likely reason for this brevity was that most of the rules were easily gleaned from archived data (Feigenbaum 1977), and only one week was spent interviewing the experts (Bramer 1982).

Apparently, if one is relying on unstructured interviews, is interviewing a large number of experts, or is working on a system that requires hundreds or thousands of rules and facts in

**TABLE 8.** Some Steps for Extracting and Characterizing the Knowledge of an Expert Prior to the Construction of an Expert System. The analysis of familiar tasks includes the analysis of texts and technical manuals. The activity designated "Special Tasks" includes limited information tasks, constrained processing tasks and analyses of "tough cases." All figures for "effort required" are approximations based on the author's experience.

| STEP | ACTIVITY | PURPOSE | EFFORT REQUIRED |
|---|---|---|---|
| 1 | Analysis of Familiar Task | Familiarizes the knowledge engineer with the domain. Yields information for the first-pass data base. | One month |
| 2 | (Optional) Unstructured Interview | Familiarizes the knowledge engineer with the domain. Yields information for the first-pass data base. Helps in determining user needs and system design. | One to two weeks |
| 3 | Preparation of First-pass Data Base | Beginnings of a computer file. | One month or more |
| 4 | (Optional) Unstructured Interview | Familiarizes the knowledge engineer with the domain. Yields information for the second-pass data base. Helps in determining user needs and system design. | One to two weeks |
| 5 | Structured Interviews | Yields information for the second-pass data base. | One to two weeks |
| 6 | Preparation of Second-pass Data Base | Refinements of the computer file. | Two weeks or more |
| 7 | Special Tasks | Yields further refinements of the data base. | One week or more per experiment. |

its data base (as in the INTERNIST system), then many years of effort are required to develop the system to the prototype stage.

In this light, a minimum of three months to build a second-pass data base seems like an underestimate. However, it cannot be a gross underestimate. The second-pass data base for the aerial-photo-interpretation project (Hoffman 1984) contained over 1400 rules and facts, and it took me about 45 days to develop it by means of structured interviews and special tasks.

AI researchers will not be eager to use all the methods and carry out all the efficiency computations presented here, but I do not propose that they should. I do not want to shoehorn the "tricks of the trade" of building expert systems into the rigid statistics-oriented structure of a psychological experiment. However, I do want to strongly recommend that developers of expert systems routinely report the methods used to extract experts' knowledge and the efficiency of the methods (that is, the amount of effort taken to construct the data base).

## SOME LINGERING ISSUES

None of the methodological ideas that are presented here is intended to be logically airtight. My categorization of methods is intended to be pragmatic rather than complete. The criteria for analyzing methods are probably insufficient. I welcome reactions and suggestions and hope that these ideas are helpful to others.

To those who have already developed an expert system, many of the research ideas I have referred to might seem detailed (if not trivial). I wanted to spill out the gory details for the sake of those who have not yet attempted to generate an expert system. As I said at the outset, I address the expert system engineering process from a nuts-and-bolts perspective. To those who are not familiar with experimental psychology, it might be surprising that experimentalists deal with minutiae such as better ways of tape recording or the variety of ways to assess the validity of a data set. However, such minutiae are precisely the sorts of things that experimental psychologists like to attend to. Thus, my discussion focused on methods and methodology (the analysis of methods). Hidden in the discussion are a few broader issues that merit explicit consideration and a wee bit of feather ruffling.

## THE SOCIAL PSYCHOLOGY OF EXPERTISE

Should the knowledge engineer be the expert? In other words, should the expert become a knowledge engineer? I do not know if there can be a principled answer to this question. Some researchers claim that the knowledge engineer should be the expert (Friedland 1981), that "expert systems are best conceived by the experts themselves" (Taylor 1985, p. 62). Some researchers claim that the situation in which experts interview other experts can be disastrous. Other researchers say the more the expert knows about AI, the more likely it is that the expert has biases (for example, about which knowledge representation format to use) (McIntosh 1986).

The answer to this question probably lies in the social-psychological dynamics of particular working groups. Certainly, the expert should know enough about AI to be skeptical and enough about expert systems to appreciate the ways in which the system can aid, rather than replace them.

## ARE EXPERT SYSTEMS AI, OR ARE THEY COGNITIVE SIMULATION?

Some expert systems have an "explanation" component; that is, one can query the system about a given conclusion or inference. Typically, the system returns with what is essentially a list or a printout of the rules involved. Such an explanation is not very adequate. Until expert systems deal with reasoning and knowledge at a semantic or conceptual level, their artificiality will remain painfully obvious, and they might not even merit being called intelligent.

Concepts are typically defined in AI using logically necessary and sufficient conditions. However, can an expert system work (or work well) without also being a "cognitive simulation?" To what degree does a given expert system need to represent conceptual knowledge? The jury is still out. We cannot be certain the purely rule-based approach will always effectively or efficiently solve the various problem that people would like their expert systems to solve.

Most concepts do not exist in human cognition in any pristine form. Experts, unlike expert systems, do not always reason in terms of a logical set of rules (Dreyfus and Dreyfus 1986). What is clear is that in many domains, experts reason in terms of their perceptual and conceptual understanding, such as their "mental models" of causal laws (Gentner and Stevens 1983; Sridharan 1985).

When the expert aerial-photo interpreter looks at a photo, the complex geo-biological events that led to the formation of the terrain are perceived (for example, mountain building, glaciation, and so on). When the expert cardiologist listens to heart sounds over a stethoscope, the complex biomechanical events that occur in the cardiovascular system are perceived (Jenkins 1985; Johnson et al. 1982). Such perceptual and conceptual understanding, the result of perceptual-learning and concept-formation processes, might be direct (Gibson 1979); that is, it might not be mediated by any analysis of naked if-then rules, serial or otherwise.

Recently, attempts have been made to incorporate conceptual knowledge into AI systems (Chandrasekaran and Mittal 1983; Kunz 1983; Pople 1982) and to define rule systems that behave like the human reasoner (Sridharan 1985). As instances of AI systems, expert systems might not need to precisely simulate cognition in order to get the job done. However, we do need to learn more about experts' reasoning through basic research if our expert systems are ever to get the job done well, which brings me to the last issue I address.

## DOES AI HAVE ITS FOUNDATIONS IN PHILOSOPHY OR RESEARCH?

The cognitive-simulation work hints at the fact that some AI workers are really closet psychologists. They rely on psychological terms and mentalistic metaphors, and they work on psychological problems. More to the point, the problems they work on often beg for an empirical answer, an answer based on research findings. However, AI workers tend to turn to computing theories and abstract concepts to produce solutions.

No better example of this tendency exists than that provided by the field of expert systems itself. Having recognized that the knowledge-acquisition process is a bottleneck, what solution do AI workers seek? Let's build another program! Davis and Lenat (1982, p. 348) assert that a system which has knowledge about its own representations can allow for "knowledge acquisition using a high-level dialog." But can't humans use dialog to extract knowledge, or did I miss something? AI really does like to put the logical cart before the empirical horse.

In the literature on expert systems, I've found numerous assertions, such as the claim that experts are better able to build good data bases than computer scientists. Such assertions might seem solid and might indeed be correct, but they are rarely empirically grounded, which causes the experimental psychologist to yank out clumps of hair.

The broader literature on AI and cognitive science is characterized by its penchant for philosophical speculation (Hoffman and Nead 1983). The typical issue of a cognitive science technical journal contains evermore clever theories, theories that combine "schemas," "scripts," "inference nets," and "labeled relations" in all sorts of clever computational ways. However, there is rarely a clear statement about whether the theory has an evidential base. Sometimes, no statement even exists about whether the theory is supposed to have anything at all to do with heads or whether it is just supposed to be about computers, which causes the experimental psychologist to yank out even larger clumps of hair.

While remembering that the roots of AI are in the philosophy of the mind (cf. McCarthy and Hayes 1969), AI practitioners seem to have forgotten about the roots in experimental psychology. It is the rare paper that acknowledges the need for basic research on cognition, that is not put off by the experimental psychologist's stubborn concern with methodological details, or that is sensitive to the difference between AI and cognitive simulation.[8]

If one is at all interested in cognition or cognitive simulation, then experiments are necessary to ensure that the model works like the mind does, or to test hypotheses about an expert's strategies. One cannot simply assert, for instance, that human or computer memories must rely on schemas because schemas are computationally elegant. Such hasty epistemological pronouncements will never do.[9]

If AI is to solve the really tough problems, it would do well to put a bit less effort into short-term solutions (for example, reliance on naked if-then rules) and premature applications (for example, expert systems that rapidly become too complex to be rapidly computable) and a bit more effort into systematic research (for example, how experts really reason). In the past few years, federal funding for basic research on cognition and graduate training in experimental psychology have suffered from much more than their fair share of cuts. Rather than just bemoaning the lack of trained knowledge engineers, anyone who is interested in making a real contribution to our needs in the field of AI might consider investing some resources in the support of basic research on human cognition and perception.

## THE BENEFITS OF COLLABORATION

The collaboration of AI researchers and experimental psychologists can be of benefit to work on expert systems. I hope my article has made this point. Benefits can also accrue for psychology, however. For example, a major theory of memory asserts that forgetting is caused by the interference of new learning with old (Reder 1987, Smith, Adams, and Schorr 1978). This hypothesis generates what is called the *paradox of expertise*: how can experts deal so adroitly with so many remembered facts? Hopefully, research on the cognition of experts can help clarify this paradox.

Expert system work also bears on theories of perceptual learning. Although it is obvious experts have special knowledge and concepts, it should be kept in mind that they also have special perceptual skills (Shanteau 1984). For example, the expert radiologist "sees" X rays differently than the first-year medical student (Feltovich 1981). Another, more commonplace example is the expert sports commentator who "sees" something that we novices can only pick up when shown the slow-motion replay. Lifetimes of good research could be carried out to distinguish experts from novices in terms of their perceptual processes, learning processes, and reasoning strategies. What information do experts focus on? What reasoning biases do they have? How can experts be identified?

What I find particularly appealing about such questions is that the research they engender is practical and basic at the same time—practical because it contributes to the solving of important problems, basic because it contributes to the body of knowledge. The collaboration of experimental psychologists and AI researchers can be of great mutual benefit.

### Acknowledgments

Most of the ideas reported here were first developed under the aegis of the U.S. Army Summer Faculty Research and Engineering Program (Delivery Order No. 0550). The work was conducted in the summer of 1983 at the Engineer Topographic Laboratories (ETL), U.S. Army Corps of Engineers, Ft. Belvoir, Virginia. The author would like to thank Olin Mintzer, master aerial-photo interpreter, for his help and guidance. The author would also like to thank all the people at the Center for Physical Science and the Center for Artificial Intelligence at ETL for their many stimulating discussions.

Clarifications and amplifications arose in discussions at the Artificial Intelligence Research in Environmental Science Conference held at the Environmental Research Laboratories of the National Oceanic and Atmospheric Administration (NOAA), Boulder, Colorado, 28–29 May 1986. The author would especially like to thank William Moninger of NOAA for his encouragement.

Many others deserve thanks for their encouragement and support of the research reported here: Gary Grann, Lieutenant Colonel John Whitcomb, Captain Eric Goepper, Captain Thomas Moran, Captain

Jeffrey Valiton, 2d Lieutenant Joseph Besselman, and Lieutenant Ray Harris of the Strategic Planning Directorate, Electronics System Division, Hanscom Air Force Base, Massachusetts; Murray Daniels of MITRE Corporation; Rodney Darrah, Susan Espy and the people at Universal Energy Systems, Inc.; Karen Thompson and Pat Carey at Adelphi University.

Preparation of this paper was supported by a grant from Summer Faculty Research Program (Contract No. F49620-85-C-0013) of the U.S. Air Force Office of Scientific Research. The U.S. Government is authorized to reproduce and distribute reprints for governmental purposes not withstanding any copyright notation herein.

## References

Bierre, P. 1985. The Professor's Challenge. *AI Magazine* 5(4):60–70.

Boose, J. H. 1984. Personal Construct Theory and the Transfer of Human Expertise. In Proceedings of the Third National Conference on Artificial Intelligence, 27–33. Menlo Park, Calif.: American Association of Artificial Intelligence.

Bramer, M. A. 1982. A Survey and Critical Review of Expert Systems Research. In *Introductory Readings in Expert Systems*, ed. D. Michie, 3–29. London: Gordon and Breach.

Buchanan, B. G. 1982. New Research on Expert Systems. In *Machine Intelligence*, vol. 10, eds. J. Hayes, D. Michie, and Y–H. Pao. New York: Wiley.

Chandrasekaran, B., and Mittal, S. 1983. Deep versus Compiled Knowledge Approaches to Diagnostic Problem Solving. *International Journal of Man-Machine Studies* 19:425–436.

Cooke, N. M. 1985. Modeling Human Expertise in Expert Systems, Technical Report, MCCS-85-12, Computing Research Laboratory, New Mexico State Univ.

Davis, J. 1986. Summary of the Workshop on Knowledge Acquisition. Paper presented at Artificial Intelligence Research in Environmental Science Conference. Boulder, Colo.: NOAA.

Davis, R., Buchanan, B. G., and Shortliffe, E. H. 1977. Production Systems as a Representation for a Knowledge-Based Consultation Program. *Artificial Intelligence* 8:15–45.

Davis, R., and Lenat, B. 1982. *Knowledge-Based Systems in AI.* New York: McGraw-Hill.

Denning, P. J. 1986. Towards a Science of Expert Systems. *IEEE Expert* 1(2):80–83.

Doyle, J. 1984. Expert Systems without Computers or Theory and Trust in Artificial Intelligence. *AI Magazine* 5(2):59–63.

Dreyfus, H., and Dreyfus, S. 1986. Why Expert Systems Do Not Exhibit Expertise. *IEEE Expert* 1(2):86–90.

Duda, R. O., and Gashnig, J. G. 1981. Knowledge-Based Expert Systems Come of Age. *Byte.* September:238–281.

Duda, R. O., and Shortliffe, E. H. 1983. Expert Systems Research. *Science* 220:261–276.

Einhorn, H. J. 1974. Expert Judgment. *Journal of Applied Psychology* 59:562–571.

Eliot, L. B. 1986. Analogical Problem Solving and Expert Systems. *IEEE Expert* 1(2):17–28.

Ericcson, K. A., and Simon, H. A. 1984. *Protocol Analysis: Verbal Reports as Data.* Cambridge, Mass.: MIT Press.

Feigenbaum, E. A. 1977. The Art of AI. In Proceedings of the Fifth International Joint Conference on Artificial Intelligence. International Joint Conference on Artificial Intelligence.

Feltovich, P. J. 1981. Knowledg-Based Components of Expertise in Medical Diagnosis, Technical Report, PDS-2, Learning Research and Development Center, Univ. of Pittsburgh.

Freiling, M., Alexander, J., Messick, S., Rehfuss, S., and Shulman, S. 1985. Starting a Knowledge Engineering Project: A Step-by-Step Approach. *AI Magazine* 6(3):150–163.

Friedland, P. 1981. Acquisition of Procedural Knowledge from Domain Experts. In Proceedings of the Seventh International Joint Conference on Artificial Intelligence, 856–861. International Joint Conference on Artificial Intelligence.

Gentner, D., and Stevens, A., eds. 1983. *Mental Models*. Hillsdale, N.J.: Lawrence Erlbaum.

Gevarter, W. B. 1984. *Artificial Intelligence Computer Vision and Natural Language Processing*. Park Ridge, N.J.: Noyes.

Gibson, J. G. 1979. *The Ecological Approach to Visual Perception*. Boston: Houghton-Mifflin.

Gorfein, D., and Hoffman, R., eds. 1987. *Memory and Learning: The Ebbinghaus Centennial Conference*. Hillsdale, N.J.: Lawrence Erlbaum. Forthcoming.

Hartley, R. 1981. How Expert Should Expert Systems Be? In Proceedings of the Seventh International Joint Conference on Artificial Intelligence. International Joint Conferences on Artificial Intelligence.

Hayes-Roth, F., Waterman, P. A., and Lenat, D., eds. 1983. *Building Expert Systems*. Reading, Mass.: Addison-Wesley.

Hoffman, R. 1986. Procedures for Efficiently Extracting the Knowledge of Experts, Technical Report, U.S. Air Force Summer Faculty Research Program, Office of Scientific Research, Bolling Air Force Base.

Hoffman, R. R. 1985. Some Implications of Metaphor for the Philosophy and Psychology of Science. In *The Ubiquity of Metaphor*, eds. W. Paprotte and R. Dirven, 327–380. Amsterdam, Netherlands: John Benjamin.

Hoffman, R. R. 1984. Methodological Preliminaries to the Development of an Expert System for Aerial-Photo Interpretation, Technical Report, ETL-0342, The Engineer Topographic Laboratories.

Hoffman, R. R. 1980. Metaphor in Science. In *Cognition and Figurative Language*, eds. R. Honeck and R. Hoffman, 393–423. Hillsdale, NJ: Lawrence Erlbaum Associates.

Hoffman, R. R., and Kemper, S. 1987. What Could Reaction-Time Studies Be Telling Us about Metaphor Comprehension? In *Metaphor and Symbolic Activity* vol. 2. Forthcoming.

Hoffman, R. R., and Nead, J. M. 1983. General Contextualism, Ecological Science, and Cognitive Research. *The Journal of Mind and Behavior* 4:507–560.

Jenkins, J. J. 1985. Acoustic Information for Objects, Places, and Events. In *Persistence and Change: Proceedings of the First International Conference on Event Perception,* eds. W. Warren and R. Shaw, 115–138. Hillsdale, N.J.: Lawrence Erlbaum

Johnson, P. E., Hassebrock, F., Duran, A. S., and Moller, J. H. 1983. Multimethod Study of Clinical Judgment. *Organizational Behavior and Human Performance* 30:201–230.

Kelly, G. 1955. *The Psychology of Personal Constructs*. New York: Norton.

Kintsch, W. 1972. *The Representation of Meaning in Memory*. Hillsdale, N.J.: Lawrence Erlbaum.

Klein, G. A. 1987. Applications of Analogic Reasoning. *Metaphor and Symbolic Activity* 2(3):201–218.

Kunz, J. 1983. Analysis of Physiological Behavior Using a Causal Model Based on First Principles. In Proceedings of the Second National Conference on Artificial Intelligence. Menlo Park, Calif.: American Association for Artificial Intelligence.

McCarthy, J. 1983. President's Quarterly Message: AI Needs More Emphasis on Basic Research. *AI Magazine* 4(4):5.

McCarthy, J., and Hayes, P. 1969. Some Philosophical Problems from the Standpoint of AI. In *Machine Intelligence*, vol. 4, eds. B. Meltzer and D. Michie. Edinburgh, Scotland: Edinburgh University Press.

McDermott, J. 1980. R1: A Rule-Based Configurer of Computer Systems, Technical Report, Computer Science Dept., Carnegie-Mellon Univ.

McIntosh, P. S. 1986. Knowledge Acquisition for THEO: An Expert System for Solar-Flare Forecasting. Paper presented at Artificial Intelligence Research in Environmental Science Conference. Boulder, Colo.: NOAA.

McNeill, D., and Levy, E. 1982. Conceptual Representations in Language Activity and Gesture. In *Speech, Place, and Action*, eds. R. Jarvella and W. Klein, 271–295. New York: Wiley.

Mintzer, O., and Messmore, J. 1984. Terrain Analysis Procedural Guide for Surface Configuration, Technical Report, ETL-0352, Engineer Topographic Laboratories.

Mittal, S., and Dym, C. L.  1985.  Knowledge Acquisition from Multiple Experts.  *AI Magazine* 6(2):32–36.

Moninger, W., and Stewart, T.  1987.  A Proposed Study of Human Information Processing in Weather Forecasting.  In *Bulletin of the American Meterological Association.*  Forthcoming.

Nii, H. P., and Aiello, N.  1979.  AGE (Attempt to Generalize): A Knowledge-Based Program for Building Knowledge-Based Programs.  In Proceedings of the Sixth International Joint Conference on Artificial Intelligence, 645–655.  International Joint Conferences on Artificial Intelligence.

Pachella, R. G.  1974.  The Interpretation of Reaction Time in Information-Processing Research.  In *Human Information Processing: Tutorials in Performance and Cognition*, ed. B. Kantowitz.  Hillsdale, N.J.: Lawrence Erlbaum.

Patton, C.  1985.  Knowledge-Engineering: Tapping the Experts.  *Electronic Design.*  May:93–100.

Politakis, P., and Weiss, S.  1984.  Using Empirical Analysis to Refine Expert Systems Knowledge Bases.  *Artificial Intelligence* 22:23–48.

Pople, H. E.  1982.  Heuristic Methods for Imposing Structure on Ill-Structured Problems.  In *Artificial Intelligence in Medicine*, ed. P. Szolovits.  Boulder, Colo.: Westview.

Posner, M. I.  1978.  *Chronometric Explorations of Mind.*  Hillsdale, N.J.: Lawrence Erlbaum.

Prerau, D. S.  1985. Selection of an Appropriate Domain for an Expert System.  *AI Magazine* 6(2):26–30.

Purves, W. K.  1985.  A Biologist Looks at Cognitive AI.  *AI Magazine* 6(2):38–43.

Quinlan, J. R.  1984.  Fundamentals of the Knowledge Engineering Problem.  In *Introductory Readings in Expert Systems*, ed. D. Michie, 33–46.  London: Gordon and Breach.

Raulefs, P.  1985.  Knowledge Processing Expert Systems.  In *AI: Towards Practical Applications*, eds. T. Bernold and G. Albers.  Amsterdam, Netherlands: North-Holland.

Reder, L. M.  1987.  Beyond Associationism: Strategic Components in Memory Retrieval.  In *Memory and Learning: The Ebbinghaus Centennial Conference*, eds. D. Gorfein and R. Hoffman.  Hillsdale, N.J.: Lawrence Erlbaum.  Forthcoming.

Shanteau, J.  1984.  Some Unasked Questions about the Psychology of Expert Decision Makers.  In Proceedings of the 1984 IEEE Conference on Systems, Man, and Cybernetics, ed. M. El Hawaray.  New York: Institute of Electrical and Electronics Engineers, Inc.

Shortliffe, E. H.  1980.  Consultation Systems for Physicians.  In Proceedings of the Canadian Society for Computational Studies of Intelligence.  Victoria, B.C.: Canadian Society for Computational Studies of Intelligence.

Smith, E. E., Adams, N., and Schon, D.  1978.  Fact Retrieval and the Paradox of Interference.  *Cognitive Psychology* 10:438–464.

Sridharan, N. S.  1985.  Evolving Systems of Knowledge.  *AI Magazine* 6(3):108–120.

Stefik, M., Aikins, A., Balzer, R., Benoit, J., Birnbaum, L., Hayes-Roth, F., and Sacerdoti, E.  1982.  The Organization of Expert Systems: A Tutorial.  *Artificial Intelligence* 18:135–173.

Sternberg, R. J.  1977.  *Intelligence, Information Processing, and Analogical Reasoning.*  Hillsdale, N.J.: Lawrence Erlbaum.

Taylor, E. C.  1985.  Developing a Knowledge Engineering Capability in the TRW Defense Systems Group.  *AI Magazine* 6(2):58–63.

Townsend, J. T., and Ashby, F. G.  1983.  *Stochastic Modeling of Elementary Psychological Processes.*  Cambridge, Mass.: Cambridge University Press.

Way, D. S.  1978.  *Terrain Analysis.*  Stroudsberg, Pa.: Dowden, Hutchinson, and Ross.

Weiss, S., and Kulikowski, C.  1984.  *A Practical Guide to Designing Expert Systems.*  Totowa, N.J.: Rowman and Allanheld.

Woods, D. D.  1985.  Cognitive Technologies: The Design of Joint Human-Machine Cognitive Systems.  *AI Magazine* 6(4):86–92.

**Notes**

1. For discussions of the psychology of expertise, see Cooke (1985), Einhorn (1974), Feltovich (1981), and Shanteau (1984).

2. One exception is the work of Boose (1984), who has adopted ideas about interviewing from psychologist George Kelly (1955). Boose's concern has been with building a computer system for interviewing experts.

3. A proposition is generally regarded as an "atomic fact"—an assertion of the existence of some entity and the predication of some property or relation of this entity. Treatments that are relevant to protocol analysis can be found in Kintsch (1972, chapter 2) and Ericcson and Simon (1984, chapters 5 and 6).

4. Tape-recording tips: (1) conduct the interview in a small, quiet room; (2) use batteries liberally so you always receive a clear signal; and (3) preface your recordings by identifying each of the participants.

5. Constrained-processing tasks can also involve the measurement of reaction time or *decision latency*. Such measures are important for the purposes of cognitive simulation and cognitive psychology, because the results can be informative about specific sequences of mental operations (such as memory encoding and retrieval). For a discussion of the logic of reaction-time experiments, see Hoffman and Kemper (1987), Pachella (1974), Posner (1978), or Townsend and Ashby (1983).

6. What is salient here is that the analogic reasoning is in terms of a comparison to previously encountered scenarios. Because reasoning by analogy pervades all problem solving, the analogy component of the method of scenarios does not seem as salient for present purposes as the reliance on scenarios to form the analogies. For reviews of the abundant literature on the role of analogy and metaphor in problem solving, see Eliot (1986), Gentner and Stevens (1983), Hoffman (1980, 1985), and Sternberg (1977).

7. Some detailed comments are in order about the transcription process for the sake of those who might choose to go this route. As I have already implied, the transcription process takes time. Without any doubt, the most time-consuming aspect of the transcription process is the time spent pausing and backing up the tape to interpret and write down the segments where more than one person speaks at a time. The moral: The examiner should consciously try to withhold comments or questions while the expert is talking. The examiner should use a notepad to jot down questions and return to them when the expert's monologue is over. The goal of any interview, whether structured or unstructured, is not to edify the knowledge engineer, but to let the expert talk and get the knowledge out so that it can be formalized (hence my earlier distinction between interviews and discussions). It also takes time to code the transcript for propositional content, anywhere from one to five minutes for each page of transcript. The coding should involve at least two independent coders (or judges) until evidence indicates that their respective codings show agreement which is high enough to warrant dropping the extra coders.

8. To be fair, some AI authors are sensitive to the difference, for example, Bierre (1985), McCarthy (1983), Purves (1985), and Woods (1985). Furthermore, the major AI conventions include sessions on cognitive research, and the AI technical journals include occasional reviews of recent cognitive research.

9. I am hesitant to attribute this particular claim about schemas to any one person. I've read so many claims about the representation of knowledge (templates, prototypes, networks, semantic features, and so on), and I've yanked out so much hair, that I'd rather ruffle everyone's feathers. I also find it worrisome when claims are made about computer or mental representations on the basis of the argument that there are "storage" limitations. Indeed, "storage" might be the wrong metaphor altogether. For further discussion, see Gorfein and Hoffman (1987).

# Appendix E

## Expert System Versus Credit Fraud

*Alan Alper*

The American Express Co. is calling on the advice of an expert—an expert system, that is—to help it weed out bad credit risks and reduce losses. The system relies on 800 rules derived from American Express' best credit authorizers.

American Express, according to expert systems watchers, thus becomes the first charge

**American Express Co.'s proposed implementation of an expert system**

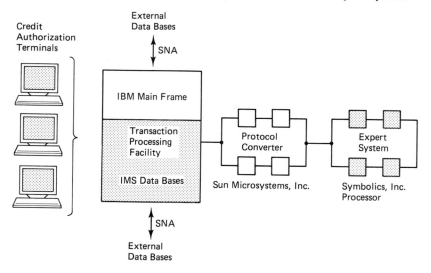

CW Chart: Susan Aldam

Reprinted with the kind permission of *Computerworld*, April 13, 1987, pp. 25, 30.

card company to utilize artificial intelligence in credit authorization applications. The expert system—called Authorizer's Assistant—was developed by Inference Corp. in Los Angeles and will be fully functional by mid-year, according to Robert Flast, vice-president of technology for American Express' Travel Services Co.

## HEAVY IMPACT SEEN

"This expert system has the ability to touch more people than any other expert system ever implemented," says Tom Schwartz, an expert systems consultant and publisher of "Who's Who in AI."

American Express had good reason to seek the assistance of an expert system. The American Express Card—unlike bank credit cards—has no credit limit. Losses caused by bad credit authorizations and fraudulent use of its charge cards have been substantial during the last few years, observers say. Flast is unwilling to quantify the losses.

Flast, however, concedes that conventional computer systems have been only partially successful in limiting bad credit risks and fraud. Moreover, such technology has been slow and unwieldy to use, he admits.

Using the old system—running on an IBM 3033 mainframe—credit authorizers first had to enter IBM's Transaction Processing Facility (TPF) and then go offline searching through as many as 12 data bases, via CICS and IMS, for additional card-holder information.

It was two years ago that Flast, then vice-president of transactional services, decided credit authorizers could benefit from better tools to make consistent decisions.

"It seemed like the perfect fit for an expert system," Flast recalls. "We decided to put all of our resources into this one major project."

In mid-1985, Flast proposed that the firm contract with an expert systems developer to build a prototype expert system to assist—not replace—authorizers.

Later that year, American Express chose Inference, developer of the automated reasoning tool, to build a prototype expert system in a little more than one year.

Inference developed the system to run on a coprocessor accessing data from the IMS data bases residing on the mainframe. A Symbolics, Inc. processor was selected to run the expert system. A Sun Microsystems, Inc. workstation—acting as protocol converter—enabled the Symbolics processor to extract data from the IMS data bases on the IBM mainframe.

## LEAST RISKY APPROACH

This approach, while not optimal, was the least risky way for American Express to test the expert system concept, Flast explains.

The biggest challenge in building Authorizer's Assistant was not getting the expert system to talk to TPF, Flast says. The difficulty arose in getting TPF and IMS to talk to one another since IBM does not provide that capability. American Express, therefore, had to build a bridge to allow TPF and IMS to communicate while Inference developed the expert system.

Inference began the development cycle by sending its knowledge engineers—software designers who, through a rule-based approach, created an expert system—to interview American Express' five best authorizers in Fort Lauderdale, Fla. It was this amalgam of information that formed the knowledge base for Authorizer's Assistant.

"It was a gradual process of building a knowledge base," notes Laurel Miller, manager of credit authorization. "We began with a finite number of situations dealing with specific customer types or cases and from there broadened the scope."

Authorizer's Assistant's function was to gather, organize and reason all data relevant to each transaction from American Express' customer files, notes Alexander Jacobson, Inference president. Factors such as a customer's outstanding charges, payment history and buying habits are used by the system to ascertain whether the charge in question should be approved.

Specifically, the system assesses the magnitude and nature of the credit risk, recommends acceptance or denial of the transaction and asks questions to resolve concerns, updates recommendations as questions are answered and provides an explanation for all recommendations.

"The expert system takes data from 10 or 12 data bases and launders the information," Jacobson explains. "It does the reasoning the authorizer does and then makes the decision to grant or not grant credit."

## CAN BE OVERRIDDEN

The system can be overridden by authorizers if they disagree with a decision to grant credit. The authorizer does this by asking the expert system for an explanation.

"If they still think it's the wrong call, they are expected to make their own decision," Flast points out. "The authorizer is still responsible for the decision."

A prototype, completed in April 1986, had 520 rules. After some refinement, a pilot version of the product debuted last November featuring some 800 rules, Jacobson says.

"Our experts have found it interesting to have their expertise played back to them," Flast says. "They're impressed with the system's authenticity."

Flast says it is difficult to quantify the projected benefits of the Authorizer's Assistant. One objective is to shorten the total handling time of each transaction by 20% to 30%. More important, Flast says, he hopes Authorizer's Assistant will reduce losses.

With the expert system's concept proven, American Express is now planning to construct what it calls the optimum architecture for Authorizer's Assistant. In the optimal approach, the authorizer will enter TPF, which will then activate Authorizer's Assistant. The expert system will then access information from the IMS data bases and make its credit authorization recommendation.

Flast is currently considering proposals to have a single vendor supply the entire system's hardware. Among the bidders for the hardware contract are IBM Sun, Symbolics and Texas Instruments Inc., Flast notes.

The optimal architecture will support up to 300 users at American Express' four authorization centers nationwide.

# Appendix F

## Expert Systems for Legal Decision Making

*Donald A. Waterman*
*Jody Paul*
*Mark Peterson*

## 1. INTRODUCTION

For over a decade the computer has been used to assist legal experts with complex decision making. Examples include the JUDITH system for assisting lawyers in reasoning about civil law cases [1], a system that helps lawyers reason about the intentional torts of assault and battery [2], a system that automates the assembly of formal legal documents [3], the SARA system for helping lawyers determine factors relevant to a case decision [4], the LEGOL language for expressing legal concepts [5], the TAXMAN system for investigating tax consequences of corporate transactions [6], and the LRS system for performing knowledge-based legal information retrieval [7].

Many of these early systems, as well as more recent ones, resulted from researchers choosing the legal domain either to 1) provide a testbed for exploring AI methods and paradigms, or 2) develop simple models to provide insight into the operation of the legal system. For example, the HYPO system uses hypothetical cases to strengthen legal reasoning and argument [8], while a legal analysis program identifies important issues for cases in contract law [9]. Researchers are also using the legal domain to explore human cognitive processes [10, 11].

Recently, AI technology has been applied to the legal area to develop expert systems that solve complex problems in the law. We distinguish here between expert systems for legal decision making and the more general class of AI programs that operate in the legal area, such as those just mentioned. The general AI work tends to focus on basic issues related to representation and search, as well as methodologies for making programs behave more intelligently. By contrast, the expert system work focuses on pragmatic issues related to acquiring

---

Reprinted with the kind permission of The Rand Corporation. Source: *Expert Systems*, Vol. 3, No. 4, October 1986, pp. 212–225.

**TABLE 1.** Selected expert system applications in the legal area.

| Expert System | Application | Developer |
|---|---|---|
| CORPTAX | Assists attorneys with a problem in federal corporate taxation: whether a stock redemption qualifies for favorable tax treatment under the provisions of IRS code section 302-b [13]. | Columbia University |
| DSCAS | Helps contractors analyze the legal aspects of differing site condition of claims, determining when additional expenses should be allowed [14]. | University of Colorado |
| EXPERT TAX SYSTEM | Provides tax inspectors with advice about apportionment of a corporation's income by applying knowledge concerning current tax legislation [15]. | University of Manchester |
| LDS | Assists legal experts in settling product liability cases by calculating defendant liability, case worth, and equitable settlement amount [16]. | The Rand Corporation |
| SAL | Helps attorneys and claims adjustors evaluate claims related to asbestos exposure by estimating how much money should be paid to the plaintiffs [17]. | The Rand Corporation |
| TAXADVISOR | Assists an attorney with tax planning for clients with large estates, including insurance purchases, retirement actions, wealth transfer, and will modification [18, 19] | University of Illinois |

and formalizing knowledge, as well as techniques for improving efficiency and system performance. The expert systems are developed around a body of expertise, usually gleaned from a small number of human experts who work with a knowledge engineer to uncover and formalize the expertise in the domain.

The majority of expert systems developed for legal applications use a rule-based knowledge representation scheme. These rules describe the conclusions that litigators draw from a limited set of facts and legal issues. The exact form of the rules depends on the structure of the knowledge engineering language or programming language used to implement the expert system.

Table 1 summarizes selected expert systems developed for legal applications. Most of these systems involve either interpreting the law, anticipating the legal consequences of proposed actions, predicting the effects of changes in legislation, analyzing and managing cases, or some combination of these tasks. The use of expert systems to analyze and explain legal reasoning is similar to other expert system applications such as those in medicine, geology, electronics and chemistry [12], although new problems are raised by the adversarial quality of the litigator's decisions and the subjective nature of legal evidence.

In section 2 of this paper we say more about the special nature of legal reasoning and the problems it raises during expert system development. Next, in section 3, we describe the design and operation of two expert systems from Table 1—Legal Decisionmaking System (LDS) and System for Asbestos Litigation (SAL). Finally, in the last section we discuss other important application areas for expert systems in law.

## 2. LAW AS AN AREA FOR EXPERT SYSTEM DEVELOPMENT

The legal area is drawing much interest as a profitable domain for expert system development. However, developing expert systems in this domain can lead to special problems and thus warrants special consideration. We now discuss characteristics of the legal domain relevant to expert system development and then describe problems one might encounter as part of such a development effort.

## 2.1 Characteristics of the Legal Domain

The law is in a constant state of change, so legal experts must work hard to stay appraised of the current legislation and its impact on their decision making. Legal experts use many different kinds of reasoning processes. These include rule-based methods centered around antecedent-consequent representations of causality and case-based methods which involve analogical reasoning and analysis of hypotheticals [20]. These methods often require the judicious use of commonsense reasoning to guide the decision making and interpret formal rules and regulations.

The legal domain has the unique property of being semi-formalized, i.e., there exists a large body of formal rules that purport to define and regulate activity in the domain. These rules are often contradictory, incomplete, and even deliberately ambiguous. Their complexity has encouraged the development of a body of informal knowledge, practices or strategies concerned with how to access and reason with the formal rules.

Concepts in the legal domain tend to be open-textured, i.e., in general one cannot state necessary and sufficient conditions for applying legal predicates or have a program assess their applicability in arbitrary factual situations [9]. Complex, ill-defined concepts (e.g., strict liability) are defined using new concepts that are just as ill-defined or vague (e.g., responsible, defective). Since there doesn't seem to be a progression toward a set of fundamental or primitive concepts, reasoning often takes place at a somewhat higher level than it might in a domain without this characteristic. This open-textured nature of legal concepts makes it difficult to avoid subjective considerations when performing legal reasoning.

## 2.2 Problems with Developing Expert Systems for the Legal Domain

The legal area poses some special problems for expert system development. Modeling what a lawyer does is more difficult than modeling what experts do in many technical or scientific domains because of 1) the complexity of the legal area, 2) the need for commonsense reasoning, and 3) the lack of a deep model of the legal process.

*Complexity.* The rules in the legal domain are more complex than informal or formal rules in most other domains. Part of this complexity has to do with the fact that the formal legal rules are expressed in lengthy natural language passages filled with jargon. This jargon is more prone to misinterpretation by novices, since the terms have meanings to the novices, but may be interpreted differently by legal experts.

But much of the complexity stems from very elaborate concepts and ideas that resist being broke down into smaller independent and self-contained concepts. This suggests the need for a representation scheme that can handle such complexity, a knowledge engineering language that provides the required degree of expressiveness.

*Commonsense reasoning.* Legal problems tend to resist partitioning into narrow, neat subproblems. Because they involve and describe our everyday activities they may require broad knowledge about the world and how things work. This need for commonsense reasoning over a broad range of activities and problems causes difficulties for expert system developers who are trying to keep the problem domain as narrow as possible and as free from the mysterious "commonsense reasoning" and "world knowledge" as possible.

*Lack of a deep model.* The legal area doesn't have a clear and well understood underlying (deep) model of many of the mechanisms involved in decision making. Some domains do have a fairly clear model that can be used to predict activity and explain reasoning. For

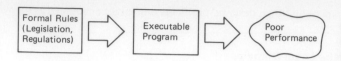

example, in the electronics area knowledge about circuits and their operation can be used for prediction and explanation. Deep knowledge of this sort is not easy to find in the legal area. This makes the task of developing competent explanation facilities for legal expert systems somewhat difficult. But in the legal area, as in other complex problem areas, it is important for the expert system not only to explain how it reached a conclusion, but also to provide a convincing argument that the method used to reach it is valid.

One might expect that the large body of legal rulings and regulations that have been accumulated and formalized in the legal domain would make expert system development easier. Unfortunately, this is not the case. Instead, this characteristic of the domain, having rules that already exist, has led to trouble. The problem this creates is the naïve notion (for some) that because a body of rules and regulations exists, all one has to do is translate them into executable code to create a program for performing complex legal reasoning. However, this fails because the rules alone do not constitute a program for producing a good solution, as Figure 1 indicates. First, the formal rules that define and regulate legal activity are often ambiguous, contradictory and incomplete. And second, there exists a body of informal rules or procedures about how to access, interpret and use the "formal" rules. Without these informal rules the formal rules cannot be used in any efficient or cost-effective way.

Still, this body of rules needs to be mapped into code and the large quantity of rules has produced a need for more efficient methods of knowledge base construction. One technique that has been tried is the assembly line approach. Here the domain expert writes the rules with the help of a "compiler" who knows something about the domain but nothing about knowledge engineering. The compiler puts the rules into a standard format devised by the knowledge engineer. The knowledge engineer then takes the formatted rules and reorganizes them so they can be integrated into the existing program. The encoder then takes the formatted reorganized rules and rewrites them as executable code. Another person, the tester (who may be the knowledge engineer or the domain expert) then tests the program, as indicated in Figure 2. This technique has its problems: 1) it assumes the rules already exist in a form (granularity, composition) required by the expert system, 2) the knowledge engineer doesn't do knowledge engineering, just programming design while the encoder does the coding, and 3) no one adequately handles conceptualization and formalization.

### 2.3 The Problem of Explanation for Expert Systems in Law

The acceptability of expert systems in the legal community depends not only on the quality of their performance but also on how easily they can be reimplemented, refined and extended. This is because legal expertise can rapidly change and become outdated. This effect may be more pronounced here than in many other domains due to the constantly changing legislation and the wealth of judicial interpretations of that legislation. The problem of refining and

**FIGURE 2**    **The assembly line approach to knowledge engineering.**

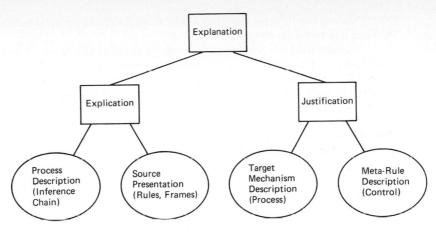

**FIGURE 3   Components of an explanation.**

extending expert systems can be addressed by providing users with sophisticated support facilities as part of the system building tool, including facilities for knowledge acquisition and explanation.

The mechanism an expert system uses to explain its performance is one of the critical factors in the construction, utilization and extension of the system. This mechanism, typically called an *explanation facility*, shows the user how the expert system reached a given conclusion and why it believes the conclusion is justified [21]. This knowledge about the system's operation can provide the user with the needed basis for deciding how to incorporate new knowledge and how to resolve conflicts arising from earlier attempts to incorporate knowledge. Although explanation facilities in current expert systems are somewhat primitive, they are crucial to system operation, speed system development and inspire confidence in the system's performance and reasoning processes.

By explanation we mean both *explication* and *justification*, as indicated in Figure 3. Explication refers to techniques for further specifying the reasoning process, i.e., answering "WHAT was done to reach a conclusion?" Justification refers to methods for describing some rationale to indicate that the reasoning process or some part of it was correct or reasonable, i.e., answering "WHY is this conclusion considered valid?"

Explication and justification are not as easy in law as they are in some other domains which have clear underlying or deep models of the mechanisms involved, mechanisms that can provide predictive and explanatory power. For example, in estate planning one might like to justify a decision about the type of trust to recommend by presenting a process model that describes the flow and control of wealth between the client and various other entities such as relatives, institutions and the IRS. What constitutes fundamental models in the legal domain and what determines real justification of conclusions are questions not easily answered. One can point to the doctrine of precedent and the use of cases for justification and argumentation as a kind of model of legal processes. Of course, this will not work for all types of legal reasoning, such as nonadversary situations that don't involve litigation.

## 3. EXPERT SYSTEMS FOR CASE EVALUATION AND SETTLEMENT

For a number of years we have been interested in how lawyers and claims adjusters evaluate product liability claims. Our extensive interviews with these legal experts have indicated that their decisions can be represented by a schema that defines the relationships existing between the facts and issues involved in a case [16].

We have used this schema as the basis for developing two expert systems in the product liability area, LDS and SAL. LDS focuses more on rules representing formal legal doctrine, while SAL focuses more on rules related to interpretation of medical evidence. Both systems are implemented in ROSIE (Rule-Oriented System for Implementing Expertise), a general-purpose knowledge engineering language developed at the Rand Corporation [22].

ROSIE was chosen as a development vehicle for our expert system applications in the legal area to promote *understandability*, i.e., readability and expressiveness. We feel these features are particularly important for legal expert systems, with their long complex rules and confusing terminology. Readability clearly speeds development and later refinement. The choice of ROSIE as the development language meant that with careful attention to programming practice, the knowledge in the resulting expert system would be accessible to those with only a minimum of specialized knowledge about the functioning of rule-based systems. Expressiveness permits the knowledge base to be organized in a way that is consistent with the actual concepts and relationships that are being represented. Again ROSIE provided the expressive power needed to ensure that the developing model bears a direct correspondence to the objects or activities it is modeling.

We now give a brief overview of ROSIE and then describe the design and operation of LDS and SAL, including an explanation facility developed for SAL.

## 3.1 The ROSIE Knowledge Engineering Language

ROSIE has evolved from a relatively simple language [23], to a sophisticated expert system building tool [24]. Its distinguishing characteristic is an English-like syntax that facilitates expressing complex concepts and permits the program to use substantially the same terminology as the domain expert.

ROSIE is a rule-based language tightly integrated into a procedure-oriented programming paradigm, where rulesets can be organized as nested, recursive procedures. As indicated in Figure 4, ROSIE rules can take many forms, not just the traditional IF-THEN form.

ROSIE permits three different types of rulesets: *procedural, predicate*, and *generator*

> Display the laboratory-test result and
>     assert that laboratory test-result was presented.
>
> For each asbestosis symptom (S) of the plaintiff,
>     check alternative-explanations for S and
>     assert S was checked for alternatives.
>
> If the plaintiff was directly exposed to asbestos and
>     the plaintiff was exposed in confined spaces and
>     the plaintiff's exposure did occur before 1965,
>     let the plaintiff's exposure history be severe exposure
>     and output (the plaintiff, "had a severe exposure to
>       asbestos.")
>
> While any background information is not determined,
>     collect the background information for the plaintiff.

**FIGURE 4   Examples of ROSIE rules for legal decision making.**

*rulesets.*  A procedural ruleset performs some activity rather than returning a result to the rule that invoked it.   An example of a procedure is shown below.

> To record a finding for a person:
> [1] If the finding is a type of medical evidence, put that finding into the medical history of the person.
> [2] If the finding is a type of legal evidence, send (that finding, "does apply to", the person).
> End.

This ruleset updates the database or notifies the user when invoked by procedure calls, like the ones shown below.

Record radiographic-evidence of asbestosis for the plaintiff.
Record the current legal-theory for the plaintiff.

Predicate rulesets provide a way of computing the truth or falsity of a *proposition* (i.e., a primitive sentence) when ROSIE cannot determine its truth value from a search of the data base.   A predicate can conclude true or false, returning a Boolean value to the calling form, or it can simply terminate, returning nothing and implying an indeterminate truth value.   An example of a predicate is shown below.

> To decide a plaintiff does manifest radiographic-evidence of asbestosis:
> If (the plaintiff does exhibit parenchymal-findings of asbestosis
>     and the plaintiff's parenchymal-findings are not explained by alternatives
>     and the plaintiff's parenchymal-findings are not contested)
> or (the plaintiff does show pleural-plaques in x-ray
>     and the plaintiff's pleural-plaques are not explained by alternatives
>     and the plaintiff's pleural-plaques are not contested),
> Conclude that the plaintiff does manifest radiographic-evidence of asbestosis.
> End.

This ruleset could be invoked by executing the following rule.

If the plaintiff does manifest radiographic-evidence of asbestosis,
        record radiographic-evidence of asbestosis for the plaintiff.

Generator rulesets produce instances of a class of items.   For example, if the database contains:

> Bilateral-fibrosis is an injury.
> Bilateral-interstitial-opacities is an injury.
> Asthma is an illness.
> Emphysema is an illness.
> John Smith's tests do indicate bilateral-fibrosis.
> John Smith does have emphysema.
> John Smith does have asthma.

then a generator ruleset, such as,

> To generate the evidence of injury for the plaintiff:
> [1] Produce every illness which the plaintiff does have.
> [2] Produce every injury which the plaintiff's tests do indicate.
> End.

when invoked by

> For each evidence of injury for the plaintiff, display that evidence.

causes each computable piece of evidence to be displayed in succession, as

> bilateral-fibrosis
> emphysema
> asthma

Note that calls to predicates and generators can be made transparent, i.e., indistinguishable from references to relations in the database.

## 3.2 The Legal Decision Making System

The LDS expert system calculates defendant liability, case worth, and an equitable settlement amount, given a description of a product liability case [16]. Its expertise includes both formal doctrine in product liability, e.g. negligence and liability laws, as well as informal principles and strategies used by legal experts. We gathered this expert legal knowledge from a variety of sources: legal texts, legislation, and interviews with legal experts such as law professors, claims adjusters and both plaintiff and defense attorneys specializing in product liability cases. Most of the system's knowledge, however, was gathered through intensive, lengthy interviews with a few lawyers and claims adjusters—the typical knowledge engineering approach to system development.

During our interviews with litigators we found that they consider a common set of issues in evaluating claims. To capture this idea we formulated a schema that describes and relates those issues. The schema breaks litigators' evaluations into five separate components, as shown in Table 2.

The plaintiff's *loss* includes both special and general damages, the latter being more difficult to formalize because of its complexity and reliance on subjective judgments. Our treatment of general damages is much more elaborate than the traditional idea of "pain and suffering." In LDS we distinguish between the trauma of the injury; the inconvenience and trauma of treatment (e.g., surgery); disfigurement; permanent disability; permanent loss of recreation; and other factors.

**TABLE 2.** Schema elements used by LDS for case evaluation.

| Schema Element | Definition |
| --- | --- |
| LOSS | Special damages (dollar value of economic losses resulting from the injury) such as medical expenses, lost income, and property damage, plus general damages (dollar value of other direct and indirect effects of the injury) such as injury trauma, fear, faculty loss, and activity limitation. |
| LIABILITY | Litigators' estimates of the probability of establishing liability against a defendant. This is affected by the particular theory of liability that applies to the case. |
| RESPONSIBILITY | An estimate of the proportion of responsibility that should be assigned to a plaintiff, such as for his or her own carelessness relative to the injury. |
| CHARACTERISTICS | The numerical adjustment for factors based on seemingly superficial aspects of the case, such as characteristics of the litigants, lawyers, judges and jurisdictions. |
| CONTEXT | The numerical adjustment for factors related to case context, such as strategy, timing and the type of claim. |

The *liability* depends on formal rules of law and their application to the facts of the case. These rules may vary among different jurisdictions, e.g. California does not require proof that a defective product was unreasonably dangerous, while other jurisdictions do require such a proof.

The issue of *responsibility* is critical, since a plaintiff's award will be reduced by the percent of his own responsibility for his injuries. Like liability, responsibility depends heavily on the facts for the specific case, which may be based on circumstantial or incomplete information.

Case *characteristics* are highly subjective but entirely necessary if we want an accurate reflection of the case value produced by experienced legal experts. For example, our interviews suggest that the skill of the attorneys involved with the case strongly affect case value. Furthermore, the defense attorney's skill seems to affect case value more than the plaintiff's attorney's skill. We can reflect this in rules that change the case value more for differences in defense attorneys' skills than for differences among plaintiff's attorneys.

Factors involving case *context*, such as strategy and timing, must also be taken into account. For example, a claim is worth less if the claimant has an immediate need for money or if the trial date is still far in the future. We found that a case may be worth as much as 20% more just before the trial than it was two years before the trial.

We combine the schema elements to produce the case value, as indicated by the formula shown below.

VALUE = LOSS * LIABILITY * RESPONSIBILITY * CHARACTERISTICS * CONTEXT

Thus, if we determined that the loss was $300,000, the probability of a plaintiff's verdict was .6, the plaintiff's responsibility for the loss was .5, the adjustment for characteristics was 1.8 (more favorable to plaintiffs than to defendants) and the adjustment for context was .7 (e.g., timing and strategy reduce the value), the resulting value for the case would be the product of these factors or $113,400.

Each of the schema elements is represented as a complex configuration of ROSIE rulesets, each containing from five to fifty rules that describe how decisions are reached about that element. The schema organizes the rules and provides a framework for controlling the application of rules to the case facts.

Figure 5 shows a portion of an LDS rule for determining whether or not an Implied

```
If the product was sold by the defendant
   and the failure of that product
       (in that product's intended use) did cause the damages
   and (the purchaser of the product did sustain damages
           (by the use of the product)
       or (a bystander did sustain damages by that use
       and that bystander's presence was
           both "reasonable and foreseeable")
       or a reasonably intended user (of the product)
       who is not equal to that purchaser
           did sustain damages by that use),
   assert that implied warranty of fitness theory
       does apply to the damages.
```

**FIGURE 5   A portion of an LDS rule for determining implied warranty of fitness.**

Warranty of Fitness theory of liability applies to the case. This rule is shown in executable ROSIE code, not an English translation of the code.

LDS contains approximately 300 ROSIE rules organized around the evaluation schema just described. The system has reached the stage of a research prototype system—it makes intelligent decisions but would require extensive field testing and refinement to carry it to the level of a viable commercial system. Our experience with LDS has led us to believe that the system would be more useful and cost effective if specialized to cover a narrower piece of the product liability area. These considerations have led to the development of an asbestos litigation system patterned after LDS but constrained to the area of asbestos claims. We discuss this system in some detail in the next section.

### 3.3 The System for Asbestos Litigation

SAL is a rule-based expert system for evaluating asbestos claims [25]. We are developing SAL to address a problem stemming from the backlog of unresolved asbestos litigation cases. With over twenty-one million exposures to asbestos and the possibility of over 200 thousand related deaths in the next thirty years, insurance companies are bracing themselves for the onslaught. When completed, SAL will help speed the litigation process by analyzing asbestos claims and producing dollar values for the cases. Although currently a research vehicle, we expect it will eventually be used on a regular basis, possibly by lawyers to guide and support settlement positions, by judges to evalute the equity of settlements, or by law firms and insurance companies to determine settlement values and train new personnel.

SAL evaluates plaintiffs' claims related to asbestos exposure. It was built utilizing the knowledge and expertise of attorneys from a jurisdiction in Cleveland, Ohio. We have restricted our analysis to just one disease, asbestosis, and to one class of plaintiffs, insulators, and those whose jobs significantly exposed them to asbestos insulation. Our approach involves applying the general schema developed for LDS adapted to asbestos litigation, as illustrated opposite.

SAL focuses more on loss than does LDS. Much of the expertise in SAL concerns the evaluation of the loss, in particular, the analysis of the medical evidence. Less attention is paid to liability, since this aspect of the problem is both more and less complex than it is for typical product liability cases. Given that a plaintiff was exposed to asbestos (usually at work) liability issues are usually the same for different plaintiffs, thus there is no value in considering this common issue separately for each plaintiff. Consideration of liability would require a separate expert system that focused on each defendant's actual sale of an asbestos product during the period of a plaintiff's exposure, as well as the defendant's knowledge of asbestos dangers.

Matters of context are probably important in evaluating asbestos claims, e.g., settlements might be smaller if plaintiffs are particularly anxious to receive a settlement, but SAL does not presently consider any such strategic or contextual issues.

SAL maintains knowledge about the medical domain at a surface level, that is, in terms of diagnostic rules and procedures. It currently contains no deep knowledge about the domain

VALUE = LOSS (The medical damages due to asbestos exposure, based on symptoms, x-rays, other laboratory results, and disability)
    *LIABILITY (The adjustment to liability based on the plaintiff's history of exposure to asbestos)
    *RESPONSIBILITY (The proportion of responsibility assigned to the plaintiff for smoking, knowledge of danger, etc.)
    *CHARACTERISTICS (The adjustment for personal characteristics such as the plaintiff's age)

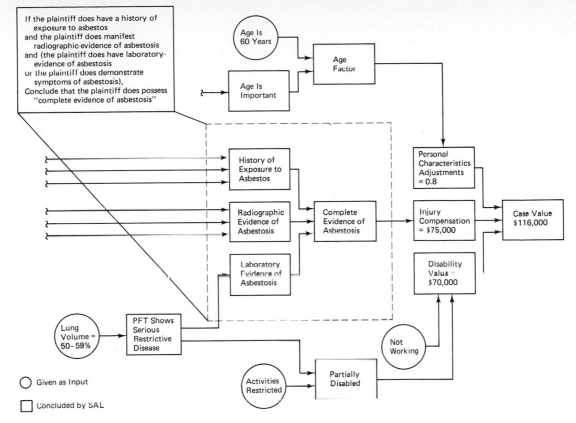

If the plaintiff does have a history of
exposure to asbestos
and the plaintiff does manifest
radiographic-evidence of asbestosis
and (the plaintiff does have laboratory-
evidence of asbestosis
or the plaintiff does demonstrate
symptoms of asbestosis),
Conclude that the plaintiff does possess
"complete evidence of asbestosis"

Age Is
60 Years

Age
Factor

Age Is
Important

Personal
Characteristics
Adjustments
= 0.8

History of
Exposure to
Asbestos

Radiographic
Evidence of
Asbestosis

Complete
Evidence of
Asbestosis

Injury
Compensation
= $75,000

Case Value
$116,000

Laboratory
Evidence of
Asbestosis

Disability
Value =
$70,000

Lung
Volume =
50-59%

PFT Shows
Serious
Restrictive
Disease

Not
Working

○ Given as Input

□ Concluded by SAL

Activities
Restricted

Partially
Disabled

**FIGURE 6    Inference chain produced by SAL.**

or basic models of disease interactions. So far, this seems to cause no problems—the only
need we have seen for deeper levels of reasoning relates to justification of rules about how
schema elements are valued and combined.

SAL is a rule-based system that generates an inference chain composed of the rules used
to reach its conclusions. Figure 6 illustrates a portion of an inference chain produced by SAL
during an asbestos case evaluation.

SAL acts as a consultant, carrying on a dialog with the user of the system to gather data
and explain what it is doing. SAL can explain why it asked a certain question, what the terms
in the question mean, and how it reached a particular conclusion, as shown in Figure 7.[1]

Some rules in SAL specify relatively complex conditions under which their conclusions
will be made. During a consultation, the user may ask to see only the precise set of conditions
that SAL used in deciding to make the conclusion, or the user may ask to see the entire rule
written in ROSIE. Figure 8 illustrates this process.

SAL has reached the stage of a research prototype. It contains approximately 400 rules

---

[1] Figures 7 and 8 contain stylized traces of SAL's output. The actual trace looks somewhat different,
since SAL operates on a Xerox 1100 series workstation and uses multiple pop-up windows and menu to
communicate with the user.

> [*Before answering a question, the user asks SAL to explain why that particular question was asked.*]
>
> SAL: Did John Smith work on board ships?
>
> USER: Why? [*Why are you asking me this?*]
>
> SAL: If the plaintiff worked on board ships the severity of exposure is greater since it occurred in a confined space.

---

> [*Before selecting an item from a menu, the user asks SAL to explain the meaning of the item.*]
>
> SAL: Which of the following parenchymal findings (if any) does John Smith have? (Select all that apply.)
>
> > 1. Bilateral Interstitial Fibrosis in Lower Lobes
> > 2. Bilateral Interstitial Opacities in Lower Lobes
>
> USER: Elaborate 2 [*What does this term mean?*]
>
> SAL: Distinctive x-ray markings showing fiber-like scarring in tissues that cover lower parts of both lungs.

---

> [*The user asks how SAL reached a particular conclusion*]
>
> USER: My conclusions are:
>
> > 1. 'John Smith' does have 'a history of exposure to asbestos.'
> > 2. The value of 'the case' is 116000 DOLLARS.
> > 3. The disability-compensation of 'the case' is 70000 DOLLARS.
>
> USER: Why 2? [*How did you reach this conclusion?*]
>
> SAL: I concluded that the value of 'the case' is 116000 DOLLARS in 'To evaluate the case, Rule 5' because:
>
> > The value of the case is the sum of the amounts awarded for injury, disability and aggravation as adjusted by considerations of the personal characteristics of the plaintiff.
>
> USER: Example [*give me an example of this*]
>
> SAL: Here we find the value of the case to be 116000 DOLLARS by combining the injury value (75000 DOLLARS), the disability compensation (70000 DOLLARS) and the aggravation value (0 DOLLARS). This total (145000 DOLLARS) is adjusted (multiplied) by the personal characteristic adjustment (.8) yielding the final value.

**FIGURE 7** **SAL can explain why a question was asked, what specific terms mean, and how it reached a conclusion.**

plus an explanation component that helps the user understand how and why it reaches its conclusions. We now discuss XPL, the explanation component of SAL, in more detail.

### 3.4 The XPL System

XPL is the explanation facility we developed for use with SAL and other expert system applications [26]. We have implemented XPL in Interlisp and imbedded it in ROSIE running on Xerox 1100 series workstations. Developing such a mechanism was more difficult than developing one for a typical rule-based language, such as EMYCIN [27] or M.1 [28]. The principal difficulty arises because ROSIE is both rule-based and procedure-oriented, allowing complex nested procedures that can be written using a variety of sophisticated syntactic constructs. Thus the technique of storing a history of all computations (and then later trying to unravel the result) has little merit. Although this works well with simple EMYCIN-like languages which are basically sets of *If–Then* statements, it is somewhat inappropriate for a more complex language like ROSIE.

The most common type of explanation mechanism used by expert systems is the *inference chain display*, where the expert system displays a chain of rules leading to a particular conclusion to explain how the conclusion was reached [12]. This is a reasonable approach for providing a very specific explanation with lots of detail. However, when used in isolation this may prove unsatisfactory, since the amount of detail can be overwhelming and the rule itself is seldom a good justification for its use.

---

[*The user again asks how SAL reached a particular conclusion*]

SAL:    My conclusions are:

> 65. "John Smith's exposure to asbestos" is severe.
> 66. "John Smith" does have PLEURAL-FINDINGS.
> 67. "John Smith" is partially disabled by ASBESTOSIS.

USER:   Why 67? [*How did you reach this conclusion*]

SAL:    I concluded that John Smith is partially disabled by asbestosis in "To decide a plaintiff is partially-disabled by asbestosis, Rule 3" because:

Since John Smith is not totally disabled but does have some disability due to asbestosis, we assert that the plaintiff is partially disabled.

USER:   Premises [*What are the instantiated premises of the rule that led to this result?*]

SAL:    ' "John Smith" is not working' and
' "John Smith's pulmonary function test" does show
   "serious restrictive disease" and
'John Smith is not diagnosed with
   "an obstructive-lung-disease" and
' "John Smith's activities" is restricted'

USER:   Rule [*What rule led to this result?*]

SAL:

IF   (the plaintiff is not working
     or the plaintiff is working-part-time
     or the plaintiff's job-status is reduced
     or (the plaintiff is retired
     and the plaintiff's age is less than 65))
     and ((the plaintiff's pulmonary-function-test does
        show "serious restrictive disease"
        and the plaintiff is not diagnosed with
        an obstructive-lung-disease)
       or the plaintiff's pulmonary-function-test does
        show "severe restrictive disease")
     and the plaintiff's activities are restricted,

Conclude that the plaintiff is partially-disabled by
     asbestosis is TRUE because, in general,
     (the partial-disability-explanation).

**FIGURE 8**   **Another example of explanation provided by SAL.**

**TABLE 3.** Various forms of an explanation.

| Explanation Type | Explanation Form |
|---|---|
| Text | "The value of a case is the sum of the values of the injury, disability compensation, and value added because of aggravated medical conditions." |
| Pattern | {"Since", the plaintiff, "has only", the plaintiff's exposure to asbestos, "we conclude that there is no history", "of asbestos exposure"}. |
| Ruleset | {the explanation for disability-compensation}. |

In XPL we use a modified inference chain display as the basis for explanation. This approach, which we call *selectable paraphrasing*, consists of marking those rules and rulesets which may be of interest to the user and then generating explanations based on only those rules in an inference chain that were pre-marked. This technique helps control the size and complexity of inference information stored as a history of the computation. As the rules and rulesets are marked, they may also be assigned specific patterns (text annotations containing variables) or procedures (executable rulesets). During the explanation process these patterns and procedures are instantiated by the current context and used in conjunction with the inference chain display to explain how the system reached particular conclusions. For problem domains having a well-understood deep model of the mechanisms underlying the surface rules, the procedures associated with rules can be used to generate sophisticated explanations or justifications describing why a particular rule is valid and why it is appropriate to use it in the current context. For problem domains having poorly formalized or no deep models, the text patterns associated with the rules can be used to produce the needed explanations.

The user may select the level of detail XPL provides by exercising different options when requesting an explanation. For example, the user may request a general explanation in terms of rulesets and their objectives, a more specific explanation in terms of rules, and their instantiated premises, or specific examples based on instantiated patterns or procedures.

The *general* and *example* explanations may either be a string of text enclosed in double quotes (""), a ROSIE pattern containing text and terms evaluated at run time when the explanation record is created, or a ROSIE pattern specifying a call to an arbitrary ruleset. Examples of each type of explanation are given in Table 3.

XPL consists of a number of components that modify and enhance the standard ROSIE 2.4 programming environment, including a history mechanism that automatically creates a history list during expert system execution. The history list contains the items that the system

**TABLE 4.** Explanation options available to the SAL user.

| Selection | Result |
|---|---|
| Description | The system presents a high-level explanation describing why the item was concluded. |
| Example | The system gives specific examples illustrating why the item was concluded. |
| Premises | The system displays the instantiated form of the premises from the rule used to conclude the item. |
| Rule | The system displays the uninstantiated rule used to conclude the item. |
| Ruleset | The system displays the entire ruleset containing the rule used to conclude the item. |
| Summary | The system presents a high-level explanation of the ruleset used to conclude the item. |
| Tutorial | The system gives information illustrating the concepts embodied in the ruleset used to conclude the item. |
| Why? | The system explains the rules that invoked the ruleset currently being examined. |
| RETURN | The user exits the explanation mode. |

can explain. For SAL it typically contains between 80 and 100 intermediate and final conclusions and actions. After SAL finishes its computation these items appear in a special overlay window and may be selected by scrolling through the list and pointing to the desired items. Once an item is selected, the user may exercise any of nine options regarding explanation (selected from a pop-up explanation menu window), as indicated in Table 4.

The *Why?* option allows the user to follow the logical chain of reasoning the system used to arrive at a particular conclusion. Each time *Why?* is selected the system moves one step up the inference chain, displaying the explanation associated with the rule that invoked the previous ruleset. At each step the user may exercise any of the options described in Table 4.

The use of the *Why?* option is illustrated below. Assume the user has indicated that the history list item of interest is the plaintiff's exposure history and now wants to trace back through the inferences leading to the conclusion that the plaintiff does have a history of exposure to asbestos.

I did conclude that JOHN SMITH does have "a history of exposure to asbestos"

in To decide A PLAINTIFF does have A
HISTORY–OF–EXPOSURE–TO–ASBESTOS rule 2

because:
By history of exposure we mean that the plaintiff experienced either a severe or significant exposure to asbestos.

> Why? [*were you trying to determine that the plaintiff had a history of exposure to asbestos*]

LEVEL 2

I needed the conclusion that
'JOHN SMITH does have "a history of exposure to asbestos' "
in order to conclude that
'JOHN SMITH does possess "complete evidence of asbestosis' "

in To DETERMINE–DOCUMENTATION–OF–INJURY rule 2

because:

We consider evidence to be complete if the plaintiff has a history of exposure to asbestos, symptoms of asbestosis, and both laboratory evidence and radiographic evidence of parenchymal asbestosis.

The selectable paraphrasing technique used by XPL, in which particular rules and procedures are defined by the expert system builder to be explainable, seemed to solve the structural complexity problem. It allowed us to build explanation into a language containing not only If–Then rules but conventional constructs as well, such as for-loops and recursive procedure calls. Its primary disadvantage came from restrictions on what we could mark as explainable. Explainable items were restricted to a set of standard, relatively simple, syntactic forms. This kept us from using esoteric but possibly more compact syntactic forms to handle the knowledge that needed to be explained.

## 4. APPLICATION AREAS FOR EXPERT SYSTEMS IN LAW

We have described a few of the expert systems currently being developed for the legal area. These systems can be grouped into four important types of applications: case management, monitoring, legal interpretation, and document generation, as shown in Table 5 [12].

**TABLE 5.** Important application areas for expert systems in law.

| Application Areas for Law | Systems Descriptions |
| --- | --- |
| Case management | Organizes case information, estimates case value, and strategies for negotiation and case disposition. |
| Scheduling monitoring and retrieval | Schedules attorneys' activities, monitors legal data bases and knowledge bases to find changes in the law that could affect active cases, and assists in retrieving knowledge from these sources. |
| Interpretation and prediction | Interprets the law (e.g., statutes, regulations) in the context of a particular question or problem, anticipates the legal consequences of proposed actions, and predicts the effects of changes in legislation. |
| Document generation | Produces legal documents (e.g., wills, contracts, draft legislation) by selecting or composing appropriate pieces of text and organizing them into document form. |

We can easily provide examples of implemented systems in each of these areas; for case management: LDS and SAL; for scheduling, monitoring and retrieval: LRS [7]; for interpretation and prediction: Expert Tax System (see Table 1); and finally for document generation: EPS, an estate planning system currently under development [29].

The term "document generation," is a bit of a misnomer, since it includes not only the physical generation of the document but more importantly assistance in acquiring, integrating, and organizing the knowledge needed to produce the document. Thus an expert system that performs this task might conduct an interview to determine the client's needs, produce a plan for addressing those needs, and then generate a document reflecting that plan. EPS performs just those steps as it develops an estate plan for a client. It first conducts an interview during which it queries the client about his or her desires and provides tutoring about estate planning terminology and concepts. It then produces a plan which the client can either approve or modify. Once approved, the plan is used as the basis for generating the client's will.

Despite the relatively small number of expert systems that now exist for the law there is much interest in developing commercial legal applications. Many law firms and insurance companies are seriously exploring this technology, some even creating expert system groups or departments to perform in-house research and development. We predict that within a few years most of the major insurance companies and many legal firms will be heavily involved in the building of expert systems.

## References

1. W. G. Popp and B. Schlink, 'Judith, a computer program to advise lawyers in reasoning a case,' *Jurimetrics Journal*, **15**, 4, Summer 1975, pp. 303–314.
2. J. A. Meldman, *A Preliminary study in computer-aided legal analysis*, Ph.D. thesis, Departments of Electrical Engineering and Computer Science, MIT, August, 1975.
3. J. A. Sprowl, 'Automating the legal reasoning process: A computer that uses regulations and statutes to draft legal documents,' *American Bar Foundation Research Journal*, 1979, pp. 1–81.
4. Jon Bing, 'Legal norms, discretionary rules and computer programs,' In B. Niblett (ed.). *Computer Science and Law*, Cambridge, England: Cambridge University Press, 1980, pp. 119–146.
5. S. Cook and R. Stamper, 'LEGOL as a tool for the study of bureaucracy,' In H. Lucas (ed.), *The Information Systems Environment*, Amsterdam: North Holland, 1980.
6. L. T. McCarty, 'The TAXMAN project: Towards a cognitive theory of legal argument,' In B. Niblett (ed.), *Computer Science and Law*, Cambridge University Press, England: Cambridge, 1980.
7. Carole D. Hafner, "Representation of knowledge in a legal information retrieval system,' In R. Oddy,

S. Robertson, C. van Rijsbergen, P. Williams (eds.) *Information Retrieval Research*, London: Butterworths & Co. 1981.

8. E. L. Rissland, 'Argument moves and hypotheticals,' *Proceedings of the First Annual Conference on Law and Technology*, University of Houston Law Center, Houston, TX, 1984.

9. A. Gardner, 'An artificial intelligence approach to legal reasoning,' Ph.D. Dissertation, Department of Computer Science, Stanford University, Stanford, CA, June 1984.

10. M. G. Dyer and M. Flowers, 'Toward automating legal expertise,' In C. Walter (ed.), *Computing Power and Legal Reasoning*, St. Paul, MN: West Publishing Co., 1985, pp. 49–68.

11. S. R. Goldman, M. G. Dyer and M. Flowers, 'Learning to understand contractual situations,' *Proceedings IJCAI-85*, 1985, pp. 291–293.

12. D. A. Waterman, *A Guide to Expert Systems*, Reading, MA: Addison-Wesley, 1986.

13. R. Hellawell, 'A computer program for legal planning and analysis: Taxation of stock redemptions,' *Columbia Law Review*, **80**, 7, November 1980, pp. 1363–1398.

14. T. A. Kruppenbacher, *The application of artificial intelligence to contract management*, **1**, Master's Thesis, Dept. of Civil, Environmental and Architectural Engineering, Univ. of Colorado, Boulder, CO, 1984.

15. A. E. Roycroft and P. Loucopoulos, 'The development of an expert tax system,' *Proceedings of the 5th International Workshop on Expert Systems and Their Applications*, Agence de I'Informatique, France, May, 1985.

16. D. A. Waterman and M. Peterson, 'Evaluating civil claims: an expert systems approach,' *Expert Systems*, **1**, 1, 1984, pp. 65–76.

17. J. Paul, M. Peterson and D. A. Waterman, 'An expert system for asbestos litigation,' Rand Paper, The Rand Corporation, Santa Monica, CA, 1986a. (in preparation)

18. R. Michaelsen, *A knowledge-based system for individual income and transfer tax planning*, Ph.D. Thesis, Univ. of Illinois, Dept. of Accounting, Urbana, IL, 1982.

19. R. H. Michaelson, 'An expert system for federal tax planning, *Expert Systems*, **1**, No. 2, 1984.

20. E. L. Rissland, 'Argument moves and hypotheticals,' In C. Walter (ed.), *Computing Power and Legal Reasoning*, St. Paul, MN: West Publishing Co., 1985, pp. 129–143.

21. D. A. Waterman, J. Paul, D. McArthur, S. Bankes, S. Kipps and H. Sowizral, 'A survey of explanation in expert systems,' Rand Paper, The Rand Corporation, Santa Monica, CA, 1986b. (in preparation)

22. H. A. Sowizral and J. R. Kipps, 'ROSIE: A programming environment for expert systems,' Report R-3246-ARPA, The Rand Corporation, 1700 Main Street, Santa Monica, CA, October 1985, 46pp.

23. D. A. Waterman, R. Anderson, F. Hayes-Roth, P. Klahr, G. Martins and S. Rosenschein, 'Design of a Rule-Oriented System for Implementing Expertise,' Rand Note N-1158-ARPA, The Rand Corporation, Santa Monica, CA, 1986b. 1979.

24. J. R. Kipps, B. Florman, and H. A. Sowizral, 'The New ROSIE Reference Manual,' Rand Report, In preparation, 1986.

25. J. Paul, D. A. Waterman, M. Peterson and J. R. Kipps, 'SAL: An expert system for evaluating asbestos claims,' Rand Paper, The Rand Corporation, Santa Monica, CA, 1986b.

26. D. A. Waterman, J. Paul, B. Florman and J. R. Kipps, 'An explanation facility for ROSIE,' Rand Report R-3406-ARPA, The Rand Corporation, Santa Monica, CA, 1986a.

27. W. van Melle, E. H. Shortliffe and B. G. Buchanan, 'EMYCIN: A knowledge engineer's tool for constructing rule-based expert systems,' In B. Buchanan & E. Shortliffe (eds.), *Rule-based Expert Systems*, Reading, MA: Addison-Wesley, pp. 302–328, 1984.

28. B. D'Ambrosio, 'Building expert systems with M.1'. *BYTE*, **10**, 6, June 1985, pp. 371–375.

29. D. A. Schlobohm, D. A. Waterman and J. Paul, 'Explanation for an expert system that performs estate planning,' Rand Paper, The Rand Corporation, Santa Monica, CA, 1986.

# Bibliography

Barnat, Andrew. 1986. "Digitalk: Smalltalk/V," *AI Expert*, November, 77ff.

Bonnet, Alain. 1985. *Artificial Intelligence*. Translated by Jack Howlett. Englewood Cliffs, N.J.: Prentice-Hall.

Bourne, L. E., R. L. Dominowski, E. F. Loftus, and A. F. Healy. 1985. *Cognitive Processes*, 2nd ed. Englewood Cliffs, N.J.: Prentice-Hall.

Bulkeley, William. 1986. "Computers Take on New Role as Experts in Financial Affairs," *Wall Street Journal*, 7 February, 23.

Charniack, E., and D. McDermont. 1985. *Artificial Intelligence*. Reading, Mass.: Addison-Wesley.

Davis, Bob. 1986. "Superfast Computers Mimick the Structure of the Human Brain," *Wall Street Journal*, 19 February, 1.

Doherty, Michael E., and William E. Leigh. 1986. *Decision Support and Expert Systems*. Cincinnati, Ohio: Southwestern.

Dologite, D. G. 1987. *Using Computers*. Englewood Cliffs, N.J.: Prentice-Hall.

Dologite, D. G. 1984. *Using Small Business Computers*. Englewood Cliffs, N.J.: Prentice-Hall.

Evanson, Steven E. 1988. "How to Talk to an Expert," *AI Expert*, February, 36–42.

Fikes, Richard, and Tom Kehler. 1985. "The Role of Frame-Based Representation in Reasoning," *Communications of the ACM*, September, 904ff.

Gevarter, William B. 1987. "The Nature and Evaluation of Commercial Expert System Building Tools," *Computer*, May, 25–41.

Gleick, James. 1987. "New Superconductors Offer Chance to Do the Impossible," *New York Times*, 9 April, A1 and D8.

Goldberg, Eddy. 1986. "How Companies Implement Artificial Intelligence Projects," *Computerworld*, 11 November, 219.

Harmon, Paul, and David King. 1985. *Expert Systems*. New York: John Wiley.

Harrison, Mark, and David Tribble. 1986. "Five-Minute Prolog," *Computer Language*, August, 65ff.

Hart, Anna. 1986. *Knowledge Acquisition for Expert Systems*, New York: McGraw-Hill.

Hayes-Roth, Frederick, Donald A. Waterman, and Douglas B. Lenat. 1983. *Building Expert Systems*. Reading, Mass.: Addison-Wesley.

Hoffman, Robert R. 1987. "The Problem of Extracting the Knowledge of Experts from the Perspective of Experimental Psychology," *AI Magazine*, Summer, 53–67.

Holsapple, Clyde W., and Andrew B. Winston. 1986. *Manager's Guide to Expert Systems Using GURU*. Homewood, Ill.: Irwin.

Kauber, Peter G. 1985. "Prototyping: Not a Method but a Philosophy," *Journal of Systems Management*, September, 28–33.

Keller, Robert. 1987. *Expert System Technology: Development and Applications*, New York: Yourdon Press.

Koff, Richard. 1984. *Using Small Business Computers to Make Your Business Strategies Work*. New York: Wiley.

Lemonick, Michael D. 1987. "Superconductors," *Time*, 11 May, 64–75.

Leonard-Barton, Dorothy. 1987. "Technology Implementation as Integrative Innovation: The Case of an Expert System," *Sloan Management Review*, October–November, 84–109.

Lewis, Peter. 1986. "A New Agenda for Tomorrow's Industry," *New York Times*, 12 November, D10.

Maeroff, Gene I. 1981. "Reading Data Indicate Decline in Reasoning Ability" and Edward Fishe, "Reading Analysis is Called Lacking," *New York Times*, 29 April, A1ff.

Mahler, Ed. 1986. "The Business Needs Approach," *Knowledge-Based Systems: A Step-by-Step Guide to Getting Started* (The Second Artificial Intelligence Symposium), Austin, Tex.: Texas Instruments Company.

Mockler, Robert J. 1971. "Situational Theory of Management," *Harvard Business Review*, May–June, 146–154.

Moore, James, John Sviokla, and Ann Lynnworth. 1985. *Situation Analyst*. Homewood, Ill.: Irwin.

Morris, Betsy. 1986. "Marketing Firm Slices US Into 240,000 Parts," *Wall Street Journal*, 3 November, 1.

Nagy, Tom, Dick Gault, and Monica Nagy. 1985. *Building Your First Expert System*. Culver City, Calif.: Ashton-Tate.

Naylor, Thomas. 1986. *The Corporate Strategy Matrix*. New York: Basic Books.

Newell, A., and H. A. Simon. 1972. *Human Problem Solving*. Englewood Cliffs, N.J.: Prentice-Hall.

Osborn, Alex. 1963. *Applied Imagination*. New York: Scribner.

Pollach, Andrew. 1986. "New Approach in Computers," *New York Times*, 1 May, D2.

Polya, George. 1957. *How To Solve It*, 2nd ed. Princeton, N.J.: Princeton University Press.

Posner, Michael I., and Peter McLeod. 1982. "Information Processing Models—In Search of Elementary Operations," *Annual Review of Psychology*, vol. 33, 477–514.

Prerau, David. 1987 "Knowledge Acquisition in the Development of a Large Expert System," *AI Magazine*, Summer, 43–51.

Rauch-Hindin, Wendy B. 1986a. *Artificial Intelligence in Business, Science and Industry (Volume I—Fundamentals)*. Englewood Cliffs, N.J.: Prentice-Hall.

Rauch-Hinden, Wendy B. 1986b. "Software Integrates AI, Standard Systems," *Mini-Micro Systems*, October, 69ff.

Rauch-Hinden, Wendy B. 1985. *Artificial Intelligence in Business, Science and Industry (Volume II—Applications)*. Englewood Cliffs, N.J.: Prentice-Hall.

Rich, E. 1983. *Artificial Intelligence*. New York: McGraw-Hill.

Rosenkranz, Friedrich. 1979. *An Introduction to Corporate Modelling*. Durham, N.C.: Duke University Press.

Rothfeder, Jeffrey. 1985. *Minds Over Matter: A New Look at Artificial Intelligence*. New York: Simon & Schuster/Computer Book Division.

Schank, Roger C., and Robert Abelson. 1977. *Scripts, Plans, Goals and Understanding: An Inquiry into Human Knowledge Structure*. Hillsdale, N.J.: Erlbaum.

Schank, Roger C., with Peter G. Childers. 1984. *The Cognitive Computer: On Language, Learning and Artificial Intelligence*. Reading, Mass.: Addison-Wesley.

Simon, H. A. 1969. *The Science of the Artificial*. Cambridge, Mass.: MIT Press.

Simon, H. A., and S. K. Reed. 1976. "Modelling Strategy Shifts in a Problem-Solving Task," *Cognitive Pyschology*, vol. 8, 86–97.

Thompson, Steve. 1986. *Seminar in GURU*, New York: MDBs, July 1 to 3.

Waterman, Donald A. 1986. *A Guide to Expert Systems*. Reading, Mass.: Addison-Wesley.

Winograd, Terry, and Fernando Flores. 1986. *Understanding Computers and Cognition*. Norwood, N.J.: Ablex Publishing Corporation.

The Yankee Group. 1986. "Business Communications to Advance Business Goals," *Forbes*, 22 September, 160ff.

# Sources for Services and Software Referred To in the Book

Although an effort has been made to verify the following reference information, the volatile nature of the field will inevitably lead to changes that may affect the currency of the following information.

## Data Base Information Services and Sources

BRS: Bibliographic Retrieval Service
   1200 Route 7
   Latham, NY 12110

CompuServ: CompuServ Information Service
   5000 Arlington Center Blvd.
   Columbus, OH 43220

Dialog: Lockheed Corporation
   3460 Hillview Avenue
   Palo Alto, CA 94304

Dow Jones News Retrieval: Dow Jones and Company, Inc.
   P.O. Box 300
   Princeton, NJ 08540

Knowledge Industries Publications Inc: Executive Guide to Online Information Sources
   701 Westchester Avenue
   White Plains, NY 10604

The Naisbett Group: The Naisbett Group
   1101 30th Street NW
   Washington, DC 20007

Nexus: Mead Data Central
   9333 Springboro Pike
   Miamisburg, OH 45342

Strategic Intelligence Systems: Wide Range of Strategic Data Sources
575 Madison Avenue
New York, NY 10022

## Software

Arborist: Texas Instruments Data System Group
Texas Instruments Incorporated
12501 Research Blvd., M/S 224
Austin, TX 78759

ART: Inference Corp.
5300 W. Century Blvd., Suite #501
Los Angeles, CA 90045

Auto-Intelligence: IntelligenceWare, Inc.
9800 S. Sepulveda Blvd.
Los Angeles, CA 90045

Businessplan: Sterling Wentworth Corp.
2319 South Foothill Drive
Suite 150
Salt Lake City, UT 84109

EMS: Econometric Sciences Corporation
One Penn Plaza, Suite 2214
New York, NY 10001

ESP (Econometric Software Package): Economica, Inc.
2067 Massachusetts Ave.
Cambridge, MA 02140

Expert Choice: Decision Support Software
1300 Vincent Place
McLean, VA 22101

EXSYS: EXSYS, Inc.
P.O. Box 75158
Contract Station 14
Albuquerque, NM 87194

Financial Advisor: Palladin Software, Inc.
Four Cambridge Center
Cambridge, MA 02142

1st-CLASS: Programs in Motion
10 Sycamore Road
Wayland, MA 01778

Focus: Information Builders, Inc.
1250 Broadway
New York, NY 10001

Forecast Master: Scientific Systems, Inc.
One Alewife Place
35 Cambridge Park Drive
Cambridge, MA 02140

Futurcast: Futurian Associates
4067 Greensburg Pike
Pittsburg, PA 15331

GUIDE: Owl International
Bellevue, WA 98007

GURU: Micro Data Base Systems, Inc.
P.O. Box 248
Lafayette, IN 47902

Idea Generator: Experience in Software, Inc.
2039 Shattuck Avenue
Berkeley, CA 94704

IFPS: Execucom Systems Corporation
P.O. Box 9758
Austin, TX 78766

Impact: Engineering Design Concepts, Inc.
160 Old Derby Street
Hingham, MA 02043

INSIGHT 2+: Level Five Research
503 Fifth Avenue
Indialantic, FL 32903

KEE: Intellicorp
707 Laurel Street
Menlo Park, CA 94025

Knowledge Craft: Carnegie Group, Inc.
Commerce Court, Suite 650
Station Square
Pittsburgh, PA 15219

KOPS: PCE, Inc.
Suite 400
6033 West Century Blvd.
Los Angeles, CA 90045

Lightyear: Lightyear, Inc.
1333 Lawrence Expressway #210
Santa Clara, CA 95051

Lotus 1-2-3: Lotus Development Corporation
55 Wheeler Street
Cambridge, MA 02138

M.1: Teknowledge, Inc.
525 University Avenue
Palo Alto, CA 94301

Operation Advisor: Palladin Software, Inc.
Four Cambridge Center
Cambridge, MA 02142

Pairs: Optical Technologies
1524 O'Block Road
Pittsburgh, PA 15239

Personal Consultant: Texas Instruments
P.O. Box 809063
Dallas, TX 75380-9063

Planning Pro: Kepner-Tregoe
P.O. Box 704
Princeton, NJ 08542

PlanPower: Applied Expert Systems
1 Cambridge Center
Cambridge, MA 02142

PSA: TSP International
204 Junipero Serra Blvd.
Stanford, CA 94305

SAGE: Systems Designers Software, Inc.
444 Washington Street
Woburn, MA 01801

SAS: SAS Institute
Box 8000, SAS Circle
Cary, NC 27511-8000

SCA: Scientific Computing Associates
P.O. Box 625
De Kalb, IL 60115

S.1.: Teknowledge, Inc.
525 University Avenue
Palo Alto, CA 94301

Situation Analyst: Center for Expert Systems
Richard D. Irwin
1818 Ridge Road
Homewood, IL 60430

Smalltalk/V: Digitalk, Inc.
5200 W. Century Blvd., Suite 250
Los Angeles, CA 90045

SPSS: SPSS International
444 N. Michigan Avenue
Chicago, IL 60611

Strategic Planning Model: William Luther
211 Riverbank Drive
Stanford, CT 06903

TSP: TSP International
204 Junipero Serra Blvd.
Stanford, CA 94305

VP-Expert: Paperback Software International
2830 Ninth Street
Berkeley, CA 94710

# Index

Programming languages (*cont.*)
  flexibility of, 84–85
  knowledge-based system, 84
Programming shells, 32–33. *See also* Expert
    system shells
PROLOG, 32, 33, 151, 152–54
Promotion decisions, 398–99
  international, 400
Promotion regulations, 406
Prototypes
  creation of, 7, 33
  descriptions of, 61–62
  initial development of, 48
  as learning and teaching tool, 11
  management decisions in, 60
  number of conditions in, 79
  of personal investment planning system
      documenting of, 177–85
    studying of situation, 170–77
  purposes of, 9–11
  role and importance of, 7–11
  testing and validation of, 39
  typical situations in, 41

# Q

Qualified audited financial statements, 196
Qualifiers, in EXSYS program, 106, 107
Quality standards, 215
Quantitative analysis tools, 354–55
Questions
  computer formatting of, 77–78
  in EXSYS, 109
  guidelines for preparing, 94–95
  in GURU, 146
  knowledge-based, 24
  in M.1, 94–95
  user, 24
  user-effective, 78
  in VP-Expert knowledge base, 129,
      134–35

# R

(R1)XCON, 20
Reasoning
  basic for, 40

Reasoning (*cont.*)
  inferential, 29–32
  paths of, 65
  process of
    for account assignment, 267–68
    for capital investment planning, 226
    in career strategy planning, 497–98
    in commercial loan approval, 204
    for computer configuration system, 317
    for customer service representative
        system, 292
    in external auditing system, 245
    for insurance claim evaluation system,
        340
    for inventory planning, 355–58, 361–63
    for marketing strategy, 413
    for media strategy selection, 441–42
    models of, 63–64
    for new venture planning, 387–88
    in personal investment planning system,
        179–80
    precisely defining of, 51
    for sale quota development, 456–57
  scenarios for, typical, 41
  techniques for, 30–31
  tracing to roots of, 51–53
  with uncertainty, 31
Recommendations, 41
  entering in EXSYS program, 105
  identification of, 49
  reasoning path to, 65
  values of, 75
Recycling, 57–58
Refinement process, 57–58
Replication model, 57
Representative form, selection of, 74–75
Research functions, 19–20
Reserved words, in Level Five, 120
Restricted words, in M.1 programming, 93
Retail stores
  opportunities in, 375
  type of, 373
Rising input prices, 166
  future impact of, 172
Risk
  analysis of for capital investment planning,
      218
  in audits, 234–36

User questions (*cont.*)
  sample of, 24
  in VP-Expert, 134–35
Users
  as co-developers, 81
  input information of, 156
Utilities, 302

## V

Valuation methods, 241–42, 243, 244, 245
Verbal threshold, 331, 334–35
  categories of, 340
Vertical integration decision, 214
VP-Expert program
  computerizing knowledge-based systems
    using, 128–42

VP-Expert program (*cont.*)
  creating knowledge base with induction
    method in, 135–40
  creating small knowledge base in, 129–35
  installation of, 128–29
  knowledge base elements of, 129–35
  running consultation in, 140–42
  split screen in, 141

## W

Weapons systems, 19
Word processor. *See also* Computers creating
  knowledge base with using Level Five,
  119
  in GURU, 147
Worlds, 150–51